HANDBOOKS

BERMUDA

ROSEMARY JONES

BERMUDA

ATLANTIC OCEAN

BERMUDA
MARITIME MUSEUM

Ireland Island
North

Royal Naval
Dockyard

Ireland Island
South

Grassy Bay

Boaz
Island

Lagoon Park

Spanish
Point Park

Clarence
Cove

PEMBROKE
PARISH

Watford Island

Spanish
Point

Admiralty
House Park

NORTH SHORE RD

MARSH FOLLY RD

Long
Bay

Mangrove
Bay

Mill Creek

Pembroke
Marsh

Somerset
Village

SOMERSET CRICKET CLUB

Fairyland
Creek

PITTS BAY RD

City of
Hamilton

FORT
HAMILTON

SANDYS
PARISH

Somerset
Island

Pitts
Bay

Hamilton
Harbour

White's
Island

Scaur Hill
Fort Park

FORT SCAUR

Great

Paget
Marsh

Hinson's
Island

RD

SOMERSET
BRIDGE

Sound

Ely's Harbour

Hog
Bay
Park

MIDDLE

WARWICK
PARISH

Belmont Hills
Golf Course

ORD RD

Elbow
Beach

RD

Little Sound

Riddell's Bay
Golf Course

MIDDLE

Warwick
Pond

Railway Trail

Astwood Park

Port Royal
Golf Course

SOUTHAMPTON
PARISH

Five
Star I

South Shore
Park

SOUTH

SHORE

RD

Warwick Long Bay

WHALE BAY
FORT

Jobson's Cove

Stonehole Bay

West Whale
Bay Park

Fairmont
Southampton
Golf Course

Chaplin Bay

GIBBS HILL
LIGHTHOUSE

Church Bay
Park

Horseshoe Bay

FORT ST CATHERINE
St Catherine's Beach
Tobacco Bay

St George's
Golf Course
Town of
St George
ALEXANDRA BATTERY
ST GEORGE'S PARISH
ST GEORGE'S CRICKET CLUB
GATES FORT
Ordnance Island
Paget Island
Town Cut
BERMUDA BIOLOGICAL STATION FOR RESEARCH
Mullet Bay
St George's Harbour
Smith's Island
ST DAVID'S BATTERY
St George's Island
Great Head Park
Ferry Reach Park
Ferry Reach
BERMUDA INTERNATIONAL AIRPORT
MARTELLO TOWER
St David's Island
ST DAVID'S LIGHTHOUSE
Coney Island Park
Coney Island
Clearwater Beach

Castle Harbour
Cooper's Island

Blue Hole Park
Nonsuch Island

HAMILTON PARISH
Walsingham Nature Reserve

Shelly Bay Beach Park
Harrington
Shark Hole
Tucker's Point Golf Course
Tucker's Town
Shelly Bay
Mid Ocean Golf Course
Sound
Trott's Pond
BERMUDA AQUARIUM, MUSEUM & ZOO
Mangrove Lake
Gibbet Island
Flatts Inlet
Flatts Village
John Smith's Bay
Penhurst Park
Watch Hill Park
RD
Spittal Pond Nature Reserve
SMITH'S PARISH
inson's y Park
VERDMONT MUSEUM
Devonshire Marsh
RD
cean View olf Course
MIDDLE
Devonshire Bay Park
Devonshire Bay
retum
SOUTH
DEVONSHIRE PARISH
otanical ardens
AGET PARISH

UNITED STATES
ATLANTIC
BERMUDA
OCEAN
CUBA
Caribbean Sea

0   1 mi
0   1 km

© AVALON TRAVEL PUBLISHING, INC.

DISCOVER BERMUDA

Bermuda is a difficult place to get a fix on, even after numerous visits. There is an ephemeral, cotton-candy element to the island with its candy-pink veneer, so ubiquitous on buses, cottages, and hibiscus blooms. Bermudians themselves struggle to describe the essence of their 21-square-mile home or their national character, if there can be such generalizations. But for Bermuda's visitors, such ambiguities are all part of the island's allure. Its fast-forward economic buzz – thanks to big business – provides an anachronistic clash with its physical self, a laid-back Xanadu that hasn't changed much since wintering tourists like Winslow Homer, Georgia O'Keefe, and Mark Twain found creative inspiration in the island's peaceful pace. Bermuda encompasses two islands: Life can be frantic for those who actually live here – and work hard to pay for it – but for the visitor, a holiday can be utterly stress-free, sampling Azorean donuts and wool sweaters, meandering by scooter along oleander-carpeted lanes. Its people, too, can seem like a throwback to a gentler time.

A bird of paradise blooms at the Botanical Gardens.

Bermudians say "Good Morning!" when passing on the street and are actually offended if you don't reply in kind.

Bermuda's intriguing qualities are best unraveled slowly, like the layers of its namesake onion. The island once exported the fragrant bulb by the thousands to winter markets of New York and other American cities, installing it so strongly in the public imagination that Bermudians describe each other as "Onions" as a token of utmost respect. The island has very few tangible exports these days, aside from the rum cakes, linen shorts, and duty-free six-packs of dark 'n' stormies carried home by travelers – and most of those items aren't even manufactured in Bermuda. Rather, the island sells its natural attributes – to travelers – and its offshore jurisdiction – to international businesses.

To the first-time visitor, a few myths should be dispelled. Subtropical Bermuda is *not* part of the Caribbean – that island group lies more than 1,000 miles to the south. Bermuda had no indigenous people. Slavery instituted by the first English settlers forms a painful, 200-year legacy that continues to feed subtle racial

Paget rooftops overlook Hamilton Harbour.

bitterness and misunderstanding in a country with a 60 percent black population but a mostly white economic powerbase. A British Overseas Territory, in the term coined for today's remaining colonies, Bermuda is neither very British nor wholly North American, but rather a complex mixture of the two – with a large dose of easygoing island cool thrown in. Bermudians may fly the Union Jack and sing "God Save the Queen" as protocol requires at official occasions, but they certainly do *not* interrupt their workday for scones and clotted cream. And while islanders watch *Oprah* religiously, run office pools for NFL games, and visit family and friends in U.S. cities several times a year, they remain entirely skeptical of a wholesale American cultural invasion.

From the moment you touch down or sail in over aquamarine reefs to its green shore, Bermuda will seduce you as the brochures promise, even if its treasures are revealed somewhat coyly. The island caters to a mixed crowd of travelers these days. While most come for beaches – and a Hamilton shopping excursion thrown in – more and more are flocking for spa weekends, golf holidays,

coral-hued flamingos at the Bermuda Aquarium, Museum & Zoo

cultural attractions, eco-tours, and a growing slate of special sports events and international festivals. Music, food and film festivals, kite-surfing, deep-sea fishing, scuba-diving, art classes, and tours of bio-diverse natural parks, both marine and terrestrial, are among the varied menu of offerings on this most northerly of coral archipelagos. Honeymooners, hikers, artists, sports aficionados, even shop-a-holics – though, it must be said, those with ample wallets – will find plenty to see and do year-round, not to mention a delightfully different island to explore at various seasons.

Many of the island's best hotel properties have spent the past few years pouring money back into renovations and updates – sometimes forced to do so through necessity after hurricanes, but also to please sophisticated travelers accustomed to Manhattan boutique hotels or London spas. The island's tourism industry has had to become more competitive to survive the onslaught of far cheaper resorts with better climates, and that has only benefited visitors to Bermuda. UNESCO's World Heritage Site at St. George is busy preserving living history. Hamilton envisions a major waterfront facelift, complete with

Pastel shops of Flatts Village sit on the edge of a tranquil inlet.

boardwalks and added parklands. And cultural tourism initiatives are forging ahead with programs to fix up historic forts, open new museums, and launch the kinds of grassroots tours that allow outsiders to truly experience a place. Notably, the island's black community is developing the underexposed story of its people and traditions, with an African Diaspora Trail that details the heroes and struggles of slavery, emancipation, and the modern black experience.

Bermuda's quirkiness – comprising a curious mixed bag of 21st-century cutting-edge commerce and sea-hewn fables – manages to enchant newcomers and hold tight to those who return again and again and again. It is a miniscule, blindingly beautiful, quirky gem of a destination – so close to the Real World, yet in mindset, so seemingly far away. "I think I could live here always and be contented," Mark Twain said during a March 1910 visit. "You go to heaven if you want to – I'd rather stay here."

gentle rollers and pink sand at John Smith's Bay

Contents

MAP CONTENTS

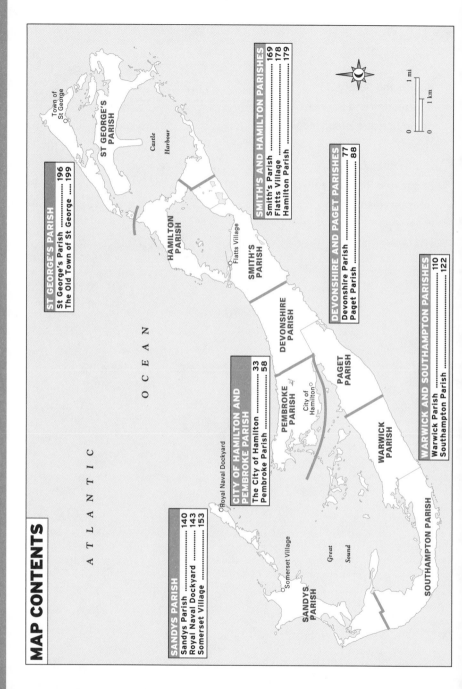

ATLANTIC OCEAN

ST GEORGE'S PARISH

Town of St George

Castle Harbour

HAMILTON PARISH

Flatts Village

SMITH'S PARISH

DEVONSHIRE PARISH

Royal Naval Dockyard

PEMBROKE PARISH

City of Hamilton

PAGET PARISH

Somerset Village

Great Sound

SANDYS PARISH

WARWICK PARISH

SOUTHAMPTON PARISH

1 mi

1 km

0

0

The Lay of the Land

CITY OF HAMILTON AND PEMBROKE PARISH

Whether you make forays into "Town" for shopping, restaurants, or nightclubs, or use the capital (since 1815) as a base from which to explore the rest of the island, the city and its environs make a logical place to start a tour of the parishes, depending on where you stay. Pembroke, a once-tranquil suburb that now absorbs an expanding urban environment, is home to several very good hotels and guesthouses, which offer a convenient access to the city and its surroundings and are within walking distance of the bus and ferry terminals for adventures beyond. The city is packed with history and culture, including art galleries, lovely parks like Victoria and Par-la-Ville, a cathedral with stunning panoramic views, and an 1870s fort with dungeons and moat gardens. Tours, water sports, and cruises to the inner islands leave from the city's waterfront. Hamilton is evolving on all sides, with major plans for a harborfront facelift, coupled with efforts to reinvigorate North Hamilton, the long-neglected "back of town"—a nonetheless thriving community with highly popular eateries, West Indian gingerbread architecture, clubs—and shops offering funkier music and fashion than any in the city center.

DEVONSHIRE AND PAGET PARISHES

The heart of Bermuda comprises scenic routes east and west, but also numerous, often free, attractions. Deep country, Bermuda style, is found in Devonshire, with old estates, farmland, and seaside communities, while Paget offers faster-paced suburban attractions such as golf, tennis, and an ultra-hip nightclub. Resorts, guesthouses, and restaurants to suit different tastes and budgets abound in Paget, while more colorful local eateries and landmarks like churches and nature reserves create Devonshire's allure. Key attractions include The Arboretum, Paget Marsh, the Botanical Gardens, and Elbow Beach.

WARWICK AND SOUTHAMPTON PARISHES

Beach bums beware: You could descend into the pink-sand environs of these western parishes and never see anything else. This is the realm of scuba, water sports, horseback riding, and snorkeling, not to mention tennis, golf, and pampering spas at several major resorts. Jocks, spa addicts, and sun-worshippers will find nirvana here. There are a few historic sites, as well, including Gibbs Hill Lighthouse—the island's best view. Both undulating parishes offer spectacular views of the South Shore and Great Sound, a plethora of gourmet and comfort food, and accommodations to suit various budgets. Day trips by bus, scooter, or ferry allow for easy exploration. These "up de country" regions also carry various routes westward to Sandys.

SANDYS PARISH

The historic military gems of the fortified Royal Naval Dockyard, including Bermuda Maritime Museum, are the biggest collective magnet of the West End, but beyond the ramparts and wharves of this fascinating peninsula, the parish has a quaint, countrified character that invites gentle exploration. Somerset Village and its surroundings provide endless rural lanes to meander, as well as local shops, restaurants, and water sports centers. Numerous deep-sea fishing boats also operate out of this area. Since the parish links several islands, bridges lead you between the bunch; Somerset Bridge, the world smallest drawbridge that opens just wide enough to let yacht masts through, is one of them. Pricey resorts and less costly guesthouses provide West End accommodation, but the fast ferries from Hamilton can get you (and your scooter) here in 20 minutes. The outer parish, with pristine wildlife areas such as the Heydon Trust and 38-acre Hog Bay Park, one of the island's largest nature reserves, is within a half-day's tour, although it would take at least two or three days to really scrape the surface.

SMITH'S AND HAMILTON PARISHES

Packed with sights and attractions, Smith's Parish and Hamilton Parish—not to be confused with the capital city—are destinations in their own right, as well as pretty pathways to the East End. A historic home, Verdmont, and the 60-acre oceanfront bird sanctuary of Spittal Pond Nature Reserve offer valuable insight into Bermuda's past and natural environment, as does the Bermuda Aquarium, Museum & Zoo in Hamilton Parish—one of Bermuda's most-visited attractions. The cave-honeycombed Harrington Sound provides a scenic route east, and several beautiful beaches—Shelly Bay, John Smith's—are inviting distractions.

ST. GEORGE'S PARISH

Declared a UNESCO World Heritage Site in 2000, the historic town of St. George and its related fortifications are the main draws of the East End. The parish incorporates the island's first capital—the oldest colonial town of the British Empire—along with the quirky island of St. David's and outlying regions such as Ferry Reach, home of the Bermuda Biological Station for Research, which continues as a pioneer in global marine science. St. George, built by the first handful of English settlers, boasts multiple attractions, including winding backstreets, centuries-old landmarks, a public square, and a yacht-laden waterfront. Surrounding coastal forts are no less striking, a tribute to the 400-year-old heritage of overseas British coastal fortifications and artillery. The nearby community of St. David's welcomes visitors with outstanding seafood restaurants, the Carter House museum, and a legacy of whaling, piloting, and lily-farming. The parish deserves at least a day's visit, more if you have the time. High-speed ferries run between Hamilton and St. George several times a day (a 45-minute voyage along the picturesque North Shore), and regular bus service also serves the East End. There are also several accommodations in this part of the island, allowing visitors to actually "live history."

Planning Your Trip

Bermuda's digestible size means even first-time visitors can cover the island end-to-end, taking in major sights and attractions like beaches, forts, and pastel towns, over a long weekend—a popular trend given Bermuda's 90-minute flying distance from the U.S. East Coast. An oft-quipped maxim goes that it's probably faster to get to Bermuda from New York City than it is to the Hamptons.

Cars are not rented to visitors because of the space crunch, but whether you rent a scooter, hop on and off the island's efficient new fast-ferries and air-conditioned buses, or hire taxis to get around, there is plenty to see and do in all nine parishes. The island's capital, Hamilton, at Bermuda's center, the old town of St. George in the East End, and the Royal Naval Dockyard spilling over the West End hook are highlights that should not be missed and, if schedule dictates, can be covered in as short a timespan as one well-planned day.

Like many small places, however, the physical geography is sometimes deceptive; around every hairpin corner, there's always more to explore. You could easily potter around the parishes for weeks on end, languidly savoring a mussel pie here, a backstreet there, with all the time in the world.

Because the regions are so easy to explore, a visitor's main decision should be the type of vacation and activities they prefer. Choosing accommodation will then follow suit, and in many cases special packages (spa weekends, for example) can be had for more economical rates. Mixing and matching activities within a Bermuda vacation's timeframe and geography is also very do-able (scuba and spa, golf and museums).

Book in advance for accommodation (you need a return airline ticket and a destination address to pass through Bermuda Customs), but also for preferred activities, especially if you plan to travel here in the busy summer months.

WHEN TO GO

Since Bermuda is further north than tropical Caribbean and Central American hotspots, don't expect perfect weather all year round. The winter off-season (November–March) has average 68-degree Fahrenheit temperatures compared to the 80s of mid-summer, along with unpredictable rainstorms. Violent wind and rain especially plague the early months of the year (January–March), but generally Bermuda's weather patterns are capriciously short-lived, meaning that a morning of hot sun and blue skies perfect for the beach can always be followed by a torrential afternoon downpour as squalls roll in. And even if it's pouring in St. George's, Hamilton may be clear and dry. Spring (April–May) and fall (September–November) witness a delightful drop in the summer-long humidity, a torpor that can hit 90-plus-percent for days on end.

Most visitors choose the summer, however, due to a preference for the hot weather, allowing them to enjoy the island's beaches and multitude of watersports. Rates at hotels and other accommodation rise accordingly, usually by at least a third, and sometimes doubling. The high season also affects availability: heavy demand in the summer months often means a hotel's best rooms, or all its rooms, become fully booked for certain periods, particularly at popular small resorts such as The Reefs or Pompano Beach, where repeat visitors book early, occasionally up to a year in advance. Such is not always the case, however, especially since the island has been suffering from low-occupancy rates in recent years.

Summer brings the cruise ships, and it is the season of numerous high-season activities laid on for visitors (beach parties, special shopping nights, alfresco restaurant seats). But summer travelers may have to contend with hurricanes, whose Atlantic season runs June–November. Bermuda lies within the hurricane belt, though it suffers far less frequently, and less substantially, than its Caribbean neighbors. If you're booking a trip in August or September, the worst hurricane months, be prepared for stormy weather that could disrupt flights, beach activities, or scuba outings.

The winter low season is cooler, quieter, and features a bigger focus on cultural attractions such as museums, historical walking tours, and art galleries. Restaurants offer dine-around programs. It is also a popular time of the year for golfing getaways. Bear in mind, the sea temperature may dip to a chilly 65 degrees in these months, although scuba-divers appreciate the ocean's clearer visibility in this season. Christmas is a particularly good time to visit—an islandwide festival of lights, the popular Boat Parade, Santa Claus parades, and other festivities make December a busy time of year.

You may want to plan your visit around the island's expanding calendar of cultural and sports events, some purely local, others big-name. Local favorites are Cup Match (a Thursday and Friday in late July or early August), when the island shuts down for a four-day weekend and hotly contested cricket match between both ends of the island. Easter brings kites and codfishcake festivals. International events include April's Bermuda International Film Festival, and the ATP-sanctioned XL Capital Bermuda Open tennis tournament; October's Bermuda Music Festival and the Culinary Arts Festival; and November's World Rugby Classic.

Keep in mind that Bermuda celebrates numerous U.K. public holidays, including Good Friday (the Friday before Easter), the Queen's Birthday (in mid-June), Remembrance Day (November 11), and Boxing Day (December 26), when everything shuts down. Sundays see retail outlets mostly closed also, except near to Christmas.

WHAT TO TAKE

For most of the year, flip-flops, leather sandals, or boat shoes will be far more comfortable than the typical North American vacation uniform of thick socks and sneakers, especially in the summer. You'll fit in far better, too. Breathable cotton outfits are good for all seasons; you can always layer up if it gets chilly. Beating sunshine, lashing rain, and high winds can accost you no matter the season. Drastic weather changes within the same day can also prove confusing. Be prepared: Pack a light, waterproof, wind-proof anorak with a hood for scooter or walking expeditions. Even in hot summer, you'll appreciate keeping dry.

Hats and shades are a must if you don't want to end up lobster red. Waterproof sunblock with a high (36 or more) UVA and UVB factor is recommended for all seasons, but it is an absolute necessity for the summer when even riding a scooter can give your hands and forearms bad burns. Mosquito repellant is also useful in the summer, as the insects come out at night all over the island.

In the winter, know that few buildings are heated, so bring along sweaters, turtlenecks, pants, and socks to keep the damp out. A breathable Gore-Tex jacket and an umbrella will shield you from the weather, and if you have rain-pants or waterproof slacks, bring them along; they'll keep you dry while driving in the frequent showers. Even a pair of gloves might come in handy (Bermuda motorbikers wear them to avoid frozen fingers).

Two pointers: Bermuda residents dress up, and they dress conservatively. Bikini tops and bare chests are not welcome at restaurants, and you'll stick out like a sore thumb riding a moped nearly naked also. When going out at night, think "urban" rather than "island," that is, smart-casual or even elegant is the rule. To fit in best, you don't need to be dripping in designer labels, but do understand that Bermuda's nightclubs and restaurants welcome a moneyed crowd: cocktail dresses, heels, button-down shirts, suits, or nice pants (no jeans) is the expected dress code.

There is little if any pick-pocketing, so body-worn passport pouches and zipped handbags are not necessary. However, bag-snatches are relatively common, so bags with straps that can be worn across the body and backpacks are useful deterrents.

You can purchase clothes, toiletries, child-care items—in fact pretty much anything you'd find in North America or Europe—but much merchandise is pricier than on the mainland. If you'll be needing electronics, computer, or camera equipment, including film, bring your own. They are routinely overpriced in Bermuda outlets (sometimes triple U.S. retail prices).

Explore Bermuda

THE 10-DAY BEST OF BERMUDA

Sure, you can laze on a beach for weeks on end, and shop till you drop—or run out of money. But with its short distances and efficient public transport, Bermuda can reveal so much more of itself to energetic travelers during a 10-day stay (a typical vacation for those seeking more than just a weekend getaway). Look below the surface of this reef-fringed paradox and you'll discover a fascinating melting pot of culture, history, and outdoor adventure encompassing all nine parishes. Split your stay between a couple of hotels or guesthouses to experience the island's very different areas.

Day 1

Arrive at Bermuda International Airport and grab a cab to your hotel. Shake off your mainland cobwebs with an afternoon at **Elbow Beach,** strolling the soft sand or testing turquoise waters. Dress up and choose a South Shore terrace, such as **Café Lido** or **Coconuts,** for an alfresco dinner.

Day 2

Head into **Hamilton** for breakfast with Bermudians of all backgrounds at **The Spot Restaurant.** Try traditional codfish and potatoes, if it's on the menu. Spend the morning exploring Front, Reid, and Church Streets' boutiques, art galleries, and churches such as **Holy Trinity Cathedral,** whose landmark tower overlooks the city. The harborfront's **Aggie's Garden Café** is the perfect lunch spot. In the afternoon, rent a moped or hop on a bubblegum bus and cruise the North Shore and Harrington Sound to visit **underground caves.** Watch the sun go down from **Shelly Bay.**

Day 3

Okay, you can laze on the beach today. Go to **Horseshoe Bay** for bodysurfing, sandcastles, and snorkeling. Follow the trail east through protected dune-cradled park to sample **Chaplin Bay, Jobson's Cove,** and

Long Bay. In the late afternoon, escape the sun and book a spa treatment at one of the many resorts (book your treatment days in advance if possible).

Day 4

Take the ferry from Hamilton across the Great Sound to the **Royal Naval Dockyard,** scooter optional. Immerse yourself in the stories of military, slaves, immigrants, and war veterans at **Bermuda Maritime Museum.** Watch a cedar craftsman at the **Bermuda Arts Centre.** Stop into **Somerset Village** for lunch, then rent a kayak or take a snorkeling or paragliding tour of the West End.

Day 5

Take the ferry along the North Shore to **St. George's.** Explore the steeped history and twisting alleys of the old town, a UNESCO World Heritage Site. Visit area forts (also UNESCO gems), including **Gates Fort,** the **Martello Tower at Ferry Reach,** and **Fort St. Catherine** with its commanding views of the bay where the first settlers landed. Mingle with fishermen at **St. David's** and sample the fresh lobster, tuna, and dark 'n' stormies at neighborhood eateries.

Day 6

Walk in John Lennon's footsteps at **Botanical Gardens,** Paget, where *Double Fantasy* was born, and pay a visit to the nascent **Masterworks Museum of Bermuda Art.** Nearby, journey to the virtual ocean floor at the **Bermuda Underwater Exploration Institute** at the foot of Hamilton Harbour. Head into North Hamilton, the city's "Uptown" district, for a West Indian-style lunch at one of the many cafés, such as **Jamaican Grill** or **Fish Hut.** Walk the pretty French Quarter-style streets here, and climb up to **Fort Hamilton** for moat gardens and panoramic views. Return to North Hamilton for a rousing evening of local jazz.

Day 7

Get a nature fix with a hike along the old **Railway Trail** from Paget or Warwick as far as you feel fit for. The outing will give you an "inside" look at Bermuda via backyards, farmers' fields, golf courses, and thick woodlands populated with island birds, lizards, and wild fruits like loquats and cherries. Tribe roads lead off the trail back to main roads and bus stops at regular intervals. The beach is never too far away; cool off with a leisurely afternoon swim. If you reach Southampton, climb **Gibbs Hill Lighthouse,** have afternoon tea, then squeeze in an hour or two at a spa to unwind.

Day 8

Take a bus or moped to the **Bermuda Aquarium, Museum & Zoo** and spend a few hours soaking in the wildlife. Have lunch in historic **Flatts Village,** then take your time exploring North Shore communities such as Devonshire Dock and Spanish Point. Fit in a swim at one of the deep, sheltered coves along the way, such as **Robinson's Bay** or **Clarence Cove.**

Day 9

Head down under to explore Bermuda's reefs and shipwrecks. Numerous scuba and snorkeling outfitters can arrange half-day or full-day expeditions, from Hamilton, Somerset, the South Shore, or East End. Popular shallow-dive wrecks, spanning the Age of Discovery to the 20th century, include the 1943 *Hermes* off Horseshoe Bay in Southampton and the 1915 German vessel *Pollockshields,* off Paget's South Shore.

Day 10

Grab an early-morning beach run and dip along the South Shore before your flight out.

UNBEATABLE BEACHES

Bermuda's beaches are world-renowned for their pristine, coral-tinged beauty, and there are hundreds of them around the island. Whether you're staying at a dedicated beach resort, or at an inland guesthouse, you are never far away from the shoreline (Bermuda is less than a couple of miles wide at its widest point). Although some are officially private, belonging to resorts or restricted neighborhoods, all of Bermuda's beaches are open to the public sunrise to sunset from the water's edge to the high-tide mark.

You can swim all year round (though Bermudians don't). Water temperatures in summer can reach a balmy 85 degrees; winter dips to an average 65. The first official beach day is May 24, when boaters take to the water to kick off the season, but most locals wait until June to make their first beach foray. Mid-summer's Cup Match holiday is the ultimate beach extravaganza, with practically every inch of shoreline occupied by family outings and elaborate seaside camping parties. Fancy Christmas Day at the water's edge? Hardy expatriate residents have long celebrated the morning of December 25 with a dip and champagne toast at Elbow Beach; some don Santa hats and bring mini trees, complete with ornaments, for the festive occasion.

Concessions—for boogie boards, noodles, masks and snorkels, hair-braiding, umbrellas, and refreshments—can be found at many major beaches, particularly those along the South Shore. Hard-core surfing is rare, because Bermuda's rollers are usually not large enough, hurricane season excepted. There are no nude or topless beaches, and baring all on this conservative island will only land you in trouble with the law.

Government lifeguards are posted on just a handful of the most popular strands, identifiable by their white huts with posted flag. Be careful of riptides and undertow on the South Shore, especially during hurricane season when swells surge the coast propelled by approaching storms.

BEACH REGIONS
South Shore
The South Shore has some of Bermuda's best-known beaches: Horseshoe Bay, Warwick Long Bay, and Elbow Beach, all stunningly panoramic, with long stretches of clean, soft sand, turquoise breakers, and boiler reefs for snorkeling just a few yards from the surf. There are also tiny gems like Jobson's Cove – sheltered swimming holes perfect for children, novices, or romantics seeking some solitude.

North Shore
The North Shore lacks surf – and often, sand – inviting swimmers to immerse themselves instead in the cerulean depths of shallow

bays or by taking off-the-rocks dips. Clarence Cove, Robinson's Bay, and Gibbet's Island are all soothing escapes.

West End
In the West End, West Whale Bay and Somerset Long Bay are worth visiting. The 9 Beaches Resort in Sandys offers water sports like kiteboarding at its multiple strands, and the Snorkel Park at Dockyard has a rare on-the-beach restaurant plus bar. Private dinners actually served on the beach – at resorts like The Reefs and Cambridge Beaches – can also be arranged.

East End
At the East End, Clearwater Beach, Tobacco

Bay, and St. Catherine's Beach are all popular among East Enders. Lesser-known swimming spots such as Devonshire Bay and the Harrington Sound public dock offer varied swimming options. If you rent a sailboat, kayak, or motorboat and explore Bermuda from the water, you will find many more tiny coves and beaches on the inner islands around Hamilton Harbour and St. George's Harbour.

BEST BEACHES
Most Beautiful Beaches

Horseshoe Bay (South Shore – Southampton): A sweeping pink stretch hemmed by emerald foliage and sparkling turquoise. . . plus showers, washrooms, a café, and beach gear rentals.

Warwick Long Bay (South Shore – Warwick): A serene antidote to neighboring beach crowds, with deep white sand and crashing surf.

Elbow Beach (South Shore – Paget): Offers pillow-soft sand and frolicking parrotfish, along with volleyball and kitesurfing.

John Smith's Bay (South Shore – Smith's): Framed by coconut palms, this picturesque bay has shady caves, a lifeguard, and nearby reefs for snorkeling.

Whale Bay (East End – Ferry Reach, St. George's): A beachcomber's treasure within a quiet nature reserve, thanks to its littering of washed-up beach glass.

Most Secluded Beaches

Astwood Cove (South Shore – Warwick): Hard to access, except by a steep cliff-side path, but the privacy and crystal-clear water are worth the trouble.

Jobson's Cove (South Shore – Warwick): A favorite of romantics and families with children due to its cliff-sheltered swimming hole.

West Whale Bay (West End – Southampton): Hidden below Whale Bay Fort with a string of coves and caves connected by pristine sand at low tide.

Turtle Bay (East End – Southside, St. David's): Situated on the former U.S. baselands, now called Southside, this small beach is tucked next to nature reserves and bird sanctuaries.

Best Snorkeling Beaches

Church Bay (South Shore – Southampton): Easy-reach boiler reefs make it a perennial top pick among devoted snorkelers.

Gibbet Island (North Shore – Smith's): A tranquil collection of shallow bays popular with boaters, snorkelers, and children.

Dockyard Snorkel Park (West End – Royal Naval Dockyard): At the foot of towering ramparts, shallow waters and reef-speckled coastline prove a hit with locals and visitors alike.

Tobacco Bay (East End): A snorkeler's heaven (when not crowded with cruise ship passengers), thanks to its natural underwater columns and reeflife.

Most Bermudian Beaches

Horseshoe Bay (South Shore – Southampton): Local teens and twentysomethings lend a beach party atmosphere to summer weekend afternoons here.

Clarence Cove (North Shore – Pembroke): A magnet for Admiralty Park neighborhood families and kids.

Robinson's Bay (North Shore – Devonshire): Deep coves, a low-tide beach, and rock ledges attract families and fishermen.

Somerset Long Bay (West End – Somerset Island): Turtles can be seen grazing in the shallows, alongside a public park and nature reserve.

Clearwater Beach (East End – Southside, St. David's): With its accessible water and nearby playground, parkland, and fast-food restaurants, this aptly-named swimming venue is a summer hotspot.

St. Catherine's Beach (East End): A sandy arc on the island's easternmost tip where shipwrecked English colonists struggled ashore.

HAUNTING HISTORY

An impressive 500 years of colonial history abounds throughout the parishes, and the island's museums and monuments are a fascinating passage back in time. Some are free and outdoors, such as Spanish Rock—the carving believed left by Portuguese castaways when they scrambled to safety along the Spittal Pond shoreline in the 1500s. Others, like the town of St. George, where modern-day Bermudians live and work amid the cobblestoned milieu of early settlers, provide a "living history" for visitors to experience. The East End town, now a UNESCO World Heritage Site, oozes a sense of the past from its cedar-clad churches and old limestone buildings that sit on a street grid mapped out in the 1600s. A brand new World Heritage Centre opened in 2006 at historic Penno's Wharf. The West End Dockyard casts a similar spell: 26 acres of fortified coastline that's home to a slew of restored military buildings, including the Bermuda Maritime Museum and spectacular Commissioner's House—a showcase of the island's nautical and Royal Navy past, including rooms of rare maps, and exhibits on trans-Atlantic slavery, Portuguese and West Indian immigrants, and Bermudian war vets.

Some 90 forts defended Bermuda and its harbors for more than three centuries, from the time of English settlement in 1612 to the last coastal defenses of 1957. With several well-preserved examples and plans to restore many others, Bermuda's forts are considered a vital record of British built heritage and intrinsic to the island's cultural tourism. Some fortifications are not accessible, due to overgrown foliage and debris, or are just archaeological remnants of their former glory. But many are in good condition and open to the public, offering a unique vantage point from bastions, ramparts, and dungeons.

You can cover the whole island with visits to Bermuda National Trust properties, including antiques-packed mansions haunted by legendary ghosts. Highlights include Verdmont and Tucker House, plus the Trust Museum in St. George, where a fascinating exhibit details Bermuda's key role in the U.S. Civil War. If you're a scuba fan, plan to investigate history from the water; several scuba companies arrange year-round daily dives on the necklace of 100 superb shipwrecks around the island, from sites of Spanish galleons to Second World War battleships and fighter planes.

Day 1

Bermuda began in the East End four centuries ago, so it's logical to begin your cultural tour of the island in the old town of **St. George.** After learning about the town's origins at the World Heritage Centre, visit some of the first stone buildings, including quaint **St. Peter's Church** and the **State House** – used for a slew of witch trials in the 17th century. Ogle the elegant antiques and artworks to get a feel for the lifestyle of Bermuda's privileged at the well-preserved **Tucker House,** then follow the fascinating adventures of U.S. Civil War "Rogues & Runners" at the **Bermuda National Trust Museum** off King's Square. The **Bermuda Heritage Museum,** which chronicles the achievements and traditions of the island's slaves and free blacks, is also worth a visit. Have lunch in one of the town's waterfront restaurants, before exploring the dungeons and ramparts of scenic **Fort St. Catherine** – where Charlton Heston once performed *Macbeth*. **Blackbeard's Hideout,** on high near the beach where first settlers landed, is the perfect place for a sunset cocktail.

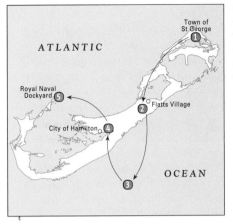

ity time investigating old paddle steamers, vintage sailing ships, and Second World War vessels. If you're not certified, operators are usually more than happy to take snorkelers out to surrounding reef preserves, too. In between dives, grab a chowder, soup, or sandwich at a local café or service station, where local fishermen often stop in.

Day 2

Conjure the ghost at **Verdmont,** Smith's Parish – an old family mansion now owned by the National Trust. It's believed the attic nursery, complete with toys and a child's cradle, is home to a benevolent spirit. The property's precious antiques, cedar-clad rooms and rose-filled gardens are just as intriguing. Nearby, at **Spittal Pond Nature Reserve,** climb the mile-long trail to **Spanish Rock** to relive the view experienced by 16th-century shipwreck survivors. Have lunch at **Aqua,** the Ariel Sands Resort restaurant owned by Michael Douglas that pays tribute to Bermuda's Shakespearean ties to *The Tempest*. Just along the coast, a reconstructed version of **Devonshire Bay**'s fortifications offer a picturesque walk in this quiet shoreline neighborhood, where fishermen sell their fresh catch – good for a barbecue dinner.

Day 3

Take a dive boat trip out to any of the fascinating **shipwrecks** encircling the island. Several operators organize full-day packages, with morning and afternoon dives to different sites. Swift access to Bermuda wrecks, and their position in relatively shallow water (60 to 75 feet) means you can spend qual-

Day 4

Spend the morning at **Fort Hamilton,** whose panoramic, bird's-eye view stretches all the way to Dockyard. The maze of limestone dungeons and munitions rooms – once manned by British garrison troops – together with the fort's bedded lawns and exquisite moat garden, provide one of the island's best diversions. Have a fish sandwich or West Indian curry in North Hamilton's laid-back neighborhood, then drop into **Bermuda National Gallery,** where a permanent collection of prestigious European oils is augmented by regular showcases of the island's best contemporary artists. Enjoy a late afternoon swim at **Admiralty House Park,** Pembroke, the former home of British Navy brass, where coastline caves and limestone tunnels carved by the military are fun to explore.

Day 5

Take a ferry ride to the West End **Dockyard,** where you can spend the morning steeped in British naval history. Climb the ramparts of **Bermuda Maritime Museum,** where artifacts like coins, pottery and slave irons from shipwrecks through the ages are on display. Outside, stroll the streets and buildings of the Dockyard, Bermuda's largest fort which was home to the British fleet for 200 years. Stop for lunch in one of the several cafés, then hop on the bus or scooter to **Fort Scaur,** on Somerset Island, whose bastions offer a beautiful view of the Great Sound. Nearby **Whale Bay Fort,** in Southampon, also boasts sweeping ocean views – and a quiet beach below for swimming.

KID-FRIENDLY BERMUDA

Being a kid in Bermuda is like stepping into *Fantasia* or *Alice in Wonderland*. There are plenty of weird animals—lizards, trilling treefrogs, yellow-bellied kiskadees. Manta rays gliding like planes under Flatts Bridge and turtles popping up behind your kayak. Roadsides are polka-dotted with trails of Technicolor blossoms, perfect for pretend princesses. And sunshine-packed days spill over with sandcastles, real-life forts, bubblegum buses, and hovercraft ferries. As for snacks, the outdoor variety are always there for the taking: sweet wild loquats, bottom-of-the-garden bananas, and fish pulled up by a handline.

It may sound like a no-brainer as a destination for family holidays, but ironically, the island has received a bad rap over the years, mainly due to transportation challenges caused by the lack of rental cars. No doubt, it can be difficult managing the logistics of toddlers and public transport, but Bermuda's payoff in terms of kiddie—and parent—satisfaction is more than worth it.

SIGHTS AND RECREATION

Even without set events or activities, there's plenty for little ones to enjoy. Visit Wahoo, the Wyndham Bermuda Resort and Spa's South Shore waterpark, for a day; its slides, waterfalls, and geysers have proven a monstrous hit with every age. Hop on to the bus or ferry to see the dolphins at Dockyard or the hokey but hilarious performance by "George the Ghost" at Fort St. Catherine in the East End. Join young islanders at the half-dozen government playgrounds around the parishes; Warwick Playground, Shelly Bay, and the mock pirate ship at Dockyard are particularly well equipped. The Saturday morning Bull's Head Farmers Market, held in the fall, winter, and spring at Bull's Head carpark in Hamilton, should also be on your hit list. Children can listen to local musicians, ride the resident pony for $1, or sample fresh-baked banana bread and island honey. Highlights like these should leave positive impressions on inquiring young minds, long after the island is a distant memory.

There are special rates for children at most museums and sightseeing attractions; kids under five are usually free. Don't miss the big favorite, the Bermuda Aquarium, Museum & Zoo in Flatts, or the Bermuda Underwater Exploration Institute on East Broadway with its giant squid and Bermuda Triangle presentations. Like these educational facilities, the World Heritage Centre in St. George also has a children's learning area, allowing kids to experience history handson. Check out the children's sections of local bookstores; most stock numerous Bermuda books for kids, well-illustrated publications which also teach about island wildlife, folklore and traditions.

BEACHES

Bermuda makes it pretty easy to entertain children of most ages, because you usually don't have to arrange anything more organized than a trip to the beach – so parents can actually have a vacation, too. Kids entertain themselves for hours at rock pools, body surfing, creating castles from the soft pink sand, spying on reef-life with a mask and snorkel, or collecting mountains of ocean-washed glass or sand shells. Even infants are lulled by the sound of surf and the sea breeze. Some of the best beaches for children are Jobson's Cove, John Smith's Bay, the "Baby Beach" at Horseshoe Bay, and Clearwater Beach (where there's also a playground and restaurant). Make sure to bring hats, shades, and plenty of sunblock. Choosing a hotel or guesthouse on the beach, or at least within easy walking distance, is probably a wise choice when vacationing in Bermuda with children of any age.

ENTERTAINMENT AND EVENTS

Certain times of the year are no-holds-barred magical for kids in Bermuda. Easter weekend kite-flying festivals, with their mandatory fishcake sandwiches; Cup Match camping and boat raft-ups; the Christmas Boat Parade – even island children accustomed to such annual rituals are enchanted by these spectacles. Kids can take part in a wacky sandcastle competition sponsored by an architects' institute in late September. They can ride the toy-like train or dance to the rhythms of gombeys at summer's stay-up-late Harbour Nights. There's also a kids' film festival in October, a spin-off of Bermuda's popular adult version. If you're staying at any of the major hotels, you'll find that several, including Elbow Beach, Wyndham, and Fairmont Southampton, have well-run summer-long kids' programs to keep little ones happy and busy while parents get some R&R.

FOOD AND SHOPPING

Lots of local restaurants, including standouts La Trattoria in Hamilton, the Paraquet in Paget, and the Frog and Onion at Dockyard, are kid-friendly to the max, easily accommodating family groups, with baby chairs, kids' menus, speedy service, and entertaining wait staff to keep young diners amused.

Kids don't have to be bored even during a shopping spree. They'll get a kick out of many kid-friendly island stores, including Treats, Jack'n'Jill's, the Annex, Pulp & Circumstance, and People's Pharmacy in Hamilton; Robertson's Drugstore in St. George; and Somerset Drug Store in Sandys. Master craftsman Chesley Trott makes delightful pull-toys of Bermuda cedar from his Dockyard studio at Bermuda Arts Centre, and little cedar cars and buses are sold in the next-door Bermuda Craft Market.

ON THE WILD SIDE

Bermuda may seem like one big manicured garden, but its limited open spaces nevertheless give a fascinating glimpse of the island's wildlife. Well-managed government national parks in many parishes, as well as nature reserves owned by the Bermuda National Trust and Bermuda Audubon Society throughout the island, offer spectacular ocean scenery, woodland, farm tracts, birdlife, insects, and geology. Contact either of these groups for seasonal information on birding tours and other eco-tour schedules. Don't forget that much of Bermuda's biodiversity is marine, not terrestrial; half-day and full-day snorkeling and scuba tours over Bermuda's renowned reefs can be arranged through several respected outfitters. The beauty of exploring by land or sea is the compact size of the island, meaning that you could be floating over seafans or inspecting mangrove dragonflies in the morning, and still have plenty of time later in the day to cool out at the beach or enjoy a shopping jaunt to Hamilton.

WILDLIFE HOTSPOTS
Bermuda Aquarium, Museum & Zoo

Spend an illuminating morning or afternoon at this historic Flatts facility, home to more than 200 local fish and invertebrate species, a 140,000-gallon reef tank, and a $1.7-million Natural History Museum that tells the story of Bermuda's origins. The zoo's parrots, monkeys, resident python, and flock of flamingos reflect links with island environments around the globe. BAMZ is a major educational center, schooling thousands of island students annually on conservation issues and Bermuda's endangered species. Ask for feeding times and the daily tour schedule when you enter. Divers sometimes give special presentations from within the giant North Rock Tank, and there is a Friday morning storytime for kids.

Bermuda Biological Station for Research

Visitors are welcome at this world-renowned institution at Ferry Reach in the East End. Take a free morning tour of the station, located here since 1932, where top scientists from around the globe now come to study global warming, natural disasters, and possible medical breakthroughs – to cure cancer, to slow aging – that might be derived from the world's oceans. Expeditions to Bermuda's reefs and parks are also offered seasonally, along with lectures on cutting-edge marine research. The BBSR runs a well-subscribed year-round Elderhostel program for senior travelers to Bermuda, including a summer snorkeling camp geared especially for grandparents and grandchildren. If you get hooked, the station also offers a slate of internships for foreign students and volunteers.

Bermuda Underwater Exploration Institute

From springtime whale-watching expeditions off the South Shore to traveling exhibits, "glow-worm" cruises, and lectures by some of the world's top scientists, BUEI is a favorite destination for the ecologically inclined. The Pembroke facility is part museum (with exhibits on Bermuda shells, geology, wildlife, and shipwrecks) and part conference center and organizational hub for ocean-based activities around the island. You can sign up for a moonlit midsummer cruise to watch the phosphorescent glow worms enacting their fascinating mating dance, see humpback whales frolic just a short distance offshore, or spend an evening hearing about the latest deep-ocean submersible adventure by BUEI's international board of scientific advisors.

PARKS AND NATURE RESERVES

Bermuda has 63 national parks, though some of these are tiny patches of preserved land, with a few located on offshore islets. The largest is South Shore Park, which at 103 acres, sprawls along the coastline of Warwick and Southampton, linking all the major beaches, dunes, trails, cliffs, and coves in these parishes. There are also some 13 national nature reserves, maintained by the government, as well as 33 properties owned by Bermuda National Trust (BNT) or Bermuda Audubon Society, though not all of these are open to the public.

Dress coolly to hike the nature reserves in summer; several, including Hog Bay Park, border the ocean, so bring a bathing suit and feel free to take a refreshing dip en route. Don't forget to wear mosquito repellent. In the winter, all-terrain shoes, an umbrella, or hooded waterproof coat are recommended to keep dry in frequent rainsqualls. Bermuda's traveling distances are short, and none of the sites are very large. So, you can cover several over the course of a weekend – two or three parks a day – depending on the pace you wish to keep and the diversions (swims, picnics) you may wish to take.

Here are 10 of the most important areas for island plants and wildlife:

Sandys Parish

Hog Bay Park: This 38-acre reserve is surprisingly little visited by Bermudians or visitors, yet it offers some of the island's most rugged and beautiful undulating trails, which wind past farmers' fields, through inland forest and along a cedar-coated coastline complete with beach and seagrass bays. Birdlife galore nests here, and various species of lizards, mice, toads, insects, and spiders can be seen. If you're lucky, you can spot turtles and parrotfish frolicking off the breathtakingly panoramic shoreline. There is also a parking lot with portable toilets.

Southampton Parish

South Shore Park: A vast spread of coastal area connecting Warwick and Southampton's most popular beaches, this public land was designated a national park in the 1990s. Included are areas for camping, trails across limestone cliffs and dunes, and shaded grassy areas for hilltop picnics. Land crabs' burrows dot the dunes and longtails soar from cliff nests. Access is easy, via any beach entrance along South Shore Road.

Warwick Parish

Warwick Pond: Once a large marshy basin which ran through the heart of the island, this reserve owned by the National Trust is a key bird sanctuary. Renovated in 2003 with trails and informative signage, the nine-acre reserve off Middle Road encircles a large pond and is bordered by agricultural land.

Paget Parish

Paget Marsh: With a quaint boardwalk leading into a small portion of this central wetland, this National Trust/Audubon Society property off Middle Road is one of the few areas where primordial Bermuda lives on in stands of ancient cedars, palmetto trees, giant ferns, red mangroves, and other rare and endemic species. Interpretive signs describe the abundant birdlife, which includes ducks, wrens, cardinals, and catbirds, as well as numerous varieties of insects, reptiles, and toads.

The Botanical Gardens: Bermuda's premier showcase of endemic and imported flora, this beautiful park offers innovatively planned areas (sensory gardens, cacti beds, kitchen gardens, and medicinal plantings), gargantuan rubber trees, rolling lawns, views of the sea, and a well-run Visitors Centre offering souvenirs, books, and snacks.

The rare eastern bluebird (now protected) can be seen nesting in the quiet lawn areas here, along with Bermuda toads, lizards, insects and creepy-crawlies, from mammoth silk spiders to monarch butterflies. Easy to get to in this central location off South Shore and Berry Hill Roads, the Gardens are also home to the Masterworks Museum of Bermuda Art, whose O'Keeffes and Homers were inspired by just such island beauty.

Devonshire Parish

The Arboretum: Somewhat under-rated by locals and visitors, this large rolling tract of meadow-dotted woodland is nonetheless a fantastic place to spot endangered bluebirds, flocks of cardinals, and other species. Hillside fiddlewood groves, avocado trees, whispering pines, newly-planted cedar stands and thick groves of cherry bushes, and carefully-planted quarry gardens make this public park a treat for outdoor enthusiasts. Access is from Middle or Montpelier Roads.

Smith's Parish

Spittal Pond: A circular trail through this premier 69-acre reserve includes a spectacular cliff outlook, a close-up look at pond-life, woodland and spray-splashed coastal trails, as well as a dairy farm. Geological formations along the hurricane-battered shoreline are fascinating. The large pond and its parkland offer an important stop-off for migratory birds, and a nesting and breeding ground for resident ducks, coots, herons, waterfowl, finches, and scores of other resident birds.

Hamilton Parish

Walsingham and Blue Hole Park: This cavern-hollowed region contains the island's oldest hard limestone, as well as several caves and sea-filled lagoons inside a quiet compound of trail-cut cherry forest. Take a dip in the forest swimming hole, which, linked by subterranean tunnels to Castle Harbour, feeds the central lagoon with fish and the occasional turtle.

St. George's Parish

Ferry Reach Park: Cut off from traffic and residential neighborhoods, this isolated tract of land cradles picturesque Whale Bay, and continues east, hugging the wide-open North Shore coast. Forested hillsides, pine groves, mangroves, a walled military graveyard, and a marine pond called Lovers Lake make this one of the best island parks to get away from civilization. Bluebird populations thrive here, and turtles, angelfish, parrotfish, and schools of silver fry frolic in the bay.

The Railway Trail

The Railway Trail, the former rail bed that runs throughout the parishes, today belongs to Bermuda's national parks system, and hiking the trail between some parks is possible. It includes a wide variety of habitats – from forest, mangrove, and golf-course to coastal cliffs – and its mostly flat, cool, noise-free surroundings offer walkers, runners, and mountain-bikers perhaps the best way to get a "behind the scenes" look at natural Bermuda, as well as farms and residential gardens along its path. The Sandys Parish stretch, from the old U.S. Naval Air Station gates to Mangrove Bay, is one of the most scenic, with longtails swooping out from Great Sound cliffs and a plethora of fiery aloes, fragrant oleanders, and cedars in garden estates along the way. Strike out on your own or take a guided tour of the Trail by pedal bike along sections of its end-to-end length.

CITY OF HAMILTON AND PEMBROKE PARISH

At the center of Bermuda, the City of Hamilton—and Pembroke, the parish in which it lies—forms the crux of island life on many levels. Home to the seat of government, including the House of Assembly and the Senate, the city is also the island's main port and its major center for local and international business, the justice system (Supreme and Magistrates' courts and legal offices), civil service, commerce, employment, restaurants, and nightclubs. The island's central ferry and bus terminals, which feed service throughout the parishes, are located here. And because it is where most Bermudians work, shop, and eat, Hamilton, and, by physical association, Pembroke are also the barometers of national mood: Here is where you'll find the political issues of the day hotly discussed, the latest gossip relayed, the merriment of an imminent public holiday bursting forth, or the staid pomp and ceremony of integral events such as Budget Day or the Throne Speech celebrated. It is where you may rub shoulders with the country's richest—the old-money merchants or new-wave CEOs—and poorest, as it is probably the only place on the island where you'll see panhandling (though it is a rarity).

Named for Henry Hamilton, its first mayor, the city's genesis came from the need for a central port, midway between St. George and the Dockyard. It was an issue both of convenience, so Bermudian merchants didn't have to travel the length of the island to get their trading done, and control, so authorities could clamp down on Bermudian vessels, which increasingly were offloading cargoes in western parishes so they could avoid paying heavy duties at

© ROSEMARY JONES

HIGHLIGHTS

(Bermuda Historical Society Museum: Two rooms of antiquities, explained by attendant historians, tell the history of Bermuda in this tiny museum inside the parkside Bermuda National Library (page 34).

(Bermuda National Gallery: Lunchtime lectures, high-profile shows, a respected Biennial, and an internationally renowned collection of artworks make this museum a shot of island culture (page 36).

(Holy Trinity Cathedral: Climb up the 155 winding stairs to the top platform of this church tower for dramatic views of Hamilton on all sides. The historic Anglican landmark's interior is breathtaking, too (page 36).

(The Sessions House: Bermuda's Italianate Parliament building holds the boisterous Friday afternoon House of Assembly meetings upstairs, and staid, bewigged Supreme Court sessions below. All are open to the public (page 39).

(Bull's Head Farmers Market: Know your paw-paw from your plantain? Find out, at this winter-through-spring showcase of island produce, baked goods, Bermuda honey, and arts and crafts (page 57).

(Spanish Point Park: A grassy promontory stretching into the main sea channel into Hamilton, this oft-forgotten park is a neighborhood favorite. Stretch out on a bench, take a dip in one of its North Shore coves, or watch the locals enjoy cards and Cockspur (page 59).

(Fort Hamilton: With a stunning panorama that stretches from Paget across the city and up the Great Sound, this well-preserved fort of the 1870s boasts historic ramparts, cannons, underground passages, and an exotic moat garden. Bagpipers play here in the winter months (page 61).

(Bermuda Underwater Exploration Institute: Join the likes of explorers William Beebe and Jacques Cousteau at this showcase of Bermuda's surrounding deep ocean, which includes a simulated 12,000-foot descent to the sea floor – plus encounters with giant squid. Kids will love the shipwreck treasure, shell collection, and pretend shark cage (page 62).

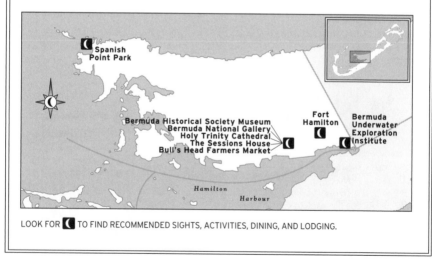

LOOK FOR **(** TO FIND RECOMMENDED SIGHTS, ACTIVITIES, DINING, AND LODGING.

the East End. Hamilton's location made such mischievous tactics far more difficult, and eventually the practice died out. Over two centuries, the city has morphed from a sleepy port for sailing ships into a global corporate powerhouse, rivaling New York and London in many respects. Indeed, it is the exponential growth in international business that has changed the city and its social dynamics more than anything in its history. Today, while quaint china and woolen stores do their business as timelessly as ever from their pastel waterfront facades, multi-billion-dollar deals are being struck in the buildings along the block. The Louis Vuitton bags and Prada suits you see parading down Reid Street at lunchtime are thanks to the latest reinsurance start-up. Gaggles of brokers and actuaries pull their lives in carry-on bags as they move between city meetings and the airport. And that *Survivor*-looking guy tooling along on a beat-up Vespa could actually be the architect of cutting-edge business that protects—financially, anyway—against terrorism or disasters in space. Meanwhile, Pembroke, once the countrified outskirts of the city, is now—with a few neighborhood exceptions—a mostly frantic suburban parish, catching Hamilton's commercial overflow, providing vital housing and schools, and playing noisy hub for public transport and private traffic to other points of the island.

Together, Hamilton and Pembroke contain numerous attractions and sights, sporting activities, entertainment, world-class restaurants, and bars that will form an integral part of a visit to the island. Pembroke's accommodations cater to a variety of budgets, though most are geared to higher-end business travelers. Theatrical events, art show openings, the annual film festival, national parades, and big sporting events are also rooted in Hamilton and Pembroke, allowing you to experience the different moods and offerings of the city and its environs.

PLANNING YOUR TIME

Unless you're staying in the Town of St. George or the West End, each with its own culinary and retail offerings, Hamilton will likely be your first point of reference as you explore Bermuda. If you are a business visitor, you would be wise to stay in outlying Pembroke, namely in the cluster of Pitts Bay hotels and guesthouses, which cater to corporate needs and schedules.

Both the East End (St. George's) and the West End (Sandys, including the Royal Naval Dockyard) are a 30- to 40-minute drive from the city (quicker if you hop on the westbound fast ferry, longer if you board a leisurely pink bus). Hamilton makes a perfect starting place to visit either by public transport or rental scooter, as its main routes run through Pembroke and launch you on your way to all the other parishes.

Sightseeing in Hamilton could take hours or days, depending on your itinerary. Spend time poking around its boutiques and art galleries, visiting a few sights and walking its busy streets, for being amid the daily hustle and bustle is a great way to get a feel for Bermudians and the way they live. You may choose to break up your Hamilton experiences by, for example, spending a morning shopping and sightseeing, then going to the beach or another parish before returning for happy hour and dinner in one of the city's many clubs or restaurants.

Hop on a ferry—around Paget-Warwick or to Dockyard and back—and see the juxtaposition of insurance towers (albeit pastel ones) and age-old landmarks; nowhere is the city's changing skyline as dramatic as from the waterfront. Ferry rides are also a good place to mix with locals and see the smaller islands of Hamilton Harbour and the Pembroke shore.

The city's size means it is entirely walkable if you are able, and, though there are a few steep hills, it is easy to cover over the course of a day. If you have a scooter here, parking may be your biggest frustration; spaces are few and far between, given the city's swelling working population. Bike theft is also a substantial problem.

A scooter tour of Pembroke Parish takes just a few hours, depending on the sights you stop to see—and there are a few fascinating things to see, including Fort Hamilton, the Bermuda Underwater Exploration Institute, Admiralty House Park, and Blackwatch Well. Pembroke has no ferry service, but buses serve various parts of the parish.

Hamilton and Pembroke are generally very safe places to walk. Take a little more caution after dark, as bag-snatchers have been a problem in quieter regions and tourist-heavy areas around Pitts Bay and western Hamilton. North Hamilton's retail and residential areas are as safe as any in the daytime; at night, avoid the area's remote streets, as visitors and locals have been accosted or robbed here.

The City of Hamilton

Bermuda's capital since incorporation in 1793, Hamilton, or "Town" in islanders' vernacular, borders the north shore of a long natural harbor at Bermuda's middle, making it the main port for cruise ships and cargo vessels that cross the Atlantic every week delivering the vital imports of food, clothing, and other goods the island survives on. The city's central location makes it the natural launchpad for explorations east and west through the parishes; no matter where you're staying, you will probably want to take a good look around Hamilton first.

Strict building codes throughout Hamilton's history have retained the city's old-time pastel facades and, for the most part, kept ugly high-rises from springing up. The 21st century is proving a battle for city planners, however, as developers scramble to take advantage of soaring demand for office space for the island's booming international business industry, whose global players are almost exclusively based in Hamilton. Indeed, mammoth insurance towers have reshaped the city's profile from east to west, and while Hamilton's official borders have not expanded, many of its businesses have spilled over in recent years to Pembroke—west along Pitts Bay, and east towards Crow Lane. The city had an estimated 3.5 million square feet of office space in 2006—and that was to jump by a whopping 14 percent in the near future due to planned or ongoing construction.

The building boom has not been confined to commercial space. The somewhat novel concept (for Bermuda) of city living is starting to take root, mostly through necessity, due to sky-high rents and a dire shortage of residential units elsewhere. New, urban-style condominiums are now pushing Hamilton north, providing apartment suites for Bermudians and expatriate city workers, and investment properties for those lucky enough to afford real estate. No tourist accommodations fall within the strict city limits, although there are numerous lodgings in Pembroke, within a 15-minute walk from Hamilton's retail center.

The city is not difficult to navigate, with a straightforward grid system of streets running east-west (Front, Reid, Church, Victoria, Dundonald) and north-south (King, Court, Parliament, Burnaby, Queen, Par-la-Ville, Bermudiana). Several are one-way streets; look carefully at signs before entering on a scooter. The main flow of traffic comes back and forth via Front Street, or down Reid's one-way lanes up Queen and back out of the city via Church Street (also a one-way passage). The actual city borders are defined by King Street to the east, Parson's Lane in the north, Bermudiana Road in the west, and Front Street, along the harborfront, to the south. Within that space are two beautiful and well-used parks—Par-la-Ville and Victoria—and numerous sights, restaurants, museums, galleries and shopping attractions.

Indeed, aside from the nine-to-five weekday, shopping is what brings most people to Hamilton, whether they're locals or visitors. Front Street—long the domain of Bermuda's white power bloc, whose key merchants were nicknamed the "Forty Thieves"—is today becoming a far more pluralistic thoroughfare. Gone are the days of Front Street's beloved multifloor department stores—century-old landmarks

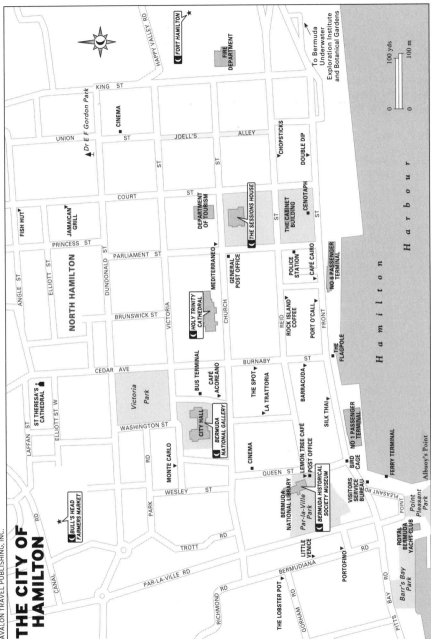

© AVALON TRAVEL PUBLISHING, INC.

THE CITY OF HAMILTON

Trimingham's and Smith's closed in 2005. But new, smaller boutiques like Max Mara and Lusso are drawing residents and their pocketbooks, while events like Harbour Nights, the Front Street Mile, May 24, and the Christmas Boat Parade bring out Bermudians from every parish and background to celebrate annual traditions along the waterfront. Front Street's retailers are mostly geared to tourists, while Reid, Queen, and Church Streets remain the major shopping destinations, connected by the rambling Washington Mall, which is poised for major expansion in 2007.

But don't restrict your visit to the city's most trafficked regions. Long denigrated as "back o' town," culturally vibrant North Hamilton is on the verge of a renaissance, with young entrepreneurs ready to take up offers by government and big business to give the area a boost. Strolling around the region's streets, you can enjoy the West Indian architecture, wooden verandas, pastel cottages, and walled gardens harking back to a quieter time in old Bermuda. Don't miss North Hamilton's boisterous clubs, retail bargains, or popular eateries, either.

SIGHTS

Hamilton's small size means there are no vastly different "neighborhoods" to explore. Sights and attractions are scattered throughout the city blocks. North Hamilton is the only really distinct section, mainly because it has not been privy to major development to date and has therefore retained more of its quaint original architecture than other areas.

Albuoy's Point

Busy Albuoy's Point is the wedge of parkland behind the Ferry Terminal and the Bank of Bermuda HSBC headquarters off Front Street. Mature baygrape trees shade the little patch of grass and benches surround the harborfront dockside—the city's main boat pickup spot for day and evening charters, including snorkeling and glass-bottom boat excursions, sailing trips, and carnival-style cruises. Public toilets are located on Point Pleasant Road, the lane linking the park to Front Street, which also has a few souve-

---

THE BIRD CAGE

Front Street's odd-looking blue and white "Bird Cage" at the junction with Queen Street has become a beloved island symbol, thanks to traffic police who, over the years, have posed for thousands of holiday snaps from the kiosk in their Bermuda shorts.

While the platform, which acts as a traffic island, *does* look like Tweety Bird's hangout, it actually got its name from a former City of Hamilton official, Geoffrey Bird, who in the 1950s devised its design to keep "bobbies" safe while directing traffic. Though it's become nothing more than a tourist-pleasing gimmick in the 21st century, the Bird Cage remains a Hamilton icon, even celebrated in the form of gold charm jewelry.

---

nir shops and charter tour company offices. On the park's western side sits the salmon-colored **Royal Bermuda Yacht Club,** its members-only clubhouse and marina the headquarters of the King Edward VII Gold Cup Match-Racing Competition and the biannual **Newport-to-Bermuda Ocean Race,** which celebrated its centennial in June 2006. Across the harbor is government-owned White's Island, where Bermuda youngsters enjoy swimming and sailing summer courses; it is also the venue for fireworks in public celebrations such as the Christmas Boat Parade. Linking to Albuoy's Point via a thin stretch of land on the north side of the Yacht Club is Pembroke's **Barr's Bay Park,** another shady lawn for watching yachts come and go up the harbor. You can also access this park from Pitts Bay Road.

◖ Bermuda Historical Society Museum

On the edge of Par-la-Ville Park in a trio of rooms inside the Bermuda National Library is the charming little Bermuda Historical Society Museum (Queen St., tel. 441/295-2487, 9:30 A.M.–3:30 P.M. Mon.–Sat., admission free). The museum is run by knowledgeable volunteers, including published historians, of the Bermuda

Historical Society, a nonprofit group dating back to 1895 that promotes interest in the island's past. Par-la-Ville, the 1814 building that now houses the library, was once a gracious Georgian homestead, like many that lined Hamilton's streets in the 19th century. It has remained intact, its wooden veranda today overlooking the crush of traffic on Reid Street. Outside, the landmark giant rubber tree also survives; it was planted in 1847 by merchant William Perot, who built and lived in the house. The museum's prize artifacts include original "Hogge" money; 18th-century cedar furniture including a cradle and prayer chair; silver flatware made in Bermuda; oil portraits of key figures, such as the island's founder, Admiral Sir George Somers; and ceramics and glassware that once belonged to local sea captains. Look at the exquisite etched-glass hurricane shades in the dining room and the carved palmetto seats of the Queen Anne cedar chairs.

Par-la-Ville Park

Beautifully landscaped Par-la-Ville Park (open 8 A.M.–sunset daily, admission free) is the city's best used green space, popular with office workers for outdoor lunches in the spring and fall (summer's torpid heat and humidity tend to discourage anyone wearing a suit from leaving the comfort of air-conditioning for more than a few minutes). Mosaic pathways lead through the oasis, connecting Queen Street with Par-la-Ville Road, which lies parallel to the west (there's a delightful moongate entrance on this side). A third entrance-exit runs through Par-la-Ville carpark from Church Street to the north. Rock gardens, flower beds, trellises, pergolas, and shady mature trees can be found throughout, as well as wooden benches. The park was once the private garden of the Perot family, and merchant William Perot's son, William Bennet Perot, served as the island's postmaster 1818–62. He designed Bermuda's first stamp, the circular Perot stamp, of which there are only 11 in the world today. Visit the quaint **Perot Post Office** (11 Queen St., tel. 441/292-9052, 8 A.M.–5 P.M. Mon.–Fri.), still a working post office on the park's eastern border.

© ROSEMARY JONES

Par-la-Ville Park provides an oasis at Hamilton's center.

City Hall and Arts Centre

Hamilton's central landmark and public gathering spot, the City Hall and Arts Centre (Church St., tel. 441/292-1234, 9 A.M.–5 P.M. Mon.–Fri., admission free) is the masterpiece of legendary Bermudian architect Wil Onions, who was renowned for adapting cottage aesthetics to almost every project he undertook. Completed in 1960, the building, whose design is basically an oversized cottage with a slate roof and tower, was inspired by Stockholm's city hall. Though Onions died before its completion, the whitewashed structure embodies his aim of simple lines and traditional features. Its 90-foot tower supports a distinctive weathervane sporting a bronze rendition of the shipwrecked *Sea Venture.* Life-size bronze statues of children by Bermudian sculptor Desmond Fountain play in fountains set in a water-lily pond. City Hall serves many functions. It is home to the offices of the Corporation of Hamilton on the ground floor, where portraits of mayors and Queen Elizabeth II hang on the stairwell. The main theater on the building's west side hosts performing arts, including dance recitals, theatrical presentations, Christmas pantomimes, and shows of the Bermuda International Film Festival. Up the grand cedar stairs is the **Bermuda National Gallery** and the **Bermuda Society of Arts.** Outside, public performances like choir recitals, Christmas marching bands, and occasional government press conferences are held on City Hall's steps.

◖ Bermuda National Gallery

Home to a fine permanent collection of artworks, and host of regularly changing shows of work by contemporary local artists, Bermuda National Gallery (Church St., upstairs in the City Hall and Arts Centre, tel. 441/295-9428, fax 441/295-2055, www.bng .bm or www.bermudanationalgallery.com, 10 A.M.–4 P.M. Mon.–Sat., closed holidays, admission free) was created in 1992 to promote public education and art appreciation through its national collection, exhibitions, and outreach programs. The original core collection comprised works of European masters—Gainsborough, Murillo, Reynolds—gifted by Bermudian Hereward T. Watlington. The Watlington Collection has since been joined by African art, a provocative collection of black and white photographs by Bermudian Richard Saunders, and Hale Woodruff linocuts. The gallery hosts seasonal exhibitions featuring artworks by international and local artists, including the popular summer-long Bacardi Limited Biennial every two years. Join a free tour of the gallery Thursday mornings at 10:30 A.M. The BNG also hosts a regular program of films, seminars, cocktail parties, and evening lectures by visiting curators and art historians, and free lunchtime lectures on Wednesdays (12:30–1:30 P.M.) by Bermudian historians and artists.

◖ Holy Trinity Cathedral

It took me until my 40th birthday to climb the 155 stairs to the top of "The Cathedral," as Holy Trinity Cathedral (Church St., tel.

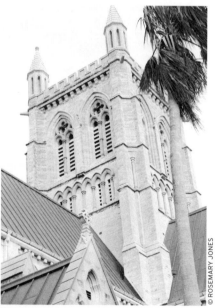

The tower of Holy Trinity Cathedral makes for a panoramic viewing spot of the city.

"GUILTY – WITH AN EXPLANATION"

There can't be a better slice of island life than an afternoon spent hearing the convoluted excuses, remonstrations, and final verdicts of **Plea Court**. The special session of Magistrates Court (23 Parliament St., tel. 441/295-5151, ext. 1230), held weekdays at 2:30 P.M., brings out every segment of the population to answer to accused crimes, both trivial and serious. Intoxication, shoplifting, handbag-snatching, assault, swearing in public – the litany of "summary-only" offenses can rarely be tried in Supreme Court and must be dealt with by a magistrate.

The courtroom exudes an almost Dickensian aura as defendants are called one by one to enter a plea to their respective charges. If they choose "not guilty," the court adjourns the case for reviews, social reports, or to fix a trial date. But it is the "guilty" pleas to trivial offenses that are most entertaining, as defendants of all social standings let their creative juices flow as they try to win a lighter sentence or fine before the magistrate's bench. "Guilty – with an explanation" is almost always the prelude to a hilarious yarn; it's met by anticipatory sniggers all around. If he's had a good lunch or it's Friday afternoon, the presiding magistrate may join the fun with snappy comebacks or personal anecdotes that delight the press box, lawyers, prosecutor, public, even the other defendants awaiting their turns. Of course, a crotchety magistrate can put a damper on the jovial proceedings just as easily.

441/292-4033, fax 441/292-5421, 8 A.M.–5 P.M. daily, admission free) is called by Bermudians, and as soon as I'd reached the tower's eye-popping view over Hamilton, I wished I hadn't waited so long. It's one of the best ways to really get a sense of the city and surrounding parishes—like looking at Manhattan from the bird's-eye view of the Empire State Building. To the north lies Government House, Pembroke Marsh, and the North Shore shipping channel;

to the east the House of Assembly, King Edward VII Memorial Hospital, and the freight docks; to the west, City Hall, Hamilton's city grid, the Great Sound, and the Dockyard; and to the south, Front Street, White's Island, and the harbor. The neo-Gothic Anglican church, whose interior has stunning stained-glass windows, flying arches, lady and warrior chapels, and a carved altar screen, was originally called Trinity Church. Its first cornerstone was laid in 1844, though construction suffered numerous setbacks over subsequent decades, including an arson fire in 1884 that forced authorities to tear down the whole structure and start again. Work began again in 1886, with imported stone from Nova Scotia, Scotland, and Indiana used with Bermuda's own limestone. Plans by Scottish architect William Hay called for a spire to rise above the 144-foot tower, but these were scrapped after various delays. The Cathedral Tower was finally completed in 1905 and is now open to the public (10 A.M.–4 P.M. Mon.–Fri., $5 adults, $2 students, children under five free). The climb—up a slightly claustrophobic spiral, followed by regular stairs to the terrace—is not for the completely unfit, but you can take breaks along the way on two spacious landings. Watch out for the piles of pigeon dung toward the end.

Victoria Park

Anyone interested in Bermuda botany should take a stroll through Victoria Park (open 8 A.M.–sunset daily, admission free), where shaded winding paths move between beds of decorative flora and mature trees and shrubs. Scented gardenia bushes, golden acacia trees, even towering Norfolk pines have found root here in this small but pretty park leading to the "back o' town." On its main lawn is a bandstand, where Sunday Concerts in the Park, sponsored by Butterfield's Bank through the summer, alternatively bring out jazz lovers, classical fans, and rock 'n' rollers. Look for ads in *The Royal Gazette*. The park is bordered by Victoria Street, Dundonald Street, Cedar Avenue, and Washington Street. There are public washrooms located here, but they

NORTH HAMILTON'S REVIVAL

"Back o' town" has long been castigated as a drug-ridden, crime-plagued neighborhood with nothing of value to Bermuda travelers. But that reputation may soon be a thing of the past as the culturally vibrant neighborhood stakes its future on celebrating the island's black culture and its residents' own architectural, musical, and political achievements.

Court Street is the oft-troubled artery that runs up from the harborfront – and rival Front Street – through the heart of North Hamilton. Like New York's Harlem, its name has become something far greater than a simple geographical locator in the public imagination, a moniker that, for black Bermudians especially, is symbolic of a society ignored during decades of white political and economic control. For many white residents, by contrast, the area is a complete enigma. Long linked to drug-selling, robberies, and dangerous elements (though the truth is those problems affect every parish), Court Street and North Hamilton are often avoided as a result.

In 2005, the energetic **Uptown Market Association** (www.uptown.bm) began moving to change those perceptions, with ambitious plans to reinvigorate North Hamilton with major cultural public events, a museum or two, new business ventures, plus initiatives to encourage residents to preserve some of the most historic and beautiful architecture on the island. Indeed, Tourism Minister Dr. Ewart Brown likes to call the neighborhood

"Bermuda's French Quarter." Between King Street to the east, Parson's Road to the north, Cedar Avenue to the west, and Victoria Street to the south, North Hamilton boasts both a vibrant business center and quaint residential lanes, where gingerbread architecture, pastel homes, and quiet walled gardens have been left so far undisturbed by the trend of rampant development. The region counts scores of clothing and shoe stores – offering bargains not found in the center of town – salons, bakeries, nightclubs, a jazz club, and numerous popular restaurants, which attract patrons from across the island for fresh fish and West Indian cuisine.

"My roots are here – my grandfather built the First Church of God on Angle Street, so I do have a heritage that binds me to North Hamilton," says Elmore Warren, the association's indefatigable chairman, who also heads up a Court Street-based television station, Fresh TV, and runs an entrepreneurial company called Fresh Creations. "I grew up here and now I work here, so I have a self-interest in figuring out ways to bring value to this area," he adds. "And I don't mean selling it off to a developer. Unity is what I would like to see happen – to get the community feeling part of this whole growth process. Changes won't happen wholesale or overnight, and people don't want it that way."

Court Street's stigma in recent history stems back to 1977 when televised race riots saw a

tend to be used mostly by homeless people who sleep on the park benches.

St. Theresa's Cathedral

Ornately contrasting its Anglican counterpart across town, Bermuda's Roman Catholic St. Theresa's Cathedral (13 Elliott St., tel. 441/292-0607 or 441/292-8486, sttheresas@northrock .bm, 6:30 A.M.–7 P.M. daily, admission free) was built in 1932 and named for St. Theresa of Lisieux, "The Little Flower." The church's tower was not finished until 1947, and 20 years later, St. Theresa's became a cathedral

when Bermuda officially was named a diocese. St. Theresa's boasts the largest weekly attendance of worshipers on the island, with numerous masses and evening services. The Portuguese-Bermudian community's religious *festas*, which honor certain saints, use the cathedral as the base for colorful spectacles. One of the best known is the procession of Santo Cristo, when hundreds gather at St. Theresa's on the fifth Sunday after Easter seeking miracles for the sick and poor during a march through the city. The cathedral's gift shop (tel. 441/292-0416, 9:30 A.M.–3:30 P.M.

showdown between crowds of fire-bombing black youth and armed police. But residents say they are tired of disparaging attitudes toward their neighborhood, and they feel North Hamilton's time for rejuvenation has come.

"This is the place where cultural tourism should begin," says Warren. "This is the place where revolutionaries were born – the black heroes of Bermuda, the ones who fought for equal rights and desegregation." A plaza at Union and Dundonald Street is dedicated to the legendary E. F. Gordon, a firebrand lawyer and black-rights pioneer of the 1950s, who rallied black Bermudians and sowed the seeds for the breakthrough Theatre Boycott in 1959, which saw segregation's barriers fall in hotels, restaurants, churches, and other public institutions. North Hamilton's **Pembroke Youth Centre** nurtured Bermuda's only Olympic medalist, boxer Clarence Hill. And the first black press, the historic *Bermuda Recorder,* was also based here.

The Uptown Market Association's hopes got a boost in 2005, when the government declared North Hamilton an "Empowerment Zone." In 2006, Bank of Bermuda HSBC – whose black CEO, Phillip Butterfield, also grew up in the area – teamed with the island's Small Business Development Corporation to help North Hamilton entrepreneurs. The partnership offers financial advice, financing arrangements, and business and management expertise – all elements that for many years were sorely unavailable to black business people in Bermuda.

A visit to North Hamilton should include a walk around the architectural history of Angle Street, Elliott Street, Ewing Street, and Princess Street, where Victorian row housing, wooden verandas, and cute-as-a-button cottages can be found around every corner. Court Street between Victoria and Dundonald Streets is home to a wonderful array of fashion boutiques, music and shoe stores, and several food outlets. Drop into **Dub City Records & Boutique** (46 Court St., tel. 441/292-6775), where owner and manager Donovan McKoy also runs Palm Rock Entertainment, a thriving talent agency and artist-management business across the West Indies. Don't miss the **Caribbean Food Market** (47 Court St., tel. 441/293-9260), where specialty items like cassava, coconut milk, yams, and green seasoning are available.

Indeed, North Hamilton's culinary offerings alone are enough to tempt visitors. **Zaki Bakery** (40 Court St., tel. 441/292-8250) is famous for its birthday cakes, pies, breads, and pastries. **Fish Hut** (Court St., at Angle St. junction, tel. 441/292-3267) and **Fish & Tings** (45 Angle St., tel. 441/292-7389) satisfy seafood-lovers. Crowds jam **Jamaican Grill** (32 Court St., tel. 441/296-6577) for jerk chicken, oxtail, and brown stew. And **Art Mel's Spicy Dicy** (9 St. Monica's Rd., tel. 441/295-3965) cooks up fish cakes extraordinaire.

Mon.–Sat.) sells rosaries, bibles, cards, candles, and English and Portuguese books.

◖ The Sessions House

From the harbor, the Italianate Sessions House (21 Parliament St., tel. 441/292-7408, fax 441/292-2006, 9 A.M.–12:30 P.M. and 2–5 P.M. daily, admission free) is the landmark building that defines Hamilton; like Toronto's C.N. Tower or the Statue of Liberty, the impressive structure identifies the city's skyline. Built in 1819, the building's tower was added decades later to celebrate Queen Victoria's golden jubilee. Today, sitting atop Parliament Street, the Sessions House contains Supreme Court on its ground floor, and the House of Assembly—one of the oldest parliaments in the world—upstairs. Parliament sits every Friday throughout the winter and spring, breaking for the summer and reconvening after November's ceremonious Throne Speech, government's promised to-do list which is read by the governor and attended by members of Parliament (MPs) in their formal finest. Like the British House of Commons, members are seated according to political party, with opponents facing each other across the floor. A speaker, sporting traditional black robes and a wig, oversees the proceedings, which count at least a couple of all-nighters every year—probably due to the fact there is no strict cutoff for debates, nor time limits on speeches. Heckling opponents while they are speaking is termed "interpolating," and allowed within reason, provided hecklers do it from their appointed seat. Famous debates have covered everything from whether to allow motor cars onto the island back in the 1940s (the yes vote finally held sway in 1946), to the Golden Arches in 1995 (a move to bring in McDonald's and other fast-food franchises was voted down). Feel free to watch the frivolity from the public gallery during parliamentary sessions (10 A.M. Fri., Nov.–June). You can also visit the empty gallery to inspect its cedarwood, portraits, and the speaker's silver mace any weekday, when sergeant-at-arms Albert Fox is happy to talk about the House of Assembly and show visitors around. Winter walking tours (Nov.–March) organized by the Cultural Affairs Department (tel. 441/292-9447) also stop in here.

The Cabinet Building and the Cenotaph

South of the Sessions House sits the Cabinet Building (105 Front St., tel. 441/292-5501, fax 441/292-8397, open 9 A.M.–5 P.M. Mon.–Fri., admission free), where the "Upper House," or Senate, meets every Wednesday morning at 10 A.M. (Nov.–July). The imposing two-story building, completed in 1833, is home to the Premier's office and headquarters of his cabinet of government ministers, whose flashy cars are usually parked outside. The Cabinet lawn is the venue of the annual November Throne Speech, which the Governor delivers before a packed crowd of dignitaries and MPs in hats, topcoats, and tails; Bermuda Regiment soldiers, band, and corps of drums; as well hundreds of public onlookers and curious tourists. Prince Andrew did the honors during a 2005 visit to the island. Along the lawn's south perimeter stands the 1920 Cenotaph, a limestone monument honoring Bermudian soldiers killed in the two World Wars and other international conflicts.

A solemn Remembrance Day ceremony is held here each November 11, when surviving war veterans parade down Front Street, wreaths of symbolic poppies are laid at the Cenotaph, and a gun salute is fired by the Bermuda Regiment. The day is a public holiday on the island, and hundreds attend the event.

ENTERTAINMENT AND EVENTS

Hamilton is the staging point for numerous big local and international events throughout the year. The city also has a busy nightlife, particularly in the summer, when visitor crowds swell the bars and clubs. Winter can be very quiet during the week, but you can usually count on Bermudians to party on Friday and Saturday nights.

Bermuda Festival of the Performing Arts

The New Year brings the Bermuda Festival of the Performing Arts (tel. 441/295-1291, www.bermudafestival.org), a two-month cultural showcase of top international acts, from contemporary dance troupes and circuses to ballet and orchestral performances. Several venues are used, but most performances take place in the evenings at Hamilton City Hall and Arts Centre.

Bermuda International Film Festival

March's Bermuda International Film Festival (tel. 441/293-3456, fax 441/293-7769, www.bermudafilmfest.com) adds an unusual touch of bohemia to Hamilton's normally conservative ambience, as black-garbed twentysomethings from Tribeca and Hollywood wander around incongruously between screenings. The showcase has made a name for itself on the world's celluloid circuit and draws not only award-winning indie directors from the United States, Africa, and eastern Europe, but international film financiers intrigued by Bermuda's offshore benefits. BIFF has also become a celebrity magnet, with appearances in the past by resident Michael Douglas, director Jim Sheridan,

© ROSEMARY JONES

Gombeys incorporate Native American dance and tradition into their performances.

Willem Dafoe, and *The Green Mile*'s Michael Clarke Duncan.

Harbour Nights

Held on Wednesday evenings 6–9 P.M. throughout the high season, this crowded street festival includes arts and crafts stalls, bouncy castles and train rides for kids, alfresco food, and live performances by Bermuda bands and gombey troupes. The fun takes place on Front Street, which is closed to traffic between Parliament and Par-la-Ville Streets. Reid Street is also shut down for the evening.

Bermuda Day Parade

The Bermuda Day Parade on May 24 is the island's version of Caribbean Carnival. Following a historic half-marathon, which runs from the West End through the Front Street's cheering crowds to a Pembroke finish, an hours-long parade of majorettes, gombeys, decorated floats, dance troupes, and other community performers winds through the city. Families stake out their seats the night before to get a good viewing spot, and then camp out on sidewalks most of the day.

Other Events

The **Queen's Birthday Parade** in June brings colonial pomp and ceremony to Front Street to mark the British monarch's special day. A gun salute is followed by a marching parade by the Bermuda Regiment Band and Corps of Drums.

In December, kids and parents pack Front and Church Streets for the festive **Santa Claus Parade,** which features colorful illuminated floats, parish majorettes, gombeys, and Santa riding on a vintage fire engine. "Elves" throw out bags of candy to onlookers. The **Christmas Boat Parade** is also a holiday must-see—a magical parade around Hamilton Harbour by yachts, barges, charter boats, and pleasure craft decked out in cleverly themed light displays. The best viewing is from Front Street restaurant terraces and along Harbour Road.

Bars

Lunch spot by day, **Lemon Tree Cafe** (7 Queen St., tel. 441/292-0235) is *the* spot to be on Friday nights, when its hugely popular happy hour (5–9:30 P.M. Fri. high season only) takes flight. A DJ spins a cool vibe as a mixed-age crowd packs the back parkside patio for sangria, free gourmet nibbles, or mulled wine when the weather turns.

Little Venice Wine Bar (32 Bermudiana Rd., tel. 441/295-3503, noon–1 A.M. Mon.–Fri., 6:30 P.M.–1 A.M. Sat.) is an offshoot of the popular adjoining restaurant, attracting a more mature hip crowd than other venues' twentysomethings, who come for fine wines, Cosmopolitans, and other cocktails. Patrons can sit at tables indoors or out on the patio.

Friday night happy hour brings regulars to **Coconut Rock** (Williams House, 20 Reid St., tel. 441/292-1043, 11:30 A.M.–3 A.M. Mon.–Sat., 6 P.M.–3 A.M. Sun.), where music videos play loudly on large screens, and clientele can partake of blue cheese burgers and other main

A NEW-LOOK HARBORFRONT?

Hamilton's waterfront has been the focus of much debate over recent years, with assorted architects, city planners, and creative members of the public venturing forth plans on how to make the area more people-friendly.

Former premier and millionaire developer Sir John Swan upped the ante in 2005 when he went as far as hiring architects to draw up a full blueprint of his vision for the harborfront area – one that would do away with the noisy cargo docks and replace them with marinas, boardwalks, and a casino.

While locals like the sound of a harborside promenade, reaction was mixed to the casino and container port relocation; the main problem with the latter is that a huge section of the island's coastline would have to be destroyed to accommodate the docks elsewhere.

While nothing is even close to being decided, the proposal spurred public brainstorming, and several rival plans were hatched, including one by the Corporation of Hamilton. Whether any drastic revamp of the waterfront will actually go ahead – and when that might happen – remains to be seen.

menu items, or the Yashi Bat, a separate sushi room in the back.

Café Cairo (93 Front St., tel. 441/295-5155, cafecairo@northrock.bm, noon–3 A.M. daily) is *the* place everyone goes for after-hours schmoozing—including staff from many other Hamilton restaurants. While the popular eatery has won raves for its menu, it is the bar's cool vibe that attracts the city's most devoted night owls. A snack menu of Middle Eastern dishes is laid on 10 P.M.–3 A.M.

The Docksider Pub & Restaurant (121 Front St., tel. 441/296-3333, www.dockies.com, 11 A.M.–2 A.M. daily) is one of the hot spots among Bermuda's youth, attracted by reasonable drink prices and pub grub. The popular sports bar opens for special games shown live on its big-screen TVs, so it's not unusual for bleary-eyed expats to head in here at 8 o'clock on a Saturday morning to catch a U.K. soccer showdown.

Front Street's **Flanagan's Irish Pub** (Emporium Building, 69 Front St., tel. 441/295-8299) and **Pickled Onion** (53 Front St., tel. 441/295-2263, www.thepickledonion.com) are both popular among both locals and visitors for nighttime carousing, and both have panoramic terraces overlooking the harbor. Flanagan's is an especially good venue for viewing the finish line of January's Front Street Mile.

Tucked down under Burnaby Hill, **Hog Penny** (5 Burnaby Hill, tel. 441/292-2534, www.hogpennypub.com, 11:30 A.M.–1 A.M. daily) is the kind of place you want to seek out when you're craving a bit of British pub life and a plate of bangers and mash. Live music is usually on the menu, too, during the summer.

Live jazz, cheap drinks, and a laid-back vibe keep the regulars returning to back o' town **Hubie's Bar** (10 Angle St., tel. 441/293-9287, Friday jazz 7–10 P.M.), where Friday nights see a packed crowd. Go early to snag one of the room's few banquettes and then people-watch all night amid the relaxed, friendly atmosphere. There are free table nibbles, but no food is served, so eat first or plan on a late dinner elsewhere.

Clubs

Splash (12 Bermudiana Rd., tel. 441/296-3849 or 441/296-3368, 5 P.M.–3 A.M. Mon.–Fri., 9 P.M.–3 A.M. Sat. and Sun.), opened in 2004, is the newest kid on the nightclub block—with lines down the block on Friday nights through the summer. The Euro-style disco, with DJs and a lounge-like interior aims for a well-dressed crowd (guys, no sneakers, jeans, or baggy pants). Guests must be 21 or over, and there's a $20 cover charge Fri. and Sat., which includes one free drink. Diners at next-door Portofino restaurant get complimentary admission.

Ozone (69 Front St., tel. 441/292-3379 or 441/333-5669) is Bermuda's largest nightclub, its Bond-like glass elevator swooshing patrons up from a ground-level Front Street mall to its bars and dance floors. A popular place for weekend late-nights, private parties, and salsa nights—with free instruction—on Thursdays, the club conveniently has a taxi stand on the street outside. The club offers free entry before midnight, and a decent dress code is strictly enforced.

An open-air plaza becomes a late-night dance floor at **Square One** (Bermuda House Ln., tel. 441/296-3849, 5 P.M.–3 A.M. Mon.–Sat.), where early-evening tapas and sushi give way to pure nightclub after 10 P.M. There is seating outdoors or inside, behind Tuscany restaurant.

The Captain's Lounge (Reid St., at Washington Ln., tel. 441/293-9546) and **Casey's Cocktail Lounge** (25 Queen St., tel. 441/293-9549) both attract a purely Bermudian crowd, especially on Friday afternoons and public holiday weekends.

North Hamilton's **Swinging Doors** (29 Court St., tel. 441/293-9267) and **Spinning Wheel** (33 Court St., tel. 441/292-7799) are busy weekend hangouts. Avoid walking in the neighborhood's quieter regions alone at night.

Cinemas

Hamilton has two cinemas, both of which show major box-office releases and the occasional Oscar-nominated indie. Twice-nightly showings, plus weekend matinees, keep movies around for a week or two. Occasionally, films will then move east or west to the island's other two cinemas. Tickets can be purchased at the door or via www.boxoffice.bm.

The Little Theatre (30 Queen St., tel. 441/292-2135, box-office hours 2–9:30 P.M. Mon.–Fri., 1:30–9:30 P.M. Sat. and Sun.) is so minuscule, it's smaller than some home theaters. The funereal flowers occasionally placed before the old-fashioned stage curtains are off-putting, but the popcorn and candy are good. Besides, it's the film that counts. Popular Little Theatre films often head east after their run in the city to Southside Cinema in St. David's.

The Liberty Theatre (49 Union Square, Victoria St., tel. 441/291-2035, www.liberty neptune.com) is a larger venue with a regular-sized screen, though its technology still lags behind the average North American multiplex.

Liberty films usually head west afterwards to sister cinema the Neptune, at Dockyard.

Theater, Music, and Dance

Plays, musicals, dance recitals, and other live performances are held in Hamilton throughout the year. Check *The Royal Gazette* and *Bermuda Sun* listings and Arts pages to see what's on. Schedules and online tickets are available on **www.boxoffice.bm.**

Daylesford Theatre (Washington St., opposite Victoria Park, tel. 441/292-0848, bar 441/295-5584 from 5 P.M. Mon.–Fri., www.bmds.bm) is headquarters of the Bermuda Musical and Dramatic Society (B.M.D.S.), which stages regular plays throughout the year, as well as the popular Christmas pantomime at City Hall.

The **City Hall and Arts Centre** is the island's major venue for theatricals and performing arts, including dance, theater, and orchestral performances, including many of the international acts in for the Bermuda Festival of the Performing Arts (Jan.–March).

SHOPPING

The bulk of Hamilton's retail stores are found along the length of Reid Street, Front Street, Queen and Burnaby Streets, as well as Court Street in North Hamilton. There are also several malls, which link these major thoroughfares and are packed with boutiques and shops of all kinds. These include the Walker Arcade (between Front and lower Reid), which also links to the Old Cellar (off Front Street); the Emporium (Front Street east of the Flagpole); the Bermudiana Arcade (off Queen Street); Windsor Place (off Queen Street), and the large Washington Mall (with two floors of shops between Reid and Church Streets).

Hamilton stores increasingly are opening at 10 A.M., though a few still open as early as 9 A.M. Most stay open until 5 or 5:30 P.M. Special Christmas season (Fri. night) and summer-long Harbour Nights (Wed. only) hours mean some Front Street, Queen Street, and Reid Street stores stay open later. Virtually all retail stores, save a few smaller, homespun outlets, accept major credit cards.

Books

Bermuda Book Store (3 Queen St., near Front Street junction, tel. 441/295-3698, www.bermudabookstore.com) has come under new ownership in the past few years, but it remains in the historic building it has inhabited for decades. A great selection of current and rare Bermuda books, plus new fiction and the island's best kids' section, is the drawing card.

As its name suggests, **Washington Mall Magazines** (lower level, Washington Mall, tel. 441/292-7420, www.bdabooks.bm) carries a vast assortment of popular weekly, monthly, or semiannual publications, from both North America and Britain. Its Bermuda book section, children's favorites, and travel guide shelves are also well stocked.

Located upstairs in the sprawling Phoenix Centre, **The Bookmart** (3 Reid St., tel. 441/295-3838, ext. 412, www.phoenixstores.bm) is a wonderful place to while away a few hours searching for the latest best-seller, or browsing the large selection of Bermuda publications, coffee-table books, cookbooks, and popular kids' series, like the U.K.'s Mr. Men collection.

Twice-Told Tales (34 Parliament St., tel. 441/296-1995) has a good selection of secondhand fiction, nonfiction, Bermuda books, and children's editions. Lawyers, police, and MPs from nearby courts and Parliament buildings gather here for coffee. There's also Internet access.

The Metaphysical Book Shop (61 Reid St., at Court St., tel. 441/295-5683) specializes in books and CDs on meditation, yoga, and spiritual healing. Incense sticks are also sold here.

Clothes and Shoes

While thousands of Bermudians beef up their wardrobes on overseas shopping sprees every

---

BARGAIN BUYS

Bargain-hunters scouting for great buys on designer labels, shoes, or cutting-edge fashions will be disappointed in Bermuda. The island carries such a limited and expensive range of clothing and footwear that even the average Bermudian travels abroad a couple of times a year to load up their wardrobes in U.S. and Canadian malls – a longtime trend the Bermuda Chamber of Commerce tries to combat with its "Buy Bermuda" campaign.

Of course, if you're simply in the mood for fashion shopping, and not too worried about comparative price tags, you will find plenty to spend on. The good news is that Hamilton's once-stuffy though beloved department stores have either gone bankrupt or are being forced to compete – both by Bermudians' foreign retail therapy and the advent of designer boutiques, which are springing up along Front and Reid Streets. **Mambo** (12 Walker Arcade, tel. 441/296-9797) stocks racks of Dolce & Gabbana and Diesel; **Lusso** (51 Front St., tel. 441/295-292) proffers Prada and Jimmy Choo – including coveted "It" bags

that mainland boutiques don't get. **Benetton, Stefanel, Kenneth Cole, Nine West, French Connection, Longchamp, Gucci,** and **Max Mara** all have stores, most opened in the last five years.

True good buys, however, are to be had in perfumes, European cosmetics, jewelry (mostly conservatively designed gold and silver), and fine china and crystal. Wedgwood, Kosta Boda, Orrefors, Hermès, Royal Doulton, and Limoges can be found at several Front Street retailers, at prices competitive with, or better than, those in the United States. Scottish woolens and hand-embroidered Irish linens, which are hard to find in North America or very expensive, are also worth stocking up on.

Although they used to be sold in Hamilton, duty-free items are now only available at **Bermuda Duty Free** (Departures Hall, tel. 441/293-2870), the retail outlet at Bermuda International Airport. Popular merchandise includes the island's hallmark Goslings Black Seal Rum, rum cakes, Outerbridge's sherry peppers, perfumes, and cigarettes.

year, there's still plenty to please fashionistas in Hamilton's stores, In fact, there's more now than ever, thanks to the arrival of popular boutiques such as Max Mara, Nine West, and Kenneth Cole. Be warned that variety and sizes are often lacking, however, compared to larger urban centers, and prices are higher due to import duties.

For that Pucci scarf or little black dress you simply must have, join local cocktail mavens at **Cecile** (15 Front St. West, tel. 441/295-1311), purveyor of the latest European catwalk designs including evening and corporate suits, slacks, bathing costumes, and handbags. Sister stores are **Boutique C.C.** (Front St. West, tel. 441/295-3935) and the ultra-chic **Lusso** (51 Front St., tel. 441/295-2928).

Popular men's stores include **Aston & Gunn** (2 Reid St., tel. 441/295-4866), **A. S. Cooper Man** (29 Front St., tel. 441/295-3961, www.coopersbermuda.com), **English Sports Shop**'s Nautica boutique (49 Front St., tel. 441/295-2672), and **Kenneth Cole** (25 Reid St., tel. 441/295-0022).

Bermudians head to **Calypso** (45 Front St., tel. 441/295-2112) every spring for their new bathing suits—from string bikinis to racing backs. **Makin' Waves** (75 Front St., tel. 441/292-4609) is another favorite swimsuit supplier for men and women.

For shoes, **Kenneth Cole** (25 Reid St., tel. 441/295-0022), **Quattro** (12 Walker Arcade, tel. 441/295-9815), and **Giorgio Beneti** (44 Reid St., tel. 441/296-8097) have the most stylish selections.

Teens and club-hoppers like **Stefanel** (12 Walker Arcade, tel. 441/295-5698), **French Connection** (Reid St. at Washington Ln., tel. 441/295-2112), and **Zig-Zag Too** (31 Dundonald St., tel. 441/295-0785).

Perfume and Cosmetics

Several stores sell well-priced, designer perfumes and cosmetics. Newest to open is the **MAC Boutique** (53 Front St., tel. 441/295-8843), staffed by six professional artists. The large department store **Gibbons Company** (21 Reid St., tel. 441/295-0022) carries most of the major cosmetics lines, at U.S.-competitive prices. **A. S. Cooper's Cosmetics & Fragrances** (7 Front St. West, tel. 441/296-8816) is a new dedicated boutique with most major brands, including Clarins, Clinique, Estée Lauder, and La Prairie.

The Perfume Shop (23 Front St., tel. 441/295-0571), directly across from the Ferry Terminal, carries Hermès, Van Cleef & Arpel, Calvin Klein, and Dolce & Gabbana. Perfume specialists **Peniston Brown & Co.** (23 Front St., tel. 441/295-0570) has the island's widest selection, with brand names such as Givenchy, Yves St. Laurent, Marc Jacobs, and Prada.

Gifts and Souvenirs

Pulp and Circumstance (10 Queen St., tel. 441/292-9586) is a mecca for soaps and bath products, bags, stuffed toys, novelty items, baby shower gifts, and beautiful wrapping paper and greeting cards.

The Island Shop (Old Cellar, 49 Front St., tel. 441/292-6307, or 3 Queen St., tel. 441/292-5292) is popular for artist Barbara Finsness's hand-designed tablecloths, ceramics, handbags, linens, and Christmas ornaments, as well as gorgeous Venetian glass jewelry.

A Front Street landmark, the quaint little **Irish Linen Shop** (31 Front St., tel. 441/295-4089, www.theirishlinenshop.com) sells Madeira hand embroideries, table and bed linens, children's clothes, and handkerchiefs by Souleiado, Le Jacquard Français, and Yves Delorme.

True Reflections (1 Chancery Ln., tel. 441/295-9424, truereflections@ibl.bm) carries African and West Indian–inspired souvenirs, silk-screen designs, T-shirts, and books by African-American authors including Maya Angelou and Bill Cosby.

Proceeds from **Trustworthy Gift Shop** (Old Cellar, Front St., tel. 441/296-4164), which stocks Bermuda books, Christmas ornaments, and local arts and crafts, help support Bermuda National Trust's historic homes and nature reserves.

Sporting Goods

Sportseller is the island's premier running gear store, with shoes by Nike, Asics, and New

CUBAN CIGARS

Cuban cigars are highly popular Bermuda souvenirs – maybe because they're illicit.

If you're American, you'll risk confiscation, mega fines, or even criminal prosecution, if you're found trying to take them back into the United States – an offense under economic sanctions enforced against Cuba since 1963. (Only licensed visitors to Cuba can bring back less than $100 worth of cigars for personal use.)

Nonetheless, retailers say Americans are some of their best customers, either taking the opportunity to enjoy their Romeo y Julietas and Cohibas during their vacation, or running the risk and sneaking them home in their luggage.

Cigar retailers include: **Chatham House** (Front St., at the corner of Burnaby Hill, tel. 441/292-8422), a specialty tobacco shop which stocks Punch, Partagas, Romeo y Julieta, H. Upmann, Montecristo, Cohiba, and Bolivar. **Churchill's** (Duke of York St., St. George, tel. 441/297-1650, open 10 A.M.-7 P.M. Mon.-Sat.) carries a full range of Cuban, Dominican, Costa Rican, Nicaraguan, and Jamaican cigars. **Cuarenta Bucaneros** (Continental Building, corner of Cedar Ave. and Church St., second floor, tel. 441/295-4523) sells boxes of 25 cigars ($175-340) in top Cuban brands, including Cohiba, Montecristo, and Romeo y Julieta.

Balance, running shorts, vests, singlets, and socks for women and men, as well as Danskin yoga gear, racing swimsuits, triathlon and cycling outfits, stopwatches, backpacks, reflector vests, and heart-rate monitors.

Pro Shop (Reid St. at the corner of Washington Ln., tel. 441/292-7487) stocks soccer, tennis, and running gear, including Adidas, Reebok, and Umbro brands.

The Upstairs Golf and Tennis Shop (26 Church St., tel. 441/295-5161, alan@upstairsgolf.bm) stocks big-name brands like Ping, Callaway, and Titleist, including clubs, rackets, and accessories for both sports.

Sports R Us (61 Church St., tel. 441/292-1891, 8:30 A.M.-6 P.M. Mon.-Sat.) is the island's largest sports store, with everything from weights equipment to running, golf, soccer, tennis, and competitive swim gear. There's also a large range of shoes, beach slippers, and waterproof slides.

Winners' Edge is a cyclist's heaven, and unofficial clubhouse of the Bermuda Bicycle Association (B.B.A.). The showroom floor includes flashy models by Trek, Gary Fisher, and Cannondale, as well as gear, clothing, and accessories to transform the average weekend pedal-pusher into a Lance Armstrong. An onsite shop does repairs.

China and Crystal

Historic **Bluck's** (4 Front St., tel. 441/295-5367) is the island's oldest vendor of fine china and crystal. Opened in 1844, the forest-green cottage-style building wedged between Front Street's financial and insurance blocks, is famous for both classic and contemporary designs by Kosta Boda, Baccarat, Herend, Royal Doulton, and Spode.

Vera P. Card (11 Front St., tel. 441/295-1729) is another family-run enterprise, with porcelain figurines, Swarovski crystal, and Lladro's version of a Bermuda moongate.

With brand new premises being built for a planned 2007 opening on Front Street, opposite the flagpole, department store **A. S. Cooper** (57 Front St., tel. 441/295-3961) is a wedding registry favorite, thanks to its major lines of china and crystal from Europe and around the world. Until the grand opening, the store's china department is operating out of temporary space (26 Church St.).

Jewelry and Watches

The island's two largest retailers for jewelry and watches are **Crisson** (55 and 71 Front St. and 16 Queen St., tel. 441/295-2351, www.crisson.com) and **Astwood Dickinson** (83–85 Front St., opposite No. 6 Shed, tel. 441/292-5805). Both carry major brand names, including Rolex, Tag Heuer, David Yurman, and Mont Blanc.

Walker Christopher (9 Front St., tel. 441/295-1466, walkerchris@cwbda.bm) is known for its own designs in fine jewelry.

Swiss Timing (95 Front St., tel. 441/295-1376) specializes in European watch brands, including Zenith, Concord, and Certina.

For Kids

Several stores will interest kids and their parents. Favorites include: **Treats of Bermuda** (7 Reid St., in the Washington Mall, tel. 441/296-1123), for candy and Thomas the Tank Engine; **Jack'n'Jill's** (7 Park Rd., tel. 441/292-3769), with a tempting old-fashioned candy bar and toys for all ages; **The Annex** (Phoenix Centre, 3 Reid St., tel. 441/295-3838 ext. 414/439), where candy and toys can also be found; **Pulp and Circumstance** (10 Queen St., tel. 441/292-9586), a treasure trove of stuffed animals, nursery lamps, and upscale baby gifts; and **Otto Wurz** (3–5 Front St., tel. 441/295-1247), at the corner of Front Street and Bermudiana Road, home of beautiful wooden handmade toys. **Bears Repeating Too** (Washington Mall, at Church St., tel. 441/295-7477) sells well-priced new and secondhand items, including toys, strollers, books, and clothes for all ages. **People's Pharmacy** (62 Victoria St., tel. 441/292-7527, www.peoplespharmacy .bm) has a children's toy store and book section as well as candy and chocolate.

For stylish European clothes, don't miss **Iana** (12 Walker Arcade, Hamilton, tel. 441/292-0002) and **Benetton** (Reid St., tel. 441/295-2112), which both stock fashionable leather shoes and durable boys' and girls' outfits. **The Irish Linen Shop** (31 Front St., tel. 441/295-4089), a fixture of Front Street for over a century, sells hand-stitched babies' layette, embroidered dresses, booties, and other precious gift items. **English Sports Shop** (49 Front St., tel. 441/295-2672) also has a children's department, with preppy woolens, golf shirts, and polo necks. (Sorry, there's no Gap on the island.)

X-Clue-Sive Creations Pottery Studio (84 Reid St., tel. 441/296-1676, excreations@logic .bm) allows children and adults to create their own ceramics (lighthouses, pirate mugs), then paint them. Collect them a few days later after glazing. Owner Doris Wade sets up "slump-and-hump" stations, where clay can be slumped in a mold to create a bowl, or humped over a bowl to make masks.

SPORTS AND RECREATION

Several water sports outfitters operate from the Hamilton waterfront, running cruises (day and evening), and sportfishing, reef snorkeling, eco-tours, sailing, whale-watching, and scuba expeditions.

Fantasea Bermuda (Albuoy's Point, 5 Point Pleasant Park, tel. 441/236-1300, fax 441/236-8926, www.fantasea.bm) is a full-service PADI and NAUI dive center offering daily one- and two-tank dives, night dives, private charters, and equipment sales. Fantasea is also popular for its kayak tours, cycling eco-expeditions along the Railway Trail, glass-bottom boat tours, plus private sailing charters.

© ROSEMARY JONES

Sailing is a popular pastime in Bermuda.

The company even offers a three-events-in-three-hours package, combining a boat cruise with cycling, kayaking, and swimming.

Jessie James Cruises (Albuoy's Point, Front St., tel. 441/236-4804, www.jessiejames.bm) is known for its daily summer tours, which take visitors to three different snorkeling locations—a beach and small islet, a historic shallow shipwreck, and a coral reef sea garden—as part of a three-hour cruise. The company also runs a two-hour daily November–May excursion aboard a glass-bottom boat that cruises over shipwrecks and throws in a bit of sightseeing.

Bermuda Island Cruises (tel. 441/292-8652, fax 441/292-5193, www.bic.bm) is known for its popular "Don't Stop the Carnival" parties out on Hawkins Island in the Great Sound. Passengers cruise from Albuoy's Point to Hawkins, where a live band and carnival dancers provide entertainment during a barbecue buffet dinner. Families might prefer BIC's twice-a-day "Reef Explorer Safari" aboard a large glass-bottom boat (departs Hamilton, next to the Ferry Terminal, at 10 A.M. and 1:30 P.M. daily).

ACCOMMODATIONS

There are presently no visitor accommodations located within Hamilton's boundaries (though many are nearby in Pembroke). There have been years of discussions linked to a proposal to turn the land now occupied by Par-la-Ville carpark into a city hotel, but so far there's been no progress.

FOOD

Hamilton's culinary scene has evolved considerably over the past decade, with an infusion of new restaurants, multiethnic menus, and chefs' innovative twists on Bermudian traditions. The result is that you can enjoy meals of the caliber you'd expect in urban centers like New York, Los Angeles, or London. Sushi has taken off in popularity recently. There's also no shortage of fresh seafood, and most restaurants, even pizza and pasta specialists, offer a catch-of-the-day that ranges from Bermuda wahoo

and tuna to rockfish, yellowtail, or grouper, depending on the weather and season. Italian restaurants have long enjoyed a monopoly on Bermuda's food industry, though many are developing more varied Mediterranean menus, and Asian influences are also strong. Several new ethnic contenders include Silk Thai and Café Cairo, which came to Front Street in the past couple of years, and a new sushi takeout place, L'Oriental Express, opened on Par-la-Ville Road in late 2005. The majority of the island's restaurants are located in Hamilton, and since 2004, many have adopted No Smoking regulations—a trend enforced by law in 2006. Credit cards are accepted by all major restaurants, and the standard dress code is smart-casual—so avoid wearing sneakers or T-shirts to dinner.

Ice Cream Bars

Double-Dip (Brunswick Mall, 119 Front St., tel. 441/292-3503) lures midsummer passersby with its frosty selection of ice creams and sorbets—including a kid-pleasing blue Smurf flavor.

La Trattoria Shop (22 Washington Ln., tel. 441/295-1877) sells decadent homemade gelato from a little outlet opposite La Trattoria restaurant.

Hamilton Ice Queen (27 Queen St., tel. 441/292-6497, 10 A.M.–midnight daily) sells soft-serve ice cream from this crowded eatery, also popular for its fried chicken.

Lunch Wagons

Office workers line up weekday lunchtimes for burgers, sandwiches, and friendly chit-chat at **DeGraff's Lunch Wagon** (City Hall carpark, tel. 441/799-3904, 9 A.M.–3 P.M. Mon.–Fri.).

Jor-Jay's Takeout (Front St., in the carpark opposite The Supermart, tel. 441/296-3114, 8 A.M.–3 P.M. Mon.–Thur., 8 A.M.–4 A.M. Fri., 11:30 A.M.–4 A.M. Sat.) is very popular with hungry late-night revelers on their way out of town. The lunch wagon makes scrumptious homemade burgers, sandwiches, fries, and fish cakes, and although the wait is sometimes a good half hour, it's worth it.

Keith's Kitchen (48 Woodlands Rds., at

B.A.A. carpark, tel. 441/295-1310) is a convenient stop for thick tuna sandwiches, BLTs, and straight-off-the-grill burgers.

Cafés and Delis

Cafés and delis are located all over Hamilton, though a few catering to the corporate crowd are closed Saturdays. Good delis are also located in supermarkets, particularly The MarketPlace (Church Street) and The Supermart (Front Street).

One of Bermuda's best truly "local" joints, **The Spot** (6 Burnaby St., tel. 441/292-6293, 6:30 A.M.–10 P.M. summer, 6:30 A.M.–7 P.M. winter Mon.–Sat.) is a Bermudian melting pot, remarkable for the way it attracts customers of all races, ages, and backgrounds, who come for great homemade dishes and the convivial atmosphere. The place is a landmark in Hamilton, having been at its present location for a good half-century. Some of The Spot's staff has been there almost as long. Try the soups (red bean, barley, split pea), hot sandwiches, and shakes. Takeout is fast, and the service is ultra-friendly (and kid-friendly).

Drop into **Rock Island Coffee** (48 Reid St., tel. 441/296-5241, 7 A.M.–6 P.M. Mon.–Fri., 8 A.M.–5 P.M. Sat.) for the island's best java and one of the city's most interestingly mixed crowd of patrons. Dreadlocked "trustafarians"—trust-funded bohemians—linger over their lattes and lemongrass salads, while lawyers and actuaries rush in for espresso and a peanut butter cookie. Staff roasts and grinds beans from Colombia, Kenya, Jamaica, and elsewhere at the popular coffeehouse and offers trays of home-baked goodies, soups, and salads daily. The artsy surroundings, a wooden-floored cottage decorated in ever-changing local paintings and photography, add to the ambience—pure Bermudian bohemia. There's a garden out front with tables, umbrellas, and views of the cruise ships in the summer. The shop also opens at night occasionally over Christmas and during the summer.

You can get a taste of Portuguese cuisine at **Café Acoreano** (Russell Eve Building, 2 Washington St., tel. 441/296-0402, 6:30 A.M.–3 P.M. Mon.–Fri., 6:30 A.M.–2 P.M. Sat.), where deep-fried *malasadas* (Portuguese donuts) are a Bermudian favorite, among other sweet treats. Great coffee and a convenient location alongside the central bus terminal also make this tiny café worth a visit.

Formerly Mannie's Snack Bar, **Soul Food Express** (18 Washington Ln., tel. 441/295-3890, 7 A.M.–3:30 P.M. Mon.–Fri., 8 A.M.–2:30 P.M. Sat.) serves breakfast and lunchtime lineups with specialties like saltfish and ackee, omelettes, egg-filled croissants, spareribs, roast chicken, curries, and macaroni and cheese.

Run by award-winning team Jean-Claude Garzia and Lee Uddin, **Lemon Tree Cafe** (7 Queen St., tel. 441/292-0235, 7:30 A.M.–4 P.M. Mon.–Fri.) tempts lunch-goers with gourmet offerings, from chicken pies wrapped with melt-in-your-mouth pastry to ciabatta sandwiches and healthy wraps. Plans to cover the outdoor patio of the park-side eatery are in the works, as Garzia and Uddin hope to morph their little gem into an evening bistro with a menu of French fare.

Family-run **Jamaican Grill** (32 Court St., tel. 441/296-6577, 6:30 A.M.–10 P.M. Mon.–Fri., 6:30 A.M.–11 P.M. Sat.) attracts aficionados of Caribbean cuisine, such as oxtail, jerk chicken, brown stew, and West Indian curries. Fast service and delicious meals keep crowds coming back. Take out or eat in the atmospheric little diner, which has a cluster of tables downstairs and a few overlooking the jovial gathering from on high.

Hidden away in the hallway of a retail building, **Donna's Café** (61 Church St., next to Sports R Us, tel. 441/292-2009, 7:30 A.M.–3 P.M. Mon.–Fri.) is a throwback to the 1950s, with fluorescent lights and simple row of revolving stools pushed up to the yellow linoleum bar. Breakfast sandwiches, burgers, and shakes are the menu favorites. Service is a no-fuss affair in the friendly hands of owner/manager Donna Warwick, who won a Best of Bermuda award for her burgers in 2005.

Another tiny coffee bar far from the tourist track is **Coffee Pot**, inside Hamilton Pharmacy (17 Parliament St., tel. 441/292-6097, 8 A.M.–3 P.M. Mon.–Thurs., 8 A.M.–2 P.M. Fri.), where lawyers from the nearby courts and bureaucrats from the civil service headquarters gobble down egg and cheese rolls for breakfast.

My favorite deli/takeout in Bermuda is ◖ **The Hickory Stick** (Clarendon Building, 2 Church St., tel. 441/292-1781, 6:30 A.M.–4 P.M. Mon.–Fri.), whose Dagwood-esque sandwiches are legendary. Construction workers, bankers, journalists, and tourists traipse in for footlong subs stuffed with deli meats and smothered in melted cheese. Hot fish cakes, hash cakes, sausage rolls, and hot dogs are also available, as well as whole-wheat rolls filled with tuna and chicken salads, deli meats, chopped egg, or crabmeat. Cold drinks, pastries, baked goods, tea, and coffee are also sold. The place is so popular, staff sets up a sandwich-making factory line to efficiently serve the lunch queue snaking through the little eatery noon–2 P.M. Go early or late to avoid the wait.

Sitting on the steep connection between Front and Reid Streets, **Dorothy's Coffee Shop** (3 Chancery Ln., tel. 441/292-4130, 7:15 A.M.–3:30 P.M. Mon.–Fri.) is best known for its award-winning homemade burgers—juicy, made-while-you-watch creations on the little diner's grill. Sit at barstools to watch the proceedings, or at the few tables. Takeouts are popular, too.

Enjoy breakfast or lunch alfresco on the napkin-sized plaza at **Bistro 12** (12 Walker Arcade, tel. 441/295-5130, 7 A.M.–5 P.M. Mon.–Sat.), one of Hamilton's best people-watching spots and a popular weekend breakfast nook. Just across the street, another fabulous people-watching perch is a window seat at **Paradiso Café** (7 Reid St., tel. 441/295-3263, 7 A.M.–5 P.M. Mon.–Sat.), owned by the Opposition U.B.P. party leader Wayne Furbert.

Island Hi Eatery (6 Parliament St., tel. 441/295-6163, 6:30 A.M.–5:30 P.M. Mon.–Sat.) makes wraps and subs, fruit smoothies, and a variety of other sandwiches and salads.

Billed as a taste of Barbados, **Spring Garden** (Washington Ln., tel. 441/295-7416, lunch 11:30 A.M.–3 P.M., dinner 6–10 P.M. Mon.–Sat.) specializes in Barbadian and Caribbean cuisine. Eat inside or out to the beat of Caribbean tunes

in the pleasant garden, tucked away in the heart of Hamilton.

Pub Fare

Technically it's a bar, but **Pickled Onion** (53 Front St., tel. 441/295-2263, www.thepickled onion.com, lunch 11:30 A.M.–5 P.M., dinner 5:30–10 P.M. daily) has a restaurant-caliber menu, with a variety of nicely presented appetizers, pastas, fresh fish, salads, steaks, and desserts. The live music and drinks are just a bonus.

You couldn't find a more British-looking establishment than **Hog Penny** (5 Burnaby Hill, tel. 441/292-2534, www.hogpennypub.com, 11:30 A.M.–1 A.M. daily), where home-cooked and typically ill-named staples like shepherd's pie and toad-in-the-hole are comfortable favorites. Its "crusted dinners" (beef Wellington, scallopini veal chop) are well liked, too.

Named for the way Bermudians say "'Em are onions," **M.R. Onions** (11 Par-la-Ville Rd., tel. 441/292-5012, www.mronions.com, noon–10 P.M. daily, brunch noon–2:30 P.M. Sunday) has great seafood (calamari, fish chowder, Cajun-style tuna, fresh lobster) as well as pasta, beef, lamb chops, barbecue, and surf-and-turf specials. Customers can also surf the Internet on the bar's computers. U.K. soccer, NFL, NHL, and major-league baseball attract couch jocks on the weekends.

All-day breakfasts, super sandwiches, and build-your-own burgers get top billing at **The Docksider Pub & Restaurant** (121 Front St., tel. 441/296-3333, www.dockies.com, 11 A.M.–2 A.M. Mon.–Fri., 10 A.M.–2 A.M. Sat. and Sun.), a crowded hangout all year around.

Asian

Bermuda's first Thai restaurant, ◖ **Silk Thai** (Masters Building, Front St., tel. 441/295-0449, lunch noon–2:30 P.M. Mon.–Fri., dinner 6:30–9:30 P.M. daily) offers diners a sleekly evocative dining room and deliciously authentic cuisine. Bamboo, dark woods, privacy screens, and a cozy upstairs nook with views of the harbor elegantly transformed the space, which was a deli previously. The menu includes curries, soups, salads, and specialties like pad Thai and beef curry, all expertly created.

Bermuda's favorite Chinese takeout, **Chopsticks** (88 Reid St., tel. 441/292-0791, www.bermudarestaurants.com, lunch 11:30 A.M.–2:30 P.M. Mon.–Fri., dinner 5–11 P.M. daily) is popular for eating in as well. The dramatically designed dining room allows for parties or dinner for two, and service is efficient and friendly. Fried rice, noodles, vegetable dishes, foo young, and a few Thai specialties are the most popular items.

Indian

Outstanding Indian fare, equal to anything I've had in little Indias in Toronto, New York, or London is the strength of **C House of India** (Park View Plaza, 57 North St., tel. 441/295-6450, lunch 11:30 A.M.–2:30 P.M. Mon.–Fri., dinner 5–10 P.M. daily), where a dedicated team of Indian chefs turns out lunch buffets and nightly feasts of tandoori, biryanai, and balti specialties. The award-winning chicken passandas, chicken and beef khormas, and chicken and lamb tikka masalas are particularly well done. There is also a wide selection of vegetarian dishes. Appetizers include bhajiyas, pakoras, and samosas.

Right next door, the newer **Bombay Palace** (60 North St., tel. 441/296-4094, 11:30 A.M.–10 P.M. Mon.–Sat.) offers an Indian and Jamaican lunchtime buffet ($12.95) that brings a steady clientele.

Italian

Leader of the pack, **Little Venice** (32 Bermudiana Rd., tel. 441/295-3503, lunch noon–2 P.M. Mon.–Fri., dinner 6:30–9:30 P.M. daily) was the vanguard of Bermuda's love-fest with Italian cuisine back in the 1960s. Today, it's still going strong, and the restaurant's owners, Capri natives, have succeeded beyond their wildest dreams, with a dozen popular restaurants and a catering arm that feeds the island's social scene. Little Venice was always the power-lunch venue, and it still attracts insurance-industry movers and shakers, as well as occasional celebrities (Michael Douglas dines here). Efficient, entertaining staff members keep the dining room buzzing. Pastas, meat dishes, and lovingly crafted desserts make up the menu.

Just down the street, **C Portofino** (20 Bermudiana Rd., tel. 441/292-2375, www.portofino.bm, lunch 11:30 A.M.–3 P.M., Mon.–Fri., dinner 6–10:45 P.M. Mon.–Thur. and Sun., 6–11:45 P.M. Fri. and Sat.) is one of the island's few Italian restaurants not owned by the Little Venice Group, and it is wildly popular. Speedy waiters, daily pasta specials, tasty salads and meats, and a cozy, red-checkered interior make Portofino a hit. Dinner reservations (for groups of more than two) are definitely recommended to avoid lining up down the street on summer weekend evenings. Diners here also get free entry to the hip Splash nightclub, which has the same owners.

C La Trattoria (22 Washington Ln., Washington Mall, tel. 441/295-1877, lunch 11 A.M.–3 P.M. Mon.–Sat., dinner 5–10 P.M. daily) got a makeover in 2004 that makes diners feel they've stepped into the terra-cotta courtyard of an eatery in Naples or Rome. The menu, which has always been a crowd-pleaser, remains excellent, with daily-changing homemade pastas, pizzas baked in the dining room oven, and great salads, breads, and desserts, including homemade gelato. La Tratt's cappuccino is the best on the island. Topping even the food is the eatery's stellar service; nothing is a problem, least of all wailing children or order-off-the-menu clientele. The professional team smoothly fulfills everyone's wishes, and fast. Kids, particularly, are well accommodated with crayons, balls of dough to play with, cost-effective smaller platters, even "white" pizzas (should they turn their noses up at tomato sauce). As a result, the place is full of families but somehow manages to attract couples and dinner parties, too.

Northern Italian dishes are celebrated at **Tuscany** (Bermuda House Ln., 95 Front St., tel. 441/292-4507, lunch noon–2:30 P.M. Mon.–Fri., dinner 6:30–10:30 P.M. Mon.–Sat.), where colorful decor—including a wall-length fresco—and comfortable booths make for relaxing meals. There is also terrace seating overlooking Front Street. The adjoining Square One nightclub is part of the same complex.

Seafood and Sushi

Possibly Bermuda's best fish sandwich and the crowning example of a good local fish cake can be found at **(Art Mel's Spicy Dicy** (9 St. Monica's Rd., tel. 441/295-3965, noon–10 P.M. Mon.–Fri., noon–9 P.M. Sat.), which, though tucked away in North Hamilton's backstreets, is searched out daily by fish-lovers, thanks to its word-of-mouth praise. The simple eatery cooks up fresh fish and crispy fish cakes on buns, as well as burgers and other fast food. Follow your nose—and the lines of people.

Another North Hamilton favorite is **Fish Hut** (Court St., at Angle Street junction, tel. 441/292-3267, 11 A.M.–10 P.M. Mon.–Sat.), where fish dinners, wahoo sandwiches, and fish cakes are all on the menu. Just down the street, **Fish & Tings** (45 Angle St., tel. 441/292-7389, 11 A.M.–10 P.M. Mon.–Thurs., 11 A.M.–11 P.M. Fri. and Sat.) specializes in Jamaican dishes, like fish curries, stews, and jerk everything.

The Lobster Pot (6 Bermudiana Rd., tel. 441/292-6898, 11:30 A.M.–10 P.M. Mon.–Fri., 5:30–10 P.M. Sat., 6–10 P.M. Sun.) has been a beloved fixture of this corner of Hamilton for decades, and it still has one of the island's most enjoyable bars, as well as an atmospheric dining room, where you might as well be below decks on a sumptuous ocean liner. Fresh Bermuda or Maine lobsters, pan-fried rockfish, snapper, and grouper make this one of the island's best seafood venues.

The sushi and tempura bar at 30-year-old **(The Harbourfront** (Front St. West, tel. 441/295-4207, 11:45 A.M.–3 P.M., 5–9:30 P.M. Mon.–Sat.) has become a veritable institution, especially the nightly happy hour (5–6:30 P.M.), which offers sushi, wine, highballs, and beer for $4.50, plus free miso soup. The sushi menu includes soft-shell crab wapari gani, vegetarian sushi, inside-out rolls, sushi boats, nigiri, sashimi, and temaki. Ask for a seat on the terrace overlooking the harborfront.

L'Oriental (32 Bermudiana Rd., above Little Venice, tel. 441/296-4477, lunch noon–3 P.M. Mon.–Fri., dinner 6–11 P.M. daily) has some of the island's best sushi and teriyaki, including Sunday night's Asian buffet ($31.75).

New in 2005, **L'Oriental Express** (ground floor, Maxwell Roberts Building, 1 Church St., tel. 441/296-7475, fax 441/295-5454, www.lorientalexpress.bm, 8 A.M.–7 P.M. Mon.–Fri.) is extremely popular with nearby office workers, thanks to its varied menu of eat-in or takeout sushi, as well as sandwiches, wraps, paninis, build-your-own salads, and breakfast specials.

Opened in 2004, **(Barracuda Grill** (Burnaby Hill, tel. 441/292-1609, lunch noon–2:30 P.M. Mon.–Fri., dinner 5:30–10 P.M. daily) made a splash on Bermuda's foodie scene, replacing the previously stuffy Fisherman's Reef restaurant with a distinctive cutting-edge interior and outstanding seafood, steaks, and chops. Tuna tartare, garlic-poached prawns, chili-rubbed lamb chops, and lobster fettucine are among the favorites. Don't miss the chocolate banana bread volcano, either.

International

"World fusion" is the menu's ambition at **(Café Cairo** (93 Front St., tel. 441/295-5155, cafecairo@northrock.bm, noon–3 A.M. daily, snack menu after 10 P.M.), where belly-dancers entertain diners seated on floor cushions in a tented room (diners can also choose to sit on the harborfront terrace). The restaurant's popularity was long proven by the crowds who used to trek west to its former location in a Southampton industrial park. Café Cairo's 2005 move to Front Street should make it a lot easier to partake of its popular Middle Eastern fare and unique decor.

After a good 20 years in the heart of Hamilton, **Monte Carlo** (9 Victoria St., tel. 441/295-5453, fax 441/295-5442, www.montecarlo.bm, lunch noon–2:30 P.M. Mon.–Fri., dinner 6–10:30 P.M. Mon.–Sat.) has cultivated a loyal clientele with its convivial atmosphere and consistently inventive menu. Fresh seafood, pastas, salads, and steaks are staples, and a tasting menu offers tapas, Moroccan dishes, and Greek specialties on different nights of the week.

ℂ Mediterraneo (39 Church St., tel. 441/296-9047, www.mediterraneo.bm, lunch 11 A.M.–3 P.M. Mon.–Fri., dinner 5–11:45 P.M. Mon.–Sat., 5–11 P.M. Sun.) is owned and run by the team behind Pembroke's popular Ascot's restaurant, including award-winning chef Edmund Smith. With a winning location and fantastic kitchen, it is shaping up to be another winner. The two-story eatery has a cool, contemporary look, its frescoes coupled with track lighting, a chic bar (open until 3 A.M.), and a strong menu featuring innovative Mediterranean dishes, from seafood to pastas, salads to more hearty meats. Mostly, it's the ambience—a muted, urbanely intimate chic—which sets it apart from so many other local restaurants.

The elegant dining room at **Port O' Call** (87 Front St., tel. 441/295-5373, lunch noon–2:30 P.M. Mon.–Fri., dinner 6–10 P.M. daily) makes a special night out, and the seafood-and-steak menu won't disappoint. Owned by the same restaurant group, tiny **Bistro J** (Chancery Ln., tel. 441/296-8546, lunch noon–2:30 P.M. Mon.–Fri., dinner 6–10 P.M. Mon.–Sat.) has a more relaxed charm, with blackboard menus offering a limited but tasty assortment of daily specials, including fish, meat, pastas, and vegetarian offerings.

Grocery Stores

One of the island's best-stocked grocery stores, **The Supermart** (125 Front St., tel. 441/292-2064, www.supermart.bm, 7 A.M.–10 P.M. Mon.–Sat., 1–5 P.M. Sun.) carries the British line of Waitrose products. Its meat department, cheese selection, and fresh produce section are also excellent. There's a liquor store here also. Parking is on the street, or opposite in the small carpark.

Flagship of the islandwide chain, the **Hamilton MarketPlace** (42 Church St., tel. 441/295-6066, 7 A.M.–10 P.M. Mon.–Sat., 1–5 P.M. Sun.) is a massive food emporium, offering full liquor store, meat department, enormous bakery, full-scale deli with hot and cold dishes and salad bars daily, and all manner of foodstuffs. Kids will enjoy the special car-like trolleys for family use and the remote control train that runs on a circuit overhead hooting its horn. There is parking outside and in a dedicated carpark beneath the store.

The **Shopping Centre** (Victoria St., tel. 441/292-4545, 8 A.M.–10 P.M. Mon.–Sat., 1–5 P.M. Sun.) is a MarketPlace branch and carries a much smaller selection of goods.

INFORMATION AND SERVICES

The **Visitors Service Bureau** (8 Front St. by the Ferry Terminal, tel. 441/295-1480) is the island's main orientation center for travelers. Staff can direct you to key points of interest, attractions, events, and services and answer questions about the island. There are also numerous informational brochures available here, as well as bus and ferry tickets, tokens, and multiday passes for sale. V.S.B. runs special desks at **No. 1 Shed** (tel. 441/292-2453) and **No. 6 Shed** (441/292-3933) during the cruise season.

Hamilton Police Station (42 Parliament St., tel. 441/295-0011, 441/292-1458, or 441/299-4538, fax 441/299-4589, hps@bps.bm) is located just across the street from Magistrates Court, where officers parade accused criminals for appearances and trials. A reception desk handles walk-in queries or problems.

The **Government Administration Building** (30 Parliament St., tel. 441/295-5151) houses numerous government departments, including Immigration, which deals with work permits and vacation extension requests.

Public toilets are located at: the General Post Office; Point Pleasant Road at Albuoy's Point; beneath No. 1 Shed on Front Street; at banks; and upstairs in the Phoenix Centre on Reid Street.

ATMs are at banking centers, the General Post Office (universal swipe card access after 6 P.M.—swipe any credit card at the door to enter), outside the Phoenix Centre's rear exit (Windsor Place Mall), and on the ground floor of the Washington Mall.

Banks

Bank of Bermuda HSBC (head office Front Street; 64 Church St.; 36 Par-la-Ville Rd., main switchboard tel. 441/295-4000, www.bankofbermuda.com) has branches in all the parishes, including the airport.

Butterfield Bank (head office 65 Front St., at Burnaby Hill; Rosebank Centre, Bermudiana Road at Richmond Road; Reid Street; main switchboard tel. 441/295-1111, www.butterfieldbank.com) has ATMs and bank branches islandwide, but its headquarters have been located here for over a century.

Bermuda's newest bank, **Capital G** (19 Reid St., tel. 441/296-6969, www.capital-g.com) offers financial services, loans, mortgages, and select banking and card services.

Bermuda Commercial Bank (43 Victoria St., tel. 441/295-5678, fax 441/295-8091, www.bermuda-bcb.com) provides fund administration, private banking, global custody, and electronic banking to personal, corporate, and international clients.

Pharmacies

Phoenix Centre (3 Reid St., tel. 441/295-3838, ext. 418, www.phoenixstores.bm, 8 A.M.–6 P.M. Mon.–Sat., noon–6 P.M. Sun. and holidays) is the island's largest general drugstore and flagship of an islandwide chain of pharmacies. The Hamilton center also has a major toy store and bookshop.

Clarendon Pharmacy (2 Church St., tel. 441/295-3838, ext. 376, www.phoenixstores. bm, 8 A.M.–6 P.M. Mon.–Sat., closed holidays) is located inside a small bank mall. The store carries chocolates, greeting cards, baby products, and other drugstore items.

Hamilton Pharmacy (Parliament St., tel. 441/295-7004, 8 A.M.–9 P.M. Mon.–Sat.) is a busy but friendly little store, complete with dispensary, small café, toys, books, magazines, and stationery. It is conveniently located, a stone's throw from Parliament, the law courts, and the main central post office.

People's Pharmacy (62 Victoria St., tel. 441/292-7527, prescriptions tel. 441/292-9261, fax 441/295-0639, www.peoplespharmacy.bm,

8 A.M.–8:30 P.M. Mon.–Sat., 10 A.M.–6 P.M. Sun.) is my favorite drugstore on the island, for its efficient, friendly staff, easy parking, and wonderful stock. The large, modern store carries loads of drugstore products, but it also has magazines, a brand new children's toy store and book section, greeting cards, gifts, candy, and household supplies.

Post Offices

General Post Office (56 Church St., at Parliament St., tel. 441/297-7893, www.bermuda postoffice.com, 8 A.M.–5 P.M. Mon.–Fri., 8 A.M.–noon Sat.) sells stamps, including first-day covers and collectors' issues, has a mail-drop, offers parcel and express post, and has ATMs.

Historic **Perot Post Office** (11 Queen St., tel. 441/292-9052, 8 A.M.–5 P.M. Mon.–Fri.) is the only sub-post office in Hamilton.

Internet Access

The **Bermuda Library** (Queen St., tel. 441/295-2905, 8:30 A.M.–7 P.M. Mon.–Thurs., 10 A.M.–5 P.M. Fri., 9 A.M.–5 P.M. Sat., 1–5 P.M. Sun.) offers the city's only free Internet access (30-minute limit) on its three PCs, all with T1 line connection. Printing costs $0.25 a page.

Twice-Told Tales (34 Parliament St., tel. 441/296-1995, 8 A.M.–5:30 P.M. Mon.–Fri., 11 A.M.–4 P.M. Sat.) is a delightful secondhand bookstore, which also happens to have a T1 connection and four PCs offering Internet access. Fresh coffee and baked goods are for sale, too.

Internet Lane (The Walkway, 22 Reid St., tel. 441/296-9972, 9 A.M.–7 P.M. Mon.–Sat.) has speedy T1 lines on six PCs ($6 for 30 minutes). Laptop access is also offered ($7 for 30 minutes), and printing is allowed in private suites.

Logic Internet Café (10–12 Burnaby St., tel. 441/294-8888, 8 A.M.–6 P.M. Mon.–Fri., 9 A.M.–5 P.M. Sat.) is a funky space built for people-watching with its bird's-eye view of the street and free coffee. With a T1 console of six PCs, the Café sells cards for long-distance phone or Internet use ($5 for 30 minutes). No printing is permitted.

Print Express (34 Burnaby St., tel. 441/295-

© ROSEMARY JONES

Historic Perot Post Office sells stamps and still operates as a working branch outlet.

3950, printexp@ibl.bm, 9 A.M.–5 P.M. Mon.–Sat.) is conveniently tucked into a steep city street leading down to the harbor. The pocket-sized shop has just two PCs, and constant people traffic, but the connection is a T1 line ($5 for 30 minutes).

M.R. Onions (11 Par-la-Ville Rd., tel. 441/292-5012, noon–1 A.M. daily) is a popular pub and restaurant with three bar-area PCs with a 128K line. No laptop access or printing are allowed, but perks include late hours, a full menu of food and drink, large-screen TV, and jovial environs.

At **TeleBermuda International** (corner of Queen and Reid Streets, tel. 441/296-9029 or 441/296-9030, 9 A.M.–4:30 P.M. Mon.–Fri.), you can go online via four T1-capable PCs (15 minutes are $2.50, an hour $10). Printing is $0.25 a page. There is no laptop access.

Gas Stations

Bermuda Industrial Union Gas Station (22 Dundonald St., tel. 441/292-2726, 7 A.M.–midnight daily) has helpful staff and a con-venience store selling hot dogs, cold drinks, snacks, newspapers, and candy.

Esso City Automarket (37 Richmond Rd., tel. 441/295-3776, open 24 hours daily) is the island's only 24-hour service station. Its busy convenience store stocks hot and cold snacks, including hot dogs, pies, coffee, and cold drinks.

Liquor Stores

You can buy beer, wine and spirits in most grocery stores, but there are also dedicated liquor merchants in Hamilton.

Historic **Gosling Brothers** (Front St., at Queen St., tel. 441/295-1123 or 441/298-7337) is famous for its Black Seal Rum and dark 'n' stormies, but also supplies much of the island's fine wines, ports, and other liquors. A short distance east is **Bermuda Wines & Spirits** (15 Front St., tel. 441/295-1919), which also stocks a full selection of alcoholic beverages.

Court Street Liquors (29 Court St., tel. 441/295-7457, 9 A.M.–9 P.M. Mon.–Sat.) is located in North Hamilton.

Queen Street Liquors (corner of Queen and Church Streets, tel. 441/295-1147) specializes in fine wines.

GETTING THERE AND AROUND

Buses
The renovated $3 million bus terminal reopened in February 2006 with a new name in honor of a longtime driver—the **Hubert W. "Sparky" Lightbourne Central Terminal** (Washington St. at Church St., tel. 441/295-4311, information and dispatch tel. 441/292-3854). This is the central hub for all bus routes running throughout the parishes. Tickets, tokens, and passes can be purchased here also.

Ferries
The island's ferry terminal (6 A.M.–11:30 P.M. Mon.–Fri., 8 A.M.–11:30 P.M. Sat., 8:30 A.M.–8 P.M. Sun. and holidays), serving Paget, Warwick, Southampton, the West End, and East End, is on Front Street. A ferry ride to Dockyard is a mere 20 minutes, to the town of St. George a scenic 45. For information, call Sea Express (tel. 441/295-4506, www.seaexpress.bm).

Scooters
Wheels Cycles (117 Front St., at Court St., tel. 441/292-2245, wheels@northrock.bm, 9 A.M.–5 P.M. daily) rents mopeds ($57 per day) and single- and double-seat scooters ($75), with lower rates for longer rentals. Pickup and delivery service is also available.

© ROSEMARY JONES

Ferries come and go from Front Street's Ferry Terminal.

Taxis
There are taxi stands along Front Street opposite No. 1 Shed. Otherwise, contact **Bermuda Industrial Union Co-op** (tel. 441/292-4476) or **Bermuda Taxi Radio Cabs** (tel. 441/295-4141, btrcabs@cwbda.bm) for pickup. Typical average taxi rates from Hamilton to the airport are $35, to St. George's $45, to the Southampton beaches $23, and to Dockyard $50.

Pembroke Parish

From back o' town to Fairylands, and everything between, Pembroke encompasses a diverse world of Bermudian culture on the city coattails of Hamilton, which sits within the parish. Encompassing the soaring insurance towers of Pitts Bay, the grandiose, old-money mansions of the harborfront, the salt-sprayed charm of Spanish Point, and the vibrantly scrappy chutzpah of the Marsh Folly community, Pembroke might be the best microcosm of Bermuda as a whole—the best, worst, richest, and poorest distilled into its coasts and valleys. Once rural environs of Hamilton, where the distant clip-clop of horse hooves or the splash of oars from a skiff rowing past were the only disturbances, Pembroke now is completely suburban, even 100 percent urban in parts, as the city's borders blur. Its once-tranquil neighborhoods now bear the aural scar of roaring traffic.

Pembroke begins where Hamilton ends: all points west of Bermudiana Road, east of King Street as far as the Devonshire border, and north of Parson's Lane to the North Shore. The main routes include Pitts Bay Road, which winds out of the city into tony residential neighborhoods, all the way to Cox's Hill and St. John's Road, which connects with Spanish Point Road. North Shore Road runs along the northern edge of the parish as far as Mission Lane, when it enters Devonshire. East Broadway leads out of Hamilton along the harbor's edge to Crow Lane. Parson's, Palmetto, and Marsh Folly Roads are major thoroughfares through the belly of the parish north of Hamilton. Langton Hill and the dramatic Blackwatch Pass cut north through the parish to the North Shore.

The variety of interesting neighborhoods make for great explorations, from Spanish Point, a self-contained community steeped in maritime history, to Fairylands and Point Shares, where high pastel walls hide centuries-old waterfront spreads, and areas of North Hamilton, where West Indian cafés and local playgrounds reveal a totally different facet of Bermudian life.

SIGHTS

Pitts Bay Road is one of Bermuda's most scenic thoroughfares; lined by guesthouses, pastel mansions, and sprawling gardens, it is one of the island's wealthiest districts. The serene residential enclaves of Fairylands, Point Shares, and Mill's Point contain centuries-old waterfront homes of Bermudian merchant families, many of whose descendents still live here. These are private property, of course, but a stroll down the network of neighborhood lanes is nevertheless peacefully revealing. In the early spring, many old homes have gardens carpeted with freesias, and the sound of traffic is nonexistent.

⟨ Bull's Head Farmers Market

Saturday mornings see scores of early birds head down to the popular Farmers Market (Bull's Head Carpark, Canal Rd., off Woodlands Rd., tel. 441/238-0059, www.bermuda farmersmarket.org, 8 A.M.–noon Sat. Nov. 1– June 30). Started in 2002, the project was a grassroots initiative to foster interest in local agriculture and farming skills. Hugely successful from the start, the alfresco market has now expanded in both customers and vendors, who include everyone from artisans and commercial farmers to backyard gardeners. The atmosphere is almost like a bohemian street festival—a wonderful way to meet interesting locals and sample everything from lemongrass hand cream to local honey. Sip coffee or hot chocolate, chew on a sweet sugarcane stick, and people-watch to your heart's content. Fresh Bermuda fish is often for sale. Fruits and vegetables range from pawpaws and pumpkins to collards and jalapeños, and Bermudians love the selection and prices. Stands also sell organic poultry and eggs, jams and chutneys made from Bermuda's wild fruits, dips, pestos, pates, and home-baked goods. Arts and crafts have become an increasingly big part of the market, with items like Venetian glass

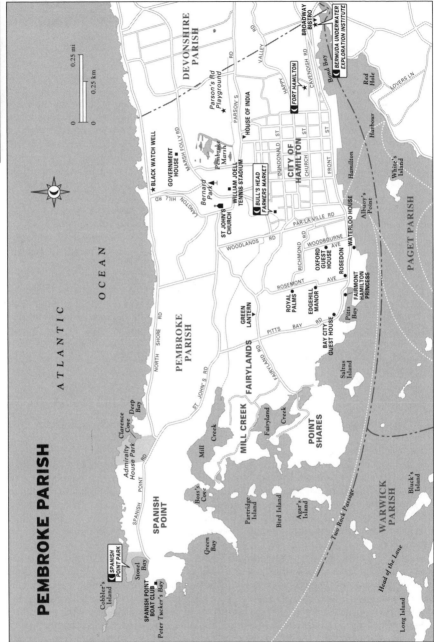

PEMBROKE PARISH

ATLANTIC OCEAN

DEVONSHIRE PARISH

CITY OF HAMILTON

PEMBROKE PARISH

WARWICK PARISH

PAGET PARISH

SPANISH POINT

MILL CREEK

FAIRYLANDS

POINT SHARES

Cobbler's Island
Stovel Bay
Peter Tucker's Bay
SPANISH POINT BOAT CLUB
SPANISH POINT PARK
Green Bay
Long Island
Bluck's Island
Head of the Lane
Two Rock Passage
Agar's Island
Bird Island
Partridge Island
Boss's Cove
Mill Creek
Fairyland Creek
Salt us Island
Pitts Bay
BAY CITY GUEST HOUSE
ROYAL PALMS
EDGEHILL MANOR
GREEN LANTERN
FAIRMONT HAMILTON PRINCESS
WATERLOO HOUSE
Albuoy's Point
OXFORD GUEST HOUSE
WOODBOURNE
BERNARD PARK
ST JOHN'S CHURCH
WILLIAM JOELL TENNIS STADIUM
BULL'S HEAD FARMERS MARKET
GOVERNMENT HOUSE
BLACK WATCH WELL
Pembroke Marsh
Parson's Rd Playground
HOUSE OF INDIA
FORT HAMILTON
BROADWAY BISTRO
BERMUDA UNDERWATER EXPLORATION INSTITUTE
Red Hole
LOVERS LN
White's Island
Harbour
Hamilton
Clarence Cove
Deep Bay
Admiralty House Park

NORTH SHORE RD
ST JOHN'S RD
SPANISH POINT RD
LANGTON HILL RD
MARSH FOLLY RD
PARSON'S RD
VALLEY RD
CAVENDISH RD
HAPPY VALLEY RD
DUNDONALD ST
CHURCH ST
FRONT ST
PAR-LA-VILLE RD
WOODLANDS RD
RICHMOND RD
ROSEDON
ROSEMONT AVE
PITTS BAY RD
FAIRYLAND RD
Bond Bay

0   0.25 mi
0   0.25 km

© AVALON TRAVEL PUBLISHING, INC.

jewelry, scented candles, greeting cards, needle-craft, afghans, and handbags. Children will love the market for the fun, relaxed atmosphere, all the nibbles, and the pony rides (in dry weather only). The market is held rain or shine; in downpours, stalls set up a few yards away on the ground floor of the carpark's indoor section.

Admiralty House Park

Once the site of an 1816 residence named Admiralty House and later a Royal Navy Hospital, Admiralty House Park (junction of North Shore Rd. and Spanish Point Rd., open sunrise to sunset daily, admission free) now belongs to the national parks system. The former mansion, torn down except for a ballroom that's used for special events, used to provide housing for British admiralty officers who worked at Dockyard. The graceful park has gorgeous old trees, nature trails, and small beaches, including shallow Clarence Cove, which, sheltered by a sturdy dock (which kids love to jump and dive off), is a popular neighborhood swimming venue. Across the cove, **Deep Bay** is also well used in

the summer, with young daredevils performing in-air stunts on their way into the turquoise depths. Notable also are the tunnels, galleries, and caves dug into the park's seaside limestone cliffs by the British military in the 1850s. The property was a Royal Navy signal center during World War II, but the British pulled out of Bermuda in 1951, turning it over to the island's government. Unfortunately, the park's upkeep has declined, with graffiti and garbage spoiling its natural beauty at times. Safety has also been an issue, as the park is sometimes a hangout for youths and unsavory elements. Women would be advised not to come here alone, except during the busy summer months. Families, groups, and couples should have no problems. The park tends to be packed when school is out and is especially crowded at Cup Match and other summer weekends.

◖ Spanish Point Park

Situated on picturesque promontory which defines the channel entrance for all ships approaching the Great Sound and Hamilton

© ROSEMARY JONES

Steeped in maritime history, Spanish Point is still home to fishermen and watery pursuits.

Harbour, Spanish Point Park (open sunrise to sunset daily, admission free) is a delightful excursion—either for a quick visit and photos or a whole day's relaxation. Utterly peaceful, it sits at the tip of Spanish Point, a historic little community whose marzipan cottages and rambling tributaries evoke a long and direct connection with the sea. Spanish Point Road twists down past the offshoots of Doubloon Lane, Stormalong Lane, and Ocean Bright to the shorefront park at the bottom. The route is fringed by gingerbread architecture, candy-pink walls, and even a few rare wooden homes. One resident has labeled his property, "The Home that Jack Built, 1924." Beside a carpark, a beach edges Stovell Bay, a tiny harbor where pint-sized fishing boats, dinghies, and ruby sailboats like the kind in kids' storybooks sit at a collection of moorings.

At the bay's mouth lies a rusty hulk and pontoons, the remains of **H.M. Floating Dock,** once a magnificent example of Victorian maritime engineering. Launched in Woolwich on the Thames in 1869, the 47,000-square-foot dry dock was towed across the Atlantic by four Royal Navy ironclads, arriving in Bermuda 35 days later. The largest drydock in the world at the time, the structure was able to heave 10,000 tons and was used by the Royal Navy at Dockyard. By the early 1900s, however, it was outdated, unable to accommodate new, larger vessels, and was sold and towed to Spanish Point to be dismantled. But the World Wars intervened, and the effort was finally abandoned. Although it's an eyesore, the hulk today provides a sheltered harbor for local boats.

The park itself lies inside a tiny gate, its shady lawns, whispering pines, and baygrapes stretching along the finger of land bordered by the North Shore and Great Sound. There are picnic tables and benches, and a sprinkling of reefs and islets just a few yards off the North Shore side has created calm, shallow coves perfect for snorkeling. Walk to the end of the park that looks out over the shipping channel toward Dockyard—a good vantage point to watch the comings and goings of ocean liners and cargo ships into port. The park attracts a local crowd who wash cars or play cards near the beach. There are public toilets near the carpark.

Black Watch Well

Ignored by passing Bermudian motorists, Black Watch Well sits at a sometimes chaotic three-way intersection between North Shore Road, Langton Hill, and Blackwatch Pass. It is marked by a sign, which explains the little structure's history. The well takes its name from the heroic Scottish soldiers of the 1st Battalion of the 42nd Regiment of Loyal Highlanders, who are forever remembered here as having come to the aid of the area's "poor and their cattle in the long drought of 1849." The limestone well they dug down to an underwater lens still bears its wooden roof, though its interior has been capped for safety reasons. Park at nearby C-Mart's parking lot, or across the road at the **Ducking Stool Park,** whose name refers to its history as a site like St. George, where 17th-century public punishments, using a seat on a log to dunk sinners, were frequently staged. These days, it is a popular Cup Match campsite, with deep swimming holes off its scenic cliffs. The dramatic Pass is also worth driving or walking through; its towering limestone walls, which were carved by hand in the 1930s, demonstrate a magnificent feat of engineering, and also show the crumbling geological strata of local limestone. The Pass links North Shore Road with Marsh Folly and Palmetto Road.

Government House

From the junction of Blackwatch Pass and North Shore Road, you can also see the impressive lawns of Government House, whose Victorian towers overlook north Hamilton and the North Shore. Not open to the public, the property is the home of Bermuda's resident British governor, currently Sir John Vereker and his wife Judy, who hold numerous official functions here. Built in the late 1800s, the house sits on 210 acres of manicured lawns and gardens, tennis courts, and an Olympic-length swimming pool, forests of cedar and spice trees, and mature plantings over the years by previous governors or royal visitors. Queen Elizabeth II and Prince Philip have stayed here, along with Prince Charles, Sir Winston Churchill, and President John F. Kennedy. The property, which flies the governor's own flag when he's on the island, was tainted with a horrific crime in 1973, when then-governor Sir Richard Sharples was shot dead while walking his dog at night, as was his aide-de-camp, Captain Hugh Sayers. Two Bermudian men were convicted and hanged for the crime, and ensuing race riots marked the most bitter, turbulent episode in the island's modern history. The property is the site of the Queen's Birthday cocktail party in June, held to honor Bermudians receiving lifetime achievement awards bestowed by Buckingham Palace on Commonwealth citizens.

St. John's Church

Built in 1621, the original St. John's Church (127 St. John's Rd., tel. 441/292-5308, fax 441/296-9173, admission free) was one of the island's first churches, with a wooden structure and thatched palmetto roof. It was destroyed less than a century later by a hurricane-fed fire and replaced by a stone church, which was demolished in 1821 for the needs of a larger congregation. Numerous additions and renovations have been done since then, but the Anglican church remains a historic and popular community landmark ministering to the parish's varied demographics. (It is also the mother church of St. Monica's and St. Augustine's mission churches in the North Village neighborhood.) The church's beautiful interior is notable for its stained glass, bell tower, and 2,418-pipe organ, rebuilt in 1989. The crowded graveyard contains historic family plots—stacked to make more room—interspersed with ancient cedars and other shady trees and shrubs. Funerals are held many weekday afternoons here; I've even seen several gombey ceremonies, with graveside performances by the colorfully garbed troupes.

Pembroke Marsh Park

Used as the island's trash dump for the latter part of the 20th century, Pembroke Marsh Park (bordered by Marsh Folly Rd. and Parson's Rd., open sunrise to sunset daily, admission free) bears the scars of longtime pollution that could take decades to erase. The good news is, that process has already begun, with trash now disposed of at the North Shore incinerator and the marsh today the focus of government plans to return them to public parkland. While scientists say pollution levels in the water are high, the area remains a popular birding site; egrets and herons are seen in the vicinity, along with endemic plant life. Access is difficult and dirty, however. A public playground, alongside the park on Parson's Road, is a popular attraction for children of all ages.

C Fort Hamilton

Built in the 1870s, Fort Hamilton (Happy Valley Rd., off King St., tel. 441/292-1234, 8 A.M.–sunset daily, admission free), like Fort St. Catherine in St. George's, remains one of the best-kept examples of the island's ancient fortifications. It's equally interesting to historians, gardeners, and sightseers, thanks to its awesome panorama of Hamilton and Pembroke, as well as the Paget shoreline. The fort served as the southern end of the Royal Navy's Prospect defensive line—intended to halt an enemy attack on Spanish Point, and thereby protect the Royal Naval Dockyard and fleet anchored at Grassy Bay. Managed by the Corporation of Hamilton, the fort is used today as a plant nursery, the reason for its meticulously landscaped gardens. Mosaic pathways lead among vibrant flower gardens, and benches are positioned on lower lawns and atop the ramparts, where cannons point out over Hamilton's corporate streets below. A wooden drawbridge leads into the fort, where a guardroom and tearoom (now closed) sit at the entrance. Inside, steps near the entrance lead down into the circular moat garden, planted with gorgeous varieties of ferns, waxy elephant ears, orchids, bromeliads, and other shade-loving species. A skinny dirt path follows the moat completely around; despite the occasional mosquito, it is one of my favorite walks. Along the way, doorways lead into the fort's dungeons, which are worth exploring if you have time. The smell of thick, damp limestone permeates this network of subterranean galleries, which kids, especially, will find fascinating, though perhaps a little frightening if they're very young. The catacomb is usually well lit, and there are various entrances and exits, including one set of stairs that must number in the hundreds. A caretaker's cottage is situated on the main lawn, and there are well-maintained toilets here. Every Monday noontime throughout the November–March season, kilted dancers and drummers perform a bagpipe "skirling" ceremony at the fort.

(Bermuda Underwater Exploration Institute

The world's last frontier—the ocean—is the domain of the Bermuda Underwater Exploration Institute (BUEI) (40 Crow Ln., East Broadway, tel. 441/292-7219, ticket desk 441/297-7314, fax 441/236-6141, www.buei.org, 9 A.M.– 5 P.M. Mon.–Fri., 10 A.M.–5 P.M. Sat. and Sun, last ride at 4 P.M., $12.50 adults, $10 seniors,

$6 children 6–17, under five free). Opened in 1997, the facility's mission to advance understanding and appreciation of the world's oceans is carried out through a small but interesting array of hands-on exhibits and eye-popping artifacts. The notable collection of early diving apparatus includes a diving bell, exo-suit, and a bathysphere replica of the famous metal pod in which William Beebe and Otis Barton descended a half-mile down off Bermuda in the 1930s (see sidebar *Beebe's Bathysphere* in the *Smith's and Hamilton Parishes* chapter). The adventure starts with a simulated (and rather hokey) submersible dive to the 12,000-foot bottom of Bermuda's seamount. The institute is a tribute to the career of world-renowned Bermudian diver Teddy Tucker, who has retrieved artifacts and dived on most of the island's 150 or more known shipwrecks. The **Tucker Shipwreck Gallery** features a map of known wrecks, and exhibits of their contents, including cannons, bottles, and clay jars. The **Treasure Room** displays Spanish gold and pirates' booty collected from local dive sites,

© ROSEMARY JONES

the Bermuda Underwater Exploration Institute

as well as a replica of the infamous "Tucker Cross," which mysteriously disappeared from Bermuda Maritime Museum shortly before the Queen's visit in 1975. **Science at Sea** uses interactive exhibits to teach visitors about the body reaction to the pressures of the deep, and a wall of bioluminescent creatures down a darkened tunnel mimics the feel of the deep ocean. Kids and ichthyologists will especially like the video-simulated shark cage that allows you to experience the charge of a Great White. Upstairs, don't miss the **Jack Lightbourn Shell Collection,** showcasing some 1,200 of the Bermudian diver's own shells, including 1,000 different species, of which 110 are Bermudian. The **Oceans Gift Shop** sells marine-inspired books, games, and toys, including pirate gear and Christmas ornaments. **Broadway Bistro** is located on the site's waterfront.

BEACHES

Clarence Cove at Admiralty Park off North Shore Road, is a delightful little beach, shallow enough for young children but overcrowded on busy summer weekends. Nearby **Deep Bay** is best accessed farther down the North Shore (via unmarked steep, stone steps cut into the hillside off North Shore Road near a bus layby). At low tide, there's a beach here, but it is most popular for diving and jumping into its deep swimming hole.

The coves and bays off **Spanish Point Park**'s North Shore edge are perfect for snorkeling or bathing when the wind's from the south (most of the summer). Shallow reefs here can be seen through clear water even from the shoreline. The No. 4 bus comes by here from Hamilton, or you can come by scooter and leave vehicles in the small carpark.

ENTERTAINMENT AND EVENTS

A tournament of 31 of the world's top squash players, the **Bermuda Masters** (tel. 441/292-6881, fax 441/2925-8718, www .bermudamasters.com) is held every April at a state-of-the-art glass court at Bermuda High School, Richmond Road. Organized by the

Bermuda Squash Racquets Association, the event offers 600 spectators perfect viewing as players battle for one of the most prestigious titles on the world circuit. The event is sanctioned by the Professional Squash Association (P.S.A.).

Weekly **skirling ceremonies** featuring the Bermuda Islands Pipe Band are held at Fort Hamilton (noon on Mon., Nov.–March only). Dancers and drummers in kilts perform for the crowd atop the fort's panoramic ramparts.

Nightlife

Friday night happy hour at the Fairmont Princess Hotel's **Heritage Court** (76 Pitts Bay Rd., tel. 441/295-3000, fax 441/295-1914, www.fairmont.com/hamilton, 5–9:30 P.M. Fridays, April–Oct. only) was the place to see and be seen in 2004–05, and there appears to be no reduction in the crowds of partygoers who stream west from Hamilton offices at the end of each week. The big attraction is the elegant hotel's lobby bar and its alfresco terrace, perfect for schmoozing at sunset on the water's edge. Happy-hour specials ($5 for beers and rum cocktails) are offered on the bar's regular sky-high drink prices. The Heritage Court bar is open year-round (10 A.M.–1 A.M. daily). It is, perhaps, Bermuda's most elegant bar, projecting an old-world feel that makes for enjoyable evenings—the $12 martinis notwithstanding.

Beebe's Lounge offers a sophisticated soiree venue inside the front section of Broadway Bistro at Bermuda Underwater Exploration Institute (40 Crow Ln., East Broadway, tel. 441/292-6122, fax 441/292-8825).

Get local with a visit to the **Spanish Point Boat Club** (Spanish Point Rd., tel. 441/295-1030, fax 441/292-8024, 11:30 A.M.–midnight Mon.–Thurs. and Sun., 11:30 A.M.–1 A.M. Fri. and Sat.), whose bar has a nightly gathering of neighborhood residents, local fishermen, and other regulars who like the $3 highballs and beer. Like its sign says, the facility is a members' club, but tourists are welcome.

The Robin Hood Pub & Restaurant (25 Richmond Rd., tel. 441/295-3314, fax 441/292-9338, www.robinhood.bm, 11:30 A.M.–1 A.M.

daily) has a lively sports-bar scene, including quiz nights and live soccer and NHL showdowns on big-screen TV. It's a favorite stomping ground for U.K. and Canadian expat residents.

SHOPPING

Jeremy Johnson's Village Carpentry (127 North Shore, tel. 441/292-2088 or 441/295-5370) has been a roadside institution since the 1960s. Today Johnson's aromatic workshop, spreading the scent of cedar along this stretch of North Shore, is worth a visit to get a glimpse of cedar craftsmen at work. He sells cedar trinkets, animals, and other sweet-smelling mementoes from the roadside building.

Casual Footware (14 Parson's Rd., tel. 441/295-9968, 10 A.M.–5 P.M. Mon.–Fri.) sells hip and comfortable Birkenstocks, Mephisto, Oakley, and Hogan footwear for men, women, and kids.

SPORTS AND RECREATION

Tennis

Anyone can play at the government-owned **William Joell Tennis Stadium** (2 Marsh Folly Rd., at Cedar Ave., tel. 441/292-0105, fax 441/292-4802, 8 A.M.–10 P.M. Mon.–Fri., 8 A.M.–5 P.M. Sat. and Sun., $8 an hour). The popular facility, named for the Bermudian recognized for knocking down racial barriers in the sport, has eight courts (three clay, five hard courts), three of which are lit for night play, for an additional $8 fee. Traditional tennis attire is required, and advance bookings are recommended. Peak times are after 5 P.M. and on Saturday mornings. Pro Eugene Woods gives lessons (adult $60 an hour, or $250 for five; juniors $45). The shop sells cold drinks and tennis balls and also rents rackets ($5).

Scuba and Water Sports

The **Bermuda Sub-Aqua Club** (Admiralty Park, tel. 441/292-6642, information line 441/291-5640) is a NAUI-registered training and diving organization, which arranges regular expeditions for its 150 members throughout the year. Club nights are held on Wednesday evenings after 7 P.M. at the clubhouse, a pink building on the right as you enter the park. Visitors are welcome.

A PADI five-star facility opened in 1981, **Dive Bermuda** at the Fairmont Hamilton Princess Hotel (76 Pitts Bay Rd., tel. 441/295-9485, www.bermudascuba.com) offers two-tank dives leaving its Hamilton center at noon daily through the summer. Snorkelers are also welcome. Popular dive sites off the island's northwest include the *Constellation,* the 1918 schooner featured in Peter Benchley's 1977 thriller, *The Deep.*

Fishing

Spanish Point Boat Club (Spanish Point Rd., tel. 441/295-1030, fax 441/292-8024) is one of the island's main sportfishing hubs, with docks and hauling equipment outside, where boats land their record catches. A members' club, it nevertheless welcomes tourists.

Veteran sportfishing king Allen DeSilva runs **Mako Charters** (11 Abri Ln., Spanish Point, tel. 441/295-0835, fax 441/295-3620, www.fishbermuda.com) aboard his 57-foot air-conditioned Carolina sportfisher, *DeMako,* the island's largest charter fishing vessel. DeSilva holds the current 1,352-pound blue marlin record, and boasts one-day hauls such as 44 yellowfin tuna. Full-day (nine hours) charters for five people cost $1,600 ($500 deposit required). Charters carry a maximum eight people.

Father-and-son team Keith and Kevin Winter operate **Playmate Charters** (4 Mill Point Ln., tel. 441/292-7131, boat cell 441/335-5172, fax 441/292-9598, playmate@logic.bm), offering full- ($1,200) and half-day ($850) charters aboard 43-foot *Playmate,* a Torres Sports Fisherman, outfitted with tournament tackle, a fighting chair, two fishing chairs, outriggers, downriggers, kites, and other accessories for modern game-fishing.

Soccer

Evening and weekend soccer games are held at the clubhouse field of **Bermuda Athletic Association** (B.A.A.) (24 Woodlands Rd., tel. 441/292-3161), an organization which has promoted a wide gamut of sports on the

MADE IN BERMUDA

There's always a T-shirt or paperweight to take home, but if you look around, you'll find far more interesting souvenirs of your trip to Bermuda.

Established in 1928, the **Bermuda Perfumery** (Stewart Hall, 5 Queen St., St. George, tel. 441/293-0627, toll-free from the U.S. 800/527-8213, www.bermuda-perfumery.com) used to operate out of rambling gardens of a historic estate in Hamilton Parish. When the land was sold in the late 1990s, the business moved to the town of St. George, and today, the popular LiLi line of fragrances, including perfume (0.25 oz./7.5 ml $29), soaps, body lotions, and bath and shower gel, is sold in stores islandwide. The scents appear to have a fervent fan base overseas, including Bermudians' friends and relatives who get hooked on the scent of bermudiana, or who *must* have a bottle of oleander to wear at their wedding. Scents include Easter lily, jasmine, oleander, passion flower, frangipani, and bermudiana. You can learn all about their production by visiting the Perfumery and its pretty little garden, now housed at a Bermuda National Trust property.

There's nothing more Bermudian than cedar – the *Juniperus bermudiana* variety, of course. Cedar trinkets are sold in stores all over the island, but you can watch the *maestro* in person at the **Bermuda Arts Centre** (tel. 441/234-2809, www.artbermuda.bm) at Dockyard. There, cedar craftsman Chesley Trott works wonders out of a pile of gnarled silver twigs or tree trunks, that today demand top prices. Pull-toys and public-art sculptures are his specialty. **Jeremy Johnson's Village Carpentry** (127 North Shore, Pembroke, tel. 441/292-2088) is also worth dropping into. The aromatic roadside workshop sells cedar animals and other hand-carved mementos.

Gosling's Black Seal Rum will ensure your enjoyment of black 'n' cokes and dark 'n' stormies long after you leave Bermuda. Bottles of rum (one-liter $12), as well as Goslings and Horton's rum cakes, can be found at **Bermuda Duty Free** (Departures Hall, tel. 441/293-2870), the retail outlet at Bermuda International Airport.

Island artworks are some of the highest quality and nicest products visitors can buy to take Bermuda home with them. **The Bermuda Society of Arts** (City Hall and Arts Centre, tel. 441/292-3824) holds regular shows where members' oils, acrylics, watercolors, sculpture, and other media are for sale. Artist Barbara Finsness's popular **Island Shop** (3 Queen St., tel. 441/292-5292, or 49 Front St., Old Cellar Ln., tel. 441/292-6307) carries her designs on linen tablecloths and place settings, handbags, Christmas ornaments, and ceramics. Around the corner, gift shop **Pulp & Circumstance** (10 Queen St., at Reid, tel. 441/292-9586) has some greeting cards by Bermudian artists and photographers.

Bermuda stamps and coins make good souvenirs. The General Post Office's **Philatelic Bureau** (corner of Church and Parliament Streets, tel. 441/297-7807) sells collections of commemorative stamps, featuring themes of cultural and historical significance to the island. Numismatists seek out the **Bermuda Monetary Authority** (43 Victoria St., Hamilton, tel. 441/295-5278, www.bma.bm) for boxed gift sets of Bermuda coins, including commemoratives such as 2005's gold and silver quincentennial issue.

Buy a CD by Bermudian **Heather Nova** (www.heathernova.com), an ethereal singer-songwriter with Lilith Fair and movie-soundtrack credits to her name. Born and raised in Bermuda and the Caribbean of a centuries-old maritime family (her ancestor was notorious privateer Hezekiah Frith), Nova's melodic songs reverberate with island references – including tree frogs, redbirds, sailboats, and the sea. She lives in Bermuda's West End when not touring Europe or recording albums (her works include *Oyster, South, Blow, Siren,* and *Redbird*). Find her music at **The Music Box** (58 Reid St., tel. 441/295-4839), on the racks in North America and Europe, or www.amazon.com.

island—football (soccer), badminton, rugby, swimming, track and field—for over a century. Admission is usually free.

Spas

Inverurie Day Spa at the Fairmont Hamilton Princess (76 Pitts Bay Rd., tel. 441/295-7016 or 441/293-3000 ext. 7811, inveruriedayspa@ tbinet.bm, 9 A.M.–6 P.M. daily, credit cards accepted) is a small spa offering facials, body treatments, waxing, manicures, and pedicures.

For Kids

The government-run **Parson's Road Playground** is a highly popular attraction for children from all over the island. Parents bring their kids after school at 3:30 P.M., and holidays find the swings, slides, tunnels, fort, and pirate ship crowded with happy youngsters. There's also a gazebo for shady picnics, and plenty of parking.

Spanish Point Park's tiny coves and quiet, shallow bays are just what children love, and kids can spend hours here exploring rock pools, snorkeling, and swimming. The park's North Shore edge, where coves are scattered, is best when the wind's blowing from the south; in the winter, the water gets choppy. Shady trees, lawns for playing and picnic tables make this a perfect family spot.

Don't miss **Fort Hamilton**'s moat garden and dungeons—one of the Hamilton area's best kid-pleasing attractions.

ACCOMMODATIONS
Under $200

Perched on the North Shore, **Mazarine By The Sea** (91 North Shore Rd., tel. 441/292-0010 or 441/292-1690, fax 441/292-9077, mazarinebythesea@ibl.bm, $135–155) has seven units looking out over turquoise horizons that stretch as far as Dockyard. There's an oceanfront mini pool, and access by steps (no beach) down to the sea, where snorkeling is very good on calm days. All rooms have private bathrooms, kitchenettes with two burners, refrigerator, microwave, and toaster, and private balconies.

$200-300

Forty-year-old **Rosemont Guest Apartments** (41 Rosemont Ave., tel. 441/292-1055, fax 441/295-3913, www.rosemont.bm, doubles $198–204) offer self-catering-style accommodations on Hamilton's doorstep. Some 47 suites and apartments with private entrances are arranged around a central swimming pool. All have balconies or patios, air-conditioning, full bath, kitchen, cable TV, hair dryer, Internet access, and daily maid service. All are wheelchair accessible. The family-run enterprise was purchased in 2006 by the longtime manager of the popular South Shore Reefs Resort. Catering mainly to business travelers, the property also makes a handy place for long-term rentals, thanks to the kitchenettes and housekeeping units.

The (**Oxford House** (20 Woodbourne Ave., tel. 441/295-0503, fax 441/295-0250, www.oxfordhouse.bm, $105 per person) has seen its city-side neighborhood drastically change in the past decade, since the Bermudiana Hotel—which once stood opposite—was closed and the huge property transformed into insurance towers for the ACE and XL companies. But the quaint, British-style, two-story guesthouse has proudly stood its ground against the corporate invasion—and benefited hugely, thanks to the influx of business travelers. Oxford's small, elegant rooms offer exactly what's demanded by anyone attending meetings within a few blocks, or a visitor who plans to spend most of their time in Hamilton or wants a central location not on a beach. Twelve guest rooms are furnished like private residences, almost dollhouse-like with dressers and curtains and floral bedspreads. Each has a private bath, coffeemaker, air-conditioning, and cable TV. Continental breakfast is served in the lounge every morning.

Renovated under new ownership in 2005 to great acclaim, (**Bay City Guesthouse** (53 Pitts Bay Rd., tel. 441/295-1275 or 441/336-5354, fax 441/295-3166, www.baycity.bm, doubles from $210) commandeers a sweeping curve of Pitts Bay Road, its dozen guestrooms offered panoramic views of the harbor. Catering mainly to business clientele, amenities in the newly refurnished and decorated rooms include high-speed Internet access, air-conditioning, digital cable TV, telephones and maid service. Hot tubs were being installed in the property's backgarden in 2006. Owner/manager Bernadette Soote serves a daily continental breakfast, and evening beverages (self-service).

Edgehill Manor (36 Rosemont Ave., tel. 441/295-7124, fax 441/295-3850, www.bermuda.com/edgehill, doubles $198–210) is a completely refurbished, colonial-style mansion-turned-bed-and-breakfast. Seven large rooms—four upstairs with private balconies and splendid views—have air-conditioning, ceiling fans, private bathrooms, cable TV, Internet access, small refrigerators, microwaves, safes, and clock radios. The property also has a large freshwater pool in the quiet neighborhood garden.

A former manor house on the edge of Hamilton, **◖ Royal Palms** (24 Rosemont Ave., tel. 441/292-1854, toll-free 800/678-0783 U.S. or 800/799-0824 Canada, fax 441/292-1946, www.royalpalms.bm, doubles $210–340, including breakfast) offers relaxing surroundings in a very convenient location. With its hallmark white shutters and wraparound veranda, the turn-of-the-20th-century property's biggest draw is its beautiful garden, which spills riotous bougainvillea over the road, as well as its standout restaurant, Ascot's. A total of 32 rooms—including seven brand new ones added in 2006—are decorated in European florals with high ceilings and classic moldings. All have cable TV, air-conditioning, and high-speed Internet access, making this a very popular business visitors' hotel. A few mini-suites have kitchenettes. Run by brother-sister team Richard Smith and Susan Weare, Royal Palms remains one of the island's best small hotels.

Elegant **Rosedon** (61 Pitts Bay Rd., tel. 441/295-1640, fax 441/295-5904, www.rosedon bermuda.com, doubles from $238) stands opposite the Fairmont Hamilton Princess Hotel, one of Pitts Bay's grand old mansions, built in 1906. Decorated like an English manor home, with rooms boasting oak, mahogany, cherry,

and redwood, the small bed-and-breakfast hotel is highly popular with business travelers, given its amenities and short walk from Hamilton. Rosedon's 47 rooms have cable TV, air-conditioning, private baths, phones, refrigerators, coffeemakers and Internet access. "Royal Rooms" are a step up, with CD players and whirlpool tubs. Same-day laundry service is available. Guests have a choice of picnic lunches or poolside à la carte service, and at 4 P.M. everyday, staff members serve a grand afternoon tea. The hotel also offers wedding and honeymoon packages.

Over $300

Entering Relais & Chateau property **◖ Waterloo House** (100 Pitts Bay Rd., tel. 441/295-4480, fax 441/295-2585, www .waterloohouse.com, standard rooms start at $380) is like stepping over the threshold of an elegant waterfront home. The tangerine property, dating back to 1815, has original artworks and antiques, fountains with real turtles sunbathing in rocky pools, beautifully landscaped gardens, a small swimming pool, interior courtyards, and terraced gardens on the Hamilton water side. Its Christmas Dinner and alfresco New Year's Day buffets are legendary. While some of the floral rooms could use an update, modern amenities such as T1 lines and WiFi have been added to all 20 rooms and 10 suites. Rooms also offer cable TV, air-conditioning, en suite bathrooms, and private balconies or terraces; some have whirlpool baths. Waterloo's staff is ultra-professional, and the property remains a beautiful and convenient nook on the city's edge—far more intimate than a larger hotel. Ask for a harbor-facing room, rather than one on the traffic-laden Pitts Bay Road side. Room rates include continental breakfast and afternoon tea. Guests also have use of the facilities (championship tennis courts, spa, squash courts, nine-hole golf course) at two sister properties on the South Shore, Horizons & Cottages, and the exclusive, members-only Coral Beach & Tennis Club.

Fondly known simply as "The Princess," the **◖ Fairmont Hamilton Princess Hotel**

(76 Pitts Bay Rd., tel. 441/295-3000, toll-free 800/330-8272, fax 441/295-1914, www.fairmont.com/hamilton, 410 rooms, doubles start at $409) has been a fixture of the Pitts Bay waterfront since Victorian times. The confectionary-pink hotel was built in honor of Queen Victoria's daughter, Princess Louise, who visited Bermuda in 1883, launching a tourism industry in her wake. The property's harborfront venue, beautiful views, and five-star amenities have made it a popular choice ever since. In 2006, the Princess and its more modern sister hotel, the Fairmont Southampton, were sold to the Kingdom Hotels International empire, owners of the Raffles group and London's Savoy—a transaction which can only mean good things for both hotels' guests of the future. The Princess, famous during World War II as an intelligence center where mail and radio communications were analyzed by more than 1,000 British "censorettes," offers traditional comforts just a 15-minute scenic walk from Hamilton's center. Guest rooms and suites decorated in pastel florals and old-time furnishings offer either garden/pool or harbor views—the latter far preferable, but also more expensive. Some have private balconies with views stretching up the Great Sound. The property is popular with Hamilton's corporate visitors, and most rooms have high-speed Internet access, dataports, spacious work desks, telephone with voicemail, and cable TV. Some offer large-screen TVs, marble bathrooms, and large, panoramic decks. "Fairmont Gold" suites offer even more business amenities. The hotel has a large heated pool, scuba center, popular lobby bar and afternoon tea area, a coffee shop, small spa, and award-winning restaurant on-site. Guests are also able to use facilities at the Fairmont Southampton, including a golf course, beach, tennis courts, and large spa.

FOOD
Cafés and Bars

For extraordinary comfort food Bermudian-style, join the local crowd at **❮ The Green Lantern** (9 Serpentine Rd., tel. 441/295-6995, 6 A.M.–8:45 P.M. Mon., Tues., Thurs.,

Sat., 6 A.M.–3 P.M. Wed.). Made-from-scratch pancakes, fresh fish dinners (wahoo), and homemade soups are the highlights of this green-painted roadside eatery that draws packed lunch and dinner crowds to its no-frills, diner-style interior. Specials, such as its American Thanksgiving Dinner of roast turkey, baked ham, farine pie (made with root vegetables), macaroni 'n' cheese, candied yams, and apple pie are popular, including takeout versions. The daily pièce de résistance is the chocolate cake made by Jamaican waitress Fay Woodley. The coconut cake slices and sticky macaroons are tasty, too.

Chef Judith Wadson's **❮ Aggie's Garden & Waterside Cafe** (108 Pitts Bay Rd., harbor level, tel. 441/296-7346, aggies@tbinet.bm, 10:30 A.M.–3 P.M. Mon.–Fri., special dinners by appointment) uses organic produce from her brother Tom's Southampton farm at this adorable waterside eatery, where your stomach feels it's checked into a spa. The property once belonged to Wadson's grandmother, Aggie. Today it attracts epicurean lunch-goers with its delicious wraps, omelettes, quiches, sandwiches, salads, homemade pizza, and lemonade, all made as you wait in the pocket-size café. Wedged between insurance towers, Aggie's sits at the foot of a long set of brick stairs from Pitts Bay Road—look for the sign at the sidewalk. You can sit outside under umbrellas on the tiny lawn and watch the yachts sail by on Hamilton Harbor—a relaxing mental escape from Hamilton's hustle and bustle.

Monty's Restaurant (75 Pitts Bay Rd., tel. 441/295-5759, fax 441/296-0166, montys@fkbnet.bm, breakfast and lunch 7:30 A.M.–2:30 P.M. Mon.–Sat., dinner 6–10 P.M. Mon.–Sat., breakfast/brunch 7:30 A.M.–2:30 P.M. Sun.) got an interior makeover in 2003, and its menu is as popular as ever. Lunch includes fish chowder, soups, sesame chicken salad, wraps and grilled sandwiches, burgers, fish 'n' chips, and Southern fried chicken. The dinner menu boasts crepes, rockfish, egg rolls, steaks, curries, bangers 'n' mash, and house creations such as hazelnut-crusted duckling. Kids will love the pancake or waffle breakfasts and the chocolate

ONION-NATION

If you're seeing giant psychedelic onions popping up around the parishes, don't reach for the smelling salts just yet.

The Masterworks Foundation, always up for a public-rousing gimmick, shipped in 50 polymer onions from Toronto in 2006 and distributed them to artists, architects, schools, graphic designers, and anyone else with a creative bent to submit ideas on how they'd decorate it. A committee chose participants to paint their onions, which were then posted to all points of the island. (In 2005, the charity did the same with polymer hogs, which have also joined the ranks of the island's public art.)

Bermuda's fascination with onions dates back to the late 1800s, when crates of the pungent bulb grown by island farmers were shipped off to winter markets in New York, Philadelphia, and other East Coast urban centers, along with potatoes, tomatoes, lilies, and arrowroot. Hamilton's docks were the major shipment hub for thousands of barrels and crates of produce. Red or white Bermuda onions – known for their mild, sweet taste – remained a major island export until cheaper produce from California and Florida, coupled with higher U.S. import tariffs, put an end to the handsome profits in the early 1900s.

"Onion" remains a popular term of endearment, however, among islanders. If you call someone a "real onion" there can be no stronger endorsement of their genuine Bermudian-ness. Numerous local businesses also use onion in their names, though none have anything to do with selling the aromatic vegetable.

fudge bomb for dessert. The traditional Sunday codfish breakfast is also a crowd-pleaser. Inconveniently, the restaurant closes 2:30–6 P.M., so late lunch-goers are out of luck.

Tasty homemade pizzas (including takeout service) and loads of beer and pub grub get crowds to **The Robin Hood Pub & Restaurant** (25 Richmond Rd., tel. 441/295-3314, fax 441/292-9338, www.robinhood.bm, 11:30 A.M.–1 A.M. daily), where British soccer and occasional quiz nights entertain regulars. Steak platters, pastas, English staples like cottage pies and Cornish pasties, even Indian curries keep customers satisfied with big helpings and reasonable prices.

Fine Dining

Award-winning chef Serge Bottelli keeps gourmands titillated at (**** **Broadway Bistro** (Bermuda Underwater Exploration Institute, 40 Crow Ln., East Broadway, tel. 441/292-6122, fax 441/292-8825, lunch 11:45 A.M.–2:45 P.M., dinner 6:30–10:30 P.M. Mon.–Sat.), where French bistro fare evokes a Mediterranean-style brasserie on the waterfront. With a new name (it was formerly La Coquille) and menu in 2006, the bistro offers comforts such as steak frites, baked goat cheese, and tarte tatin. The adjoining Beebe's Lounge (10:30 P.M.–1 A.M.) serves late-night snacks from the same menu.

Harley's Restaurant at the Fairmont Hamilton Princess Hotel (76 Pitts Bay Rd., tel. 441/295-3000, fax 441/295-1914, www.fairmont.com/hamilton, noon–10 P.M. daily, entrées start at $23) is famous for its aged-beef prime rib and porterhouse selections, the omelettes to order, and its decadent Sunday brunch. Its menu also offers creative Bermuda fish selections (rockfish glazed with bananas and almonds) and pure comfort food, including one of the best versions of mashed potatoes around (full of onions, squash, and skins). There are also lots of vegetarian options. Harley's dining room is elegant, but if the weather's right, choose lunch or dinner on the terrace. Here, next to the endless swimming pool, overlooking the harbor, the food is almost immaterial.

(**** **Ascot's** at Royal Palms Hotel (24 Rosemont Ave., tel. 441/295-9644, 441/292-4986, or 441/296-0831, fax 441/292-1946, lunch noon–2:30 P.M., dinner 6:30–10 P.M. Mon.–Sat.) is where Northern Ireland's Edmund Smith cut his chef's teeth, before winning international awards with his fresh take on Bermudian cuisine. Smith has now taken over a second restaurant in Hamilton, Mediterraneo, and expanded Ascot's in a major 2006 face-lift that added more space. Entrées include dishes such as blackened mahimahi, port-glazed sirloin, and grilled portobello mushrooms. Lunch on the veranda of this 19th-century manor house is also very popular, overlooking gardens spilling with bougainvillea, shady poincianas, and citrus trees.

The 【 **Wellington Room and Poinciana Terrace** at Waterloo House (100 Pitts Bay Rd., tel. 441/295-4480, fax 441/295-2585, www .waterloohouse.com, lunch noon–2:30 P.M., dinner 7–9 P.M. daily) have won numerous awards for service, menu, and elegant style—not to mention one of the island's most scenic dining venues, inside and out. The main dining room, with its antiques and chandeliers, recalls a formal manor home. The menu is outstanding, particularly on special occasions such as Christmas or Thanksgiving. Regulars also attend the outdoor New Year's Day buffet lunch, featuring a feast of salads, fish, meats, and desserts, enjoyed at harborside tables. Dress code for the dining room is listed as casual, though jackets and ties are definitely encouraged at night. Reservations are recommended.

Tearooms

An over-the-top afternoon tea is served daily in the 【 **Heritage Court** at Fairmont Hamilton Princess Hotel (76 Pitts Bay Rd., tel. 441/295-3000, fax 441/295-1914, www.fairmont.com/ hamilton). A Best of Bermuda Award winner, and repeatedly recognized as one of the top 10 afternoon teas in the world, the feast includes finger sandwiches, scones with jam and clotted cream, pastries, sorbets—and 14 teas, including several loose-leaf black varieties, green, herbal, and fruit teas. The tea ($29 plus gratuities) is served 2:30–5:30 P.M. daily in the lobby-area Court.

Grocery Stores

To describe 【 **Miles Market** (The Waterfront, Pitts Bay, tel. 441/295-1234, customer service fax 441/296-4537, www.miles.bm,

7:30 A.M.–7 P.M. Mon.–Sat., 1–5 P.M. Sun.) as a mere grocery store is a cruel insult. The specialty food store—owned by the Cox family, to whom the entire surrounding waterfront complex belongs, Miles has been a fixture of the gourmet scene since 1862. Today, in a modern headquarters, it boasts highly professional staff and pretty much any foodstuff an epicurean could desire. Of course, you need a trust fund to shop here: it's hard to escape without spending at least $100 just on sundries. Miles's meat department is the island's best, with melt-in-your-mouth cuts and both wet-aged and dry-aged beef selections. Treats include cheeses from around the world; fresh croissants, muffins, and pains du chocolat; a menu of olive oils and marmalades; ethnic sections; wines from France, Napa, and Lebanon; and organic everything—dinner-party hostesses live here. Miles also has a coffee bar, Café Godiva, so you can sip a latte or cappuccino while you shop. The store's Miles To Go deli offers takeout feasts (salads, fish cakes, polenta, grilled vegetables), and staff pack up lunch boxes or gourmet picnics to order (smoked salmon, grilled chicken, fresh fruit platter, strawberry tartlet). Picnic menus start at $19.95; to order call tel. 441/295-1234, ext. 255.

The Garden Market (13 Serpentine Rd., tel. 441/292-7000, fax 441/295-1260, 7 A.M.– 7 P.M. Mon.–Thurs., 7 A.M.–8 P.M. Fri. and Sat.) is a family business with friendly staff, vegetables from local farmers, flowers, wine, and liquor. A 2005 renovation updated the store and added new parking.

Arnold's Family Market (113 St. John's Rd., tel. 441/292-3310, 6:30 A.M.–midnight daily) is a bustling neighborhood hub that has gone in a few short years from a tiny, cramped grocery to a modern expanse. There's a large liquor section, meats, produce, baked goods, magazines, and pharmaceuticals. The place is a zoo on Friday and Saturday nights.

With ample parking on the stretch of North Shore leading east from Hamilton, **C-Mart** (96 North Shore Rd., at the corner of Blackwatch Pass and Langton Hill, tel. 441/292-5332, fax 441/292-4245, 7 A.M.–6 P.M. Mon.–Thurs.,

7 A.M.–7 P.M. Fri. and Sat., 8 A.M.–12:30 P.M. Sun.) makes a convenient stop for snacks, drinks, newspapers, or liquor. The tiny outlet, a favorite with Cup Match campers who set up in the seafront park opposite, also sells fresh baked goods, hot pies, sodas, and dry and frozen goods.

Point Mart (Cox's Hill, tel. 441/292-0342, 8 A.M.–9 P.M. Mon.–Sat.) is tiny but well stocked.

Manuel Soares & Son (Old House Ln., Spanish Point, tel. 441/292-1426, 7 A.M.–8 P.M. Mon.–Sat.) is the only grocery store down in the heart of Spanish Point.

Formerly Dismont Robinson, **Arnold's Express** (135 Front St. East, tel. 441/292-4301, 6:30 A.M.–midnight daily) has joined the successful island-wide grocery store chain.

Carousel Liquors (137 Front St. East, tel. 441/292-2559, 10 A.M.–9 P.M. Mon.–Sat.) sells wines, beer, and spirits.

INFORMATION AND SERVICES

Woodbourne Chemist (Woodbourne Ave., tel. 441/296-1073, 8 A.M.–6 P.M. Mon.–Sat.) is Pembroke's only pharmacy, conveniently located near several hotels and guesthouses.

Gas stations around the parish include: East Broadway Shell Station (25 Crow Ln., tel. 441/296-7225); St. John's Road Station (61 St. John's Rd., tel. 441/296-6732); The Waterfront Shell (2 Waterloo Ln. at The Waterfront, tel. 441/295-3185); and Village Gate Service Station (114 North Shore Rd. at Government Gate, tel. 441/295-8294).

Public toilets are in Spanish Point Park, Admiralty Park, Fort Hamilton, hotels, and restaurants.

ATMs are located at the Butterfield Bank Waterfront branch (Pitts Bay Rd., tel. 441/294-2071).

GETTING THERE AND AROUND

The beauty of staying in Pembroke is that all points in Hamilton are walkable. Pembroke has no ferry service.

Buses

Numerous bus routes serve Pembroke, all departing from the central bus terminal in Hamilton (Washington St. at Church St., tel. 441/295-4311, information and dispatch 441/292-3854, www.bermudabuses.com). To visit Spanish Point, take Route No. 4 (buses run every 20 minutes). Routes 10 and 11 (every 15 minutes) head north through Pembroke on their way to St. George's; 10 takes North Shore Road (Blackwatch Pass) and 11 goes via Palmetto Road. Route No. 5 (hourly, or every half hour at peak commuter times) travels to Pond Hill via Glebe Road. Route No. 9 (hourly) runs between Hamilton and Prospect, Devonshire. Bus Routes 2 (hourly) and 3 (every half hour) head east out of Hamilton, the No. 2 along East Broadway (Bermuda Underwater Exploration Institute), and the No. 3 along Cavendish Road into Devonshire (Fort Hamilton). Fares to Hamilton Parish and St. George's are $4.50, to all other areas on these routes $3 (exact change, or tokens, tickets, or passes required).

Scooters

Oleander Cycles (15 Gorham Rd., tel. 441/295-0919, www.oleandercycles.bm, 8:30 A.M.–5 P.M. daily, closed Sun. in winter) is a first stop for visitors keen to hop on a rental scooter to tour the island. The livery rents standard scooters or bigger, more powerful "deluxe" models, advised if carrying a passenger. Rates ($50 for one day, $212 per week, $16 per day after seven days) include scooter delivery and pickup (or hotel pickup), first tank of gas, helmet, lock and basket, $25 third-party insurance, and islandwide roadside service for breakdowns.

Smatt's Cycle Livery (74 Pitts Bay Rd., tel. 441/2951180, fax 441/295-2539, mssmatt@ northrock.bm, 8 A.M.–5 P.M. daily) is located directly outside the Fairmont Hamilton Princess Hotel.

Taxis

There are taxi stands outside the Fairmont Princess Hotel. To order a cab, call **Bermuda Taxi Radio Cabs** (tel. 441/295-4141) or

HORSE AND BUGGIES

Horse-and-carriage rides have been a popular way to go sightseeing for more than a century. Even today, visitors jump aboard the quaint carriages lined up on Front Street and get a tour of the city and its environs. But as Bermuda's fast-forward development continues, the clip-clop of meandering buggies could soon be a thing of the past. Carriage drivers have received a slew of criticism in the past few years from motorists, who claim carriages hold up traffic and are accidents waiting to happen, and veterinarians and animal-rights activists, who say horses working in the city suffer amid the traffic, stifling heat, pollution, and noisy construction.

There have been several accidents involving horses and vehicles over the past decade, including one in which the animal died. The Society for the Prevention of Cruelty to Animals is now pushing for better monitoring of commercial stables and a rethink of horse-and-carriage service, suggesting it could be restricted to cooler evening hours. The S.P.C.A. also wants to see a shade put up for horses working in the town of St. George (Hamilton's horses got one a few years ago).

Commercial stables are inspected by the government annually. In 2005, a new set of standards was made law to improve stables and facilities within the carriage industry.

Bermuda Industrial Union Taxi Co-op (tel. 441/292-4476), both based in Hamilton.

Horse and Carriage

Horse and carriage can be hired on Front Street for tours around the parish, though the industry could be in for changes. If you do hire a carriage, make sure you get a scenic route, and one that's comfortable for the horse, too. Ask the driver not to be taken around the back of Belco, the island's only power plant. Carriage drivers putting their horses and passengers through this high-decibel ordeal of barbed-wire fences and deafening turbines is nonsensical; the prettier, quieter route past Belco's facade on Serpentine Road, leading back to Par-la-Ville and Front Street, is far preferable. Even better is a meander through the residential lanes of Fairylands and Pitts Bay Road.

DEVONSHIRE AND PAGET PARISHES

Like sisters who may look alike but behave entirely differently, Devonshire and Paget share common traits but occupy divergent places in the collective imagination. Both with verdant valleys, rolling farmland, old estates, centuries-old churches, and nature reserves, the regions are fairly similar in appearance and incorporate a variety of geography, from coastal regions to inland farms. Both are heavily residential, and steeped in history—Paget's of the seafaring variety, Devonshire more military-minded. Unfortunately, both parishes have also borne the brunt of modern-day progress, serving as conduits for ever-increasing streams of traffic moving between the city and the rest of the Bermuda.

Yet the parishes' differences become more apparent by spending time in each. Devonshire is deep-country in the most laid-back sense, with deserted coast-view trails, quiet cedar-fringed farms, stables, and tucked-away family estates where, amid walled meadows and wooded drives, you might imagine you were in the heart of the English countryside. Its shoreline communities are just as relaxed, with fishermen's stalls and dry goods stores that belong to another century. Noisier, more developed Paget has its quiet spots, certainly, but overall, it proffers a more suburban edge—no surprise, since it gazes across the narrow foot of the harbor at the city, and its coveted Harbour Road properties were earned long ago by merchants and traders, yesterday's movers and shakers. Together, both parishes encompass central Bermuda and, along with Pembroke, are generally considered the most desirable areas in real estate. They boast a

© ROSEMARY JONES

DEVONSHIRE & PAGET

HIGHLIGHTS

◖ **The Arboretum:** Quiet trails wind through fiddlewood forests and meadows alive with bluebirds and cardinals, yet this undulating 22-acre park is surprisingly underused. Don't miss the limestone quarry gardens and ornamental bridges near the Middle Road entrance (page 78).

◖ **Old Devonshire Church:** Centuries old, this whitewashed, pocket-sized church is notable for its traditional architecture, cedar-fused interior, and quaint gardens that burst with roses and poinsettias (page 79).

◖ **Devonshire Bay Park:** This bay encompasses a tiny beach that's great for kids and nonswimmers and a small national park with a ruggedly spectacular outlook on the South Shore. The park also contains the ruin of an early coastal forts (page 80).

◖ **The Botanical Gardens:** Bermuda's favorite park has rolling lawns, storybook trees, gardens boasting roses, herbs, and medicinal plants, and a visitors center offering tea, sandwiches, and souvenirs (page 87).

◖ **Camden House:** The Premier's official residence is open for public tours (page 89).

◖ **Masterworks Museum of Bermuda Art:** This groundbreaking institution is the work of a nonprofit agency that has spent two decades repatriating Bermuda artworks by Winslow Homer, Georgia O'Keeffe, and other luminaries. Local artists' work is also on display in this former arrowroot factory (page 90).

◖ **Waterville:** Antiques and oils adorn the interior of this gracious waterfront homestead, headquarters of the Bermuda National Trust, but the roses, mangroves, and gardens outside are even more spectacular. Watch ducks and boaters in the tranquil Foot of the Lane, or picnic in the quaint gazebo (page 92).

◖ **The Birdsey Studio:** From her bottom-of-the-garden studio, watercolorist Jo Birdsey-Linberg she dispenses practical advice, witty anecdotes, local knowledge – along with landscapes and beautifully whimsical portraits, just like her famous father, Alfred, did (page 93).

◖ **Paget Marsh:** Teeming with birdlife, this former peat marsh can now easily be explored via a quaint boardwalk. See original stands of cedars and palmettos, and enjoy benches provided for restful interludes (page 93).

◖ **Elbow Beach:** One of Bermuda's most famous pink stretches, this beach links several private South Shore resorts, but you're still free walk from end to end and swim in the clear turquoise rollers (page 95).

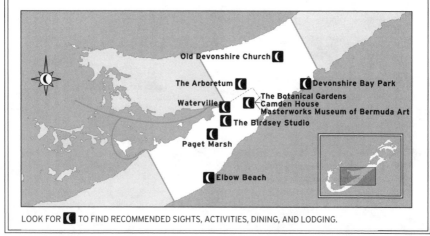

LOOK FOR ◖ TO FIND RECOMMENDED SIGHTS, ACTIVITIES, DINING, AND LODGING.

massing of old money and a convenient proximity to Hamilton (five to 10 minutes, with fewer traffic jams than other areas en route to the city)—factors which have served to boost already-exorbitant land values here over the past decade. The surge is particularly due to Hamilton's burgeoning international business sector, which constantly seeks executive rentals not too distant from corporate headquarters.

Devonshire's bucolic borders begin northeast of Hamilton, touching Pembroke at the junction of Spruce Lane and North Shore Road, and continuing south along Glebe Road to Paget's edge at Foot of the Lane. Devonshire's contents then spill east, spreading between South and North Shores as far as Collector's Hill and Cable Hill. Undulating Middle Road rambles through the parish center, while North Shore and South Shore Roads hem its edges on both sides. Devonshire includes large tracts of farmland, including the lovely Orange Valley and Locust Hall Nature Reserve, owned and managed by the National Trust, where acres of lilies and snapdragons spring from the earth at Easter.

Paget, meantime, moves west from the ludicrously named Happy Talk Drive, continuing past the Botanical Gardens and Hungry Bay Fort and Nature Reserve. Trimingham Hill, a highway hub from Hamilton, channels traffic westward through Paget via pretty, winding Harbour Road, central Middle Road, or South Shore Road, all of which connect with and continue through Warwick Parish after the north-south boundary of Cobb's Hill. Paget's north boundary includes several islands in Hamilton Harbour, namely White's, where children learn to sail in summer camps; large residential Hinson's, which has a ferry stop on the Paget-Warwick run; and smaller outcrops such as Doctor's and Burnt Islands.

PLANNING YOUR TIME

Unless you're ensconced in a resort, it's likely you will pass through the central parishes of Devonshire and Paget many times on your way into or out of Hamilton, or moving between the East and West Ends. Both parishes provide a highly scenic passageway, but both also offer sights, restaurants, bars, and beautiful outdoor spaces in their own right and are certainly worth dedicated visits. Buses run several regular routes through Devonshire and Paget, and ferries are a scenic way to explore Paget's harborside and beyond. The old tribe roads in both parishes also make for interesting tangents, linking east-west main roads via these skinny north-south divisions past red fields of newly sown soil, schoolyards, or Bermudian backgardens.

Devonshire, the more rural of the two, with little shopping or accommodation, is an oasis of historic family estates, tracts of farmland and forest, a marsh protected as a nature reserve, and an 18-hole golf course, with the majority of land taken up with residential property. While Paget also lays claim to important natural spaces, the parish houses the island's major hospital, King Edward VII Memorial, with its expanding medical environs; several major hotels, beaches, bars, restaurants, and a popular nightclub also lie within the parish. Wrapped around the bottom of Hamilton Harbour, it is closely connected to the city physically and philosophically.

Outdoor and sports enthusiasts will find plenty to do in both Devonshire and Paget, thanks to numerous resorts' tennis facilities, two nine-hole golf courses (at Ocean View Golf Club and Horizons), and walking, riding, and running trails, not to mention two of the island's most expansive public parks, the Arboretum and Botanical Gardens. Stretches of the Railway Trail in both parishes are great for exploring the countryside. Either parish is good for simply sampling Bermuda's garden-like atmosphere. Buy sunflowers or fresh honey from a farm stand on Saturday morning. Stop for a "Foot of the Lane" picnic along Pomander Road's harborside, or walk the Railway Trail from Barker's Hill, the glistening North Shore panorama laid out before you like a movie backdrop.

Devonshire Parish

As a born-and-bred Devonshire resident, I must admit the bucolic, valley-dotted parish, infused as it is with childhood memories, is my favorite of the bunch. Spend time here, and you find yourself not only in the physical crux of Bermuda, thanks to its central position, but also in the heart of the island's "country" roots. Devonshire conjures old gardens on rambling estates that tumble down gentle hills and fenced meadows; North Shore cottages clustered in salt-sprayed pastels; the echo of surf on South Shore verandas; lily fields and footpaths through fiddlewood forests. Historically, Devonshire (pronounced DEV-on-sure, not "shire" as North Americans are tempted to say) is named for the southwest corner of England, birthplace of William Cavendish, the first Earl of Devonshire and one of the prominent London investors behind Bermuda's early development.

Sparsely populated until the 20th century due to its lack of natural harbors (and therefore disconnected from the boom in maritime industry), Devonshire prospered primarily through farming. Military history runs deep here, too. It was the British Army that effected the greatest impact on the parish from the mid-1800s, after appropriating a quarter of the land and establishing forts, a military hospital, and a garrison at Prospect. Montpelier (today the home of the Deputy Governor) and the neighboring Arboretum became part of a huge military complex that covered Fort Hill—a vantage point chosen for its commanding view of land and sea stretching as far as the Royal Naval Dockyard. When the Army pulled out of Bermuda in 1951, the area became headquarters for the Bermuda Police Service. Today it is also home to one of the island's largest public high schools (CedarBridge Academy) and a well-used cultural center, the Ruth Seaton James Center for the Performing Arts.

Centuries-old families such as the Cox, Watlington, and Dill clans—the latter, actor Michael Douglas's relatives—have managed to preserve from destruction or development

their impressive historic mansions and large landholdings. Today, these, along with government lands held as open space, contribute to the sense of natural beauty in the parish and help offset eyesores such as the Tynes Bay Incinerator, an ugly tower rising off former North Shore farmland, where the island's garbage is trucked and burned.

With just one hotel property (the Dills' Ariel Sands Resort), few dedicated attractions, and no village or commercial center for shopping or dining out, Devonshire can be considered the least tourist-focused parish. Without hoopla, residents live and work and enjoy outdoors pursuits here, but despite the lack of advertised sights, visitors will find many corners worth spending time in. Lying on the western outskirts of Hamilton, Devonshire is wedged snugly between Pembroke and Smith's. Its western border, with Pembroke, runs from Cavendish Heights to the North Shore; southward, it connects with Paget at the foot of Hamilton Harbour and follows Middle Road nearly to Tee Street, then continues east, spanning both shorelines. Navigate its hilly terrain via a few main roads: sea-swept North Shore Road and Palmetto Road to the north, Middle Road through the center, and South Shore Road as far as the Smith's Parish border.

It might be true to say Devonshire is a state of mind rather than a destination. It demands slowing down, kicking back, soaking in a different time when rhythms of life were connected to the earth rather than the minute or the dollar.

SIGHTS

If you take Cavendish Road out of Hamilton continuing east via Middle Road (Bus Route 3), you'll end up in the heart of Devonshire. From here, you can explore the parish's diverse nooks and crannies, where many of the sights are not posted attractions, but the comings and goings of regular daily life. Montpelier Road and Frog Lane lead to North Shore Road, passing circuitous Happy Valley before

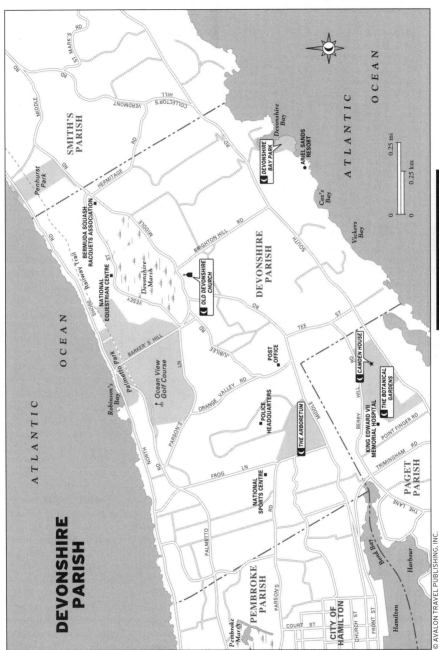

DEVONSHIRE PARISH

HOUSE NAMES

If a foreign postman had been dropped into Bermuda not so long ago, he or she might have been totally perplexed by the island's archaic address system. Until the 1980s, Bermudians generally relied on identifying properties by house names, because private residences throughout the parishes rarely had numbers. Letters, therefore, simply went to "Anstey," Middle Road, Devonshire, or "Windswept," Southampton. Making matters more confusing was that many of the more remote lanes and neighborhood roads had no names at all, at least not officially. The government changed all that over the past couple of decades, methodically giving all roads a title – though sometimes rather curious ones (Happy Talk Drive, Frolic Lane, Pain Lane, and Stepmother's Drive among the oddities) – and numbering every house. Today everything is clearly identified, but Bermudians still like to name their houses (as well as their boats), and most homes have decorative nameplates prominently displayed.

climbing past the grand National Sports Centre (a multi-million-dollar work in progress, though the track is open for runners). Frog Lane connects with Dock Hill, a short, steep exit onto North Shore Road. Take time to hang out at the former military cargo port Devonshire Dock, now a public dock where Rastafarian fishermen gather in the afternoons to cut up their catch and sell fresh fillets of snapper, rockfish, and other sweet-meated specialties from roadside coolers. Many of the ancestral homes in this area—some garnished with gingerbread verandas, gazebos, even a crenelated tower—belong to the Dill family, built in the 1700s by privateers and merchants. All along the North Shore, far less affluent homes boast rich traditional features, including front-door fanlights, keystones, parapets, and welcoming-arms stairways.

Staying on Middle Road will lead you past farms, churches, and inland neighborhoods.

Rolling Orange Valley, largely consisting of age-old family estates, connects to major Palmetto Road, or switches back along delightfully rural Parsons Lane towards Devonshire Marsh and Jubilee Road, Old Devonshire Church, Locust Hall Nature Reserve, and Vesey Street's equestrian areas.

If you head east along the South Shore, you can stroll the gardens of Palm Grove or Devonshire Bay—another public park and swimming area where some of the best fresh fish is sold straight off the commercial fishing boats on Fridays. Look for the hand-drawn roadside sign.

◖ The Arboretum

The Arboretum (entrances on Middle Road or via the carpark on Montpelier Road, open sunrise to sunset daily, admission free), a 22-acre expanse of meadows, palms, and fiddlewood forests, is one of Bermuda's best parks, though quite underused. Unlike Botanical Gardens, it consists not of ornate planted beds but wild tracts of wooded hillsides, large soft lawns, and stands of interesting plants and trees, including cedars, flowering golden acacias, avocados, and acres of mature Surinam cherry forest. The reserve—owned by the government since the Army pulled out of Montpelier and Fort Hill in 1951—is an important bird sanctuary, and flocks of trilling cardinals and rare bluebirds can be seen feeding and nesting in meadows off Middle Road. A giant olive tree at the roadside spreads its dark foliage over the sidewalk, and gargantuan rubber trees with endless root systems and hanging tendrils bear testimony to the centuries-old age of the park. Also off Middle Road, an ornamental bridge crafted with rustic cedar planks and railings leads into the park, and two quarry gardens inside, one with tiny pools, are planted with interesting ferns and other shade-loving flora. Running clubs use the park for afternoon workouts, and joggers, birders, families, and dog-walkers come for the tranquil trails, grassy spaces, and birdsong. In 2005, many Bermudians were horrified to hear plans that could jeopardize much of that serenity: Canadian consultants hired to assess the future revamp of King Edward VII Memorial

© ROSEMARY JONES

A rustic cedar bridge leads into the Arboretum, an oasis of rolling lawns and fiddlewood forests.

Hospital in Paget suggested the facility be torn down and rebuilt on part of the Devonshire site instead. An area in the Botanical Gardens was also put forward as an alternative, but local environmentalists decried both suggestions.

(Old Devonshire Church

Cute as a button, Old Devonshire Church (106 Middle Rd., tel. 441/236-4906 after 5 P.M., tours 10:30 A.M. Wed., admission free), a pint-sized, whitewashed example of pure Bermudian architecture, dates back to 1624, when the original structure was built. The first was thatched in palmetto and destroyed by the hurricane of 1715, but the current version was rebuilt of limestone the following year. Interestingly, the church's construction demonstrates the same techniques employed by those who crafted ships of the era. Various enlargements were made over the years, but the plain style beloved by early parishioners was kept. Centuries later, the old church suffered severe damage in a 1970 fire, but reconstruction was faithful to its original and very simple de-

sign—a marked contrast to the Gothic revival of the nearby Christ Church, built by the parish in 1851 when the old church was too small to hold the growing congregation. Notable in the historic building's interior is a Bermuda cedar screen decorated with quaint hearts and *fleurs-de-lis*. The pulpit and pews are also of cedar. Outside, the graveyard holds the tombs of parish residents and an 1817 hearse house built in the style of the church. Surrounded by climbing roses, flaming poinsettia plants, and old cedars, the church is popular for candlelit weddings—Michael Douglas's mother Diana married her third husband here in 2002—and carol services are an annual calendar staple.

Devonshire Marsh

Botanists and bug-lovers will want to visit Devonshire Marsh (open sunrise to sunset daily, admission free), a protected wetland cradled in the Middle Road valley and once dubbed "Brackish Pond"—which became a popular nickname for the whole parish in centuries past. A 10-acre segment of the marsh, named the **Firefly Nature**

Reserve and the **Freer Cox Nature Reserve,** has been set aside by Bermuda National Trust as a special sanctuary for birds and endangered island fauna. Waterways meander through the marshland, leading past natural orchids and a wealth of insect and birdlife. Unlike Paget Marsh, it remains largely the realm of scientists or birders, as the ground is deep and boggy; to date, no boardwalks or educational signage have been erected to guide public visits. The effects of a fire, which ravaged a large portion of the area in the 1990s, can still be spotted in some parts, though the marsh mostly recovered from the blaze. The grassy borders of the marsh are harvested for fodder for the island's dairy cows.

Palm Grove Gardens

Owned by the Gibbons family, this beautifully landscaped 18-acre estate (38 South Shore Rd., tel. 441/295-0022, 9 A.M.–5 P.M. Mon.–Thurs., admission free) stretches from the main road to the sea. A private home, it is opened to the public in daytime hours most of the week. The property is very popular for staging wedding photos, thanks to its well-planted gardens, complete with water-lily ponds designed in the shape of a miniature map of the island, statues, stunning night-blooming cereus blooms, sago, coconut and Canary Island palms, ivy-coated butteries, and a traditional Bermuda moongate—said to bestow good luck upon newlyweds. There is also a tropical bird aviary with a collection of parrots.

Historic Military Buildings

A scattering of historic military buildings once used by the British Army can still be seen around the Fort Hill-North Shore area. At **Prospect,** former military barracks today belong to **Police Headquarters,** where the complex of buildings is used for executive offices, cadet training, media relations, and traffic squad police offices. An Edwardian officers' mess with views of Hamilton and the Great Sound is now the Police Recreation Club. On Fort Hill, the **Prospect Cemetery** contains the graves of soldiers posted on the island through the 19th and 20th centuries. Farther north, where Orange Valley meets

Palmetto Road, an old military hospital, like the barracks displaying hallmark iron verandas, is now a government office building overlooking the North Shore.

BEACHES
Robinson's Bay

Below hilly Palmetto Park on North Shore Road (just west of the Palmetto Road roundabout), Robinson's Bay is a perfect place for a quick dip in the heat of summer, when parish children dive from the high rocky ledges into an azure natural swimming hole. With its rocky formations and reefy edges, there are several areas to swim here, and snorkeling in and out of the tiny bays amid yellowtail, butterfly fish, and stripy sergeant majors is a great way to while away a morning or afternoon. As a child, I enjoyed many waterlogged birthday parties here, and my brother and I considered an after-school dip here the ultimate treat. The property, now public, bears the telltale signs of British military use in years past: steps carved into the water at various points, natural stone bridges between rocky outcrops, and old changing huts made of thick limestone. Locals can often be found line-fishing off the rocks.

🄲 Devonshire Bay Park

Tucked away at the end of a narrow South Shore lane, Devonshire Bay Park is easy to miss. But don't—because this scenic little corner of Bermuda offers a perfect place to relax, swim, picnic, explore, and meet Bermudians who frequent a decidedly non-touristy venue. There's a clean beach fringed by baygrapes and palmettos, and the quiet bay is good for swimming, except on very windy days when surf rolls through the channel into the natural harbor. Nearby residents keep small boats here, as do fishermen, who return to clean and sell their catch on weekday afternoons. Friday is usually a sure bet to find them chopping up fillets for a loyal crowd of customers. A hand-drawn sign is usually posted at the main road to advertise the catch. One of Bermuda's many coastal fortifications, **Devonshire Bay Battery,** a rebuilt version of "Brackish Pond Fort," as it was once known,

SHAKESPEARE AND *THE TEMPEST*

There's a certain theme to Bermuda nomenclature, which will gradually become apparent as you explore Hamilton and the parishes. In the city, one of the large international re-insurance entities calls itself "TempestRe." Over in Devonshire, Michael Douglas's resort, "Ariel Sands," sports a bronze statue of the namesake sprite leaping from the South Shore rollers. At least one home – Ross Perot's three-acre spread in Tucker's Town – is named "Caliban." And various businesses carry stormy appellations (Tempest Employment Agency, Tempest Housekeeping Services). If you're starting to feel the slightest bit Elizabethan, you're on the right track. Legend has it that William Shakespeare's play, *The Tempest*, has Bermuda to thank for its creation.

The violent 1609 shipwreck of the *Sea Venture* and its would-be colonists was chronicled in crewman Silvester Jordan's highly descriptive account, *A Discovery of the Barmudas*, published in 1610. The play was first performed in 1611. It is known that Jordan's and another eyewitness account of the disaster and enchanting island whetted English enthusiasm for New World discoveries. Shakespeare undoubtedly would have been privy to the writings; among other connections, one of his major patrons was the Earl of Southampton, Henry Wriothesley, an investor in both the Virginia and Bermuda Companies. So experts believe it's no coincidence that his verse depicts a fanciful island, supposedly in the Mediterranean, but described in historically accurate terms for Bermuda as having "hogges of force and bignesse," "a pleasant drinke" made of cedarberries, and raucous seabirds whose tongues could "walke as fast as any Englishwomen's."

The allegorical romance featuring characters Prospero, his daughter Miranda, the elf Ariel, and savage Caliban also happens to be launched by a monstrous storm whose "dreadful thunderclaps and sulphurous roaring" mirror the *Sea Venture's* nemesis. "Enter Mariners, wet," the first act begins. Certainly the work's main themes – the role of destiny and chance – also tie in appropriately to Bermuda's own story and its eventual Latin motto, *Quo Fata Ferunt* (Whither the Fates Carry Us).

is located here, on a promontory in the adjacent park. The original was built in the 1750s, a square-shaped redoubt with a parapet and a central magazine—now archaeological remains. Around the shoreline of the national park, bordered by boiler reefs, you can see the whole south coast and wade in pools where trapped crabs, shrimp, and tiny jewel-like fish dart until high tide returns them to the ocean.

ENTERTAINMENT AND EVENTS

Parish events are mostly of the sporting nature, including regular soccer and cricket matches at Devonshire Recreation Club, squash tournaments at the Bermuda Squash Racquets Association, and track and field and other events at the National Sports Centre. Check the daily newspaper or www.bermudatourism.com for details of scheduled events.

World Rugby Classic

Launched in 1988, the popular World Rugby Classic (Windsor Place, third floor, Queen St., Hamilton, tel. 441/295-6574, fax 441/296-7318, www.worldrugby.bm) attracts thousands to the National Sports Centre at Prospect to watch a weeklong showdown of former top international players. Teams from Canada, Australia, New Zealand, Scotland, Wales, England, South Africa, Argentina, Spain, and the United States face off in what has grown into a veritable Seniors World Cup of Rugby. Stars including Willie McBride, Matt Dawson, Olivier Roumat, and Joost Van Der Westhuizen have entertained crowds over the years; celebrity Catherine Zeta-Jones sometimes turns up to support her Welsh roots. Daily admission is $25, weeklong passes $100, and gold passes (with access to hospitality tents and nonstop cocktail parties) $900.

Nightlife

Despite Devonshire's tranquility, there are several parish bars, which deliver very different nightlife experiences. **Caliban's** at Ariel Sands Resort (34 South Shore Rd., tel. 441/236-1010) is the most elegant of the bunch, serving up rum swizzles and other concoctions from noon daily. The walls of the snug, paneled bar are lined with photographs of famous co-owner Michael Douglas, with family and Hollywood friends.

The bar at **Ocean View Golf Club** (2 Barkers Hill, tel. 441/295-7041) is a friendly place to stop in, if only to inhale the gorgeous North Shore view. Visitors are welcome at **Police Recreation Club** (Headquarters Hill, Prospect, bar tel. 441/299-4261), where members of the Bermuda police service socialize after hours. Somewhat rowdier are **Mid-Atlantic Boat & Sports Club** (37 North Shore Rd., tel. 441/295-0172 or 441/296-2697) and the bar at **Devonshire Recreation Club** (20 Frog Ln., tel. 441/292-5539), with festivities peaking on Friday and Saturday nights.

SHOPPING

With no central community or village, Devonshire is not a shoppers' paradise. One quirky exception is **The Barn** (53 Devon Spring Rd., tel. 441/236-3155, open 9 A.M.–2 P.M. Thurs. and Sat.), a bargain-hunter's treasure trove, spilling over with secondhand toys, collectibles, and an impressive stock of books, from vintage and just-released fiction to kids' mystery series from the 1970s and 1980s. Items cost just a quarter or two sometimes, and nothing is more than a few dollars. The nonprofit facility raises funds for several island charities. Opposite The Barn stands Bermuda's other hospital, the Mid-Atlantic Wellness Institute, a psychiatric treatment facility.

SPORTS AND RECREATION

Devonshire has plenty for the active traveler, including a golf course, tennis, and several dedicated sports centers—the National Sports Centre, the National Equestrian Center, the Bermuda Squash Racquets Association—but the parish is also full of outdoor spaces in which you can work out while getting back to nature.

Running and Walking

Site of the former National Stadium, the government's new **National Sports Centre** (50 Frog Ln., tel. 441/295-8085) promises world-class facilities for track and field, cricket, soccer, rugby, swimming, concerts, and special events—if it's ever completed. Over the past five years, many millions of taxpayer dollars have been poured into the project, which stretches north from Parson's Road to Devonshire Recreation Club over several acres. By 2006, a running track with lights and bleachers was complete, and the island's running clubs and track program was making good use of it in the evenings. Runners of all abilities looking for a safe, soft-surface site to put in some mileage can also join the many locals, especially women, who head to the track before work in the mornings, even in the darkness before sunrise. Washrooms are on-site, and there is no admittance charge. Park on the grassy verge on Parson's Lane and enter via the turnstiles.

The **Devonshire Railway Trail** is one of the most panoramic stretches of this national park, with elevated, 180-degree views of the main shipping channel into the Great Sound and Hamilton Harbour. Much of the North Shore is visible, from Dockyard to Shelly Bay. It is a particularly good spot to watch cruise ships and tankers moving through the channel into port or back out to the open ocean. Starting at Barker's Hill (leave scooters in the roadside Ocean View Golf Club carpark), you can trek a good mile along the shady tarmac path, past Loyal Hill Playground, historic Bermudian cottages such as Firefly Hall—a private home—and through busy pastel communities peppered with children, dogs, and clotheslines. The trail continues through Smith's, past more lush vegetation, all the way to Gibbet Beach—a good run of about four miles from Barker's Hill and back, even offering a refreshing swim mid-route.

Golf

With a spectacular view of the North Shore channel, **Ocean View Golf Club** (2 Barker's Hill, tel. 441/295-9092, fax 441/295-9097, oceanview@northrock.bm) is one of three government-owned courses on the island, along with championship Port Royal and St. George's Club. Well maintained, the nine-hole course (with 18 tee positions for a double round) offers a leisurely though not challenging outing and is best suited to mid-handicappers. With a putting green, well-stocked pro shop, and a comfortable clubhouse with well-run bar and restaurant, plus a panoramic terrace, the club has benefited from many improvements over the past few years. Pro shop hours are 7:30 A.M.–6:30 P.M. April–October and 7:30 A.M.–5:30 P.M. November–March. Daily greens fee is $65, golf carts $16, and club rentals $27. The club offers reduced "sunset" fees after 3 P.M., plus a "golf-around package" for $250, with two rounds at Ocean View and St. George's golf courses and one round at Port Royal. For lessons with pro Dwayne Pearman, call tel. 441/295-9077. The dress code calls for collared shirts, Bermuda shorts or long trousers, and soft spikes.

Riding

With its relaxed country atmosphere, Devonshire is the perfect parish in which to go horseback riding, and it has a long equestrian history. The wooded hills, paths, and valleys, as well as its scenic stretch of Railway Trail, provide rare peaceful paths for riding in Bermuda's overdeveloped environment.

Competitive harness pony racing is a popular spectacle held most weekends September–May at the new **National Equestrian Centre** (48 Vesey St., Bermuda Equestrian Federation president Dennis Cherry tel. 441/234-0485, or 441/505-0903, www.bef.bm). Formerly called the Vesey Street Racetrack, the center has an egg-shaped track, a few bleachers, washrooms, and a canteen that's open during races, which are held evenings (under lights) or Sunday afternoons and are usually advertised via the hotels and Tourism Department's events calendar. Admission fee is $7 adults, $4 children. Horse shows are also held at the center, where local riders vie for honors in dressage, equitation, jumping, and hunter class.

Squash

Visitors can play on any of four courts at the **Bermuda Squash Racquets Association** (111 Middle Rd., tel. 441/292-6881, fax 441/295-8718, www.bermudasquash.com, 10 A.M.–10 P.M. Mon.–Fri, 10 A.M.–5 P.M. Sat. and Sun.) for a guest fee of $10. Contact the club if you need a partner. Lessons ($45 for one hour) are available from two club pros, including club director and former Australian doubles champ Ross Triffitt. As well as showers, changing rooms, and a licensed bar, the club has a small, well-equipped gym, with Cybex bikes and equipment, dumbbells, and Stairmasters, included in guest fees. The association is best known for hosting the Bermuda Masters (www.bermudamasters.com), which brings 30 international top players to the island every April to battle for the prestigious world tour title. Event games are held at the Bermuda High School's glass court in Pembroke.

Soccer and Cricket

Crowds flock to **Devonshire Recreation Club** (20 Frog Ln., tel. 441/292-5539), dubbed "Devonshire Rec," for evening and weekend soccer games (the resident team is the green-and-gold Cougars) over the fall and winter, and cricket showdowns all summer long. Few of the sports fans who party here may appreciate it, but the building that houses the club, with its billiards hall, bar, and canteen, is actually a historic Georgian structure, built in 1760 as one of the Dill family's ancestral homes.

Spas

The Spa at Ariel Sands (Ariel Sands Resort, 34 South Shore Rd., tel. 441/232-5300 spa direct, or 441/236-1010, www.arielsands.com, 9 A.M.–7 P.M. daily) is a tiny beachside day spa and hair salon for men and women, offering facials, manicures, pedicures, skin and beauty treatments, and a full massage menu (Swedish 50 minutes, $85). One of the most popular spa packages is the Deluxe Body Facial, complete with Yon-Ka seaweed mask (80 minutes, $160) and the Chocoholics' Dream, a chocolate body scrub with mud mask (one hour, $120).

DEVONSHIRE & PAGET

For Kids

The Arboretum is a dream environment for children whose imaginations need nothing more than woodlands for hide-and-seek and shady trees to picnic under. There are no facilities at the park, but kids don't seem to mind. Large enclosed meadows and soft dirt paths make safe tumbling areas for tots.

Devonshire Bay is an ideal beach for children to wade, swim, or explore rock pools. They'll also be fascinated by the fishermen who come in daily with boatloads of fresh catch, which they cut up and sell parkside.

ACCOMMODATIONS
Over $300

Owned by one of the island's oldest clans—Michael Douglas's relatives, the Dills—**Ariel Sands Resort** (34 South Shore Rd., tel. 441/236-1010, toll-free reservations in the U.S. 800/468-6610, in the U.K. 800/917-0548, fax 441/236-0087, www.arielsands.com, high-season doubles starting at $350) enjoys a heavy dose of Hollywood cachet. Douglas and his wife, Catherine Zeta-Jones, socialize with friends and family here when they jet into the island—she's been known to use the spa and lead sing-alongs at the bar. He is a shareholder and sometimes comes with well-known friends (Jack Nicholson) in tow. Celluloid icons—Nicholson, Martin Scorsese, Karl Malden, Jane Fonda—smile down from the paneled walls in the lobby and lounge. It wasn't always that way. The 14-acre property has been owned by Dills for five generations (Douglas's mother Diana was born into the family and raised in Bermuda); until the 1940s, it was a sleepy corner of Bermuda's quietest parish, covered with cedar trees that later were victims of an islandwide blight. In 1954, the family decided to build a hotel, named for the mercurial sprite in Shakespeare's play *The Tempest* (a bronze statue of Ariel rises from the waves out in the bay). Among the resort's attractions are its two enormous ocean-fed pools and an award-winning fusion restaurant, Aqua, which has a terrace within a few yards of the surf.

In the late 1990s, Douglas got personally involved and the property underwent a makeover, adding a spa, high-end restaurant, and update of all rooms and cottage suites. But bigger changes are ahead. In 2006, the resort signed a deal with the Hilton Grand Vacations Club that looks likely to take the property to another level. The partnership will see the current hotel and cottage colony demolished and rebuilt into a five-star $170 million development featuring vacation villas, a world-class spa, fitness center, restaurant, and conference center. The number of units, currently 47, would be upped to 214 rooms. The move allows Bermuda to tap into a pool of 100,000 vacation club owners who holiday at Hilton properties around the world. Construction is set to begin by the end of 2006.

Ariel had already been hedging its tourism bets by developing a chunk of its land for luxe condominiums—six 3,500-square-foot "villas," with infinity plunge pools, private gardens, and ocean views, an example of the fractional ownership trend driving the industry's future on the island. Selling at $3 million apiece, they won't solve Bermuda's housing crisis anytime soon, but they could cushion Ariel's stakeholders from the uncertainties of the industry.

FOOD
Delis and Takeout

If you can have a favorite gas station, the new **Esso Collector's Hill Tigermarket** (65 South Shore Rd., next to Collector's Hill, tel. 441/236-6574, 6 A.M.–11 P.M. daily) might be the perfect candidate. The friendly professionalism and spotless interior of the facility's convenience store are factors, but the deli's fried chicken alone would be enough to score top points for popularity. Melt-in-your mouth chicken tenders ($12 for a dozen), chicken legs, pizza, hot dogs, and coleslaw, all made fresh daily at the on-site kitchen, are perfect for picnics and beach outings. Trail mix and homespun glass candy (colorful hard candy the shape of a hockey puck) are sold at checkout. The cappuccino-to-go is the icing on the cake. You can even enjoy coffee and snacks on site; grab a stool at the prime people-watching window counter.

Bermudian

Fat Man's Café (1 Track Side Ln., tel. 441/292-0361, 11 A.M.–7 P.M. Tues.–Fri., 11 P.M.–7 A.M. Sat.) is a popular roadside takeout for fish cakes, hamburgers, chicken burgers—and codfish potato breakfasts that are snapped up by hung-over Hamilton revelers on weekends.

€ **Sammy's Kitchen** (Mid-Atlantic Boat & Sports Club, 34 North Shore Rd., tel. 441/295-0172 office or 441/296-2697 kitchen, open for lunch and dinner noon–9:30 P.M. Mon.–Sat., 8 A.M.–noon Sun.) serves up chicken, burgers, and island comfort food like peas 'n' rice and macaroni 'n' cheese during the week and draws a loud, jovial bar crowd on Friday nights. But the roadside club is best known for its authentic Sunday morning codfish and potatoes breakfasts, appreciated by members and other regulars who gather here for a laid-back café-style spread at the popular social and boating club, which sits a few feet from the water's edge. Be warned: breakfast starts early and only lasts "until it's all gone," says a club staffer.

Take in a bird's-eye view of the North Shore seascape with lunch, dinner, or snacks at **Water Hazard** (Ocean View Golf Club, 2 Barkers Hill, tel. 441/295-7041, fax 441/292-2651, breakfast 8 A.M.–11:30 P.M., lunch noon–4 P.M. Mon.–Sat., brunch 8 A.M.–1 P.M. Sun.). The licensed club bar and restaurant has a full breakfast menu (eggs, pancakes, meats), and a lunchtime offering of soups, salads, burgers, codfish cakes, fish tacos, shrimp po'boys, and vegetarian wraps (dishes $7–16). Golfers, caddies, local regulars, and visitors also drop in for tasty nibbles such as popcorn shrimp, codfish balls, and conch fritters. The restaurant has an inside dining area, but the best tables are on the terrace overlooking the greens and the azure swath of ocean beyond. Locals also swarm here for an out-of-town Friday happy hour (4–8 P.M.) and for the popular Sunday brunch of codfish and potatoes, dished out with the staple accompaniments: bananas, avocado, tomato sauce, eggs, bacon, and toast.

International

€ **Aqua** (Ariel Sands Resort, 34 South Shore Rd., tel. 441/232-2332 or 441/236-1010, fax 441/236-2208, www.arielsands.com, breakfast 8–10 A.M., lunch noon–3 P.M., dinner 6:30–10 P.M. daily) is the only gourmet offering in Devonshire, a hip, upscale dining room with a covered oceanside terrace and imaginative menu. Owner Claudio Vigilante opened Aqua in 2002, and it instantly became a public favorite, winning *The Bermudian* magazine's Best of Bermuda Gold Award. Aqua's multi-blue decor, mirroring the nearby surf, is soothing, as is its wine list and selection of Asian-influenced dishes, including a wide selection of vegetarian choices (rare in Bermuda). Starters such as shrimp kabuki with bamboo shoots ($15.95), ginger pork-belly spring roll ($13), and Thai-spiced rare tuna niçoise ($15.50) are elegantly presented. Entrees, starting at $23.50, include a daily fresh catch, roast rockfish, beef tenderloin with wasabi mash, and Oriental vegetable strudel. The sound of South Shore breakers rolling in and the wind whispering through the coconut palms puts you in a holiday frame of mind, even if you've only come for dinner.

Grocery Stores

Belvin's Variety (1 Vesey St., tel. 441/236-6644, 6 A.M.–midnight daily) stocks beer, liquor, dry and frozen goods, and also sells fresh-baked hot beef, chicken, and mussel pies.

Empire Grocery (12 North Shore Rd., tel. 441/292-0277 or 441/295-2625, 8 A.M.–6 P.M. Mon.–Thurs., 8 A.M.–8 P.M. Fri. and Sat.) has been part of the North Shore community since 1927 when the DeSilva family first opened its doors. Relatives still run the friendly, efficient convenience store, packed with "as much as we can fit," says an employee. That includes liquor, beer, grocery products, and deli meats.

Howard's Mini Mart (99 Middle Rd., tel. 441/236-7037, fax 441/236-7000, 7 A.M.–9 P.M. summer, 7 A.M.–8 P.M. winter Mon.–Sat., 6 A.M.–1 P.M. Sun. year-round) is a family-owned roadside grocery offering all the basics, including some straight-from-the-farm fruits and vegetables.

Lindo's Market (4 Watlington Rd. East, tel. 441/236-5623, www.lindos.bm, 8 A.M.–7 P.M. Mon., Tues., and Thurs., 8 A.M.–8 P.M. Wed., Fri., and Sat.) is the only major supermarket in Devonshire, and one of the island's biggest and best stocked. Now owned by the Italian-Bermudian Zanol family, the modern floor space includes a harvest of organic foods and Bermuda-grown produce, cheeses from around the world, a carefully stocked wine section, magazines and children's books, and an outstanding fish and meat department boasting fresh-caught Bermuda wahoo, tuna, traditional Bermuda codfish cakes, as well as a wide selection of imported fish and meat.

INFORMATION AND SERVICES

Bermuda's second hospital, the **Mid-Atlantic Wellness Institute** (formerly St. Brendan's Hospital) (44 Devon Springs Rd., tel. 441/236-3770, www.bermudahospitals.bm) is a psychiatric treatment facility with 130 inpatient beds.

Lindo's Pharmacy (Lindo's Market, 4 Watlington Rd. East, tel. 441/236-7732, 8 A.M.–7 P.M. Mon., Tues., and Thurs., 8 A.M.–8 P.M. Wed., Fri., and Sat.) is a handy stop-in located inside the main grocery store, just left of the main entrance area.

Devonshire Post Office (2 Orange Valley Rd., tel. 441/236-0281, 8 A.M.–5 P.M. Mon.–Fri.) is another friendly parish outlet with helpful staff. There is plenty of parking outside.

ATMs are located at Lindo's Market, Watlington Road, and ESSO Collector's Hill Tigermarket.

Public toilets are located at Robinson's Bay, the Arboretum, and area restaurants.

GETTING THERE AND AROUND

There is no ferry service to or from Devonshire.

There are no livery services based in Devonshire, but all the scooter rental companies provide a free shuttle service to their nearest outlets (in Hamilton or Paget).

With no taxi stands and just one resort (Ariel Sands), hailing a cab in Devonshire is hard work. A better strategy is to call one of the cab companies to arrange a pick-up.

Buses

Regular bus service runs every half hour through Devonshire between Hamilton and Grotto Bay (Route No. 3) in Hamilton Parish via Middle Road, Devil's Hole, and the caves, making for convenient sightseeing transport. Other Devonshire bus routes include South Shore Road (No. 1) between Hamilton and St. George's every half hour via Spittal Pond and the Tucker's Town golf courses, and North Shore Road (No. 10 and No. 11) to and from St. George's every 15 minutes via the Aquarium and Bailey's Bay. Bus fare to Devonshire falls into the three-zone tariff, which is $3 adults, $2 children 5–16, under five free (exact change, or tokens, tickets, or passes required). Transfers are free.

Paget Parish

Hemmed by the South Shore on one side and Hamilton Harbour on the other, most of Paget is contained within what on a map looks like a trouser leg on a pair of sideways pants (matched across the harbor by the spread of Pembroke and the city). As the outskirts of Hamilton, Paget is a bustling, thriving community passed through every morning by thousands of city-bound commuters from the western parishes, and every night by the same residents heading home. The river of traffic has brought noise and congestion to what once were peaceful country lanes leading horses and carriages, bicycles, and pedestrians into a very different Bermuda. But beyond the main thoroughfares, Paget's charm endures, and the beauty of its historic places, family estates, nature reserves, beaches, and meandering harborfront make it a treasure trove of discoveries around every hairpin corner.

Off the South Shore Road, for example, take a tangent down neighborhood lanes and feel manmade turbulence evaporate into the sound of blue surf instead. Tool down Middle Road, bordered by elegant old homes and their impossibly green gardens; dawdle down narrow lanes which roll into valleys or over hills where silence is, finally, golden. Of course, there's plenty to occupy a visitor who wants to be busy in Paget—hot new restaurants, the coolest bars, top-quality sports facilities, and events to go with them.

Named for William Paget, the fourth Lord of Paget, the parish is changing as speedily as the rest of Bermuda, with new hotel properties planned, along with residential complexes. Notably, Harbour Road's Newstead Resort & Spa is slated for a 2007 opening, on the site of the long-beloved Newstead guesthouse, now torn down except for its gracious old facade, which will be incorporated into its successor.

And then, there is the Paget that never seems to change—the quaint stone limestone walls of seafaring Salt Kettle, the ducks of Foot of the Lane, the Elbow Beach breakers, the herb gardens of Camden, and, of course, Johnny Barnes's smile.

SIGHTS
The Botanical Gardens

Bermuda's most popular and historic park, the Botanical Gardens (tel. 441/236-5902, open sunrise to sunset daily, one-hour guided tours from visitors center carpark at 10:30 A.M. Tues., Wed., and Fri. weather permitting, admission free) encompasses 36 acres of rolling lawns, horticultural halls boasting orchids and cacti, and myriad outdoor gardens planted with exotica (ficus, rubber, and cotton trees) and down-home varieties (medicinal herbs). Opened in 1898, the original "Public Gardens" totaled just 10 acres and served as an agricultural station in the 1930s. They were renamed and expanded to their current size in 1965 when the government bought the Camden estate to the east from the Tucker family. Since then, specimens from around the world have been gathered and planted here, making the property the biggest and best natural showcase of both endemic and non-native flora on the island. The gardens are maintained by the government's Parks Department. There are three entrances: North Gate on Berry Hill Road, South Gate at 183 South Road, and West Gate on Point Finger Road next to the King Edward VII Memorial Hospital. The visitors center (tel. 441/236-5291, 9:30 A.M.–3:30 P.M. Mon.–Fri.), with a café, washrooms, and gift shop, is staffed by volunteers from the Bermuda Botanical Society; it's near North Gate, off Berry Hill Road, but can be accessed from any entrance. All proceeds are used for park projects or student scholarships.

Highlights of the gardens in the North Gate area include a cacti hillside, with alien-looking aloes, agaves, and other succulents that occasionally sprout spectacular blossoms; a collection of subtropical native conifers, including Bermuda's own cedar; and a "blue garden" featuring plants with blue fruit, flowers, or foliage.

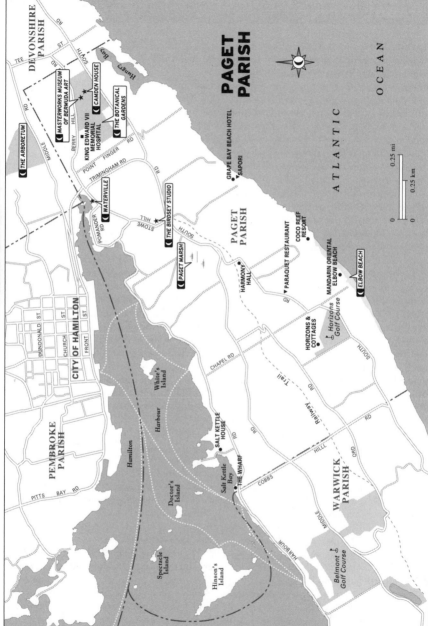

PAGET PARISH

DEVONSHIRE PARISH

ATLANTIC OCEAN

PEMBROKE PARISH

CITY OF HAMILTON

WARWICK PARISH

THE ARBORETUM

MASTERWORKS MUSEUM OF BERMUDA ART

CAMDEN HOUSE

KING EDWARD VII MEMORIAL HOSPITAL

THE BOTANICAL GARDENS

WATERVILLE

THE BIRDSEY STUDIO

PAGET MARSH

GRAPE BAY BEACH HOTEL

SAPORI

PARAQUET RESTAURANT

HARMONY HALL

COCO REEF RESORT

MANDARIN ORIENTAL ELBOW BEACH

ELBOW BEACH

HORIZONS & COTTAGES

Horizons Golf Course

SALT KETTLE HOUSE

THE WHARF

Belmont Golf Course

White's Island

Hamilton Harbour

Doctor's Island

Spectacle Island

Hinson's Island

Salt Kettle Bay

Hungry Bay

BERRY HILL

BURNT HOUSE HILL RD

TEE ST

RD

MIDDLE RD

POMANDER RD

POINT FINGER RD

TRIMINGHAM RD

STOWE HILL

SOUTH RD

CHAPEL RD

RAILWAY TRAIL

HILL RD

COBBS HILL RD

MIDDLE RD

HARBOUR RD

PITTS BAY RD

DUNDONALD ST

CHURCH ST

FRONT ST

0   0.25 mi

0   0.25 km

Behind Camden House, a new display developed in 2006 showcases a kitchen garden, with edibles and cut flowers; an economic garden, with tobacco, arrowroot, cotton, and indigo, which early settlers cultivated to survive; and medicinal herbs used in old-time Bermuda. This area also has aviaries with peacocks, ducks, parrots, doves, and budgies, and a delightful walled rose garden, one of Bermuda's best.

Hilly lawns spill down from Camden to South Shore Road, peppered with mature trees such as acacias and cedars. Bordering the top lawns are wide beds planted with bulbs that flower at different times with colorful lilies, freesias, dahlias, and others. This was the famous site where John Lennon saw a freesia named Double Fantasy during a 1980 visit to the island—and left a lasting legacy.

The western section of the gardens contains a wealth of miniature environments, from butterfly gardens and subtropical fruit and palm collections, to mammoth rubber and ficus trees that send down aerial roots to support their huge overhanging branches. There is also a lovely walled "sensory garden" planted with rosemary, jasmine, and other sweet-scented flora, with a gurgling fountain in the center, and several slathouses containing orchids, bromeliads, ferns and cacti. Another interesting feature nearby is a tiny whitewashed Bermuda cottage, built for the 2001 Smithsonian Folklife Festival to showcase island architecture. Thousands of Bermudians come to the Gardens every April for the three-day **Bermuda Annual Exhibition,** a cultural and agricultural fair that's one of the island's biggest events.

C Camden House

An elegant landmark visible from South Shore Road atop the Botanical Gardens' rolling lawns, Camden House (183 South Rd., tel. 441/236-5732, open for free public tours noon–2 P.M. Tues.–Fri.) is definitely worth a visit. The 18th-century mansion has an imposing wooden facade comprising a two-story veranda offering sweeping views of the distant seascape. Official residence of island premiers since 1979, government-owned Camden is

sometimes described as Bermuda's counterpart to 10 Downing Street or the White House (and, yes, it is white), but the head of state doesn't actually live here. Instead, the building is used for occasional public events and VIP receptions; foreign dignitaries including Princess Margaret, former U.S. secretary of state General Colin Powell, ex-U.K. prime minister Margaret Thatcher, and civil rights leader Reverend Jesse Jackson have all dined in the house. One of the favorite public events held here is a yearly carol service, a free, festive occasion staged on the front lawn in early December featuring local choirs and bands, and attended by the premier and governor.

Camden is an example of Georgian architecture; while it is not known exactly when it was constructed, the main structure and some additions were completed between 1714 and 1830. The first owner of the house, Francis Jones, died of yellow fever in 1795. The home passed to the Tucker family, and Hamilton mayor Henry James Tucker lived here until his death in 1870. It was during this time that an arrowroot factory was opened in buildings behind the main house (now the headquarters of the Masterworks Foundation). In 1966, Camden was sold to the government as part of the Botanical Gardens and has been a public treasure ever since; the huge facing property on South Shore Road is still owned by Tucker descendents.

Camden's interior is all the more impressive after its designer makeover of 2003, when much of its plumbing, upholstery, and woodwork—including mountains of cedar—was refurbished. In the dining room, where carved paneling reportedly took a mid-1800s cabinetmaker 30 years to finish, walls set off a stunning handcarved Bermuda cedar table and chairs (to seat 22); *boite*-like powder rooms recall a gentler age of tea parties and parasols; and expansive drawing rooms and studies, accented by historic antiques, artworks, books, crystal chandeliers and gilded mirrors, make this one of the finest restored stately homes open to the public. One special feature on carved panels is the "bird's-eye" cedar, prized for its eye-catching grain. The William and

Mary cushion-molded mirror over the dining-room fireplace is also worth a close look. Another gem of the building is curator-housekeeper Alfred Ambrose Scott, a gracious character who answers visitors' questions or simply offers witty greetings. On Sunday afternoons, his lively jazz can be heard spilling down from a stereo on the balcony.

◖ Masterworks Museum of Bermuda Art

Scheduled to open its doors in 2007, the Masterworks Museum of Bermuda Art (MMBA) is the brainchild of the **Masterworks Foundation** (Arrowroot Building, Botanical Gardens, 183 South Rd., tel. 441/236-2950, fax 441/236-4402, www.bermuda masterworks.com, 10 A.M.–4 P.M. Mon.–Fri., 9 A.M.–noon Sat., call for admission), an indefatigable nonprofit whose *raison d'etre* since 1987 has been the repatriation of Bermuda artworks by famous artists including Winslow Homer, Georgia O'Keeffe, and Charles Demuth. The group's Tom Butterfield and

Elise Outerbridge have since gathered an impressive collection of more than 1,000 paintings, drawings, photographs, maps, and memorabilia, which will be showcased in the new museum. After various headquarters, Masterworks moved in 2003 to the Botanical Gardens, where it now rents a former arrowroot processing factory for $1 a year from the government. Hemmed by a walled rose garden, the rear portion of the building is the site of a $6 million, two-story, purpose-built art gallery for the valuable collection, set to open in time to celebrate Masterworks' 20th anniversary. Until then, the facility has two existing galleries open, which show rotating works by contemporary local artists or the group's annual artist-in-residence. After years of acclaimed shows in the United States, Canada, and beyond, the "Bermuda Collection" will finally return to the island. It is the culmination of a dream for foundation director Butterfield, who hopes the museum becomes "a home for history, culture, education, and some of Bermuda's greatest treasures."

painted tributes by the Masterworks Foundation to Bermuda's beastly icon, the wild hog

PAINTERS IN PARADISE

Bermuda is a place "to hide and hush," wrote American painter Marsden Hartley after a 1917 visit – a sentiment that would have found favor with other art-world luminaries, including Winslow Homer, Georgia O'Keeffe, and Charles Demuth, who all found the island a calm and creative inspiration.

O'Keeffe recovered from a nervous breakdown during her 1933-34 sojourns in Somerset, where she eschewed her typical explosive colors for charcoal sketches of banana flowers and banyan trees. Fauvist E. Ambrose Webster (1869-1935) was struck by the island's palette of purples, blues, and oranges, which he used to capture evocative landscapes as well as bold portraits of native Bermudians. And Homer, one of the most influential American painters of the 20th century, enjoyed exploring the coastline by horse-and-buggy, foot, and ferry when he visited Bermuda in 1899 and 1900, recording his sightseeing in 21 known watercolors of the island, which he proclaimed "as good an example as I have ever done."

Today the works of Bermuda by these and other internationally renowned artists from North America and Europe are being brought back to the island, thanks to the efforts of the Masterworks Foundation, a nonprofit group that will open a dedicated museum in the Botanical Gardens, Paget, to showcase the collection in 2007. Among the stars of the nearly 1,000 artworks, photos, and artifacts Masterworks has gathered are two O'Keeffe charcoals; two of Homer's seascapes, *Inland Water* and *Bermuda (The S.S. Trinidad)*; Ross Sterling Turner's impressionist views of gardens and neighborhood cottages; and photographer Karl Struss's three-dimensional color record of a post-war island in the 1950s.

Scores of artists made their way to Bermuda in the 18th, 19th, and 20th centuries, finding respite from Real World challenges in the island's sea, sun, tropical colors, unusual light, flora and fauna, and human personalities. In the process, many found fresh energy to paint and draw, reviving stalled careers or launching new artistic avenues that would win them further celebrity back in their home environments.

The museum will have a café and gift store on-site. The Masterworks Foundation has an active calendar of events and outreach and educational programs, including art camps for kids, painters' picnics, Art in the Park festivals, workshops, and biweekly openings of temporary shows during the summer. Check the schedule on the website. Masterworks published a book of its collection in 1994, and another coffee-table edition is planned.

King Edward VII Memorial Hospital

On the northeast side of Botanical Gardens is Bermuda's main healthcare facility, the King Edward VII Memorial Hospital (two entrances: 7 Point Finger Rd. and via Berry Hill Rd., tel. 441/236-2345, www.bermudahospitals.bm). Opened in 1920, the 327-bed hospital offers medical, surgical, and critical care. It also has a

gift shop, washrooms, and a public cafeteria on the ground floor, and a second cafeteria on the first floor. Over the past decade, the hospital neighborhood has undergone a dramatic transformation, with once-residential homes being converted or torn down and rebuilt for use as doctors' offices and headquarters for medical support services.

Crow Lane

Crow Lane Park (open sunrise to sunset daily, admission free), at the foot of Corkscrew Hill near the parish boundary with Devonshire, has a small lawn tucked long the waterside of "Foot of the Lane," the bottom of Hamilton Harbour. It's a good place for picnics or watching the sun set. A multitude of small pleasure craft are moored here next to the mangroves. But despite the sunny surroundings, the park has a sordid history. In 1730, slave Sally Bassett was publicly

© ROSEMARY JONES

Waterville, headquarters of the Bermuda National Trust

executed by burning here after being accused of poisoning a slave-owning Sandys couple. Her case was the most notorious of many so-called poison plots used as a form of rebellion by slaves who practiced the religious art of Obeah. Bassett has been remembered in island folklore, and the park is now one of the sights on the African Diaspora Trail through the island.

His bronze statue stands just 50 yards away, but you can see **Johnny Barnes** in person every morning, rain or shine, at the Crow Lane roundabout. With his white beard, straw hat, and a smile to stop traffic, the octogenarian Bermudian waves rigorously to motorists on their way to work, shouting out loudly, "I love you!" While many thought Johnny was plain nuts when he first began his morning ritual in the 1980s, commuters now have come to expect and even look forward to his beaming face. Indeed, when Johnny misses a rare day, hundreds of calls flood local media to find out if he's okay. A group of area citizens decided to honor his goodwill with the statue, erected in 1996 along the garden verge at the start of East Broadway.

◖ Waterville

A rambling 1725 homestead set on parkland that curls around the foot of the harbor, Waterville (corner of The Lane and Pomander Rd., tel. 441/236-6483, www.bnt.bm, 9 A.M.–5 P.M. Mon.–Fri., admission free) is the headquarters of the Bermuda National Trust. Its elegant Georgian proportions ensure the building's status as a listed property, and stepping inside makes for instant time travel back to the 18th century. Somber oil portraits grace the walls in the lounge and dining room near the trellised entrance, and antiques, china, and a grandfather clock carry visitors back to early Bermuda. Originally a private home, Waterville belonged to the Trimingham family and later was the site of the first Trimingham's (the legendary but now defunct Front Street department store).

Waterville's gardens and surrounding park are even more stunning. A landmark tamarind tree blew down in Hurricane Fabian, but the Heritage Rose Garden, established in 1988 by the Bermuda Rose Society and showcasing many old Bermuda varieties, lights up the front lawn with color. Waterville Park includes Duck Island, a low, mangrove-covered islet where herons and waterfowl nest and ducks alight on the boats moored at Foot of the Lane. Neighborhood boaters access their vessels via this park, making it a hive of activity on summer weekends. A dirt path winds through thick cherry hedges along the waterfront and past an old horse watering station to the main road sidewalk.

Pomander Road

Meander by scooter or foot along the quaint harborside edging Pomander Road, a one-way, largely residential lane that slips off the bustle of The Lane into yesteryear. Ducks paddle by the mangroves and moored pleasure boats, wooden dinghies sit on the shoreline, and grassy nooks invite roadside picnics.

Despite its tranquility, there are a few enterprises along the loop back to Harbour Road. **Aberfeldy Nurseries** (tel. 441/236-2927), one of the oldest and largest plant retailers, is a good place to look at hundreds of the island's endemic and ornamental garden plants. Two guesthouses, Little Pomander and Erith, have waterfront properties. And the **Royal Hamilton Amateur Dinghy Club** (tel. 441/236-2250, www.rhadc.bm) can be found at the western end of the lane, home to hundreds of motorboats and fine yachts, which have docking rights and moorings. Hugged by serpentine Harbour Road, **Red Hole** is the name for the sheltered bay here, home to a working boatyard and a tiny beach, where dinghies used to ferry boat-owners to their yachts are pulled up on the sand at low tide.

◖ The Birdsey Studio

Bermuda travelers who met Alfred Birdsey (1912–1996) would not easily forget him. The unassuming but prolific painter welcomed thousands of visitors over the years to his Paget studio, where he often treated them to tea and a chat, no matter whether any art changed hands. Renowned outside of Bermuda, his Impressionistic, even Asian-in-fluenced brushstrokes of island landscapes, yachts, harbors, and backstreets revolutionized the way Bermuda was captured in art and caught the imagination of collectors worldwide. Today, his daughter, Jo Birdsey-Linberg, carries on the family tradition at The Birdsey Studio (Rosecote, 5 Stowe Hill, tel. 441/236-6658, linberg@northrock.bm, 10:30 A.M.–1 P.M. Mon.–Fri., appointments recommended). Like her father, she breaks artistic conventions—and makes guests feel entirely at home. Linberg's breezy watercolor landscapes and whimsical animal portraits—popular children's gifts—range $80–450; oils are priced $400 and up. The studio also sells note cards of Birdsey Sr.'s work, which she hopes one day to memorialize in a book. Park scooters in front of the house and follow the path on the left to the back garden, where the studio is located amid roses, lilies, cacti, and paw-paw trees. Birdsey-Linberg, a Latin scholar, musician, and mother, can be found here most weekday mornings, with her "assistant managers"—two miniature dachshunds, Mango and Chutney.

◖ Paget Marsh

A 25-acre natural wetland lying in the ample valley between the South Shore and Hamilton Harbour, Paget Marsh (Lovers Ln., off Middle Rd., open sunrise to sunset daily, admission free) is jointly owned and managed by the Bermuda National Trust and Bermuda Audubon Society. Today a highlight on any island eco-tour, the marsh was long neglected and inaccessible until 1998, when the two agencies launched an innovative conservation project that re-created the pond, rid the area of much non-endemic plantlife, and encouraged the return of native and migratory birds. The entrance is on Lovers Lane; go down the steep hill and park at the bottom, where banana groves and adjacent agricultural lands form a barrier against the nearby intersection. Informative signage on birdlife and plantlife leads the way to a charming wooden boardwalk that winds through the mangroves into the marsh. Benches have been built into the

DEVONSHIRE & PAGET

Waterfront homes at Salt Kettle date back to the days of pirates and privateers.

walkway at intervals, allowing for restful communing with nature.

Paget Marsh is special among Bermuda's nature reserves because it is essentially a remnant from a previous era, much of its interior virtually untouched by man. As a result, it is home to centuries-old stands of cedar and palmetto forest, ancient mangrove forests, native wax myrtles, and Bermuda sedge, which is unique to the island and found only in this reserve. All are sustained by a primordial anchor of peat, which also serves to keep down mosquito populations. The marsh supports varied birdlife, including green and night herons, great egrets, kingfishers, moorhens, and yellowthroat warblers, which feed on the abundance of insects and larvae. The wetland is also a breeding ground for the giant toad, which was introduced to Bermuda in 1885.

The marsh consists of several interesting micro-habitats. Ancient red mangroves overhang the first section, their distinctive boughs and prop roots creating a tunnel-like effect over the walkway. With the water glistening around their silver root tangle, they represent relics from an era when the marsh was a tidal saltwater pond. This first section of the marsh is flooded, and ducks and other waterfowl can be seen here gathering food. Moving forward, huge vine-covered cedars, rustling palmettos, giant ferns, and bulrushes create a thick forest wall on both sides, but as the creaky boardwalk turns a corner, there emerges an open area of sawgrass savannah, similar to vegetation in the Florida Everglades. Serrated leaves poke through the boardwalk like green swords, grassland stretching like a sea on either side. This is a seasonally flooded area, where heavy rains drastically raise water levels in the winter. The boardwalk's end, reaching into the belly of the marsh, brings you to forests of original cedars and palmettos—a scene not unlike what the first settlers of 1612 would have encountered. In their shade grow cinnamon, royal, and sword ferns, along with southern bracken and rare sedge. Constant culling of invasive species such as the guava, Brazilian pepper, and Chinese fan palm continues by environmentalists to preserve the reserve's important endemic populations.

Visible from Paget Marsh is the silver spire of **St. Paul's Anglican Church** (Middle Rd. at Valley Rd. junction, tel. 441/236-5880), an area landmark. Inside the church are beautiful stained-glass windows, old wooden pews, and cedar accents; outside, a historic graveyard with cedars and bougainvillea vines contains the whitewashed tombs of parishioners.

Salt Kettle

The spirits of pirates and privateers inhabit the tidy pastel lanes of Salt Kettle, home to Bermudian mariners and merchants over hundreds of years. Turn off Harbour Road onto Salt Kettle Road and follow it down into the intriguing promontory, which, now laden with historic homesteads, waterside gardens, and picturesque bays, is invested with the island's maritime history. Two guesthouses are located here, Salt Kettle Guest House and Greenbank Guest Cottages. The Paget-Warwick ferry stops regularly at the public dock at the farthest point.

HOMES AND GARDENS

Sotheby's antiques. Mystery roses by the dozen. Art by Warhol, Rembrandt, and El Greco. These are the treasures to be found at the ancestral homes that welcome visitors every spring in the popular **Open Houses and Gardens**. The program, organized by **The Garden Club of Bermuda** (tel. 441/232-1273), every year showcases a different parish whose elegant – sometimes unbelievably extravagant – properties provide a revealing behind-the-scenes look at privileged Bermuda. A half dozen or so homes throw open their doors to the public one day a year (usually a Wednesday) to raise money for club scholarships given to Bermudians studying horticulture or the environment. The homes and gardens selected are usually in the same neighborhood, so visitors can walk easily between the featured properties. While centuries-old homes and no-holds-barred interior design makes for eye-popping walkabouts, visitors will usually find the featured gardens no less spectacular, works of art in themselves. Feel free to photograph the flora and outdoor areas; no photography is allowed inside homes for security reasons. Check the club's tour brochures, distributed annually to hotels, guesthouses and Visitors Service Bureaus, for details of dates, times, and locations.

BEACHES
C Elbow Beach

Originally called Elba Beach, before the Elbow Beach Hotel opened its doors in 1908, this prime stretch of South Shore strand curves a good half mile, incorporating three private beachfront hotel properties (Elbow, Coco Reef Resort, and Coral Beach Club) as well as a public section, accessible by Tribe Road No. 48. Signs point to the beach from the main South Shore Road. Since all Bermuda beaches are public below the high-tide mark, locals enjoy this one as much as resort guests, and joggers, swimmers, and snorkelers can feel free to make use of the entire length of the beach. Elbow is a popular site for kitesurfers (www.bka.bm) when the wind swings around to the south, and regular volleyball tournaments are held on the sand near the public steps. Elbow's clean, soft sand, cerulean breakers, and mostly gentle surf (hurricane season notwithstanding) make it a perfect beach for all swimming abilities, but note that there are no lifeguards at the public section.

Private **Grape Bay** is restricted to guests of area hotels and homeowners in the tony neighborhood nearby. While the water is legally public, access is difficult, with no direct main roads leading to this quiet bit of coastline.

ENTERTAINMENT AND EVENTS

Social butterflies and night-owls can party to their hearts' content in Paget, home of nightclubs, bars, and several big annual sporting and cultural events.

Bermuda Annual Exhibition

If you're planning a trip to the island near the end of April, don't miss the Bermuda Annual Exhibition (Botanical Gardens, 169 South Shore Rd., tel. 441/236-5902 ext. 2351, fax 441/236-4812, agshow@ibl.bm or exhibition@logic.bm, 9 A.M.–6 P.M. Thurs.–Sat., $7 adults, $3 seniors and children 5–15, under five free), a truly local event that is one of the highlights on Bermudians' social calendars. For decades purely an agricultural competition, the beloved "Ag Show" got a new name and makeover in the past few years, evolving into a broader cultural celebration showcasing island traditions like kite-making and cedar craftsmanship, as well as horticulture, culinary arts, and sports. Entrants compete for prizes for the best artworks, cakes, roses, and vegetable critters, to name a few. Real animals—farmyard pigs, cattle, harness ponies, pet rabbits—are highlights for children, and a foreign troupe of clowns or acrobats is usually invited to perform. The three-day fair also offers a sampling of foodstalls selling cotton candy, fish sandwiches, fruit kabobs, and other favorites. Everyone from politicians and the governor to buses of grandmothers and society rose-growers comes out to support what has become a true island institution. For the fair at its best, go on Thursday (schoolchildren get a day off class to attend on Friday, and Saturday is a complete zoo).

The XL Capital Bermuda Open

A premier tennis event, sponsored in April by one of the largest Bermuda-based reinsurance companies, the XL Capital Bermuda Open (tel. 441/296-2554, fax 441/296-2551, www.xlcapitalbermudaopen.bm) brings male players ranked 50 or higher on the ATP Tour to the island to battle it out in nine days of clay-court action, including qualifiers. Organized by the Bermuda Tennis Federation (tel. 441/296-2554 or 441/296-2551) and held in the cushy environs of Coral Beach & Tennis Club, which opens its doors to the public for the occasion, the event provides a great opportunity to see tennis's top young turks up close and personal—box seats can be booked at courtside, and cheaper bleacher seats also offer a good view. Exhibition matches are thrown in for good measure: in past years, spectators have been treated to the likes of Michael Chang, Jim Courier, Mats Wilander, and John Lloyd. Plan early if you want tickets to the final—they sell out months in advance.

Nightlife

With one of the plushest venues and state-of-the-art light and sound systems, **The Deep** (Elbow Beach Hotel, 60 South Shore Rd., tel. 441/236-9884 or 441/236-3535, 6:30 P.M.–1 A.M. Mon.–Thurs. 6:30 P.M.–3 A.M. Fri. and Sat., admission $30 Fri. and Sat.) is on the hit-lists of local hipsters. The cool factor doesn't come cheap, though. Atop the steep cover charge, champagne ($15 a glass) and cocktails ($10–14) carry grown-up prices—and that's the point. Renovated in early 2006, the club is geared to those who dress up properly for a night out—and can afford to. Nevertheless, members' areas, private tables, a mezzanine lookout, elegant lounge area, and music ranging from Euro dance and house to Latin pop bring out summer crowds. Diners at adjacent Café Lido receive complimentary access. Dress code is "smart-elegant," no jeans.

Located off the main lobby at Elbow Beach Hotel, the panoramic **Veranda Bar** (60 South Shore Rd., tel. 441/236-3535, cocktails 11 A.M.–1 A.M., dining noon–11 P.M., snack menu 5 P.M.–1 A.M.) attracts a Friday night exodus from Hamilton for its popular summer happy hour (5–9 P.M.), where visitors and local corporate types mingle in the cozy lounge and on the covered terrace as the sun sets over the beach below. A rum bar offers more than 50 brands, including Bermuda's Goslings Black Seal, and snacks are served all night long, with tapas on Fridays.

SHOPPING

Named for the flower that inspired the John Lennon album (he saw it in the park during his summer 1980 Bermuda visit), the **Double Fantasy Gift Shop** at Botanical Gardens visitors center (183 South Rd., tel. 441/236-5291, fax 441/236-8970, 9:30 A.M.–3:30 P.M. Mon.–Fri.) stocks an assortment of whimsical, garden-inspired treasures. Bermuda books, cedar souvenirs, and knickknacks such as candles, games, toys, light plates, floral stationery, croquet sets, even gardening tools. An image of Lennon's famous freesia is branded on T-shirts, tea towels, and cutting boards. Cold drinks and snacks are also sold at the center, which has a large room with tables and chairs and vistas of the rolling lawns outside.

SPORTS AND RECREATION

Paget is one of the sportiest parishes, packed with running trails, a nine-hole golf course, tennis galore, volleyball, water sports like kayaking and kitesurfing, and a scuba and snorkeling outlet.

Tennis

Paget resort properties have numerous tennis courts that can be rented by nonguests at an hourly rate. Some of the best are the five Plexi-pave hard courts at **Mandarin Oriental Elbow Beach Resort** (30 South Shore Rd., tel. 441/236-3535); two of these have floodlights for night play. The resident pro is David Lambert—Bermuda's Davis Cup team coach—who gives lessons, and there's a pro shop with equipment, balls, outfits, and cold drinks.

Home of the annual XL Capital Bermuda Open, **Coral Beach & Tennis Club** (34 South Shore Rd., tennis shop tel. 441/236-6495, www.coralbeach.com) is a private members' club and the premier tennis facility on the island, with eight clay courts monitored to ATP standards. Three courts have lights. Visitors who are not club members can book lessons here ($95 per hour), or games with club members. The tennis shop stocks clothing emblazoned with the club's insignia, plus racquets and balls. Note that all-white tennis attire is required. Four club pros, including veteran Derek Singleton, give private lessons or group coaching.

Horizons & Cottages (33 South Shore Rd., tel. 441/236-0048) has three championship courts ($10 an hour). Contact the main reception for booking.

Golf

Horizons (33 South Shore Rd., tel. 441/236-0048) has a nine-hole "mashie" golf course—a Scottish word for a golf club, of which a 7-iron is recommended. For pure fun, a bit of practice, and spectacular ocean-view scenery from every hole, a round here makes for a great afternoon (the longest shot is 122 yards). There are no carts, and reservations are required for tee times. The greens fee is $20 per person weekdays, $25 on weekends; club rentals are $2.50, balls $1.

Scuba and Snorkeling

Blue Water Divers & Watersports (tel. 441/234-2909, www.divebermuda.com) operates a year-round snorkel and scuba outlet at Elbow Beach, offering snorkel tours on the nearby boiler reefs, James Bond–style waterscooter tours, and beach dives around the fringe reefs that lie just a few hundred yards from shore. You can also kayak out to *Pollockshields*, a 1915 German wreck that lies within swimming distance from the beach. Scuba certification by instructors trained in PADI, NAUI, and SSI is also available. Reservations by credit card are recommended.

Running and Walking

It's hard to get away from traffic in Bermuda, and Paget's busy, hilly, narrow roads, often lacking sidewalks, are far from ideal for running and walking. **The Railway Trail** is the perfect escape from the hubbub, a flat, shady path cutting through scenic neighborhoods. The Paget trail starts at the top of Trimingham Hill on South Road, where signs and a zebra crossing lead to the entrance. Passing through a short tunnel and between thick limestone cuts in the hillside, the trail runs past Grape Bay, with wide-open views of Paget Marsh and the city of Hamilton's skyline beyond. Although the trail occasionally hits tarmac sections and has to cross a couple of main roads, it soon enters a long, wide tranquil stretch that passes through thick cherry woods, past farmers' fields and spice forests, all the way to Warwick and beyond. If you keep going, you can actually make it all the way to Mangrove Bay in Sandys—this I know from many a marathon training session!

For nearly 30 years, members of the Mid Atlantic Athletic Club (tel. 441/236-9586, www.maac.bm), the island's largest running club, have met at the Botanical Gardens for a two- or four-mile **"fun run"** at 6 P.M. Tuesday evenings through the summer months. Meet in the center of the Gardens just past the main carpark. The loop route leaves North Gate and follows the park's perimeter along Point Finger Road, South Shore Road, Tee Street, and Berry Hill Road.

Spas

Cream of the crop of Bermuda's resort spas, **The Spa at Elbow Beach** (60 South Shore Rd., tel. 441/239-8900, fax 441/239-8906, www.mandarinoriental.com/bermuda, 9 A.M.–9 P.M. Mon.–Sat., 9 A.M.–8 P.M. Sun.) is the newest facility to open on the island—and the most luxurious. How luxurious? A basic manicure and pedicure combo will set you back $200. But then again, the facility's wow factor is pretty impressive. If you feel like treating yourself, this is the place to go. Six private spa suites (including couples' suites) offer daybeds, granite baths, pebble-lined showers, bamboo floors, and glittering ocean views from private balconies. Thai, Balinese, and Tibetan influences permeate the facility, located in a separate building near the hotel's entrance. Massage, face, and body treatments include deep tissue massage (80 minutes, $225); a petal bath (20 minutes, $75), an "age-defying" facial (80 minutes, $225), a marine mud, algae, and clay body wrap (50 minutes, $150), and signature body treatments of two hours or more, ranging from $320 to $900 (for a three-hour couples' treatment). Forty-eight-hour advance bookings are highly recommended. Minimum age for spa access is 18.

Samadhi (27 Harbour Rd., second floor, Shoreby Building, tel. 441/236-6060 ext. 23, samadhi-spa@belmonthills.com, 9 A.M.–5 P.M., by appointment only) opened at the site of the Newstead Resort & Spa in the fall of 2005, while it was still in the throes of major construction. Promising "a fusion of East and West," the spa offers body treatments such as the sugar glow (90 minutes, $155), using turbinado sugar, lavender, aloe, and rosemary, as well as detoxifying seaweed and mud masks and aroma wraps. Massages range from the "Four Hands," carried out by two therapists (90 minutes, $270) to couples' massage ($285), deep-tissue and prenatal massages. A 15 percent gratuity is added to your final balance, which can be settled with cash, MasterCard, or Visa only.

For Kids

Paget kid-pleasers include **Botanical Gardens, Paget Marsh,** picnics and wading along **Pomander Road,** and boat-watching at **Red Hole.** Children will adore the bunnies, ducks, and peacocks at Botanical Gardens, in enclosures behind Camden House. Camden's grassy hills are great for tumbling down, and the lawns invite impromptu games of football or hide-and-seek. On the western side of the Gardens, gargantuan ficus and rubber trees

with hollow insides—the kind that inhabit fairy tales—serve as make-believe treehouses. Kids of all ages will want to walk inside, climb their low branches, and swing on the hanging roots. Directly opposite Camden, there are more ducks to feed and follow on the Tucker property, a vast estate owned by the Tucker family, who open the lawns to catch football games and Saturday morning kids' soccer practices. Visitors are welcome to stroll the lawns and inspect the natural canal under a roadside rubber tree, where the ducks hang out with fleets of ducklings in the spring.

As always, **beaches** often make for the best play areas, and Paget's Elbow Beach will not disappoint with its soft sand and easygoing surf. In addition, the three-day **Bermuda Annual Exhibition** at Botanical Gardens is a must-see if you're vacationing in April.

ACCOMMODATIONS
$100-200

Opened in 1970, **◖ Salt Kettle House** (10 Salt Kettle Rd., tel. 441/236-0407, fax 441/236-8639, cottages $70 per person, main house rooms $60 per person, breakfast included; lower rates Dec. 1–March 1) has been the kind of place many Bermuda visitors prefer to keep secret. Maybe it's the fact you can't help but thoroughly believe her when innkeeper Hazel Lowe says she loves what she's doing. Maybe it's the restful hammock between the waterside whispering pines, or the resident duck, or the turquoise shutters, but the quaint property breathes utter peace. With five rooms in the rambling house with use of the main kitchen, and four simple but nicely appointed cottages with full kitchens, the property delivers an affordable opportunity to experience life in one of Bermuda's most historic neighborhoods. It can accommodate a total of 22 guests. Trellised gardens, a gracious old homestead, and a serene bay with boats bobbing at their moorings make Salt Kettle House a winner. The ferry stop is within easy access, at the end of Salt Kettle Lane.

"Please remove tar from feet with Lestoil," cautions a front-door sign at **Little Pomander Guest House** (16 Pomander Rd., tel. 441/236-

7635, fax 441/236-8332, info@littlepomander.com, $140 doubles with breakfast), a clue to the quaint whimsy of this waterfront property. Perched on the edge of Foot of the Lane, where boaters meander past on their way up the harbor, it's hard to imagine a more intimate place to kick back in Bermuda. Just five minutes around the harbor's edge to Hamilton, with lovely views of the water and cityscape across the way, Little Pomander may not be high-tech or five-star, but it offers a homey and very convenient island retreat. The cottage-style home is such a delectable icing-like shade of pink, you almost feel you could reach out and break off a corner to nibble. Five air-conditioned rooms all have private bath, cable TV, microwave, refrigerator, phone, and harbor views. The harborfront garden, with deck chairs shaded by a brilliant poinciana tree, is a perfect spot to sunbathe or people-watch. Credit cards accepted.

Next to the private Pomander Tennis Club sits **Erith Guest House** (15 Pomander Rd., tel. 441/232-1827 or 441/535-6369, erith@therock.bm, $155 standard room, $175 superior, $225 suite), a renovated old Bermuda home with six rooms, a one-bedroom suite, a swimming pool, and hot tub. All rooms have air-conditioning, cable TV, Internet access, phones, microwaves, coffeemakers, irons, hair dryers, and a refrigerator. The superior room has a kitchenette, while the suite offers a full kitchen and private balcony. Ground-floor units have private entrances.

Tangerine-bright **Dawkins Manor** (29 St. Michael's Ln., tel. 441/236-7419, www.dawkinsmanorhotel.com, $150 doubles) may be a too-imposing appellation for this cozy, family-run guesthouse, but it captures the imagination. Located on a busy residential street, with a grocery store at one end and a primary school at the other, the house is nonetheless a calm respite for travelers. Run by Celia Dawkins, the business thrives on repeat visitors and word-of-mouth praise for the careful hospitality, neat rooms, and handy location (near beaches, bus stops, cycle liveries, and Hamilton). Eight standard rooms are located in the main house, with private bathrooms,

refrigerators, coffeemakers, and microwaves. One- and two-bedroom apartments with full kitchens are in a complex across the road. The property also has an unheated pool.

Sun-worshippers choose **Paraquet Apartments** (South Shore Rd., tel. 441/236-5842, fax 441/236-1665, starting at $155 doubles) for their affordable proximity to Elbow Beach. Set on a hillside above the busy main road, three basic units include private bathroom with shower, small refrigerator, and patio. There are nine larger units with full kitchens. The popular Paraquet Restaurant sits on the same property.

$200-300

A salmon-pink landmark for more than a century, **◖ Harmony Hall** (109 South Shore Rd., tel. 441/236-3500, toll-free 888/427-6664, www.harmonyclub.com, $210 high season, $155 low season) retains much of the old-time elegance that brought generations of Bermuda-lovers back to the property over the years. Perhaps hoping to live up to its name, the resort makes no apologies for its adults-only policy, so families with kids can cross this hotel off their list. The resort offers one of the island's best bargains; for its price, few properties can match the cottage-style elegance, mature garden setting, proximity to Hamilton and the beaches, plus facilities such as tennis courts, hot tub, sauna, and heated freshwater pool. Harmony's 68 double units, all situated around a central lawn—a onetime croquet pitch—have roomy bedrooms and bathrooms, cable TV, coffeemakers, and garden views dripping with bougainvillea, lilies, and flaming poinciana trees. Guests receive free passes to use the beach and its facilities at Mandarin Oriental's five-star Elbow Beach Hotel just around the corner. The Paget Railway Trail runs along the southern border of the resort, providing a flat, shady route for walking or running.

A reincarnation of the former Inverurie Hotel's west wing, **The Wharf** (1 Harbour Rd., tel. 441/232-5700, toll-free 866/782-9232, www.wharfexecutivesuites.com, studios $260, one-bedroom suites $420) opened in 2003, offering simple but modern suites and studios. Geared mainly to business travelers housed here by Hamilton corporations for weeks or months at a time, the hotel's main draw is the view—the blue expanse of Hamilton Harbour from every room's king-size bed. The adjacent ferry dock, Darrell's Wharf, allows easy access to Hamilton via a seven-minute ride. The decor of both studios and suites is uninspired but functional, with desks, ergonomic chairs, two-line speakerphones, data ports, DSL lines, fax machines, printers, and copiers, plus cable TV and concierge service when necessary. Studios contain galley kitchens, while suites, which have separate sitting rooms plus office space, have fully applianced kitchens for self-catering. Wooden decks front each of the rooms over the water. A small front desk foyer, breakfast room, and laundry are the hotel's only public areas. The Wharf belongs to a Paget/Warwick hotel group (www.bermudaresorthotels.com) incorporating Harmony Hall, Grape Bay Beach Hotel, and Surf Side Resort, so guests can use pools, beaches, and other facilities of those properties.

Named for the waxy paddle-leafed bush that hugs Bermuda's shoreline, the **Grape Bay Beach Hotel** (White Sands Rd., tel. 441/236-2023, fax 441/236-2486, www.grapebay.com, ocean-view rooms $265, garden view $235) is the former White Sands Hotel, which was sold to new owners and renovated in 2003. With a choice of king beds or two doubles, all rooms are located in the somewhat sterile apartment block attached to the quainter main building, where public areas include a lounge with fireplace and sea views. All rooms are simply outfitted with tile floors and small bathrooms. But the reason to stay here would be outside, not in. While the hotel does not sit directly on the oceanfront, beautiful, private Grape Bay Beach lies just a few hundreds meters down a sandy lane. There is also a lovely swimming pool at the hilltop property, which is blissfully free of traffic noise. The popular restaurant Sapori, which specializes in seafood and Italian fare, is also on-site, adjacent to the pool.

Over $300

For anyone seeking a little more solitude than a hotel or guesthouse can offer, **(Grape Bay Cottages** (Grape Bay Dr., off South Shore Rd., tel. 441/236-1194, one to four people $315 per night April–Nov., $210 winter) may offer the perfect solution. Two cottages, Beach Crest and Beach Home, each with two bedrooms, a kitchen, a living/dining area, and one bathroom, sit on ultra-exclusive, absolutely tranquil Grape Bay Drive (address of millionaires and bigwigs, including the former U.S. consul general). Especially popular in summertime, the cottages lie just a few minutes from private Grape Bay Beach, and each has its own small garden and barbecue for self-catering. Other amenities include cable TV, phones, and air-conditioning.

When it comes to blending monied colonial style with modern comforts in Bermuda, **(Horizons & Cottages** (33 South Shore Rd., tel. 441/236-0048, toll-free reservations 800/468-0022, fax 441/236-1981, www.bermudasbest.com, rooms $400, cottages and suites $450–700) is in a realm of its own. Once an 18th-century plantation, the powder-pink resort sprawls over a 25-acre hilltop estate, complete with manor house, quaint cottages, a nine-hole golf course, tennis courts, a croquet lawn, mature gardens, and, around every hibiscus or honeysuckle, breath-catching ocean views. Passing through its limestone pillars, emblazoned with the brass Relais & Chateaux crest, is akin to entering a privileged, tranquil world of past years. Mourning doves coo from the orchards, a golf cart putters across a green, and the silver sheen of the far-off reef surf fills you with a giddy, "king-of-the-world!" euphoria. It will cost you to partake of this tony time-travel, but from all accounts, it is worth any money spent. Nothing is too much trouble for the cheery, gracious staff, and the surroundings are quintessential Bermuda—from the cedar fireplaces to the pastel views from every window.

Thirteen cottages with 45 rooms and three suites grace the property, which underwent a thorough refurbishment over the past two winters. Four-poster king-size beds in some rooms, tasteful floral linens, and artworks ranging from original local watercolors to botanical prints lend style and comfort. Families or couples can be accommodated in cottages where several bedrooms can be linked or divided with separate entrances. In the main house, guests can relax amid Wedgwood, endless Bermuda cedar, whitewashed architecture, red-brick terraces, and welcoming arms stairways leading to the large, heated freshwater pool. Quaint rooms in the house, all with tiny brass doorknockers, have eclectic, individualized decor. The main dining room offers afternoon tea, silver-service dinners, leisurely lunch on the patios, and a popular Friday night barbecue in high season. Horizons guests also can enjoy the beach and facilities of the neighboring sister property, the exclusive Coral Beach & Tennis Club, which has dramatic alfresco dining, top-rated clay tennis facilities, a squash court, fitness spa, and health club.

The fine **◖ Mandarin Oriental Elbow Beach Hotel** (30 South Shore Rd., tel. 441/236-3535, toll-free 800/223-7434, doubles from $475) has poured millions of dollars into a redesign of many of its 235 rooms and suites over the past two years, and it shows. The makeover has been targeted to the higher-end suites to date, but plans to update mid-range rooms are under way. Unlike the often-tacky florals and frills that garb so many hotel properties in Bermuda and the tropics, M.O.'s M.O., so to speak, has been to modernize its decor with neutral tones and high-end minimalist furnishings and amenities. The result is five-star stunning and no doubt makes guests feel that the lofty rates they pay for such luxury are worth it. The 60-acre seafront property is one of Bermuda's premier resorts, offering a wish-list of amenities, including a deluxe spa which opened in 2005, five top-rate tennis courts, a climate-controlled pool, fitness center, putting green, beauty salon, lobby shops, a summer-season Kids' Club, a scuba outlet, five restaurants, and a hip nightclub on-site. Among its rooms and suites, the hotel has 104 cottages set in the lush grounds, one- and two-bedroom beachfront suites, and a spectacular split-level penthouse ($4,000 per night), with

Jacuzzi and private patios, where Arab sheikhs have stayed. Luxury suites come with LCD flat-screen AV systems, limestone bathrooms, feather duvets, and private sundecks. More economical rooms in the main building include those facing the rear garden, available with king or twin beds ($475), high-speed Internet, 24-hour room service, air-conditioning, in-room safes, bathrobes and slippers, hair dryers, and Molton Brown products. The property's beach is its crown jewel, stretching outside the hotel in a pristine, half-mile arc linking to next-door Coral Beach. Between them, a public access section makes this one of the most popular in the summer, but the hotel's beach facilities (deck chairs, umbrellas, pedal boats, kayaks, snorkeling, showers, and changing rooms) are reserved for paying guests.

Government-owned **Coco Reef Resort** (Stonington Circle, College Dr., off South Shore Rd., tel. 441/236-5416, fax 441/236-0371, www.cocoreefbermuda.com, doubles from $443) came under new management in 2003, when Bermudian hotelier John Jeffries won a 50-year lease to operate the property. Formerly the Stonington Beach Hotel, the oceanfront resort with 60 units plus two one-bedroom suites has undergone recent renovations, including a revamped lobby with 50-foot atrium and crystal skylight. With far fewer facilities or high-end amenities, the property isn't in the same league as neighboring Elbow Beach Hotel, but rates are slightly lower and the beach outside is shared with the Mandarin Oriental hotel. Coco Reef has two free-use tennis courts, a heated swimming pool overlooking the ocean, a bar and restaurant, and wireless and high-speed Internet service in the lobby, bar, and terrace areas. It continues to act as a training ground for students of hospitality enrolled in the next-door Bermuda College, a junior college that awards Associate degrees.

FOOD

Paget enjoys a thriving restaurant scene, thanks to the plethora of hotels and guesthouses, and its vicinity on the outskirts of Hamilton. From burgers and comfort food to beachside

Mediterranean menus, cutting-edge Bermudian cuisine and à la carte silver service, foodies of all tastes will find plenty to sample.

Cafés, Takeout, and Snacks

Pastries, sandwiches, coffee, ice cream and cold drinks are sold at the **Double Fantasy Café & Gift Shop** inside the Botanical Gardens visitors center (183 South Rd., 9:30 A.M.–3:30 P.M. Mon.–Fri.), a renovated space that provides a welcome air-conditioned respite for park visitors in the summer. Sit down at teak tables and chairs, or take your snack with you as you stroll around the gardens. The center is near the park's Berry Hill Road entrance and has ample parking right outside.

The Pink Café (King Edward VII Memorial Hospital, 7 Point Finger Rd., ground floor, tel. 441/239-2057, 9 A.M.–3:45 P.M. Mon.–Fri., 9 A.M.–1:30 P.M. Sat., closed public holidays) is partly run by the facility's ubiquitous "Pink Ladies" and teenage "Candy Stripers"—volunteers from the charitable Women's Hospital Auxiliary, who, identifiable in their hallmark rosy uniforms, work in virtually every department of the hospital aiding nurses with patient care. Their much-loved little coffee shop, which shifted locations after many decades and underwent renovations in 1998, serves up local favorites like fish cakes, black-eyed pea soup, gingerbread, and chicken pies to a constant crowd of medical staff, hospital visitors, and drop-in passersbys. Hot lunch specials range from $8.50 to $12.

The hospital's **cafeteria** (first floor, open for breakfast 7:30–9:30 A.M., lunch noon–2 P.M., dinner 5:30–7:30 P.M., tel. 441/236-2345) is also open to the public and offers a truly local experience, complete with loads of well-priced comfort food (burgers, chicken legs, macaroni 'n' cheese).

Like its after-hours Hamilton counterpart of the same name, **The Ice Queen** (Rural Hill Plaza, South Rd., tel. 441/236-3136, 10 A.M.–5 A.M. daily) sees lines out the door for its takeout cheeseburgers, mozzarella sticks, chicken, and fries when Hamilton bars close on Friday and Saturday evenings. Things can get rowdy,

even dangerous—in July 2001 a young man was fatally stabbed before a crowd of 100 onlookers. Lunch brings a calmer clientele—construction workers, school kids, seniors in search of a delicious fish sandwich. Prices are reasonable and the offerings hearty.

(The Paraquet Restaurant & Takeout (68 South Shore Rd., tel. 441/236-9742, 8 A.M.–midnight daily) is more public forum than restaurant, a welcome roadside drop-in for taxi drivers, police patrols on coffee breaks, flip-flopped beachgoers, senior citizens, and families with children. The Portuguese-owned eatery has been around for as long as most locals can remember. Today, it keeps on serving favorites like the delectably crusted fish cake on a bun (at $5, far cheaper than its ridiculously priced counterpart, the $17 fish cake dinner), hearty soups, hot and cold sandwiches, wraps, meatloaf, chicken dinners, cakes, pies, and thick milkshakes. Special holiday menus are popular during the Easter, Christmas, and Thanksgiving seasons. The Paraquet's bakery offerings are also worth sampling: banana bread, gingerbread, rolls, and hot-cross buns (at Easter) are stacked daily on shelves near the entrance. Bermudians also bulk-order their Christmas cassava pies and Easter fish cakes (arguably the best on the island) from here. Opt for a stool at the foyer bars to get the full experience: cabbies and other regulars hold debates on the political issues of the day here most afternoons.

Blue Point (Mandarin Oriental Elbow Beach Hotel main lobby, 60 South Shore Rd., tel. 441/236-3535, lunch noon–4 P.M., bar 11 A.M.–5 P.M. daily) serves salads, seafood, gourmet pizzas, burgers, spa cuisine, and other casual fare at the hotel poolside during the summer season.

Mediterranean

Situated on a hilltop above the South Shore at the Grape Bay Beach Hotel, **(Sapori Restaurant & Terrace** (55 White Sands Rd., tel. 441/236-7201, sapori@northrock.bm, lunch noon–3 P.M., dinner 6–10 P.M. daily, Sunday brunch 11 A.M.–4 P.M.) changed ownership in the spring of 2006 and its menu was amended accordingly. New boss Paolo Schulz opted for a refocus on all things Mediterranean in the ocean-view dining room, which spills out onto a breezy poolside terrace. As a result, starters include Italian favorites such as *timballo di salmone* (smoked salmon envelopes filled with mascarpone cheese) and *campagnola* (chargrilled seasoned vegetables), while a wide menu of pastas is followed by main courses featuring fresh seafood, steak, and chicken. "Anything-goes" pizzas are also proving popular. Sapori's vodka bar, boasting martinis of all flavors, also attracts a following, especially on Friday nights.

Reopened after a massive 2004–05 overhaul caused by Hurricane Fabian's devastation, the new (**Café Lido** (at the beach, Mandarin Oriental Elbow Beach Hotel, 60 South Shore Rd., tel. 441/236-9884, fax 441/236-8496, www.lido.bm or www.mandarinoriental.com/bermuda, 6:30–10 P.M. daily, $40 buffet brunch 11:30 A.M.–3 P.M. Sundays) is as elegant and sophisticated an oceanfront dining room as any of its previous incarnations. With large windows looking out to Elbow Beach's blue horizons, and the surf just a staircase away, the restaurant oozes modern ambience with its terracotta and wood decor and very professional service from manager Ennio Lucarini and his attentive staff. The award-winning menu is outstanding, loaded with fresh fish and seafood. Appetizers include fresh oysters ($3.50 each) and crustacean salad with avocado and white asparagus ($16). Entrées offer a choice of fish (roasted spiced monkfish $29), meat (angus beef tenderloin with foie gras medallion $38), and a daily-changing pasta special ($26). Diners can dance their calories off afterwards; they are admitted free into adjoining The Deep nightclub.

Sister to Café Lido on the terrace above, (**Mickey's Beach Bistro** (at the beach, Mandarin Oriental Elbow Beach Hotel, 60 South Shore Rd., tel. 441/236-9107, open May–Oct. only, lunch noon–2:30 P.M., dinner 6:30–11 P.M. daily, bar service 10 A.M.–1 A.M.) sits on the sand within a few yards of the thunderous surf under a custom-made tent. The casual chic eatery offers a simpler vibe than Lido, but some of the same specialties—salads, pastas, steaks, and

seafood—at near-parallel prices (main courses $25–29). But service is stellar, the dishes beautifully concocted, and the alfresco surroundings utterly relaxing, even by Bermuda standards.

Tearooms

Afternoon tea at **Veranda Bar** (Mandarin Oriental Elbow Beach main lobby, 60 South Shore Rd., tel. 441/236-3535, tea 3–5 P.M. daily) includes a choice of teas and a spread of tea sandwiches and tea cakes, served on a tiered tray, like something out of *Alice in Wonderland*.

Fine Dining

Attentive staff and outstanding architectural creations distinguish (**Seahorse Grill** (Mandarin Oriental Elbow Beach Hotel, 60 South Shore Rd., tel. 441/239-6885 or 441/236-3535, dinner nightly 6:30–10 P.M., Sunday brunch noon–3 P.M.). Fresh produce from local farmers is conjured into delectable fusion offerings such as ravioli of goat's cheese, black rum and soy-glazed pork tenderloin, loquat chutney, and caramelized Bermuda onion tart, lifting the island's culinary traditions to new levels of innovation. The contemporary-designed restaurant, which wraps around one of the hotel's lower levels, won the People's Choice Award for Best Overall Restaurant at the 2005 Bermuda Culinary Arts Festival, and chef, Terence Clark, has also been lauded. It bills itself as the birthplace of "New Bermudian Cuisine," which includes lighter-fare spa dishes. Two-course prix fixe menu $45; three-course prix fixe $53.

Bearing the Relais & Chateaux stamp of approval, the gourmet production of (**Horizons & Cottages** (South Shore Rd., tel. 441/236-0048, fax 441/236-1981, www.bermudasbest.com, lunch 12:30–3 P.M., dinner 7–9 P.M. daily) is a silver-service, jacket-and-tie favorite, but not just for the food. The setting—in summer, outdoors on the hillcrest patio or pool terrace, overlooking the coconut palms of the shoreline; in winter, inside the cozy cedar environs of the Middleton Dining Room—rivals even the carefully prepared menu, which chef Graham Fyfe changes daily. Starters include salmon gateau ($14.50) and Bermuda banana salad with tiger shrimp ($16). Main courses range from flame-broiled swordfish ($32) and baked corn-fed chicken breast with a truffle-tossed fig salad ($27) to homemade fettucine ($23). The locale is one the island's most popular romantic dinner spots for Bermudian couples as well as visiting honeymooners.

Boasting a fabled, 300-year-old reputation, 【 **Fourways Inn** (1 Middle Rd., tel. 441/236-6517, fax 441/236-5528, www.fourways.bm, dinner only 6:30–9:30 P.M. daily, Sunday brunch 11:30 A.M.–2:30 P.M.) offers a hefty spoonful of history along with its gourmet menu. Built in 1727 by John Harvey of the Bristol Cream clan, Fourways has been a private home, a restaurant, and a guesthouse over the years. Steeped in cedar and stuffed with antiques, narrow hallways, and low doorframes, it retains a charming character and is a noted architectural landmark. The restaurant's award-winning kitchen has for decades won international accolades for its gourmet creations. Champagne-strawberry soup, shellfish risotto, fresh lobsters, herbs from the garden, a wine list to get lost in—suffice it to say Fourways provides a dining experience you won't soon forget. It is not a cheap date, however; dinner for two with wine will cost about $200. Eat in the historic interior, where grandfather clocks and the Peg Leg Bar recall earlier times, or outside in the garden-fringed courtyard. Service is impeccable; dress code is smart-casual, with a previous jacket-and-tie rule recently relaxed. The popular Sunday brunch is a good way to sample Fourways's menu cost-effectively. The spread of sushi, roast meats, fresh fish, seafood, pasta, and omelettes-to-order is $39.75 for adults, $20 children 6–11, under five free.

Grocery Stores

Tucked behind Paget gas station, the small **A1 Paget Market** (Middle Rd. at Valley Rd. junction, tel. 441/236-0351, 8 A.M.–10 P.M. Mon.–Sat., 1–5 P.M. Sun.) is a convenient stopping place for wines, liquors, fresh fruit and vegetables, frozen meals, deli meats, and baked goods. One of the MarketPlace store chain, it is most popular for its rotisserie chicken and takeout chicken fingers, located near the back of the store. Friendly staff and easy parking attract a regular parish clientele.

The large, busy **Modern Mart** (104 South Shore Rd., tel. 441/236-6161, 8 A.M.–10 P.M. Mon.–Sat., 1–5 P.M. Sun.) offers everything from groceries to foreign and local newspapers, greeting cards, toiletries, and pet paraphernalia. An extensive variety of Canada's President's Choice product line is carried here; the store's substantial wine selection is also worth a visit. Modern Mart's butchers are particularly helpful and professional.

INFORMATION AND SERVICES

One of the islandwide Phoenix Stores chain, **Paget Pharmacy** (Rural Hill Plaza, 130 Middle Rd., tel. 441/236-2681, fax 441/236-9057, 8 A.M.–8 P.M. Mon.–Sat., 10 A.M.–6 P.M. Sun. and holidays) offers newspapers and magazines, makeup, beach supplies, candy, greeting cards, postcards, and a prescriptions counter.

The cheery staff at pocket-sized **Paget Post Office** (108 Middle Rd., tel. 441/236-7429, 8 A.M.–5 P.M. Mon.–Fri.) know the locals by name, making this tiny outlet a hub of the parish community, especially during the busy Christmas season.

Paget Shell Service Station (65 Middle Rd., at the corner of Valley Rd., tel. 441/236-1691, 7 A.M.–11 P.M. Mon.–Sat., 9 A.M.–6 P.M. Sun.) is run by a friendly team who know the regulars by name. The on-site shop sells newspapers, cold drinks, and baked goods.

Paget Drycleaners and Mailboxes Express (2 Lovers Ln., at the junction with Middle Rd., tel. 441/236-5142, 8 A.M.–7 P.M. Mon.–Sat.) offers full dry-cleaning services, plus a FedEx, DHL, and TNT mail-drop for overseas mail (documents only). Residents can rent mailbox suites here also.

ATMs can be found at Paget Pharmacy, Modern Mart, and at the hospital.

Public toilets are located at area restaurants and hotels, Botanical Gardens visitors center, and King Edward VII Memorial Hospital.

GETTING THERE AND AROUND

Buses

Paget is dotted with bus stops, making for easy public transport around the parish. Take the No. 2 bus (hourly) through the parish center between Hamilton and Ord Road (north of Elbow Beach). To go to Sandys or the South Shore beaches farther west, hop on the No. 7 (every half hour) or No. 8 (every 15 minutes), which take South Shore Road and Middle Road respectively to the Royal Naval Dockyard. Travel within Paget qualifies for the three-zone tariff of $3 (exact change, or tokens, tickets, or passes required).

Ferries

The quaint iron ferries of the Paget-Warwick route are worth experiencing, especially for the breezy harbor-hop to the Ferry Terminal in Hamilton. Paget has three very scenic stops along narrow Harbour Road, where you can either jump aboard or get off and explore. Farthest down the harbor is Lower Ferry (between Highwood Lane and Valley Road); Hodgson's Ferry opposite the Chapel Road junction is next, followed by Salt Kettle, situated at the foot of this charming old seafaring neighborhood. Corporate commuters use the service; in the mornings, you can see suits, skirts, and heels scampering along serpentine Harbour Road to catch the vessels after they pull out of the city's Ferry Terminal. If you board in Hamilton, the short circuit out and back takes about a half hour; ferries leave Hamilton every 30 minutes or less at commuter times, otherwise every 45 minutes. Fares are $5 round-trip, $2.50 one-way. For information, call Sea Express (tel. 441/295-4506, www.seaexpress.bm) or check the schedules available at Visitors Service Bureaus and hotels or printed in the back of the phone book.

Scooters and Bicycles

Paget is the headquarters for **Oleander Cycles** (6 Valley Rd., tel. 441/236-5235 or 236-BIKE, fax 441/236-1949, www.oleandercycles.bm, 8:30 A.M.–5:30 P.M. daily), the island's largest scooter livery, with six other outlets around the island. Standard or deluxe (two-person) scooters can be rented by anyone aged 16 or older; no driver's license is required, but instructors carry out a mini-tutorial on Valley Road before letting visitors loose on two wheels. Rates ($50 for one day, $212 for seven days, $16 per day after seven days) include delivery and pickup (or hotel pickup), first tank of gas, helmet, lock, and basket, $25 third-party insurance, and islandwide pickup service for breakdowns.

Eve's Cycle (114 Middle Rd., tel. 441/236-6247, fax 441/236-5464, www.evecycles.bm, open 8 A.M.–5 P.M. daily) offers a complimentary shuttle to and from its shop near the Paget traffic lights (it has another outlet in St. George). Rates for automatic double-seat ($45 a day, $193 seven days) and single-seat scooters ($38, $143) include mandatory $15 insurance. Online reservations and special corporate rates are available. Mono Shock 21-speed mountain bikes can also be rented here ($25 per day, $110 for seven days).

Taxis

There is a taxi stand outside the main entrance of the Elbow Beach Hotel. Otherwise, book a taxi via telephone.

Tour Train

The **Bermuda Train Company** (6 Valley Rd., tel. 441/236-5972) owns and operates two toy-like engines, which run regular one- and two-hour tours with commentary, from Hamilton and Dockyard during the summer and fall. The Hamilton engine, which picks up passengers outside Number-Six Shed on Front Street, offers a one-hour loop ($25) through the city, along East Broadway to Botanical Gardens, around the park, and back to Hamilton. A two-hour version ($32) includes a one-hour tour of the Bermuda Underwater Exploration Institute (BUEI). Look for the train-stop marker and climb aboard, though most seats are sold out in advance to cruise ship passengers. The driver's yarn, which describes sights and local traditions, is entertaining, though based more on folklore than fact.

WARWICK AND SOUTHAMPTON PARISHES

Bermuda's most panoramically scenic parishes, with cliff-top views of surf-tossed coastlines on one side and the Great Sound's archipelago on the other, Warwick and Southampton project the quintessential Bermuda experience. The most recognizable images, those that sell the island in magazine layouts, TV ads, and postcards are often captured here. Full-blast Waikiki-esque fun in the sun? Check. Secluded azure grottoes? Check. Kitesurfing, golf, tennis, scuba, spas? Ditto. Beaches, water sports, and big-resort indulgences are the key draws for these parishes, whether you're stopping off for a swim while driving west, or choosing them as home base for a Bermuda stay. While shopping is limited to convenience stores, groceries, and retail outlets within hotels, and entertainment is almost exclusively of the out-

door variety, both parishes offer food, sports, and accommodations galore.

Sprawling westward between Paget and Sandys, Warwick and Southampton encompass undulating terrain scattered with residential neighborhoods, farmland, nature reserves, hotels, guesthouses, and national parks, to which the miles of south-facing beaches and coastal dunes belong. The two parishes are dotted with historic properties (Michael Douglas and Catherine Zeta-Jones spend time at their 2.5-acre, Georgian hilltop estate in Warwick), as well as modest cottages tucked down meandering tributaries bearing soporific names like Sleepy Hollow Lane, Rose Glen, and Tamarind Vale.

When Bermudians talk about going "up de country," they mean heading west to Somerset through these parishes. There is a choice of

© ROSEMARY JONES

HIGHLIGHTS

◖ Warwick Pond: Newly added signage and cleared trails make this nature reserve, containing the second-largest freshwater pond in Bermuda, an attraction for anyone interested in eco-walks or island birdlife (page 111).

◖ Warwick Long Bay: As its name suggests, this is officially Bermuda's longest beach, its soft pink stretches typically less crowded than that of nearby Horseshoe Bay, which is connected by trails through the dunes (page 112).

◖ Jobson's Cove: Romantics – and families with small children – will appreciate this postcard-pretty retreat from the hubbub of neighboring Horseshoe Bay. It's also a haven from

the occasional force of breakers and riptides (page 112).

◖ Gibbs Hill Lighthouse: Even the Queen deigned to stop here (in 1953), and that was before scones and Earl Grey were served. Today, the quaint tearoom, perched on the steep hilltop alongside the historic lighthouse, offers bird's-eye views with a creative all-day menu (page 121).

◖ Horseshoe Bay: Bermuda's answer to Bondi, this tamer version of surf and sand attracts crowds through the summer. Cruise ship passengers flock here during the week, but its beauty and access to miles of other beaches and coves make it worth a visit (page 124).

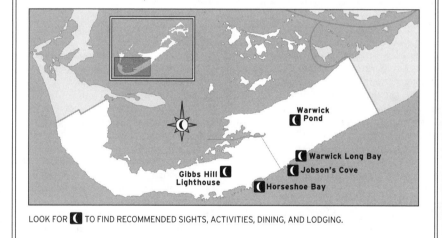

Warwick ◖ Pond

◖ Warwick Long Bay

◖ Jobson's Cove

Gibbs Hill ◖ Lighthouse

◖ Horseshoe Bay

LOOK FOR ◖ TO FIND RECOMMENDED SIGHTS, ACTIVITIES, DINING, AND LODGING.

WARWICK & SOUTHAMPTON

routes to do this. Warwick's main arteries include Harbour Road on its northern boundary, a wall-hugging route reminiscent of narrow, sidewalk-free lanes in British seaside towns, which snakes quaintly from the end of Hamilton Harbour around part of the Great Sound's southern rim. The serpentine journey poses a dilemma for scooter drivers: Sure, the scenery is alluring, but take your eyes off the road for a second, and you might miss the next hairpin turn—a not-infrequent occurrence, based on the number of patched holes in the road's low wraparound wall. Harbour Road represents one of the island's most sought-after addresses; hemmed by centuries-old mansions, the drive offers coveted water views and spectacular sunsets.

Near the Southampton border, Harbour Road connects via Burnt House Hill to Middle Road, which, as its name suggests, runs through the belly of the parish. The busy, low-lying route offers few pretty vistas but lots of local interest as traffic whisks Bermudians to and from sports clubs, grocery stores, schools, and residential neighborhoods. South Shore Road, with its wide curves and convenient hilltop lay-bys for pulling over, is the most dramatic vantage point from which to admire both parishes' tumbling dunes, sweeping beach views, and reef-dotted ocean expanses that reveal an intoxicating palette of blues, from swimming-pool turquoise to midnight navy. Migrating humpback whales—or at least their blowholes—are sometimes visible on the horizon beyond the inshore reefs during the spring.

South Shore Road continues west through half of Southampton before cutting north across the parish to Barnes Corner, where it ends at the harbor. From here, Middle Road becomes the only route west, running to Somerset Bridge in Sandys. Dissecting both parishes north-south are historic tribe roads, skinny, dead-straight, mostly pedestrian-only right-of-ways running shore to shore—necessary for parish access before larger thoroughfares and motorized vehicles. Indeed, early law dictated tribes measure the width of a barrel, to allow transport of commodities like rum, foodstuffs, and gunpowder. Parallel to the main east-west roads runs the scenic old Railway Trail, accessible via the tribe roads and sign-posted points off Middle Road.

PLANNING YOUR TIME

If you're staying at a hotel or guesthouse in Warwick or Southampton, you will find yourself close enough to the beaches or Railway Trail for early-morning dips and evening strolls any season of the year. Most Bermudians swim strictly June–October, but visitors will find the ocean's average 65°F winter temperature quite balmy, especially if escaping winter snow. There are more than a dozen beaches, bays, and coves lining the southern side of both parishes, offering the island's best variety in swimming and beach venues. Depending on how much of a beach bum you are, you can enjoy a different spot every day of your trip. Outdoorsy types will enjoy activities like diving, whale-watching (in season), snorkeling, and horseback-riding on the dunes.

The area is a magnet for golfers, thanks to four major courses in the two parishes, including the 2003-redesigned Belmont Hills Golf Club and the world-renowned Port Royal championship course.

Warwick and Southampton make convenient starting points for excursions to other parts of the island; they're well served by the island's buses, taxis, rental scooter outlets, and ferries. If you're staying elsewhere on the island, you will definitely want to visit Warwick and Southampton, if only for the views. Beach aficionados can do what the locals do, and make day trips to these parishes to swim and sunbathe. Some of the best-known restaurants and spas, located in hotels and equally patronized by Bermudians, are also reason enough to come here. Travelers heading west on excursions to Somerset and the Royal Naval Dockyard can make the most of the panoramic scenery, various eateries, and sights like Warwick Pond and Gibbs Hill Lighthouse en route.

Warwick Parish

Warwick, like the county of Warwickshire in England's West Midlands, is properly pronounced WAH-rick, its silent, middle "W" usually proving confusing for American tongues. The parish was named for the Earl of Warwick, Sir Robert Rich, one of the original "Adventurers" or London investors in the colony in the 1600s and a key player in New World expansion during the Elizabethan Age.

Today, Warwick's residential neighborhoods are heavily populated and have suffered the pressures of drug-driven crime and occasional youth gang violence. Yet the parish also contains beautiful national parks and rambling historic estates, often located cheek by jowl with lower-income areas. Perhaps as a result, there are no areas considered truly off-limits; aside from telltale groups of wall-sitters and graffiti in some places, a visitor would be barely aware of social dysfunctions beneath the pretty facade.

Warwick's key draws for visitors, like Southampton's, are its beaches (arguably Bermuda's best) and its wide assortment of walking-distance accommodations. For anyone whose chief aim is to relax, swim, and get a tan, there's no better area of the island. If you're staying here, the 20-minute drive into Hamilton for shopping and entertainment is hardly arduous, either.

SIGHTS

There are far fewer sights of specific interest in Warwick than general scenic beauty, and the latter can be appreciated by simply traveling along either **Harbour Road** or **South Shore Road** as you explore the parish (Middle Road is busier and less scenic). From the harborside, the expansive **Great Sound,** stretching from the harbor entrance to the fishhook of Dockyard, offers a pristine panorama, its waters sprinkled with mostly private smaller islands where Bermudians live full-time, keep summer cottages, or camp in August and September. Weekend yacht-racing and scheduled Bermuda dinghy-racing take place out here, as do impromptu public-holiday "raft-ups" of sometimes a dozen

vessels or more, as local boaters tie up together at anchor for cockpit cocktails, picnics, and off-the-stern swims. Evening barbecue cruises to several islands can be arranged through Hamilton-based tour operators and boating outlets.

At **Darrell's Wharf,** the border of Paget and Warwick, ferries shuttle business people and tourists to and from Hamilton, a 15-minute ride. This is a good spot to watch the cruise ships sail by twice a week (Monday mornings and Thursday afternoons), dwarfing the distant Pembroke shore and the Hamilton skyline. Tugboats escort the ships through the narrow channel of Two Rock Passage into the harbor, where they dock, and out again at week's end to the North Shore channel. Harbour Road's tony properties, with brick drives, pergolas, spilling bougainvillea, and freesia-carpeted lawns, are also eye-catching.

Wide viewing spots on South Shore Road allow for frequent stops, if you're going by scooter or taxi. Populated by whispering pines, bay-grape trees, goldenrods, and dramatic white-flowering Spanish bayonets, this route is also popular for local runners and walkers. Its high vantage point gives a spectacular aspect of the whole shoreline, as well as the boiler reefs, which lie exposed at low tide.

Cobb's Hill Methodist Church

Among Warwick's specific sights is this seemingly nondescript church (off Cobb's Hill Rd. on Moonlight Ln., tel. 441-236-8586, fax 441/232-4806, open for Sunday services from 9:30 A.M.). With a steeple and tiny sanctuary dating back to 1827, the church "built by slaves in moonlight"—a truism proudly carried on its sign and in its literature—holds a symbolic spot in the hearts of the island's black community. At a time when blacks were banned from worshiping in white churches, slaves and free blacks of the early 19th century constructed their own church in their spare time, including at night, using block from nearby quarries. (Slavery was abolished in Bermuda in 1834.)

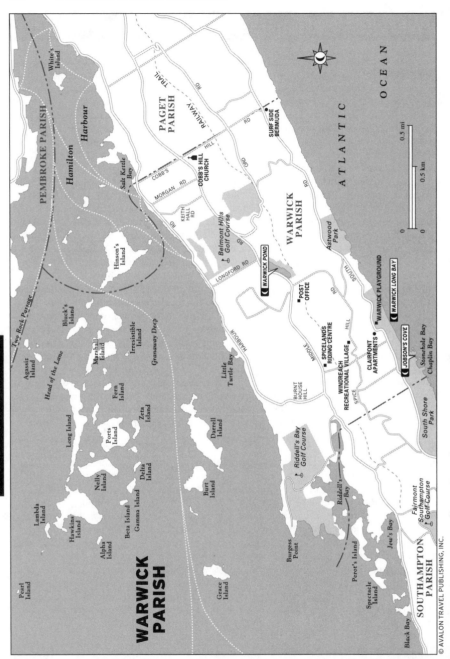

WARWICK & SOUTHAMPTON

Thanks to its proud past, the church is a point of interest noted on the Bermuda Tourism Department's African Diaspora Trail, but the building is open only during Sunday worship and Wednesday prayer evenings. Visitors are welcome to these weekly events.

An addition to the building was erected in 1967, which now serves as the church hall. The most interesting section of the church from an architectural and historical perspective is the old sanctuary, where cedar beams and limestone slate and block were used to build a simple but sturdy structure that has withstood natural tempests and changing political times.

Warwick Academy

Bermuda's oldest surviving school (117 Middle Rd., tel. 441/236-1917, fax 441/236-9995, www.warwickacad.bm), west of Cobb's Hill, was established in 1662 by early settlers on property designated as school lands from the colony's earliest days. Bermuda's 17th-century surveyor, Richard Norwood, was the first headmaster. Once government-owned, it is now one of several private schools on the island, with a longstanding reputation for high academic standards and a racially mixed student body representative of Bermuda's own diverse population. Indeed, Warwick was the first of the white segregated institutions to admit blacks, in 1962. The original two-room schoolhouse remains visible in the current building, laid out around a small, shady quadrangle of palms. While the cloakrooms, corridors, and curricula retain much of their British grammar school roots, Warwick Academy's International Baccalaureate graduates today mostly go on to North American colleges and universities. The school is open 8:30 A.M.–4:30 P.M. Monday–Friday while in session September–June. The office is open 9 A.M.–2 P.M. during holidays, including the summer. Tours can be arranged by contacting Nancy Steynor (nsteynor@warwickacad.bm) or Mair Swift (mswift@warwickacad.bm).

◖ Warwick Pond

This under-visited wildlife reserve (open sunrise to sunset daily, admission free) stretches for nine acres along Middle Road, its marshy ponds, farm fields, and woodland reserves lying in a wide central valley coated by endemic Bermuda cedars and allspice trees. Recognized as a wetland of international importance by the World Conservation Union, the pond was once part of a chain of wetlands through Bermuda's center, linking Southampton to Spittal Pond in Smith's. It is Bermuda's second-largest freshwater pond (after Spittal) and a sanctuary for resident and migratory waterfowl, including barn swallows in the fall, common snipes in winter, and mourning doves year-round. You might also spot resident roosters; until recently, there was a lone flamingo—a bright-coral specimen nicknamed "Flo," which escaped the large flock at the Bermuda Aquarium, Museum & Zoo in 1987 but was eventually recaptured.

The Bermuda National Trust acquired most of the Warwick Pond reserve that same year but made the site more accessible late in 2003, when it was reopened with a better parking area, cleared trails, and educational panels describing habitats and wildlife found along a circular path. The pond's fertile wetland borders are rented from the Trust by farmers for cattle-grazing or agriculture. Warwick Pond's entrance is well marked by a Trust sign on Middle Road at the turnoff to Tribe Road 3, which also connects to the Railway Trail. For more information, contact the Trust (tel. 441/236-6483, www.bnt.bm).

Khyber Pass

Cut through this dramatically named access route to get from Middle Road to the South Shore. At the foot of the steep hill, near a landmark rubber tree outside Warwick Post Office, a memorial remembers the island's slaves. The site of a local slave market, in recent decades the corner had become an eyesore, marked with gang-related graffiti. In April 2006, neighborhood residents decided to claim back the space, launching the "We Love Warwick Rubber Tree Festival"—a monthlong series of Saturday markets selling everything from homemade jams to African clothing and secondhand CDs. The group hopes to make the festival an annual rite of spring. To reach the beaches, continue over Khyber Pass, bordered by soaring limestone quarries used for past building works. Spice Hill Road, on the other side, winds down to South Shore Road.

Warwick Camp

The headquarters of the Bermuda Regiment (1 South Shore Rd., at Camp Rd., tel. 441/238-1045) covers a large property west of Warwick Long Bay and opposite the entrance to Stonehole and Chaplin Bays. Although not generally open to the public, special tours or visits to the hillside site can be arranged. Built in the 1870s, Warwick Camp was chosen for its strategic location to foil potential beach invasions and now comprises barracks, an officers' mess, a canteen, and firing range. Regiment recruits conduct training exercises on the nearby dunes, allowing passersby the rather incongruous scene of soldiers playing war while beachlovers frolic in the surf a short distance away. (For more information on the Regiment, see *The Regiment and Police* under *Government* in the *Background* chapter.)

BEACHES

Warwick is synonymous with beaches, and what the parish lacks in shopping or five-star restaurants, it more than compensates for with its glorious stretch of coastline. Walkers, runners, sunbathers, swimmers, kitesurfers, and volleyball enthusiasts will find all they need here. Lifeguards are posted at the most popular areas (including Warwick Long Bay) during the summer season, and Bermuda's Parks Department ensures the soft, pink sand is combed of washed-up seaweed, jellyfish, and tar every morning. Do, however, watch for Portuguese man-of-wars. Warning signs are clearly posted during hurricane season, warning off swimmers when approaching storms bring dangerous swells—a big attraction to daredevil windsurfers and kitesurfers.

Astwood Cove

Severely battered by the hurricane surge of recent summers, this little beach is beautiful but hard to get to. Still, if climbing down cliff-top trails isn't a problem, you will find privacy once you get down to this, Warwick's first public beach as you head west. Surrounded by agricultural land and a seaside park that's a favorite for family picnics and wedding photographs, the beach itself sits at the foot of steep cliffs that have been badly eroded. Massive boulders, the work of several seasons' storms, have tumbled onto the beach and shoreline in places. Storms perennially claim the sand as well, leaving just a field of underlying rocks, though seasonal tides return it every year. Picnic tables can be found in the park, and ample parking is also available.

🄲 Warwick Long Bay

Like neighboring Horseshoe, this is one of the island's most dramatic beaches, spanning a half mile of coast. A concession stand in the carpark rents swimming and snorkeling gear during the summer. The beach's thick, coral-sprinkled sand, boiler reefs, and surrounding dunes and parkland makes it a popular venue, yet it is never as crowded as Horseshoe, perhaps due to the lack of a café or very shallow bathing areas.

🄲 Jobson's Cove

West of Long Bay and connected via the dune trails is a tiny gem of a swimming hole, nestled between cliffs and boasting swimming-pool-clear water. Honeymooners and children make a beeline for this beach, though, so you may find it busy later in the day, especially when cruise ships are in port. A horseshoe of tall limestone cliffs creates this perfect swimming hole, no more than 40 feet across. Shallow water near the sand, plus reefs encircling the foot of the cliffs makes it good for novice or young swimmers, and for snorkelers, too. Access Jobson's Cove via the lane down to Warwick Long Bay (park at the bottom and walk a few hundred meters in along the west trail), or go a little farther west on the main road and drive down the lane opposite Warwick Camp. You will see signs for both Jobson's and Chaplin Bays, and sandy dune trails lead to both. It's a short walk down from the main road bus stop.

BERMUDA'S "PINK" SAND

No need to don rose-colored glasses in Bermuda, at least on the beaches. The island's iconic pink sand, touted from brochures to tacky bottled souvenirs, is as curious to visitors as tales of the Triangle.

The sand, most noticeable on the South Shore, especially on surf-heavy beaches like Warwick Long Bay, is the result of constant wave action on the nearby reef. Single-celled organisms called Foraminifera or red foram, grow on the underside of Bermuda's reefs, their bodies peppered with holes through which they extend sticky threads to consume bacteria and other food. When they die, their bright red skeletons erode from the rock, drop to the sea floor, and wash up on beaches. Here they mix with white sand, composed of particles of shells, coral, seaweeds, mollusks, and other marine detritus.

While the phenomenon happens all over the Caribbean and other reef areas worldwide, the result is most obvious on Bermuda's beaches, perhaps because the South Shore reefline, in particular, is so close to the shore. The island's sand is mostly soft and fine, though some patches are made gritty with larger particles of shell, coral, and foram.

Bermuda tourist trinkets have long incorporated the famous pink sand, and you can find tiny bottles of the stuff in souvenir shops around the island. Local artists and craftspeople also find inspiration in the beach sand, using it in souvenirs and artworks.

Stonehole and Chaplin Bays

These twin coves lie farther west, again connected by the South Shore's public park system and an easy trail through the dunes. Chaplin sits on the Warwick-Southampton parish border below Warwick Camp, and beachgoers may sometimes spot Bermuda Regiment soldiers taking part in military training exercises on the dunes. Both beaches offer good swimming and snorkeling areas and walkable access to Horseshoe Bay in the next parish.

ENTERTAINMENT AND EVENTS

Warwick is weak on organized entertainment or events of any kind, and if you're staying in the parish, you will likely want to seek out nighttime activities at nearby hotels or head into Hamilton. There are a couple of bars, however, that attract a busy local and tourist crowd, mostly on Fridays and Saturdays.

Warwick Workman's Club (42 Cobb's Hill Rd., tel. 441/236-7470, noon–midnight, except Christmas Day) is a favorite with local cab owners, construction workers, and other area Bermudians, as well as its 100-plus membership. Friday afternoons are boisterous, when, as in many parish bars, the weekend starts early. But the atmosphere is always cordial. "We cater to the oldie-goldies, not troublemakers," says bartender "Coolie."

The 13th Frame Lounge and Bar (47 Middle Rd., tel. 441/232-3839, 7 P.M.–1 A.M., except major holidays) is found inside Warwick Lanes, the island's only bowling alley. Friday happy hour starts at 4 P.M., and the bar also welcomes a busy Sunday night crowd.

Visitors and locals alike flock to **The Swizzle South Shore** (formerly PawPaws, 87 South Shore Rd., tel. 441/236-7459, 11:30 A.M.–1 A.M. daily), the new Warwick branch of Hamilton Parish's landmark Swizzle Inn. Writing on the bar's walls is encouraged here also.

SHOPPING

Shopaholics will find precious little to spend on in Warwick, other than tie-dyed T-shirts and other items sold from roadside stands, and a sparse collection of stores, most of them convenience marts.

The Sports Source (49 Middle Rd., tel. 441/236-9981, 10 A.M.–8 P.M. Mon.–Thurs., 9 A.M.–8:45 P.M. Fri.–Sat.), a branch of a Hamilton store by the same name, is a rare exception, offering shoes and fashions with street cred (Nike, Adidas, Reebok, Puma, Jordan, and Pepe) to a loyal following. Easy parking in a small plaza.

SPORTS AND RECREATION
Bowling

Warwick Lanes (47 Middle Rd., Warwick, tel. 441/236-5290) is the island's only bowling alley, attracting a crowd, including members and local teams, as well as novices and corporate parties enjoying a cheap night out, especially during the winter. The air-conditioned facility is owned and operated by the Bermuda Bowling Club, which hosts the Professional Bowlers' Tour every February. It has 24 lanes, all computerized to take the work out of scoring. A bar and open-plan restaurant, serving hamburgers, sandwiches, soups and salads, are also on-site. Winter hours (Sept. 1–April 30) are 4 P.M.–midnight Monday–Friday, 9:30 A.M.–midnight Saturday, 2 P.M.–midnight Sunday. Summer hours (May 1–Aug. 31) are 6 P.M.–11 P.M. Monday–Saturday, 2–11 P.M. Sunday. Fees are reasonable: $4 a game, children $2.75, shoe rental $1.50.

Golf

Warwick is home to two respected golf courses—one a time-worn country club, the other reopened in 2003 after a multi-million-dollar redesign and reconstruction.

Tennis ace (and former Bermuda resident) Pat Rafter tested the links here, and Michael Douglas is one of 300 members at **Belmont Hills Golf Club** (97 Middle Rd., tel. 441/236-6400, fax 441/236-0694, www.belmonthills.com). Once the site of the Belmont Hotel, the club is open to visitors. The main footprint of the former golf course remains, though some holes were reshaped and new ones created. A waterfall and two lakes were built, new turf laid to meet USGA standards, and a tee-to-green irrigation system installed. Handicappers call it a "shot-maker's course," thanks to tricky pin placements and challenging greens. Dress code is strictly club-style: collared shirts and slacks for men, "Bermuda-length" shorts for men and women accepted. Ferry and private boat service to and from Hamilton from the Harbour Road dock.

Bermuda's oldest golf course, **Riddell's Bay Club** (Riddell's Bay Rd., tel. 441/238-1060, www.riddellsbay.com), dates back to 1922. A visit to its elegant Georgian clubhouse, set in a multi-million-dollar enclave, is like stepping into a tourist brochure of the 1950s or 1960s. The private club's golf course, which has seen the likes of crooner Michael Bolton and Olympian Jim Thorpe, is touted as a scenic challenge, with holes mapped out over an ocean peninsula that measures 600 yards at its widest point. At a total of 5,800 yards, the 70-par, 18-hole course falls short of the island's three championship courses (Mid Ocean, Tucker's Point, Port Royal), but its meticulously kept greens are challenging to mid-handicappers, particularly on windy days. The club makes an effort to accommodate visitors. Call ahead to set a tee time.

Riding

Exploring the Railway Trail and beachside dunes can be a leisurely outing on horseback through **Spicelands Riding Centre** (50 Middle Rd., west of Warwick Pond, tel. 441/238-8212, spicelands@northrock.bm). The center runs five guided trail rides on weekdays, but times vary according to season and sunrise time (summer's first ride usually starts at 6:30 A.M., winter's at 7:30 A.M.). Mornings-only outings go on Saturdays. Each ride is 75 minutes long and costs $65. Private rides, like the one former Bermuda resident celebs David Bowie and his wife Iman enjoyed, are 90 minutes for $130. Moonlight rides and special group rides are also popular. Early birds will prefer the first ride of the day—it's the only one that leads along the water's edge of Warwick Long Bay. Horses are generally banned from beaches May–October—a law owner Judy Baum is battling the government to reverse. Western saddles are used for comfort, but English-style tack is also available. Helmets are provided. Wear sneakers and pants or shorts. The facility, home to 63 horses and ponies, also offers riding instruction.

Bermuda Riding for the Disabled, at Wind-Reach Recreational Village (57 Spice Hill Rd., tel. 441/238-7433, fax 441/238-7434, www.brd.bm), provides therapeutic riding free of charge to children with special needs. The nonprofit

CAMPING OUT

Crowds of locals lounging under roadside tarpaulins, blasting their stereos and barbecuing four-course meals... no, it's not squatters or a sudden outbreak of homelessness, just the start of camping season, Bermudian-style.

The island may lack North America's natural drama and absolute serenity of the great outdoors, but camping is a beloved summer ritual nonetheless. True, it's difficult to retreat far from the madding crowd in an island with so little undeveloped land, but for islanders, that's not really the point. Bermudians simply enjoy the change of scenery and routine, coupled with the camaraderie of outdoor living, even if they do they take all the comforts of home with them – everything including the kitchen sink.

"I saw one guy with his laptop and a 52-inch TV, which he was running from the battery of his dump truck," recalls Craig Burt, camping coordinator for the Parks Department. "Bermudians don't like to leave anything behind."

Come July and August, particularly the four-day Cup Match public holiday that falls between these months, Bermudians set up camp all over the island – in public parks, on roadsides, and along the South Shore dunes. At the height of camping season, virtual tent villages sprawl along the North Shore waterfront, along Kindley Field Road at Ferry Reach, between Warwick Long Bay and Horseshoe Bay, and everywhere in between. Whole families turn out, with camping accoutrements and picnic fare galore, to swim, rest, spend time with friends and relatives, wave to passing traffic, and generally enjoy time off work. While camping is technically restricted to Bermuda residents, cruise ship workers and visitors are allowed to camp if they register with the Parks Department and are staying in a hotel, guesthouse, private residence, or on a ship.

Camping season runs from the first Saturday in May through the third Sunday in September. Permits are issued on a first-come, first-served basis, and fees ($100 refundable deposit, and $10 a night per site) must be paid at booking. There are four designated government campgrounds: Ferry Point Park, St. George's; Higgs and Horseshoe Islands, St. George's; Coney Island, St. George's; and Chaplin Bay, Warwick. Campsites managed by private groups are also open at various islands in Hamilton and St. George's Harbors and the Great Sound, including Hen Island and Paget Island in the East End, and White's Island, Darrell's Island, Ports Island, and Burt Island. Camping is permitted at all parks and beaches over major official holidays such as Cup Match.

Conditions of camping in Bermuda include:

- The use of proper tents

- Three tents of 180 square feet each are allowed per site

- No wood fires are permitted; charcoal, propane, or liquid fuel stoves are allowed in metal containers, but ashes should be soaked with saltwater and disposed of

- Cooking in tents is prohibited

- Maximum stay on any site is six weeks

- Garbage should be bagged and dumped at the nearest trash can

- Cutting of trees and branches, or excavation of the ground, is forbidden

- A maximum of eight people per site is allowed

- Generators are not permitted in government campgrounds

- Dogs are not allowed

- "Checkout" is 4 p.m. and the site must be vacant for 48 hours

For more information or to report problems, contact the **Park Ranger Office,** tel. 441/236-5902 or 441/239-2355, or fax 411/236-3711.

group, funded by public donations, has five horses and ponies and two full-time staff members, at a newly expanded Equestrian Centre, complete with stables and show-ring. Visits and rides should be arranged well in advance.

Snorkeling

The coral reefs of the South Shore are arguably some of the most beautiful in the world, and close enough to shore to make them easily accessible. You don't even need to be a full-fledged scuba diver to enjoy them. Several beachside concessions, including an outpost at Warwick Long Bay during the summer, rent masks, snorkels, and fins, as well as ubiquitous polystyrene "noodles," allowing for hours of easy floating over boiler reefs and sea grass beds and around the edges of sheltered coves and bays. Here, you can watch exquisitely multihued parrotfish nibbling on the reef, ethereal angelfish, anemones, speckled morays, cheeky sergeant majors, schools of jacks, and even endangered green turtles in some areas.

Running and Walking

Walking enthusiasts will find plenty of off-road trails in Warwick, namely throughout the coastal parklands and along the Railway Trail. On the dunes, twisting sand or dirt trails, hemmed by oleanders, bay-grapes, prickly pears, and Spanish bayonets, are occasionally nosebleed-steep (one hill north of Chaplin Bay is dubbed "Kilimanjaro" by local runners). The trails are also pitted by knee-deep crab holes, so watch your step.

The **Warwick Railway Trail** goes from Cobb's Hill past Belmont golf course, a picturesque stretch of jasmine and fiddlewoods, quarries, local neighborhoods, and farmland frequented by runners, walkers, and cyclists, particularly in the evenings.

South Shore Road, unlike many other major roads on the island, has ample grassy verges for safe walking and running.

For Kids

Children adore **WindReach Recreational Village** (57 Spice Hill Rd., Warwick,

tel. 441/238-2469, fax 441/238-2597, www.windreach.org/bermuda), a nine-acre oasis with an air-conditioned activity center, petting zoo, sensory trail, campground, and fully accessible playground and picnic area. Opened in 1999, the facility promotes activities for people of all ages with disabilities and special needs, but has become a regular visiting spot for all children on the island. The zoo, with its menagerie of guinea pigs, goats, parrots, miniature horses, rabbits, a donkey, and lamb, is especially popular. The playground, a shady, tree-house-style set-up of slides, swings, stairs, and ramps under a giant poinciana, is also a must-visit. Wheelchair-accessible bathrooms are on-site. Tours and visits must be booked in advance.

Warwick Playground (South Shore Rd., east of Warwick Long Bay), one of a half dozen government-owned venues around the island, is a favorite among expat moms and nannies, though its lack of breeze or ample shade makes it almost unbearable throughout the summer. Run by the Parks Department, the dog-free playground is kept scrupulously clean and well maintained, with soft white sand surrounding equipment suitable for kids of all ages, from infants to middle-schoolers. Swings, slides, tunnels, poles, rope ladders, and a wooden fort and train are among the equipment. Kids also enjoy feeding and chasing the resident flock of chickens. A portable toilet and ample parking are available. A path on the playground's southern edge leads down to beachside parkland and Warwick Long Bay.

ACCOMMODATIONS
Under $100

For adventurous travelers, **WindReach Recreational Village** (57 Spice Hill Rd., Warwick, tel. 441/238-2469, fax 441/238-2597) offers cabins or camping on its peaceful nine-acre property—a novelty in Bermuda, where camping is prohibited without season-specific permits and mostly restricted to locals. The charity, which runs programs and events for people with special needs, is just beginning to market its accommodation services, but so far it's winning positive feedback for both affordability and facilities. Two wooden cabins, with bunks to sleep five each, cost $50 per night. Visitors can also pitch their own tents for $25 per night in the same picnic area, with access to barbecues, kitchen facilities, and washrooms. Cabins, showers, and bathrooms are wheelchair-accessible. Families with children will appreciate the playground and petting zoo on-site.

$100-200

Guests return again and again to **Granaway** (1 Longford Rd., tel. 441/236-3747, fax 441/236-3749, www.granaway.com, high season $130–180, off season $100–160), the elegant 1734 manor-turned-guesthouse that offers lushly mature gardens, a large pool surrounded by shady palms, and eye-popping views of the Great Sound from its five main house guest rooms. All rooms have private bathrooms and air-conditioning, and breakfast is laid on in the mornings. A separate cottage on the property (formerly a slave quarters) has a well-equipped kitchen, bathroom, and private patio with view of the Sound; the cottage is $200–280 high season, $150–200 off season.

C Clairfont Apartments (6 Warwickshire Rd., tel. 441/238-3577, fax 441/238-3503, www.clairfontapartments.com, $130–150) is spared the noisy main road location of several of its competitors. Instead, the peachy complex, run as guest quarters for 30 years, sits high on a hill along a residential lane, a short walk from Warwick Long Bay, Jobson's Cove, and other South Shore beaches. Energetic new manager Corinne Simons took over in January 2004, full of innovative ideas after a hospitality career spent in senior roles at many of the island's major hotels. Since her arrival, extensive repairs have been made and professional-standard conveniences added to the eight self-contained units (six one-bedroom, two studios), including mounted hair dryers, voicemail, Internet connections, security locks and lights, credit-card safes, first-aid kits, and new kitchen appliances. Business has boomed as a result. Spotlessly clean, modern, and airy, Clairfont offers an attractive alternative to pricier establishments that may have fewer amenities. Welcome letters, air-conditioning, maid ser-

vice (except Sundays), cable TV, and a newly revamped pool make guests feel pampered. Special winter monthly rates are so popular, locals and temporary workers sick of soaring rents sometimes book into Clairfont pads as a cheaper alternative.

Brenda's Apartments (93 South Shore Rd., tel. 441/236-7807) is "not the Ritz-Carlton, but we keep the rooms neat and try to make it a home away from home," says its eponymous owner, Brenda Augustus-Spencer, a feisty grandmother of five. After Hurricane Fabian demolished the roof of her complex in 2003, she decided it was time to downsize after three decades in the tourism business. The result is the reopening of seven of 17 guest apartments at the electric-blue roadside landmark, comprising a poolside diner, ice cream parlor, barbershop, and launderette, along with apartments. All rooms are now nonsmoking. One-, two-, and three-bedroom units ($130, $220, $310 per night, respectively) have air-conditioning, private bathrooms, and kitchenettes with refrigerators and microwaves; studios ($115) have fully equipped kitchens. Bonuses include the beautiful 25-meter pool (also open to the public for $10.50 a day) and laundry facilities.

The Sandpiper (103 South Shore Rd., tel. 441/236-7093, fax 441/236-3898, www.bermuda.com/sandpiper) suffers from its proximity to the main road, but with simple, airy rooms, garden, pool, and hot tub, it's a good option for families, students, and anyone looking for affordable quarters near the beaches. Fourteen rooms include five one-bedroom suites (with extra futons for additional guests) and studios with full kitchens. Barbecues are provided for poolside use. An office on the premises is staffed 9 A.M.–8 P.M.

Over $200

Spectacular cliff-top views and quiet surroundings compensate for the fading florals, outdated TVs, and ubiquitous wicker-and-tile interiors of **Marley Beach Cottages** (Marley Close, South Shore Rd., tel. 441/236-1143, fax 441/236-1984, marleybeach@therock.bm, $210–290). The property, one of Bermuda's longtime "cottage colonies," took a beating in Hurricane Fabian and could use some reinvestment. Six self-contained units, with a/c, cable, kitchen facilities, and hibachis, mean guests have to fend for themselves, but repeat visitors swear by the privacy and lack of big-hotel commercialism. The property includes a cliff's-edge heated pool with whirlpool, and a winding trail down to the private beach.

C Surf Side Bermuda (90 South Shore Rd., tel. 441/236-7100, fax 441/236-9765, www .surfsidebermuda.com, $275–500) holds a panoramic perch over the South Shore stretch of reefline. With a pool, hot tub, and sauna, the much-lauded restaurant Palms, and a pristine private beach, it is extremely popular among honeymooners, wedding parties, and romantics of all persuasions. Oceanfront rooms range from basic bed and bath to penthouses with private lawn patios and cliff-side suites boasting living rooms, dining rooms, and fireplaces. Coin laundry, beauty salon, and mini spa are also on-site. The hotel has its own wedding coordinator. Breakfast and dinner plans are available.

FOOD
Cafés, Bars, and Pubs
For a quick "greeze" (grease), as Bermudians call their soul-food lunches, drop in to **C The Upper Crust** café at **Warwick Workman's Club** (42 Cobb's Hill Road, tel. 441/232-0123, 11 A.M.–11 P.M. Mon.–Thurs., 11 A.M.–midnight Fri. and Sat., 7 A.M.–10 P.M. Sun.). Line up with the local crowd for pan-fried wahoo, pizzas, pastas, sandwiches, wraps, salads, onion rings—even Indian curries—at this longtime Warwick café now run by the efficient islandwide chain. Codfish breakfast with Johnny bread and "all the trimmings" is served every Sunday morning.

Brenda's Poolside Diner & Ice-Cream Bar (93 South Shore Rd., tel. 441/236-7807, 10 A.M.–10 P.M. daily) has a full slate of fast-food treats, including "Whatever-You-Please" burgers, hot dogs, scallops, fries, onion rings, and ice cream. Eat under umbrellas at tables around the inviting pool, or take out.

Warwick residents got a boost to their

SUMMER SNOWBALLS

Summertime lineups at small roadside stands near the South Shore beaches usually mean just one thing: snowballs.

When temperatures soar and school's out, the crushed-ice-and-syrup confections sold June–September are a tempting way to cool off. Seasonal permit-holders – often students – set up carts daily to dole out the popular treat islandwide. Many choose spots along South Shore Road to catch traffic traveling to and from the beaches. After-work rush hour also sees a booming business, as locals snap up snowballs for the drive home.

Snowballs demand few tools or ingredients: ice cubes, an ice crusher, and special syrup, for which each vendor uses a different recipe of sugar and mix. Costing $1 for small, $2 for medium, or $3 for a large, snowballs come in every flavor of the rainbow. If you want to taste the full gamut, ask for a "'Round the World" – a combo of everything on hand, generally raspberry, strawberry, apple, cherry, and the all-time island favorite, ginger beer.

---

parish entertainment scene in 2006, when the longtime PawPaws roadside eatery was bought by owners of Bermuda's most popular pub, The Swizzle Inn. When it reopened, **The Swizzle South Shore** (87 South Shore Rd., tel. 441/236-7459, lunch 11:30 A.M.–5 P.M., dinner 5–10 P.M., bar 11:30 A.M.–1 A.M. daily) immediately drew crowds of Swizzle aficionados, who come for the namesake drink, but also the convivial party-like atmosphere. Like its Hamilton Parish landmark, this Swizzle offers a full menu of comforting pub grub (burgers, nachos, spicy fries), as well as local seafood and pizzas. Barbecues through summer weekends offer pork ribs and steaks galore.

International
C Palms Restaurant & Bar (Surf Side Bermuda, 90 South Shore Rd., tel. 441/236-7100,

ext. 258, fax 441/236-9765, www.surf sidebermuda.com, breakfast 8–10:30 A.M., lunch noon–3:30 P.M., dinner 6–8:30 P.M. daily) is highly recommended, both for its delicious menu and the dramatic alfresco setting. Tables are arranged inside a cabana-like dining room, or, if weather permits, poolside overlooking the precipitous South Shore—where the 180-degree horizons and sound of rolling surf would be awesome even without a first-rate menu. But manager Llew Harvey, who used to run the beloved Once Upon A Table in Hamilton, oversees a gourmet operation. The restaurant's wide assortment of offerings include oysters Rockefeller ($13), Bermuda fish chowder ($6), poached wahoo ($29.50) or rack of lamb ($31) among entrées, and tempting crème brûlées, tarts, and spice cakes ($8) for dessert. Especially popular for romantic dinner dates, the restaurant encourages reservations.

A rare culinary addition to the island in 2006, **⬛ Blu Bar & Grill** (Belmont Hills Golf Course, 97 Middle Rd., tel. 441/232-2323, fax 441/232-6464, www.blu.bm, lunch noon–2:30 P.M. Mon.–Sat., noon–3 P.M. Sun., dinner 6 P.M.–9 P.M. Mon.–Sat.) opened in the property's panoramic clubhouse overlooking the greens and the Great Sound. Breakfast is to be added to the menu later in 2006. The latest jewel in the Little Venice Group's tiara (which owns a half dozen restaurants and runs the island's largest catering service), Blu certainly makes a welcome entrée to a parish sparse on gourmet fare. A southwestern flair distinguishes its menu, which includes appetizers like barbecue chicken quesadillas ($11) and warm spinach salad ($7.75) and inventive entrées such as Long Island duck ($26.75), bourbon-marinated chicken and suckling pigs grilled in the rotisserie ($21.75), and cornmeal-crusted salmon with black bean sauce ($24.75). Comfort food reigns with no end of sides like sweet potato gratin and jalapeño corn bread. Desserts ($8.50) have a N'Awlins twist, with offerings like bourbon pecan tart and crème caramel. Kids' menu is available before 7:15 P.M. An outstanding wine list, with close to 100 well-selected California vintages, is another good reason to stop by.

Grocery Stores

Bermudians flock to **Lindo's Family Foods** (128 Middle Rd., tel. 441/236-1344 or 441/236-1346, 8 A.M.–7 P.M. Mon., Tues., Thurs., 8 A.M.–8 P.M. Wed., Fri., Sat.), a large renovated grocery stocked with pretty much everything, including wines and liquors (not for sale Sundays), baked and frozen goods, pharmaceuticals, and a particularly appealing butcher department offering freshly caught Bermuda fish and imported meats.

White's Supermarket (22 Middle Rd., tel. 441/238-1050 or 441/238-1051, 8 A.M.–9 P.M. Mon.–Sat., 1–5 P.M. Sun.) is a modern, one-stop shop outside Hamilton where you will find food, liquor (a wines and spirits store is located within), housewares, and a pharmacy. There is ample parking in front.

Hayward's Supermarket (49 Middle Rd., tel. 441/232-3995, 7 A.M.–7 P.M. Mon.–Sat.) is a small, modern grocery stocked with all the staples, as well as fresh fruit, cold drinks, magazines, and a self-service deli offering island choices like baked chicken legs, macaroni 'n' cheese, salads, and sandwich fillings. The adjacent liquor store, **Hayward's Liquor Mart** (49 Middle Rd., tel. 441/236-8610, 8 A.M.–8:45 P.M. except Sun.), is a handy stop outside Hamilton.

INFORMATION AND SERVICES

Terceira's Shell Service Station (72 South Rd., tel. 441/236-4158, 6:30 A.M.–midnight) makes a convenient stop for bottled water, sodas, ice, ice cream, snacks, and newspapers, along with gasoline.

The expansive new **Warwick Esso Tigermart** (66 Middle Rd., tel. 441/236-2595, 6 A.M.–10 P.M. Sun.–Wed., 24 hours Thurs.–Sat.) does a lot more than gas. The supersized structure, which wouldn't look out of place in U.S. suburbia, opened in late 2005 and includes a large, modern store with deli offerings, fresh-baked pastries, hot and cold snacks, as well as magazines, toiletries, and basic grocery items. There's an ATM, too.

Warwick Post Office (70 Middle Rd., just

WARWICK & SOUTHAMPTON

west of Khyber Pass, tel. 441/236-4071, 8 A.M.–5 P.M. Mon.–Fri.) sells stamps and bus and ferry passes, and it also offers Internet access.

White's Pharmacy (29 Middle Rd., tel. 441/238-1145, 8 A.M.–9 P.M. Mon.–Sat., 1–5 P.M. Sun.), located inside White's Supermarket, is the only pharmacy between Paget and Somerset Village.

Mix with the locals at **Warwick Laundromat and Dry-Cleaning** (15 Ten Pin Crescent, behind Hayward's Supermarket, tel. 441/236-5403, 6:30 A.M.–9 P.M. Mon.–Sat.). On Sundays, last wash starts at 4 P.M. (closes at 6 P.M.).

ATMs are located at Lindo's Market, White & Sons Supermarket, and the Warwick Esso Tigermart service station, all on Middle Road.

Public toilets are located at Astwood Park, Warwick Long Bay, and area restaurants.

GETTING THERE AND AROUND
Buses

Buses are a convenient way to get up and down the South Shore Road between resorts and beaches (No. 7, every 15 minutes), and along Middle Road (No. 8, every 15 minutes), though bus routes do not include the parish's pretty Harbour Road. The three-zone tariff for both routes is $3 (exact change, or tokens, tickets, or passes required).

Ferries

Ferries crisscross Hamilton Harbour throughout the day from the main Ferry Terminal in town to two stops in Warwick—Darrell's Wharf and Belmont Wharf. The scenic Paget-Warwick ferry route has kept its chugging, ironclad veterans, *Corona, Georgia,* and *Coralita,* quaint throwbacks to the days before the ad-

vent of speedy, air-conditioned, quieter vessels now used on longer routes such as Hamilton-Dockyard. The Paget-Warwick ferries provide service every half hour at commuter times on weekdays, or 45 minutes at other times, including weekends. Fares are $5 round-trip, $2.50 one-way. For information, call Sea Express (tel. 441/295-4506, www.seaexpress.bm).

Scooters

Scooters, both double-seaters and single-seaters, and less-powerful mopeds can be rented from outlets at major hotels, as well as from liveries in Hamilton, Paget, Southampton, Flatts, Sandys, and St. George's. It's an easy way to beach-hop independently, if you are a confident, safe biker.

Taxis

Taxi stands are located at the major hotels, and most guest properties can quickly arrange for taxi transport. Hailing cabs from the roadside is less successful, since most are run via central dispatch and are usually en route somewhere and averse to extra pick-ups. Taxi tours and wheelchair-accessible taxi service is also available.

Bicycles

Bicycles up the adventure quotient for travelers who want to get some exercise with their sightseeing. Bermuda's hilly terrain and the ever-popular Railway Trail have attracted increasing numbers of cyclists, including off-road mountain-bikers. Bikes can be rented from some hotels and liveries, including **Eve's Cycle Livery** (114 Middle Rd., tel. 441/236-6247, 8:30 A.M.–5:30 P.M.), but unless you are Ironman-fit, you might want to opt for motorized transport in the torpid heat of midsummer.

WARWICK & SOUTHAMPTON

Southampton Parish

Southampton lays claim to a close Shakespearean connection: Like the island's eight other parishes, it was named for one of the colony's original investors, in this case, the Earl of Southampton. Henry Wriothesley was a nobleman, soldier, and courtier, as well as a patron of William Shakespeare. In turn, Wriothesley had a poem dedicated to his generosity by the Elizabethan playwright, whose play *The Tempest* was supposedly inspired by the 1609 shipwreck that led to Bermuda's colonization by the English. If he had actually laid eyes on the parish, Shakespeare would not have been disappointed. Southampton is Bermuda's most sweepingly scenic region, a crescendo of breathtaking seascapes, azure reeflines, heartbreakingly beautiful beaches, and top-of-the-world lookouts like Gibbs Hill Lighthouse.

The parish is heavily populated with residential neighborhoods, many capitalizing on the unrivaled views and rugged coastline. It is also home to two large chain hotels (the Fairmont Southampton Princess and the Wyndham Bermuda Resort & Spa), as well as award-winning smaller resorts (The Reefs, Pompano Beach Club), all claiming stunning beachfront properties or precipitous Malibustyle real estate. In fact, South Shore Road through Southampton could be considered Bermuda's version of California's Pacific Coast Highway, a curvaceous thoroughfare hugging the shoreline and hemmed by horizons worthy of a movie set.

Southampton extends west from Chaplin Bay on the South Shore and Riddell's Bay on the north-side Great Sound as far as Tribe Road No. 6, which runs along the western edge of Port Royal Golf Course at the Sandys border. The parish's two main arteries are South Shore Road and Middle Road, which becomes, after exiting Warwick, a very scenic harborfront drive to the Barnes Corner junction with South Shore Road. From here, only Middle Road continues west through the parish.

Beaches, scuba diving, spas, tennis, golf, and hotel-based cuisine and entertainment make Southampton the premier parish for visitors of all ages and interests.

SIGHTS
◖ Gibbs Hill Lighthouse

The main sightseeing attraction of the parish is 117-foot Gibbs Hill Lighthouse (68 St. Anne's Rd., tel. 441/238-8069 or 441/238-0524, www.bermudalighthouse.com, 9 A.M.–4:30 P.M. daily except Christmas, closed for February renovations, $2.50 per person, under five free), good for a dedicated visit or a stop on your drive west. Built of prefabricated cast iron shipped from England, the historic landmark's 26-mile lamp was first lit on May 1, 1846, as a navigational marker for approaching

WARWICK & SOUTHAMPTON

© ROSEMARY JONES

Gibbs Hill Lighthouse, with its adjoining tearoom

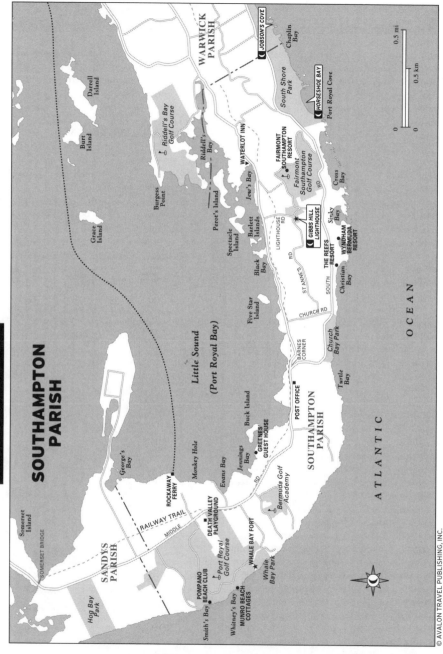

WARWICK & SOUTHAMPTON

SOUTHAMPTON PARISH

WARWICK PARISH

SANDYS PARISH

*Little Sound
(Port Royal Bay)*

OCEAN

ATLANTIC

JOBSON'S COVE

HORSESHOE BAY

Chaplin Bay

South Shore Park

Port Royal Cove

WATERLOT INN

FAIRMONT SOUTHAMPTON RESORT

Fairmont Southampton Golf Course

Cross Bay

Sinky Bay

GIBBS HILL LIGHTHOUSE

WYNDHAM BERMUDA RESORT

THE REEFS RESORT

Christian Bay

LIGHTHOUSE RD

ST ANNE'S RD

SOUTH RD

CHURCH RD

Church Bay Park

BARNES CORNER

Turtle Bay

POST OFFICE

GREENE'S GUEST HOUSE

Buck Island

Jennings Bay

Evans Bay

Monkey Hole

ROCKAWAY FERRY

George's Bay

Bermuda Golf Academy

DEATH VALLEY PLAYGROUND

RAILWAY TRAIL

MIDDLE RD

SOMERSET BRIDGE

Somerset Island

Hog Bay Park

Smith's Bay

POMPANO BEACH CLUB

Port Royal Golf Course

MUNRO BEACH COTTAGES

Whitney's Bay

WHALE BAY FORT

Whale Bay Park

Darrell Island

Burt Island

Riddell's Bay Golf Course

Riddell's Bay

Burgess Point

Grace Island

Perot's Island

Jew's Bay

Spectacle Island

Bartlett Islands

Black Bay

Five Star Island

0.5 mi

0.5 km

0

0

ships. It was a revolutionary method at the time for diminishing the number of shipwrecks around the island's treacherous necklace of reefs; before its construction, some 39 vessels had foundered or sunk on reefs, which extend 16 miles offshore in some areas. While shipping now employs higher-tech navigation methods, such as GPS systems, the lighthouse offers a backup method of shoreline navigation still appreciated by modern mariners. The flash of its light can be seen as far as 180 miles by planes flying at 10,000 feet or higher. For generations, lighthouse-keepers ran the property, now operated electronically and maintained by the government's Marine and Ports Department.

At 10-second intervals, the light emits a two-second-long flash that is visible from most parts of the island. Its 1,000-watt bulb is housed within a revolving beehive lens.

The whole hillside is panoramic—Queen Elizabeth II visited in 1953 shortly after her coronation, and today a bronze plaque on the roadside below the lighthouse marks where she stopped to gaze over the Great Sound's scattering of islands. But the best view, if you can muster the energy, is from the windswept balcony atop the structure's 185 stairs. The climb is not as tough as it might appear; eight floors, with mini exhibits that describe the tower's manufacture as well as general Bermuda history, provide resting platforms on the way up and down. Climb past the gargantuan lamp to the high-railed balcony with its 360-degree views—a spectacular vantage point from which to spy the South Shore horizons, the West End as far as the Royal Naval Dockyard, the Great Sound with Hamilton Harbour and the city in the distance, and the homes, swimming pools, farm fields, and seascapes of Southampton and Warwick. Indeed, the view demonstrates well Bermuda's crowding of residential neighborhoods and the lack of substantial greenbelts. Alongside the lighthouse, in a former signaling station used by the British Army, is a quaint tearoom (which doubles as one of Bermuda's most unique restaurants), open for breakfast, lunch, and weekend dinners in season, and a gift shop.

St. Anne's Church

A historic site responsible for the names of Church Bay (opposite) and several vicinity streets, St. Anne's Church (13 Church Rd., tel. 441/238-1864, 10 A.M.–4 P.M., Sunday services) makes a quaint stop en route west. One of the original parish church sites, St. Anne's today stands where a cedar version called "Port Royal Church" was built in 1620 by the first settlers. Structural additions over the years are said to have incorporated some of the original cedar wood. The nave and chapel were built 1716–17, while the west-end tower was added in 1905. Its new bell, replacing one from 1780, could be heard as far away as Hamilton in those days. The old bell can also still be seen in the vestry. The whitewashed building, one of the best examples of Bermudian ecclesiastical architecture, is surrounded by a picturesque graveyard that includes numerous tiny headstones marking the graves of infants and children. Park in the lot opposite the church on Church Road.

Seymour's Pond

Surrounded by marshland, with nearby pockets of woods and farm fields, tiny Seymour's Pond (open sunrise to sunset daily, admission free) is tucked into the Barnes Corner junction of Middle and South Shore Roads. The half-acre reserve, owned and maintained by the Bermuda Audubon Society, is a natural freshwater pond, like Warwick Pond, and both belonged to the same connecting band of peat-marsh basins that once ran through Bermuda's central parishes. Described by Canadian biologist and author Dr. Martin Thomas as "the best example of a freshwater pond in Bermuda," the pond is known by nature-lovers as a good place to find a wide variety of animals and plants. Bird-watchers, in particular, will see many resident and visiting species. Coots, ducks, and common moorhens make their home here, and herons can also be spotted, usually sitting in trees and bushes around the pond edge. Dragonflies and damselflies swoop over the water, and diving beetles and other insects, including mosquitoes, hang out here—though large numbers of the eastern mosquito fish, a freshwater guppy look-alike, keeps their numbers in check.

© ROSEMARY JONES

St. Anne's Church

Whale Bay Fort and Battery

Whale Bay Fort and Battery, in West Whale Bay Park (at the end of Whale Bay Rd., open sunrise to sunset daily, admission free), makes a beautiful sidetrack from a trip west. Once known as Fort Newbold for its commanding officer, Captain William Newbold, the half-moon-shaped fort was constructed in the mid-1700s, when the several small coastal forts were built on the South Shore before the American Revolutionary War. Today, its actual walls are gone, but the flag-stoned gun floor where it once stood remains a spectacular vantage point, overlooking West Whale Bay and the dramatic sweep of ocean on the southern face of the island. Both the fort and nearby battery, built a century later, guarded the entrance to Hogfish Cut, a channel for small boats that was of value to local shipping as vessels traveled the western coast toward Dockyard. The battery's impressive walls, barracks, and underground magazine rooms are still standing and can be explored. Leave mopeds at the beach parking lot, and climb the hill to the forts.

Evans Bay Nature Reserve

Access is difficult, but diehard naturalists will enjoy plodging around Evans Pond Nature Reserve (open sunrise to sunset daily, admission free), a small tract of private land that contains one of the island's saltwater ponds (connected to the sea by subterranean channels). The pond, nestled in woodland, is probably best viewed from a farm track off the busy main road. Fringed by black mangroves, this pond contains a rich ecosystem that often includes endemic species. Among the critters here are giant toads, night herons, lizards such as the Jamaican anole, bonefish, bream, mullet, flatworms, sponges, seaweed, algae, and sea grass—though you'd have to don a mask and snorkel to actually see many of these. Eels and green turtles find their way to the pond occasionally, clambering overland to get there. Turtles are only temporary visitors, though; they breed in more southern climes.

BEACHES
◖ Horseshoe Bay

The most-photographed beach in Bermuda, Horseshoe Bay is equally popular among locals and visitors, its various moods appealing to a diverse range of beach-lovers. Arguably Bermuda's number-one tourist attraction, it welcomes shiploads of tourists taxied here the moment their vessel makes port throughout the summer cruise season. As a result, weekday afternoons May–October see the half-moon-shaped bay packed with bodies soaking up the soft sand, balmy water, and picturesque surroundings. Flotillas of cabs descend to ferry them back to Hamilton's docks around 4:30 P.M. every day.

Staffed by lifeguards May 1–October 1, the beach itself is alluring, but its on-site services allow for a full day's outing. A concession at the entrance sells towels, beach mats, sunblock, sarongs, souvenirs, and flip-flops. Rentals from 9:30 A.M. include lounge chairs ($10), umbrellas ($10), rafts ($12), and body boards ($8.50). Hair-braiding à la Bo Derek, formerly a Caribbean tourist highlight, finally made it to Bermuda in the 2000s, and local women and girls posted at Horseshoe in the summer will twist your locks into elaborate cornrows—be careful

© ROSEMARY JONES

Horseshoe Bay's "Baby Beach" is popular for children.

of scalp sunburn afterward. A bonus of Horseshoe is the café, where waterlogged beach bums can slake their thirst and heat with sodas and ice cream, as well as fast-food meals. Baby-changing facilities, showers, spacious sky-lit bathrooms, and outdoor showers and taps for washing sandy feet before the ride home, are also laid on.

Locals head to Horseshoe Bay year-round at dawn on Saturday mornings to swim, run, and walk, enjoying the serenity of the beach and its dune trails before the day's later crowds. Horseshoe is a favorite hangout of Bermudian teens and twentysomethings on Saturday afternoons, when night-owls nurse their hangovers with pizza, cheeseburgers, and eyefuls of beach-trotting fashionistas.

Families with young children also choose Horseshoe for its cliff-sheltered ends, which offer shade and paddling pools. Horseshoe's beach has less of a steep surfside drop-off than next-door Warwick Long Bay's, lessening the undertow and allowing for wading farther out. There is also a kid-perfect adjoining cove, officially named Port Royal Cove but locally dubbed "The Baby Beach," to the west of the main stretch. A turquoise swimming hole encircled by cliffs that keep its waters flat, this little gem is a big draw for moms and nannies with toddlers or infants.

Church Bay

Rounding the last bend off South Shore Road as you head west, Church Bay's cliff-top park offers a scenic stop for a picnic, and its reef-encircled bay has long been considered the best snorkeling spot on the island. But Hurricane Fabian's coastal damage in 2003 closed down the main entrance and access for two years, due to instability of the cliffs around the path down; a new timber boardwalk and fence have been completed. The shady park at the top has a convenient pull-in and parking lot. Portable toilets are on-site, though like many public washrooms throughout the island, they are not well maintained.

West Whale Bay

Surprisingly under-visited by locals or crowds of visitors, West Whale Bay (at the end of Whale

Bay Rd., off Middle Rd.) is one of the island's best, offering pristine pink sand, clear turquoise water, safe coves, and a sense of undisturbed privacy, as if it were a resort property rather than a public one. Follow Whale Bay Road to the end, where a quiet parking lot stands. A manicured lawn hemmed by whispering pines leads down to the beach under towering cliffs. Dramatic boulders, tumbled into the bay, separate the beach into a string of shady, private coves. Golfers can be seen down the distant shoreline, teeing off the world-famous 18th green at Port Royal Club. Portable toilets are in the parking lot.

ENTERTAINMENT AND EVENTS

Good Friday brings the popular **Bermuda Kite Festival** to Horseshoe Bay, an Easter weekend spectacle not to be missed. Organized by the Opposition United Bermuda Party, the event, held noon–3 P.M., is nonetheless a nonpartisan affair, drawing hundreds from all over the island for a colorful showdown of kites both store-bought and homemade in traditional island styles. Kite-flying is practically an art form in Bermuda, and traditionalists turn tissue paper and sticks into kaleidoscopic flying contraptions, complete with tails and "hummers." Islanders come to check out the best designs (judged in various categories), fly their own kites, enjoy kids' games and music, and share Easter picnics of sticky hot-cross buns and cod fish cakes. Kite-making demonstrations are often the highlight. For information, call the U.B.P. office at tel. 441/295-4597.

Horseshoe Bay is also the site for the annual **Bermuda International Sand Sculpture Competition,** run by the Tourism Department. The creative contest is fun for both entrants and spectators, with five categories open to children, adults, families, teens, and tourists. Held on the first Saturday of September, noon–4 P.M., the competition's past crowd-pleasers have included mermaids, sea creatures, and cartoon characters like Sponge-Bob SquarePants, all built from the bay's coral-specked sand. For information, contact vleader@gov.bm.

Nightlife

Time slips away amid the mellow environs and generously poured cocktails of the **Southampton Arms** (215 Middle Rd., next to the gas station, tel. 441/238-9809, 10 A.M.–10 P.M. Mon.–Sat.), a truly local taste of island camaraderie. A favorite hangout of taxi drivers (hopefully off-duty), the nondescript roadside bar is an oasis of tall tales and jovial spirits—including those dispensed into the Cockspur 'n' Cokes and dark 'n' stormies. On Friday and Saturday nights, games of billiards and cards get into full swing. No food is served, but feel free to bring your own.

Several bars in Southampton hotels offer live entertainment throughout the week. **The Cellar** (Fairmont Southampton Resort, 101 South Shore Rd., tel. 441/238-8000, 9 P.M.–3 A.M., closed in winter) attracts as many locals as visitors to its cavelike interior, next to the hotel spa's indoor pool. The club encourages a 30-plus crowd, who dance to local DJs and bands like the popular Prestige. Local musicians perform from 9:45 P.M. Wed.–Sun. at **Henry VIII Pub & Restaurant** (56 South Shore Rd., tel. 441/238-1977, henrys@ibl.bm). Happy hour at the **Lounge Bar** (The Reefs, 56 South Shore Rd., tel. 441/238-0222, www.thereefs.com) runs 5:30–7:30 P.M. and boasts 37 different cocktails, endless tapas, and a dance floor. Live entertainment includes DJs and salsa on Saturdays, 6:30–11:30 P.M.

SHOPPING

Like Warwick, Southampton is hardly a shoppers' mecca, offering only hotel-lobby boutiques and the occasional souvenir outlet. Label-conscious travelers will appreciate Longchamp and Rolex at the **Fairmont Southampton Resort,** home to a microcosm of Front Street's top-end retailers. The **Wyndham Bermuda Resort & Spa** also has outlets of several Hamilton branch stores in its lobby.

The **Lighthouse Gift Shop** (68 St. Anne's Rd., 9 A.M.–5 P.M. daily except Christmas) is good for postcards, film, disposable cameras, and the tackiest of Bermuda memorabilia. Steer clear, unless you really can't leave the island without a clay ferry, baseball cap, or pirate flag.

SPORTS AND RECREATION

Southampton is an outdoors enthusiast's nirvana, with great conditions and facilities for swimming, body-surfing, kitesurfing, horseback riding, scuba, snorkeling, tennis, and golf. The large stretches of public parkland, including the Railway Trail, offer traffic-free space for walking, running, and mountain-biking. Soccer and cricket fans can catch evening and weekend matches, in each sport's respective winter and summer seasons, at local sports grounds. Hotels have their own dive shops or liaisons with scuba outfits that operate off Southampton's reefline.

Diving

One of three locations run by 30-year veteran and PADI five-star recipient **Blue Water Divers & Watersports,** the operation at Wyndham Bermuda Resort & Spa (6 Sonesta Dr., tel. 441/232-1034, www.divebermuda.com) offers several daily expeditions for experienced or novice divers. Choose a two-tank morning dive departing by boat at 9 A.M. ($100) or a single-tank guided afternoon excursion at 1:30 P.M. ($65). The company offers PADI, NAUI, and SSI facility certification courses and referrals, and scuba lessons for 10-year-olds and up. Noontime snorkel trips ($45) to South Shore reefs are also offered throughout the summer season, and kayak rental is available.

Dive Bermuda (101 South Shore Rd., tel. 441/238-2332, www.bermudascuba.com) operates out of the Fairmont Southampton Resort, offering introduction scuba dives, full PADI training, underwater "scooters," and guided outings to notable wreck sites.

Water Sports

Based at the Fairmont Southampton Resort, **Sea Venture Watersports** (Waterlot Inn Dock, Jews Bay, Middle Rd., tel. 441/238-6881, www.jetskibermuda.com) offers an adrenaline-packed way to see Bermuda from the water by Jet Ski, water skis, wakeboard, or tube. Skiboat charters with a captain/instructor cost $170 per hour. Polaris and Yamaha personal watercraft rentals (the driver must be 16 or older) cost between $60 (half hour) and

WHALE-WATCHING

Whale-watching has become a spring ritual off Bermuda's South Shore, the migration route for humpbacks as they travel from the Caribbean to north Atlantic feeding grounds. Between March and April, pods of humpback whales can be spotted, even from the shoreline (you may see a line of motorists pulled over to ogle the distant spouts or flukes beyond the reefline).

Found throughout the world, most humpbacks follow regular migration routes. In the Atlantic, they tend to spend winters mating and calving in tropical zones, then move north to polar waters in the summer to feed. Unlike other species, they are highly acrobatic, breaching (throwing their whole bodies out of the water), swimming upside down with flippers raised in the air, or slapping the surface with their huge tails, called flukes. Scientists believe these may all be forms of communication between pod members, along with the species' characteristic singing.

Several charter boat companies organize special whale-watching tours in these months. One of the best is **Fantasea Diving** (5 Albuoy's Point, Hamilton, tel. 441/236-1300 or 441/295-0460, fax 441/236-8926, info@fantasea.bm), which takes five-hour trips aboard glass-bottomed vessels through which whales and their calves can sometimes be seen frolicking. **Blue Water Divers & Watersports** (Robinson's Marina, Somerset Bridge, Sandys, tel. 441/234-1034, www.divebermuda.com) offer charters on request.

WARWICK & SOUTHAMPTON

$300 (half day), with higher rates for two- and three-person vehicles. Two-hour and half-day personal watercraft tours around the West End, Great Sound, and myriad islands between can also be arranged. Instruction is provided for novices. Reservations are suggested, and rentals must be secured by credit card.

Golf

The executive par-3 18-hole course at the

Fairmont Southampton Resort (101 South Shore Rd., reservations tel. 441/238-8000, direct tel. 441/239-6952, fax 441/238-8479, www.fairmont.com, $70 for 18 holes, $45 for nine, 20 percent discount on five rounds) was designed by Ted Robinson, with a lofty, palm-studded layout rambling over the South Shore property. Its 2,684 yards (longest hole is 215 yards) include manicured hills, 60 bunkers, and three water hazards, making a course that takes an average 2.5–3 hours to play—appropriate for beginners, couples who want to play together, or as a warm-up for longer courses. Unpredictable winds make it a highly challenging short course. Lessons, clinics, rentals, practice putting green, and pro shop are on-site. Summer hours are 7 A.M.–6:30 P.M., winter 7 A.M.–5 P.M.

Designed by Robert Trent Jones, **Port Royal Golf Course** (5 Middle Rd., tel. 441/234-0974, fax 441/234-3562, $150 for 18 holes, golf carts obligatory) is widely regarded as one of the best government-owned courses in the world. Greg Norman played here. Jack Nicklaus sang its praises. Hollywood's Samuel L. Jackson chose Port Royal to host his celebrity tournament for several years in the 1990s. One of three public courses on the island, together with St. George's Club and Ocean View in Devonshire, Port Royal's fairways wind along dizzying cliff-tops; its greens are set against the ocean's dazzling turquoise. The 18-hole, 6,561-yard course is not, however, as well maintained as it once was. Bermuda's perennial lack of water often gets the blame, though the government invested in an osmosis plant in 2002, which still is not operational. But while the greens and fairways may not be as pristine as those of some of the private courses, Port Royal remains a challenging world-championship course with breathtaking views of the southwest shoreline.

The **Bermuda Golf Academy** (Industrial Park Rd., off Middle Rd., tel. 441/238-8800, fax 441/232-0034) is a good place for tuning up your tee-off or simply having fun. The facility is home to Bermuda's only all-weather, 320-yard driving range. The range features 40 practice bays, 25 of which are covered, and night lighting is offered until 10:30 P.M. An 18-hole practice green, eight target greens, and a chipping/bunker play area also attract golfers, especially given the difficulty of landing tee times at favored clubs around the island. Tokens for a bucket of 40 balls cost $4.50, or $5.50 after 5 P.M. Private lessons ($70 an hour, $40 half hour) can be booked with three PGA pros. Children and adults also love the facility's mini golf course, which has waterfalls, bridges, and Bermuda-style butteries. Mini golf costs $9 for adults, $7 for children under 13. During the high season, the academy is open 9 A.M.–10 P.M. Monday–Thursday plus Sunday, and until 10:30 P.M. Friday and Saturday. Winter closing time is 9 P.M.

Tennis

The **Whaler Inn Tennis Club** (Fairmont Southampton Resort, 101 South Shore Rd., tel. 441/239-6950, witc@logic.bm, 8 A.M.–midnight) has six Plexi-pave hard courts, three lit for night play. Daily court rental for resort guests or any visitor to the island is $15, or $12 after noon; per-hour rental for locals is $20. Half hour and hour-long lessons are also offered by three full-time pros. The club shop (8 A.M.–7 P.M. through the summer) stocks one of the island's best selections of men's and women's Nike tennis gear, along with other select brands.

Four all-weather tennis courts are run by the **Port Royal Tennis Club** (5 Middle Rd., manager Stan Smith tel. 441/234-2516 or 441/337-1806, pro Steve Bean 441/234-3594), which leases the facility from government. Located on the Port Royal Golf Club property, the courts have not been resurfaced recently, and Hurricane Fabian destroyed their lights, wiping out night play. Although their condition is not pristine, they are safe and playable. The club holds clinics for area children on Saturday mornings, but the facility is not staffed during the day. To book a court ($10 per hour) or a lesson, contact Smith or Bean. Guests at neighboring Pompano Beach Club or Munro Beach Cottages should contact their resorts' receptions, which have special arrangements for use.

Soccer and Cricket

Football (a.k.a. soccer) fans enjoy the weekend action at **Southampton Rangers Sports Club** (1 Middle Rd., tel. 441/238-0058) all winter long. The same grounds convert to a cricket pitch May–September for the very competitive County matches, a series that pits teams in various zones of the island (Eastern, Central, Western) against each other, drawing spillover crowds throughout the summer.

Spas

The 2002 opening of the 15-room **Willow Stream Spa and Health Club** (Fairmont Southampton Resort, 101 South Shore Rd., tel. 441/239-6924, www.willowstream.com, day spa and fitness center 6:30 A.M.–9 P.M., salon 10 A.M.–7 P.M.) upped the ante among spa additions to island tourism. The spa is one of six Willow Streams at Fairmont hotels around the world, and one of the chain's most successful, thanks partly to a devoted island clientele. Bermuda residents rave about Willow Stream's hot stone massages, rose hip body wraps, shiatsu, acupressure, and hydrotherapy treatments, not to mention the setting: terraced gardens, ocean-facing hot tubs, and an indoor pool with waterfalls. *Sex in the City*-style girlfriends' retreats fill the place year-round on weekends. The 31,000-square-foot spa has made strong overtures to male patrons as well, with exclusive den-like lounges for guys, sports massage treatments, a "Gentleman's Barber Facial," and a "Keep Your Shorts On" allowance for novice spa-goers. Specialities include the Sea Splendor Body Oasis, with eucalyptus foot soak, exfoliation, aromatherapy bath, massage, and body wrap (two hours, $279), and Island Inspiration Body Sorbet, a massage followed by sorbet application and body wrap (one hour, $139). The spa offers a hair and nail salon, steam room, sauna, women's and men's lounges, and couples' lounge and treatment room. The fitness center has a full range of Cybex cardiovascular and weight-training equipment and a personal trainer.

Small but professional, **La Serena** (The Reefs, 56 South Shore Rd., tel. 441/239-0184, www.thereefs.com, 8 A.M.–8 P.M. daily) opened in 2003. With five therapists and two treatment rooms, it is open to guests of The Reefs as well as outside clients. The beauty menu includes aroma-massage (85 minutes, $135), pregnancy and sports massage, facials, hot rock therapy, Thai bodywork, and reflexology for couples. Body wraps and other treatments use Thalgo products, made with algae and sea minerals. Special packages include a daylong treatment with lunch at the resort restaurant ($270).

Serenity (Pompano Beach Club, 36 Pompano Beach Rd., tel. 441/234-0222, www.pompanobeachclub.com) expanded as part of the 50-year-old resort's renovation in 2005–06. The spa has three therapists providing a menu of hot stone facials and massage, body, and mud treatments. Some of the more intriguing are the Whipped Milk Bath (25 minutes, $55) and the Ginseng and Spirulina Mask (45 minutes, $75), gratuities not included. Treatment rooms are in a glass-front space overlooking the ocean.

The Cedar Spa (Wyndham Bermuda Resort & Spa, 6 Sonesta Dr., off South Shore Rd., tel. 441/238-8122, fax 441/238-8463, toll-free from the U.S. 877/999-3223, www .wyndhambermuda.com) opened in April 2005 after the property's massive renovation. With separate facilities for male and female clients, the spa features a gym, sauna, and steam bath, and full offering of manicure and pedicure services, Golden Door Spa facial treatments, deep-tissue massage, and body exfoliations. A spa sampler offer, with room and spa menu combined, is also available.

Running and Walking

Southampton's **Railway Trail** includes some of the route's most deeply forested stretches, tunneling through spice tree and fiddlewood groves on a high ridge above Middle Road. It cuts across the Fairmont Southampton Princess Hotel property and then meanders beneath Gibbs Hill Lighthouse (a tribe road cuts up from the trail to the lighthouse for easy access). A couple of breaks in the trail heading west mean you have to cross Middle Road and stay on the main road for a half-mile section after Barnes' Corner before a paved stretch of the trail picks up again, leading into the rural beauty of Sandys.

The wide, grassy verges of **South Shore Road** make it safe from traffic for walking and running. Fringed by spider lilies, goldenrods, and Spanish bayonets, the route sweeping high above the beaches makes for dramatically scenic territory.

For Kids

Southampton beaches are free, nonstop attractions for children—and usually more than enough to occupy all ages. Whether they're swimming, snorkeling, body-surfing, building sandcastles, or simply pottering about between surf and sand, children seem to be perfectly content to spend days on end at the beach, even after their parents may have had enough. Horseshoe's "Baby Beach" and main arc and shallow West Whale Bay are two kid favorites. Memo to parents: don't forget the sunblock!

Wahoo, the spectacular waterpark that opened in 2005 at Wyndham Bermuda Resort & Spa (6 Sonesta Dr., off South Shore Rd., tel. 441/238-8122, fax 441/238-8463), will win you major brownie points with the kids. With its waterfalls, geysers, slides, and fountains, a day at the four-pool extravaganza makes for giddy, waterlogged family fun. If you're not staying at the resort, day passes are expensive: $50 per person, including children. But when you see your child's eyes light up at the 110-foot translucent body slide, it just might be worth it.

Its unfortunate name notwithstanding, **Death Valley Playground** (Middle Rd., opposite Terceira's Port Royal Esso Station) is a fun, safe place for kids to let off steam. Maintained by the Parks Department, the small site entertains kids with swings, slides, and activity frames for both toddlers and older children. Shady benches and a picnic table sit alongside, and a large playing field lies adjacent. Located next to the busy main road, there's no peace and quiet here, but the little ones don't seem to mind. There is plenty of parking space, but no public toilets.

ACCOMMODATIONS

Southampton is home to the majority of the island's high-end resorts, but there are also more affordable cottage colonies and guesthouses.

$100-200

Greenes' Guesthouse (71 Middle Rd., tel. 441/238-0834 or 441/238-2532, fax 441/238-8980, www.greenesguesthouse.com, $150 doubles, including full breakfast) is a family-run bed-and-breakfast in a panoramic property overlooking Jews Bay and the Great Sound. Jean and David Greene have turned their very large house into comfortable, modern guest accommodations complete with ample lounges, a home theater area, and a large dining room for guests to enjoy the full breakfast Jean cooks up every morning (she also bakes gingerbread for afternoon tea). The six spacious rooms, each with private bathroom, have air-conditioning, heating, telephone, refrigerator, and cable TV. The main kitchen is open for use by guests; Jean just asks that they wash up afterwards. While the sprawling property sits just a few yards off busy Middle Road, its rear side is serene with quiet lawns, patios, and a 40-foot pool overlooking the ocean. A public bus stop is just down the main road, though Jean often transports guests to nearby shops or the Rockaway ferry dock in her car.

$200-300

Established in 1963, **Munro Beach Cottages** (2 Port Royal Golfcourse Dr., off Middle Rd., tel. 441/234-1175, fax 441/234-3528, www.munrobeach.com, 16 units, $235–289) is a family enterprise whose five-acre property spreads atop bluffs edging the 18-hole Port Royal Golf Course, commanding a spectacular view of the western South Shore over Whitney Bay. There are few facilities—no restaurant, pool, or cable TV—but the awesome vantage point and the pristine private beach more than make up for that. "My father always said, 'I have the biggest swimming pool in the world,'" says Norma McAndrew of her dad, hotelier Burton Munro. Though boxy and identical from the outside, the no-frills, ground-floor duplex units all have full kitchens equipped with fridges, microwaves, stoves, oven/broilers, toasters, and coffeemakers for self-catering (restaurants at next-door Pompano Beach Resort and Port Royal Golf Club are also handy). Each unit has a bathroom with tub and shower, a combined living-room/bedroom (with either king or twin beds, plus a sofa bed for a third person for an additional $40 per night), a barbecue grill on a backdoor patio, and sliding front glass doors to take in the breezy panorama of coconut palms and turquoise shallows that stretch a few hundred yards out to the reefline.

Over $300

A $3.9 billion buyout in 2006 could spell even more improvements for the five-star ◖ **Fairmont Southampton Resort** (101 South Shore Rd., tel. 441/238-8000, toll-free reservations 800/441-1414, www.fairmont.com, high season $549–2,900, low season starting at $209). Along with its sister Hamilton Fairmont Hotel, it was sold to a global luxury empire that includes the famed Raffles Hotel in Singapore and London's Savoy. The Southampton property had already undergone a slew of renovations in recent years. Hurricane Fabian in 2003 forced a $43 million refurbishment of guestrooms, corridors, and public spaces—including installation of a 100,000-square-foot hurricane-resistant roof. The latest deal will only add to the property's bragging rights.

Built in 1972 and encompassing 100 acres, the Fairmont Southampton is the island's largest luxury resort hotel property, perched on a high ridge that overlooks both the South Shore and Great Sound. Saudi sheikhs and their entourages have booked penthouse floors here, and celebrities like Michael Bolton have spent holidays at the property. Private jets special-order menus from the hotel's kitchens, and even visiting celebrities who don't happen to stay here hire out its chefs. And when Bermudians want to "go away" without leaving the island, a weekend at the Fairmont Southampton is considered the superlative escape. The decor—a 1970s confection of chandeliers, powder rooms, soaring staircases, and several hundred miles of

carpet—is over-the-top in a 007 sort of way, but every service is available and staff are professional. If you enjoy large resort hotels and don't mind being 20 minutes from Hamilton, this is the island's best choice.

Guest rooms include standard to one- and two-bedroom suites and duplexes, plus a couple of penthouses overlooking the South Shore or Great Sound. All rooms have private balconies, in-room safes, air-conditioning, minibars, private baths, walk-in closets, cable TV, voicemail, dataport with Internet access, and hair dryer. Four floors are nonsmoking. The resort has six restaurants (including two rated AAA Four and Five Diamond Awards), two bars, and a 31,000-square-foot spa and fitness club. It can accommodate convention groups of up to 1,500, with 16 meeting rooms and a multimedia amphitheater. Recreational amenities include two swimming pools (outdoor heated and indoor, both with hot tubs), an 18-hole par-3 golf course, 11 all-weather tennis courts, and a private beach. Other diversions include a year-round complimentary Kids Explorers Camp for children four and up with supervised activities, a cycle shop, dive shop, and Jet Ski rentals. There's free ferry service across the Great Sound to Fairmont Hamilton Princess dock.

◖ **The Reefs** (56 South Shore Rd., tel. 441/238-0222, fax 441/238-8372, toll-free from the U.S. or Canada 800/742-2008, www.thereefs.com, doubles from $474, cottages $548–908) consistently rakes in international awards (like *Condé Nast Traveler*'s Gold List in 2006) for privacy, professionalism, and its well-appointed property. Nestled in the cliffs above its own beautiful beach, the resort is owned by Bermuda's former tourism minister, David Dodwell. The Reefs surpasses many other Bermuda resorts by reinvesting in its coral-pink property; it recently updated three top-end point suites ($854 a night, with private outdoor hot tubs) in the urbane decor of a SoHo loft—a play on neutrals that makes a refreshing change from the wicker-and-floral epidemic afflicting many island accommodations. There are seven cottage suites, the best located on the ocean-facing side of the property. In 2003, The Reefs

© ROSEMARY JONES

an infinity pool at The Reefs

opened a spa, La Serena, and also converted its pool to an infinity version, its horizon blending with the South Shore's. Meticulous landscaping makes every planted palm appear freshly scrubbed, and a razor blade may have been used to trim the lawn edges. Honeymooners, families, and guests of every age bracket seem to enjoy the place equally. Bermudians flock here for weekend getaways in the off-season, and to the property's restaurants year-round. There is a five-night minimum stay mid-April–November. All 65 rooms have private balconies. Wedding, honeymoon, and anniversary packages are offered. Three restaurants, a gym, pool, kayaks, croquet, shuffleboard, and tennis courts make this a property you might never want to leave.

Named for the schools of long-finned surf fish, **(** **Pompano Beach Club** (36 Pompano Beach Rd., tel. 441/234-0222, 508/358-7737, toll-free 800/343-4155, www.pompanobeachclub.com, doubles from $460) commands one of the island's most dramatic seascapes. Ensconced in the cliffs of the southwest shoreline, the resort overlooks an atoll-like bay where low tide al-

lows you to wade out some 250 yards over a shallow sandbar, called Pompano Flats, to the surrounding reefline. Sea turtles frolic here, and the wide-open azure horizons and rolling breakers give the illusion of looking out from the top deck of an ocean liner at sea. A family-owned and -run resort, Pompano's casual atmosphere attracts kid-toting couples as well as honeymooners. Staff members boast about its 58 percent rate of repeat guests and the ultra-personalized service. Rooms are of the usual Bermuda mold, with tiled floors, potted plants, floral decor, and pastel watercolors, but private balconies with uncommon surf views make up for the lack of interior inspiration. Golf, honeymoon, and anniversary packages are offered. The hotel closed in late 2005 for a $5 million renovation that added 16 rooms (for a total of 74), a revamped spa and gameroom, oceanfront hot tubs, and a glass-enclosed, 60-seat restaurant. The resort reopened in 2006, in time to celebrate its 50th anniversary. Other amenities include the private beach, water sports, spa, gym, pool, five tennis courts—not to mention the adjoining world-championship Port Royal Golf Course.

Like the Fairmont Southampton, **Wyndham Bermuda Resort & Spa** (6 Sonesta Dr., off South Shore Rd., tel. 441/238-8122, fax 441/238-8463, toll-free from the U.S. 800/996-3426, www.wyndhambermuda.com, 311 rooms, including 32 suites, $272–425) is poised to reap the benefits of a major cash injection. In 2006, Windwalker Bermuda LLC acquired a controlling stake in the company that owns the 32-acre resort and spa and promised $200 million in refinancing—to elevate the resort from three- to five-star status. Development plans include a condo-hotel, fractional ownership accommodations, renovations to several guest wings, and revamped recreational areas and activities, including an expanded spa. The deal ended a period of uncertainty since 2003's Hurricane Fabian, when the property was closed for 18 months for renovations after suffering extensive damage. The site, formerly the Sonesta Beach Hotel, has long been a popular destination, particularly for families. Located on a peninsula fringed by three beaches, it is the island's only large oceanfront resort—a plus, except when hurricanes hit.

All rooms have private patios or balconies, satellite TV, and Golden Door toiletries in the bathrooms. The oceanview rooms, though more pricey, are best, looking south out to sea, rather than over the hotel's property. Ideal for families with children, one of the resort's most notable features is the highly popular waterpark, Wahoo—the only one of its kind in Bermuda. The 230,000-gallon attraction comprises one main pool and three family activity pools, with slides, fountains, and other diversions kids love. Among the highlights are a 110-foot translucent body slide, a 140-foot "lazy river" for tubing, a hot tub, and cascading waterfalls. Even Bermudian families check in by the dozen to let their kids frolic in the Disney-esque attraction (day passes cost $50 per person, including children). The main pool, for adults, has a swim-up bar. The resort also has a full-service spa and fitness center; a hair salon; tennis courts; a water sports center offering kayaking, pedal boats, and snorkeling equipment; a scuba center run by Blue Water Divers & Watersports; and a June–Labor Day activities program for children.

FOOD
Cafés and Bars

For authentic Bermudian favorites such as pan-fried grouper, meat loaf, liver and onions, plantains, peas 'n' rice, macaroni 'n' cheese, and bread pudding, drop into **Island Cuisine** (235 Middle Rd., tel. 441/238-3287, 6 A.M.–10 P.M. Mon.–Sat., 6 A.M.–1 P.M. Sun.). The roadside diner is simple but super-clean; it's had keen new owners since the spring of 2004. All-day breakfast is served daily, and traditional codfish and potatoes on Sunday.

Horseshoe Bay Beach House (at Horseshoe Bay, 94 South Shore Rd., tel. 441/238-2651, 8 A.M.–8 P.M. daily weather permitting) serves hamburgers, veggie burgers, fish 'n' chips, chicken nuggets, tuna sandwiches, pizza, sodas, lemonade, and ice cream. Enjoy the outdoor patio with tables and shady umbrellas, or eat your picnic on the beach. In 2005, Bermuda's Tourism Minister suggested the Horseshoe concession should get a liquor license as a pilot project that might pave the way for legalizing alcohol on public beaches like in the Caribbean—a scenario he endorses. But vociferous anti-drinking lobbies on the island were poised to oppose such a move at press-time.

Lunch can be enjoyed in the air-conditioned comfort of a hotel lobby at the **Jasmine Lounge** (Fairmont Southampton Resort, 101 South Shore Rd., tel. 441/238-8000, 11 A.M.–1 A.M. daily), with all-day cocktails, snacks, burgers, and afternoon tea. Watch the comings and goings of guests and golfers, including the occasional celebrity as you nibble pizza or sip a martini.

Similarly, the **Tip-Toe Lounge** (Wyndham Bermuda Resort & Spa, 6 Sonesta Dr., off South Shore Rd., tel. 441/238-8122, fax 441/238-8463, www.wyndhambermuda.com, 10:30 A.M.–1 A.M. daily) allows for casual lobby dining.

Italian

Bacci (Fairmont Southampton Princess, 101 South Shore Rd., tel. 441/238-8000 or 441/239-6966, www.fairmont.com, dinner only 6–10 P.M. daily) is the latest incarnation of the now-defunct Rib Room of many decades. Located next to the hotel's golf course, a good trek from the main entrance (take the hotel trolley or drive past the hotel to the golf club), the restaurant was renamed (Italian for "kiss") and reopened as a reasonably priced, family-friendly Italian restaurant in 2004. Appetizers feature favorites such as calamari ($9), fresh mussels ($15), and garlic shrimp ($15). Pastas and pizzas ($15–18) include a create-your-own category. Main courses are classics like osso buco ($32) and stuffed roast chicken breast ($22). One of its most popular offerings is the antipasti bar, serving sun-dried tomatoes, sardines, grilled vegetables, bocconcini cheese, prosciutto, anchovies, and cured meats ($14, or $24 as an entrée).

The stone lions, red-and-white awnings, and bright tablecloths scream "Mediterranean!"

and **Tio Pepe** (117 South Shore Rd., tel. 441/238-1897 or 441/238-0572, fax 441/238-4966, maresma@northrock.bm, lunch noon–5 P.M., dinner from 5 P.M. daily) has the feel of a Spanish or Italian roadside pizzeria or seaside pasta place. The menu is packed with Italian specials, but dinner items, in particular, are pricey for the venue ($29.50 for grilled wahoo, $23.50 for chicken breast parmigiana)—but that's nothing new in Bermuda. Inside, where Chianti bottles swing from the ceiling and waiters breeze around with trays of sangria and swizzles, smoking has been banned (one of the first island restaurants to lay down the law). Cozy, table-packed rooms are ideal for families or groups. Outside, there is seating under umbrellas on roadside terraces. Located directly opposite the entrance to Horseshoe Bay, Tio Pepe is a favorite with beachgoers and Bermudian regulars.

Japanese

Sazanami (Wyndham Bermuda Resort & Spa, 6 Sonesta Dr., off South Shore Rd., tel. 441/238-8122, fax 441/238-8463, www.wyndhambermuda.com, 6–10 P.M. Tues.–Sun.) opened in 2005 in the resort's refurbished lobby, offering a tasty menu of sushi, nigiri, sashimi, tempura, and other dishes. At the revolving sushi bar, diners help themselves to platters of their liking as they sail by floating boats. Ordering dishes à la carte in the shoji-screened dining room is another option. Sake and Japanese beer are also served.

International

Seafood—and lots of it—is the draw at **The Whaler Inn** (Fairmont Southampton Resort, 101 South Shore Rd., tel. 441/239-6968, www.fairmont.com, open in summer, dinner only 6–9:30 P.M. daily). Located in the Fairmont Beach Club (accessible by hotel trolley), the seasonal restaurant overlooks the hotel's private beach and South Shore breakers, its patio a perfect alfresco venue. The menu features traditional dishes such as Bermuda fish chowder ($8), island rockfish with Portuguese chorizo and black rum broth ($29), yellowfin tuna fillet ($28), as well as steaks, pastas, and surf and

turf specials (the lobster is from Maine—not Bermuda's spiny version). There's a children's menu, and suggested dress is smart-casual.

Henry VIII Pub & Restaurant (69 South Shore Rd., tel. 441/238-1977, henrys@ibl.bm, lunch noon–2:30 P.M., dinner 6–10:30 P.M., bar noon–1 A.M. daily) looks as if it might date back to Tudor times, though it's been a Southampton roadside fixture only since 1970. Permeated with the aroma of prime rib and spilled draught beer, the low-ceilinged eatery is Bermuda's best example of an English-style pub. A strong local following keeps the place lively even in off-season, especially on Sunday nights when a raucous crowd enjoys dinner and live entertainment until 3 A.M. The kitsch plays to serious Anglophiles, but if you don't cringe at the sight of strolling minstrels in the dining room, the menu is heartily enjoyable. Highlights are the Bermuda rockfish ($29.50), rack of lamb ($32), steak and kidney pie ($23.50), and 14 different ales. Minimum food charge $20 per person. Wednesdays through Sundays bring live entertainment from 9:45 P.M., including local calypso kings Stan Seymour and Duke Joell, and Canadian keyboardist Dave Bootle, who keeps the crowd lively with rock 'n' roll favorites.

Right next door to Henry VIII Pub is **Henry's Pantry** (69 South Shore Rd., tel. 441/238-1509, 10 A.M.–7 P.M. Mon.–Sat.), which sells cold drinks, chocolate bars, snacks, batteries, and a few deli items like chicken legs, hot pies, beef patties, fish chowder, and sandwiches.

◖ **Coconuts** (The Reefs, 56 South Shore Rd., tel. 441/238-0222, www.thereefs.com, lunch noon–3 P.M. daily April–Dec., dinner 7–9 P.M. daily May–Nov.) wins the hearts of alfresco diners and numerous awards for the island's best lunch venue, most romantic restaurant, and table with a view. Set on a treehouse-style covered deck below tumbling cliffs overlooking the surf, it has managed to be consistently competitive for more than a decade. Lunch offers light but creative dishes like corn-crusted calamari ($8.95) and oak leaf and roasted pumpkin salad ($8.95) and burgers ($10.95), while a typical four-course dinner menu might include tortilla soup, sea bass, rack of lamb, or pan-fried wahoo, and tangerine crème brûlée ($64, plus 15 percent service charge). No matter how scrumptious the food, it will always be eclipsed by the spectacular thunder of the surf and the glittering turquoise reefline just a few meters away.

Greg's Steakhouse (Port Royal Golf Club, 5 Port Royal Dr., off Middle Rd., tel. 441/234-6092, fax 441/234-6100, gregssteakhouse@ logic.bm, lunch 11 A.M.–4 P.M. daily, dinner 6:30–8:30 P.M. Tues.–Sun.) wins high praise for its T-bone, filet mignon, and New York strip from both visitors and locals. The menu also features specialties such as Bermuda fish chowder, pastas, and vegetarian dishes. Friday nights during the spring and summer are the most popular, thanks to the barbecue buffet and live music.

Fine Dining

Dating back to 1670, the historic **Waterlot Inn** (Fairmont Southampton Resort, Jews Bay, Middle Rd., tel. 441/239-6967, www.fairmont .com, dinner only 6–10 P.M. daily, jacket required) is a Bermuda landmark, beloved as much for its indulgent menu as for its resident ghost. Local lore says the spirit of pioneering owner Claudia Darrell still stalks the building that was home to generations of her seafaring ancestors, as well as a blacksmith shop and parish post office over the years. In the early 1900s, Darrell inherited the house and converted it into an English-style tavern where she befriended visiting celebrities like Mark Twain, Eugene O'Neill, James Thurber, and Eleanor Roosevelt, becoming something of an island legend. Hamilton's flags flew at half-mast when she died in 1949. Now owned by the Fairmont Southampton Resort, the harborside Waterlot remains steeped in history, its cedar beams, thick limestone walls, and low ceilings converted to intimate dining rooms. Patrons often arrive by boat, and nothing is more bucolic than sunset cocktails and dinner on Waterlot's dockside on a summer evening. Winner of the AAA Four Diamond Award for the past 11 years, Waterlot underwent a thorough up-

date in 2004, and its menu is now more in keeping with an upscale American steakhouse than a U.K. tavern. Vegetarians might think twice about dinner here; while the Caesar salads (prepared tableside, $14), oysters on the half shell ($18), and Bermuda onion soup ($10) may be scrumptious, the star of the show is the USDA steak, aged a minimum of three weeks. Tenderloin, strip loin, loin chop, Porterhouse, rib eye, and prime rib cuts ($28–57, side orders $8) are chef's specialties. Bermuda-style baked and stuffed spiny lobster ($60, in season) is also worth the steep price.

Long revered by gourmands, **[The Newport Room** (Fairmont Southampton Resort, 101 South Shore Rd., tel. 441/239-6964, www.fairmont.com, 6:30–10 P.M. daily, jacket required, tie suggested) is a Bermuda culinary icon—and the place for a serious proposal, anniversary, or deal clincher. In 2005, it won kudos for its refined menu and impeccable European-style silver service, with an upgrade to AAA Five Diamond Award status, becoming the only restaurant in Bermuda or the Caribbean to hold such distinction. Within its intimate navy and varnished-teak interior, bone china, and crystal, you'd be hard-pressed to believe you weren't in the dining room of a well-endowed private yacht. Named for the century-old Newport-Bermuda Ocean Race, the restaurant opened in 1972 with the hotel, whose then-owner, the late multi-billionaire Daniel Ludwig, was passionate about sailing.

The prix fixe menu (four courses $75, five courses $85, plus 15 percent gratuity) by chef Michael Scott draws heavily on seasonal produce from Bermuda's farms and ocean combined with en vogue imports. The result is a selection of elegant modern French dishes: Hudson Valley foie gras brûlée, porcini-dusted monkfish, Scottish langostines, tomato risotto and garlic froth, quail filled with boudin noir. The restaurant has partnered with uber-chef Terrance Brennan, owner of trendy Manhattan bistros Picholine and Artisanal and founder of the Artisanal Cheese Center in Hell's Kitchen, to bring in 15 handpicked varieties of cheese weekly. The Newport Room's cheese course

WARWICK & SOUTHAMPTON

now offers a sampler of three ($15) or six ($25) with quince jelly, fig loaf, fresh fruit, and nuts. Choose the side banquettes for maximum privacy and people-watching.

There's a $48-per-person seafood buffet every Friday evening at **Grill 56** (The Reefs, 56 South Shore Rd., tel. 441/238-0222, www.thereefs.com, lunch noon–3 P.M., dinner 6:30–8:45 P.M. daily, Sun. brunch noon–2 P.M.), the reinvented restaurant that opened at The Reefs in 2004. Its specialties the rest of the week are those of a true steakhouse (14-ounce New York sirloin, filet mignon, and grilled chops), yet it's a carefully crafted minimalist menu. Dinner entrées include Australian rack of lamb served with orzo, feta, mint and plum tomatoes ($32); grilled veal chop with Italian couscous ($38); or pan-roasted mahimahi on sweet potato mash ($19). Lunch is more relaxed, with favorites like the smoked salmon club ($11.75) and the Christian Bay fish sandwich ($12.75). The dining room is split between an interior high-ceilinged fireplace setting and a glass-fronted ocean view.

Tearooms

Tucked into a historic cottage at the foot of Gibbs Hill Lighthouse, the ◖ **Lighthouse Tearoom** (68 St. Anne's Rd., tel. 441/238 8679, www.lighthousetearoom.com) is a charming out-of-the-way addition to the island's restaurant scene—a must for romantics or anyone aching for homespun cooking. Owner and chef Heidi Cowen is the granddaughter of the last lighthouse-keeper before the structure turned electronic, and she spent much of her childhood living in what is now the restaurant. She has created a whimsical menu using fresh island produce and inventive combinations: starters like cream of pumpkin and banana soup with a splash of rum ($5.50) and portobello quesadillas ($8.75); entrées such as guava-glazed lamb lollipops ($25.75) and rockfish laced with Pernod ($24.75). Breakfast (9–11:30 A.M.) and lunch (until 4:45 P.M.) served daily; dinners are available on Friday and Saturday 6:30–8:30 P.M. (May–Sept.). Dinner seating is limited. Call for a reservation.

Grocery Stores

Heron Bay MarketPlace (Middle Rd. at Heron Bay, tel. 441/238-1993, 7 A.M.–10 P.M. Mon.–Sat., 1–5 P.M. Sun.) is one of the larger members of the MarketPlace chain, stocking a large array of foodstuffs fresh and unperishable, and including a bakery on-site. A small mall attached to the grocery has a pizza restaurant, a florist, and other retail outlets.

Markets

Organically grown fruit and vegetables, chickens, fresh eggs, and Bermuda honey make ◖ **Wadson's Farm Stand** (at the junction of Middle Rd. and the Railway Trail, opposite Whale Bay Rd.) a mecca for area residents and passing motorists. Farmer Tom Wadson hails from a centuries-old Bermudian family and now focuses his energies on all things organic; he supplies his sister Judith's award-winning Pitts Bay Road, Pembroke, restaurant, Aggie's Garden Café. The stand is open 3–6 P.M. Monday, Wednesday, and Friday and 8 A.M.–noon Saturday at the Bull's Head Farmers Market in Hamilton.

INFORMATION AND SERVICES

The parish has one mail-drop at **Southampton Post Office** (2 Church Rd., off Middle Rd., tel. 441/238-0253, 8 A.M.–5 P.M. Mon.–Fri.).

Parish gas stations include **Terceira's Port Royal Service Centre** (31 Middle Rd., tel. 441/234-0090), a busy outlet with pleasant staff that sells newspapers and basics, along with hot dogs, fresh pies, sodas, and fruit drinks. **Raynor's Shell Service Station** (217 Middle Rd., near Heron Bay, tel. 441/238-3492, 6:30 A.M.–9 P.M. Mon.–Sat.), a once-tiny service station with a few snacks sold from its cash register, was undergoing a complete face-lift in 2006, with plans to include a full convenience store.

ATMs are at Heron Bay MarketPlace, Middle Road; Wyndham Resort & Spa; and Terceira's Port Royal Service Centre, 31 Middle Road.

Public toilets are located at Horseshoe Bay, and at the major hotels, restaurants, and golf clubs. Portable toilets are at Warwick Long Bay and Church Bay.

GETTING THERE AND AROUND
Buses

Catch the No. 7 (Hamilton–Barnes Corner/Dockyard via South Shore) to get to the beaches or the lighthouse, or the No. 8 (Hamilton–Barnes Corner/Somerset via Middle Road) for points along the parish's harborside (buses on both routes run every 15 minutes most of the day). The fare to all points in the parish is $3.

Ferries

To encourage local commuters back in 2003, the fast ferry service Sea Express (tel. 441/295-4506, www.seaexpress.bm) initiated a stop at Rockaway, Southampton, accessible off Middle Road, opposite the Port Royal Golf Club, near the parish border with Sandys. Weekday service offers an express route (20 minutes) to Hamilton leaving Rockaway at 7:25 A.M. The evening's last ferry leaves Rockaway at 7:30 P.M. There is also 8:25 A.M.–6 P.M. Saturday service. The 4:30 P.M. ferry departing Rockaway Monday–Saturday loops into the West End and Dockyard before returning to Hamilton. Ferries depart Hamilton every 15 minutes at peak commuter times, every 90 minutes at other times (no service Sun.). The fare is $4 adults, $2 children 5–16, under five free (no cash or change accepted; tickets or tokens only).

Scooters

Oleander Cycles (Southampton branch, 8 Middle Rd., tel. 441/234-0629, 8:30 A.M.–5:30 P.M.) rents scooters for exploring the parish.

Taxis

Taxi stands are located at all the major resorts and are easily arranged to and from restaurants, but the logistics of catching cabs to the beach and back are more difficult, without prior arrangements. Buses are far more convenient.

WARWICK & SOUTHAMPTON

SANDYS PARISH

The distinctive "fishhook" of Bermuda is the island's charismatic West End, Sandys—an undulating patchwork of geography, in which the rugged South Shore coastline on one side and the mirror-like Great Sound bays on the other sandwich a rural bosom of onion fields, towering cedars, and loquat woods. The West End is all about peace and quiet; perhaps more than in any other parish, you can actually find loads of both here. Winding country lanes littered in oleander petals invite leisurely strolls past miles of red-earthed farms, avenued estates, and craggy islets where whalers once lived. You can watch old-time dinghies with billowing sails scoot across wide-open ocean or hang out with fishermen as they clean their catch in the afternoon. The fact that Sandys is so detached from the rest of Bermuda—a 40-minute drive from the bustle of Hamilton—lends serenity to any time spent in then parish. No wonder that a traveler would encounter places called Tranquillity Hill, Pinkhouse Lane, and Daisyfield Drive around here.

The parish name may conjure a delightful image of nonstop beaches—which wouldn't be deceiving—but Sandys (pronounced Sands) actually is derived from Sir Edwin Sandys, one of the colony's first Virginia Company investors. To keep your bearings, it helps to remember the parish comprises a string of five islands—plus a chunk of mainland bordering Southampton at Port Royal Golf Course—which curve around in an arc. That may help explain all those bridges you're crossing. From the west, the islands are: Ireland Island North, Ireland Island South, Boaz Island, Watford Island, and—the

© ROSEMARY JONES

HIGHLIGHTS

■ **Bermuda Maritime Museum:** The most visited Bermuda attraction, the museum is housed inside the tall ramparts of the six-acre Keep, the Royal Naval Dockyard's citadel. Learn about the island's sea-swept history through exhibits on ancient shipwrecks, pirates, the Royal Navy, and the story of trans-Atlantic slavery. Commissioner's House offers the island's best view (page 144).

■ **Bermuda Dinghy Races:** Somerset Village is the best place on the island to witness this hugely popular spectacle throughout the summer. Cute as a button, the pastel village on the shore of Mangrove Bay is itself worth a stop on a tour through Sandys, inviting languorous afternoons spent strolling its winding country lanes (page 154).

■ **Fort Scaur and Park:** Talk about lunch with a view! With panoramic views of the Great Sound and Dockyard, this fort and surrounding parkland make a great stop for a picnic or photo op. They also have access to the Railway Trail. Climb into the ditch leading from the 1870s fort right across Somerset Island (page 159).

■ **Hog Bay Park:** The island's third-largest park is a loner's paradise – 38 acres of trails through farmland, woods, and coastal scrub. A pristine beach pops up on the shoreline at low tide, and snorkelers can wade out hundreds of yards to inspect reefs and sea grass (page 160).

■ **Railway Trail:** Arguably the finest stretch of Bermuda's old railway bed to walk along is the section between the gates of the former

LOOK FOR ■ TO FIND RECOMMENDED SIGHTS, ACTIVITIES, DINING, AND LODGING.

U.S. Naval Air Station at Morgan's Island and Somerset Village. The trail's cool cut-limestone walls, backlane gardens, sweeping ocean views, and trails down to the rocky shoreline, where you can take a cooling dip, are unbeatable (page 161).

largest—Somerset Island, named for the English county. Somerset Island connects to the rest of the parish at its western tip via Somerset Bridge, the world's smallest drawbridge. Quaint Somerset Village is found on Somerset Island—a point of confusion when Bermudians talk about "Somerset." Sometimes, they may mean the village itself, but they could be referring to anything in the larger area. In fact,

many locals tend to call all addresses farther west than Somerset Bridge, including the other islands and Dockyard, Somerset.

Steeped in both early colonial and British military history, Sandys is historically important, as its stunning fortifications, military cemeteries, and cultural heritage museums will attest. It is also a nature-lover's destination, with two of Bermuda's most extensive

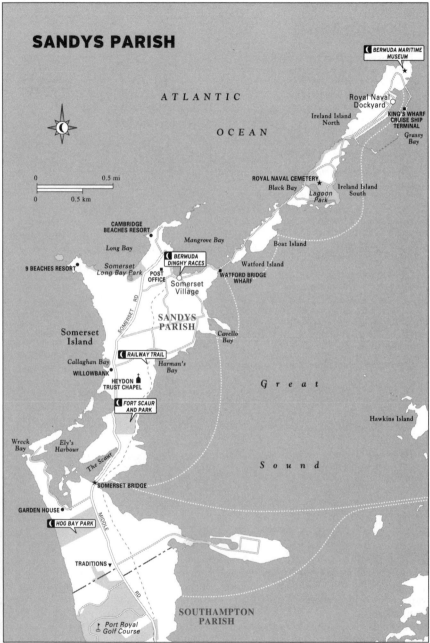

national parks, plus several smaller ones, dramatic coastal landscapes, and endless shallow reef systems you can spend full days exploring. Quintessential Bermudiana is everywhere here—in the village verandas, cricket matches, and cottage-fringed lanes, and in the cheerful homespun eateries you may choose to visit. Like the other parishes, it is not without its social troubles—gangs, drug-dealing, and graffiti are particularly overt on sections of the main road here where idle groups of young men hang out—but visitors are rarely bothered. The center of attention is the awesome Royal Naval Dockyard—an unbeatable combination of maritime endeavors, arts and crafts, beach fun, and hearty menus. Somerset Village, with its infectious lethargy, is a West End gem. The surrounding parish—including the old Railway Trail, whose Sandys stretch is one of the island's most scenic—should not be overlooked, either; with memorable sights, loads to do, accommodations, restaurants, and laid-back whimsy, it will entice you to linger just that little bit longer.

PLANNING YOUR TIME

Ferries are a highly recommended way to travel to the West End, particularly if your vacation is a short one. The fast-ferry fleet of Sea Express, launched over the past five years, has revolutionized access to the Dockyard and the way people visit the area, not to mention area residents' commute to work. The service, which zips between Hamilton and the Dockyard in a mere 20 minutes, has made it possible for visitors who might have previously skipped the West End to spend a few hours in Sandys. That said, while the Dockyard is a true gem, Sandys has so much more to see and experience (fast ferries, which carry scooters, also run to other points in the parish). If your schedule permits, I recommend a full day or two's excursions to its various nooks and crannies. For example, if it's utter relaxation you're after, you could easily spend an entire day at Hog Bay Park, hiking and then swimming or snorkeling at its pristine shoreline, where a little-known beach offers secluded beauty. Another more time-consuming

but worth-it adventure: forgo the high-speed (Hamilton-Dockyard direct) ferries and jump on the milk run instead. Ironclad veterans, including *Deliverance* and *Patience,* operate during the high season, chugging across the Sound from Hamilton to several stops along the Sandys shore, including Dockyard, and back—a 60–90 minute jaunt. Forgotten treasures, these old vessels will no doubt be retired before too long in favor of more of the air-conditioned hovercraft, but in the meantime, they stretch the enjoyment of a scenic ferry journey (and you can always disembark at Dockyard and take the speedy return to the city if you've had enough or are pinched for time).

In terms of must-see value, Dockyard rates at the top of the West End's offerings, worth a few hours at least. Next would be Somerset Village, with its charming shops, cafés, and backstreets, as well as the picturesque lanes leading off Mangrove Bay. Finally, if you have time to explore farther afield, the rest of the parish leading right up to the Southampton border is full of worthwhile sights and experiences—huge nature reserves (Hog Bay Park, Heydon Trust), one of the island's most scenic forts (Fort Scaur), ultra-Bermudian eateries (Traditions) and myriad water sports, from waterskiing to scuba on some of Bermuda's most interesting shipwrecks. Notably, the Sandys Railway Trail is a major highlight—one of the most scenic and peaceful stretches of the old rail bed–turned–walking route, running from George's Bay Lane, at the parish border with Southampton, all the way to the Somerset Police Station at Somerset Village, Mangrove Bay. Along the way, walkers or cyclists can enjoy bucolic residential neighborhoods, tracts of farmland, soccer pitches, and trails leading down to quiet docks and picnic areas on the Great Sound (the very best stretch is from Somerset Bridge westward).

Dockyard is perfect for a family visit, with enough sights, attractions, and eateries to appeal equally to toddlers or seniors. The Hamilton-Dockyard ferry run allows scooters on board, so it's easy to explore Dockyard on foot, then drive out to see Somerset Village and the rest of the parish. There are several different transport combos you might choose to get to Sandys, around the parish, and back. You could take a one-way ferry from Hamilton, then ride the bus or drive a scooter back through the parishes. The bus ride to Hamilton takes about an hour, with numerous stops included; if you're traveling by scooter, count on a half-hour to 45-minute journey to the city or central parishes. Or, take the bus or drive out via Harbour Road or the South Shore Beaches and ride the ferry back (driving both ways makes for a lot of scootering—unless you *really* want to. Another option would be to go by ferry, explore, then take a Dockyard bus as far as Somerset Bridge to catch the Green Route Sea Express back to Hamilton.

Middle Road is the main parish artery for vehicles, continuing from Southampton. Its name changes as it passes through Sandys: becoming Somerset Road after Somerset Bridge; Mangrove Bay Road at Mangrove Bay; Malabar Road after Watford Bridge; Cockburn Road until Cockburn's Cut; and finally one-way Pender Road to the Clock Tower buildings (Freeport Drive is the way out).

Royal Naval Dockyard

Like the old town of St. George in the East End, the Royal Naval Dockyard on Bermuda's western point is crucial to understanding what shaped the political and social history of Bermuda. It's also loads of fun to visit. The 24-acre area—the largest and best preserved of Bermuda's fortifications—is a working community with shops, restaurants, a marina, and working boatyards. It also embodies the fascinating maritime history of the island, including its 150-year Royal Navy connection. "Dockyard," as it's simply called by locals, sits on Ireland Island North, the westernmost of Sandys's five islands, its tip forming the entrance to the main shipping channel into the Great Sound. Towering stone pillars stand at its entrance on Pender Road, where the notorious Casemates Prison also looms, and thick limestone walls and ramparts edge the site. Dockyard's waterfront is a hive of activity, with ferries coming and going, cruise ships (the largest liners, including Panamax liners, dock here), a marina packed with yachts and other pleasure craft, and myriad marine businesses operating out of historic former military buildings. Public washrooms and ATMs are located in the distinctive **Clocktower Building,** air-conditioned home to a plethora of shops, a restaurant, and ice cream bar. A **Visitors Service** Bureau and useful convenience store are located across the central Camber on Dockyard Terrace, a few yards from the ferry stop. Buses are lined up outside Bermuda Maritime Museum for journeys back to Hamilton. Bear in mind that Dockyard's retail and restaurant businesses may operate on a more restricted schedule in the winter months, when cruise crowds disappear; call ahead to check opening and closing hours.

HISTORY

On the heels of America's successful revolution against Britain in 1783, Bermuda's role in the maritime geopolitics of the day suddenly gained new stature. With the loss of its chain of North American ports (other than Halifax), Britain urgently needed a winter anchorage and dockyard to supply and repair its fleet, in the event of war with America or France. It also needed to protect its political and trade interests in the Caribbean. Efforts were begun immediately to transform once-sleepy Bermuda into a "Gibraltar of the West," transforming the island into a well-fortified Western Atlantic British naval base and dockyard. Royal Engineers designed breakwaters, boat slips, barracks, wharves, a victualing yard, and a fortified Keep. Construction—including massive land reclamation—began in 1809 and continued

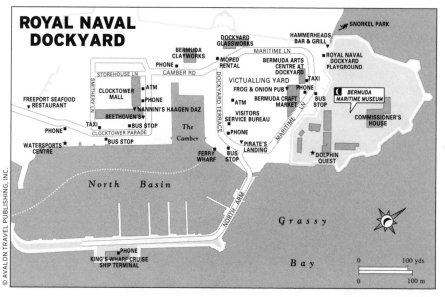

through to the 20th century. Initially, work was carried out by black slaves, but after Emancipation in 1834, Britain shipped over thousands of convict laborers from England and Ireland. Housed in converted warships called prison hulks off His Majesty's Dockyard, convicts quarried the region's hard limestone, and, block by hand-sawn block, built what eventually became a self-contained "Little England" of military barracks, a prison, a hospital, warehouses, and munitions storage buildings, encircled by massive bastions, gun placements, and ramparts.

The payoff was immediate for Britain. In the War of 1812 with the States, Britain launched its attack on Washington from the Bermuda Dockyard, its Ships of the Line successfully sacking and burning the city. Over the next century and a half, Dockyard's Grassy Bay anchorage and sheltered docks catered to Britain's greatest warships, which evolved from tall-masted men-of-war and ironclads armed with cannons to steam-driven dreadnoughts and diesel-turbine frigates bearing World War II torpedoes. The area also supported thousands of naval personnel and civilian staff.

The British operated an apprentice scheme at Dockyard in the 20th century, training a generation of Bermudians in the skilled trades of masonry, engineering, and electrics, some of whom are still alive today. The Royal Navy finally pulled up stakes in 1951, closing its operations at the Dockyard. The area became public land, but it was not until the 1970s and 1980s that a major renovation campaign transformed the Victorian military buildings into retail centers, restaurants, and artists' studios. Responsibility for the area now lies with the semipublic West End Development Corporation (WedCo), which plans, under a hoped-for long lease deal from government, to restore more of Dockyard's historic buildings, perhaps convert some for loft-living, and encourage further revitalization of the peninsula.

The Bermuda Maritime Museum, located in the six-acre fortress Keep at Dockyard's westernmost section, was opened in 1975. The museum's Commissioner's House, a landmark 1820s building made of limestone and prefabricated iron, was restored and finally opened in 2000 as a cultural heritage museum.

SANDYS

© ROSEMARY JONES

All things military and marine come together at Dockyard.

SIGHTS

The entire Dockyard, with its historic wharves and restored military buildings is an attraction unto itself—even without its shops and museum. Feel free to stroll around the whole area, where tourist attractions sit cheek by jowl with working boatyards, sail-makers, and marine service centers. Most of the shops and visitor services hug the waterfront, along Clocktower Parade, the Camber Road, Maritime Lane, and Dockyard Terrace. You can watch glassblowing demonstrations, see ceramics being fired, and watch a cedar craftsman work beauty from gnarled tree limbs. Walk out along **King's Wharf,** where scores of vessels, from fishing craft to private sailing and motor yachts, sit in a marina near giant cruise ships at the West End terminal throughout the April–November season. Opposite the entrance to Bermuda Maritime Museum is the 1831 **Cooperage,** a historic building where barrels for preserving foodstuffs in salt were manufactured. Today it houses the Frog & Onion Pub. Two forges are on display in the atrium by the cinema and

craft market. On the other side of the atrium lies the **Victualing Yard,** where high walls protected the Royal Naval fleet's food and drink from theft. Today, picnic benches by the wide-open lawns make it a good lunch spot.

◖ Bermuda Maritime Museum

Bermuda's largest and most-visited attraction, Bermuda Maritime Museum (tel. 441/234-1333, fax 441/234-1735, www.bmm.bm, 9:30 A.M.–5 P.M. daily, last admission 4 P.M., closed Christmas Day, $10 adults, $5 ages 5–15, under five free) combines a spectacular property with historic buildings and fascinating exhibits, artifacts, and cultural heritage displays. Its six acres of grounds lie within the "Keep," a stronghold built within the fortified Dockyard to protect the entire Dockyard against attack by land or sea (though it never had to). The citadel had seven bastions and ramparts, reinforced by casemated gun emplacements with lines of sight sweeping the Great Sound and North and South Shores.

Begin your tour on the lower grounds, where

SANDYS

SPIRIT OF BERMUDA

In the "Age of Sail," Bermudians were renowned for innovative methods of boatbuilding and their sailing prowess. A nonprofit group aims to rekindle those talents in a new generation of Bermudians. Based in Dockyard, the **Bermuda Sloop Foundation** (tel. 441/236-0383, www.bermudasloop.org) has spent much of the past decade raising funds to design and build an 85-foot (107 feet with bowsprit) sail-training schooner, which it hopes will inspire maritime interest in young Bermudians and also teach visitors about the island's proud past.

The design of *Spirit of Bermuda* is based on the rig of an actual vessel that sailed out of Bermuda in the mid-19th century. It features three heavily raked masts, the tallest in the middle, and a single boom on the mizzen. The main and foresail sheet like a jib, slightly overlapping the mast, and another jib is set forward on the schooner's long bowsprit. It has been adapted for safety reasons from the original Bermuda sloop design, which, while fast, challenged crews with its massive amount of sail – a huge, gaff-rigged mainsail and a square topsail.

By contrast, *Spirit*'s design is nimble but more akin to the "Bermudian schooner" hull whose design evolved into the modern yacht.

Noted for their speed and durability, cedar-made Bermuda sloops were the envy of the Atlantic maritime world throughout the 18th century, with many countries adapting the rig for their own use. Such sloops were used in trade throughout the Caribbean and North Atlantic, privateering, and illicit pirating; in fact, they were often captured by pirates who coveted their getaway abilities.

Spirit of Bermuda was launched in August 2006 from a boatyard in Rockport, Maine, for her inaugural journey to the island, where she will be docked outside the Clocktower and used as an expeditionary learning school for Bermudian teens. The ship will also be hired out for corporate teambuilding initiatives and private group charters (maximum 45 people). The Bermuda Sloop Foundation's headquarters on Camber Road, next to Bermuda Clayworks, will include a retail store selling maritime-themed books and gifts, and information on the ship and its mission.

seven historic buildings detail the island's maritime past and Royal Naval history. In the cavernous beauty of **Queen's Exhibition Hall,** where 4,860 kegs of gunpowder were once stored, exhibits trace Bermuda traditions such as whaling and piloting, and the story of Bermuda sloops, flying boats, and cruise ships like the beloved liner, *Queen of Bermuda.* The building's floor is made of nonsparking bitumen. In the facing Forster Cooper Building, Gibraltar of the West showcases the Royal Navy at Bermuda. Exhibits describe the creation of Dockyard, including the story of its convict laborers and the lives of the Royal Navy captains and crews who lived here.

The next-door Shifting House, where ordnance was shifted to and from naval vessels, today houses an interesting display about the *Sea Venture,* the ill-fated 1609 vessel that carried the first accidental colonists to Bermuda.

Included are 17th-century artifacts like bellarmine jars, coins, and candlesticks, excavated from the shipwreck site off Bermuda's East End. A cannon off the ship is here, along with a model of *Sea Venture.* Across the lawn is the **Boatloft,** where traditional Bermuda fitted dinghies are on display, along with other island craft. The famous pilot gig *Victory,* fully rigged, and the century-old racing yacht *Dainty* are prize maritime treasures. There are also exhibits on fishing and turtling in this building, distinguished by its clock tower. Children like to climb on the regal statue of Neptune, Greek god of the sea, out in the Keep Yard.

The crown jewel of the museum, however, is **Commissioner's House** on the upper grounds, the grand home of the Dockyard's civilian commissioner. It's a building unlike any other in Bermuda, and one, which—even if you're not interested in its exhibits—offers a spectacular

SANDYS

vantage point. From the top-floor wraparound veranda, the sweeping panorama of the entire Dockyard is revealed, as well as the glistening turquoise seascapes of both the North and South Shores. The world's first cast-iron building, its girders, red brick, and flagstones were shipped from England in the 1820s, while its three-foot-thick walls consist of hard limestone quarried from the Dockyard. Restored in a mammoth 20-year campaign, the building reopened in 2000 as a museum. Three floors of exhibits fill Commissioner's House, from rooms of rare Bermuda maps to those showcasing notes and coins, including historic Hogge money—the island's first currency. Other rooms on the first floor are dedicated to exhibits detailing topics of cultural and social importance: the trans-Atlantic slave trade and slavery in Bermuda; the Newport-Bermuda Ocean Race; and the stories of Portuguese and West Indian immigrants. The second floor's dining rooms pay tribute to the various military in Bermuda, with both the British Navy and U.S. Navy highlighted with photographs and artifacts. Take a look also at the stunning 36-seat dining table in the Commissioner's Room, once a wartime mess hall, which now houses a collection of contemporary maritime art on loan from the Bank of Bermuda Foundation.

Downstairs on the ground floor, a dozen interlocking rooms contain the exhibit Bermuda's Defence Heritage, detailing the story of local defense, from the forts and cannons of the 17th century through to Bermudian vets of World War II. Military uniforms, medals, and munitions vividly depict the role tiny Bermuda played on the world stage. A documentary film here includes interviews with local vets. There's also the story of women at war: the island's female military members who served overseas and the famous "Censorettes"—young Englishwomen headquartered at the Hamilton Princess Hotel who were trained to sift through incoming mail and telecommunications, checking for coded messages being sent to Germany.

A major player on the island's heritage protection scene, Bermuda Maritime Museum is also home to a conservation center, where artifacts found on local shipwrecks or terrestrial sites are preserved. The museum coordinates archaeological field trips and dives throughout the year with local historians and archaeologists and teams from visiting universities from Canada, the United States, and Britain. Books published by Bermuda Maritime Museum Press are sold in island bookstores.

Museum visitors can explore the historic windblown ramparts and gun placements around the Keep's perimeter, where Bermuda's only flock of sheep graze—natural lawnmowers for the property. Museum admission also allows you to view the dolphins of **Dolphin Quest** (see *Sports and Recreation*), located at the Keep Pond on the lower grounds.

Casemates Prison

Looming over the southern side of Dockyard is Casemates Prison, a former military barracks for Royal Marines built by convicts in the 1830s. The grim two-story structure is made of hard area limestone, its thick walls and vaulted roof built to sustain enemy cannon and mortar fire. When the British Navy left Dockyard in 1951, Casemates became the island's main prison for housing convicted criminals over the next four and a half decades. Casemates closed in 1995, when a new prison facility, Westgate, was built just outside the Dockyard gates on Pender Road. Casemates is not open to the public, but there have been talks about turning it into a museum, or even a hotel.

BEACHES

Run by Windjammer Watersports, which also operates out of Dockyard on the Great Sound side, **Snorkel Park** (31 Maritime Ln., tel. 441/234-6989) is the Dockyard's only beach. While, technically, the ocean is free, the park expects visitors to either rent its water sports equipment or eat and drink at Hammerheads, the on-site café and bar. As a result, those toting their own picnic lunches who hope to spend the day here will encounter some confrontation with staff. The park may even charge an admission fee in the future. The beach is small but clean, and its waters offer good snorkeling at the foot of Bermuda Maritime Museum's towering ramparts. Reef areas farther out in the shallow bay are great for snorkeling. Kids love the pontoons, which have small slides leading into the water. You can also rent noodles, pedal boats, and masks, snorkels, and fins. Snorkel Park has large bathrooms as well.

ENTERTAINMENT AND EVENTS
Cinema

Owned by Hamilton's Liberty Theatre group, **Neptune Theatre** (4 Maritime Ln., tel. 441/234-2923) is the West End's only cinema; it usually gets movies after they have shown at the Liberty. Friendly staff sell popcorn and candy, but don't expect IMAX-style professionalism here—sound and projection problems are often part of the experience.

Events

Launched in 1995, the **Bermuda Music Festival** (www.bermudatourism.com/musicfest, $60 general one-night admission, suites $300, three-day passes $160–270) has become one of the island's premier international events, highly popular with both Bermudians and overseas visitors who travel to the island for the three-day October showcase of top jazz, soul, and R&B performers. Joss Stone, Al Green, Patti LaBelle, and the Manhattans are just a few of the big-name acts who have wowed crowds in the alfresco Dockyard setting, which has bleachers and a stage erected next to the Camber waterfront. For tickets, call Ticket Web, tel. 866/666-8932, www.ticketweb.com. In Bermuda, tickets can be purchased at Sound Stage (Washington Mall, mezzanine level, Hamilton, tel. 441/292-0811, soundstage@northrock.bm).

Destination Dockyard is the West End equivalent to Hamilton's Harbour Nights, a street-festival extravaganza of food, outdoor arts and crafts, and live entertainment. Ferries lay on special service for the evening, and the Clocktower's shops stay open, too.

Nightlife

Islanders crowd into **Hammerheads** (Snorkel Park, 31 Maritime Ln., tel. 441/234-6989) for regular happy hours and beach parties throughout the summer months. Tuesday nights are the biggest draw, when Destination Dockyard brings scores of people to the West End. The bar is closed November–April.

Dockyard's problem child, **Club Malabar Nightclub & Lounge** (16 Freeport Rd., tel. 441/234-6199) has brought more trouble than fun to the West End, with an often unsavory crowd, accusations of gang attendance, and even stabbings. While there's a sad lack of nightlife in Dockyard, you'd be advised to skip this joint.

SHOPPING
Clocktower Mall

Clocktower Mall (open summer 9:30 A.M.–6 P.M. Mon.–Sat., 10 A.M.–5 P.M. Sun., winter 10 A.M.–5 P.M. daily) is the West End's main shopping center, with more—and busier—retail outlets than Somerset Village, particularly on weekends and during the cruise ship season, when the mall gets swamped with passengers. Note that many stores here keep shorter winter hours, as the Dockyard reverts to quiet maritime enterprises once cruise season is over—to shopkeepers' chagrin.

Beautiful kilim rugs, bags, and slippers from **Turkish Imports** (tel. 441/234-4646) are chosen by husband-and-wife team Bulent and Teresa Ganal.

Newcomer **Iana** (tel. 441/234-1194), which opened late in 2005, offers Euro-style panache to young fashionistas with its Italian-made clothing for girls and boys.

Gift-hunters love **Pulp & Circumstance** (tel. 441/234-1698), whose two Hamilton stores are hugely popular. Stocked with stationery, Kate Spade wallets, Jellycat soft toys, baby gifts, CDs, candlesticks, picture frames, and soaps and bath bombs, the Dockyard outlet is a gift to West Enders.

Bermuda Bookstore (tel. 441/234-4065) also opened an outlet here in 2005, offering a wide selection of Bermuda books, adult fiction and nonfiction, plus a good kids' books section.

Photographer Roland Skinner and artist Michael Swan have their own stores here.

SANDYS

© ROSEMARY JONES

Dockyard's Clocktower Mall is a Victorian masterpiece that today contains retail stores.

Skinner's **Picturesque** (tel. 441/234-3342, www.picturesquebermuda.com, 9 A.M.–5 P.M. Mon.–Sat.) sells Ilfochrome prints of his Bermuda images, from rustic cedar gates to beach scenes and sweeping aerials. The **Michael Swan Gallery** (tel. 441/234-3128, www .michaelswan.com) sells his distinctive airbrush art portraying abstract island snapshots, as well as a wide assortment of jewelry and other gift items and CDs.

Follow your nose to **The Littlest Drawbridge** (tel. 441/234-6214 or 441/335-8074, fax 441/236-0075, www.littlestdrawbridge.free. bm), where cedar trinkets and handmade gifts are a tribute to Bermuda's woodwork tradition.

West End branch stores of Front Street's **Makin' Waves, Cooper's, Crisson Jewellers,** and **Calypso** are also located here.

Camber Road

On Camber Road, just around the corner from the Clocktower Mall, **Bermuda Clayworks** (tel. 441/234-5116, fax 441/234-3136, www.bermudaclayworks.com, summer 9 A.M.–5 P.M. daily, winter 10 A.M.–4:30 P.M. Mon.–Sat., 11 A.M.–4:30 P.M. Sun.) has a floor full of bright ceramics for sale, and a worldwide shipping service so you don't have to lug breakables home. You can also paint your own piece in the shop's pottery studio (and pick it up a few days later after glazing).

You can watch free demonstrations at **Bermuda Glassworks** (tel. 441/234-4216, fax 441/234-3813, www.dockglass.com, 8 A.M.– 6 P.M. daily), where artists create beautiful art glass in the Venetian tradition. An adjoining retail gallery sells the rainbow of glassworks, which make elegant souvenirs and gifts, including Christmas ornaments. Next door, sample nine different flavors of the island's favorite dessert at the **Bermuda Rum Cake Company** (tel. 441/234-4216, fax 441/234-3813, www.bermudarumcakes.com, 8 A.M.– 6 P.M. daily). Varieties include black rum, rum swizzle, dark chocolate rum, and banana rum.

Maritime Lane

Opposite the entrance to the Bermuda Mar-

SANDYS

itime Museum the 20-year-old **Bermuda Craft Market** (4 Maritime Ln., tel. 441/234-3208, fax 441/234-0823, summer 9:30 A.M.–5 P.M., winter 10 A.M.–5 P.M.) is a cooperative selling the work of more than 60 artists, including cedar crafts, candles, Christmas ornaments, needlework, quilts, ceramics, and batiks. There's also a section full of rare Bermuda books (Bermudaphile treasures) and contemporary editions.

Next to the Craft Market, with a cherry-red English phone box outside, is **Bermuda Arts Centre** (tel. 441/234-2809, www.artbermuda.bm, 10 A.M.–5 P.M. daily, admission free, wheelchair-accessible), one of the key venues for showcasing island artists. Regular seasonal shows (art is for sale), as well as a retail store and six resident artists' studios give visitors a true sense of the vibrant local arts scene. One of Bermuda's best oil painters, popular Jonah Jones, keeps a studio here, as does renowned cedar craftsman Chesley Trott. Drop into his sweet-smelling workshop, where rough boughs lay ready for transformation into polished works of art. Trott, who also teaches in the prison system twice a week, has an impressive collection of cedar pull-toys, including crickets and frogs. A recent work is somewhat larger—an eight-foot totem pole, intricately carved with Bermudian icons, now on display in the Arrivals Hall of Bermuda International Airport.

SPORTS AND RECREATION
Water Sports

Located in the grounds of Bermuda Maritime Museum, **Dolphin Quest** (15 Maritime Ln., tel. 441/234-4464, fax 441/234-4992, www.dolphinquest.org, 9:30 A.M.–4:30 P.M., entrance included with museum admission $10 adults, $5 children 5–15, prepaid reservations admitted free) is part of a U.S.-based for-profit group that runs interactive dolphin encounter programs on the Big Island of Hawai'i, Oahu, Moorea, and Bermuda. Different programs are geared to various ages, including young children, and include programs where participants can get in the water and touch and swim with the boisterous mammals. The cost ranges

$125 (30 minutes) to $975 for family groups (maximum five). Reservations can be made two months in advance for the popular program and can be booked online via the Dolphin Quest website, or through its central reservations office (800/248-3316 or 540/687-8102).

Windjammer Watersports (Building 41, Freeport Rd., tel. 441/234-0250, windjammerbda@northrock.bm, closed Nov.–March) rents out Jet Skis, kayaks, sailboats (Lasers and Daysailers), motorboats (17-foot Powercats) able to accommodate six people, and Windsurfer boards by the hour, or for half- or full-day excursions around the Great Sound and Somerset area.

Skyrider Bermuda (Building 41, Freeport Rd., tel. 441/234-3019, skyriderbda@northrock.bm, closed Nov.–March) gives a maximum two passengers at a time an exhilarating bird's-eye view of the whole West End, hitched to a parasail towed by a speedboat. There's no age limit and no skills required for the adventure, which promises soft, dry takeoffs and landings.

Fishing

Captain Russell Young Jr.'s **Sea Wolfe Sportfishing Bermuda** (tel. 441/334-8353, seawolfe@sportfishbermuda.com, open March–Oct. only) offers charters aboard his renowned 43-foot Sportfisher, which departs from the Watersports Center at Dockyard (alternate pick-ups can be arranged). The boat is air-conditioned, with three fighting chairs and Penn and Shimano tackle and equipment for chasing the *really* big ones (blue marlin, yellowfin tuna, and wahoo). Rates, for a maximum of six people, are $850 half day, $1,250 full day, $1,550 deluxe full day, including unlimited hours, lunch and cocktails, or a tournament. Children must be seven or older. A $500 deposit is required, refundable in the event of bad weather or cancellation at least 10 days prior to the departure date. Water and sodas are provided on all trips.

For Kids

Dockyard's tiny-town sort of feel is just the right scale for kids. Getting there is half the fun. Depending on where you're starting from,

SANDYS

the Sea Express fast ferry from the Hamilton Ferry Terminal ($8 return adults, $4 children 5–16, under five free) is a blast, even for grown-up kids, darting across the breezy Great Sound with lots of boats, houses, and skylines to take in along the 20-minute ride.

At Dockyard, exit the ferry and head right, following the main road around to **Bermuda Maritime Museum,** where kids can learn loads about pirates, shipwrecks, and gold treasure in Bermuda waters over the centuries. The lower floor of **Commissioner's House** appeals to young museum-goers with its cave-like maze of interlocking rooms, where exhibits feature giant cannons, forts, and local soldiers from the 1600s to the 1900s. Upstairs, kids can admire sweeping views of the entire North Shore from the building's king-of-the-mountain upper balcony. Don't let them climb the railing!

Dolphin Quest (15 Maritime Ln., tel. 441/234-4464, www.dolphinquest.org) is located on the southern part of the lower grounds. The mutual appeal of dolphins and kids is adorable, and while actually swimming with the clever mammals is a wonderful experience, just watching them cavort in the Keep Pond is almost as much fun. It's free with admission to the museum.

Outside, to the right of the museum gates, is the **Dockyard Playground** (admission free), complete with pirate ship apparatus to scramble aboard, turn captain's wheels, and descend via a tunneled slide. There are swings, too. Kids can spend a good couple of hours here, except in the heat of summer when it's grilling by mid-morning. If they get too hot, there's a fountain designed perfectly for youngsters to get soaked in.

Through the adjacent gate is the **Snorkel Park** (31 Freeport Rd., tel. 441/234-6989, closed Nov.–March), a great little beach for kids, with tons of amenities and playthings. Rent a noodle, mask and snorkel, or floating chair, or swim out to the pontoons and climb up a slide to whoosh into the bay. Adults like the beachside bar, just a few meters from the water's edge. There are large washrooms and a café serving hot dogs, burgers, and other lunchtime staples sure to please waterlogged youngsters.

Alternatively, the **Frog & Onion** serves up hearty pub grub inside, or under umbrellas on the indoor terrace. There's a large games room in the back, with coin-operated video games and a pool table. If they save room for dessert, don't miss **Nannini's Haagen Dazs,** a popular ice-cream bar in the **Clocktower Mall.** Bermuda kids make Mom and Dad drive the length of the island just to come here for the two-scoop sugar cones, numerous rich flavors—and rainbow sprinkles.

Several new branch stores in the mall will be of interest to parents and kids: **Iana** stocks colorful, well-made Italian togs for girls and boys; **Pulp & Circumstance,** like its popular Hamilton outlets, has stuffed animals, baby gear, and gift items; and **Bermuda Bookstore** has great kids' books, like Julia Donaldson's *Gruffalo* series.

Finally (if they're still awake), **Neptune Cinema** occasionally shows children's matinees, mainly during midterm breaks and Easter and summer holidays. Get some popcorn and candy and relax in the air-conditioned interior, which is smaller than some home-theaters.

ACCOMMODATIONS

There are no visitor accommodations in the Royal Naval Dockyard, though the past few years have seen much talk about the need for a boutique hotel in the vicinity, and even suggestions that the menacing-looking Casemates Prison—Bermuda's answer to Alcatraz—be restored as a resort.

FOOD
Cafés and Pubs

Pub grub reigns at the popular **Frog & Onion Pub** (The Cooperage, Maritime Ln., tel. 441/234-2900, www.frogandonion.bm, lunch 11:30 A.M.–4 P.M., dinner 6–9:30 P.M. Mon.–Sat., lunch noon–4 P.M., dinner 5:30–9 P.M. Sun.), which serves fish 'n' chips, steaks, pizza, salads, meat pies, seafood, and lobster in season. It also offers Thursday night quiz challenges, Friday night carvery, seafood Saturdays, and kids activities on Sunday afternoons (magic shows, free ice cream, kids' menus).

Hammerheads Bar & Grill (Snorkel Park, 31 Maritime Ln., tel. 441/234-6989, 9 A.M.–5 P.M. daily, bar 11 A.M.–3 A.M. daily, closed Nov.–March) sells burgers, sandwiches, fries, snacks, cold drinks, and alcoholic beverages at this very popular beach park facility.

Fish sandwiches, fish cakes, fish 'n' chips— you get the picture, although **Freeport Seafood Restaurant** (1 Freeport Rd., just inside Dockyard's main gate, tel. 441/234-1692, fax 441/234-3605, 11:30 A.M.–10 P.M. daily) serves burgers and meat dishes, too.

They line up out the door all summer long for cold scoops of decadence from **Nannini's Haagen Dazs** (Clocktower Mall, tel. 441/234-2474, summer 9:30 A.M.–6 P.M. Mon.–Sat., 10 A.M.–5 P.M. Sun., winter 10 A.M.–5 P.M. Mon.–Sat., 11 A.M.–5 P.M. Sun.).

International

Swiss-run **C Beethoven's** (tel. 441/234-5009, breakfast 9–11:30 A.M., lunch 11:30 A.M.–3 P.M., afternoon tea 3–5 P.M. daily, dinner 6–9 P.M. Tues. and Thurs.–Sat. April–Oct. only) is located in non-fancy premises in the western corner of the Clocktower, but the tiny restaurant is by far the best in the West End. In fact, it's one of the island's standouts, thanks to sophisticated but well-priced lunch and dinner menus incorporating light tangy salads, fresh breads, innovative sandwiches and wraps, fish dinners, steaks, pastas, and rich desserts. Even the coffee is perfect.

Pirate's Landing (6 Dockyard Terrace, tel. 441/234-5151, lunch 11:30 A.M.–4 P.M., dinner 6–10 P.M. Mon.–Sat., noon–6 P.M. Sun.) serves up tasty pastas, steak dinners, fish 'n' chips, and sandwich specials, along with an impressive wine list, at a choice of alfresco benches on its front patio, air-conditioned seating inside, or on the back bar terrace.

INFORMATION AND SERVICES

Dockyard's **Visitors Service Bureau** (tel. 441/234-3824, 9 A.M.–5 P.M. daily) is conveniently located just across from the fast-ferry dock. Ferry and bus tickets, tokens, and passes

a typical British red phone box at Dockyard

© ROSEMARY JONES

are sold here, and staff can fill you in on all area sights and attractions.

You can find everything from fishing rods to lifejackets, cold drinks, and nonfiction at the packed little **Dockyard Store** (tel. 441/234-0300, 8 A.M.–6 P.M. daily).

For Internet access, there's **Swiss Connection** (Clocktower Mall, 5 Freeport Rd., tel. 441/234-6480, 9 A.M.–6 P.M. Mon.–Wed., 10 A.M.–6 P.M. Thurs.–Fri., 10 A.M.–6 P.M. Sat., 10 A.M.–5 P.M. Sun.), which has four PCs with T1 connections. Printing is $0.50 a page, or $1.25 in color. The store also offers reproduced images on mugs and T-shirts for sale.

ATMs are outside the western entrance to the Clocktower Mall, and on the other side of the Camber in a building near the Visitors Service Bureau on Dockyard Terrace.

Public toilets are located inside the Clocktower Mall, in a small building on Dockyard Terrace, outside Bermuda Craft Market,

SANDYS

© ROSEMARY JONES

The fast ferry offers a 20-minute ride from Hamilton to the West End.

inside the Bermuda Maritime Museum lower grounds, and on two upper floors of Commissioner's House.

GETTING THERE AND AROUND
Buses

Bus service to the Dockyard is efficient, frequent—and scenic if you take Route No. 7, which goes via the South Shore beaches (No. 8 also travels between Hamilton-Dockyard via Middle Road). Buses leave Hamilton every 15 minutes for the West End. The 14-zone journey ($4.50) takes about an hour. Bus stops are located in front of the Bermuda Maritime Museum and in front of the Clocktower Mall. For more information, contact the central terminal (tel. 441/292-3851, www.bermudabuses.com).

Ferries

The **Sea Express** (tel. 441/295-4506, www.sea express.bm) Blue Route operates regularly between Hamilton and Dockyard from 6:50 A.M.

to late at night on weekdays (last ferry leaves Hamilton at 11 P.M.), with less-frequent service on Saturdays, Sundays, and public holidays. The service runs at least once an hour, with more ferries in the morning and midday hours. Most runs are Hamilton-Dockyard direct (both ways). Along the way, see Front Street's facade; the lavish harborfront mansions of Pembroke's Fairylands and Point Shares neighborhoods; landmark Two-Rock Passage, where the liners come through; and the islands of the Great Sound. The breezy ride takes just 20 minutes; sit up on the sunny top deck (which gets sprayed with salt on very windy days), or escape the heat in the main air-conditioned cabin. The other option is to take one of the older breed of ferries for a leisurely, scenic ride out to stops at Cavello Bay, Watford Bridge, Boaz Island, then to Dockyard and back to Hamilton, a journey ranging 1–1.5 hours. The Sea Express Green Route runs from Hamilton to Somerset Bridge (also stopping at Rockaway, Southampton) all day long, except Sundays. Cash is not accepted on ferries; buy tokens, tickets, or cost-effective one-day or multiday passes from the Ferry Terminal or Visitors Service Bureau in Hamilton or Dockyard. Regular ferry fare to Dockyard is $4 adults, $2 children 5–16, under five free.

Scooters
Oleander Cycles (The Clocktower, Royal Naval Dockyard, tel. 441/234-2764, 8:30 A.M.–5:30 P.M. daily) rents single- and double-seater scooters.

Electric Bicycles
Easy Rider (tel. 441/777-3500, www.easyrider.bm) offers 2.5-hour tours ($65 per person) on its electric unisex bicycles, which make the pedaling a breeze—even up Bermuda's killer hills. The tours, launched in 2005, take partic-

ipants through Dockyard, around Ireland Island's Lagoon Park and Royal Naval Cemetery, to Somerset Village, on to the Railway Trail as far as the Heydon Trust, up to Fort Scaur, and on to Cavello Bay, where riders can hop on the ferry back to Dockyard. The tours have been geared to cruise passengers to date, with pick-ups at the King's Wharf Terminal, but owner Jay Anderson can accommodate other groups and individuals if they call in advance.

Tour Train
The Bermuda Train Company (6 Valley Rd., Paget, tel. 441/236-5972) offers an hour-long tour ($27) of Dockyard and nearby Lagoon Park aboard its colorful open-air mini-train in the high season. Reservations are suggested.

Somerset Village

So small, you might whiz right by it if you're not paying attention, Somerset Village is a quaint, historic little community hugging picturesque Mangrove Bay. Mangrove Bay Road slopes through it to Dockyard. Pastel storefronts, wooden verandas and the kind of old-time languor you thought the Internet had forever vanquished, make Somerset a relaxing little gem. Lanes like "Tween Walls," which run off on either side of Mangrove Bay Road, are worth strolling. Take a swim in the palm-fringed bay, like a mirror when the wind is

right, or from the public dock, where freight was once offloaded from ships onto horse-drawn carts here. Like Flatts Village, Somerset was a key maritime port for trade and boating around the island, in the days before roads and motorized vehicles linked the parishes. Illicit cargo was often taken to harbors like these to evade custom duties in Hamilton or St. George. Today, Somerset doesn't seem capable of such energy. Sample the several eateries, and mosey around the sleepy shops. As part of a West End tour, the village only takes

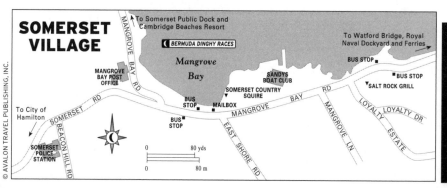

a few hours to soak in properly, though you might end up staying longer.

BEACHES

Mangrove Bay Beach, with its line of coconut palms and pile of wooden dinghies, is a slice of the way much of Bermuda used to be, and still is in these parts. Swim in the shallow, clear bay where schools of fry jump at dawn. There's plenty of parking in front of the post office.

ENTERTAINMENT AND EVENTS

"Anything but a boat" is the battle cry of participants vying for honors in Mangrove Bay's annual July **Non-Mariners Race** (tel. 441/236-3683). Organized by Sandys Boat Club, the Sunday afternoon affair features teams of Bermudians gussied up as pirates or in top hats, trying to sail across the bay in assorted craft made from anything you might least imagine had the ability to float. Needless to say, most end up in the drink. It's a laugh, for participants and the crowd of onlookers.

Nightlife

There's not much going on in Somerset, aside from lively bars at two village establishments, **Somerset Country Squire** (10 Mangrove Bay Rd., tel. 441/234-0105, 11 A.M.–1 A.M. daily) and **Salt Rock Grill** (27 Mangrove Bay Rd., tel. 441/234-4502, bar 441/234-4503, fax 441/234-4504, saltrockgrill@transact.bm, noon–1 A.M. daily).

SHOPPING

Dub City Records (23 Somerset Rd., tel. 441/234-3737, 10 A.M.–10 P.M.) opened a West End outlet in Somerset in 2006, offering the same good selection of reggae, soul, R&B, and urban hit music as its popular Court Street store.

Knowledgeable friendly staff people make shopping a delight at **Somerset Pharmacy** (49 Mangrove Bay Rd., tel. 441/234-2484, 8 A.M.– 6 P.M. Mon.–Fri., 8 A.M.–5 P.M. Sat., noon– 2 P.M. Sun.), which, aside from its dispensary and regular drugstore items, sells tourist items

such as postcards, towels, and souvenirs. But its best stock is the well-chosen toys, loads of them, for girls and boys of all ages, rivaling Hamilton stores of quadruple the size. Major-brand dolls, action figures, arts and crafts, balls, board games, baby toys—it's a child's heaven.

Genuine Bermuda linen-blend shorts (pink, yellow, red, $49) can be found at the Somerset branch store of **English Sports Shop** (Somerset Rd., tel. 441/234-0770, 9:30 A.M.–5 P.M.), along with linen and wool blazers ($199–225), Bermuda silk ties (sporting longtails, horse and carriages, and Hamilton's pastel skyline), and conservative women's fashions.

SPORTS AND RECREATION
◖ Bermuda Dinghy Races

Mangrove Bay and the nearby shoreline is one of the best vantage points to watch the Bermuda dinghy races. The much-loved tradition, featuring the island's trademark vessels vying for weekly honors amid mountains of sail and a flotilla of spectator boats, is one of the summer's highlights. Dinghy races are held every Sunday afternoon, alternating between different parts of Bermuda, namely St. George's Harbour, Granaway Deep in the Great Sound, and Mangrove Bay, where they sail from **Sandys Boat Club** (tel. 441/234-2248). The best part is when crew members jump overboard to lighten the load (they usually get rescued by passing friends or swim to raft-ups, where they can cheer on their boat with a beer or rum. Call the club for schedule details. Just around a few corners, on Watford Island, the **West End Sailboat Club** (tel. 441/234-1252, kitchen 441/234-2523) organizes the annual East-to-West Comet Race.

Water Sports

Take to the water in a kayak, sailboat, or motorboat from **Windjammer Watersports** (Cambridge Beaches Resort, reservations tel. 441/234-0250, windjammerbda@northrock. bm, closed Nov.–March), which offers rentals by the hour or the half and full day from this resort outlet. It's a perfect way to spend a day in the West End, because there are so many tiny coves, beaches, islands, and islets around this

Traditional Bermuda fitted dinghies race in Mangrove Bay through the summer.

part of the island. Pack a picnic and go exploring the reef-laden South Shore flats or around Mangrove Bay and the Great Sound coastline.

Fishing

Baxter's Reef Fishing (tel. 441/234-2963 or 441/234-9722, baxtersreef@northrock.bm) departs daily from Mangrove Bay public dock at the foot of Cambridge Road. Captain Michael Baxter's 32-foot Cape Islander, *Ellen B.,* offers half- and full-day reef-fishing charters, in which you can catch and release or take your fish home for dinner. Typical catches are chub, grouper, trigger fish, snapper, porgy, shark, and barracuda. The boat can accommodate up to 10 people.

Railway Trail

You can get on the Sandys Railway Trail just behind the Somerset Police Station. The trail runs through the parish, hugging the Great Sound shoreline through to Somerset Bridge—the most scenic stretch in Sandys, and possibly the whole island.

Spas

In 2006, Cambridge Beaches Resort took over operation of its property's **Ocean Spa** (30 Kings Point, tel. 441/234-3636, www.cambridgebeaches.com), whose seven rooms, with sauna, offer a full menu of face and body treatments for men and women, as well as massage therapy. A Marine Detoxifying Mask (70 minutes, $133), Bermuda Shorts cellulite treatment (60 minutes, $109) and Lift 'Yeux' Deluxe Facial (55 minutes, $121) allow clients to tap into the fountain of youth. Packages such as the full day spa ($419) allow use of the sauna, steam room, lockers, showers, robes, and slippers. Upstairs, Aquarian Baths, a luxurious indoor heated pool with retractable roof, is also available to spa clients. The daily admission fee for nonguests is $30.

For Kids

Children will enjoy the restful pace of Somerset, where they can take a swim, watch a dinghy race, or explore old-time lanes without keeping time. Check out **Somerset Pharmacy**'s

SANDYS

© ROSEMARY JONES

great toy selection, or nibble a macaroon from **Dean's Bakery.**

ACCOMMODATIONS
Over $300

Historic (**Cambridge Beaches** (30 Kings Point Rd., tel. 441/234-0331, toll-free 800/468-7300, fax 441/234-3352, www.cambridgebeaches.com, doubles from $430, no children under five) is one of the island's premier "cottage colonies," resorts in which cottage units are arranged around a central clubhouse, amid many other facilities. The five-star, 30-acre resort has 94 rooms, five private beaches, a putting green, a croquet lawn, tennis courts, a water sports center, two restaurants, two bars, and a spa. A new pool with an infinity edge and a waterfall feature was added in summer 2006. In the main house, a paneled library and stuffed floral sofas conjure the ambience of a grand English manse gone tropical. Old-style rooms and suites in cottages, or slick, recently added condo-style units overlooking Mangrove Bay, are furnished in an island-chic style—mahogany, sisal rugs, rattan, and bold florals leading the way. Amenities include cable TV, Internet hookups, air-conditioning, and king-size beds. Bette Midler, Kenny G., and Natalie Cole have all stayed here over the years.

FOOD
Cafés and Pubs

Tucked away in a concealed plaza on a treacherous bend, (**Dean's Bakery & Deli** (23 Somerset Rd., tel. 441/234-2918, 6 A.M.–6 P.M. Mon.–Sat.) is where locals go for Johnny Bread; chicken legs; beef, turkey, and veggie patties; and the baked goods which it now sells at grocery stores and gas stations throughout the island. The bakery, a 30-year institution, has a few tables inside, and sells sandwiches made with its famous fresh-baked bread. Parking is in the plaza.

Formerly Thel's Café, **The Purple Cow** (19 Somerset Rd., tel. 441/234-1767, 7 A.M.–9 P.M. daily) opened in April 2006 with a funky new interior and comfort-food menu dedicated

to all things bovine. The barstools are actually old milking cans, now sporting black and white spots, and the menu includes an appropriately violet Purple Cow milkshake, along with meatloaf, oxtail, seafood, chowder, burgers, and curried lamb.

Home turf of yachties and other neighborhood regulars, the **Somerset Country Squire** (10 Mangrove Bay Rd., tel. 441/234-0105, lunch 11:30 A.M.–4 P.M., dinner 6:30–9:30 P.M. daily) has a cave-like bar and dining room downstairs that's used throughout the winter, and an alfresco bar and terrace, where fish dinners, fresh lobster, burgers, steak and kidney pies, and filet mignon are popular fare all summer long. A children's menu is offered, too.

International

Somerset residents can't stay away from the (**Salt Rock Grill** (27 Mangrove Bay Rd., tel. 441/234-4502, bar 441/234-4503, fax 441/234-4504, saltrockgrill@transact.bm, lunch noon–3 P.M., light snacks 3–5 P.M., dinner 5:30–10 P.M. daily), where wide-open views of Mangrove Bay—and outstanding sushi—are the big crowd-pleasers. Indeed, even if they don't live nearby, boaters like to zoom across the Great Sound for summertime family brunches at this renovated establishment (formerly the historic Loyalty Inn). A full sushi and tempura bar serves appetizers like fried yellowtail and spicy tuna salad ($6–9), nigiri and sashimi, and six-piece maki mono rolls ($5.95–14.50). Pub fare includes chicken curry, beef pie, and the popular West End fish sandwich. Lamb, steak, and filet mignon grill, salads, grilled Bermuda tuna, and pastas are also well done.

Fine Dining

Candle-lit dinners are served in **The Tamarisk Room** at Cambridge Beaches Resort (30 Kings Point Rd., tel. 441/234-0331, toll-free 800/468-7300, fax 441/234-3352, www.cambridgebeaches.com, dinner only 7–9 P.M. daily), where cedar-steeped surroundings, dark coral walls, and silver service make for a formal treat. In the old Bermudian tradition, jacket and tie are invited, though no longer required attire for male guests. During the summer, meals are also served outside on the terrace, overlooking Mangrove Bay and the string of nearby islands. Chef Harald Klement's five-course menus change daily, along with recommended selections from the vintage wine cellar.

INFORMATION AND SERVICES

Mangrove Bay Post Office (55 Mangrove Bay Rd., tel. 441/234-0423, 8 A.M.–5 P.M. Mon.–Fri.) offers snail-mail and Internet service, under a new government initiative to bring technology to the public. It is the island's most picturesque post office, in a restored historic building a few feet from the sand of Mangrove Bay Beach.

Somerset Pharmacy (49 Mangrove Bay Rd., tel. 441/234-2484, 8 A.M.–6 P.M. Mon.–Fri., 8 A.M.–5 P.M. Sat., noon–2 P.M. Sun.) offers a dispensary and regular drugstore items, as well as postcards, beach towels, and lots of toys.

One of few independent pharmacies on the island, **Caesar's Pharmacy** (30-32 Somerset Rd., tel. 441/234-0851 or 441/234-0987, fax 441/234-0783) has an efficient dispensary and all the drugstore basics in its small store.

Somerset Police Station (3 Somerset Rd., atop the hill entering Mangrove Bay, tel. 441/234-1010 or 441/234-1011, sps@bps.bm)

is the regional detachment with responsibility for the West End.

Goslings Wines & Spirits (tel. 441/298-7338) stands at junction of Cambridge and Somerset Roads opposite Dean's Bakery on the way into the village.

Bud's Wines & Spirits (10 Mangrove Bay, tel. 441/234-1740, 8:30 A.M.–8 P.M. Mon.–Sat.), on the main village street, alongside the Somerset Country Squire, stocks ice, cigars, bait, beer, and wine.

ATMs are located outside both Butterfield Bank and Bank of Bermuda HSBC branches in the village.

Public toilets are at Mangrove Bay Post Office and next to Somerset Police Station. Dean's Bakery & Deli has restrooms for customers.

GETTING THERE AND AROUND

Buses Nos. 7 and 8, which travel every 15 minutes between Hamilton and Dockyard, service the village.

The Watford Bridge stop is the closest to Somerset Village, served by the Sea Express Blue Route **ferries** with scheduled stops within every two hours throughout the day. The adult fare is $4 one-way (tokens or tickets required, no cash or change accepted).

Oleander Cycles has an outlet at Cambridge Beaches Resort (30 Kings Point Rd., tel. 441/234-0331), renting single-and double-seat scooters.

SANDYS

Around Sandys

The environs of Somerset Village and points east as far as the Southampton border encompass a wonderful array of places to let time evaporate. Swim at the countless little coves, hike the several beautiful parks, ogle spectacular ocean views on both shores—and let the hours slide easily by. The region is best seen in a flexible time-frame; even a day's tooling around on moped or walking the Railway Trail will give you a truer sense of real life "out West."

SIGHTS
Lagoon Park and the Royal Naval Cemetery

Beyond Dockyard's gates and over one-vehicle-wide Grey's Bridge on Ireland Island South is Lagoon Park (open sunrise to sunset daily, admission free), a large, quiet chunk of parkland that has a spectacular islet-sprinkled coastline on the Great Sound. Named for the central lagoon, which attracts birdlife, insects, toads, and frogs,

the park has lots of picnic tables and grassy lawns, as well as coves and bays for swimming. Nestled alongside the parkland is a large meadowed valley that contains the Royal Naval Cemetery. The early 19th-century graveyard contains intriguing headstones and above-ground cemetery plots, where the lives (and often sorry deaths) of naval officers, crewmen, and their families were honored with touching inscriptions. Easter lilies pop up here around Easter, and wildflowers are scattered over the hillside.

Somerset Long Bay Park

Lovely Somerset Long Bay Park and Nature Reserve (Daniel's Head Rd., off Cambridge Rd., open sunrise to sunset daily, admission free) is co-owned by the Bermuda National Trust and the Bermuda Audubon Society, a coastal mangrove area that is a sanctuary for resident and migratory birds. A plot of adjoining private land was recently purchased to expand the protected

The world's smallest drawbridge can be found on Somerset Island.

© ROSEMARY JONES

zone, which now includes a stretch of pristine coastline. Plans are in the works to restore the reserve by culling invasive species and replanting endemics, as well as clearing garbage and debris. Located on a quiet stretch far from the noise of main road traffic, the grassy park is a shady place to relax, and the shallow beach, with turtle grass and reefs just a few yards out, is a good spot for snorkeling. It's a popular local beach, too; Bermudian families congregate here for picnics, swimming, and games throughout the summer.

Somerset Bridge

The smallest drawbridge in the world, Somerset Bridge has become a quintessential Bermuda icon, featured on postcards and the island's banknotes for almost a century. The bridge's central plank can be raised, an opening just wide enough to permit a yacht's mast to be eased through by someone standing above, thereby allowing vessels to pass between the Great Sound and Ely's Harbour (though this is a rare occurrence in modern times). Built in the 17th century, the structure is one of the most historic points in the parish, connecting Somerset Island to the mainland.

◖ Fort Scaur and Park

One of the loveliest views can be had from a quiet bench atop Fort Scaur (Scaur Hill, Somerset Rd., open sunrise to sunset daily, admission free), overlooking the whole Great Sound and Dockyard. A telescope allows you to see as far Fort St. Catherine and St. David's Lighthouse. The West End fort and its surrounding 22 acres of parklands are one of the island's most scenic and well-preserved fortifications. Built in the 1870s, the fort was intended to guard the crossing at Somerset Bridge—and thereby protect against a landward approach by an enemy toward the Dockyard. It was used through the 1920s; later the American 52nd Coast Artillery mounted two eight-inch railway guns at Scaur Park. The fort, with ramparts, cannons, and gun placements, is surrounded by a defensive ditch, which extends across the length of Somerset Island. There is a steep trail leading east-

BUY BACK BERMUDA

A Somerset Long Bay property was the lightning rod for a populist campaign to win back open space for Bermudians.

Bermuda National Trust and Bermuda Audubon Society joined forces in the fall of 2004 to launch the "Buy Back Bermuda" campaign, an effort to inspire Bermudians to fight for land that would otherwise fall into the hands of developers – an all-too-common scenario amid the island's ultra-hot real estate market. When a three-acre Sandys property was made available by its owner for a friendly price of $1.7 million – half what it might have won on the open market – Bermudians rallied to raise the money. The land lay next to Somerset Long Bay, an Audubon nature reserve and national park, and its addition would protect the length of the shoreline, creating a public park of almost 10 acres.

In less than a year, the campaign had achieved its goal – and sparked such grassroots enthusiasm that organizers set about looking for other sensitive properties to target under the Buy Back banner. More than 400 people, including schoolchildren, took part in the drive. "We believe it shows the high value Bermudians put on preserving open space," said a Trust spokesman, adding that an ensuing cleanup and restoration plan, including fencing and planting of endemic flora, aimed to make the site an important nature reserve and bird sanctuary in the future.

ward through the woods to the Railway Trail on the shoreline below. You can also walk into the hillside flanking galleries and go through the sally port into the ditch—an impressive feat of engineering. Picnic tables and lawns invite relaxation in the adjoining park.

A property on the left as you descend the other side of Scaur Hill, heading out of the West End, is **The Parapet,** the mustard-colored home where artist Georgia O'Keeffe stayed during her visit to Bermuda in the early 20th century. O'Keeffe was recovering from depression at the time, but her charcoal drawings of a banyan tree and banana flowers helped restore her creative energies.

Heydon Trust Estate

Open to the public, the private Heydon Trust Estate (Heydon Dr., off Somerset Rd., opposite Willowbank Resort, open sunrise to sunset daily, admission free) is a natural enclave of protected woodland, farmers' fields, a couple of private homes, and the charming **Heydon Chapel** atop the hill. Turn in off the main road and follow the country lane all the way to the tiny whitewashed building, which overlooks the Great Sound. It dates back to a 1616 survey of Bermuda, and today it is still used for religious services. Nearby, a walled rose garden contains numerous chinas, teas, and mystery species, one of Bermuda's best collections. There are also trails rambling through the extensive cherry forests around the property. The land is a noted birding location.

◖ Hog Bay Park

One of Bermuda's most spectacular wild parks, government-owned Hog Bay Park (open sunrise to sunset daily, admission free) comprises some 38 acres of open space, leading from a roadside carpark on Middle Road to the coast. Between, there are undulating, shady dirt trails leading past an ancient lime kiln near the entrance, then rising past numerous tracts of agricultural fields and cherry, loquat, and spice tree forests, before descending to serpentine seaside trails past prickly pears and the silvery skeletons of Bermuda cedars. While it is Bermuda's third-largest park, and one of its most untamed, Hog Bay is underused; you can find remarkable solitude exploring it in any season, though because of the steep hills, you need to be fairly fit. Follow the main trail down to the shoreline, where there's a tiny beach at low tide, and a beautiful area for swimming. Sea grass attracts turtles here, and rock pools contain crabs and sergeant majors. You can actually explore a long section of the coastline here, with the wide-open horizon of the South Shore flats stretching out as far as

you can see. At low tide, the shallows extend some 300 meters, good for snorkeling.

The park, which is used occasionally for cross-country races and mountain-biking, is named for Bermuda's wild hogs, which were roaming the island when the first settlers arrived in the early 17th century. It's believed passing mariners in previous years had offloaded the animals to multiply and create a natural larder at Bermuda to serve castaways wrecked on the island's treacherous reefs. The former Hog Bay, where settlers found a large herd of the swine in the West End, is now called Pilchard Bay.

BEACHES

Somerset Long Bay is a perfect place to cool out, far from traffic or the crowds who frequent the larger South Shore beaches (including Warwick Long Bay) most weekdays. On weekends or public holidays, Somerset Long Bay sees lots of local families come for picnics and swimming.

Black Bay on Ireland Island South, opposite the Royal Naval Cemetery, has a gem of a beach that appears only at low tide. Night herons can sometimes be seen standing like statues on the coastal rocks—until they dart for crabs in the shoreline rock pools. It's a good place for a shallow, calm swim throughout most of the summer, and there are picnic tables, too.

ENTERTAINMENT AND EVENTS
Cup Match

Thousands pour into Sandys every other summer for the cricket showdown and carnival atmosphere of Cup Match. The island's favorite holiday sees club teams from both ends of the island, St. George's and Somerset, meet for a two-day contest, held in alternate years at each club's headquarters. The **Somerset Cricket Club** (6 Cricket Ln., tel. 441/234-0327) sports its team colors (red and blue) to welcome the masses, who fill bleachers and camp out with enough supplies to support the 48-hour hoedown. Gambling, in the form of Crown & Anchor game tables, is legalized for the occasion and tens of thousands of dollars change hands—along with gallons of rum and other spirits. Amid the blazing heat, Cup Match draws everyone from politicians to schoolchildren to celebrate the century-old festival.

SPORTS AND RECREATION
Water Sports

Blue Water Divers & Watersports (Robertson's Marina, Somerset Bridge, tel. 441/234-1034, www.divebermuda.com) has been leading dive expeditions for more than 30 years. Their qualified guides lead a two-tank dive ($100), which departs at 9 A.M. daily, followed by a one-tank dive ($65) in the afternoon. Scuba enthusiasts often want to do both, with a soup lunch at the marina in between. Dive packages can also be arranged (five two-tank dives, or 10 dives, $400). There are numerous interesting wrecks, many in shallow reef-laden waters, off the West End, including the 1881 *North Carolina,* the 1943 *Hermes,* and the *Maria Celestia,* a U.S. Civil War blockade-runner that sank in 1864 (the vessel's paddlewheels remain intact).

Somerset Bridge Watersports (Mangrove Marina, Somerset Bridge, tel. 441/234-0914) rents Boston Whaler motorboats and personal watercraft by the half and full day, great for exploring the West End by water.

Bermuda Waterski Centre (Mangrove Marina, Somerset Bridge, tel. 441/234-3354, open May–Sept.) is run by Bermudian uber-athlete Kent Richardson, an accomplished triathlete and expert skier. He gives group or individual lessons aboard his Ski Nautique in the Great Sound or off the West End, depending on the weather. Lessons are $40 for 15 minutes, $120 for an hour-long session.

Surfshack at 9 Beaches Resort (tel. 441/239-2999, www.9beaches.com) is the newest addition to the West End's water sports scene—and now the largest such facility. The water sports center boasts kiteboarding, windsurfing, kayaking, motorboat rentals, personal watercraft, sailboats, snorkeling gear, rafts, pedal boats, and floating lounges. Located off Daniel's Head, a stunning peninsula with, yes, nine beaches, the area has shallow bays and crystal-clear water perfect for any of these activities.

◖ Railway Trail

The Railway Trail in outer Sandys Parish is one of the nicer stretches to walk, with a flat shady trail passing farmlands, residential neighborhoods, forts, and dramatic seascapes. Get on at George's Bay Road (at the former U.S. Naval Air Station Annex; the trail leads all the way to Mangrove Bay, with wonderful views of the Great Sound, and tributaries that allow you to break off and visit sights along the way, like Fort Scaur. Be careful of locals on speeding motorbikes along the tarmac sections; while the trail is supposed to be off-limits to motorized traffic, residents are allowed access, but many take advantage of that loophole to break the speed limit away from the main road.

ACCOMMODATIONS

Accommodations in Sandys are few, but varied. Coming soon in the upscale department is **Sanctuary Spa and Resort** on the former Lantana property. The development, slated for a 2007 opening, plans a wellness center, spa suites, private residences, and beachfront villas, as well as a marina and yacht club. The sprawling waterfront property used to be a favorite place for Bermudians to pull up in their yachts for an alfresco lunch.

$100-200

Garden House (4 Middle Rd., tel. 441/234-1435, fax 441/234-3006) is a true gem, tucked up a limestone drive just footsteps south of Somerset Bridge. Owned by Rosanne Galloway, two studio units ($75 and $115 doubles) are attached to the main house in a wing that was once the three-acre property's coach house and stables. Each has a private bathroom—one with a bathtub, the other with a shower—and full kitchens. A separate one-bedroom cottage ($125 doubles) sits among citrus groves. Manicured gardens surround the home, which also has a pool. Persian carpets, antiques, TV, and private phone lines make guests feel quite at home.

With its cedar interiors, traditional moongates, and mature gardens, **Willowbank** (126 Somerset Rd., tel. 441/234-1616, toll-free

SANDYS

from the U.S. 800/752-8493, fax 441/234-3373, www.willowbank.bm, high season rates $139–177 per person double occupancy, with breakfast, afternoon tea, and dinner included) somehow manages to create an oasis of peace beside the very busy main road. The 45-year-old cottage colony was created by a group of nondenominational Christian businessmen who hoped to offer guests a respite from the stresses of regular life. Today, the nine-acre resort retains a religious aura, with daily prayer sessions, lectures, and grace said before dinner in the "Loaves and Fishes" Dining Room. It is popular with church groups, but nonreligious guests are also welcome. A choice of ocean, pool, or garden views from the 67 no-frills units affords a range of prices. Amenities include air-conditioning, private bathroom, hair dryers, coffee pots, and small refrigerators. The main clubhouse is an elegant Bermudian homestead, its open-beamed lounge boasting cedar beams, an old library, and since the fall of 2005, a quaint tearoom. The property also has a heated swimming pool, two tennis courts, a private dock, and a couple of beaches on the Ely's Harbour coastline.

$200-300

Owned by the multi-award-winning operators of The Reefs Resort in Southampton, **9 Beaches** (4 Daniel's Head Ln., tel. 441/232-6655, toll-free 866/841-9009, fax 441/232-6634, www.9beaches.com, cabanas $240–375, children 15 and under stay free) opened in 2005 on a divinely beautiful peninsula called Daniel's Head. Once the base of the Canadian military in Bermuda, the 18-acre waterfront property lay deserted for years until another cabana-style hotel group took it over for a short spell but eventually closed. 9 Beaches sells itself as a different kind of Bermudian holiday, where you can wear flip-flops and thumb your nose at stuffy formality. Critics argue prices should correspond or five-star amenities be offered. Still, you can't beat the location. The resort's 84 cabanas are picturesquely situated on stilts, scattered over bluffs and coves with unobstructed views of the ocean; some huts actually stand over the water, connected to land by boardwalks, and have innovative Plexiglas

floors so guests can watch the reef fish swim by. The cabanas' walls and roofs are made of canvas, but somehow all managed to survive Hurricane Fabian. With interiors by designer Lynn Wilson, each cabana has a small bathroom with shower, queen-size bed, a futon sofa, table and chairs, and mini veranda. A cooler, hair dryer, and beach towels are supplied. Air-conditioning was installed for the 2006 season to ease the torpor of summer, even though the cabanas catch the sea breezes. The property also has a large residential building for family rentals: the two-story, three-bedroom Commander's House ($799 per night, or $2,999 weekly).

FOOD
Cafés and Pubs

It doesn't get more Bermudian than **C Traditions** (2 Middle Rd., tel. 441/234-3770, 6 A.M.–8 P.M. Mon.–Thurs., 6 A.M.–9 P.M. Fri. and Sat.), a roadside restaurant that draws local farmers, retirees, neighborhood residents, and passing motorists. Some sit at the diner-like bar to chat with kitchen staff; tables are set out in three other rooms. The menu, as its name suggests, offers island staples like homemade red bean soup, as well as delicious burgers and sandwiches. If you come here more than once, the friendly staff will remember you.

Tucked behind the legendary Somerset Cricket Club (home of Cup Match every other year), **Shabazz Bakery & Deli** (15 Cricket Ln., tel. 441/234-1601, 11 A.M.–6 P.M. Mon.–Thurs., 11 A.M.–7 P.M. Fri. and Sat.) is famous for its sweet yellow pound cake, for which islanders come from all over. Baked goods, including gigantic birthday cakes and cherry nut loaf cakes, are the main line of business, but the shop also serves up delicious trays of hot dishes, including fish dinners, broasted chicken, fish boats (fish in wheat rolls), soups, and curries. Locals line up out the door at lunchtime. The bakery is run by Bermudian Muslims who follow the Farrakhan ministry. Copies of his *Final Call* newspaper are available inside.

Gloria's Kitchen at West End Sailboat Club (Watford Island, tel. 441/234-1252, 10 A.M.–3 P.M. Mon.–Fri.) serves up loads of fresh fish, plus chicken salads and peas 'n' rice, among other daily dishes.

Standing on the edge of a harborside inlet where convict laborers were once held in jails, popular local watering hole **Woody's Drive-In Two Bar & Restaurant** (1 Boaz Island, tel. 441/234-2082, restaurant 441/234-6526, 10 A.M.–6 P.M. daily) offers typical Bermudian comfort food. Most popular are its fish cakes and burgers.

Takeout
Formerly Four-Star Pizza, **The Upper Crust** (65 Somerset Rd., tel. 441/234-2626, 7 A.M.–11 P.M. Mon.–Thurs., 7 A.M.–midnight Fri. and Sat., 7 A.M.–10 P.M. Sun.) has expanded the menu somewhat to incorporate subs, wraps, Indian curries, and Asian rice dishes, in addition to the popular pizza.

International
Flip-flop casual is the vibe at **Hi Tide**, a new restaurant for the West End opened on the 9 Beaches Resort (tel. 441/232-6655, www.9beaches.com, 6:30–10 P.M. Tues.–Sun.). Szechuan pumpkin soup, beef tenderloin ravioli, seafood ragout, pan-seared yellowtail snapper, and wild berries with raspberry granita are some of the delightful gastronomic concoctions whipped up by the resort's celebrity chef, John Pritchard.

Tearooms
Doilies and clotted cream, china dolls and Princess Di trinkets…. If the sun weren't blazing down and mopeds whizzing past outside, you could easily think you were deep in the English countryside once you step into **(Mrs. T's Victorian Tearoom** (Willowbank, 126 Somerset Rd., tel. 441/234-1374, noon–5 P.M. Tues.–Sun., except holidays). Relocated to Willowbank in late 2005, the tearoom had enjoyed huge success for several years on Middle Road in Southampton. When owner-manager Penny Terceira decided to retire and close up shop, Willowbank incorporated the beloved tearoom—along with much of the memorabilia and collectibles—in a converted library, where the eatery now looks perfectly at home alongside cedar furniture and a quaint old bread oven. Homespun soups, salads, sandwiches, quiches, fish cakes, and, of course, scones and tea remain highlights of the menu. Meals are served on a delightfully mixed array of china, also part of Terceira's collection, adding to the dollhouse-like surroundings.

Grocery Stores
The aroma of fried chicken draws folks to the **Somerset MarketPlace** (48 Somerset Rd., tel. 441/234-0626, 8 A.M.–10 P.M. Mon.–Sat., 1–5 P.M. Sun.), the largest area grocery store and part of an islandwide chain. President's Choice products from Canada are sold, among a full array of frozen and dry goods; wines, beer, and spirits; and dairy, meat, and deli products.

Arnold's Supermarket (41 Somerset Rd., tel. 441/234-2237, 7 A.M.–10 P.M. Mon.–Sat., 7 A.M.–midnight Sun.) sits just down the road east of MarketPlace but offers a much smaller selection of goods. The next-door **Arnold's Liquor Store** (tel. 441/234-0963) does a roaring trade.

Maximart (42 Middle Rd., tel. 441/234-1940, 6:30 A.M.–midnight Mon.–Sat., 7 A.M.–5 P.M. Sun.) is a small modern supermarket, owned by the Arnold's group. It has lots of parking and all the basics, including fresh fruits and vegetables.

INFORMATION AND SERVICES
Robinson's Marina Shell Station (176 Main Rd., at Somerset Bridge, tel. 441/234-0709, 7 A.M.–10 P.M. Mon.–Thurs. and Sun., 7 A.M.–10:30 P.M. Fri. and Sat.) is a year-round hub of visitor and local activity. The small station shop cooks up a cauldron of fish chowder daily, plus other soups such as chicken barley and vegetable. It also sells shades, fishing supplies, cold drinks, and snacks. The plaza outside is home to several water sports outfitters and deep-sea fishing operations, and the dockside is also used by area anglers.

The line-ups at **Boaz Island Shell Station** (28 Malabar Rd., tel. 441/234-0128) are for the Transport Control Department's special vehicle licensing satellite program for the

West End. The small shop sells cold drinks, cookies, potato chips, and some canned goods. There is also a marine station behind on the waterfront for boat fuel refills (tel. 441/235-2794).

Sandys Esso Service Station (37 Somerset Rd., tel. 441/234-1542) is a handy little outlet on the main road into the West End.

Sandys Hardware (66 Main Rd., tel. 441/234-1448) also sits on the main drag leading through the parish. There is usually a lawnmower or two outside.

Two laundries within a half mile of each other are **Sandys Laundromat** (at the MarketPlace Plaza, off the main road, tel. 441/238-9455) and **Somerset Laundromat** (57 Middle Rd., tel. 441/234-3361).

Somerset Bridge Wharf Post Office (1 Middle Rd., tel. 441/234-0220) is located on the roadside tucked against the waterfront. It backs onto a scenic point on the Sandys Railways Trail.

ATMs are located outside Maximart and Somerset Marketplace grocery stores.

Public toilets are located at Hog Bay Park and at area gas stations and restaurants.

GETTING THERE AND AROUND
Buses
Buses Nos. 7 and 8 run via Middle Road through Sandys every 15 minutes through-out the day, with the first bus leaving Hamilton at 7 A.M. and the last departing Dockyard at 10:20 P.M. Monday–Friday, first bus at 9:30 A.M. and last departing Dockyard at 11:59 P.M. on Saturday. Sunday and public holidays schedules run every half hour 9:30 A.M.–6 P.M.

Ferries
The **Sea Express** (tel. 441/295-4506, www.seaexpress.bm) Blue Route runs between Hamilton and Watford Bridge and Cavello Bay, as well as Dockyard, several times a day. While Dockyard service operates every hour, ferries travel to Watford Bridge and Cavello Bay less frequently (with gaps of two hours or more) between commuter periods. The Green Route runs from Hamilton to Somerset Bridge (also stopping at Rockaway, Southampton) all day long, except Sundays. Ferries depart Hamilton every 15 minutes at peak commuter times, every 90 minutes at other times (no service Sun.). Fare is $4 adults, $2 children 5–16, under five free (no cash or change accepted; tickets or tokens only). The 4 P.M. daily ferry also stops in at Dockyard.

Taxis
Sandys Taxi Company (Hook & Ladder Ln., tel. 441/234-2344) is conveniently based in the West End, meaning a faster pick-up in most cases.

SMITH'S AND HAMILTON PARISHES

Stamped with some of Bermuda's most rugged scenery, Smith's and Hamilton Parishes will appeal to outdoors enthusiasts seeking Bermuda's less-manicured face, as well as history buffs, birders, naturalists, and beachgoers. Families with children will find plenty to entertain youngsters, from caves and beaches to playgrounds and the island's only aquarium and zoo.

Two beautiful bodies of water shape the contours of these parishes—Harrington Sound and Castle Harbour. Each is ringed by stunning homes, often hidden from the main road, and a honeycomb of limestone caves, including two open for public tours. Both parishes feature sections of the South and North Shores, scenic stretches of the Railway Trail, wide farmland tracts, beaches, swimming coves, nature reserves, historic sites, and must-see attractions.

The southern coast of both parishes was one of the areas hardest hit by Hurricane Fabian in 2003. Exposed limestone cliffs and beaches were ravaged, and low-lying residential neighborhoods were evacuated as terrific rollers swamped shoreline homes, tore slate off hundreds of roofs, and destroyed sections of South Shore Road, crumpling the tarmac like a kicked-up carpet. Little evidence of such destruction remains, aside from visibly eroded limestone cliffs and hilltop views of the sea where there were none before. South Shore Road, which looked like an earthquake victim post-Fabian, has been rebuilt, and restoration of beachfront and affected nature reserves continues.

There are several routes to travel through the two parishes, the most scenic being South Shore Road and Harrington Sound Road. In

© ROSEMARY JONES

HIGHLIGHTS

◖ Spittal Pond Nature Reserve: Heavily battered by 2003's Hurricane Fabian, the island's premier nature reserve underwent the start of a full-scale restoration in 2005. Explore the sprawling 60-acre bird sanctuary via rolling coastal trails with unparalleled views of the South Shore (page 170).

◖ John Smith's Bay: A family favorite, this small half-moon bay is good for a day's retreat or just a dip while touring the eastern parishes. It is one of the few beaches with lifeguards on duty through the summer (page 174).

◖ Gibbet Island Beach: A safe, idyllic swimming and snorkeling spot, especially for children, though the main island across the bay has an unsavory past (page 174).

◖ Bermuda Aquarium, Museum & Zoo: Long Bermuda's favorite attraction, this waterfront facility's lushly exotic grounds and modern exhibits offer an up-close look at Bermuda's diverse marinelife, plants, conservation projects, and intriguing creatures from oceanic islands around the world. Kids of all ages will love the activity room (page 180).

◖ Blue Hole Park and Walsingham Nature Reserve: For a rejuvenating escape to nature, head to the little-visited forest reserve commonly known as Tom Moore's Jungle, with winding trails through cherry bushes, mangroves, and sunken caves. Fish and turtles can sometimes be seen in one of its pocket-size lagoons – a delightful swimming hole connected to the sea (page 183).

◖ Crystal Cave and Fantasy Cave: Discovered in the early 1900s, Crystal Cave and Fantasy Cave are but two grand examples of a honeycomb which riddles the parish. The caves themselves offer spectacular interiors, but their garden estate's royal palms and

LOOK FOR ◖ TO FIND RECOMMENDED SIGHTS, ACTIVITIES, DINING, AND LODGING.

behemoth Indian laurel trees are equally fascinating. The property's well-run café is open seven days a week (page 184).

◖ Shelly Bay Beach and Nature Reserve: There's nothing more beautiful on a summer day than the mirror-flat turquoise shallows of this roadside beach. Surrounded by sports fields, a playground, a grassy picnic area, and nature reserve, it's popular with families, romantics – and windsurfers, when the breeze picks up (page 186).

Smith's, South Shore Road leads east from Collector's Hill, up McGall's Hill, and past the wooded splendor of Spittal Pond to John Smith's Bay and Mangrove Lake, Bermuda's largest saltwater pond. Continuing east on the South Shore, you enter a small chunk of Hamilton Parish, most of it cushioned by the undulating greens of the world-famous Mid Ocean Golf Club. Briefly crossing the parish boundary (into Tucker's Town, St. George's), it's necessary to cut through Paynter's Road to return to Hamilton Parish via picturesque, serpentine Harrington Sound Road.

From the eastern reaches of Hamilton Parish, you can take the Causeway into St. George's or explore North Shore neighborhoods, such as Coney Island, Bailey's Bay, and Crawl. North Shore Road also hugs the cove-sprinkled coast through Smith's to the border of Flatts Village, before linking to a narrow, postcard-pretty stretch of Harrington Sound Road—another pleasant way east, particularly on dead-calm days when the North Shore horizon looks like a lake, and arriving cruise ships can be seen following the distant channel into the Great Sound. Middle Road is a third route through Smith's, traversing the parish's residential interior, where schools, a riding stable, farm fields, and grazing pastures reveal Bermudians' busy daily lives. Interconnecting roads like precipitous Harrington Hundreds, St. Mark's Road, farm-dotted Verdmont Road, or Knapton Hill with its moongates and modern, middle-class spreads, are also worth meandering if you have the time.

PLANNING YOUR TIME

Both Smith's and Hamilton Parish are full of attractions—historic, eco-oriented, and recreational. You could spend several days'

outings exploring this region, particularly since some sights, such as the Aquarium & Zoo, Spittal Pond, Crystal and Fantasy Caves, and certain beaches, offer hours of possible exploration and enjoyment. Any of these could also be visited as part of a drive east to St. George's, since all are easily accessible from the main roads. Cafés, restaurants, and ice cream parlors, like those at Flatts Village, Collector's Hill, Crawl, or Bailey's Bay, offer many options for libation and meals en route. Kayak and sailboard rentals, scuba, snorkeling, and sport-fishing outings can also be arranged through several operators located here.

Beginning in Flatts, a whole day's outing could be tailored to a circuit of Harrington Sound itself, encompassing visits to the Aquarium & Zoo, the caves, parks, beaches, or historic sites like Holy Trinity Church, and any number of restaurants or cafés along the way. Shopping and organized entertainment in both parishes, however, are slim pickings, with only a handful of retail outlets, mostly tiny stores inside key attractions. Accommodations are also few, so it's likely you would venture here from other parishes. Mopeds, taxis, and buses are efficient ways to get around; well-marked bus stops are outside most of the main sights.

As elsewhere, the Railway Trail offers lovely out-of-the-way views, coastal serenity, and glimpses of genuine Bermudian life, though the trail is broken by main roads at a couple of points. Several of Bermuda's best swimming areas are located in these parishes, a mixture of South Shore's surf and sand and North Shore's calmer, sometimes beachless rocky coves, snorkeling areas, and deep swimming holes.

Smith's Parish

The dramatic lookouts, diverse plants and animals, and the coastal trail of Spittal Pond alone would be enough to make Smith's worth visiting, but the parish has much more, including a historic—some say haunted—house that's now a museum, beautiful beaches on both shores, panoramic stretches of the Railway Trail and Harrington Sound, and a few good restaurants. The parish is named for London power-broker Sir Thomas Smith, a key figure in the colonization efforts of London's East India Company, Russia Company, and North West Passage Company, as well as a stakeholder in early Bermuda. Smith's is largely residential, with a busy community hub at Collector's Hill, offering a grocery, pharmacy, restaurants, and essential services like gas and ATMs.

The parish also claims a large farming community, with substantial parcels of land harvested for onions, strawberries, carrots, and other seasonal produce sold in island supermarkets. A dairy farm sits next to Spittal Pond, one of just two on the island. Smith's is home to many Portuguese residents, some of them newly arrived Azorean contract workers, others naturalized immigrants, and many more, full-fledged Bermudians, whose families have been here for generations.

Driving through the rolling parish, you can't help but be wowed by spectacular views of all kinds: Longtails arching from sheer cliff faces. Red dawn lifting over the glass of Harrington Sound. Sapphire depths of a favorite swimming hole. Smith's has as much to offer as any of the parishes, yet, without a single big-buzz attraction, the parish maintains an out-of-the-way quietude, a rural modesty that lets one imagine Bermuda as it used to be.

SIGHTS
Verdmont Museum
High on a hill overlooking the South Shore, Verdmont Museum (6 Verdmont Ln., off Collectors Hill, tel. 441/236-7369, 10 a.m.–4 p.m. Tues.–Sat., $5 adults, or $10 combo ticket for three Trust museums, $2 students) is a historic home that offers a glimpse of old-time colonial life—as well as a neck-prickling ghost legend. Flanked by sentry-like palmettos and surrounded by rambling lawns and rose beds leading up its garden paths, the Bermuda National Trust treasure sits at the end of a quiet lane off heavily trafficked Collector's Hill. The home's distinctive architecture, with four grand chimneys and a fine cedar staircase, excites historians, for it incorporates elements of both 17th- and 18th-century building design. Unlike most Bermudian houses, which typically exhibit a hodge-podge of structural add-ons, Verdmont has remained structurally unchanged for 300 years.

Historians guess Verdmont was built around 1710. The home's English-influenced layout includes a formal drawing room and parlor on the ground floor and a charming nursery at the top of the house, displaying a rocking horse, Victorian dollhouse, and other time-worn toys. The home's collection of furniture, assembled by the Trust in the 1950s, is impressive; fine Bermuda cedar cabinets, desks, and a Chippendale-style tallboy with marching legs are among the standouts. Several imported furnishings were brought to the island by early sea captains, including Chinese porcelain and English hurricane shades. Portraits of several former Verdmont owners hang throughout the house.

Some believe the phantom of one 1930s resident, Spencer Joell, remains in the house. Several tour guides over the years have reported experiencing strange feelings, finding furniture inexplicably moved around, and say they have felt an odd chill in various rooms, including the attic nursery. Visitors, too, often ask whether the house is haunted. One incident involved a New Jersey couple who took a snapshot of the nursery in 1976, and later mailed back the photo, along with an alarmed letter, to Verdmont's then-curator. The room was empty, they said, when they took the picture, yet the photo showed a man sitting at a table.

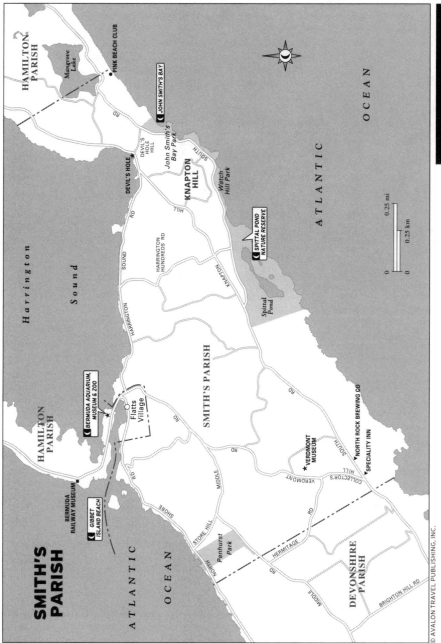

SMITH'S PARISH

HAMILTON PARISH

Mangrove Lake

PINK BEACH CLUB

JOHN SMITH'S BAY

OCEAN

ATLANTIC

H a r r i n g t o n   S o u n d

Devil's Hole Hill

DEVIL'S HOLE

John Smith's Bay Park

KNAPTON HILL

SOUTH HILL

Watch Hill Park

SPITTAL POND NATURE RESERVE

SOUND RD

HARRINGTON HUNDREDS RD

KNAPTON HILL

ATLANTIC

Spittal Pond

0   0.25 mi
0   0.25 km

HAMILTON PARISH

HARRINGTON

BERMUDA AQUARIUM, MUSEUM & ZOO

Flatts Village

SMITH'S PARISH

RD

RD

VERDMONT MUSEUM

COLLECTOR'S HILL

VERDMONT

SOUTH RD

NORTH ROCK BREWING CO

SPECIALITY INN

BERMUDA RAILWAY MUSEUM

GIBBET ISLAND BEACH

SHORE RD

MIDDLE RD

STORE HILL

NORTH

Penhurst Park

HERMITAGE RD

DEVONSHIRE PARISH

MIDDLE RD

BRIGHTON HILL RD

ATLANTIC

OCEAN

© AVALON TRAVEL PUBLISHING, INC.

Verdmont, a historic manse owned by the Bermuda National Trust, contains priceless antiques – and a resident ghost.

The curator, so the story goes, recognized the figure immediately, because she had known him well—it was Joell.

St. Patrick's and St. Mark's Churches

Continuing from Collector's Hill along South Shore Road up McGall's Hill area, the Portuguese influence is strong. The large, circular Roman Catholic church, **St. Patrick's** (23 South Shore Rd., tel. 441/236-9866, stpats@ logic.bm), conducts special masses in Portuguese (7:30 A.M. Sundays). Gardens carefully planted with Easter lilies, vegetables, or brilliantly hued flower beds, speak to the community's agricultural legacy, and the names of so many neighborhood residents—Moniz, DeSilva, Cabral, Furtado—reflects the waves of Portuguese immigration to Bermuda over the past 150 years. Azoreans were invited to the island in the mid-1800s to help spur a farming revival; within a couple of years, Bermuda was benefiting from the influx in laborers, as well as innovative farming methods and equipment.

By the 1870s, annual exports of Bermuda onions (70,000 barrels and 350,000 crates), arrowroot, potatoes, and tomatoes to U.S. East Coast cities had revitalized the island's economy and begun paving the way for Bermuda's cultural face to change.

At the top of McGall's Hill sits **St. Mark's Church,** a quaint parish landmark built in 1847 whose spire can be seen down the valleys on both sides. Inside, its cedar altar and pulpit are good examples of Bermudian workmanship. The graveyard, draped with riotous bougainvillea at certain times of year, is also worth a wander, past tombstones of seafaring, old-family islanders dating back a century and a half.

◀ Spittal Pond Nature Reserve

This rugged, 60-acre coastal reserve (open sunrise to sunset daily, admission free), co-owned by the Bermuda National Trust and the government, has two entrances along South Shore Road. Both have parking lots and lead to the circuitous trail around the park, though the eastern entrance offers a more direct entry

BERMUDA'S PORTUGUESE

On November 6, 1849, a sailing ship made port in Hamilton carrying 58 men, women, and children – the first Portuguese immigrants to Bermuda. "We sincerely trust this importation of laborers will answer the end contemplated," read a dispatch in *The Royal Gazette,* "and we hope they will be the means of inducing the cultivation of the wine more extensively than at present."

Vineyards never did become a thriving enterprise in Bermuda, but those first farm workers from the island of Madeira were the vanguard of waves of Portuguese immigration to the island. Their journey would be repeated by thousands of Portuguese, mostly from the remote Azores islands, who headed to Bermuda to fill a dire need for agricultural expertise and carve out a better life for themselves. Their efforts paid off, and farming – and the export of onions, arrowroot, tomatoes, and other products – became a lucrative economic generator for the island in the second half of the 19th century. Today, as lawyers, bankers, and tenacious entrepreneurs, generations of Portuguese-Bermudians have called the island home; their community makes up an estimated 25 percent of the population.

It wasn't always smooth sailing for Portuguese immigrants. Bureaucratic and social discrimination relegated them to the status of second-class citizens, even into the 1960s and 1970s. Strict government regulations attempted to bar the immigration of whole families, and restricted job classes to menial labor. Like blacks until desegregation in the 1960s, the Portuguese were banned from many of the island's social clubs. But the community was a strong and self-supportive one; established Portuguese helped new immigrants find their footing and lobbied for their rights. In the 1980s, the Portuguese-Bermudian Association pressed the case of long-term residents, including numerous Portuguese who had lived or even been born in Bermuda but had no legal right to stay on the island. The group's efforts finally nudged the government to grant long-term residency to many people of all nationalities who have made a significant contribution to Bermudian society.

Portuguese-Bermudians keep their culture vibrantly alive on the island, linking the island to the vast diaspora of Portuguese civilization around the world. Their club, the **Vasco da Gama Club** (51 Reid St., Hamilton, tel. 441/292-7196), has been a social and political hub for both new immigrants and later generations. Portuguese is now considered a second language on the island, where for the past decade, government departments, banks, and some businesses have begun to provide translated signs and customer information on official forms, websites, and in retail centers. The **Portuguese Cultural Association** promotes beloved age-old traditions by teaching dances, cooking, and other arts to younger generations, who perform at national events such as the May 24 Bermuda Day Parade.

Religious *festas* also make colorful public spectacles throughout the year, with ornate costumes and processions in which church elders and citizens walk on carpets of petals to celebrate important Roman Catholic saints and the Holy Trinity. In the procession of Santo Cristo, held on the fifth Sunday after Easter, hundreds gather at St. Theresa's Cathedral in Hamilton for a solemn march through the city's streets to seek miracles for the sick and needy. In June, Portuguese-Bermudians celebrate the Festa do Espiritu Santo (Festival of the Holy Spirit) in King's Square, St. George. An elaborate pageant paying tribute to the legendary charity of Queen Isabel includes a feast for participants who are served bowls of *sopa* (soup) and *pao dolce* (sweet bread).

Portugal has established a **Portuguese Consulate** in Bermuda (Melbourne House, 11 Parliament St., Hamilton, tel. 441/292-1039), which currently is staffed, but the community is waiting for a full-time consul to be appointed to the island.

and faster access to some of the most dramatic viewing spots. The reserve is the island's premier nature reserve, a sprawling sanctuary that includes a valley cradling the large brackish pond, several freshwater ponds, and surrounding marsh and woodland through which meandering trails climb to spectacular outlooks over the South Shore. Notably, the reserve's varied habitats provide a refuge for resident and migratory birds, including woodland cardinals, finches, mallards, turnstones, sandpipers, cliff-nesting longtails, blue herons, white egrets, occasional visiting hawks, and the ubiquitous yellow-crowned night herons, which devour crab populations throughout the island.

The park's highlights include the "Spanish" Rock—a historic carving on an exposed rocky cliff face, originally believed to have been left by Spanish mariners before the island's colonization. The inscription, now cast in bronze, includes letters that look like "RP" (possibly for *Rex Portugaliae,* referring to Joao III, Portugal's monarch) and the date 1543. Historians now think the markings were the work of 32 Portuguese castaways who escaped their shipwreck off Bermuda that year and spent time on the island fashioning a new vessel from cedar timber. Up here, atop cliffs tumbling down to frothy boiler reefs below, the flat rock face surrounded by a cedar fence gives a breathtaking view of the whole southern coastline. Assorted contemporary graffiti has been carved in the outlook's limestone.

Just down the trail from Spanish Rock is Jeffrey's Hole, a cave with an overhead entry hole, which, according to local lore, became a temporary shelter for an escaped slave. Another oddity, at the western end of the park, is the "Checkerboard"—a large, flat square rock surface near the water's edge bearing crosshatch markings. Experts can't decide whether it was crafted by human hand or the sea, which sprays over the edge and pounds the rock on stormy days.

Descending from Spanish Rock, follow a skinny coastal trail edged by prickly pears and baygrapes to a wind-battered promontory—a salt-licked plateau over the roiling surf where parrotfish can sometimes be seen nibbling the reef edges. Turning inland past a small pond where egrets nest and ducklings learn to paddle, the woodland trail is laced with banks of Kermit-green flopper plants, a succulent whose lantern-like flowers bob by the hundreds over assorted ferns and wild blossoms. Continuing past fiddlewood groves, aromatic spice trees, and sugarcane, the trail leads past a dairy farm to the western parking lot; exit onto South Shore Road and follow the grassy verge east for about 50 meters until a set of wooden steps leads under a hedged arch back into the reserve. The woodland trail continues around the large pond's northern rim back to the east parking lot.

Hurricane Fabian sent towering waves over the cliffs into the valley and pond, the salt leaving a swath of dead vegetation in its wake. The terrific storm surge ate away chunks of the South Shore limestone cliffs; fences, signage, and a wooden pedestrian bridge were completely wiped out. Hillsides of whispering pines were ripped from their roots and acres of plant life destroyed, leaving most trails unnavigable for months. Since then, government conservation crews have cleared all trails and carried out a major restoration—culling invasive species and replacing them with hardy endemics like palmettos and cedars. As fundraising for the large project continues, plans call for more improvement of trails and new fences and interpretive signage around the park.

The park's steep trails and hour-long circuit restrict access to the able-bodied, but good views of the South Shore can be had from the wooded trailhead alongside the eastern parking lot. There is a portable toilet here, too.

Watch Hill Park

Just east of Spittal Pond, looking out over one of Bermuda's most dramatically spectacular stretches of coastline visible from the main road, tiny Watch Hill Park (open sunrise to sunset daily, admission free) offers a peaceful stopping place for a picnic or rest while heading east. Anglers come here after work and on weekends, casting their lines for pompano and "good-eating" reef fish like snapper, rockfish, triggerfish, and hogfish. The park is located on a peaceful stretch of South Shore Road, where traffic is generally very light. The main road east from here is the quintessential "scenic route," leading far from rush hour destinations—to leisurely Tucker's Town and its private-club golf courses. The low-lying area near Watch Hill Park and beyond to John Smith's Bay was one of the hardest-hit by Hurricane Fabian, whose destruction can be seen in the eroded shoreline. The road itself underwent a mammoth restructuring to repair major damage and shore it up against future marine onslaughts; the work, including a sidewalk and railing, was completed late in 2004.

Penhurst Agricultural Park

When Michael Douglas's Bermudian mother, Diana Dill Darrid, married President Nixon's former Treasury chief of staff Donald Webster over the Christmas holidays of 2002, the wedding couple asked guests to donate toward the preservation of Penhurst Agricultural Park (Middle Rd., west of Store Hill, open sunrise to sunset daily, admission free) in lieu of wedding presents. They held a publicized ceremony to plant cedar saplings on Christmas Eve inside the 14-acre reserve, which rambles from Middle Road down across the Railway Trail to North Shore, encompassing farm fields and dense woodland that few Bermudians have ventured to explore. Visible from the park entrance area are the communications tower and giant satellite dish on the next-door property of Cable & Wireless, on which the lion's share of Bermuda's telecommunications depends. The park gives easy access to the Railway Trail in Smith's; south of the Trail, it descends to a grassy spread where a bench overlooks the North Shore. Bluebirds, cardinals, mourning doves, and finches can all be seen and heard here, amid the fiddlewoods, palmettos, and cedars. Parks Department crews spent early 2005 culling invasive species such as Mexican pepper bushes and planting replacement endemics.

Harrington Sound

This inland sound, favored by boaters and anglers, is considered by naturalists to be biologically unique in the world, because of its necklace of underwater caves, tidal currents, submerged notches, and the abundance of marinelife found here. Calico clams, black mussels, purple urchins, harbor conches, squids, and spiny lobsters can all be seen, not to mention rays that occasionally lift out of the water like speckled Stealth bombers before coming down in a loud splash—a heart-pumping experience for any nearby swimmer.

Measuring some three square miles, the sound is deep, extending down to 80 feet in some places, and ringed by steep cliffs and sheer shores, the highest point lying at Abbot's Cliff in Hamilton Parish. Below these, numerous caves provide fascinating exploration for cave-divers, kayakers, and snorkelers, though the mouths of some, such as Green Bay Cave on the western shore, lie underwater. (Inside this particular cave, however, stalactites hang from the ceiling above the surface.) Another example is Shark Hole Cave, in the emerald-hued southwest corner, which extends under the traffic of Harrington Sound Road. Swimmers can often feel patches of cool water throughout the sound, as seawater from the outer shore enters through hundreds of fissures.

Scattered around the sound are various private islands (Rabbit Island, Cockroach Island), where Bermudians keep summer cottages. Sporting events such as Zoom Around the Sound (a run/walk/cycle/in-line skate event), the Round-the-Sound Swim, and the Trunk Island Swim also take advantage of the sound's scenic loop and its mostly calm waters in the summer and fall. Flatts Bridge is a great vantage point to view most of the Sound, and swimming is popular off the rocks at Shark Hole—the only soft landing is a small beach on the property of the Palmetto Gardens condominiums, at the three-way junction of North Shore, Middle, and Harrington Sound Roads. But the high cliffs and private properties encircling much of this body of water prevent easy access, unless by boat. Organized tours are rare, but select private tours can be arranged through Paul Pike of **Bermuda Bell Diving** (5 North Shore Rd., Flatts, tel. 441/535-8707 or 441/292-4434, fax 441/295-7235, belldive@logic.bm).

Devil's Hole

The historic value of Devil's Hole (92 Harrington Sound Rd., tel. 441/293-2072, 9 A.M.–4 P.M. daily, closed Oct.–April, $10 adults, $5 children 6–12, under 6 free)—whose neighborhood takes the same name—far outweighs its contemporary offerings. The hole itself is a curious roadside site, considered Bermuda's first tourist attraction. Dating back more than 150 years, it was a must-see for Victorian visitors such as Princess Louise (Queen Victoria's daughter). "One moment was quite enough," noted American visitor Julia Dorr, who dropped in the same year to take a look at Devil's Hole. "No rendezvous for gods or fairies this, but a natural fish pond," she sniffed. Inside the walled entrance is a pond, set in a large cavern and fed by ocean currents through a subterranean connection to the South Shore—hence the groupers, snappers, and other reef fish that dart about its depths along with a collection of turtles. The hefty entry charge of $10 per person buys a bucket of squid and a "fishing pole" with alligator clip to dangle over the railing and feed the marinelife below. Feeling turtles yanking the line is vaguely entertaining (especially for children), but the creatures soon lose interest, and appetite, after a few groups of daily visitors. Generally a letdown, the whole experience lasts only 20 minutes or so. A small on-site eatery, **Angel Wings Café,** serves sandwiches, sodas, and snacks. A better choice is the never-advertised down-home diner, Woody's Café, across the street.

BEACHES

◖ John Smith's Bay

The lifeguard station posted at this crescent-shaped cove attests to its popularity, particularly among families with children. Nestled between two promontories, the beach—named for pioneer Captain John Smith of the Virginia Company, which administered early Bermuda—is usually fairly protected from high waves and winds. Hurricane Fabian was an exception, however, throwing towering waves over the beach as far as South Shore Road and eating away huge portions of the limestone cove, coastal vegetation, and beach sand. Today, only vestiges of this destruction remain… a rockier beach than before, and updated landscaping in the small park.

Ample parking, toilets, and a friendly daily lunch wagon that doles out drinks, burgers, fish cakes, and fries to hungry swimmers make John Smith's a top beach choice for locals, and anyone who wants a change from the beach crowds of Warwick and Southampton.

Coconut palms and baygrapes frame the beach, where jutting rocks have created convenient mini-coves that provide a measure of privacy even when the beach gets busy. Tucker's Town's sweep of surf along the private Windsor and Mid Ocean beaches can be seen in the distance. On Sunday mornings, the beach attracts a group of recreational swimmers who meet for spiritual gatherings at dawn throughout the year. Easter Sunday also sees a special beachside service.

◖ Gibbet Island Beach

The beauty of Gibbet Island and its idyllic facing coves belies an ugly past. Its name refers to the gallows post that once stood on the island, a site where slaves and criminals were hanged, their bodies on public display as a warning to passing maritime traffic. Such history remains a sore spot for the island's black—and white—communities in the ongoing effort to foster harmonious race relations over 170 years after Emancipation in Bermuda. If there is any peaceful closure, it is the happy laughter of children of both races who mingle all summer on this popular, though private, little atoll, generally called "Gibbet's," but officially named Gibbons Bay. There are actually two islands (the smaller is Little Gibbet), each with tiny coves and reefs separating the area into sheltered swimming and anchoring spots. Longtails nest in the roadside cliffs, and kingfishers sit on the power line between the islands, eyeing their fish prey before darting over the water beneath.

While the majority of the property is owned by a private family trust, numerous groups have been granted access in the past, including families of police officers in the 1970s and 1980s when Gibbet's was known as the "Police Beach." (My father, a Welsh-born sergeant, was a member of the local Force for two decades, so I practically grew up here.) General access to the property is today possible via the restored Railway Trail, since Gibbet's sits at the end of the Smith's Parish section of this popular walking route. Indeed, the old concrete supports remain above the beach on its grassy verge, and two large bridge pylons stand in the water at the mouth of Flatts Inlet—over which the train used to travel to and from Shelly Bay and points east.

The area's trio of bays have become favorite stopping places for pleasure craft, day cruises, even fishermen who come to gather schools of silver fry in large nets. Snorkelers and scuba-divers also come here, since the sides of Flatts Inlet and the two islands offer reams of fish, rays, and reeflife, including anemones, eels, sea fans, corals, and occasionally, for patient observers, rare glimpses of a seahorse. Be careful of the current flowing in the Inlet, especially at peak tidal times, as well as boats, for it is a major thoroughfare to Flatts Village moorings and Harrington Sound. A locked roadside gate prevents vehicular access to the beach, so parking is a problem. Locals tuck mopeds into the hedge at the top, or park in the Jennings Land estate opposite.

SPORTS AND RECREATION
Railway Trail
The Smith's Parish Railway Trail is short in comparison with stretches in Paget, Warwick, and the West End, but it offers views of the North Shore, a shady fairyland of forest and easy access to the Penhurst Agricultural Park. Banks of nasturtium and asparagus fern line the muddy path, hemmed by steep limestone walls where the Trail was cut through the hillside. This stretch of Trail is a popular route for equestrians on their daily outings from nearby Hinson Hall Stables. Enter halfway up Store Hill. You can walk west to adjoining Penhurst, or about a half mile east to Gibbet Island, where the trail breaks at the water's edge. To continue east from Gibbet's, you have to follow North Shore Road into Hamilton Parish through Flatts Village and around the other side of the Inlet, picking up the trail again along the Shelly Bay stretch of North Shore (the small Bermuda

Railway Museum is located here). For a longer excursion, experience the other two-thirds of the western North Shore stretch by starting in Devonshire, where the trail can be accessed from Barker's Hill or Palmetto Road. Try an out-and-back walk from here, returning for lunch at Ocean View Golf Club.

ENTERTAINMENT AND EVENTS
Amphibious athletes take to the waters of Harrington Sound for the **Round-the-Sound Swim,** held in the fall, usually in mid-October. The charity event is competitive, with staggered starts beginning at 10 A.M. for five distance categories, from 0.8K to 10K. The joint finish is at the private Palmetto Bay Beach on Harrington Sound Road. The event awards trophies for speed, position, and money raised from pledges, but visitors to the island can participate by simply paying the entry fee. Kayaks, paramedics, and police keep participants safe. For information, contact Reeve Trott (tel. 441/292-1661) or Kevin Insley (tel. 441/292-9169).

ACCOMMODATIONS
Over $300
Built in 1947, the 13-acre **◖ Pink Beach Club** (116 South Shore Rd., Tucker's Town, tel. 441/293-1666, toll-free 800/355-6161, fax 441/293-8935, www.pinkbeach.com, doubles $420–825) oozes the type of old-style exclusivity Bermuda once banked on to attract the rich and famous. Nothing much has changed at this elegant, reef-fringed enclave, a "cottage colony" of 94 suites surrounding a main clubhouse. John Travolta and Kelly Preston brought an entourage, including children and nannies, to the resort in the summer of 2004. LeAnn Rimes came for R&R between concerts, as did Bruce Springsteen. Location, location, location is the resort's trump card. For while suites' interiors are a mostly unimpressive mix of cherrywood and marble, all boast views of one of the prettiest and most secluded sections of the South Shore coastline. European-style concierge service and large beachfront suites with names like "Baygrape" and "Seasweep" deliver utter privacy

and relaxation, a winning combo which has won perennial kudos for Pink Beach from *Conde Nast Traveler* and *Gourmet* magazines, among other publications.

Schools of parrotfish sway in the surf off private balconies, while queen angelfish dart around the nearby boiler reef, one of the best snorkeling areas on the island. Food and beverage service and snorkeling gear is available on the 1,800 feet of private, and very pink, beach. Afternoon tea is served daily. Five-course gourmet dining is offered in the clubhouse restaurant, or lunch poolside all spring and summer. The property, a member of the S.L.H. group (Small Luxury Hotels of the World), includes two all-weather tennis courts and a moped-rental outlet. Guests also enjoy privileges at nearby Mid Ocean Golf Club and Tucker's Point Club, both with private championship golf courses. Pink Beach carried out major renovations after its surfside suites took the full brunt of Hurricane Fabian in 2003. The only remnant of the disaster now is a hillside of casuarinas tree trunks—opening up an ocean view for the garden cottages.

FOOD
International

The panoramic **(Bermudiana Dining Room** at Pink Beach Club (116 South Shore Rd., Tucker's Town, tel. 441/293-1666, fax 441/293-8935, www.pinkbeach.com, dinner only 7–9:30 P.M. daily) attracts both locals and visitors with five-course gourmet cuisine ($20 for guests) nightly. Intimate lamp-lit tables look out from the high, glass-fronted room over Tucker's Town's reefy shoreline. Appetizers like tamarind-painted Virginia quail with shiitake mushroom slaw ($13.95) and entrées such as lavender honey-glazed Barbary duck breast ($30) are inspired and priced in the same league as dishes in far inferior establishments. The restaurant also has one of the island's largest wine cellars, with more than 212 wines, 10 by the glass—recognized with an award of excellence in 2004 by *Wine Spectator* magazine. Dress code is jacket required, tie optional. Reservations necessary.

Alfresco lunch is a quiet escape at Pink Beach Club's **Ocean Terrace** (tel. 441/293-1666, lunch noon–3 P.M., dinner 6:30–9:30 P.M., May–Oct.), thanks to the resort's peacefully upscale neighborhood and wide-open views of the South Shore. Salads, sandwiches, soups, and pastas are among the offerings.

Cafés and Pubs

A local favorite, **(Speciality Inn** (4 South Shore Rd., tel. 441/236-3133, fax 441/236-2929, 6 A.M.–10 P.M. Mon.–Sat.) serves up home-style comfort food, including the creamiest mac 'n' cheese, in a casual, cafeteria-style diner/pizzeria where the folks are friendly and fast. Maybe that's what brought Clint Eastwood here during a golfing holiday in 1996, or Jimmy Carter and his son Jack (a Bermuda resident) in 2000. Grab a barstool in front of the grill for a quick Bermudian-style breakfast (bacon, egg, and cheese on a coffee roll). The wide lunch and dinner menus offer everything from sandwiches and burgers ($3.20) served on freshly baked rolls to pastas ($10.75), island fish specials ($10), pizzas (starting at $7.75), calzoni, and stromboli, plus a separate kids' menu. A full sushi menu is also available, prepared at a separate bar by dedicated sushi chefs. Home-baked loaves of banana bread and gingerbread are often sold at the checkout counter. The only thing missing is a liquor license.

Billed as Bermuda's "first" (and only) brewpub, **North Rock Brewing Co.** (10 South Shore Rd., tel. 441/236-6633, fax 441/236-2288, lunch 11:30 A.M.–3 P.M. Mon.–Fri., 11:30 A.M.–4 P.M. Sat., dinner 6–10 P.M. Mon.–Sat.) is a British-style pub, complete with dark-hued interior, booths, and a bar. The menu is pricey but varied. Seafood, burgers, sandwiches, pastas, ribs, and pub staples like steak-and-ale pie ($21.95), bangers and mash (sausages with mashed potatoes) ($18.95), and fish 'n' chips ($18.50) are all available. Bermuda fish and lobster (in season) are also offered, as well as kid-friendly platters and vegetarian dishes. The bar has wines by the glass, and specialty 20-ounce pints or 12-ounce half pints of ale brewed on the premises, with

Bermudian monikers like St. David's Light and Blackwatch Stout.

Two Canadian Ironmen friends swore by the thick chocolate milkshakes at **Woody's Cafe** (59 Harrington Sound Rd., tel. 441/293-8869, 8 A.M.–8 P.M. Tues.–Sun.), where they would regularly drop in after five hours of cycling or a 20-mile run. Who can argue with such maestros of carbo-loading? Don't be put off by the corner café's dingy exterior, or the youths loitering on nearby walls; once inside, you will be welcomed with Bermudian good humor and hospitality. Try the hamburgers, fish cakes, chicken—and shakes.

Groceries

At the hub of routes east, west, and north, **A1 Smith's Market** (10 South Shore Rd., at the foot of Collector's Hill, tel. 441/236-6673, 8 A.M.–10 P.M. Mon.–Sat., 1–5 P.M. Sun.) is a busy little grocery stocking most of the basics. One of seven groceries that belong to the MarketPlace chain islandwide, it is a purveyor of President's Choice products out of Canada but also has Bermudian bakery items, a full dairy and butcher's counter, fresh fruit and vegetables, and a wide, well-priced wine selection. Cheerful checkout clerks make it a neighborhood stopping place.

Serving the billionaires of Tucker's Town and the nouveau riche of Knapton Hill, **Harrington Hundreds Grocery & Liquor Store** (99 South Shore Rd., opposite Spittal Pond, tel. 441/293-1635, fax 441/293-3136, 8 A.M.–8 P.M. Mon.–Sat., 1–5 P.M. Sun.) is a foodie oasis far from Hamilton. Unfortunately, its prices reflect the clientele's deep pockets. But while much is overpriced, some things are worth the markup—particularly the store's superior selection of Bermuda-grown fruit and vegetables (sweet local strawberries, ripe-on-the-vine tomatoes, melt-in-your-mouth melons) and its wide selection of organic fare, including specialized items for vegans and folks with wheat allergies and other dietary challenges. The store carries a good wine selection, from California to the Continent, fresh-baked stick loaves, Ben & Jerry's ice cream… who could want more?

INFORMATION AND SERVICES

Collector's Hill Apothecary (7 South Shore Rd., at Collector's Hill, tel. 441/295-3838 ext. 303, prescriptions tel. 441/236-4499, www .phoenixstores.com, 8 A.M.–8 P.M. Mon.–Sat., 11 A.M.–7 P.M. Sun.) is well stocked with makeup and toiletries, sweets and snacks, toys, gift cards, newspapers and magazines, and a large pharmacy offering online prescription refills.

Smith's has just one gas station, with a small convenience store attached: **Terceira's Shell Service Station** (2 North Shore Rd., tel. 441/292-5130).

Flatts Post Office (65 Middle Rd., next to Whitney Middle School, tel. 441/292-0741, 8 A.M.–5 P.M. Mon.–Fri.) is a tiny parish landmark and convenient mail-drop.

ATMs are located outside Collector's Hill Apothecary (7 South Shore Rd. at Collector's Hill) and at Harrington Hundreds Grocery (99 South Shore Rd. opposite Spittal Pond).

GETTING THERE AND AROUND

There are no moped rental outlets or ferry service in Smith's. Mopeds can be rented elsewhere and are a good way to scoot around the parish, especially off the main thoroughfares. Buses are also an efficient way to travel the main arteries of Smith's. Bicycles, rentable from hotels and liveries, are great for exploring the Railway Trail.

Buses

Buses travel all three routes through the parish: South Shore Road, North Shore Road, and Middle Road. Take the No. 1 for South Shore Road destinations (Hamilton–Grotto Bay/ St. George's, buses run every half hour). Take the No. 3 for points on Middle Road (Hamilton–Grotto Bay/St. George's, every half hour), traveling through Flatts Village and along picturesque Harrington Sound Road. The No. 10 or 11 is your bus for North Shore Road (Hamilton–St. George's, every 15 minutes). Fares from Hamilton to points throughout Smith's are $3 adults, $2 children 5–16, under five free.

Hamilton Parish

Though it carries the same name as Bermuda's capital, Hamilton Parish is totally distinct from the City of Hamilton, which lies about five miles away, in Pembroke Parish. The two Hamiltons are not named for the same person, either; the parish, like the other eight, took the name of an early investor, in this case, James Hamilton, the second Marquis of Hamilton, while the city was named for Governor Henry Hamilton nearly 200 years later. The Bermudian lexicon distinguishes clearly between the two: when someone says, "Let's go to Hamilton," they mean "Town," or the city. By contrast, locals normally describe Hamilton Parish locations within their neighborhood context ("Bailey's Bay," "Crawl," "Harrington Sound"). Indeed, historically, Hamilton Parish was simply known as Bailey's Bay by most islanders, since the North Shore community was a hub of trade and travel (by boat) around the island in its early colonial days.

Today, Hamilton Parish, wrapped like a half-doughnut around Harrington Sound, is largely residential, with impressive, mostly hidden waterfront homes, as well as several public parks, one large resort (Grotto Bay Beach Resort), and popular attractions such as the Bermuda Aquarium, Museum & Zoo and the Caves. Unless you are staying in St. George's, your tour of the parish will begin immediately after arrival, since you have to travel from the airport through Hamilton Parish to reach any other part of the island.

SIGHTS
Flatts Village

Flatts Village (North Shore Road), or "Flatts" as everything in the general vicinity is located in local lingo, has enjoyed a renaissance of sorts over the past decade, with a tasteful renovation of its smattering of shops and architecturally interesting cottages, as well as the addition of new restaurants, much-needed sidewalks, and a revamped marina. The tiny community lies on the eastern band of Flatts Inlet, a finger of shallow-edged turquoise harbor that links Harrington Sound to the ocean. Directly opposite Flatts on the inlet lies the Bermuda Aquarium, Museum & Zoo, the area's main attraction. Aside from the few restaurants and an ice cream parlor, there's virtually nothing to do in Flatts Village itself except ogle the tide as the ocean sweeps in and out of the pristine Sound twice a day, the two-knot current creating the nearest thing to river rapids for wannabe whitewater kayakers. Sport anglers return to port at sunset, while those with less high-tech accoutrements simply cast their lines over Flatts Bridge and nearby docks when weather permits. Fishing is supposedly illegal off island bridges, but the rule seems to be widely ignored and, judging by the pastime's popularity, rarely enforced. Line fishing is allowed from the rocks beneath the bridge, however, and containers for disposing of old fishing line—a

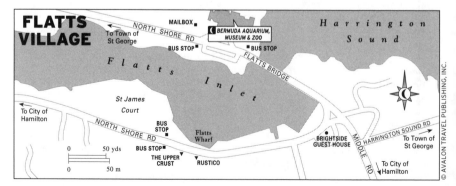

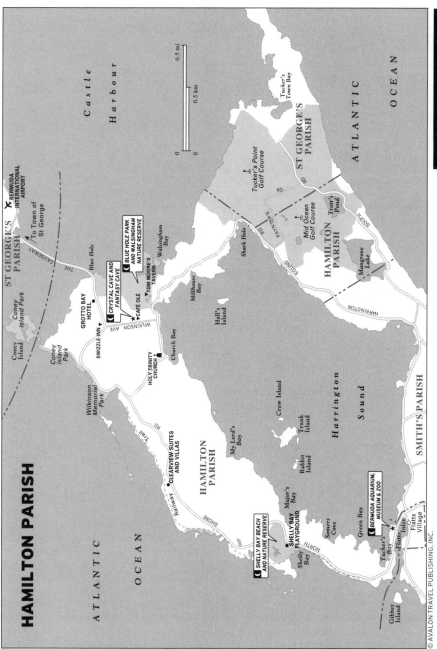

HAMILTON PARISH

ATLANTIC OCEAN

Castle Harbour

St GEORGE'S PARISH

BERMUDA INTERNATIONAL AIRPORT

To Town of St George

THE CAUSEWAY

Coney Island Park

Coney Island

Coney Island Park

Blue Hole

Wilkinson Memorial Park

Trail

GROTTO BAY HOTEL

CRYSTAL CAVE AND FANTASY CAVE

CAFÉ OLÉ

BLUE HOLE PARK AND WALSINGHAM NATURE RESERVE

TOM MOORE'S TAVERN

SWIZZLE INN

WILKINSON AVE

Walsingham Bay

Shark Hole

Tucker's Town Bay

Tucker's Point Golf Course

ST GEORGE'S PARISH

PAINTER'S RD

RD

Mid Ocean Golf Course

Trott's Pond

HAMILTON PARISH

Mangrove Lake

SOUND RD

HARRINGTON

ATLANTIC OCEAN

Millhouse Bay

Hall's Island

HOLY TRINITY CHURCH

Church Bay

Crow Island

Trunk Island

Harrington Sound

SMITH'S PARISH

CLEARVIEW SUITES AND VILLAS

SHORE RD

Railway

My Lord's Bay

Rabbit Island

HAMILTON PARISH

ATLANTIC OCEAN

Major's Bay

Somers Cove

Green Bay

Tucker's Bay

SHELLY BAY BEACH AND NATURE RESERVE

SHELLY BAY PLAYGROUND

Shelly Bay

NORTH SHORE RD

BERMUDA AQUARIUM, MUSEUM & ZOO

Flatts Inlet

Flatts Village

Gibbet Island

0   0.5 mi
0   0.5 km

© AVALON TRAVEL PUBLISHING, INC.

© ROSEMARY JONES

the waterside at Flatts Inlet

hazard for turtles and other marinelife—have been installed here. Jumping and diving off the bridge into the rushing tide is a favorite activity of daredevil youth in the summer holidays. In the early mornings or evenings, spotted eagle rays and larger manta rays can be seen swooping beneath, as they commute between the Sound and the shore beyond.

The area is historically important, since Flatts was one of Bermuda's earliest and busiest settlements of the 17th and 18th centuries, when travel and communication between the parishes was primarily by boat. Like other sheltered harbor settlements, including Crow Lane, Ely's Harbor, and Riddell's Bay, Flatts became a center for trade—and a refuge for smugglers fleeing custom duties levied by Hamilton and St. George. "Later, when Bermudians turned to shipbuilding and overseas trading, these villages took on the significance of home ports," wrote historian William Zuill in his 1946 parish tour, *Bermuda Journey*. The former sleepy whimsy in Flatts has been mostly lost in the noise and speed of

today's nonstop traffic, which flows through the village via North Shore Road—as well as summer's marine rush hour at day's end in the inlet. Two nearby sprawls of condominiums don't increase the quaint quotient, either. Area residents and businesses have tried to win it back; a lobby group created in the late 1990s launched a Flatts Community Festival, and even suggested building a new causeway to divert North Shore traffic east before the village—a bid to restore old-time tranquility. Such a plan is not likely to happen, though the group won government support in 2006 for Thursday-night "family fun festivals" in the village through the summer.

◖ Bermuda Aquarium, Museum & Zoo

Bermuda's best-known, bona fide attraction, the Bermuda Aquarium, Museum & Zoo (BAMZ) (40 North Shore Rd., tel. 441/293-2727, fax 441/293-3176, www.bamz.org, 9 A.M.–5 P.M. daily except Christmas Day, last admission 4 P.M., $10 adults, $5 seniors and children 5–12, under 5 free) sits opposite Flatts Village on the facing shore of Flatts Inlet, attracting crowds of visitors and locals alike. In fact, some 15 percent of Bermuda's population are members, and more than 100,000 people visit annually. Supported by the Bermuda Zoological Society with government and private funding, the facility fulfills many roles, offering a fun recreational venue but also conservation programs, curricula, natural history and aqua camps and special courses for some 9,000 schoolchildren, and a center for environmental research on endangered regional species like the endemic skink (or Rock Lizard) and green turtle. Raising awareness of the fragile ecosystems of oceanic islands is its key role—not only the delicate balance of Bermuda's own flora and fauna, but also that of Australasia, the Caribbean, and other archipelagos of the world. BAMZ is headquarters for the government's newly created Department of Conservation Services, as well as the Bermuda Biodiversity Program, an eight-year effort to catalog all island species.

Opened at the present site in 1928, BAMZ

BEEBE'S BATHYSPHERE

In August 1934 Bermuda made global headlines when two scientists achieved a pioneering feat that stunned the world of science and captured the public imagination: they descended a record-making 3,028 feet (a nautical half mile) off the island encased in a steel contraption called a bathysphere. Naturalist William Beebe, a former assistant curator of birds at the New York Zoological Society, and bathysphere inventor Otis Barton, had spent several years in area waters, establishing the Bermuda Oceanographic Expedition in 1928. The island made an ideal laboratory thanks to its biodiversity, year-round mild climate and easily accessible depths of more than 12,000 feet. It was the perfect testing ground for the steel pod, which was lowered by steel cable from a ship at the surface into the black reaches of the deep ocean, where two tall men curled up like spiders would stare from a glass porthole at the most wondrous specimens the world had ever seen.

"Here I was privileged to peer out and actually see the creatures which had evolved in the blackness of a blue midnight which, since the ocean was born, had known no following day," later noted Beebe in his 1934 book, *Half-Mile Down*. Electricity and a phone line were run into the bathysphere, allowing Beebe's observations to be relayed to an artist at the surface who made fantastic drawings of the iridescent fish, silvery eels, flying snails, and mists of crustaceans for the world to ogle. "We are still alive," was his comment to the anxiously waiting team at the surface when the pair dipped for the first time to a depth of a quarter mile.

Beebe, who had switched his scientific focus from birds to tropical studies in the 1920s and begun his diving quest with a homemade helmet, had an uncanny ability to describe the eerie netherworld of the deep in a way that was entirely factual, yet read like science fiction.

"To the ever-recurring question, 'How does it feel?' I can only quote the words of Herbert Spencer: I felt like 'an infinitesimal atom floating in illimitable space,'" he noted. "No wonder my sole contribution to science at the time was: 'Am writing at a depth of a quarter of a mile. A luminous fish is outside my window.'"

Beebe continued his research at Bermuda through World War II, carrying out scores of dives in the submersible chamber. He also wrote numerous popular works on his discoveries, inspiring laymen and scientists alike with his detailed descriptions of "the last frontier." Life-size replicas of his 5,000-pound bathysphere – which measured just four feet, nine inches in diameter – can be found at both the Bermuda Aquarium, Museum & Zoo and the Bermuda Underwater Exploration Institute.

was born of a collaboration between the Bermuda government, island environmentalists, and American scientists from Harvard and New York Universities who, together, set up a biology and zoology research station at Flatts as early as 1903. After various relocations during the two World Wars, the aquarium and the Bermuda Biological Station for Research became established as separate entities, though they continue to work together on many projects.

BAMZ offers an up-close look at Bermuda's marinelife, especially that of its precious coral reefs—some of the most northerly in the world. The aquarium's main hall contains many of the original tanks, displaying large moray eels, schools of silver minnows and squid, spiny lobsters, gigantic groupers, beaked parrotfish, an octopus, and a total of 200 species of fish and invertebrates. The pièce de resistance is the 140,000-gallon North Rock Exhibit—the first living coral-reef exhibit of this scale in the world. Created in 1996, it occupies the whole western side of the main aquarium building. The tank is actually two interlocking tanks naturally lit from above, cleverly mimicking what you might see by diving on North Rock, a reefy outcrop some 10 miles north of the facility on the North Shore. Inside the smaller front tank, tiny jewel-like reef fish dart among anemones, queen angelfish sway like ballerinas, and sponges, corals, and sea fans all can be seen up close. Behind this, the larger tank offers floor-to-ceiling viewing of sharks, barracuda, schools of pompano, golden-frilled triggerfish, and a mammoth black grouper. Benches are provided, and children—even babies and toddlers—can commune at floor-level with the various curiosities, making this a popular place for playgroups and family outings.

The $1.7 million Natural History Museum, opened in 2003, explores the geology and biodiversity of Bermuda with audio-visual and interactive exhibits, as well as lab-style drawer displays of preserved animals. Outside, the zoo contains more than 300 birds, mammals, and reptiles, in exhibits that aim to teach about the habitats of life on oceanic islands. Red-brick paths, rest areas and lookouts over Harrington Sound, and beautifully landscaped gardens featuring some of Bermuda's most exotic flowering plants and trees, encourage a leisurely visit that can easily span a couple of hours. The Australasia Exhibit re-creates the humid interior and landscape of a rainforest for the menagerie of tree kangaroos, wallabies, and a python that live here. Parrots squawk loudly in the cliff-style rock-faces above them.

A flock of 65 pink flamingos lives in a large open area at the zoo, where they have bred successfully. Inside the adjoining Caribbean Exhibit, cardinals and other birds dart freely among bamboos and other tropical forest plants, along with pairs of Golden Lion Tamarins. The monkeys are part of an international conservation program, the Species Survival Plan (SSP), which links Bermuda to an organized effort to boost the number of endangered animals. Bred in captivity, many tamarins are released back into the Brazilian rainforest. You will also see spoonbills, scarlet ibis, a two-toed sloth, and endangered Haitian sliders (terrapins) in this exhibit.

Young visitors love the air-conditioned Discovery Room, a hands-on exhibit center where they can touch starfish and sea urchins, feed fish, and pick up sea cucumbers, or sea squirts. Educational exhibits teach about man-made threats to Bermuda's critically endangered spe-

cies, and the easy-to-spot differences between, say, the endemic palmetto and run-of-the-mill fan palms. Storytelling for two- to six-year-olds is held on Fridays, 11:15–11:45 A.M., with critter tales, songs, and the occasional animal visitor. A playroom offers wildlife videos, a Lego table with zoo pieces, jigsaws, puppets, and live rabbits, guinea pigs, and hamsters. Outside, kids can shovel sandcastles in the playground, climb a rope "spider web," and make believe inside a hands-on shipwreck of concrete.

The lively seal exhibit, with five longtime Western Atlantic harbor seals, is located near the entrance and you can watch daily feedings at 9 A.M., 1:30 P.M., and 4 P.M. Archie, the 34-year-old patriarch, may be one of the oldest surviving harbor seals in captivity. Beyond the Aquarium's front entrance, in an outdoor pool next to the bus stop, swim a collection of green turtles, some rescued after being injured in boating accidents. The Bermuda Turtle Project, now in its third decade, tags and tracks members of the species as they migrate between the island and breeding areas like Nicaragua and the Caribbean. BAMZ also has a gift shop, selling eco-friendly items, and a small on-site café, the Peacock's Pantry, open 10 A.M.–4 P.M. General admission is needed for both, though ambitious development plans now under way hope to offer free access to these outlets in the future. Guided tours of BAMZ are offered at 1:10 P.M. daily April–September, Saturday and Sunday only October–March.

Bermuda Railway Museum

The story of the island's now-defunct Railway of the 1930s and 1940s is told at the Bermuda Railway Museum (37 North Shore Rd., tel. 441/293-1774, fax 441/293-4753, 10 A.M.–4 P.M. Tues.–Fri. weather permitting, admission free), where memorabilia from the train, dubbed "Old Rattle and Shake," is exhibited. Listen to an audio history of the Railway amid the quaint clutter of model trains, authentic old signs, rails and spikes, as well as books, maps and prints and other Railway-related items. The tiny building itself is historic; now situated along the Shelly Bay stretch of the walking trail, it was once the "Aquarium" Railway Station. Bermuda cedar and china antiques and collectibles are also for sale. Proprietor Rosa Hollis (tel. 441/337-9297, rosa@northrock. bm) lives across the street; call her to arrange a tour, or to open the museum if it happens to be closed during quieter months.

◖ Blue Hole Park and Walsingham Nature Reserve

This vast property (open sunrise to sunset daily, admission free), held largely by a private family trust but open to the public, incorporates coast and forested land from Blue Hole Park to Tom Moore's Jungle (as Walsingham Nature Reserve is more frequently called). Of the whole area, government-owned Blue Hole Park is the only designated public park, with the best access and parking. Although each area of interest can be accessed by its respective entrance—a half mile or so apart—all are linked, so they can be explored on foot from any entry point.

Tom Moore's Jungle (Walsingham Ln., off Harrington Sound Rd.) is a tangle of cherry forests and mangroves surrounding Tom Moore's Tavern, a four-star restaurant housed in a 1652 waterfront inn. Both the tavern and jungle take the name of Thomas Moore, an Irish poet-bon vivant whose mediocre romantic verse during a brief stay as court registrar (January–April 1804) managed to keep him very much alive in local legend. One of the highlights of the so-called jungle is a swimming grotto, fed via subterranean tunnels by the tides of Castle Harbour; turtles and fish can often be seen in its turquoise depths, and it is deep enough to snorkel and swim in, though it is not advertised and gets few visitors. Bird-watchers will enjoy spotting not only the many herons that stalk crabs on the shore, but finches, cardinals, and doves. Part of this chunk of land, the 1.25-acre Idwal Hughes Nature Reserve, is owned by the Bermuda National Trust and contains indigenous palmettos and cedars, along with unique geological formations.

The region is also riddled with underwater caves, including the most famous, Crystal and Fantasy Caves, which are open to the public.

Tom Moore's Jungle connects to Blue Hole Park through a woodland trail leading under diminutive bush archways, quaint enough to have been fashioned by fairy folk. Blue Hole Park, home to a popular Dolphin Show in the 1970s, is honeycombed with caves, including a cave mouth called Causeway Cave and caverns along the shoreline filled with seawater. Bermuda's oldest rock, a very hard limestone estimated to be 800,000 years old, can be found at the surface in the Walsingham area.

Don't miss the celebrity calabash—possibly Bermuda's most famous tree. Tom Moore sat in its generous shade to compose his poems, and on November 4, 1844, members of the nascent Royal Bermuda Yacht Club held their first meeting and a celebratory lunch under its branches; the iconic club has celebrated key anniversaries at the spot ever since. Tragically, Hurricane Emily in 1987 nearly destroyed the tree, but cuttings were replanted and it has now sprouted to about four feet in height. Follow the trail left of the Tavern about 200 yards to a clearing, where you will see the surviving sapling.

Holy Trinity Church

On a picture-perfect setting, Holy Trinity Church (Trinity Church Rd., off Harrington Sound Rd. or North Shore Rd.) also happens to be historically important. The current building, or at least part of the nave, dates back to 1660–70, but historians believe there was an even earlier stone structure on the site that bore a palmetto-thatch roof. Regardless, Holy Trinity is one of the oldest church buildings in the Western Hemisphere, having survived hurricanes, storm damage, and numerous alterations and additions over the centuries.

Perhaps the church's most notable feature is its 28 stained-glass windows, most of them English and installed since the 1890s. Five of these were designed by Sir Edward Burne-Jones, a noted pre-Raphaelite artist who designed for the William Morris Company. Experts have declared the quintet the best collection of his work anywhere in the world. Holy Trinity's furnishings are also impressive, including its mahogany pulpit, the 200-year-old

© ROSEMARY JONES

historic Holy Trinity Church in Bailey's Bay

Bevington-built organ, and a bronze baptismal font made in the 1970s by a resident sculptor (the original 1840s stone font can be seen in the churchyard). The church's silver collection is valuable, with the oldest piece, a handsome tankard, dedicated to "the church of Hambleton Tribe, 1677." Outside, wander through the churchyard with its roses and royal palms, and view gravestones bearing the names of this parish's hallmark families and seafarers—Outerbridge, Trott, Vesey—many of whose descendents still live in the area. The church is open for cleaning on Saturdays and for Sunday services, but contact the parsonage (tel. 441/293-5366 or 441/293-1710) if you would like to arrange a visit at other times.

Crystal Cave and Fantasy Cave

While the group tour experience is tacky, and the guided chit-chat pleasant but mostly uninformative, the actual geological phenomena visible in these two dramatic caves is worth the price of admission. While Crystal Cave and

Fantasy Cave (Wilkinson Ave., tel. 441/293-0640, 9:30 A.M.–5:30 P.M. daily May–Sept., until 4:30 P.M. Oct.–April, by guided tour only) are but two of hundreds of caverns around Harrington Sound and Castle Harbour, they are the largest and the only ones open to the public. Guided tours are carried out at regular intervals throughout the day; in the winter, when visitor numbers dwindle, you might be lucky enough to get a private viewing. Admission to each cave is $14 for adults and $8 for children ages 5–12 (under five are free); a combination ticket for both attractions costs $20 adults, or $10 children. If you visit just one, Crystal Cave is the most eye-popping and features a greater variety of formations.

Island folklore tells how Crystal Cave was discovered in the early 1900s by two boys playing a game of cricket. When they lost their ball down a hole, they found a subterranean wonderland beneath their feet. A 25-minute tour leads 80 feet down into the earth by way of a steep set of stairs cut into the hard limestone rock. At the bottom, the well-lit series of caverns opens up to expose a sapphire-bottomed lagoon, some 55 feet deep, over which a "floating trail" of pontoon bridges has been erected. Walk across the water, past soaring stalagmites and spear-like stalactites dripping like incessant taps into the pool. The water is incredibly inviting, especially in the torpor of summer, but swimming is not allowed.

A brief "nature walk" leads through an avenue of royal palms and down a red brick path through the estate gardens to Fantasy Cave. Avocado trees, sprawling Indian laurels, fiddlewood forest, and mature cherry groves nearly drown out the traffic at the busy intersection beyond. This cave's 88 steps wind down to another subterranean wonder, an open area dense with crystalline columns and more stalactites and stalagmites. Narrow walkways allow you to explore various underground nooks and crannies before climbing back to the surface, a 30-minute adventure.

The property has picnic tables under awnings, a café, a gift shop selling (imported)

BERMUDA TURTLE PROJECT

In the summer of 2005, a handful of baby turtles hatched from eggs on an East End Bermuda beach and laboriously wobbled their way down to the nearby surf. Not so exceptional, perhaps, for waters frequented by marine turtles, except for the fact it was the first time in almost a century that eggs had actually been laid and successfully hatched on the island. The phenomenon was celebrated by local naturalists involved in the Bermuda Turtle Project (www.cccturtle.org/bermuda), one of the world's longest-running tagging and research programs, established in 1968.

While the baby turtles in question were loggerheads, the Bermuda Turtle Project is mainly focused on the critically endangered green turtle (*Chelonia mydas*), once so plentiful on the island, colonists would gather hundreds of eggs at a time and capture 40 adults per boat per day. The species diminished almost immediately as a result; as early as 1620, the Bermuda Assembly moved to prevent turtle killing. Modern threats, despite legal protection, are no less severe. Turtles fall victim to boat collisions, as well as ocean debris such as plastics, Styrofoam, tar, and balloons, which fatally clog their digestive tracts. Entanglement in fishing gear, including discarded nets and lines, also kills marine turtles.

The Bermuda Turtle Project, through the Bermuda Zoological Society and the Bermuda Aquarium at Flatts, and linked to a similar Caribbean initiative, works to educate Bermudians about these dangers, as well as to gather and share vital information on turtles' life history. Green turtles are carried by ocean currents for the first years of their life, until they mature enough to feed off the bottom in inshore habitats. Bermuda's green turtles are such juveniles, who spend up to 15 years in this "developmental" stage, grazing on lush sea grass beds amid the coral reefs over the island's surrounding atoll. Once adult, averaging 300 pounds, green turtles migrate south to foraging and mating grounds.

Ultimately, the Turtle Project hopes to encourage a return of nesting populations on the island. In the 1970s, more than 25,000 green turtle eggs were brought to Bermuda from Costa Rica and buried on isolated beaches. Some 16,000 hatched and swam away. Since turtles are known to return to nest at the beach where they were born, scientists hope that when these offspring reach maturity (age 50 in green turtles whose lifespan reaches a century), they will come back to Bermuda.

Green turtles tagged or recorded in Bermuda have been traced back to origins in Costa Rica, Florida, Mexico, Surinam, and Venezuela, showing the vast ocean ranges covered by the species. Unfortunately, the size of its habitat poses dangers: many turtles mature safely in Bermuda only to be slaughtered in the Caribbean or Central and South America – a problem the project is working to change. "Bermuda can be proud of the protection it offers turtles, and the fact it has one of the healthiest reefs in the region," notes Jennifer Gray, coordinator of the Bermuda Turtle Project. "We hope to spread the word through the Caribbean and push for regional and international protection, as well as our local protection. Only then will the green turtle truly be protected."

gemstones, rock crystal, and quartz, and some of the nicest pubic bathrooms around.

Coney Island

Coney Island Park, a rugged neighborhood peninsula east of Bailey's Bay incorporating parkland, beach coves, a cricket club, and various government outposts such as the Fisheries Department, is worth a visit if you are exploring Hamilton Parish on foot, bicycle, or moped.

BEACHES

North Shore Road's rocky shoreline throughout Hamilton Parish—from Flatts Inlet to Coney Island—provides plenty of quiet coves, fishing spots, and swimming holes for adventurous travelers. The beauty of this shoreline is the lack of beach crowds (for there are few beaches). Instead, deep pristine water falls away from low rocks, which can be dived off. The shoreline, calmest when the wind is blowing from the south, is blanketed in reeflife, making it ideal for snorkeling or kayaking.

Shelly Bay Beach and Nature Reserve

Incorporating a lovely beach, a first-rate playground, a cricket pitch, soccer fields, and a protected nature reserve, this chunk of coastal Hamilton Parish invites hours of recreation. It is a favorite spot for family get-togethers and children's parties on weekends throughout the spring and summer months.

The soft white sand and gentle slope of the beach makes it a perfect spot for small children or swimmers who lack confidence. Although the busy North Shore Road is all too near, the beach's beauty on a summer morning is enough to tune out any traffic noise. Due to its easy access, the beach is also a magnet for windsurfers when the breeze swings around to the northwest. A concession serving the park, beach, and playground area offers sandwiches, hot dogs, burgers, and fries. Picnic tables are situated on the grassy lawns bordering the beach to the east. Access to and through the area has become a lot easier, and more scenic, thanks to a new boardwalk linking the old Railway Trail's Hamilton Parish start outside the Railway Museum with the beach, a half mile away. The wooden walkway, constructed by the Parks Department in 2005, allows walkers, runners, and bikers to stick to a safe, coastal path all the way.

The Railway Trail continues through a protected nature reserve, northeast of the beach and picnic park, which contains mangrove-fringed tidal pools and many indigenous plants.

Shark Hole

A dock at the ominously named Shark Hole (there's virtually no risk of the toothy reality) allows easy access to swim or snorkel in the emerald waters of this corner of the Sound. Encircled by cliffs and bypassed by a hairpin section of Harrington Sound Road, the invit-

ing grotto is also the site of a cave that extends beneath the main road. If you venture inside, you can hear the passing traffic above.

SPORTS AND RECREATION

Hamilton Parish offers a world of outdoors spaces and pursuits, from organized underwater tours to trails and parks for independent exploration. Soccer fields and a cricket pitch are at Shelly Bay Beach Park and the charming Sea Breeze Cricket Oval on Coney Island. Both are good spots to watch island teams of both sports (depending on season) and mix with avid local fans, who are usually more than happy to explain the complexities of the games.

Riding

English-saddle lessons are available inside the arenas at **Inwood Stables** (36 Radnor Rd., tel. 441/293-4964, fax 441/293-5215). A half-hour lesson is $30. This stable is mostly geared to local dressage borders and racing ponies, and no trail or beach rides are offered.

Helmet-Diving

It might look like something out of *Star Wars,* but helmet-diving is an easy way even for non-swimmers to walk the ocean floor and view the island's intriguing reeflife. **Bermuda Bell Diving** (5 North Shore Rd., Flatts, tel. 441/535-8707 or 441/292-4434, fax 441/295-7235, belldive@logic.bm) takes groups of 12–18 (maximum) participants on daily expeditions to inner-coastal reefs. The business was established back in the 1940s, but former carpenter Paul Pike has been running things for the past two decades aboard his 40-foot admiral's barge, *Cameron,* which he named for his daughter. Helmet-diving, as its name suggests, involves a heavy (50-pound), astronaut-style helmet with glass viewing window, which rests on your shoulders—and, naturally, feels lighter underwater. It is attached to a hose-pipe that runs to the surface, pumping in fresh air as you walk freely on the seafloor. Pike's 2.5-hour tours ($65) include the half-hour trip out and back to reefs at Shelly Bay, Admiralty House, and other venues. Maximum depth is 18 feet,

OLD RATTLE AND SHAKE

Bermuda's onetime Railway was a short-lived initiative, which nonetheless offered a popular mode of transport in the years before private cars were allowed on the island.

Opened in October 1931, the train – whose common nickname was "Old Rattle and Shake" – carried passengers in first- and second-class carriages the length of the island. At a time of racial segregation, the higher-priced sections were outfitted with wicker chairs and reserved for whites, while cheaper seats, for blacks, consisted of simple benches. Thirty-three bridges linked Bermuda's islands for the 22-mile line, an end-to-end journey that gave passengers accustomed to horse-and-carriage, bicycle, or boat travel a whole new perspective of the island.

The privately financed venture suffered from continual delays, breakdowns, and other snafus, however, running up large debts and eventually becoming unworkable. Notably, the train's key components – iron and diesel – were found utterly incompatible with Bermuda's rust-inducing climate, and the cost of shipping fuel to the island was prohibitive. The Bermuda government took over the line for a few years but finally closed it down in 1948, selling it off to British Guyana.

The advent of automobiles in Bermuda was the final nail in the Railway's coffin. After high-profile protests, including a petition signed by Mark Twain and Woodrow Wilson (both fond Bermudaphiles) led to a government ban on cars early in the 20th century, automobiles for private use were finally made legal and available in 1946, along with taxis. Though legislators assumed duties and licensing would restrict vehicle numbers, they underestimated the American-style consumer tastes of Bermuda residents; before long, the once peaceful crushed-coral roads had been asphalted, and locals were enjoying their newfound speed and mobility.

Neglected for decades afterwards, the old Railway Trail was rehabilitated by the Bermuda government in the 1990s as a pedestrian walkway through the island as part of the public parks system. Over the next 15 years, it became a highly popular route with walking clubs, joggers, horseback riders, and mountain bikers. Former parish stations, housed in Trailside cottages, can be seen en route. In early 2005, the Parks Department announced a major improvement plan for the Trail and asked for public input on signage, access, security, and vehicle bans that would make the route safer and easier to navigate. Sponsoring the project was the End-to-End Charity – a group which hosts a springtime St. George's-to-Dockyard fundraising walk that attracts Bermudians by the thousands.

though 10 to 12 feet is the norm. Tours leave from the Flatts wharf at 10 A.M. and 2 P.M. on Monday, Tuesday, Friday, and weekends. Pregnant women, or people with certain medical conditions, are not permitted to take the tours for safety reasons.

Diving and Water Sports

Triangle Diving (Grotto Bay Beach Hotel, 11 Blue Hole Hill, tel. 441/293-7319, www.triangled iving.com) is a five-star PADI dive center, offering certification and advanced courses, night dives, one- and two-tank dives, and private charters. The facility also sells diving equipment. Its location allows for excursions to the many East End dive sites, including Spanish shipwreck *Cristobal Colon,* some 10 miles offshore near North Rock Beacon, and the popular "Cathedral," a towering coral reef preserve you can swim through, situated just off the St. David's Island shore.

Blue Hole Watersports (Grotto Bay Beach Resort, 11 Blue Hole Hill, tel. 441/293-2915, fax 441/293-8333 ext. 37, bluehole@northrock.bm) has a wide assortment of stress-free water sports, including paddle-your-own Sunkats, sit-on-top kayaks, and snorkel gear, as well as sailboard, sailboat, and small motorboat rentals (13-foot Boston whalers). Windsurfers and sailboats are $25 an hour, motorboats $110 for four hours.

All are perfect ways to explore the turquoise calm of Ferry Reach and Castle Harbor.

Railway Trail

The Hamilton Parish section of the Railway Trail makes an interesting and highly scenic hike, with highlights like the Shelly Bay Park and Nature Reserve and Crawl Waterfront Park. The trail follows the coastline to Burchall Cove, and then leads past craggy limestone formations, inlets, and bays as it passes into the neighborhood known simply as "Crawl." This is one of the trail's most beautiful sections, with tiny gospel halls, seaside cottages, and charming old butteries in tow as it hugs the ocean on its way to the dramatic island-dotted seascape of Bailey's Bay. While the noisy main road runs parallel nearby, the thick limestone walls of the railway bed shut out most of civilization, allowing for a tranquil escape.

ENTERTAINMENT AND EVENTS

Runners, walkers, cyclists, and in-line skaters turn out for **Zoom Around the Sound,** a 7.2-mile circular course around Harrington Sound via Harrington Sound Road and North Shore Road. Held in March to raise money for the Bermuda Aquarium, Museum & Zoo, the race starts and finishes at BAMZ. Entry fee is $10, late entry $15. Refreshments are served, and T-shirts and goody bags go to all participants. For information, call tel. 441/293-2727, ext. 130, or email volunteers.bzs@gov.bm.

Open (free admission) days, kids' storytime (11:15 A.M. Fri.), yoga classes, lectures, and themed events are held regularly at **Bermuda Aquarium, Museum & Zoo** (40 North Shore Rd., Flatts, tel. 441/293-2727, www.bamz.org).

SHOPPING

Hamilton Parish shopping is limited to small gift and souvenir stores inside several of the main attractions and restaurants, including the Swizzle Inn, the Caves, the Grotto Bay Beach Resort, and the Bermuda Aquarium, Museum & Zoo. The latter is probably the most interesting, with its eco-friendly inventory, such as stuffed toys and quality plastic animal toys for kids (including dinosaurs and endangered species); soothing classical CDs with environmental recordings; and a good collection of Bermuda books, including the comprehensive coffee-table edition, *The Natural History of Bermuda,* by Canadian biologist Martin Thomas, published by the Bermuda Zoological Society in 2004.

ACCOMMODATIONS
$100-200

Clearview Suites and Villas (Sandy Ln., off North Shore Rd. at Crawl Hill, tel. 441/293-0484, fax 441/293-0267, www.bermuda-online/clearview.htm) has a cluster of suites, all air-conditioned, self-catering units with kitchenettes—and bird's-eye views of the sweeping Bailey's Bay shore. Bermudian owners Ruth and Gerald Paynter live just across North Shore Road; daughter Carollee and her painter husband Otto Trott run his artist studio nearby. The large cliff-hugging property has two outdoor saltwater pools, a tennis court, a barbecue area, and access to the shore, for swimming as Bermudians do—off the rocks. There is no beach, but two little islands offshore, reachable by able swimmers, reveal small beaches at low tide. High-season (April–Nov.) rates are $182 for garden-view suites, $210–250 for ocean-facing units, and $352 for a two-bedroom villa. Winter rates drop as low as $150.

Brightside Guest Apartments (38 North Shore Rd., Flatts Village, tel. 441/292-8410, brightside@cwbda.bm) have been a fixture of Flatts since 1979. The family-run property, owned by Willard and Michael Price, commands the southwest corner of so-called Lazy Corner—the busy junction of Middle Road, North Shore Road, and Harrington Sound Road—so tranquility is not its biggest drawing card. However, the guest units are cushioned by beautifully landscaped gardens, and there's a large swimming pool in the center of the complex. Units, all with basic decor, range from a room with double bed ($100) to a cottage accommodating four people ($340). All rooms have a microwave, refrigerator, coffee pot, phone, cable TV, and air-conditioning. The location is handy for sights (the Aquarium, the Caves), restaurants, beaches, and bus routes.

Over $300

The **Grotto Bay Beach Resort** (11 Blue Hole Hill, tel. 441/293-8333, fax 441/293-2306, toll-free in the U.S. 800/582-3190, www.grottobay.com, single/doubles $290–330) covers a lush hillside above the Causeway, giving panoramic views of Castle Harbour, Coney Island, Ferry Reach—and the airport less than a mile away. The resort's many yards of coastline encompass sheltered coves, an east-facing main beach, and a dock with water sports center offering scuba, snorkeling, water-skiing, sailing, windsurfing, pedal boating, and parasailing. The property claims its own crystal cave, nestled in landscaped grounds, an updated pool, and four tennis courts, two lit for night play. The casual atmosphere, coupled with a playground and children's program during the high season, make the resort a good choice for family vacations.

The property made major renovations in 2002, a vast improvement on the unintentionally retro decor of the 21-acre resort over the past quarter-century. Under the careful eye of general manager J. P. Martens, the large lobby-clubhouse has been expanded and transformed into a space reminiscent of a comfortable hunting lodge, or possibly a Polynesian loft, with open-beamed ceilings, solid oak floors, knotty pine columns, a cozy winter fireplace, and numerous nooks and crannies on two floors for reading, meeting friends, or surfing the Internet. Two dining rooms—one formal, the other laid-back tropical—were also reinvented. However, the rather boxy suites themselves, with tiny bathrooms and tired furnishings, could use a similar makeover, despite lovely views of the bay below. The planned addition of 71 rooms and suites is slated to begin in the fall of 2006.

FOOD
Cafés and Pubs
Pizza House Restaurant (at the Shelly Bay MarketPlace, North Shore Rd., tel. 441/293-8465, fax 441/293-1290, 10:30 A.M.–10 P.M. Mon.–Sat., 1:30–9 P.M. Sun.) is one of a three-outlet chain (also at Southside and Heron Bay) offering pizza slices, sandwiches, cold drinks, and snacks.

A welcome addition to parish eateries, **Café Olé** (8 Crystal Cave Rd., off Wilkinson Ave., tel. 441/293-7865, 9 A.M.–4:30 P.M. daily) attracts local clientele by offering breakfast and opening on Sundays. Service is super-friendly and fast, the restaurant spotless, and the menu tasty. Breakfast includes a choice of eggs, bacon, or a combo sandwich, while the lunch menu has hot dogs, hamburgers ($6.50), ice cream ($2.50 a scoop), sandwiches, cookies, and other snacks. The property is a good place to stop while heading east—for its quaintly tiled, powder room–style bathrooms alone.

A local institution, the **◖ Swizzle Inn Pub & Restaurant** (3 Blue Hole Hill, tel. 441/293-9300, www.swizzleinn.com, 11 A.M.–10 P.M. daily) is as much a Bermudian hangout as a tourist magnet, thanks to its lively social calendar, satisfying menu (including all-day breakfast), and deadly pitchers of rum swizzle. The Swizzle's caloric masterpiece, the Bailey's Bay Fish Sandwich ($14.50), seems to have reached legendary proportions, and regular visitors commonly stop for lunch on their way to or from the airport—just a few minutes away. "I have missed this so much, I couldn't leave the island again without one," confided a former resident, who now lives in Los Angeles, during a recent pit stop for the Dagwood-size creation (chunks of battered local fish fillet, topped with melted cheese, tartar sauce, lettuce, and tomato, stuffed precariously inside pieces of white toast). The swizzle, made from a closely kept combo of Goslings Black Seal Rum, Gold Rum, and fruit juices, is the sort of refreshing but potently mind-liberating concoction that makes it dangerous to get on a moped afterwards. Take a cab to lunch and back instead. The Swizzle offers nightly entertainment, including live bands, trivia nights, and Mardi Gras, St. Patrick's Day, and (American) Thanksgiving celebrations. The on-site Swagger Out Gift Shop is popular for hangover souvenirs, accessible for online shopping via the pub's website.

The Ice-Cream Parlour (2 Blue Hole Hill, tel. 441/293-8605, summer 11 A.M.–9 P.M., winter 11 A.M.–7 P.M. daily, closed Jan.) is a hot spot throughout the summer months, thanks to its 40-odd flavors of Bermuda-made cool stuff, namely the award-winning Bailey's ice creams, yogurts, and sorbets. Summertime sees lines of people waiting for scoops of chocolate-chip cookie dough, butterscotch crunch, Oreo sweet cream, and mango-passion fruit—all available by the tub in several island supermarkets that stock Bailey's products. Sit in the air-conditioned interior, or outside on the brick patio. The 20-year-old eatery expanded its menu in 2005 to include more snacks and sandwiches, and an array of popular hot items, such as chicken legs, fish cakes, peas 'n' rice, meat pies, and meatball subs—a move sure to garner a larger local clientele and cover the winter months.

Bermuda's only pizza-delivery chain, **The Upper Crust** (6 North Shore Rd., Flatts Village, tel. 441/292-9111, 11 A.M.–11 P.M. Mon.–Thurs., 11 A.M.–midnight Fri. and Sat., noon–10 P.M. Sun., $10 minimum order, $2 delivery charge) delivers deep-dish, low-carb, and 10- and 14-inch specialty pizzas, as well as calzones, sub sandwiches, salads, chicken wings, breadsticks, and desserts. If you're accustomed to North American fast food, you might be shocked by the steep prices ($27.50 for a 14-inch pizza, gratuities not included). You can take out or dine in.

Daily specials like roast lamb, oxtails, curried goat, and pork chops attract takeout aficionados to **The Village Grill** (6 North Shore Rd., Flatts Village, tel. 441/296-3634, 7 A.M.–10 P.M. Mon.–Thurs., 7 A.M.–11 P.M. Fri. and Sat., 7 A.M.–3 P.M. Sun.). Comfort-food sides featuring Bermudian staples such as peas 'n' rice, macaroni 'n' cheese, mashed potato, and baked pumpkin keep the little roadside eatery busy. Good-sized portions and reasonable prices also win customers. There are a couple of tables outside if you want to eat on the premises, but the noise and vehicle fumes may prove major deterrents.

International

Tucked into the busy curb-edge site of a couple of failed recent restaurant ventures, **◖ Rustico** (8 North Shore Rd., Flatts Village, tel. 441/295-5212, www.primaverarestaurant.com, lunch 11:45–2:30 P.M., dinner 6–10 P.M. daily) breathed new life into Flatts Village when it opened in 2001. Longtime Bermuda visitors will remember the erstwhile Halfway House, which, before its late-1990s demise, was a Bermudian burger and fish cake greasy spoon, beloved for decades by drop-in motorists—despite the glacially slow service. Subsequent restaurants opened, then closed, before Flatts finally got a venue able to attract a dining crowd all year around. Rustico, sister restaurant to Primavera in Hamilton, is a world apart from its Flatts predecessors; lovers of Italian cuisine will not be disappointed. A well-chosen wine list, and menu staples like crisp calamari, inventive salads, pastas ($12.50), pizza (starting at $11.50), and one of the island's best mahimahi fish sandwiches ($8.75), cause lines for parking on the narrow street outside. Devotees swear by the suave, super-friendly, and efficient service—a hallmark of all the island's Italian eateries. Eat inside or out, where a tent room tucked into the limestone cliff-side is heated with lamps during the winter.

Bermudian

Overlooking the spectacularly rugged Bailey's Bay coastline, **Landfall Restaurant** (Sandy Ln., off North Shore Rd. at Crawl Hill, tel. 441/293-1322 or 441/293-0484, breakfast/lunch 7:30 A.M.–3 P.M., dinner 6–11 P.M. Mon.–Sat., breakfast/lunch 7:30 A.M.–4 P.M., dinner 7–11 P.M. Sun.) is a family-run establishment linked to the next-door Clear View Suites and Villas. Both are owned by Ruth and Gerald Paynter, and their daughter Carollee and son-in-law Otto Trott, a well-known Bermudian artist whose oils of local scenes grace the walls of Government House and island homes. Needless to say, they also hang in the restaurant's three simply furnished dining rooms. The changing menu features fresh fish, lobster, steak, rack of lamb, and Bermuda-grown farm produce.

Fine Dining

⚫ **Tom Moore's Tavern** (Walsingham Ln., off Harrington Sound Rd., tel. 441/293-8020, fax 441/293-4222, www.tommoores.com, dinner only 6:30–10 P.M. daily, closed Cup Match Thursday, Christmas Day, and month of January) is a AAA four-star restaurant, housed in a historic setting, deep in the forested Walsingham Nature Reserve. The intriguing waterfront building, an old homestead built in 1652, became an inn during the 19th century and is named for Irishman Thomas Moore, who lived on the property briefly in 1804 and penned a collection of love poems beneath a calabash tree. The restaurant, colloquially referred to as "Tom Moore's," still inspires romanticism; its silver service, elegant multicourse menus, and hushed interiors make it a favored spot for very special nights out. If you pine for a $2,500 Chateau Lafitte-Rothschild, an $85 glass of "pudding wine," or fountains of Cristal champagne, general manager Bruno Fiocca will make it happen. The restaurant's celebrity guests include Prince Charles, who ate lunch here on an October 1970 visit to the island, and Tucker's Town homeowners oil magnate Ross Perot, New York mayor Michael Bloomberg, and former Italian prime minister Silvio Berlusconi.

Canadian chef Robert Nicolle's menu has appetizers like pinot noir–steamed mussels ($16.50), pan-seared scallops ($15.75), and smoked mackerel, trout and salmon roulade ($18.75); main courses ranging from rack of lamb ($34.50) to oven-roasted veal loin ($35.50) and warm mushroom strudel (21.50); and desserts to fulfill the comfort quotient (passion fruit and raspberry basked Alaska ($11.50), lemon-scented panna cotta with mulled wine jus ($10.50). Your pocketbook will undoubtedly groan (15 percent gratuities not included), but the experience is worth it. The restaurant seats up to 160 in five rooms on two floors, making it a top choice for weddings and group parties, as well as intimate dinners-for-two. (Special bookings are not restricted by the dinner-only schedule.) Since 2004, Tom Moore's has followed the island trend and relaxed its strict dress code to "elegant-casual," with no jacket required.

Groceries

Teetering halfway up Flatts Hill, **Twins Variety** (5 Middle Rd., tel. 441/292-4583, 6 A.M.–midnight daily) would be easy to miss were it not for all the truck drivers, cabbies, and neighborhood residents angling for a parking spot outside. Named for owners, twins Peter and Paul Adderley, the pocket-size convenience store is perfect for picking up a daily newspaper, cream bun, cat food, or any assortment of other basic necessities.

Long checkout lines at weekends and evenings are the only downside of **Shelly Bay MarketPlace** (110 North Shore Rd., tel. 441/293-0966, 8 A.M.–10 P.M. Mon.–Sat., 1–5 P.M. Sun.), a superstore with everything you could want for food or drink, as well as toys, kitchen supplies, beachware like towels and coolers, party balloons, and many other products.

Tony's Fine Foods (202 North Shore Rd., at the Coney Island junction, tel. 441/293-3354, 7 A.M.–7 P.M. Mon.–Sat., 8 A.M.–7 P.M. Sun.) is where Bermudians drop into at lunchtime for their chorizo-on-a-bun (a grilled Portuguese sausage delicacy). The recently renovated grocery also stocks fresh fruit, vegetables, cool drinks, and basic foodstuffs and toiletries.

INFORMATION AND SERVICES

Hamilton Parish has three gas stations: **Van Buren's Marine Station** (3 North Shore Rd. at Flatts Village, tel. 441/292-2882, 7 A.M.–9 P.M. daily); **Crawl Hill Esso Tigermart** (North Shore Rd. at Crawl Hill, tel. 441/293-6491, 6 A.M.–11 P.M. daily) and **Causeway Shell** (15 Blue Hole Hill, tel. 441/293-0621, 6 A.M.–10 P.M. Mon.–Fri., 8 A.M.–10 P.M. Sat., 8 A.M.–8 P.M. Sun.).

You won't have a problem finding a mailbox in Hamilton Parish; there are three post offices: **Harrington Sound Post Office** (19 Harrington Sound Rd., tel. 441/293-0500), **Crawl Post Office** (42 Radnor Rd., tel. 441/293-1400) and **Bailey's Bay Post Office** (2 Wilkinson Ave., tel. 441/293-0305). The last is a stamp-size outlet at the North Shore junction—and a convenient place to post your mail on the way to the airport. They are open 8 A.M.–5 P.M. Monday–Friday.

ATMs are located outside The Village Grill (6 North Shore Rd. at Flatts Village); at Causeways Shell (15 Blue Hole Hill), Shelly Bay MarketPlace (North Shore Rd., tel. 441/293-0966), and Crawl Tigermart (tel. 441/293-6491).

GETTING THERE AND AROUND
Buses
Buses are an easy way to travel through Hamilton Parish, with frequent, well-marked stops at all the major attractions, including the Aquarium, Shelly Bay, the Caves, and Grotto Bay Beach Resort. Take the No. 1 (via South Shore Road, Tucker's Point and the Caves) every half hour or the No. 3 via Harrington Sound Road every 15 minutes (both run city of Hamilton–Grotto Bay/St. George's). Nos. 10 and 11 travel North Shore Road (via the Aquarium and Shelly Bay) every 15 minutes, between City of Hamilton and St. George's. The parish like St. George's and Sandys qualifies as a 14-zone area, with a tariff of $4.50 from Hamilton.

Scooters
Wheels Cycles has an outlet outside Grotto Bay Resort (15 Blue Hole Hill next to the gas station, tel. 441/293-2378, 9 A.M.–12:30 P.M. and 1:30 P.M.–4:45 P.M. daily). It rents single-seat and double-seat ($75) scooters.

ST. GEORGE'S PARISH

Bermuda's old-time soul can be found in St. George's Parish, landing point of the first settlers and home to the oldest permanent English town in the New World. Wandering its shady backstreets, where peeling pastel walls, hidden gardens, and signs such as Old Maid's Lane and Featherbed Alley invite soporific afternoons, visitors get a sense of traditional island life a world away from Hamilton's singing cash registers, bustling sidewalks, and corporate milieu.

Both the parish and the old town are called St. George's. The 400-year-old town, seat of Bermuda's government for two centuries, was named a UNESCO World Heritage Site in 2000, along with related fortresses. The parish encompasses parkland and residential areas around the town, plus areas farther afield such as the airport, Southside, St. David's, and Tuck-er's Town. All of these sit on an amalgam of islands joined by bridges to form the eastern chunk of Bermuda's mainland—the so-called East End. The town and its immediate environs, as well as Ferry Reach Park, sit on St. George's Island; the parish's other main islands are St. David's Island, which is attached to the former U.S. baselands, now called Southside, and Cooper's Island, a nature reserve and beach area also attached to the former military air station. Scattered offshore islands and islets also belong to the parish, including Smith's, Paget, Hen, and Governor's Island in St. George's Harbour, and Nonsuch and Castle Islands spanning the channel into Castle Harbour.

Any tour of the parish should begin in the old town, whose tangle of skinny streets, including the original town grid of the early

© ROSEMARY JONES

HIGHLIGHTS

◖ **King's Square:** Any tour of St. George and the East End logically begins here, where cedar stocks and a ducking stool hark back to less-civilized times (page 201).

◖ **The State House:** The only surviving structure from the first years of settlement, this landmark building enjoyed myriad roles, including a gunpowder storehouse, the first parliament, and a court for witch trials (page 202).

◖ **St. Peter's Church:** Although its wooden predecessor was destroyed by a 17th-century hurricane, this remains the oldest continually used Anglican church site in the New World. The church's segregated graveyards – one for slaves, one for white dignitaries – are fascinating (page 202).

◖ **Bermuda National Trust Museum:** Once a Confederate headquarters, the historic Globe Hotel is home to Rogues & Runners, an entertaining exhibit about the East End's key role in the U.S. Civil War (page 203).

◖ **Bermuda Heritage Museum:** The story of abolition, black enterprise, "Friendly Societies," and gombeys is told in this showcase of black heritage, housed in the historic Samaritans' Lodge (page 204).

◖ **Tucker House Museum:** Looking inside this former homestead of one of Bermuda's most prominent 18th-century citizens is an enlightening step back in time (page 204).

◖ **Fort St. Catherine:** Peer over the ramparts at the very stretch of ocean the first castaways saw after escaping the shipwrecked *Sea Venture*. This large fort is one of the best-kept on the island, with exhibits on early Bermuda and military life, replicas of the Crown Jewels, and even a kid-pleasing George the Ghost (page 214).

◖ **Bermuda Biological Station for Research:** This world-renowned research center hosts pioneering studies on global climate changes, genome mapping, predicting disasters, and possible medical breakthroughs derived from the oceans. Free tours give a behind-the-scenes look at "science in Bermuda shorts" every Wednesday morning (page 215).

◖ **Cup Match:** Don't miss this annual cricket extravaganza if you happen to visit over the July–August cusp. Staged in St. George's every other year (it's held in Sandys in alternate years), the two-day festival represents an immediate initiation into island life. And don't worry if the game leaves you cold; the gambling, rum, fish sandwiches, and convivial crowds will more than make up for it (page 217).

◖ **Carter House:** This 300-year-old home-turned-museum tells the intriguing story of St. David's, from the neighborhood's days of whaling and harvesting Easter lilies to the advent of the U.S. baselands (page 221).

◖ **St. David's Battery and Great Head Park:** Clinging to a towering, remote cliff-top, this national park boasts dizzying views alongside historic battlements used for coastal defense up to World War II (page 222).

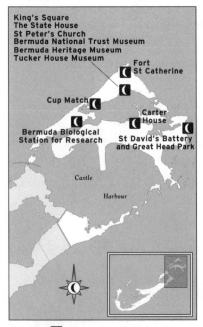

King's Square
The State House
St Peter's Church
Bermuda National Trust Museum
Bermuda Heritage Museum
Tucker House Museum
Fort St Catherine
Cup Match
Carter House
Bermuda Biological Station for Research
St David's Battery and Great Head Park
Castle
Harbour

LOOK FOR ◖ TO FIND RECOMMENDED SIGHTS, ACTIVITIES, DINING, AND LODGING.

1600s, juxtaposes immensely historic sites with the contemporary homes of St. Georgians tackling 21st-century lives. In a nation where consumerism is king, St. George stands apart as an anachronistic getaway offering amusements that often demand neither transport nor a fat wallet. A stroll around its harborside square evokes images of the rowdy days of American Civil War smugglers, whose latter-day counterparts are laid-back yachties on their way to a winter in the Caribbean. The old town is the kind of place where one can idle away the hours without achieving more than some serious people-watching and an ice-cream cone.

Thanks to its newly recognized historic status, St. George's is poised for a renaissance, with new stores and restaurants and ambitious plans for restoration of the forts, a waterfront boardwalk, and installation of cobblestone streets with new signage. An interactive World Heritage Centre opened on the harborfront in 2006 to guide modern explorers to points of interest in St. George's and beyond.

Key attractions include St. Catherine's Fort, perched above the beach where shipwrecked *Sea Venture* castaways rowed to safety, and Ferry Reach Park, a national reserve where Easter lilies and cherry hedges line the eastern stretch of the old Railway Trail. Then there's St. David's, a quirky community long detached from the rest of Bermuda, which remains quite unto itself, both physically and as a state of mind. Once home to Native American slaves whose descendants today proudly trace their lineage to Pequot roots, St. David's swirls with tall tales that linger from a heyday of whaling and pirating, its residents still innately tied to the sea.

Indeed, it is wholly understandable why the air pervading St. George's harks back to another time; it was only during the Victorian era that the parish was finally linked to mainland Bermuda by a half-mile Causeway—and even that connection is at times tenuous. In 2003, when Hurricane Fabian's surges swept over the winding roadway, hurling down walls and killing three Bermudians who were on it, St. Georgians, confined to the parish, found themselves once again fending for themselves. In January 2005, a day of high-force winds forced the government to close the Causeway for several hours, and less than a month later, a motorcycle crash on the skinny thoroughfare resulted in another fatality and shut down access to the rest of the island once again. It is one of the only times you are fully aware Bermuda is not a single island, but numerous smaller ones linked by man-made mechanisms.

Despite recent problems with youth gangs and petty crime, the parish remains a distinct society where neighbors generally know everyone's business and the rhythms of life invite small-town generosity, candid opinion, and an utterly fatalistic humor.

PLANNING YOUR TIME

St. George's may be your first point of contact with Bermuda, whether or not you plan to visit the parish: Bermuda International Airport is located here, cruise ships berth weekly in the old town, and private yachts arriving at Bermuda are required to clear Customs at the East End. Visitors tend to fall into two distinctly different categories in terms of how they spend their time here. Cruise passengers of the summer and fall flock to the town's beaches and water sports centers, of which there are many. Kayaking, personal watercraft riding, glass-bottomed boat tours, and snorkeling are all great ways to tool around St. George's Harbor and its picturesque islands. Deep-sea fishing and scuba outfitters also operate from the town. Winter visitors tend to seek out the town's historic and natural highlights—its forts, museums, churches, and parks. With a few days to play with, it's easy to combine the best of both worlds.

The old town alone is worth at least a full day's exploration if you intend to properly visit its landmark buildings and stroll intriguing backstreets, not to mention its landmark forts. Exploring on foot is the best strategy. Within the town, King's Square, St. Peter's Church, State House, Tucker House, and the Bermuda National Trust's Rogues & Runners exhibit are vital to understanding the colorful past of St. George. Grand Fort St. Catherine and its beach

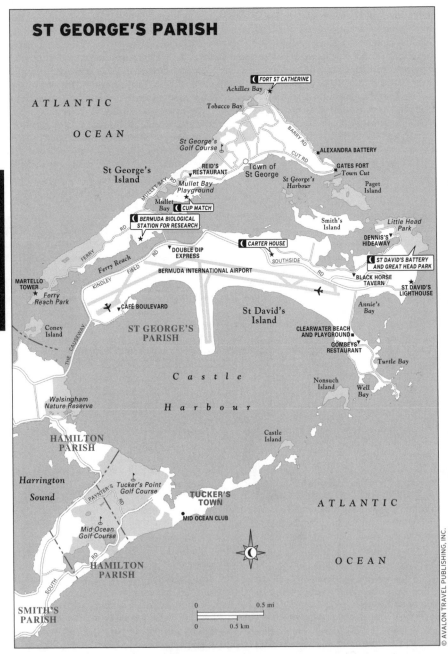

ST GEORGE'S PARISH

should not be missed, either, and along the way are Alexandra Battery and the compact Gates Fort, teetering over the pencil-thin Town Cut, where liners pass, sometimes precariously, into St. George's Harbour from the open sea. With more time, you should expand your tour of the whole parish; if nothing else, a hike through Ferry Reach Park—home of the 1820s Martello Tower and two other forts, a lovely beach and a scenic stretch of Railway Trail—and a fish sandwich or lobster feast in St. David's are well worth the sidetracks. You can get to St. George's by fast ferry from Hamilton (a 45-minute journey), by scooter (a 25-minute ride from the center of the island), or via several bus routes from the capital (Nos. 1, 3, 10, and 11). Don't disregard the possibility of staying in the East End; although there are far fewer accommodations here than in other parishes, there are several well-run bed-and-breakfasts as well as self-catering apartment rentals, allowing travelers to experience St. George overnight and soak in more of its living history. Town authorities are looking forward to a revival of the major hotel property that has sat empty and derelict above Gates Bay, north of the town, for 20 years. The government-owned property, with a multistory hotel, swimming pools, tennis courts, and several acres of land, was a Holiday Inn that shut down in the 1970s. It passed to the Loews group and then operated as a Club Med before finally closing down in 1989 and falling into serious disrepair. After on-again, off-again talks between the government and various groups, including the Four Seasons, a Connecticut-based developer, KJA Inc., was named in 2006. The site will likely be bulldozed and rebuilt as a five-star hotel and golf course.

The old town is revamping itself for the next decade, since winning UNESCO World Heritage status in 2000. Changes have been slow to date, and St. George in winter is still almost a ghost town, its streets so quiet, you can hear a dog's bark or the honk of a car horn several blocks away. However, the next few years promise dramatic updates and additions to the sleepy center. Kicking it off, the nonprofit St. George's Foundation, which drove the UNESCO campaign, opened a World Heritage Centre on historic Penno's Wharf in 2006—a logical starting place for any tour of the parish, with exhibits, informational booths, and helpful staff. The foundation would like to see motor traffic limited in the town and hopes to encourage a more dynamic program of walking tours for pedestrians. Several restaurants in the town center have changed hands and reopened, a tearoom is planned, and a waterfront boardwalk is even being considered—something St. George's mayor, Mariea Caisey, hopes might encourage Bermudians to reacquaint themselves with the town. A draft master plan published in late 2005 included an ambitious wish-list of ideas to transform the town, including a waterfront hotel, on-street alfresco dining, two giant marinas, and a pedestrianized town square and Water Street (the town's main retail artery extending to the Penno's Wharf cruise dock).

Summerlong Harbour Nights on Tuesday evenings bring out locals and visitors galore to buy arts and crafts and listen to local entertainment; retailers stay open until 9 P.M. St. George's is a very festive place to visit over the end-of-year holiday season; the Bermuda National Trust's Christmas Walkabout in early December—a buzzing Friday night street festival attended by thousands—is one of Bermuda's favorite events. And on New Year's Eve, you can watch a mammoth onion drop into King Square as the old town jauntily mimics Manhattan in lively fashion.

The Old Town of St. George

Bermuda's first capital, St. George has remained a living town from its earliest days. Never ruined or rebuilt, like Virginia's Jamestown or Williamsburg, it has retained the look and feel of its 17th-century origins, representing an impressive 400 years of domestic, religious, and military architecture. Because the town was the island's major port and capital for nearly 200 years, the story of St. George is essentially the story of early Bermuda and the island's drastic reversals of fortune that alternately shaped St. George as a boomtown or backwater.

HISTORY

The town was named for England's patron saint and dragon-slayer, Saint George, by an English admiral who claimed Bermuda for the Crown in 1609. Sir George Somers headed the English relief fleet, which in July 1609 was crossing the Atlantic with supplies for James Fort, Virginia, when it was hit by a hurricane. The flagship *Sea Venture*, carrying Somers and 150 men, women, and children, wrecked off St. Catherine's Beach. Miraculously, no one perished in the disaster, nor did the ship sink. Wedged between Bermuda's offshore reefs, *Sea Venture* and her contents were salvaged by the survivors, who spent the next 10 months as castaways on the island, feasting on cahows (a seabird), turtles, and wild hogs. Under Somers' leadership, they fashioned two new ships of island cedar, *Deliverance* and *Patience*. All but three men continued their journey to the New World in 1610, Somers among them. But when the admiral later sailed back to Bermuda to gather more supplies for the starving Virginia settlers, he died, purportedly after eating contaminated meat. His body was returned to his birthplace, Lyme Regis in Dorset, England—now also a World Heritage Site and twinned with St. George since 1996. As was custom, the admiral's heart was left behind, buried in what today is the site of the pretty park, Somers' Garden, near the town center.

The physical town itself began as a collection of palmetto-thatched wooden huts built by the

A Penny Farthing stands outside a scooter livery in St. George, where history merges with the 21st century.

first official settlers, who sailed from England in 1612 aboard the *Plough*. Erected around a market square, the community was first dubbed New London. The colonists, mostly middle-class English from London and surrounding counties, had to learn how to adapt to life in the tropics, including exotic foods such as plantains and pawpaws, and different farming seasons, soils, and climates. Building methods and materials also had to be improvised; by the close of their first century, colonists' huts had been replaced by sturdier limestone buildings. Tobacco farming flourished, land was divided into "tribes," and bridges were built, connecting Bermuda's main islands. In the town, St. Peter's Church and the State House—the colony's first stone building—were landmarks.

Fortifications were important to the fledgling community. Governor Richard Moore put the colonists to work building coastal towers

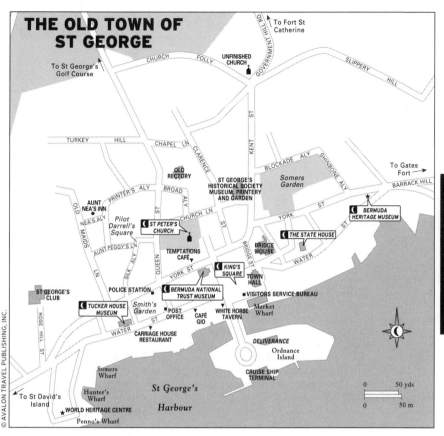

and forts as soon as basic housing had been taken care of. His efforts resulted in Paget and Smith's Batteries, on Paget and Governor's Islands; Pembroke Fort on Cooper's Island; Charles Fort on Charles Island; St. Catherine's Fort on the mainland; and King's Castle on Castle Island—all in St. George's Parish. Indeed, more than half of Bermuda's 90 fortifications were erected here, surviving virtually intact as the earliest English masonry forts of the New World (most in the Americas were constructed of timber). Though always ready for attack, Bermuda never came under enemy fire; cannon shots were fired on a single occasion—in 1614, against a pair of approaching Spanish ships, which immediately fled.

Today, St. George and its related fortifications can rest easy against enemy bombardment. The UNESCO site is considered "a place of cultural heritage of the greatest importance for humanity" and under the Hague Convention of 1954, military generals who bomb such historic treasures can be thrown in jail.

A pattern of economic stagnation, disease, and starvation interspersed with periods of immense prosperity characterized the development of the old capital, and Bermuda as a whole. As the second century of colonization began, Bermudians turned to the sea for their livelihoods, giving birth to a maritime economy that shaped St. George as never before. Whaling, shipbuilding, piloting, privateering, and maritime trade built immense benefits for entrepreneurial islanders. Bermudian shipyards began producing cedar sloops whose sleek, innovative design—long bowsprits, mountains of sail—became world-famous. Before long, the speedy, durable craft were a major export and the vessel of choice among merchants and privateers. Shipbuilding provided thousands of jobs for blacksmiths, shipwrights, carpenters, masons, and caulkers, and throughout the first half of the 18th century, the old town's docks bustled with activity as it grew into a thriving port.

Agriculture suffered as a result, and by the mid-1700s, islanders were on the brink of famine, totally at the mercy of trade with America. That lifeline was cut off in 1775 when Britain's rebellious North American colonies halted exports to British territories and also barred Bermudian ships from East Coast ports. Bermuda was caught between its loyalty to the Crown and its strong commercial and family ties to America. Those conflicting loyalties came to a head in St. George in August 1775, when a group of islanders crept ashore at Tobacco Bay and stole more than 100 casks of gunpowder from an unguarded magazine. The ammunition's destination? George Washington's Continental Army. Just weeks earlier, Washington had mentioned the magazine in a letter sent to "the inhabitants of Bermuda, " praising their "favor and friendship to North America and its liberties" and promising their support would be mutually beneficial: "Be assured the whole power and exertion of my influence will be made with the honorable Continental Congress, that your island may not only be supplied with provisions," he wrote, "but experience every other mark of affection and friendship…"

The successful "Gunpowder Plot" rescued Bermuda from starvation but also underscored the island's weak military protection. After the close of the American Revolutionary War in 1783, Britain, reeling from the loss of all its ports between Canada and the Caribbean, began to focus on turning Bermuda into a "Gibraltar of the West." At the West End, work began on a naval dockyard for the British fleet, while military activity in the East End signaled

a boon for St. George, which remained a strategic military point for the next 200 years. It became a key garrison town, with barracks for British soldiers built on "Barrack Hill" in the late 1700s, as well as residences for senior officers, messes, hospitals, and a garrison church. Like their counterparts at Prospect, Devonshire, many of these old military buildings can still be seen today.

St. George lost its status as capital in this period. A lot of shipping and trade had shifted to the Great Sound, and public pressure demanded a more conveniently located port at the island's center. Authorities also wanted a central entrepôt to thwart local smugglers who could offload merchandise in other parishes before going to the old town to declare their cargoes. Pembroke Parish was chosen for the new town, officially incorporated in 1793. The General Assembly's first meeting in Hamilton's Town Hall was held in 1815, moving the seat of government after 200 years.

Yellow fever epidemics and economic slumps intervened in the mid-1800s, but war would once again rescue the town. The bitter four-year U.S. Civil War (1861–65) pumped money, people, and industry into St. George, as, once again, Bermudian loyalties took advantage of economic opportunity. While the island, like Britain, was officially neutral, Bermudian sympathies lay heavily with the South—as did Britain's for its mills' badly needed shipments of "White Gold," or Southern cotton. From the war's earliest days, therefore, St. George became a staging post for blockade-runners, fast gunboats that dodged Union ships to deliver arms, food, and luxury goods to ports like Wilmington, North Carolina, in return for cotton. St. George became a trans-shipment port, its wharves used to hold Southern cotton sent on to England. It was a major turning point for the East End; isolation and poverty gave way to a hive of cosmopolitan activity. Spies, Confederates, Union soldiers, and political agents filled the town, making it the "principal depot of arms and munitions of war," in the words of Union commander Charles Wilkes.

Tourism did the same for St. George in the

20th century, as international visitors came to soak up its history and quaint surroundings. The development of Tucker's Town—the brainchild of island businessmen and the Furness Withy cruise line—turned 500 rural acres of St. George's Parish into a glitzy resort, the Mid Ocean Club, that attracted the rich and famous to Bermuda in the 1920s and 1930s. It has remained an exclusive enclave ever since, though the controversial buyout of 24 black landowners who fought to stay on the Castle Harbour peninsula remains a sore point in the island's racial history.

Another major conflict—World War II—changed the face of St. George's forever. Under a land-lease deal between Britain and the United States, the islands of Castle Harbor were joined in a massive landfill project to create an airfield for the U.S. Army. Cooper's Island, Longbird Island, and St. David's were linked together, and by the project's conclusion in 1941, an additional 750 acres of land had been added to the parish for the creation of the U.S. Naval Air Station and its Kindley Field Airbase—a civilian airport after the war. After the American military left Bermuda in 1995, the East End baseland around the airport was renamed "Southside" and opened for public use. Beaches, a cinema, a supermarket, and sports areas sit on the land, vast by Bermuda's standards, which is also being used to build affordable housing.

SIGHTS

The old town has a plethora of public museums and historic sites open to visitors most of the year, but bear in mind as you stroll around that the entire community lays claim to the World Heritage designation. As a result, the bank where you get your cash advance, the store where you buy a cashmere sweater, the home where your bartender lives may all be immensely historic as well. Scores of pre-1800 structures are scattered throughout the town, and many are marked with their own World Heritage plaques. These include **Stockdale,** a private home on Printer's Alley; **Esten House** on King's Square, now home to an art gallery

and shops; **Stiles House,** the Bank of Bermuda HSBC's branch on Water Street; the postcard-pretty **Fanny Fox's Cottage** at the top of Duke of Clarence Street; and many others that aren't marked at all.

King's Square

A tour of St. George should begin at King's Square, which like every other market square in the world has long been the hub of its community's life. Emblazoned with the town crest, the **Town Hall** (tel. 441/297-1532, 10 A.M.–4 P.M. Mon.–Sat., admission free) is the meeting place of the mayor, aldermen, and town councilors who represent the Corporation of St. George (whose offices are housed in modern premises on Ordnance Island). The building is furnished in cedar, and its walls pay tribute to past mayors, their portraits gazing down on visitors. On the northern edge of the square, you can't miss a couple of **Stocks and Pillory**—contraptions used in past times to publicly embarrass citizens guilty of minor transgressions from petty theft to cheating on a spouse. Tourists typically pose for photos here, their necks and arms stuck through the now easily liftable wooden frames to mimic 17th-century citizens who would have been pelted with rotten fruit or eggs by the watching crowd. Near the water's edge, the historic **Ducking Stool** dunked women accused of being "nags and gossips." Popular 15-minute re-enactments are held several times a week for the amusement of modern-day tourists.

Attached to the square by bridge is **Ordnance Island,** once the British military's storeplace for munitions, as well as a gallows site. Now it is home to a cruise-ship wharf and small harbor-front park, where a bronze statue of Bermuda's founder, *Sir George Somers,* by Bermudian sculptor Desmond Fountain, throws arms to the sky in apparent relief at reaching land at the island in 1609. Also here is a replica of *Deliverance* (tel. 441/297-1459, 9 A.M.–5 P.M. April–Oct., $3 adults, $1 children)—the ship built by Somers and the other shipwrecked *Sea Venture* castaways to sail on to Jamestown, Virginia. The life-size model contains cabins that demonstrate the claustrophobic nature of life aboard

© ROSEMARY JONES

King's Square is hemmed by historic buildings and stocks and pillories.

such vessels. Climb onto the decks and imagine tossing on 20-foot seas for the full effect.

❰ The State House

On a hilltop over King's Square stands the distinctive white State House (corner of King St. and Princess St., 10 A.M.–4 P.M. Wed., except holidays, admission free), the 17th-century colony's first stone building—and the only structure of the period that survived. Built in 1622, it was used alternately as a munitions storage depot, a courthouse, and home of the world's oldest parliament outside of Britain. For 200 years, the State House was the seat of government for the colonial General Assembly's meetings. It is constructed of sturdy limestone blocks set in a mortar of turtle oil and lime; it's believed some of the island's first West Indian slaves may have helped to build it, introducing new methods at a time when cedar-framed structures were the norm. An original third story used for holding gunpowder was removed during 1730 renovations. It was restored again in 1969. Most notoriously, the State House was

the venue for more than two dozen witch trials over the colony's first century, which, as in similar instances throughout Europe and America, resulted in the public hanging, burning, or torture of innocent women. Since 1816, the State House has been rented for the annual sum of a single peppercorn by Bermuda's oldest Masonic lodge, St. George No. 200 of the Grand Lodge of Scotland. The paltry due is paid at a colorful public ceremony in the town square every spring, attended by the Governor and Bermuda Regiment.

❰ St. Peter's Church

One of Bermuda's most famous hallmark buildings, St. Peter's Church (Duke of York St., tel. 441/297-0216, 10 A.M.–4:30 P.M. Mon.–Sat., 11 A.M. service on Sunday) is a favorite venue for local weddings and funerals, where attendees crowd into the quaint, cedar-packed interior. The original church on this site was made of wood and thatched in palm fronds by the first settlers in 1612. It was here that the first meeting of the fledgling Assembly was

© ROSEMARY JONES

the landmark State House, Bermuda's first stone building

held on August 1, 1620, two years before the State House was built as the government's dedicated headquarters. Among the items on that inaugural agenda: a ban on both "idle and unprofitable persons" and the slaughter of turtles. Although the first structure did not survive, St. Peter's is built on the same site, qualifying it as the oldest Anglican church in the Western Hemisphere. St. Peter's was rebuilt in stone in 1713, and its tower was added in 1814. Inside, its exposed cedar ceiling beams and pews, cedar altar table, and dole cupboard (used to store donations of bread for the parish poor) are all excellent examples of early craftsmanship; the furniture is believed to be the oldest on the island. St. Peter's collection of communion silver is also notable; the St. George's Chalice belonged to Charles I (1625–26), while the King's Set Chalice bears the royal arms of William III (1697–98). There is also a rare piece of 1616 Hogge money on display, an example of the island's earliest coins, decorated with the iconic image of the wild pigs that roamed Bermuda in the first years of settlement.

The church graveyards are almost as fascinating. In the eastern graveyard, notable townsfolk are buried alongside modern VIPs; an example of the latter is Sir Richard Sharpes, Bermuda's Governor who was assassinated in 1973. He lies here alongside his aide-de-camp, Captain Hugh Sayers, of the Welsh Guards, who was slain by the same gunman in the shocking episode. Under the shade of coconut palms, a western graveyard separated from the other, holds the bodies of town slaves and free blacks. Even after Emancipation on August 1, 1834, Bermuda's black and white societies remained divided until official segregation was outlawed in the 1960s. A solemn walk and ceremony is held at this site every year on the eve of Cup Match, whose Thursday public holiday in late July or early August celebrates Emancipation Day.

◀ Bermuda National Trust Museum

Few Americans realize the strategic role tiny Bermuda played in the U.S. Civil War (1861–65). The Bermuda National Trust Museum

(Globe Hotel, King's Square, tel. 441/297-1423, 10 A.M.–4 P.M. Mon.–Sat., $5 adults, $2 children 6–18) tells the dramatic story of blockade-runners, spies, and international subterfuge when the town was a hotbed of Southern sympathies, Union authorities, and British cotton smugglers. The four years' war activity brought a torrent of unprecedented wealth to St. George, marking a heyday in its history. The Globe Hotel dates back to around 1700, when the island's governor Samuel Day sparked a bitter court battle when he tried to claim it for his own; he later died in prison. The building later became the headquarters of Confederate agent Major Norman Walker, who lived here with his wife Georgiana and their three children while he masterminded the flow of guns and war supplies through Union blockades. The museum's exhibit, Rogues & Runners, details the complex web of loyalties in Bermuda in that era and how the town became a major port for rebel Southern captains and a trans-shipment center for U.K.–bound cotton. Included in the admission is a brief film about Bermuda and St. George. The museum shop sells Bermuda books, souvenirs, and arts and crafts.

(Bermuda Heritage Museum

A tribute to black Bermudian history, the Bermuda Heritage Museum (Samaritans Lodge, tel. 441/297-4126, 10 A.M.–3 P.M. Tues.–Sat., closed holidays, $3 adults, $2 children, under five free) opened in 1998 in a historically relevant building. The 19th-century lodge belonged to the Grand United Order of Good Samaritans, one of the largest so-called "Friendly Societies," which aided newly freed blacks before and after Emancipation in 1834. The museum records the story of slavery and these societies, as well as related symbols and other folklore such as the gombey tradition and the origins of Cup Match. One of the recommended stops on the African Diaspora Trail, the museum highlights historical milestones of black pride, notably the 1959 Theatre Boycott, a protest by black moviegoers that brought about the end of official racial segregation in

restaurants, hotels, and schools. Black entrepreneurs, sporting figures, and politicians are also honored.

(Tucker House Museum

Built as a merchant's house, this simple whitewashed building takes its name from Henry Tucker, one of the colony's most important figures as president of the Governor's Council. Walking through its elegant interior takes you back to the time of candlelit chandeliers, brick ovens, and four-poster beds. Tucker House Museum (Water St., at the junction of Barber's Alley, tel. 441/297-0545, 10 A.M.–4 P.M. Mon.–Sat., $5 adults, $2 children 6–18) is a treasure trove of priceless antiques, including English mahogany and Bermudian cedar furniture, family portraits by American artist Joseph Blackburn, and domestic items such as handsewn quilts and kitchen utensils. On the lower floor, visit the archaeological display, which chronicles recent years' excavations and the artifacts found below the cellar floor. Also particularly notable is the kitchen, where Joseph Hayne Rainey, a freed South Carolina slave and later the first black member of the U.S. House of Representatives, operated a barbershop for several years. The adjoining **Barber's Alley** pays tribute to Hainey and his seamstress wife, who both escaped to Bermuda during the American Civil War and set up successful businesses before returning to the United States. Off this alleyway, there is a pocket-sized public garden, Smith's Garden, which Princess Anne officially opened in 1991.

Somers' Garden

For a tranquil break between museum tours or a shady lunchtime picnic, visit Somers' Garden (open sunrise to sunset daily, admission free), the town's largest public park. Bordered by Duke of York Street, Shinbone Alley, Blockade Alley, and Duke of Kent Street, the park has a fine collection of palms and other plants amid its manicured lawns and flower beds. The oasis is named for Sir George Somers, whose heart was buried here, commemorated by a stone monument in the park's center.

St. George's Historical Society & Museum, Printery, and Garden

Tucked away in the backstreets, the headquarters of the St. George's Historical Society (Featherbed Alley, tel. 441/297-0423, 10 A.M.–3 P.M. Mon.–Fri. April–Dec., 10 A.M.–3 P.M. Wed. only Jan.–March, $5 adults, $2 children under 12) is home to an intriguing little museum, a historic printery, and a pretty garden. The building itself is an 18th-century gem, complete with traditional "welcoming arms" stairway. Like Tucker House, its rooms are full of interesting possessions that give us a sense of life long before email, television, and motorized transport. The building's lower floor is especially historic: it was the site of the island's first printing press, operated by the King's printer, Joseph Stockdale, to produce the colony's original newspaper. Inside is a working replica of a 15th-century Gutenberg Printing Press, like the one Stockdale used.

The Old Rectory

The Old Rectory (Broad Alley, behind St. Peter's Church, tel. 441/297-4261, 1–5 P.M. Wed. Nov.–March only, admission free) is a Bermuda National Trust property rented as a private home, but it is open to the public at certain times. One of the most photographed facades on the island, the quaint homestead with its rose-dotted gardens is one of Bermuda's oldest buildings, dating back to 1699. It once belonged to infamous Bermudian pirate Captain George Dew, and later to Parson Alexander Richardson, who was nicknamed the "Little Bishop."

The Unfinished Church

Like Gaudi's unmistakable Sagrada Familia Cathedral in Barcelona, Bermuda's Unfinished Church (Government Hill Rd., at top of Duke of Kent St., admission free) is a story of half-done architectural artistry. Leased by the Bermuda National Trust, the Victorian Gothic structure was the victim of financial problems, infighting by its congregation, and a series of vicious storms. Begun in 1874, it was intended as a grand replacement for St. Peter's Church but was never completed. The structure's soaring arches, cruciform shape, and imposing—but roofless—tower give a hint of the grandeur the architects hoped to achieve.

ENTERTAINMENT AND EVENTS

Top hats and bonnets come out amid full pomp and regalia for the annual **Peppercorn Ceremony,** held in mid- to late April. The tradition dates back to 1815, when the seat of the island's government finally moved to the new capital, Hamilton. As a conciliatory gesture, the Assembly, which was vacating its longtime home at the State House, symbolically passed on the building to the mayor, aldermen, and councilors of the new Corporation of St. George. The yearly rent requested for Bermuda's oldest Masonic Lodge, St. George No. 200 of the Grand Lodge of Scotland, was one peppercorn. Every year, government dignitaries drive to the East End en masse to join the Governor, who, in feathered helmet, presides over the official handover ceremony on King's Square. A 17-gun salute heralds the Governor's arrival, and the Bermuda Regiment's Band & Corps of Drums also performs. The 45-minute spectacle, watched by schoolchildren and crowds of curious tourists, includes the high-decibel proclamations of the Town Crier of St. George, who rings his bell and yells loudly enough to bring the entire congregation to immediate silence. The peppercorn is presented on a velvet cushion laid out on a silver platter, like the princess's pea of the Hans Christian Anderson fairy tale. For annual dates, contact the Corporation of St. George (5 Ordnance Island, tel. 441/297-1532).

Held the first Friday evening in December, the Bermuda National Trust's **Christmas Walkabout** in St. George's has become a calendar institution. Thousands pour into the old town after work to sip cider and meet old friends while strolling the historic streets, strung with festive illuminations. Stores stay open late to sell Christmas gifts, candle-lit museums offer free admission, and carolers fill King's Square with song. For information, contact the Trust (tel. 441/236-6483).

ST. GEORGE'S

Other holiday events in the town include the annual **Santa Claus Parade,** with majorettes, elves, and child-pleaser St. Nick, and the **New Year's Eve** celebrations at King's Square, complete with the dropping of a giant (fake) Bermuda onion.

Throughout the April–October high season, Tuesday **"Heritage Nights"** celebrations are held around King's Square, the East End counterpart to Hamilton's Wednesday Harbour Nights. The lively street festival includes gombey displays and a showcase of arts and crafts for sale.

Pretend you're a 17th-century plebeian at the weekly **Ducking Stool** (Wed. and Sat. year-round, with extra days added according to cruise-ship schedules) re-enactments on King's Square. The bellowing Town Crier calls everyone to order at 11:45 A.M. before the volunteer "wench" gets her due in the harbor to the delight of onlookers at the stroke of noon. The 15-minute demonstration harks back to the days when women were punished for crimes like gossiping and nagging.

Nightlife

It has to be said—St. George is dead in winter. "We roll the streets up after 6 P.M.," jokes one resident. But summer is a different story, with hundreds of partying cruise-ship passengers and crews creating a hopping little nightlife scene.

Harborfront sports bar **White Horse Tavern** (8 King's Square, tel. 441/297-1838, www.whitehorsebermuda.com, 10 P.M.–3 A.M. Mon., Tues., Wed., Thurs.) gets especially lively during the summer cruise season, morphing into a packed nightclub with DJs and specials like ladies' and crew nights.

SHOPPING

St. George has a fraction of Hamilton's shops, and many are branch stores, but there's plenty of retail therapy to enjoy regardless. Shops around King's Square sell T-shirts and other tacky tourist mementos, but Water Street and Duke of York Streets have worthwhile perfume, clothing, and shoe stores, toy stores, and a highly recommended bookstore. Somers

Shops, restaurants, and museums line Water Street in St. George.

Wharf, west along Water Street, has a small shopping complex on the waterfront.

Formerly located on a massive property in Hamilton Parish, where several acres of manicured gardens and towering trees made one of Bermuda's best nature walks, **The Bermuda Perfumery** (Stewart Hall, Queen St., tel. 441/293-0627, 9 A.M.–5 P.M. Mon.–Sat.) relocated to St. George in 2004 when the historic garden property was sold to a developer. The perfume business was sold separately, to Kirby and Isobel Brackstone, who have reopened in the history-steeped surroundings of Stewart Hall, a Bermuda National Trust property. The building houses their production center and retail outlet, where the world-famous bottles of White Oleander, Bermudiana, Frangipani, and other varieties of perfume are sold. There are also talcum powders and body creams in the same hallmark scents. Free tours are given to visitors interested in how the fragrances are made.

Designer perfumes can be found at **Peniston Brown** (6 Water St., tel. 441/297-1525), many of them at U.S. prices. Guerlain makeup products are also sold here.

Artists **Carole Holding** (King's Square, tel. 441/297-1833) and **Jill Amos Raine** (Bermuda Memories, 7 King's Square, tel. 441/297-8104) sell their works from respective retail outlets and can sometimes be seen painting alfresco around the town.

One of my favorite bookstores anywhere, **The Book Cellar** (Tucker House Basement, Water St., tel. 441/297-0448) boasts well-stocked shelves of fiction, including British best-sellers, classic literature, coffee-table editions, gift books, and a small kids' section. The standing-room-only space, squeezed beneath Tucker House Museum, also carries a full selection of Bermuda books.

Aside from the expected toiletries and candy, **Robertson's Drug Store** (24 York St., St. George, tel. 441/297-1828, pharmacy 441/297-1736, 8 A.M.–7:30 P.M. Mon.–Sat., 4–6 P.M. Sun.) also stocks a wonderful array of well-chosen toys, beach gear, children's books, pulp fiction, magazines, newspapers, greetings cards, and children's art supplies.

Cigar-lovers will want to seek out **Churchill's** (27 Duke of York St., tel. 441/297-1650, fax 441/297-0814, churchills@myoffice.bm), home of fine Cuban cigars and a good selection of wines, spirits, and gift items, including an array of wine-bottle openers and other bar essentials.

SPORTS AND RECREATION
Scuba and Water Sports

Summer brings an explosion of water sports to St. George, from kayak tours and glass-bottomed boats to snorkeling, scuba, personal watercraft riding, parasailing, helmet-diving, and motorboat rentals. You can take part in an organized tour, or rent a boat and do your own thing. There are so many bays, coves, harbors, and islands in the East End—from St. George's Harbour to Castle Harbour, Ferry Reach, and Coney Island—and exploring them from the water brings a whole new perspective, even for Bermudians. Paddling a kayak is a particularly good way to get around; the wildlife, including turtles, is least disturbed, and you'll see things the Jet Ski speed demon won't. Some outfitters have centers on the St. George's waterfront; others based in nearby Hamilton Parish set up transport or information outlets at Ordnance Island.

K.S. Watersports & Jetski Tours (8 King's Square, in front of the White Horse Tavern, tel. 441/297-4155, fax 441/297-2771, 9 A.M.–6 P.M. daily in season) rents Jet Skis by the hour or half day for zooming around St. George's Harbour.

Blue Hole Watersports (Grotto Bay Beach Resort, Blue Hole Hill, tel. 441/293-2915 or 441/293-8333 ext. 37) has sit-on-top kayaks, Sunfish sailboats, sailboards, or bimini-topped Boston Whaler motorboats for exploring the waters of Castle Harbour and its history-laden islets, Ferry Reach, St. George's Harbour, or the islands of St. David's.

Scuba outfitters **Triangle Diving** (Grotto Bay Beach Resort, 11 Blue Hole Hill, Hamilton Parish, tel. 441/293-7319) offer one- and two-tank dives, including wreck dives, and PADI courses.

RETURN OF THE CAHOW

The Bermuda petrel or cahow (*Pterodroma cahow*) is the island's most famous endemic species. Its return from the brink of extinction is the stuff of a Hollywood comeback classic.

Gadfly petrels are specific to a single oceanic island or group of islands – in the cahow's case, Bermuda. While they nest on land, the powerful, agile fliers spend most of their lives at sea, returning to lay eggs and hatch a single chick that spends the first eight years of life far from land over the open ocean. In the 1500s, the nocturnal birds were so abundant, their high-pitched courtship calls scared off passing mariners who believed the islands inhabited by devils. "A kind of web-footed fowl there is, and hovering in the air and over the sea, made a strange hollow and harsh howling," wrote shipwrecked English colonist William Strachey in his epic 1610 account. Fossil remains indicate up to a half million pairs were nesting on Bermuda, inhabiting rock crevices or burrows on the forest floor. Tragically, however, castaways and wild hogs landed as food supply by passing ships destroyed the cahow population. By the time colonists arrived a century later, with rats and domestic animals, they fed in such large quantities off the tame birds that within a decade, reports of the time indicate cahows were almost nonexistent.

In January 1951, after an absence of more than 300 years, seven breeding pairs were discovered by Robert Cushman Murphy, curator of birds at the American Museum of Natural History, and Bermudians Louis S. Mowbray and David Wingate. The trio found the gray and white birds living on the East End islets of Castle Harbour, which were immediately declared wildlife sanctuaries. "It was kind of like rediscovering the dodo," remembers Wingate, a 15-year-old student at the time, who made the cahow his life work. After graduating from Cornell University, he returned to Bermuda, where he was named the island's first conservation officer in 1966, a post he held until he retired in 2000. During that time, he was almost solely responsible for the cahow's return, creating a "living laboratory" of endemic species at Nonsuch Island, as well as overseeing cahow nests on other isolated islets and even creating artificial burrows to encourage nesting. Today, another Bermudian, Jeremy Madeiros, continues his work.

Cahows have been the subjects of numerous documentaries and media coverage in the past few years, including a feature-length film, *Rara Avis*, released in 2006 by Bermudian filmmaker Lucinda Spurling, which made the rounds of international film festivals. The birds remain exceedingly rare – just 60 breeding pairs are known to exist. But conservationists are confident that if protective measures continue, the bird once thought gone for good will keep flourishing.

Adventure Enterprises (Ordnance Island, tel. 441/297-1459, adventure@cwbda. bm) runs sightseeing and snorkeling tours around Tucker's Town and Castle Harbour, aboard its two powerful motorboats, 25-foot Nautica RIB *Argo I,* which can carry up to 15 people, and the larger 36-foot Timaran *Argo II,* for 36 people.

Husband and wife team, and co-captains, Virginia and Stephen McKey, operate **Kayak Bermuda** (Ordnance Island, tel. 441/505-2925 or 441/737-7378, March–Nov.), offer a combined three-hour kayaking and sightseeing tour aboard their 33-foot Safari motor yacht, taking passengers to outlying islands, where they can paddle around on glass-bottomed kayaks before returning to the boat.

St. Georgian skipper **Beau Evans** (tel. 441/335-2425, www.charterbermuda.com) offers snorkeling, sightseeing, sailing, and private charter tours aboard 65-foot glass-bottom motor yacht *Coral Sea* (departs King's Square 1:15 P.M. Mon.–Sat., 11 A.M. Thurs., $30 adults, $15 children 12 and under) and 60-foot catamarans *Rising Son II* and *Sundeck II.*

NONSUCH ISLAND

Its evocative name is alluring enough, but what the East End's Nonsuch Island represents in the environmental world is akin to a scientific miracle. Starting in the 1960s, David Wingate, the island's first conservation officer, almost single-handedly re-created Bermuda's original habitats on Nonsuch Island, bringing back the cahow, or Bermuda petrel, from near-extinction in the process.

The island is the largest of several that sit off Castle Harbor, including Governor's Island, Castle Island, and Southampton Island – where the first settlers built landmark forts in the 17th century. In the 1930s, Nonsuch served as the marine research station headquarters for American deep-ocean pioneer William Beebe's expeditions off Bermuda. But it was in 1951 that Nonsuch and the other islets won world renown when they were found to be the last nesting habitats of the cahow.

Nonsuch at the time was covered in invasive plant species, though introduced animals such as toads and rats had not made it across the bay from the mainland. Through Wingate's efforts, Nonsuch was immediately declared a protected nature reserve, and over the decades, with much culling and re-planting, it was transformed into a "living laboratory," in his words, of the island's indigenous flora and fauna. Wingate – whose daughter Janet recounts life as a 12-year-old on the island in her 2005 memoir, *Nonsuch Summer* – re-created pristine wetlands, mangroves, cedar and palmetto forests, as well as shoreline coastal habitats and bird-viewing areas. Nonsuch has remained an oasis for nature amid Bermuda's drastically changing environment.

In the past few years, special eco-tours to Nonsuch arranged through the Bermuda Biological Station for Research became very popular. But these were halted after hurricane surges destroyed the island's main dock in 2003. Special visits can now be arranged by appointment only through Pam Wade at the Department of Conservation Services (tel. 441/293-4464, ext. 145, pwade@gov.bm).

ST. GEORGE'S

Spas

Tucked into a mini-plaza, **Bersalon Cool Waters Spa Salon** (Water St., tel. 441/297-1528, 9 A.M.–6 P.M. daily) offers well-priced face and body treatments for men and women, including massage (Swedish, 50 minutes, $85), manicure (60 minutes, $60), as well as waxing and hair services.

Tours

East Ender **Alison Outerbridge** (tel. 441/297-2086, by appointment) conducts informative walking tours throughout the World Heritage Site, throwing in history, folklore and modern-day anecdotes.

For Kids

Children love the old town of St. George—even without the gombeys, Christmas walkabouts, or Heritage Nights street festivals. Watching anglers clean their catch off Ordnance Island or a raucous Ducking Stool performance is free outdoor theater for children. They also may enjoy exploring the zanily named backstreets, seeing just how old-time colonists lived during tours of historic gems like Tucker House, and romping on the green lawns of Somers Garden. The laid-back nature of the town seems to appeal to children, and most of the cafés and restaurants have kid-friendly items on the menu.

ACCOMMODATIONS

While there are few hotels and resorts in the East End, a growing number of very reasonable, family-run bed-and-breakfast accommodations and self-catering apartment rentals offer travelers an inexpensive but comfortable way to experience living in St. George.

Under $100

Like his parents, St. Georgian Brian Oatley has been providing travelers with a comfortable, cost-effective place to stay in the old town for a few seasons now. A studio apartment attached to his home, **Gobblers Corner** (1 Turkey Hill, tel. 441/297-2519 or 441/337-0561, oatley@ northrock.bm, doubles $95) has a single bed and a queen pullout sofa, a large bathroom with shower, air-conditioning, cable TV, washer and dryer, and a kitchen with refrigerator, stove, and microwave. A private backyard has a barbecue for self-catering. Located just two minutes away from the town center, in the picturesque backstreets, the apartment makes a handy little pied-à-terre for travelers who don't seek resort-style amenities.

$100-200

You couldn't find a more historic place to lay your head than the **Old Rectory Bed and Breakfast** (1 Broad Alley, tel. 441/297-4261, oldrectory@northrock.bm, doubles $100–150). Muriel Scott-Smith, who rents the historic homestead from Bermuda National Trust, runs a bed-and-breakfast in the 1699 former pirate's abode, whose traditional architecture and picturesque backstreet garden has made it a popular target of passing photographers. There are two guest rooms, one with a queen-size bed and fireplace, the other with twin beds. Both share a bathroom with bath and shower and a living room and dining room. Guests can meet the resident ghost and Muriel's Burmese cat.

It's worth staying at **Crooked Elbow** (5 Shinbone Alley, tel. 441/297-0898, $140 doubles) for the address alone. Residents Clifford and Anne Rowe rent out the lower apartment of their historic home. Included are a bedroom with queen-size bed, living room, full kitchen, bathroom, and dining room.

Even the name sounds welcoming at ◀ **Aunt Nea's Inn at Hillcrest** (tel. 441/297-1630, fax 441/297-1908, www.auntneas.com, summer rates $190–230 doubles), and the rooms don't disappoint. The homestead's 15 units invite relaxation, thanks to their decor (four-poster, canopy, and sleigh beds) and historic location, tucked on a quiet backstreet and surrounded by walled gardens. Innkeepers Delaey Robinson (a former Opposition Finance Minister) and his wife Andrea Dismont run the place with professional calm, the third generation of Wright-Robinsons since 1900 to do so (the well-traveled couple, who have two young sons, also rent out a vacation home—La Casa de Bermudez—in Santa Fe, New Mexico). Aunt Nea's, built in the 1700s, was named for the love interest of Irish poet Tom Moore—a married teenager who did not return his affections. The property also served as the home of the American Consul in Bermuda at one time. Nonsmoking rooms have en suite bathrooms, cable TV, air-conditioning, and telephones. Dismont and Robinson make guests feel completely at home, right down to the chocolate-chip cookies served in the parlor.

Over $300

The St. George's Club (6 Rose Hill, tel. 441/297-1200, fax 441/297-8003, www .stgeorgeclub.com, rates start at $325, plus $9 per person per day housekeeping charge) is a cottage complex time-share facility that also offers short-term rentals for travelers, space permitting. The club has a total of 25 air-conditioned cottages, all with cable TV and fully equipped kitchens. Guests enjoy the use of a private beach club, three freshwater pools (one is heated), an on-site convenience store, three tennis courts, a putting green, and the next-door St. George's Golf Club—a par-62 Robert Trent Jones course owned by the government. There is also a business center with Internet access, photocopier, fax machine, and FedEx services. Cut into the hillside, the resort's one- and two-bedroom cottages have spectacular views of the old town.

FOOD
Cafés and Pubs

At the foot of the stairs leading up to St. Peter's Church, **Temptations Café & Bakery** (31 York St., tel. 441/297-1368, 8:30 A.M.–5 P.M. Mon.–Fri., 8:30 A.M.–4 P.M. Sat. and Sun.) serves up sinful treats in its simple interior, including cakes, pastries, and muffins, as well as sandwiches, hot soups, coffee, and cold drinks. Sit at banquettes with views out to Duke of York Street, or farther inside at tables. Be careful when you step outside, too; the sidewalk is so skinny, you risk falling into the busy thoroughfare's traffic.

The East End outlet of popular islandwide fast-food chain **The Upper Crust** (14 Duke of York St., tel. 441/297-3434, open 11 A.M.–10 P.M. –Thurs., 11 A.M.–11 P.M. Fri. and Sat., noon–10 P.M. Sun.) serves up pizzas, calzones, salads, wraps, soups, sandwiches, and Indian and specialty dishes, even fish 'n' chips. It also delivers.

Renamed to pay tribute to one of the town's namesakes (the dragon-slayer), **The George and Dragon** (3 King's Square, tel. 441/297-1717, open noon–midnight daily), formerly Freddie's Pub on the Square, reopened in the summer of 2006 with a new menu and owners—the successful Henry VIII Pub/Robin Hood Pub group. Two entrances divide the site's twin spaces: a serious sports bar with multi TV screens and takeout deli offerings on the ground floor, and a more upscale, though comfortable, restaurant serving pastas, seafood, steaks, and other hearty pub fare upstairs.

◖ Angeline's Coffee Shop (48 Duke of York St., tel. 441/297-0959, breakfast and lunch 8 A.M.–3 P.M. Mon.–Fri., 8 A.M.–noon Sat.) is the kind of place where time slips effortlessly away. Tucked into the busy main street, the tiny eatery serves up java and plenty else, including Western omelettes, sandwiches, macaroni 'n' cheese—and lots of local atmosphere. Try the juicy, homemade burgers.

White Horse Tavern (8 King's Square, tel. 441/297-1838, www.whitehorsebermuda.com, all-day breakfast and lunch 11 A.M.–5 P.M. Mon.–Fri., breakfast 9–11 A.M. Sat. and Sun., dinner 5–9:30 P.M. daily) is a waterside sports bar offering a codfish breakfast on Sundays. It specializes in pub and seafood dishes, and takeout is available.

Formerly The Wharf Tavern, **Tavern by the Sea** (14 Water St., tel. 441/297-3305, fax 441/297-3227, tbts@therock.bm, 11:30 A.M.–10 P.M. daily, happy hour 5–7 P.M. Mon.–Fri.) is a perfect spot to sit outside on the harbor's edge and watch visiting yachties load up provisions or work on their boats. The menu offers local reasonably priced specialties and pub favorites, including nachos, fish chowder, satisfying hot and cold sandwiches, grilled wahoo, fish 'n' chips, burgers, pizzas, salads—and swizzles, if you *really* want to relax. There are vegetarian and children's menus, and takeout service.

The view is the main attraction at **Griffin's Bar & Grill** (St. George's Club, 6 Rose Hill, tel. 441/297-4235 or 441/297-1200, dinner 5 P.M.–1 A.M. Mon.–Fri., breakfast and lunch 9 A.M.–2:30 P.M., dinner 5–9 P.M. Sat.), a lively sports bar–style restaurant with a popular Sunday brunch buffet.

Sushi

For an East End sushi fix, try **Sushi Tei** (16 Duke of York St., tel. 441/297-5085 or 441/297-5086, 11 A.M.–10 P.M. Mon.–Sat.), where the takeout menu features regular rolls ($5.75), 12-piece special rolls ($14.95), nigiri, sashimi, salads, tempura, Japanese grill, noodles, and side orders such as eel tofu and stir-fry.

Mediterranean

The People's Choice Award-winner at the 2005 Bermuda Culinary Festival, **◖ Café Gio** (36 Water St., tel. 441/297-1307, www.portocall.bm, lunch 11:30 A.M.–2:30 P.M., dinner 5:30–9:30 P.M. Mon.–Sat.) received kudos for service, food, and overall excellence—no real surprise, given the restaurant's popularity. Formerly San Giorgio, it was bought by the highly successful Port O' Call restaurant group in 2004 (sister eateries are Port O' Call and Bistro J in Hamilton). Sit inside the bistro-style dining area, or out on the harborside deck or terrace. The menu is Mediterranean-meets-Asian fusion, with appetizers such as goat cheese bruschetta ($8.50) or Bermuda fish cakes in coconut reduction ($9.50), and entrées including mahimahi with cumin-scented couscous ($22.50). Chocoholics, beware the hot chocolate bake for dessert.

Fine Dining

After a near washout in Hurricane Fabian and a major renovation afterwards, the historic **◖ Carriage House Restaurant** (Somers

Wharf, off Water St., tel. 441/297-1730, car-riagehouse@northrock.bm, lunch 11:30 A.M.–3 P.M., dinner 5:30–9:30 P.M. Mon.–Sat., brunch noon–3 P.M., dinner 6–9:30 P.M. Sun.) is housed in an 18th-century wharfside build-ing once used as a warehouse in the busy ship-ping trade. Vaulted ceilings, exposed bricks, and wooden floors in the main dining room, coupled with the elegant menu and service, make meals here a special treat. There is also the option of eating alfresco on the harborside terrace. Fish chowder here is particularly good. Light pastas and salads are popular lunch fare. Dinner entrées ($17–32) include fresh catch of the day, Bermuda lobster (in season), rack of lamb, and prime rib carved at the table.

Grocery Stores

Now owned by Hamilton's Supermart group, **Somers Supermart** (41 York St., tel. 441/297-1177, fax 441/297-0827, www.supermart.bm, 7 A.M.–9 P.M. Mon.–Sat., 8 A.M.–8 P.M. Sun.) has sat at the same busy intersection for de-cades, the only grocery store in town. The small store offers all the basics, though if you're look-ing for deli items or more variety, Southside Supermarket (logically located in Southside), a new modern food mart, is a better option.

INFORMATION AND SERVICES

Created in 1995, **The St. George's Foundation** (15 Duke of York St., tel. 441/297-3370, fax 441/297-2479, www.stgeorgesfoundation.com) is the independent nonprofit group that drove the UNESCO campaign; since then, it has raised funds and orchestrated capital improve-ments to the old town. The group, which works with St. George's residents and businesses to stimulate tourism in the area and encourage educational projects, has partnered with nu-merous related overseas entities, including the Colonial Williamsburg Foundation, the James-town/Yorktown Foundation, and the Historic Charleston Foundation.

The Visitors Service Bureau (tel. 441/297-1642) is located on King's Square.

St. George's Police Station (22 Duke of York St., tel. 441/297-1122 or 441/297-1124, fax 441/297-0461, sgps@bps.bm) is on the main drag just around the corner from King's Square.

St. George's Post Office (11 Water St., be-hind St. George's Police Station, tel. 441/297-1610, 8 A.M.–5 P.M. Mon.–Fri.) is housed in a historic building near the center of town.

For Internet access, there's **Caffe Latte** (York St., tel. 441/297-8196, caffelatte@logic.bm, 7 A.M.–6 P.M. Mon.–Fri., 7 A.M.–4 P.M. weekends), a relaxing, well-run outlet offer-ing T1 lines on eight PCs, along with pastries, beer, and coffee. Plop down in a comfy sofa and join the Internet-surfing yachties who fre-quent this hangout.

St. George's Esso Service Station (2 Rose Hill, tel. 441/297-1622) is near the entrance to town, on the drive leading up to St. George's Club. **Dowling's Marine Shell Station** (12 Water St., tel. 441/297-1914) sits along the harbor next to Tavern on the Sea.

Bank of Bermuda HSBC (tel. 441/297-1812) and **Butterfield Bank** (tel. 441/297-1277) are conveniently located near each other at King's Square and the junction with Water Street.

ATMs are at bank branches on King's Square and Water Street.

Public toilets are on King's Square, St. Catherine's Beach, and at area restaurants.

GETTING THERE AND AROUND
Buses and Ferries

Several bus routes from Hamilton serve St. George's Parish, and the advent of fast ferries from Hamilton via Dockyard in the past few years has added the efficient and scenic option of getting there by water. Buses Nos. 1, 3, 10, and 11 travel between the capital and the town of St. George daily. The No. 1 runs every half hour, the other routes every 15 minutes. The Sea Express fast-ferry service leaving Hamilton five times a day (9:30 A.M., 10:15 A.M., noon, 1:30 P.M., 2 P.M.) is currently restricted to the summer months (April–Nov.), but the govern-ment hopes to launch a commuter service that could mean more frequent ferries in all seasons.

Since Hurricane Fabian destroyed the town's front-loading dock in 2003, the fast-ferry service to St. George has not allowed scooters onboard, somewhat restricting the freedom of travelers who might choose to explore the parish by bike. A temporary fix allowed side-loading (passengers only) at Market Wharf, but talks to build a new dock are still ongoing. In the meantime, a private **mini-bus service** runs between King's Square and points around the town and outer parish April–November, including Tobacco Bay and Fort St. Catherine ($3), Ferry Reach ($5), and Southside. Public buses are an even cheaper way to reach some of these areas, especially if you opt for a transportation pass, allowing unlimited access to buses and ferries (one-day pass $12, multiday passes also available). Bus No. 6 runs between the town of St. George and St. David's (including Southside); a transfer allows you to board another bus at Southside's first gate down to go the mile to

Clearwater Beach and back every half hour. Hamilton-bound buses Nos. 1, 3, 10, and 11 all cross the Causeway into Hamilton Parish, home of the popular caves.

Scooters

Oleander Cycles (26 York St., tel. 441/297-0478, www.oleandercycles.bm, 8:30 A.M.–5:30 P.M. daily) rents single- and double-seater 50-cc scooters.

Eve's Cycles (1 Water St., tel. 441/236-0839, www.evecycles.com, 8:30 A.M.–5:30 P.M. daily) is housed in a historic building that used to attract nonstop photos when the company placed a Penny Farthing bicycle outside. Today, Eve's rents 50-cc motorbikes and offers pickup and delivery service.

Both liveries have representatives at St. George wharfs when cruise ships are in port. Rental rates start at around $50 per day. Major credit cards including MasterCard, Visa, and American Express are accepted.

ST. GEORGE'S

Around the Old Town

The environs of St. George's Parish beyond the old town are not part of the World Heritage Site—except for the many interesting forts—but its parkland and various neighborhoods are worth visiting and can be covered in any daylong visit to the East End. Most visitors will at least explore the rest of St. George's Island north and east of the town, a circular loop that heads up Cut Road and along Barry Road, incorporating three important fortifications—Gates Fort, Alexandra Battery, and Fort St. Catherine. Continuing on, Coot Pond Road meanders past Achilles Bay and Tobacco Bay (a prime snorkeling spot) on the North Shore, then back to the town's exit via Government Hill Road.

West of the town, past Mullet Bay, is the extensive Ferry Reach Park, home to a nature reserve, hiking trails, including a scenic stretch of the Railway Trail, and three forts, the Martello Tower, Ferry Island Fort, and Burnt Fort. Across the Swing Bridge, there's the large St. David's

and Southside community to explore. And there's also a section of the parish completely removed from the rest due to the vagaries of land division and the layout of islands; crossing Longbird Bridge and the Causeway into Hamilton Parish, a chunk of St. George's lies west of Shark Hole on Harrington Sound, encompassing most of the golf-coursed splendor of exclusive Mid Ocean Club and the new Tucker's Point Club. Tucker's Town continues east along South Road past mansions and private beaches to the tip of Frick's Point, where Castle Island, Nonsuch Bay, and other rocky guardians of Castle Harbor lie in a chain all the way back to St. David's.

SIGHTS
Gates Fort and Alexandra Battery

Two easy-to-visit forts that belong to the World Heritage Site are Gates Fort and Alexandra Battery (open sunrise to sunset daily, admission free), located within a few hundred yards of each other along Barry Road, on the easternmost flank of St. George's Parish. Perched on the picturesque **Town Cut**—the main shipping passage into the harbor—sits tiny Gates Fort, named for Sir Thomas Gates, a key figure aboard the ill-fated *Sea Venture* who went on to become deputy governor of Virginia. The original fort was built in the 1620s and rebuilt in 1700 as a parapet for guns. Down the road, Alexandra Battery overlooks Frobisher's Bay, where Gates supervised the construction of the ship *Deliverance* in 1610. The fort was built in the 1840s, though various later reconstruction efforts created a concrete emplacement for four guns.

❰ Fort St. Catherine

If you only see one fort in Bermuda, Fort St. Catherine (15 Coot Pond Rd., at St. Catherine's Point, tel. 441/297-1920, 10 A.M.–4 P.M. daily, $5 adults, $2 children) should be the top choice (Fort Hamilton's a close second). Fort St. Catherine's historic, well-preserved interior, exhibits, and artifacts make it well worth an hour's stop on your East End tour. On the northern tip of St. George's Island, the fort stands above St. Catherine's Beach on one side and Achilles Bat on the other. Built during the year of settlement in 1612, its ramparts gaze over the stretch of ocean where *Sea Venture* hit reefs in 1609, causing England to finally claim Bermuda for its own. Inside, rather dated dioramas tell the story of Bermuda's early years. Enter by the wooden drawbridge over a dry moat to a reception area and ticket office. Guides will point the way down steps and tunnels leading into the bowels of the fort, where magazines have displays and even uniformed mannequins to illustrate the mechanisms of military life inside a fort. Other rooms have replicas of the Crown Jewels, as well as various armaments, including swords, muskets, pistols, and giant rifled muzzle-loaders weighing 18 tons each. The fort saw military use by the British Army and through the World Wars, when local forces were trained here. Children will thrill to listen to the spooky incantations of "George the Ghost" amid a brief Halloween-inspired light

Fort St. Catherine stands above Gates Bay, where the first colonists struggled ashore.

© ROSEMARY JONES

show inside one of the lower chambers, believed to be haunted (an exorcism was held at the fort in the 1970s). Incidentally, Fort St. Catherine's main terrace—a lofty plateau rimmed by ramparts overlooking the reefs below—has been the setting for several theatrical displays—the most notable by Hollywood's Charlton Heston in a 1950s production of *Macbeth*.

◀ Bermuda Biological Station for Research

Located on the north shore of Ferry Reach, and visible from Kindley Field Road, the Bermuda Biological Station for Research (BBSR) (17 Biological Ln., tel. 441/297-1880, fax 441/297-8143, www.bbsr.edu, free tour 10 A.M. Wed. only) was established in 1903 in Flatts. Scientists from Harvard and New York Universities, together with the Bermuda Natural History So-

ciety, decided Bermuda was a fitting place to set up a marine research facility, due to its balmy climate, biodiverse reefs, and relatively easy access to ocean depths of 12,000 feet. The BBSR has been at its present location since 1932, after an endowment and facilities provided by the government and the Rockefeller Foundation. Today, it is a world-renowned nonprofit center for pioneering marine science and regularly hosts visiting scientists and student interns who join local counterparts in projects ranging from global warming studies to research on possible medical applications of sealife.

The station also runs a popular year-round Elderhostel program for senior travelers, who get an inside look at "Science in Bermuda Shorts" going on around the station and island.

The Wednesday tour gives visitors a look inside the station's many laboratories, where

RISKY BUSINESS

Bermuda engineered the unlikely pairing of scientists and insurance companies in 1994, when the Risk Prediction Initiative (R.P.I.) was established at the East End's Bermuda Biological Station for Research. The program brings together the latest findings on climate change, weather patterns, and disasters by the world's leading scientists with corporations whose business it is to insure the risk of hurricanes, tornados, tsunamis and earthquakes.

The benefits work both ways: scientists at top institutions around the globe receive funding for research on destructive weather phenomena, while sponsor companies get back cutting-edge data that allows them to better value and package risk as a commercial commodity and determine future payouts. Specifically, weather research helps provide insurers, governments, and others with a vested interest with more accurate estimates of the probability and path of future catastrophes. In return, scientists see their years of study help communities in very practical ways. Days before Hurricane Katrina's arrival along the U.S. Gulf Coast in 2005, for example,

hurricane forecasters, including members of R.P.I., had pinpointed its trajectory and most likely point of impact, allowing corporations and government agencies to brace for the onslaught. "Those of us watching felt an intense dread because the hurricane was by then a recipe for disaster," noted the R.P.I.'s Dr. Kerry Emannuel, a professor at the Massachusetts Institute of Technology, which runs a Program in Atmosphere, Oceans, and Climate.

Among other projects, R.P.I. scientists have developed a computer program that uses current and past data to plot trends and make predictions on the likelihood of weather phenomena striking particular locations around the globe. Their data is also being used to assess whether such catastrophes are the result of global warming or pure chance.

Bermuda remains a perfect forum for such synergy between science and commerce, given its reinsurance juggernaut and its location smack-dab in the path of hurricane alley. Workshops held on the island bring together the two fields to discuss their findings and new areas where further research could be useful.

ST. GEORGE'S

they can meet international scientists who have achieved breakthrough discoveries here, in fields such as pharmaceutical research and climate studies.

The atmosphere at BBSR these days is akin to a college campus; in effect, the facility acts as one. Undergraduate and graduate internships, distance-learning programs, and initiatives like the JASON Project are all carried out here, along with summer courses and workshops. Notably, the station is one of two centers for studies on the impact of the ocean on climate change, and in 1998 it established the International Center for Ocean and Human Health. Under that program, scientists are involved in a range of leading-edge research, including studying marine uses in pharmaceuticals and what the genetic makeup of corals and sea urchins can tell us about curing cancer and Alzheimer's disease, and learning more about the human aging process. The Risk Prediction Initiative, a partnership with the global reinsurance industry, is also based here.

Ferry Reach Park

For hikers and history buffs, Ferry Reach Park (Ferry Rd., off Mullet Bay Rd., open sunrise to sunset daily, admission free) is one of Bermuda's treasures. The stretch of Railway Trail here is one of the more remote, far away from main-road traffic or the hustle of residential neighborhoods. The trail runs beside the North Shore, banked by a nature reserve, mangroves, and a brackish pond called Lovers Lake. Easter lilies and silver cedar skeletons pepper the landscape, and, on stormy days, sea spray washes across the dirt path. In the western section of the park, three forts, **Martello Tower, Burnt Point Fort,** and **Ferry Island Fort,** belong to the World Heritage Site. You can cross the small drawbridge over the ditch and climb up the 1820s Tower, made of hard Bermuda limestone. Burnt Point Fort is older, built in the 1600s to defend the western approach to Bermuda. Ferry Island Fort, built in the 1790s, is named for the boat service that used to carry St. Georgians to the mainland at Coney Island, before bridges linked the parish to the mainland.

© ROSEMARY JONES

Trails meander through Ferry Reach Park, a preserved natural space.

Tucker's Town

Created in the 1920s when 500 acres of land were forcibly bought from a rural black community, Tucker's Town quickly became the enclave of the rich and famous. The exclusive Mid Ocean Club demands an initiation fee of $30,000, and members include those who own multi-million-dollar homes on the manicured peninsula dubbed "Billionaire's Row": Texas billionaire Ross Perot, former Italian prime minister Silvio Berlusconi, and New York mayor Michael Bloomberg. Of course, most of what lies here is off-limits to visitors, including the breathtakingly beautiful Windsor Beach (a manned roadblock only allows residents through). But you can visit the public dock on Tucker's Town Bay to get a view of the Beverly Hills–like neighborhood (and Bloomberg's lavish spread on an opposite hillside). The dock is a nice picnic spot, and you can even swim in the sheltered bay, where area boaters keep their craft moored. Take Paynter's Road to cut through the Tucker's Point property, an enclave of palm-flanked golf course, then follow Harrington Sound Road through Hamilton Parish to its junction with North Shore Road. Once this meets the Causeway, you have once again entered St. George's Parish.

BEACHES

St. Catherine's Beach, Achilles Bay, and **Tobacco Bay** are the three main beaches of St. George's, all located north of the town. St. Catherine's is the largest, a stretch of white sand below the fort, with music and a concessions stand selling burgers, fish cakes, sandwiches and cold drinks. Tiny Achilles Bay and Tobacco Bay are better known for snorkeling—the latter, with its natural stone columns rising from the bay, is one of the best areas in Bermuda for watching fish and reeflife in a clear setting.

Farther afield, **Whale Bay** at Ferry Reach Park has one of the best washed glass collections on the island. Its shallow waters, glassy calm when the wind is blowing from the south, are good for children and novice swimmers.

ENTERTAINMENT AND EVENTS

◖ Cup Match

Aside from sporadic reggae and soca concerts held at Tiger Bay in the summertime, the biggest event in St. George's happens every other year—at Cup Match. Bermuda's favorite public holiday is held the last Thursday and Friday of July or the first Thursday and Friday in August to celebrate **Emancipation Day,** marking the freedom of Bermuda's slaves, followed by **Somers Day,** in honor of island founder, Sir George. With the weekend tacked on, Cup Match makes a four-day extravaganza loosely revolving around a historic and hotly contested cricket match. For over a century, St. George and Somerset have battled for victory—and major bragging rights—in a two-day tournament that draws thousands of spectators to either end of the island (teams alternate years playing host). But Cup Match is so much more than cricket. Many attend the game at Somerset Cricket Club or **St. George's Cricket Club** (54 Wellington Slip Rd., tel. 441/297-0374) simply to socialize with friends and family or feast on the piles of homemade treats—mussel pie, fish sandwiches, peas 'n' rice—sold from stalls dotting the ground. Others come to try their luck at Crown & Anchor on the only two days of legalized public gambling the government permits. The game presents a who's who of Bermuda, and a slice of true island life, making it imperative to experience if you're vacationing here at that time.

Nightlife

The name says it all at **Blackbeard's Hideout Grub & Grog** (Achilles Bay, next to Fort St. Catherine), where latter-day buccaneers can party into the wee hours. It is one of Bermuda's few beachside bars, to the chagrin of those who would like to shake up the island's stuffy image.

SHOPPING

For last-minute black rum (Goslings Black Seal, $12 for one-liter bottle), cigarettes ($23 a carton), makeup, perfume, or candy, visit

Bermuda Duty Free (Departures Hall, Bermuda International Airport, tel. 441/293-2870, 5:30 A.M.–3:30 P.M., reopens for evening flights) before flying home.

SPORTS AND RECREATION
Golf
One of three government-owned golf courses, **St. George's Golf Club** (1 Park Rd., tel. 441/297-8067, fax 441/297-2273, sggc@northrock.bm) is just north of the old town, bordering with the St. George's Club resort. Designed by Robert Trent Jones, the par-62 course has winding fairways and undulating terrain stretching down to the North Shore, providing superb ocean views. Golfers get a taste of history, too: Fort St. Catherine sits at the 16th hole, the hard-to-access Fort George at the 14th. The clubhouse has a pro shop, locker facilities, restaurant, and lounge—again with panoramic views. In 2005, members complained about the poor state of parts of the course, ravaged by ocean spray over the years; turf is now being replaced by salt-resistant grass.

The crème de la crème of Bermuda golf courses, the revered **Mid Ocean Club** (tel. 441/293-0330, fax 441/293-8837, www.themidoceanclubbermuda.com, greens fee $200 per person) is *the* place to play, a highly challenging 18-hole championship course. PGA great Ben Crenshaw called it one of the best small courses in the world. Though a private club, guests of members are allowed to play on Mondays, Wednesdays, and Fridays, including guests of several hotels on the island (check with your concierge to see if arrangements can be made). Designed in 1921 by Charles Blair Macdonald, considered one of the world's top designers, the course was altered slightly by Robert Trent Jones in the 1950s. It boasts spectacular views of the reef-dotted ocean, its rolling greens and immaculately maintained fairways teetering over the South Shore cliffs. You might run into Jack Nicholson or Catherine Zeta-Jones at the colonial-style clubhouse. Over the years, players have included Babe Ruth, Dwight Eisenhower, Sir Winston Churchill, the Duke of Windsor, and George

Bush (Sr.). The club atmosphere is very formal: jacket and tie attire is expected for dinner.

The longtime Castle Harbour Hotel property underwent a massive redevelopment under new ownership in the early 2000s and now is home to **Tucker's Point Club** (tel. 441/298-6915, golf club 441/298-6970, fax 441/293-5149, golf@tuckerspoint.com, greens fee $185). A private residences club, the 18-hole championship golf course, like Mid Ocean, is open to guests of members and certain island hotels. Great vistas, a redesigned course, and high elevations over Harrington Sound and Castle Harbor make playing here a memorable experience.

Sailing
Yachties local and visiting congregate at **St. George's Dinghy & Sports Club** (Cut Rd., tel. 441/297-1612). The club is far smaller than its Hamilton cousins, the Royal Bermuda Yacht Club and the Royal Hamilton Amateur Dinghy Club, but it is very involved in the local sailing scene and acts as local host for several international events, including a cruising rally from Virginia.

For Kids
Mullet Bay Playground is a popular stop for neighborhood and visiting children. Cradled in a grassy park near the moored boats of Mullet Bay, the playground has a wide assortment of climbing frames, swings, and slides, usually well maintained. There is a parking lot at the site.

ACCOMMODATIONS
Under $100
Born-and-bred St. Georgian, part-time dockmaster Bernard Oatley and his wife Lily rent out a well-equipped **studio apartment** (2 Secretary Ln., tel. 441/297-0629, doubles $90 for the first two nights, $80 thereafter) attached to their hilltop home on the North Shore side of the old town of St. George. The apartment, with private entrance, has a single bed and double pullout, a kitchen area with stove, fridge, microwave and washer and dryer, a bathroom, cable TV, VCR, fan, and air-conditioning. Sliding glass doors open onto a patio

with views of the sea. Dishes, sheets, and towels are all provided.

Mike and Debi Montgomery's **Le Roux Inn** (14 Secretary Ln., tel. 441/292-9212, monty@ibl.bm, doubles $90) was, indeed, a *ruin* when they bought their property, hence the play on words. But today, guests will find utter homestyle comfort in the refurbished, cute-as-a-button cottage, where almost every need has been thought of. Games, linens, a library of Bermuda books, even staples have been provided by the couple who began renting out to travelers in 2001. The studio-style cottage, which sits apart from the main house, has a high open-beam ceiling, Mexican-tile floors, air-conditioning (and heat for the winter), a kitchenette with small fridge, toaster oven, hot plate, and microwave, a queen-size bed, a bathroom with shower, an eating area, and a barbecue. Only cash or travelers checks are accepted.

FOOD
At Bermuda International Airport

Fresh sushi is the draw at **Café Boulevard** (Lower Concourse, Bermuda International Airport, tel. 441/293-1321, 10:30 A.M.–5:30 P.M.), the last stop for travelers to snack with relatives before heading through security to the airport's upstairs departure lounge. St. Georgians also like the café for takeout on their drive home. Renovated in 2005, the café stays open later on evenings when British Airways flies out. Sit inside or out in the hallway terrazzo, a busy people-watching perch.

Like its sister restaurant in Hamilton,

Trattoria Café and Sports Bar (Upper Departure Lounge, tel. 441/505-8784, restricted to air passengers, open 7 A.M.–4 P.M. daily) has hot and cold dishes, including pizza and daily pasta specials. It also offers takeout to travelers who prefer not to dine on airlines' mystery chicken.

On Mullet Bay Road

For the best pies on the island, pop into **◖ Reid's Restaurant** (109 Mullet Bay Rd., tel. 441/297-1039, fax 441/297-2264, 6:30 A.M.–6 P.M. Mon.–Thurs., 6:30 A.M.–9 P.M. Fri. and Sat., 8 A.M.–1 P.M. Sun.), a family-run enterprise that's been turning out flaky-pastry treats for decades. Sample sweet or savory varieties, including mussel, fish, chicken, beef, and lamb pies, and the heart-stoppingly delicious lemon pies. There are a few roadside tables at the little eatery, or enjoy a takeout picnic.

Grocery Stores

Friendly **Cousins Variety** (123 Wellington Rd., tel. 441/297-1752, 7:30 A.M.–11 P.M. daily) is located next to Reid's Restaurant on the winding main road out of town. Hands of freshly picked Bermuda bananas and baked goods, including gingerbread, are among its best offerings.

INFORMATION AND SERVICES

The **Airport Mail Facility** (2 Kindley Field Rd., tel. 441/293-1767) is a handy post office for passengers at Bermuda International Airport.

ST. GEORGE'S

St. David's Island and Southside

"You got your passport?" locals jokingly rib Bermudians who stray from other parishes into the distinctive neighborhood—for fresh lobster, sightseeing, or rum-rich nights out at the parish's single tavern. Indeed, St. David's stands out for feeling utterly apart from the rest of Bermuda, even to born-and-bred residents. Even areas farther east in St. George's don't manage to evoke such a quirky sense of individuality, stoic humor, and catchy turn of phrase as St. David's folk seem to have. Maybe it's because the island was disconnected from the main part of Bermuda until the 1930s. Today a perimeter road leads off airport-hugging Kindley Field Road, past Southside, and finally into the serpentine collection of country lanes that bear curious names such as So Far Drive and Tranquillity Lane. Here, the sea-swept hillsides are peppered with marzipan pastel homes.

St. David's begs one to slow down, linger, hang out, and ease into the community mindset. It's a corner of St. George's Parish that many visitors either skip completely or gloss over, but for those who look beyond the rather tatty surface of the neighborhood, the rewards are rich. It is the people who make St. David's a unique community, and it is they who have fueled the folklore and legends of the original 500-acre island. It is a community where far-fetched tales—and everyone here has one—sometimes turn out to be absolutely true. St. David's folk cherish their family heritage and love to share their neighborhood with "outsiders," whether in the form of a fish sandwich or a tall tale about their ancestors. Either way, sit back, relax, and soak it in; there's every chance you'll never stumble upon such an unusual community again.

With Carter House, St. David's Lighthouse, St. David's Battery, and Great Head Park, not to mention the down-home bars and eateries that might snare you for several hours, you could easily while away a day here, but an afternoon would suffice. Take Bus No. 6 from the town of St. George, or transfer from any of the Hamilton–St. George routes (1, 3, 10, 11) onto the No. 6 after Kindley Field Road.

HISTORY

Named for the patron saint of Wales (though there's no trace of Welsh culture here), St. David's swirls with maritime legends that can be traced back to the community's immersion in whaling, boatbuilding, fishing and piloting—the practiced art of guiding ships into port safely through the skinny channels between reefs. There's the story of Tommy Fox, who climbed into a whale's belly to prove he could. Or the tale of "wreckers" who cheered a "turtle in the net"—their euphemism for luring ships onto reefs with coastal fires so they could be plundered. Residents believe to this day some of that treasure is buried beneath the soil of farmers' fields in the neighborhood. Lily-growing was also a staple of life here, when the fragrant white blooms were shipped overseas by the thousands at Easter-time.

St. David's also stands apart due to its Native American links. Indians from various tribes were shipped to the island as slaves, starting in the 17th century. Many ended up living in St. David's, marrying Bermudians and gradually becoming part of the social and ethnic mix of the area. Today, many St. David's residents claim Native American family roots, particularly among the Pequot tribe of New England. Over the past decade, the St. David's community has made strong efforts to revive these links, forging cultural alliances with U.S. Native American groups whose members have visited the island several times to attend festivals and exchange genealogical history.

But World War II would change St. David's drastically, in both physical and less tangible ways. The island's original size was expanded by 150 acres when the U.S. Army descended in 1941 to undertake a gargantuan project: obliterating Cooper's Island, Longbird Island, and a large part of St. David's Island to form Fort Bell and Kindley Field Air Force Base, later called the U.S. Naval Air Station. The Severn Bridge, which had linked St. David's to the mainland in 1934, was dismantled, and once again, St. David, tucked behind the new sprawling foreign entity, was separated from the rest of Bermuda.

The lands were returned to St. David's in the late 1990s and renamed Southside, incorporating the Cooper's Island beaches and nature reserve. Notably, this section was used as a NASA tracking station from 1960 to 2000, one of 18 radar and telemetry outposts around the world, which provided vital communications links between the Kennedy Space Center and Cape Canaveral and the astronauts on various space missions.

While St. David's belongs to St. George's Parish, its separate identity is recognized by the fact it claims its own electoral constituency.

SIGHTS

Until 1995, the large tract of St. David's land now called **Southside** belonged to the U.S. Naval Air Station and was not open to the general public. When the American military pulled up stakes in 1995, locals finally got access to the lands bordering Bermuda International Airport. While the whole area still has the look and

feel of a military base (wide concrete avenues, military style building construction) rather than a typical Bermudian aesthetic, Southside offers much-needed recreational space for East Enders and all Bermudians. Home to a cinema, bowling alley, supermarket, launderette, and fast-food restaurant, most locals flock to the neighborhood for its beaches—**Clearwater Beach** and **Turtle Cove**—its recreational areas (noisy go-karting clubs come to let off steam here), and for the excellent **Clearwater Playground.** Environmentalists are excited about the possibilities for the adjacent **Cooper's Island Nature Reserve,** which has long been a birding habitat, and in 2005, was discovered to be a nesting ground for at least one loggerhead turtle. Plans are under way to develop the reserve for eco-tours and educational outreach programs in local schools.

◖ Carter House

The oldest dwelling in St. David's, Carter House (Southside Ave., tel. 441/293-5960, 10 A.M.–4 P.M. Tues., Wed., Thurs., and Sat., $2 adults, children under 12 free) is believed to have been built around 1640. With its sloping

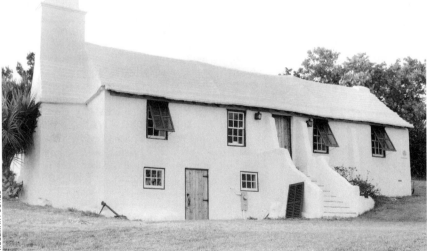

© ROSEMARY JONES

Traditional Carter House at Southside is today a museum of St. David's life and folklore.

ST. GEORGE'S

limestone roof, original hand-cut cedar beams, buttresses, and "welcoming arms" stairs, the whitewashed cottage looks completely out of place amid the sterile development of the former baselands. It was built by the descendants of Christopher Carter, a member of the *Sea Venture* crew who stayed behind on Bermuda when the other colonists continued on to Virginia. Carter's descendants lived in the home for centuries, and, as was custom in rural areas, many were buried on the land. When the U.S. Forces took possession of the property, they were exhumed and buried at the Chapel of Ease Church in St. David's. Used as a home for military officers, Carter House was renovated after it was returned to the St. David's community in the late 1990s. Today, it is run by the St. David's Historical Society as a museum to celebrate the history of the unique community, including traditions of whaling, piloting, fishing, boatbuilding, and farming.

the Chapel of Ease

© ROSEMARY JONES

Chapel of Ease

Down the pretty lane bearing the same evocative name, the Chapel of Ease (near the junction with Tranquillity Ln., tel. 441/297-1231) captures the maritime history of this East End community. The simple Anglican church is decorated nevertheless with stunning stained-glass windows portraying Bible stories and figures linked to the sea. The whitewashed graves outside hold the bodies of sailors, soldiers, and maritime pilots and the surnames of centuries-old families—Lamb, Fox, Hayward, and Pitcher.

St. David's Lighthouse

Like its Gibb's Hill counterpart in Southampton, St. David's Lighthouse (Lighthouse Hill Rd., Parks Department tel. 441/236-5902, 9:30 A.M.–4 P.M. daily mid-May–mid-Aug., 10 A.M.–4 P.M. Mon.–Fri. mid-Aug.–mid-May, admission free) is a landmark to guide ships safely past the island's treacherous reefline. Built in 1879, the structure rises 55 feet to a fixed-light lantern. It was purportedly erected here as a foil against St. David's "wreckers"—

nefarious locals who would purposely lure ships on to the reefs to loot their cargoes. Though its hours can be irregular in the winter season, the lighthouse is worth a visit; if you think the view from its base is good—overlooking the windswept pastel cottages of St. David's—just wait until you climb to the top. Mid-August–mid-May, ask the concession operator to let you in. Call the Parks Department to confirm opening hours.

◖ St. David's Battery and Great Head Park

St. David's Battery at Great Head Park (southeast end of St. David's Island, off Battery Rd., open sunrise to sunset daily, admission free) commands one of the most dramatic vantage points in Bermuda—and for good reason. The clear sightlines from this cliff-top park—across the entire East End—were chosen so this 1910 fortification could help defend the Narrows Channel in conjunction with Alexandra Battery across St. George's Harbour. The last major fortification to be built in St. George's

Parish, the battery was manned for coastal defense until 1957, including stints by the Bermuda Militia Artillery during World War II, when Bermuda was a strategic mid-Atlantic base for the Allies. Four large gun emplacements, with two British breech-loading guns still in situ pointing out to sea, sit above magazines and storerooms, which unfortunately have been marred by modern graffiti and garbage. The 9.2-inch guns had a range of about seven miles, easily capable of stopping an enemy vessel before it ventured too near the island. But despite the neglect, the park, towering over the eastern cliffs where you can watch longtails soaring over the reefs, remains a top-of-the-world place for a picnic or a photo opportunity. A bronze memorial to Bermudians lost at sea was erected in the park in 2005; the 16-foot-tall monument, by Bermudian sculptor Bill "Mussey" Ming, depicts an upturned rowing boat attached to symbolic sea-related items such as a life jacket, paddle, hourglass, and nautical dividers (navigational plotting instruments).

BEACHES

Clearwater Beach and adjacent **Turtle Bay** are highly recommended for swimmers of all abilities, including children. This is one of a handful of beach areas with government lifeguards on duty throughout the summer season. The wide bay of Clearwater is shallow and usually calm throughout the summer, its long arc of white sand facing southeast toward the islets guarding Annie's Bay. Just across the lawn, well-maintained **Clearwater Playground** has boldly colored climbing frames, ropes, tunnels, swings, and slides that make it a hit with kids of all ages.

ENTERTAINMENT AND EVENTS

Get "shipwrecked" at **Black Horse Tavern Bar & Restaurant** (St. David's Rd., tel. 441/297-1991, noon–10 P.M. Tues.–Sun.), where owner Gary Lamb, of centuries-old St. David's stock, may even drive you home if you end up having too many dark 'n' storm-ies. The waterside bar, overhung with assorted fishing tackle and stuffed game-fish prizes from Gary's expeditions, is *the* life of the parish, attracting locals as well as a devoted flock from "the rest of the country" on Friday and Saturday nights.

Housed in a former baselands movie theater used by the U.S. military, **Southside Cinema** (tel. 441/297-2821, advance tickets tel. 441/295-9789, available 9 A.M.–5:30 P.M. Mon.–Fri., 10 A.M.–5 P.M. Sat.) brought some welcome celluloid culture to the East End when it opened in the late 1990s. It's far from luxurious, with a drafty hall and creaky old seats—and they may forget to launch the soundtrack in sync once in a while—but who's complaining? Staff members are super-friendly, and there's a concessions stand selling candy and popcorn, as well as washrooms in the building.

SPORTS AND RECREATION

Cricket is a big passion in this parish neighborhood, home of the loftily named **Lords Oval** at **St. David's County Cricket Club** (52 Great Bay Rd., tel. 441/297-0449). Located on a plateau below Battery Park, where the ocean breeze whips in from the cliff-side, the club welcomes visitors to watch hotly contested games before a knowledgeable crowd during the sport's summer season. County cricket tournaments against rival island clubs are exciting to watch—even if you're clueless about the ins and outs of the game.

Bowling nights are popular at **Southside Family Bowl** (Southside, tel. 441/293-5906, fax 441/293-5907, haywire@northrock.bm), one of two bowling centers on the island.

Four asphalt tennis courts, **Kindley Community Tennis Courts** (Southside, tel. 441/293-5791), which formerly belonged to the U.S. military are now open to the public.

FOOD
Cafés and Bars
Near the busy junction of Kindley Field Park, Swing Bridge, and St. David's Road, **Double Dip Express** (1 Kindley Field Rd., tel. 441/293-5959, 9:30 A.M.–11 P.M. Mon.–Sat.,

FORTS AND GUNS

Anyone touring Bermuda's surviving forts can trace the rise and fall of the British Empire. Built from 1612 through to the 1950s, the structures tell us much about world history, Bermuda's changing role over the centuries, and the evolution of global superpowers. The fascinating chain of defense also reflects the metamorphosis of military warfare itself, since historic artillery for which specific forts were made has also weathered the test of time.

Bermuda once counted a total of 90 fortifications throughout the parishes, but, today, many of these exist only as buried archaeological remains or are inaccessible to the public because of overgrown vegetation or trash-dumping. Vandalism has also marred some of these historic sites. A survey commissioned by the government in 2003 recommended the establishment of a National Forts System, to restore as many structures as possible to their former glory and thus enhance cultural tourism. The P.L.P. government agreed an ambitious forts face-lift was needed, and discussions were ongoing in 2006.

A dozen impressive examples of forts scattered through the main island are in good condition and open to the public. From the east, around the town of St. George, these include: Fort St. Catherine, Alexandra Battery, Gates Fort, and Fort George. At nearby Ferry Reach, the Martello Tower, Burnt Point Fort, and Ferry Island Fort are all worth visiting, as is the park where they are located. In St. David's, the dramatic St. David's Battery, with its cannon and cliffs, makes a panoramic place for a picnic, and Fort Popple next to St. David's Cricket Club, is also scenic. In Hamilton, don't miss a visit to Fort Hamilton, one of the best-kept forts, with moat gardens, dungeons, and a plateau of lawns overlooking the city. Farther west, Whale Bay Battery commands views of the South Shore's turquoise horizons, while Fort Scaur's benches give a peaceful vantage point over the Great Sound. At Bermuda's westernmost point, the island's largest fortress – the cannon ramparts, casemates, magazines, and bastions of the Royal Naval Dockyard, including the six-acre Keep of Bermuda Maritime Museum – are perhaps the island's most notable historic landmarks.

A couple of the early forts built on the outer islands of St. George's are considered immensely valuable in heritage terms. Fort Cunningham, on Paget Island in St. George's Harbour, and King's Castle on Castle Island,

---

11 A.M.–11 P.M. Sun.) does a roaring trade, selling ice cream of all flavors, fish cakes, hot dogs, baked goods, chicken legs, and other short-order treats for passersby.

The canteen at **St. David's County Cricket Club** (52 Great Bay Rd., tel. 441/297-0449) serves up a small menu of fresh fish sandwiches, fish cakes, and burgers during cricket tournaments, football (soccer) games, and other community events on the panoramic oceanfront field. Call the club for schedule information.

At the site of a U.S. Naval Air Station McDonald's franchise that closed when the U.S. forces left Bermuda in 1995, **Pizza House** (106 Southside Rd., tel. 441/293-5700, 10:30 A.M.–9 P.M. Mon.–Wed., 10:30 A.M.–10 P.M. Thurs.–Sat., noon–9 P.M. Sun.) delivers burgers, fries, pizza, and soft drinks.

Gombeys Restaurant and Bar (Clearwater Beach, tel. 441/297-8177 or 441/237-1358, 10 A.M.–7 P.M. Mon.–Thurs., 10 A.M.–midnight Fri.–Sat. April–Nov. only) cooks up burgers, hot dogs, fish sandwiches, and fries for hungry swimmers. It is also a licensed bar, drawing a late crowd on weekends.

Bermudian

Tuna steaks, rockfish, and sweet lobster just a half hour out of the ocean are what bring the crowds to Gary Lamb's **(Black Horse Tavern Bar and Restaurant** (St. David's Rd., tel. 441/297-1991, noon–10 P.M. Tues.–Sun.),

at the entrance to Castle Harbour, are accessible by boat, though a tour boat and guide are advised, since Castle Island is very difficult to land at, and Fort Cunningham can only be reached via a tunnel (flashlight required). Southampton Fort and Smith's Fort lie on protected nature reserves and are therefore out of bounds. A handful of other forts, including Fort Victoria in St. George's and Fort Prospect in Devonshire, are in a bad state of repair and therefore currently inaccessible, but that may change if restoration plans finally get the green light from Bermuda's government.

The forts encompass an interesting variety of ages and styles that reveal much about the world in which they were built. The first forts were small limestone constructions, most of them built on outer islets of St. George's Parish in the 1600s. They were intended primarily for local defense (against pirates, for example), since Bermuda was not considered valuable property from a 17th-century geopolitical perspective. That changed radically, however, after the close of the American Revolutionary War (1783), when Britain lost all her American ports between Halifax and the West Indies. Bermuda then became a strategic possession, and fortifications were considered vital for Britain's Empire-building. Fortified commands were put up throughout the length of the island, and a Royal Naval Dockyard was built as a mid-Atlantic hub for the British fleet. By the mid-1800s, "Fortress Bermuda" had become a bastion of the British Empire.

"The 'enemy' up to the first decade of the 1900s was the United States," writes Dr. Edward C. Harris, director of Bermuda Maritime Museum in *Bermuda: Five Centuries*. "With [one exception], all the great forts built in the 19th century were intended to hold Bermuda from an American conquest. That the Americans ended up assuming the coastal defence of Bermuda forts from 1941-45 is perhaps the greatest military irony of our history."

The impressive legacy of Bermuda's fortifications includes gun placements, historic cannons, and other artillery. St. David's Battery, for example, was built in 1910 and kept in use as late as 1957, when the British military finally pulled out of the colony. Today, a pair of 1890s rifled breech-loader guns manned in both World Wars still point out to sea here – a telling tribute to the importance of the island's coastal defenses even in modern times.

---

a fixture of St. David's quirky social scene for decades. Lamb and his sons Chris and Brian are avid fishermen in their spare time, so, chances are, what's on your plate was hauled up by the trio on one of their frequent deep-sea expeditions. The waterfront, family-friendly restaurant pleases celebrities and common folk alike with its no-frills decor and down-to-earth service from the sweethearted Judy and her team. You can sit inside amid the noisy chatter or at picnic tables next to the water on the grassy lawn out back—a prime spot on summer evenings. Bermuda spiny lobsters, half or whole, are available in season (September 1–March 31), baked in butter and served on the shell. The on-site bar is a hive of activity on Fridays and Saturday nights, when area party-goers and Bermudians from the rest of the island come for rum—and lots of it.

Lamb's cousin, Dennis Lamb, who once ruled the roost at the infamous nearby **Dennis's Hideaway** (55 Cashew City Rd., tel. 441/297-0044, 10 A.M. onwards, daily), died in 2003, but his son "Sea Egg" runs the show these days, offering the same popular seafood feast at the world-famous outpost as his daddy did since 1967. Order "The Works": a sampler menu ($38.50) that, though served in small portions, fills you to overflowing with conch stew, mussel stew, fish chowder, conch fritters, shark hash on toast, a main fish dinner (usually porgy, hind, or grouper), shark steak, scallops, shrimp, and "a little squid if we have it," in that order. B.Y.O.B. welcomed. The venue stays open until the last diner leaves. "When they leave, the show is up," says Sea Egg. "They can lock up after themselves if they want to."

Grocery Stores

Southside Supermarket (26 Southside Rd., tel. 441/297-3959, 8 A.M.–9 P.M. Mon.–Sat., 1–5 P.M. Sun.) is Bermuda's newest grocery, a modern, wide-aisled behemoth, including a pharmacy and liquor store, which was desperately needed in the East End.

INFORMATION AND SERVICES

Southside Pharmacy (26 Southside Rd., tel. 441/297-3959, 11 A.M.–9 P.M. Mon.–Sat., 1–5 P.M. Sun.) is inside Southside Supermarket.

St. David's Esso Marine Station (107 St. David's Rd., tel. 441/297-1996, fax 441/297-1611) is busy with boaters all summer long. The attached store sells candy bars, snacks, and cold drinks.

St. David's Post Office (103 St. David's Rd., tel. 441/297-0847, open 8 A.M.–5 P.M. Mon.–Fri.) is located on the main road leading into the neighborhood, right next to the gas station.

BACKGROUND

The Land

An archipelago arranged as a fishhook, Bermuda comprises a total of more than 100 islands encircled by a collar of coral. Wary Spanish mariners of the 16th century dubbed them *Las Islas de Demonios* (Islands of Devils), while the English preferred the more benign moniker "The Summer Islands." Today, eight of the largest islands—St. George's Island, St. David's Island, Bermuda Island, Somerset Island, Watford Island, Boaz Island, Ireland Island South, and Ireland Island North—are connected by bridges and a causeway to form a single entity, which locals simply call "The Island." Within the many picturesque harbors, bays, and sounds are scatterings of smaller is-

lands and islets, some public, others privately owned, many just rocky uninhabited outcrops lacking structures or vegetation. The main island is relatively small at 21 square miles (22 miles end to end, and never more than two miles wide), with the hook's western third curling around to the northwest. But due to its varied and hilly—though not mountainous—terrain, Bermuda from the ground is rather deceptive, leading one to believe that, just around the next corner, there might be more than the sum of its compressed vital statistics. An aerial view is more revealing: As you descend for a landing at the East End airport, sweeping from violet deep-ocean across reef-dotted aquamarine

shallows, the island appears almost fragile in its entirety—an oceanic oddity whose geographic isolation has shaped a distinct survival.

Bermuda's unique, seemingly contradictory characteristics have long intrigued scientists. A subtropical island about 600 miles from the nearest mainland (Cape Hatteras, North Carolina), it bears little resemblance to Caribbean cousins in climate, biota, or geology. Instead, Bermuda is bathed by the balmy Gulf Stream, which exerts a moderating influence on its climate, just as the easterly trade winds do down south. Yet, unlike the tropical Indies, Bermuda's winters are damp and storm-wracked. There is no typical wet or dry season; indeed, the island's weather habits are so capricious, a thunderstorm can let loose on one parish while sparing all the others.

Geologically, the island's core is soft, white limestone, despite violent volcanic origins. There are no rivers, lakes, or streams. The topography is neither towering, nor dangerously low (Town Hill in Smith's Parish is the highest point of land at 259 feet above sea level). And though tiny, Bermuda's landmass holds an astonishingly diverse range of natural habitats—from marshland to sand dunes and cedar woodland—which support an equally varied ecology.

Visitors, of course, are tantalized by such offerings. Bermuda's geologic permutations have left a place characterized by mostly welcoming temperatures; by floral eye-candy found throughout its undulating length; by soft, rosy-hued beaches and turquoise swimming holes; by saltwater sounds that provide perfect natural harbors; by pastel homes hewn from the very rock they sit on; and by a necklace of bio-diverse coral reefs—some of the most northerly in the world.

THE BERMUDA TRIANGLE

If there's one thing most everyone knows about Bermuda – even if they've never set foot on the island – it's that the archipelago lies in the maw of a spooky phenomenon dubbed the "Bermuda Triangle." Bermudians who live or travel overseas get peppered with questions about the popular myth, and it is a favorite topic of discussion among tourists, but locals tend to dismiss it with humor and skepticism. Despite the Triangle's perennial appearance in books and science fiction TV series, scientists agree it is nothing more than an enduring legend fueled by deadly coincidence.

Conspiracy theorists have devoted seas of ink to explaining why ships and aircraft have sunk, caught fire, or vanished without a trace within an area of Atlantic Ocean spanning Bermuda; San Juan, Puerto Rico; and Miami, Florida. Some believe these were the victims of paranormal occurrences, blaming malevolent sea creatures, time warps, UFOs, aliens, and the lost city of Atlantis. Others speculate natural sources such as fog fields, magnetic anomalies, or methane bubbles popping up from the sea floor might have caused planes' instruments to malfunction or vessels to sink.

Empirical data suggests a far simpler explanation – that such "mysteries" aren't really mysterious at all. Given the fact that many Triangle incidents took place during raging storms or in the 1940s and 1950s before the advent of high-tech navigation equipment such as global positioning satellites (GPS), basic human error or the whims of Mother Nature could easily account for disasters. In fact, Lloyd's of London accident records were shown to prove the Triangle's geographic area is no more dangerous than any other part of the ocean – a conclusion confirmed by the U.S. Coast Guard.

Still the world's fascination with the Triangle continues, particularly with the story of Flight 19, the unsolved disappearance of five Avenger torpedo bombers on December 5, 1945. The Triangle's best-known tale describes how the aircraft left Fort Lauderdale's Naval Air Station on a routine practice mission with 13 student pilots, accompanied by their Commander, Lt. Charles Taylor. The flight plan called for a test bombing run followed by a triangular course east and north, a distance of 120 miles. But about 90 minutes after leaving the base,

Except for the ferocity of its storms, including seasonal hurricanes, Bermuda's environment is indeed charmed. Immune to natural disasters such as earthquakes, volcanoes, mudslides, or floods, devoid even of dangerous plants or animals, its appearance conjures a manicured country garden rather than a mid-Atlantic atoll.

GEOGRAPHY

Bermuda lies at 32 degrees, 17' north, 64 degrees 46' west, along the latitude of Savannah, Georgia. The nearest point of land is Cape Hatteras, North Carolina, 590 miles to the northwest. Roughly the size of Manhattan, Bermuda is 2,100 miles west of the Azores and 910 miles north of the Bahamas. There are no distinct topographical regions on the island, but rather, a variety of natural habitats, which can be found in most of the nine parishes (see *Flora*).

Bermuda consists of a limestone cap sitting at the pinnacle of a submerged volcanic seamount. Its geological origins can be traced back 110 million years to the Mid-Atlantic Ridge, a volatile, mostly submerged division between the divergent American and European tectonic plates. Scientists believe "Mount Bermuda" was the byproduct of a massive volcanic eruption just west of the ridge, which moved slowly westward over the next 80 million years. A second eruption caused the volcano to enlarge into the Bermuda Seamount, incorporating a trio of peaks: The Bermuda Pedestal (on which the island now sits), the Challenger Bank, and Argus Bank. Of these, only the 13,000-foot Bermuda Pedestal now extends above sea level. The seamount moved a further 500 miles west

the squadron found itself in trouble. Taylor sent a radio transmission reporting his compasses were malfunctioning, and it soon became clear he was hopelessly disoriented. As night fell and a storm approached, communications faded and finally stopped, presumably when the planes ran out of fuel and plunged into the sea.

One of two Martin Mariner search planes that went to look for the missing squadron also disappeared, though there were reports of an explosion after it took off, and airplane debris was spotted nearby. Nothing was seen of Flight 19, however. The Navy, pressured by Taylor's family, cited "causes or reasons unknown" for the disaster, rather than pilot error. In subsequent decades, the story of Flight 19 became the focus of Triangle speculation, which heightened after Charles Berlitz's sensational bestseller of 1974, *The Bermuda Triangle*. Flight 19's planes and pilots even enjoyed a reappearance in Steven Spielberg's 1977 UFO classic, *Close Encounters of the Third Kind*.

One of the most lauded books on the Triangle attempts to lay such fantasies to rest. *The Bermuda Triangle – Solved* was written by Arizona librarian Larry Kusche, who in 1975 decided to investigate claims put forward by the plethora of articles and books on the Triangle's unsolved mysteries. Digging into contemporary accounts and other primary sources, he discovered factual material other writers had overlooked or ignored, much of it pointing to entirely rational explanations for unusual events. His book catalogs his findings, offering in-depth detail about some of the myth's highlights and ultimately refuting many outlandish claims.

Surprisingly, Bermuda has never made much of the legend, even as a potential tourist attraction. Eponymous cocktails took the name, and several island companies pay tribute to the folklore with "Triangle" monikers, including retail stores, a now-defunct microbrewery, and at least one investment company (though one might question the wisdom of linking a financial entity with connotations of disappearance and disaster). Indeed, Tourism Department officials have qualms about marketing the Triangle to the world at large, despite calls from some in the industry for Triangle-themed travel ads, a museum, or boat tours.

in the following 30 million years, leaving the island currently situated in a stable area of the earth's crust.

The seamount's limestone cap was formed biologically over the last million years as seaweeds, algae, corals and other shallow-water marine organisms laid down deposits. A 350-foot-deep layer of calcium carbonate was formed, and as sea levels fell, this was exposed to air, about 100,000 years ago. The result was the formation of many tons of sand, which wind blew across the island to form rolling dunes that eventually hardened into what geologists term "Aeolian" limestone, meaning "created by wind." Remnants of these old dunes, sometimes even dunes atop dunes, can be seen along the shoreline of Bermuda or in road cuts such as the dramatic Blackwatch Pass in Pembroke. Soft, porous limestone rock now makes up Bermuda's entire surface and has been quarried over the centuries for roof slate and building blocks used for Bermuda's characteristic island homes.

The porous nature of the limestone helped shape Bermuda's geological identity. It allowed rain to soak into the surface rock, deterring freshwater runoff that would have created streams, rivers, and lakes. Instead, rainwater burrowed deep into the earth, forming a network of twisting underground tunnels, caverns, and caves, which still honeycomb certain parishes and give Bermuda one of the highest concentrations of caves in the world. Some are found underwater, becoming refuges for rare species. In the best known, you can find stalactites and stalagmites, columns, flow stones, and soda straws.

Bermuda's biological history begins about 800,000 years ago—the date of the oldest terrestrial fossils, belonging to a petrel, found in Hamilton Parish. But climatic changes and the dramatic rise and fall of sea levels over time played havoc with the survival of habitats, animals, and plantlife that may have lived on an ancient Bermuda far larger than its current form. As Canadian research scientist Dr. Martin Thomas points out in his book, *The Natural History of Bermuda,* observations from deep-ocean submersibles examining the Bermuda Pedestal have revealed former beaches

at a depth of 315 feet—a fascinating clue to the island's previous life. It was not until about 10,000 years ago that rising sea levels stabilized and Bermuda took its present shape. Marine and terrestrial organisms then arrived as larvae, spores, or adults, transported by wind or carried on debris propelled by the powerful Gulf Stream. Against big odds, these first forms of life would slowly spawn the rich environment to which Bermuda is home today.

Beaches

Bermuda is renowned for its scores of beaches, which vary considerably around the island. Those responsible for most of the rave reviews are located on the South Shore, where sweeping tracts of coral-tinted sand are pounded by turquoise surf populated by iridescent parrotfish and schools of pompano and amberjack. The surf is relatively gentle, thanks to the protection of reefs that lie a stone's throw from shore (a mere few yards in some areas) on this side of the island.

The North Shore, including areas of the Great Sound and St. George's, though less of a tourist attraction, is just as beautiful for swimming, snorkeling, kayaking, and scuba diving. In contrast to the sand and surf of the South Shore, this side of the island is punctuated by small rocky coves and azure bays, some without beaches at all, and there is no surf. Local youngsters practice their high-diving here, and deep grottoes invite plunging in. The reefline exists, but since it sits 10 miles offshore, it is barely visible, and divers need a boat to get out there.

All the island's beaches are covered in the same white or pinkish sand, scattered with shells and seaweed, but with none of the pebbles or dark grit of Caribbean volcanic islands such as Montserrat or Guadeloupe. In the winter, prevailing northeast winds can make the North Shore choppy, but throughout most of the summer northern horizons are calm as a lake.

CLIMATE

Bermuda's climate is subtropical and influenced by two major factors: the Gulf Stream and the Bermuda-Azores High. Like a giant

DAMP NATION

One of the hallmarks of Bermuda weather is its year-round humidity, which makes summers seem hotter and winters chillier. Aside from the physical discomfort, humid conditions spawn fast-spreading mold and mildew – the bane of local householders. Bermuda residents know all too well they must heat their closets to prevent leather jackets and shoes from turning green and lock dry goods such as crackers and cereals in Tupperware or these items lose their crunch in a matter of hours. Metals rust. Books warp. Watercolors ruin. Glued fixtures come unstuck. As Canadian expat Tracey Caswell bemoans in *Tea With Tracey*, her tell-it-all survival guide to island life, "Humidity is the instigator of a zillion problems."

One particularly moist morning Caswell describes in her book might sound exaggerated to the uninitiated, but, unfortunately, it's an accurate portrayal of daily Bermuda life. "I thought, I'll spend the day writing letters," she recounts. "The paper was damp; the ink smeared, but I did get a letter written. However, when I went to put it in the envelope, I found all 250 of my new envelopes had self-sealed. The humidity alone had done this for me. Okay, I thought, just calm down, have a cigarette and ponder these problems one by one. My matches wouldn't light; they were too wet."

Most visitors on short trips to the island will not be taxed by such aggravations, but if you rent a self-catering apartment, be aware that dry foodstuffs (potato chips, cookies, crackers) need to be air-locked, and everything else, including bread, salt, herbs, drink-mix powders, and ground coffee, should be refrigerated to avoid mold or clumping. Avoid bringing leatherwear to the island – it's not practical in winter's frequent rain showers, anyway. Makeup is also best kept in the fridge; lipsticks, mascara, and eye pencils quickly turn smudgy otherwise, although air-conditioning usually prevents this. As for hair-styling products and tools, you may find them nearly useless; Bermuda's damp air runs riot with any attempts to keep hair straight; if you do succeed, a scooter ride – and its resulting "helmet head" – is enough to convince you the effort was wasted.

---

security blanket, the Gulf Stream flows northeast from the Gulf of Mexico—from which it takes its name—through the Straits of Florida to an area northeast of Bermuda, channeling warm equatorial water northward on its journey. The Gulf Stream moderates temperature, bringing mild weather throughout the year and preventing Bermuda from getting as hot or cold as mainland areas of the same latitude. Frost is not found here, though winter gets the occasional hailstorm.

The Bermuda-Azores High is a high-pressure zone, which also exerts a welcome influence on Bermuda's climate. In the summer, the zone lies east of Bermuda, bouncing storm systems north of the island and causing light southerly winds to blow throughout the season. In the winter, though, the high sits too far southeast to make a difference, allowing northerly gales to pummel the island with cooler temperatures. Unlike the Caribbean, Bermuda has no trade winds or monsoons, and its isolated position brings a lower risk of hurricanes.

Seasons

Officially, Bermuda has two seasons, summer and winter, which also define the tourism industry. Summer, the "high" season for visitors, runs April–October, while winter, once snubbed as the "off" or "low" season, runs November–March.

Most Bermudians, however, would argue the island actually does enjoy four seasons like its mainland counterparts. Locals can immediately discern the first breath of fall in the second week of October, when temperatures dip from the torpor of summer, or the sweet calm of spring in early April after the windy barrage of New Year storms.

The island has no rainy season; instead, rain tends to be spread throughout the year, with January being the wettest month on average, with 150 millimeters, or six inches of rain. Typically, even torrential rainstorms peter out after an hour or two, and rare are the days when the sun does not make a single appearance. The hour-by-hour changes can prove challenging to packing clothes for a Bermuda holiday in any season; choose a mix of outfits and layers to accommodate the unexpected.

True summer can be counted on May–September, with temperatures peaking in July and August. Relative humidity (ranging between 75 and 85 percent all year, but occasionally spiking to 90 in midsummer) makes Bermuda feel uncomfortably like a greenhouse, draining energy—and buckets of sweat—particularly in the summer. Hydration is key to doing anything active in these months, and swimming is the most refreshing way to cool off. October–December marks one of the most pleasant times of the year, when cool breezes prevail, but the sun can be hot enough that you'll want to swim. The windy season usually takes control after Christmas, bringing storms, cold winds, rain, and damp days and nights from January to March; this is, perhaps, the most unpredictable season, for there can often be long spells of sunshine amid the tempestuousness. Ignore the euphemistic descriptions on tourist brochures, though; it can get *very* chilly by Bermudian standards, and many homes and hotels have no heating, aside from fires and electric heaters. Remember, too, a modest 60 degrees Fahrenheit can feel downright frigid if you happen to be driving a scooter on a windblown winter's night; wear gloves like Bermudians do. Spring signals a drop in winds, and a resulting rebirth in garden growth and blossoms, as calm, sunny weather prevails and temperatures begin their inevitable rise toward the end of May. Bermuda Day (May 24) is the traditional first day of summer, though islanders usually refuse to swim until at least a month later.

Temperatures

Bermuda's summer and winter temperatures differ considerably, though the yearly average is a balmy 76 degrees Fahrenheit. Monthly variations are more telling: average temperatures

range from 66 degrees in February to 85 degrees in August, the effects heightened considerably by summer's humidity. Annual lows and highs normally range from 55 to 95 degrees.

Seawater temperatures hover around 65 degrees in the winter, but warm to a bath-like 83 degrees by August. Visitors often swim and scuba dive year-round, however.

Rainfall

Bermuda's rainfall is fairly evenly distributed throughout the year, with no true rainy season, though rain is more likely to intrude on outdoor activities if you visit between January and March. Even then, Bermuda rainfall tends to be in the form of a quick downpour rather than daylong drizzle, so barring a hurricane, weather rarely ruins a Bermuda vacation. Indeed, it's typical to have torrential rain in Paget, while St. Georgians simultaneously bask in the sun.

Hurricanes

The hurricane season officially runs six months, June 1–November 30, but Bermudians consider themselves safe until the seawater temperature hits 85 degrees, usually in July, and it remains that warm through September.

Bermuda escapes most of the annual roster of storms, most of which miss the island due to its tiny landmass, though severe storms have scored direct hits—on average every half dozen years. The last—and worst on record—was Category 3 Fabian, in 2003. More common are huge storm swells off the beaches, which whip up surf and prohibit swimming, and heavy rain and wind when hurricanes are in the vicinity. Storms have also spawned tornadoes that twist across isolated areas of the island, ripping off the odd roofs before vanishing out to sea.

Hurricane near-misses have occurred some seasons, as these violent vortexes sideswipe the island; very rarely, hurricanes bounce back eastward after first careening towards the U.S. East Coast. Particularly after the fury of Fabian, however, Bermudians are highly appreciative of a hurricane's destructive force and monitor the track of every single storm during this season, no matter how large, small, or apparently distant.

PREPARING FOR A HURRICANE

Bermudians can reel off the dates and names of worst-offending hurricanes like a list of wayward relatives they would have preferred had not visited: Emily (a Category One Hurricane, which caught the island off guard on September 24, 1987, causing $35 million in damage); 1995's Felix (which swept away surfside restaurants and swiped the island back and forth three times); and Fabian (a Category Three, which scored a rare "direct hit" on Bermuda on September 5, 2003, killing four people, closing several hotels, knocking out power for several weeks, and causing an estimated $300 million in damage.)

While most hotels and guesthouses will make safety and logistical arrangements for guests in the event of a hurricane, it helps to be prepared if you're staying in a private home or renting an apartment. A hurricane checklist should include candles, canned goods (including pet food), flashlights, propane lanterns, batteries, battery-powered AM/FM radio, propane stove, tarpaulin (in case roof slate blows off), and a bucket and rope for hauling freshwater from the tank. Secure all moveable objects from the garden or yard (garbage cans, garden furniture). Secure storm shutters, and tape or board up windows. Clear out roof gutters and put strainers in down pipes. Make sure pets are kept indoors. Stock up on emergency supplies, including medications. Fill the bathtub to enable flushing of toilets. Make sure vehicles have full gas tanks.

Weather updates and community news are provided by the Government Emergency Broadcast Facility is FM 100.1 MHz.

During a storm, do not go outside, and stand clear of the windows in case flying debris smashes the glass. If you must go out, watch for falling branches and power lines. When the eye of the storm passes over the island, the weather will calm down dramatically, but do not assume the hurricane is over. Remain inside, as the storm will resume from the opposite direction.

After the storm, report any fallen trees or downed power lines and do not drive about unless absolutely necessary. To save food as long as possible, try not to open the fridge or freezer for long periods.

Call 911 for an emergency, or 955 to report a power outage.

The government and media communicate the details of approaching storms, and Bermuda's Emergency Measures Organization is well prepared to orchestrate recovery and clean-up efforts in the event of severe damage. After Fabian killed four Bermudians, the government has cracked down with stricter storm preparations, including closing the mile-long Causeway to St. George's when big storms draw too close. Yet, Bermuda generally fares far better than Caribbean islands in the event of a direct hit, thanks to its sturdy limestone or cement-block buildings, well-developed infrastructure, and modern communications system. Most householders stock up every summer with hurricane supplies (tarpaulin, torches, batteries, and buckets).

Emergency broadcasts by police and government media relations officers are made via 100.1 FM, when other stations are knocked off the air during power outages. Weather warnings, including marine forecasts, are broadcast by the Bermuda Weather Service (tel. 977, www.weather.bm), or via Bermuda Harbour Radio (www.rcc.bm). You can look up photos and climate data for any date since 1996 on www.bermudaweather.bm. During hurricane season, both the National Weather Service (www.nws.noaa.gov) and The Weather Channel (www.weather.com) track developing storms and their movements through the Caribbean and Atlantic with satellite images and forecasts.

Another useful site to learn about hurricanes and Bermuda folklore is www.sharkoil .bm, named for the homespun meteorological indicators many locals still consult when bad weather looms. Even in the 21st century, orthodox science sometimes takes a backseat to these

HURRICANE STRENGTH

Bermuda uses the American Saffir-Simpson Hurricane Scale to judge the strength and property-damage potential of approaching storms.

- **Category 1:** winds 74-95 miles per hour (minor damage)

- **Category 2:** winds 96-110 miles per hour (roof, window, vegetation, and small-craft damage)

- **Category 3:** winds 111-130 miles per hour (structural damage to homes, vegetation)

- **Category 4:** winds 131-155 miles per hour (extensive damage)

- **Category 5:** winds 155-plus miles per hour (catastrophic damage)

traditional barometers—sealed bottles of fatty hydrocarbons extracted from a shark's liver. For centuries, Bermudians have hung "shark oil" in a sheltered spot outdoors, where they check its content to predict a storm's ferocity. While younger generations now turn to CNN, old-timers swear the bottle's contents turn cloudy during disturbances, and if it's actually a hurricane, a spiraling plume will be visible inside.

ENVIRONMENTAL ISSUES

Bermuda may look like a pristine paradise, but pollution, pesticides, and overdevelopment are wreaking havoc on the island's ecosystems.

Warning signs are alarming scientists, who note that reductions in plant and animal species, as well as the ebbing health of some species, are important barometers of environmental degradation. Since 1997, the island's sea grass beds—vital habitats for conch, sea urchins, rockfish, turtles, and spiny lobsters—have drastically declined; marine biologists say 20 percent of the 5,100 acres have been eradicated in the last decade alone. Leaching cesspits and

dredging are blamed for the loss, but authorities promise sea grass beds will now be added to the list of protected areas of the island.

Disposal of waste, including sewage, is one of Bermuda's biggest problems, and, with talks on the island's sustainable development launched in 2005, the issue has become one of the most prominent on the minds of environmentalists. The island burns its garbage at an incinerator constructed for $64 million in 1992; its tower, at Tynes Bay, Devonshire, is visible along the North Shore. Sewage waste, dissolved and pumped three miles out to sea from the South Shore, Paget, has caused a growth surge in marine weeds that choke slower-growing corals—an ecological imbalance scientists are monitoring.

Pollutants in ponds and nature reserves—evident in resulting deformed toad populations—are also raising concern. A large part of the problem may be the lackadaisical attitude Bermudians have long held towards pesticides. For decades, householders have liberally sprayed bug-killers such as Baygon and Raid, prompting an organization called Pesticides Focus Group to push for the ban of such insecticides and the use of less-toxic alternatives.

Even Bermuda's air quality is not immune from modern contaminants. The large number of high-emission motorbikes, as well as cars, has raised air pollution to dangerous levels in some areas around the City of Hamilton, even exceeding annual readings of some European cities, scientists report. These are issues Bermudians must grapple with and find solutions to as island development, traffic, and population—along with their ugly fallout—seem only certain to worsen.

Water Conservation

Rainwater is at a premium on an island, as households depend on it as their main source of freshwater—at least to run faucets, showers, baths, and toilets, if not for drinking. Large water tanks are built under every home, and rain is caught as it has been for centuries—on traditional white limestone slate roofs, whose pipes and gullies channel it to a subterranean tank. From there, water is pumped into domestic plumbing systems. There are also large public water-catchments for government use. Not surprisingly, water conservation is the rule amid chronic droughts. The summer of 2005 saw an extreme period of drought, with just 0.64 inches of rain in June causing the worst shortage in 50 years.

Conservationists have sounded warnings about the problem of increasing water consumption on the island, particularly the pressure it exerts on underground lenses, which supply larger private users, such as hotels, as well as the City of Hamilton. Bermuda residents consume an estimated 1.58 billion gallons of water annually; cruise ships alone consume up to 50,000 gallons each daily in port. The island has just one reverse-osmosis plant, to supply the hospital and offset shortages, but experts argue several more plants are needed to avert future crises.

Cruise Ships

The extent to which the cruise industry benefits Bermuda has generated much debate on the island, but perhaps even more controversial is the question of whether Bermuda's infrastructure could support the inevitable advent of far bigger ships. The world's cruise liners are estimated to have nearly doubled in size every decade. The current generation of Panamax vessels launching from shipyards are longer (965 feet), wider (106 feet), and have a deeper draft (39.5 feet) than conventional ships; they are named for an enlarged superstructure design that fits maximum lock dimensions of the Panama Canal. Such ships can carry 3,000–4,000 passengers, double that of standard ships. However, critics question whether Bermuda could absorb that many cruise visitors without a negative impact on other tourists and residents. Another concern is the strain on the island's already stretched transportation, garbage, sewage, and water systems, given that ships in port make liberal use of those services. Opponents also argue that while King's Point, Dockyard, at the island's West End, can accommodate mega-vessels, the island's other key ports, Hamilton and St. George, cannot—meaning harbor channels would have to be re-cut and docks overhauled, with resulting destruction of marine environments. In 2005, the Bermuda government created a special committee of power brokers, including senators and corporate leaders, to deliberate the issue and make recommendations on the industry's best path forward.

Flora and Fauna

HABITATS

The island's habitats are not so numerous or exotic as many in pure tropical regions such as the Caribbean and Central America. Yet, Bermuda's ecosystems are interesting in their more subtle variety, as well as in their increasing fragility due to rampant development. The main habitats are the rocky shore; beaches and dunes; inland forest; marshes, ponds, and mangroves; karst and caves; sea grass beds; and coral reefs. All areas can be seen and explored around the island. Interpretive displays complete with audio at the Bermuda Natural History Museum (part of the Bermuda Aquarium, Museum & Zoo) at Flatts, Smith's Parish, describe habitats and common species found in each.

The Rocky Shore

Some of the most impressive aspects of wild Bermuda are its rocky shore and coastal environments. Climbing up and down the spray-bashed coast, where bio-diverse tidepools are often large enough to swim in, you can imagine the natural setting that greeted so many castaways to reach Bermuda's shores. When the first humans arrived on the island's shoreline in the 1500s, they encountered a reef-necklaced oasis of endemic cedar forests and palmetto palms, both of which were beneficial

BERMUDIANA

Come springtime, carpets of purple wild-flowers cover rocky hillsides and sandy shores around the island. Bermuda's national flower, the Bermudiana (*Sisyrinchium bermudiana*) is also known as Bermuda iris or blue-eyed grass. It grows wild in dry, sunny, windswept, seemingly harsh areas, such as Spittal Pond. Standing about eight inches high, its slender stem and leaves are waxy and grass-like, its small flowers sporting violet petals and yellow centers. Though related to North American species, the Bermuda variety is endemic – it does not grow wild elsewhere.

© ROSEMARY JONES

to survival in myriad ways: for timber to build huts and ships, for roof thatch, for berries to mull wine, and for hearts of palm, which shipwreck survivors roasted or baked.

The rocky shoreline is home to a wealth of plants and animals, a unique bridge between marine and terrestrial environments. Algae, lichens, and rockweeds drape the intertidal zone, where they have adapted to a hybrid environment with features such as attachments, or "holdfasts," to the rock. The band lying between the lowest tide and the spray zone is darkened and made slippery by blue-green bacteria, which provide a larder of food for other animals. Among the various species found here, rainbow-hued parrotfish can be found grazing, gnawing on reef and rock with their hallmark beaked mouths. Crabs, snails, urchins, anemones, and seaweeds also thrive. The banded West

Indian Top Shell (*Cittarium pica*) can sometimes be found; a protected species, it is illegal to remove it. Growing profusely atop the wind- and sea-eroded limestone shore are hardy, salt-resistant succulents, such as the sea purslane, coast spurge, and seaside oxeye, whose vibrant yellow flowers dot the landscape. Prickly pears, spiky Spanish bayonets with luxurious towers of white blossom, baygrape brushes, fennel, and fields of seaside goldenrod, waving feathery, butter-colored wands, cover areas above the tidal shore.

Beaches and Dunes

Sand dunes harbor a similarly tough variety of plants, whose growth effectively serves to anchor the dunes and prevent sand masses from shifting too far. Dune vegetation is peppered with the type of bright blossoms that are so striking in desert environments, although here, they are totally different varieties; these include the purple-flowered vine, seaside morning glory, wild stock, sea lavender, and the buttercup-like seaside evening primrose. Land crabs dig long burrows in dune areas to escape the prying beaks of hunting night herons; be careful when hiking the dunes not to twist your ankle in their exit holes.

Sargasso weed washes up in piles on the beaches year-round, depending on wind direction. These floating mats of brown seaweeds are found in the Sargasso Sea, a vast area east of Bermuda stretching to the Azores. Fed by the warm waters of the Gulf Stream, the seaweed got its name from Portuguese mariners of the Age of Discovery who dubbed it *sargaco* or "grape" since its air sacs and structure resemble the fruit. The weed comprises a self-sufficient food web that supports abundant small marinelife, including slugs, crabs, and shrimps. It often traps garbage, oil, and tar emitted by marine traffic, washing up sticky pollutants onto the sand.

Inland Forest

Thanks to residential and urban development, Bermuda's original woodland comprising endemic cedars, palmettos, and olivewood has been whittled down over four centuries to mere remnants of its former expanse. Today,

THE BERMUDA CEDAR

The Bermuda cedar (*Juniperus bermudiana*) is a symbol of survival for islanders, who have depended on the sturdy evergreen from the first days of human habitation on Bermuda. The endemic cedar, with the palmetto and olivewood, covered the island in thick woods during the 1500s and early 1600s, and later sustained generations of English colonists. They used its timber for constructing homes, churches, and forts after colonization in 1612. They chose cedar for building light, rot-resistant Bermuda sloops – vessels that fueled a whole maritime industry for over a century in the 1700s. The cedar tree's aromatic, red-hued wood was much sought-after for crafting cabinetry and fine furniture, including chests, tables, and four-poster beds, much of which graces modern Bermudian homes. Early Bermudians even produced liquor by fermenting the cedar's blue-gray berries and had medicinal uses for its dark-green foliage and hairy bark.

With salt-tolerant foliage and long roots anchored in the island's limestone-rich soil against hurricanes, cedars were so abundant that islanders squandered the wood, burning cedar forests in vain attempts to rid the island of rats. Colonists also shipped it carelessly overseas in the form of expendable crates to hold exports. Bermuda cedar was soon in such short supply, it became immensely valuable. Indeed, by the 18th century, island properties were valued by the number of cedars growing on them. Protection laws enacted over the years bear testimony to the iconic worth of the beloved cedar in the eyes of local residents.

But Bermuda's landscape changed drastically in the 1940s when an environmental tragedy nearly wiped out the cedar. An invasion by two scale insects, the oystershell scale and the cedar scale, spread a virulent form of cedar blight that eradicated 90 percent of the island's cedar trees within a mere decade. As the infestation continued, Bermudian officials tried to curb the pests with introduced species such as the ladybug, but efforts were ineffec-

tive and too late. Silvery hillsides of skeleton trunks – some of which remain – underscored the enormity of the outbreak; by the time authorities had a handle on the problem, just 1 percent of the original forest remained.

It has taken the species decades to recover, but the cedar is slowly making a comeback, thanks to strong reforesting efforts by the island's parks department and conservation services, using insect-resistant trees. Every September, Bermudian schoolchildren are encouraged to gather the tree's bluish-green berries to grow cedar saplings for dispersal around the island. The government is also pushing ahead with a long-range program to replace invasive species with cedars and palmettos in national parks – an effort to reclaim the look of Bermuda's first forests.

Cedars still hold a special place in Bermudian hearts. Planting a cedar tree on your property remains a popular wedding tradition, symbolizing the growth of the bride and groom's relationship. Bermuda cedar wood is coveted in the construction industry for doors, window frames, and beams, though it is now so hard to get, and therefore so expensive ($42 a board foot), many homeowners opt for Virginian cedar instead. (Indeed, cedar trees are in such demand, they have been illegally cut down and stolen from nature reserves in recent years.)

Visitors can find carved cedar trinkets for sale around the island, either in stores or from outdoor vendors, at Dockyard, for example. But the best examples of Bermuda cedar are found at auction. Check the daily paper; if your visit happens to coincide with one of the annual major auctions of contents from grand island homes, exquisite cedar heirloom chests or coffee tables will no doubt be among the offerings. Be prepared to put your pocketbook up against those of local aficionados, however; genuine Bermuda cedar treasures may appear the epitome of rustic beauty, but they cost the crown jewels.

© ROSEMARY JONES

The endemic Bermuda cedar has become an icon of the island. For centuries, its aromatic wood was highly prized for cabinetry and shipbuilding.

true remains of the old forest are almost nonexistent, since woodland is now dominated by introduced species. Many have proven detrimental to endemics; examples such as the Mexican pepper, whispering pine or casuarina, and the Chinese fan palm have competed for space and nutrients with cedars and palmettos—usually successfully. Yet inland forests covering uplands and interior valleys contain dense evergreen coverage, providing vital breeding and nesting areas for birds, insects, and other species.

Surviving native trees include the Bermuda cedar *(Juniperus bermudiana)*, the palmetto *(Sabal bermudiana)*, the yellow wood, olivewood, and hackberry. Nonendemic fiddlewoods, allspice, Surinam cherry, and Indian laurel trees are much more common and can be found in forested hillsides and valleys and in the woodland tracts of most nature reserves. The East End's Nonsuch Island Nature Reserve,

which can be visited through special tours, is the only area of the island where endemic forest has been totally restored over the past three decades. The government's Parks Department now has embarked on an islandwide restoration effort in many other protected areas to replace invasives with endemic and native saplings, a program that will take many years to achieve maturity.

Marshes, Ponds, and Mangroves

Peat marshes, freshwater and salt ponds, and mangroves are some of the most fascinating natural environments for amateur or professional biologists to explore. Such wetlands provide a vital feeding ground for bird species and also nurture insects, toads, lizards, and other animals. Bermuda's mangrove swamps—wet forests that can tolerate saltwater—are the Atlantic's most northerly.

Red and black mangrove trees, with a dense tangle of roots, many submerged, thrive in coastal swamps such as Hungry Bay on the South Shore, Blue Hole Park, and Ferry Reach Park. There are also brackish pond mangroves at Spittal Pond and Walsingham. Bees and other insects are attracted to the yellow or white flowers of mangroves. Black mangroves have air-breathing roots, which rise like alien fingers from the water. These atmospheric environments are home to numerous species of snail, mollusk, and crab, as well as lizards, crab spiders, large hurricane spiders, dragonflies, tiny whistling frogs, and giant toads. Birdlife includes herons, kiskadees, migrating warblers, and waterfowl. The only plant to avoid when exploring nature reserves, particularly swamp forests, is poison ivy *(Rhus radicans),* a red-veined crawling vine that can leave a nasty rash after contact with skin.

Karst and Caves

Scientists have discovered diverse plant and animal life inside the island's honeycomb of marine and terrestrial caves. Most are located in Smith's and Hamilton Parishes, where karst scenery is characterized by limestone terrain containing sinks, underground caves, and pinnacle rock. The dark, still, isolated environment inside caves has fed interesting biological adaptations and fostered endemic forms of life, some of which may have evolved from deep-sea creatures that inhabited Bermuda's seamount in prehistoric times. Unusual crustaceans, similar to shrimp, have been found in marine caves, and numerous more common biota, including sea squirts (sea cucumbers), sponges, and mollusks, also make their homes here. Cave mouths on land have helped keep alive many endemic species and are populated by ferns, herbs, and mosses.

Sea Grass Beds

Many of Bermuda's bays and shallow offshore areas are covered by sea grass beds, which are prime nurseries and feeding grounds for fish, turtles, invertebrates, and other species. Flounders, crabs, and crustaceans—and often protected green turtles—can be spotted feeding on sea grass. The mud underlying sea grass beds is home to marine worms and other species. Snorkeling over sea grass beds can be fascinating, but watch out for spiny sea urchins if you put your feet down in these shallow areas.

Coral Reefs

The marine equivalent of rainforests, coral reefs are precious ecosystems whose rich biodiversity of plants and animals supports a complex web of interdependence. Coral reef organisms, including hard and soft coral species, construct their own environment and thrive in areas near the Equator that receive even temperatures and sunlight year-round. Fed by the warm Gulf Stream, Bermuda's coral reefs are the world's most northerly; thanks to legislative protection, they have not been destroyed like so many in other diving resorts.

Bermuda's coral reefs take various forms. Rim reefs encircle the island inside a shallow plateau that drops off beyond to the deep ocean. This reefy necklace, bane of ships over the centuries, lies fairly close to the South Shore coastline, a few hundred meters off in places; on the North Shore, by contrast, rim reefs are located about 10 miles out. Patch reefs are scattered across the shallow plateau, covering some 290 square miles around the island. Boiler reefs are "micro atolls"—wineglass-shaped structures that rise from the sea floor and harbor coral-based ecosystems in miniature. They are particularly visible just a few meters off the entire length of the South Shore and West End. At low tide, boiler reef rims can sit just above the surface. At high tide, you can actually swim down inside these mushroom-like formations to investigate various plant and animal life within.

Bursting with life, coral reefs are continually decaying and rebuilding naturally, as organisms such as stony corals create the framework that other limestone-skeletoned creatures like forams, sea mosses, and bristle worms cement together. Anemones, sea fans, and soft corals then fill in the gaps—in turn, providing food on which other creatures come to graze. Boring clams, sponges, and barnacles are meantime undermining the reef structure, a process that sees honeycombed chunks break off, providing fresh surfaces for new growth.

FLORA

Bermuda's manicured environs are the product of its hothouse climate, a subtropical mixing bowl of high humidity, loads of sunlight, and brief, torrential rainfall that makes greenthumbs of even neophyte gardeners. Not much is difficult to grow here, and garden clubs and horticultural societies devoted to raising roses, orchids, cacti, island endemics, and other dedicated plant varieties have flourished as a result. Yet, while gardens thrive, Bermuda's wild spaces are few. More than 75 percent of the island's landmass is developed; of that, over 10 percent is covered by concrete, roads, and buildings. Open space in the form of nature reserves and national parks makes up just 7 percent of all Bermuda's land and is therefore strictly protected. It is in these reserves that various habitats, including inland forest, mangroves, and coastal zones can be seen as they have existed for centuries. But mixed-use areas such as agricultural land, hotel properties, forts, or golf courses, though designed for different purposes, are also important breeding and nesting areas for bluebirds and other species and are home to many different types of both wild and planted flowers, bushes, and trees.

Flora blossom throughout the year (there is no autumnal fall of leaves here), infusing the island with deep color and scent. Lanes infused with the prolific oleander *(Nerium oleander)* turn pink with perfumed petals starting in June. Midsummer carpets of flaming royal poinciana *(Delonix regia)* splash the landscape red in July. Riotous magenta bougainvillea vines paint parks and gardens showily year-round, while waxy frangipani trees *(Plumeria rubra* and *Plumeria alba)* and lady-of-the-night turn evenings sweet with fragrant flowers throughout the summer. Morning glory vines laden with blue-violet blossoms creep over walls and fences, and banks of red, yellow, and orange nasturtium hem the roadsides. Trumpet lilies tumble onto sidewalks in October like a pile of golden goblets. And hedgerows of ubiquitous hibiscus *(Hibiscus rosa sinensis),* hillsides of February freesias *(Freesia refracta-alba),* and Bermuda Easter lily *(Lilium longiflorum)* fields stretching as far as the eye can see are iconic to the landscape.

Bermuda has 17 surviving endemic (or unique) plant species, some 150 native, or naturally occurring, species, 1,000 introduced species, and an estimated 900 cultivated plants. Such abundance has always entranced visitors. Former Beatle John Lennon was so taken by a particular species of yellow freesia he encountered in the Botanical Gardens during a June 1980 sojourn—six months before his murder—he named his most famous album for it, *Double Fantasy.* (More recently, Gardens staff planted a lily, suitably named Strawberry Fields Forever, where the freesia had once grown, though, predictably, the sign vanished almost immediately.)

Much of Bermuda's plantlife can be seen without special visits to nature reserves— along city streets, hemming roadways, and on public properties and attractions. The island's 130 miles of roadsides alone offer an eclectic mix of most island plants, from wild flowers to aloes and agaves, bamboo thickets to herbs and exotic trees. Similarly, Hamilton's streets are lined with ornamental trees, including

flamboyantly hued varieties such as the lilac jacaranda *(Jacaranda mimosifolia),* the cassias (golden and pink showers), and the African tulip tree. Reid Street's parade of sweet-smelling black ebony sends down cascades of fragrant powder-puffs in early summer. Outside the Bermuda Library on Queen Street, a centuries-old Indian Laurel welcomes visitors to Par-la-Ville Park; it looks like a tree from a storybook, thanks to its vast canopy, wide-stretched limbs, and gnarled spread of roots. In Flatts, a similarly historic mahogany tree stands at the junction of Middle Road and Harrington Sound, while a gargantuan banyan tree spreads over nearly an acre of land at the Southlands property in Warwick. Many of these landmarks are protected by law under Tree Preservation Orders. Hamilton's Victoria Park and Fort Hamilton property are also beautifully planted; the latter's highlight is a circular moat garden accessed through limestone dungeons and boasting a bedded jungle of towering ferns, sprawling vines, locust and wild honey (or "Swiss cheese") plants, elephant ears, bromeliads, life plants or "floppers," and other shade-loving species.

Bermuda's natural harvest of wild fruit is just as impressive. At different times throughout the year, roadsides, reserves, gardens, and trails are littered with abundant piles of fruit, lots of it collected by locals and used for making preserves—or eaten on the spot. Surinam cherries, produced twice a year, in the spring and fall, can be seen thick on evergreen bushes bordering many properties; the fruits are good to eat, though more sour than North American cherry varieties. Loquat trees are heavy with fat, yellow fruit in January and February—a favorite after-school treat for passing children. Guava plums and prickly pears, though difficult to pick from thorn-infested plants, are commonly eaten or boiled for jams. Bay grapes ripen in the autumn along waxy-leafed coastal bushes. Summer storms shake down plump avocados en masse. Towering pawpaw trees, palm-like in appearance with large, round yellow fruit that are good for baking and renowned as meat tenderizer, can be found everywhere. Local bananas also grow abundantly; small and thin, they are sweeter than imported counterparts.

Roses

Bermuda's British inclinations are nowhere so beautifully on display as in the parishes' many rose gardens. Indeed, the island has been proclaimed "a living museum of roses" by one garden historian, with more than 140 different varieties noted. Tea roses, Chinas, bourbons, noisettes, hybrid musks, climbers, ramblers, and miniatures—old garden roses are prolific on the island. Perhaps the most intriguing group is the so-called mystery roses, whose original name and provenance are not known. Instead, these sometimes-unusual blooms have been given the name of the place or owner of the garden where they were found, and most commonly are simply labeled "Bermuda roses."

Roses have been part of the Bermuda landscape since early settlement. In 1639, a visiting Spaniard noted that many gardens were full of roses, and since then, numerous references point to the popularity of the rose here through the centuries. The Bermuda Rose Society (P.O. Box PG 162, Paget, PGBX, tel. 441/236-0215 or 441/292-4575), founded in 1954, today is affiliated with similar societies in Britain, North America, Australia, and New Zealand and is a member of the World Federation of Rose Societies. Its 100 members work to encourage the cultivation of roses, conserve old garden roses, and import others suitable to the island's climate and conditions.

Society members propagate hundreds of rose bushes for sale every year and also care for several dedicated rose gardens around the island, where all varieties can be appreciated free of charge. These include the rose garden at the Botanical Gardens, Paget; another at the Heydon Trust Property in Sandys; and the Heritage Rose Garden at Waterville, Paget, the Bermuda National Trust headquarters. Old garden roses can often be found in sheltered church gardens, too, such as Christ Church, Warwick; Holy Trinity Church, Bailey's Bay; and old Devonshire Church. Somers Garden in St. George is another showcase for almost two dozen types of Chinas, teas, and mystery roses. The flowering season for most roses in Bermuda is October–May, though, depending on weather conditions, some varieties bloom throughout the year.

Interestingly, through the exchange of cuttings between society members and overseas colleagues, Bermuda roses such as the "Smith's Parish," "Emmie Gray," "Miss Atwood," "St. David's," and "Bermuda Kathleen" have taken root around the world, including several U.S. locations: Huntington Botanic Gardens, San Marino, California; Antique Rose Emporium, Brenham, Texas; and the Brooklyn Botanic Gardens, New York.

Medicinal Plants

Island folklore has enshrined the healing and nutritive value of many Bermuda plants. The practice of herbalism dates back to the colony's earliest days, including the use of poisonous

Aloes known as "red hot pokers" bloom over Christmas in Bermudian gardens.

species as a form of revolt by black slaves against their owners. Nontoxic plants also fueled a plethora of uses: the large red leaves from match-me-if-you-can bushes were soaked in whiskey or vinegar and wrapped over the body to relieve measles and fevers; plantains were believed to heal sexual diseases; allspice leaves were antioxidants; a bath of chicory and herbs could combat eczema and diabetes; the raw pulp of prickly pears was said to stop diarrhea; and cedar berry syrup was a common cold remedy.

A small medicinal garden, planted in 2005 next to the kitchen beds behind Camden House, can be found at the Botanical Gardens. Herbalist Juliet Duncan lectures and writes on the therapeutic value of local plants. Her publication, *Historic and Edible Herbs & Berries of Bermuda* can be found at some related retail outlets, including Brighton Nurseries (12 Brighton Ln., Devonshire, tel. 441/236-5862, brighton@logic.bm).

Gardening Clubs

Gardening clubs include the Bermuda Botanical Society (Visitors Centre, Botanical Gardens, Paget, tel. 441/236-5291); The Garden Club of Bermuda (tel. 441/232-1273); the Bermuda Rose Society (P.O. Box PG 162, Paget, PG BX, tel. 441/236-0215 or 441/292-4575); the Bermuda Orchid Society (P.O. Box HM 3250, HM PX, tel. 441/293-2035); and the Bermuda African Violet Society (P.O. Box HM 1112, Hamilton, HM EX, tel. 441/236-5669 or 441/234-1050). Most clubs meet once a month through most of the year and welcome visitors.

FAUNA

Like any isolated oceanic island, Bermuda is a biologist's nirvana, not because of the number of species or habitats (for there are fewer than in many Caribbean islands), but for the interesting way its ecology has evolved. Separated from natural competitors and predators that wiped out mainland counterparts, numerous marine and terrestrial species that arrived in Bermuda thousands of years ago have weathered the ages and today count as precious endemics, unique to the island.

The island has long drawn scientists to its mid-Atlantic location, unique marine habitat, geological phenomena, mild climate, coral reef accessibility, and unusual forms of marine and terrestrial plant and animal life. The island lays claim to more than 8,300 known species, half of which are marine. About 3 percent are endemic. Bermuda's biologically isolated ecology has posed intriguing questions to naturalists, particularly those interested in the development and survival of endemic species.

By its very geography, separated from the mainland by vast stretches of ocean, Bermuda's biological character is unique. From its earliest days, the Gulf Stream acted as a massive conveyor belt, carrying seeds, plantlife, and marinelife to the limestone-covered former volcano; animals able to swim or fly from mainland habitats also arrived, and life gradually took root. Cut off from predators and other factors that shaped the evolution of mainland counterparts, animal- and plantlife, along with the habitats they clung to, survived or developed differently. Before humans arrived on the island in the early 1500s, abundant turtles, cahows (Bermuda petrels), and fish made the archipelago an Edenic natural larder. Rats and hogs arrived with the first passing sailors, who, it is believed, offloaded swine to multiply for future provisioning. Rodents, domestic animals, cockroaches, and other pests multiplied with the waves of English colonists who followed, from 1612 onwards, setting loose a domino effect of natural destruction that has continued to the 21st century.

Today, Bermuda's wildlife remains under the international microscope. The Bermuda Biological Station for Research (www.bbsr. edu) attracts world-class scientists who use the island as a laboratory for global investigations, including studies on climatological risk prediction and the use of certain species, such as sea sponges, in pharmaceuticals. The Bermuda Zoological Society (www.bamz.org) funds conservation research projects on endangered creatures such as seahorses, turtles, and toads. The Bermuda Biodiversity Project (www.biodiversityactionplan.bm), established

PROTECTING VANISHING SPECIES

Bermuda has a checkered past when it comes to protecting its natural heritage. Destruction of habitats and species began as soon as humans began arriving in the 16th century. The "Isle of Devils" was actually a lifesaving larder for castaways and passing mariners, who feasted on everything from turtles and cedar berries to fat petrels, or cahows, which were captured and killed to the point of near-extinction. Hogs set ashore to multiply foraged the early forest floor, while rats, cockroaches, and domestic animals brought disease and destruction.

Legislative measures were taken as early as 1615 to control the exploitation of species such as the green turtle and later, the native Bermuda cedar (*Juniperus bermudiana*), a staple for shipbuilding and furniture. In later centuries, cultivation, overdevelopment, and pesticide use have had a severe effect on the island's fragile ecosystem. Human efforts to intervene have more often than not resulted in a spectacular comedy of errors. Such was the case with the Jamaican anole, a lizard brought to Bermuda in 1905 to combat the Mediterranean fruit fly. The anole quickly adapted but preferred ladybugs to fruit flies, setting off a destructive domino effect. A belated attempt in the 1950s to control the lizard with the great kiskadee was similarly disastrous; the raucous birds may have nibbled on reptiles, but they also attacked bluebird nests and other natives.

In 2003, the Bermuda government took decisive action to protect and restore disappearing species and habitats, passing the Protected Species Act, which created a recovery plan and made it a crime to harm or capture certain listed plants and animals. The legislation is vital to endangered species, particularly those that live outside national parks and have never been protected. Those with special status include the white-tailed tropicbird (Bermuda's graceful harbinger of spring, also called a longtail), the skink (a rarely seen lizard), the land hermit crab, and the cahow, whose fragile population is being nurtured with special nesting habitats on off-lying islands.

Hurricane Fabian drove home the importance of encouraging endemic species. After 120-mile-per-hour gales blasted the island for 24 hours on September 9, 2003, flowering trees and ornamental plants were ravaged, while areas of sturdy cedars and palmettos stood virtually intact. As residents stocked up on tarpaulin, roof slate, and generators in the aftermath, they also began investing in more down-to-earth gardening choices: cedar saplings and palmetto berries.

The government created a Department of Conservation Services in 2003, which now works actively with resident and visiting scientists to protect island species and habitats. Initiatives call for installing moorings at popular dive sites to minimize anchor damage on coral reefs and erecting canisters at coastal fishing areas so anglers can properly dispose of nylon line — a major killer of sea turtles.

Bermuda's conservation organizations actively work to protect vanishing species, manage nature reserves, preserve open spaces and landmark buildings, and educate the public, particularly school students. The **Bermuda Zoological Society** (16 North Shore, Flatts, tel. 441/293-2727 or 441/293-4464, ext. 121, fax 441/293-4014, membership.bzs@gov. bm) runs the Bermuda Aquarium, Museum & Zoo and related education and species conservation programs; the **Bermuda National Trust** (Waterville, 29 The Lane, Paget, tel. 441/236-6483, fax 441/236-0617, www.bnt. bm) preserves historic homes and buildings, manages nature reserves, and raises funds to buy tracts of undeveloped land for public use. The **Bermuda Audubon Society** (P.O. Box HM 1328, Hamilton HM FX, tel. 441/292-1920 or 441/238-3239, www.audubon.bm) keeps several nature reserves, runs birding tours, educates on birdlife, and works to protect wildlife habitats. **Save Open Spaces** (Stuart Smith, smitty@ibl.bm) is a grassroots organization that lobbies against development of wild areas. **Keep Bermuda Beautiful** (P.O. Box HM 2227, Hamilton HM JX, tel. 441/295-5142, www.kbb.bm) organizes annual trash cleanups and education campaigns.

through BZS in 1997, has generated important baseline studies of the island's species and habitats, with a focus on those considered critically endangered. Among other aims, its team of scientists works to record data on caves, coral reefs, and other special habitats; define major threats to the island's ecosystems; and develop education and public awareness programs.

Birds

Bermuda's fearsome early reputation as a haunted "Isle of Devils" is blamed on the eerie cry of the nocturnal cahow *(Pterodroma cahow),* or Bermuda petrel, which populated the island in the 1500s. Sailors heard the plaintive call of the large oceanic birds and believed the island was home to supernatural creatures. Unfortunately, the endemic cahow's placid nature and lack of agility when not in flight made it so easy to catch, early colonists were able to literally pluck the bird from nests by the thousands, pushing cahows to the brink of extinction within a scant decade of their 1612 settlement (see the sidebar *Return of the Cahow* in the *St. George's Parish* chapter).

While the cahow is undoubtedly Bermuda's most famous avian resident, the island claims 22 breeding bird species (three of which are seabirds, not resident year-round). Migrants and vagrants bring the tally to 360 species, though only an estimated 132 are commonly seen, according to author Andre Raine in his 2003 publication, *A Field Guide to the Birds of Bermuda.* Bird-watching enthusiasts will find plenty to marvel over. The gracious longtail, or white-tailed tropicbird *(Phaethon lepturus),* is Bermuda's national bird, featured on the local quarter; it can be seen swooping elegantly from nests in South Shore cliff-tops throughout the spring and summer. The raucous kiskadee, whose yolk-colored chest and bossy behavior makes it perhaps the most noticeable local bird, is entertaining to watch. Pairs of melodic northern cardinals or redbirds *(Cardinalis cardinalis)* frequent gardens and parks; the male's crimson plumage with tufty crest is unmistakable, as is its repetitive trilling song (females are smaller and more brown than red,

but both have red beaks). Another treat is a shy beauty, the eastern bluebird *(Sialia sialia).* The only other endemic species is the small greenish-yellow Bermuda white-eyed vireo, or chick-of-the-village, whose chirpy song mimics its name. Common sparrows, barn owls, mourning doves, sandpipers, finches, moorhens, herons, and numerous species of waterfowl can all be frequently seen. Most originated from the eastern and central United States, as well as the Caribbean.

Spring and fall are the most popular birding seasons, as thousands of migratory species travel north and south respectively in these months, using Bermuda as a convenient stopover, or wintering on the island. Migrants can be seen as early as February. The aftermath of storms and hurricanes sometimes finds more exotic species from further afield, after they are carried off-course by prevailing wind patterns. After the frantic 2005 season, for example, when Hurricane Katrina wreaked havoc on the U.S. Gulf Coast, scores of large frigate birds were suddenly spotted gliding high over the island—a species rarely found in the area.

Sadly, the bluebird—which flashes vivid cornflower as it flits between trees—is becoming something of a rare treat to see, usually near shady lawns or meadow areas of quiet parks such as Devonshire's Arboretum or Ferry Point Park, St. George's. It also feeds and nests on golf courses. Flocks of bluebirds were once common throughout the island, nesting in cedar trees. In recent decades, Bermudians have rallied to protect the declining species (an estimated 500 birds remain), which has fallen prey to domestic and feral cats, lost vital habitat to development, and had to compete with the more adaptable sparrow for food and nesting sites. A widespread campaign distributes wooden bluebird nest boxes, with entry holes small enough to prevent larger intruders, such as the pushy starling or kiskadee. Bluebird nest boxes can be seen islandwide, in gardens and parks and along trails of hotels and golf courses.

Some of the island's best bird-watching locales include Spittal Pond, Smith's Parish, whose range of habitats attracts diverse species, from oceanic birds to waterfowl; Hog Bay Park, Sandys, a large tract of isolated land that includes coastline, wooded hillsides, and agricultural areas; Paget Marsh, with its endemic cedars and palmettos; and the undulating Arboretum. The Bermuda Audubon Society (P.O. Box HM 1328, Hamilton, HM FX, tel. 441/292-1920, www.audubon.bm) leads birding field trips, including sea-watching tours, throughout the year at parks and nature reserves. Check the society's website for tour details. *A Bird-Watching Guide to Bermuda* (2002), by society president Andrew Dobson, is another good source of information on Bermuda bird species.

Insects and Spiders

The island has a robust population of creepy-crawlies, with more than 1,200 insects and over 1,000 other arthropods. Some are irksome, like mosquitoes, fleas, and mites, but none are very dangerous, though one rarely seen spider, the brown widow, is venomous.

The cockroach is one of the more conspicuous local insects. Bermuda has 11 species, including the large American cockroach *(Periplaneta Americana)*. They're harmless and can be found absolutely everywhere—from garbage dumps to the swankiest homes, where they fly in on summer nights like some kind of bizarre, wind-up toy.

Bermuda's butterflies are perhaps not so exotic as those of more tropical areas, but there are some beautiful varieties that frequent flower-packed gardens throughout the island. The gulf fritillary, cloudless sulphur, buckeye, cabbage white, and monarch are all fairly common. Some 200 moths seen on the island include the great grey sphinx or frangipani hawk moth, whose large red and black caterpillars feast on the fragrant frangipani trees.

Beekeeping is popular in Bermuda, and honeybees are found buzzing around most gardens and park beds. Delicious Bermuda honey is sold in supermarkets and the weekly winter farmers market in Hamilton. Other common insects include beetles, wasps, dragonflies, damselflies, grasshoppers, ladybugs, church

worms, and centipedes—the largest of which is the St. David's centipede, or giant centipede, that can grow to a foot in length.

Some 59 different spiders can be found on the island. Of these, the colorful, spiny-bellied orb weaver, or crab spider—beloved by children for its clown-like red spines and black polka-dots—can be seen in trees and bushes. More dramatic is the golden silk spider, or hurricane spider, a hand-sized bright yellow creature that drapes diaphanous webs in woodland areas. Island folklore says that when these webs are spun close to the ground, a hurricane is imminent.

Frogs, Toads, and Lizards

Bermuda's treefrog, the common whistling frog *(Eleutherodactylus johnstonei)*, came from the lesser Antilles in the 1800s. A second whistling frog species that also arrived from the Caribbean has not been seen in recent years, and scientists believe it may now be extinct. Treefrogs are delicate creatures, less than an inch long, with large black eyes and suction pads on their toes. Hidden away in damp areas of forest or garden during the day, they emerge on balmy nights or during rainstorms, singing loudly, their echoing call aptly described by naturalist Martin Thomas as a "bell-like 'gleep-gleep.'" It is one of the most distinctive sounds of Bermuda.

Whistling frogs are among the two amphibians and eight reptiles, all introduced species, that now inhabit Bermuda. The giant toad, also called the cane toad or Surinam toad *(Bufo marinus)*, is an iconic resident of all parishes, and unfortunately often is seen splayed on the tarmac as roadkill. Both the frogs and toad are insectivores. Declining numbers of frogs and toads have worried scientists over the past two decades; amphibians are considered barometers of environmental health, as their permeable skin allows contaminants to pass through. Tissue samples of both frogs and toads indicate the creatures are absorbing significant amounts of metals, pesticides, and petroleum hydrocarbons from Bermuda wetlands. The Bermuda Amphibian Project, sponsored by the Bermuda Zoological Society, is now trying to determine

© ROSEMARY JONES

Giant toads are welcomed by homeowners, as they eat pesky insects like mosquitoes and cockroaches, but they are suffering from pollution and overdevelopment on the island.

the source of these contaminants and their risks to the environment generally.

Four lizard species live in Bermuda, including the critically endangered skink, or Rock Lizard, which has been on the island so long, it is now considered endemic. The bronze skink is easily recognizable, with shiny, scaled skin and clawed feet, but its numbers have been so drastically reduced, you may never see one. Just a few decades ago, skinks were found in most coastal and wooded areas but are now confined to remote sections of the shoreline with low-lying vegetation, such as the islets of Castle Harbour or forested parks like Spittal Pond. They are also found in larger numbers on Nonsuch Island. Skinks do not climb trees like other lizards; by contrast they scramble along coastal rocks or underbrush, burrowing and feeding on fruit and arthropods including beetles, spiders, and crustaceans. The reasons for their demise are not completely known, though cats and kiskadees are considered major culprits, along with overdevelopment and the impact of humans on their habitat. Roadside

trash, for example, creates lethal traps for the clawed skinks, who crawl into empty bottles and soda cans but cannot escape the slippery interiors. An education campaign funded by the Environment Ministry and geared toward educating Bermudians about skinks appears to be succeeding, and scientists hope these efforts, plus the animal's protected status since 2003, will help halt any further deterioration of skink populations.

The other three lizards, all originally from the Caribbean, include the blue-green Jamaican anole, which was brought in to control the insect infestation of cedar trees but soon moved on to other prey like bluebird eggs and ladybugs. Males put on a decorative courtship display, extending a large orange lobe from their throat while bobbing on walls and tree trunks. The yellow-green Barbados anole, at a maximum 14 inches, is the island's largest lizard, and its numbers are increasing; the aggressive creature feeds on birds' eggs and insects. The coppery Antiguan anole is far shyer, preferring deeply shaded areas.

Whales and Dolphins

Humpback whales migrate north to the U.S. East Coast and Canada in the springtime. Their pods can sometimes be seen from land along the South Shore on a clear day. Eco-tours run by the Bermuda Biological Station for Research, the Bermuda Zoological Society, and the Bermuda Underwater Exploration Institute and charter boat companies take passengers out on whale-watching expeditions in March and April. Check the daily newspaper for advertisements, or the websites of BBSR (www.bbsr.edu), BZS (www.bamz.org), and BUEI (www.buei.org) for details. Pilot whales, sperm whales, minke whales, and cuvier's beaked whale are also seen in local waters. Wild dolphins occasionally are found offshore, including the common ocean dolphin, but rarely venture within the reefline to beaches or bays.

Marine Turtles

There's nothing more magical, when kayaking around West-End sea grass beds or dropping anchor in the sheltered chain of bays between Great Sound islands, than hearing a turtle flipper slap the surface or catching the glint of its shell in the sunset as it dives back down again. Turtle populations are now a fraction of what they were in centuries past (see the sidebar *Bermuda Turtle Project* in the *Smith's and Hamilton Parishes* chapter), before human exploitation for meat and shells devastated nesting populations, particularly those of the green turtle. Today, all species of marine turtle in Bermuda waters are protected under law.

Five species are found here; the most common are the olive-brown green turtle, which grazes on sea grass beds, and the smaller, ornately shelled hawksbill, which feeds on reef sponges. The large reddish loggerhead, which lives in the Sargasso Sea for its first years of life, occasionally ends up in coastal waters; by contrast, the deep-diving leatherback never ventures into shoreline areas, but Bermuda happens to lie on the edge of its oceanic migratory route and breeding ground. Kemp's Ridley, a rare and critically endangered species

usually found in the Gulf of Mexico, occasionally makes its way to Bermuda waters.

Tragically, motorboats have killed and maimed numerous turtles in recent years, though some injured animals have been rehabilitated and released back into the wild by the Bermuda Aquarium.

Sharks and Sportfish

Bermuda's waters are spawning grounds for several larger fish, including commercial species such as yellowfin tuna, white marlin, blue marlin, wahoo, dolphin fish, and swordfish, making the island a popular deep-sea fishing destination. Of all the gamefish, marlin and swordfish are the most powerful speedsters, able to exceed 70 miles per hour (faster than a cheetah). Slashing their pointed bills to stun schools of fish, they pass by Bermuda on annual summer migrations.

More than 20 shark species, including tiger sharks and dusky sharks—and docile whale sharks, the world's largest at 40 feet long—have been recorded off Bermuda, though divers do not usually see them. Sharks tend to frequent the reef platform at night, though many stay in deep ocean beyond the reefline. They are rarely seen inshore or off beaches, although old or sick sharks seeking easy meal pickings occasionally have followed cruise ships into port at Hamilton Harbour. Shark attacks in Bermuda, however, are all but unheard of.

Other Fish, Shellfish, and Reeflife

Bermuda is renowned for its coral reefs and abundant fish and crustacean species. More than 430 marine species have been recorded from the island, and simply donning a mask and snorkel reveals the rich diversity of fish. Spend a few hours floating over reefs, and you will discover a symphony of shape and color, from jewel-like wrasses and tangs to elegant blue angelfish and spotted butterfly fish, iridescent turquoise parrotfish, gliding silver barracudas, and inquisitive bee-striped sergeant majors. Amid the delicate beauty of sea fans, corals, and anemones, you frequently will see trumpetfish, clown-like cowfish, moray eels (green and spotted varieties), groupers, snappers, red hinds, triggerfish, hogfish, spiny lobsters, and many more varieties.

Prized for its sweet meat, the Bermuda rockfish is a reef inhabitant and a staple of local seafood menus. The longsnout seahorse used to be another common reef area inhabitant, but its numbers have declined recently. You may see it, tail wrapped like an anchor around seaweed or sea grasses. Sheltered bays are home to peacock flounders, odd-looking puffers, balletic squid, urchin-eating porgy, Bermuda chub, grunts, and bottom-feeding bream. Spotted eagle rays make for a dramatic sight as they sweep under Flatts Bridge into Harrington Sound, some measuring six feet in length. And common, but no less breathtaking, are the schools of thousands of tiny "fry" or minnows, which leap in unison to create silver arcs as they try to evade predators. Fishermen typically set nets to catch fry for bait.

Portuguese man-of-wars are probably the most dangerous species you'll encounter. For more information on this and other beach dangers, see *Beach Hazards* in the *Essentials* chapter.

After a severe decline in fish stocks over the 1970s and 1980s, the Bermuda government slapped a ban on the use of fishpots, which succeeded in increasing threatened populations. Spearfishing within the reefline or with scuba gear is also banned. You can see examples of most local fish species in the eye-popping tanks at the Bermuda Aquarium in Hamilton Parish.

History

Bermuda's history is the story of unlikely survival—and remarkable economic success—against daunting odds. Geography was the first immense hurdle for the tiny speck of land isolated from the rest of the world by 600 miles of ocean. Perhaps as a result of such distance from the North American mainland, Bermuda had no indigenous people; its first inhabitants were shipwrecked English colonists of the early 17th century. Although Spanish mariners discovered Bermuda more than a century before the English ever set foot on the island, it was the English who eventually claimed the island. Bermuda's destiny and heritage could have been far different, had the Spanish considered the island useful enough to colonize.

How did Bermuda evolve from such a miniscule mid-Atlantic outpost into one of the world's wealthiest countries? A mixture of very good luck and islanders' ability to take advantage of any and all opportunities. Living by their wits, Bermudians dabbled in piracy and pirateering, benefited from the conflicts of larger warring nations, developed successful export farming, and later traded on their small landmass's natural beauty and offshore tax laws. Bermuda's course through 500-plus years of history, from discovery through the first decade of the 21st century, was not without failures, periods of pestilence, or turbulent growing pains. But the society, economy, and standard of living that resulted are today one of the globe's most envied. Bermudians are well aware of their collective serendipity and unique identity.

THE AGE OF DISCOVERY

Bermuda's early reputation was that of a fearsome devils' haunt, likely owing to tropical storms, animal shrieks, and the necklace of treacherous reefs. Yet those who did manage to make it safely ashore were uniformly surprised by what they found: a peaceful paradise with a rich larder of seabirds, turtles, fish, fruit, and wild hogs—believed to have been set ashore by passing mariners as food for castaways. "All the island and keys are covered with cedar forests and tufted palmetto palms," noted Spain's Diego Ramirez in 1603 after his galleon ran aground. "There are great droves of hogs in the island which have over-run it and trodden wide paths like well-travelled roads to the watering places."

THE LEGACY OF JUAN DE BERMUDEZ

Bermuda's discovery date has long been a point of intrigue and uncertainty among historians, and the man who discovered and lent his name to the island is just as much of an enigma.

What is known is that Spanish seafarer Juan de Bermudez was a pioneer during the Age of Discovery, a golden era of exploration and colonization by Spain and Portugal throughout the 1500s. Bermudez, born in 1449 in the port of Palos on Spain's east coast, came from a seafaring family. Though he did not participate in the iconic 1492 voyage to the Americas by Christopher Columbus, he was a seasoned navigator who distinguished himself even among other mariners of the time through the sheer number of his pioneering trans-Atlantic voyages. Between 1495 and 1519, he made a total of 11 crossings, back and forth between Europe and the Indies; in ship records, he is named in expeditions of 1495, 1498, 1502, 1503, 1505, 1509, 1511, 1512, 1513, and 1519, when he finally died in Cuba.

It was on one of his journeys that Bermudez first spotted Bermuda and named the island – but all concrete evidence ends there. The date of the milestone is unclear, though historians have recently tried to nail it down through a process of elimination. The mystery owes much to the fact that so little is known about Bermudez himself. Like many mariners of the time, he was probably illiterate and left no letters, diaries, logbooks, or written testimonials – at least none that have been found. Nor does there exist a portrait, written description, or any physical image of the man to whom Bermuda owes its nomenclature.

Historians in the United States, Britain, and Bermuda now lean toward 1505 as the most likely date of discovery. Using Spanish sources, experts have analyzed the dates of Bermudez's trans-Atlantic crossings, matching them with the voyages of one particular vessel, *La Garza* (Heron). It was this ship, a caravel, of which Bermudez was said to have been captain when he sighted the island – and 1505 was the only year he sailed the vessel. A telling clue comes from 16th-century courtier, Gonzalo Fernandez de Oviedo y Valdes, who wrote the first history of the Indies. "I sayled above the island Bermuda, otherwise called Garza," he wrote in *La Historia General y Natural de Las Indias*, "being the furthest of all the islands that are found at this day in the world." Unfortunately, although Oviedo noted Bermudez had given his name to the island, he failed to provide a date.

Bermudez would have been 56 in 1505, and in the prime of his career. It is thought he stumbled on Bermuda by venturing too far north during a return voyage to Europe. While Bermuda did not appear on a map until 1511, the island became a key navigational marker for homeward-bound mariners throughout the rest of the century.

Spanish and Portuguese castaways, and at least one Englishman, landed on the uninhabited island during the 1500s, but no one claimed Bermuda for another 100 years. Historians attribute the paucity of interest to the island's lack of freshwater and natural resources, compared to the allure of gold and silver in other parts of the New World. Bermuda's reefline also posed daunting navigational challenges, which, coupled with superstitions of the time, earned it the nickname "Isle of Devils." It was not until 1609 that Admiral Sir George Somers recognized the colony's potential, after shipwrecking en route to Jamestown, Virginia. Before long, the tiny outpost would become one of Britain's most valued possessions.

After Italian pioneer Christopher Columbus forged the way to the New World in 1492, numerous mariners began traveling back and forth between Europe and the Americas on state-funded voyages. It was one such captain, Spaniard Juan de Bermudez, who happened upon Bermuda by accident in 1505 and gave his name to the island. Although Bermudez is not known to have actually landed, several subsequent trans-Atlantic captains and crews did, by accident or necessity. During the 1500s, mariners usually made every effort to avoid Bermuda, the "Isle of Devils." England's maritime hero Sir Walter Raleigh noted his Spanish counterparts feared fictitious spirits and "durst not adventure [there] but called it *Demoniorum Insulam.*"

"It almost always rains there, and thunder is so frequent, that it seems as if heaven and earth must come together... the waves as high as mountains," wrote French explorer Samuel de Champlain in 1600. Gradually, after Ramirez's account filtered back to Spain, the archipelago became better known as a useful stop-in for provisions by anyone who dared land there. Bermuda was also used as a navigational landmark for ships homeward-bound to Europe; vessels would venture north from the Americas and West Indies until they spotted the island, then veer east, carried home by prevailing winds.

Ramirez's false assumption that Bermuda's waters were rich in pearls raised the island's allure. Yet its lack of natural resources such as freshwater or gold made Bermuda far less attractive to conquistadors of the time than the wealth-laden territories farther west. As a result, Bermuda sat virtually untouched until 1609, when the first English colonists arrived—and then only by profound accident.

THE FIRST COLONISTS

"We found it to be the dangerous and dreaded islands of Bermuda... the Isle of Devils, and are feared and avoided of all sea travelers alive, above any place on earth," commented Englishman William Strachey, secretary-elect of Virginia and a passenger aboard the ill-fated *Sea Venture.* The 300-ton, 108-foot vessel, flagship of the Third Supply relief fleet to Jamestown, became separated from the rest of the fleet after encountering a ferocious hurricane off Bermuda. Its crew and passengers battled the storm for several days until, eventually, it drove the ship onto rocks less than a mile off the island's East End—at the point now called St. Catherine's Beach. Admiral Sir George Somers and Sir Thomas Gates orchestrated the safe escape of all 150 survivors: men, women, and children who had left behind middle-class lives in southern England to live out New World dreams.

Like a real-life episode of *Survivor,* the castaways stripped the *Sea Venture* of rigging, weapons, food supplies, and timbers, some-

thing settlers would continue to do until the wreck sank from sight many years later. They fended for themselves over the next 10 months, building temporary shelters and constructing two new ships of Bermuda cedarwood to continue the voyage they had originally planned. "The Bermooda is the most plentiful place that I ever came to, for fishes, hogs and fowl," Sir George Somers would write. After much bickering among the group, all but three left Bermuda in 1610 aboard the newly built *Deliverance* and *Patience* for Jamestown, where the supplies they'd gathered from the island proved salvation for the American colony's starving residents. Sir George returned to Bermuda for more goods but died here later in 1610. His heart was buried in St. George.

It was not until 1612 that England's first official settlers arrived aboard the *Plough,* after a decision by the Virginia Company to include Bermuda among its American enterprises. London-based investors, called "Adventurers," realized the new acquisition, with its safe harbors and lack of inhabitants, might prove advantageous for their New World exploits. Sixty people arrived at Bermuda, among them a carpenter named Richard Moore, selected by the Company to be Bermuda's first governor. Bermuda was dubbed "Virginiola" and later, the "Somers Islands" or "Summer Islands," after Sir George and its balmy climate. The first settlement was initially called "New London" but later changed its name to St. George—the oldest surviving English town in the Americas after Jamestown fell into ruin.

The first settlers would lay the foundations for a colony that would develop into one of England's key possessions over the next 400 years. They fashioned palmetto huts and dug wells, creating a community around a market square at the East End, which, despite the subtropical setting, was as English as any in the motherland. The colony's laws and government were English, along with its judicial system, Church of England religious beliefs, education methods, and loyalty to King James. Great pressure was laid on Moore and the settlers to produce riches like pearls, silk, tobacco, and ambergris (a highly prized substance derived from whales' intestines and used in medicines and fragrances) to send back to the London investors, little of which ever materialized. Instead, the Virginia Company, and later the Crown, had to support the struggling colony with constant shiploads of food and supplies for most of the century.

Ironically, Bermuda's inhabitants were restricted from becoming self-sufficient by a monopolistic regimen; they were forced to trade only with Company ships and were barred from whaling or shipbuilding. Forts and bridges were built, and the main island divided into "tribes" or privately owned parishes, creating Bermuda's first infrastructure. But the colonists felt stifled by the oppressive rules laid down by the Company, and rebelled. Finally, in 1684, trade restrictions were lifted when the Company of investors was dissolved and Bermuda became a genuine Crown colony. Commercial independence was encouraged, and Bermudians looked to the sea to forge a lucrative livelihood that would endure for the next 200 years.

MARITIME TRADITIONS

Bermuda's residents quickly forfeited lackluster farming efforts to undertake all things maritime instead. Shipbuilding, piloting, whaling, and trade with nations to the south and east allowed entrepreneurial talent to flourish in the 1700s, and the colony finally began to thrive. In an era of constant wars among European nations, Bermudian privateers prowled shipping lanes in search of enemy vessels to capture with the approval of the island's royal governors. Many of the island's most prominent families—Frith, Trimingham, Cox, Durham, Joell—were engaged in privateering, though sometimes their attacks on foreign vessels were simply in defense of shipping interests.

Native cedar was used to innovatively craft speedy sloops that became the envy of larger maritime nations. The vessels were heavily used for sea-borne commerce; of Bermuda's 8,000-strong population in the early 1700s, a third of local men were constantly at sea. Unlike refuges in the Caribbean and Far East, Bermuda never became a hotbed of pirates, though it's easy to argue Bermudians exhibited more than a modicum of buccaneering behavior in many of their pursuits. "Wrecking," for example, was a nefarious pastime in which islanders would lure passing ships on to reefs with strategically placed fires aimed at disorienting them; salvagers would then row out to plunder the stricken vessels. The island also boasted a handful of homegrown bandits who became notorious for wicked deeds in other regions.

Most maritime ventures were above board, however. Salt-production and trade from the Turks and Caicos islands became a major industry for Bermudians and their ships in the 1800s. Bermudian captains would journey south for summers in the Turks, then spend the winter trading their haul of salt for grain, tobacco, or meat in American ports. Whaling was a tough but profitable enterprise of the period, one that demanded talented seamanship. Humpback and sperm whales were hunted offshore for their "sea beef," oil from blubber, and occasional ambergris.

Bermuda became a marine hub of utmost importance to the British after its defeat in the American Revolutionary War stripped the Crown of a string of ports between Halifax and the Caribbean. Britain decided Bermuda was a strategic location for a Royal Naval Dockyard—a fortified harbor where the royal fleet could anchor and re-provision. Work began on the facility at Bermuda's West End in the early 1820s and continued for several years, using mostly convict labor shipped out from Ireland and England. Forts throughout the island were enhanced or added to over the century, and the fortified Dockyard, a penal station for 40 years, became a military gem nicknamed "Gibraltar of the West." The Royal Navy remained here until 1951.

SLAVERY IN BERMUDA

Slavery existed in Bermuda for some 200 years, beginning in the early days of colonization—when blacks and some Native American slaves were brought from the West Indies and the Americas—and lasting until Emancipation in 1834. It evolved from the insidious roots of indentured servitude into full legal enslavement. Though the culture of Bermuda slavery differed greatly from the plantation system of the Americas' sugar and cotton economies, the prejudices that allowed its existence were the same. Slaves frequently rebelled against their owners, staged revolts, and ran away in protest.

Bermuda's slaves were natives of the West Indies, Central America, and Africa, who arrived at the island in many ways. Some were sold off by captains to pay debts when they made port. Most were brought here from the Caribbean. Female slaves were generally kept busy with domestic work, including the care of children of white families; male slaves were commonly house servants, gardeners, or farmers. Slave families were housed in cottages or cellar-like quarters attached to the main house of Bermudian estates. Slaves were also master artisans and craftsmen. Notably, many of Bermuda's ship crews were black—slaves or free men, who worked in overseas maritime trade, or as pilots trained to guide ships through reef-lined channels. Sometimes, slaves who excelled at such work were granted their freedom in exchange. After Emancipation in 1834, many slaves continued to work in maritime trades, running their own businesses and participating in the Atlantic trade network.

In the 1700s, Draconian laws were laid down to control Bermuda's slaves, who by then made up a third of the population. Banishment to other islands was not uncommon for certain crimes, including any form of rebellion, and men, women, and children were sold, hanged, and punished at public venues such as King's Square, St. George.

Due to its geographical location, Bermuda was intimately tied to the trans-Atlantic slave trade. The island's reefs are a graveyard of ships, including slavers traveling from Africa's Gold Coast via the infamous Middle Passage. In recent years, items found at these wreck sites have included shackles used to restrain captives on voyages and beads and other artifacts used for barter in the slave trade. Many of these are now on display at heritage institutions such as the Bermuda Maritime Museum, a site on the island's African Diaspora Trail.

By the 1800s, blacks had their own churches, graveyards, and schools, some of which were run by Methodist missionaries who came to the island. Britain abolished the slave trade in 1807, and after a massive humanitarian lobby effort by the Anti-Slavery Society, finally outlawed slavery itself in 1833. Bermuda followed suit the next year, and the island's blacks celebrated Emancipation Day on August 1, 1834. Freedom brought its own challenges, however, and blacks heavily relied on their communities' "Friendly Societies" as a welfare net to help raise funds, facilitate moneylending, and encourage education and arts. Long after slavery ended, racial friction and legal segregation continued in Bermuda until the 1960s—still a sore point in black-white relations.

BACK TO THE EARTH

Emancipation was the final nail in the coffin of Bermuda's dependence on maritime activities. The island had lost control of the salt trade in the Caribbean, along with its monopoly on the carrying trade after conflicts between Britain and America eased, allowing North American traders back into West Indian ports. The advent of steam power in the 19th century also put the swift Bermuda sloop out of business. When slave labor dried up, it was time for Bermudians to find another way of life.

Agriculture, long abandoned in favor of nautical pursuits, became the new focus. Progressive governors pushed for immigrants from farming societies in Madeira and the Azores to revitalize local farming. From 1849 onward, the arrival of Portuguese, with their strong work ethic and generations of agricultural know-how, changed the face of Bermudian society and the direction of its economy. Potatoes, arrowroot, tomatoes, and the world-famous Bermuda onion fast became lucrative exports to winter markets in New York and other East Coast centers. Over the second half of the 1800s, farming drove Bermuda's fortunes. The Easter lily also became a popular crop, and springtime harvests of the waxy white bloom were shipped overseas for sale.

Farming exports began to decline at the start of the 1900s, thanks to protective American tariffs and new competition from mainland farmers. Exports collapsed, though small-scale sales of lilies continued into the 20th century. Once again, Bermuda needed to reinvent itself.

TOURISM TAKES OFF

The island's saving grace came in the form of tourism, as wintering Victorian visitors proved the vanguard of a whole new industry. Travel as a recreational pursuit was a fairly new idea, but the island's quiet beauty attracted artists, writers, and the rich and famous, who traveled to the island for months at a time to escape the snowbound East Coast. Mark Twain, Woodrow Wilson, Babe Ruth, Winslow Homer, Georgia O'Keeffe, the Rockefellers, and the Vanderbilts lent cache to the tiny island just a few days' steamship cruise from New York. "What a contrast to the icy mountains and valleys of drifted snow," enthused early American visitor Julia Dorr after an 1883 sojourn. Over the first decades of the 20th century, Bermudian merchants set about investing in new hotels, restaurants, golf courses, and tennis courts, and the seeds of a century-long industry—as well as a new way of life for Bermudians—were sown. The era also brought the novelties of electricity, telephones, and elevators, technology that Bermuda embraced to improve the visitors' experience.

Bermuda forged agreements with major steamship lines to bring foreigners to the island through the 1920s and 1930s, when the industry truly came of age following the close of World War I. Bermuda was marketed as an upscale paradise. During Prohibition, Bermuda was "one continual carousal," according to one British visitor. The advent of air travel and luxury cruises following World War II dramatically opened Bermuda to the masses; inside the island, the motor car was finally permitted for residents, and new technology like televisions, record players, and washing machines became must-haves in Bermudian homes as islanders embraced the "American Dream." Tourism would continue to drive the economy nearly exclusively through the late 1980s, when international business became a greater economic engine. Today, the two coexist.

MILITARY INFLUENCES

The British, and later American, military have played a large part in Bermuda's evolution, security, and economic success over the centuries. The Royal Navy ran its business at Dockyard through the first half of the 20th century, pouring a welcome sum into the island's coffers. British military forces manned island defenses during both the First and Second World Wars, though an attack on Bermuda never came. Bermuda's own militia groups, divided by race, also took part in fighting overseas in both conflicts. In World War II, some 500 local men and women left the island to join British, American, and Canadian forces to fight around the world. Bermuda became a bastion of Allied defense in these years also, when the government signed a 1941 deal to provide America with 99-year leases for two baselands—one in the East End, the other in Southampton. A massive land reclamation project by the U.S. Army created a military airfield and naval base in these areas. Anti-aircraft artillery were installed, and anti-submarine patrols used the island as a base from which to scour the Western Atlantic. Bermuda also became a headquarters for the British Imperial Censor in the war years, as censorettes intercepted Nazi contraband.

After the Royal Navy and British Army garrison pulled out of Bermuda in the 1950s, the American and Canadian military continued to operate from the island. During the Cold War, Bermuda became a refueling station for U.S. nuclear bombers, and U.S. forces carried out aircraft missions from the island. Americans remained on the island until budget restrictions forced the bases' final closure in 1995.

TURBULENT TIMES

Despite its peaceful facade, Bermuda has suffered its share of social and racial conflicts. In the 20th century, women led a decades-long campaign for equality, seeking specifically the freedom to vote. Suffragettes, like their American and British counterparts, held rallies, marches, and protests in a bid to force lawmakers to grant them voting rights, which, in an archaic island system, were restricted to male owners of land of a certain value. While British women won suffrage in 1919, their Bermudian sisters had to battle old-fashioned notions for another quarter-century. When women finally won their fight in 1945, their victory opened the door for universal adult suffrage later in the century, though black Bermudians had a long fight for equality ahead of them.

The first labor union, formed by black teachers in 1919, was the vanguard of a bitter civil-rights struggle that would last many decades. Activists, including labor hero Dr. E. F. Gordon, spent the 1950s and 1960s agitating for change, inspired by the rhetoric of Malcolm X, Martin Luther King Jr., and the black civic-lobby campaigns in Britain and North America. Bermuda's white establishment continued to hold the bulk of power and wealth, and black resentment built to a boiling point. The black-led Bermuda Industrial Union took shape in the late 1940s, representing the rights of mostly black blue-collar workers for the next several decades. In 1959, blacks staged the "Theatre Boycott," a successful stand against racial segregation in cinemas, which also spread to restaurants, hotels, churches, and schools. As a direct result of the protest, discriminatory racial practices gradually ended, and blacks finally won the right to vote in 1963. However, black Bermudians continued to be largely shut out of economic power-sharing until the 1980s and 1990s.

Riots in 1965 and 1968 underscored the racial unrest, as did the violent upheavals of the 1970s, when British Governor Sir Richard Sharples and his aide-de-camp Hugh Sayers were assassinated in 1973 while walking in the grounds of Government House. Two black Bermudians were convicted and hanged in that shooting, sparking an overflow of racial tensions in the form of violent street riots in 1977, when British forces were brought in to quell the disturbances. Capital punishment remained on the island's lawbooks until 1999, though no one was ever hanged again.

The national crisis took a toll on Bermuda—financially, and in far more lasting ways—but change, while slow, did result, along with government promises to heal the island's social wounds. Royal commissions looking into the unrest pointed to gross racial inequality and recommended better housing, education, and more support for black businesses. Bermuda evolved into a more democratic and inclusive society, though members of the black community argue true economic equality will take many more decades to achieve.

MODERN PROSPERITY

Today, Bermuda's booming economy, fueled by international offshore business—and tourism to a far lesser degree—supports an enviable standard of life. Bermudians of all races and backgrounds travel overseas frequently; attend top universities in America, Canada, and the United Kingdom; and benefit from Bermuda's increasing need for highly skilled labor—in law firms, accountancy practices, banks, insurance companies, and other fields.

Bermuda has become part of the global community, and while social pressures—ironically those aggravated by the island's own success—continue, it prides itself on being a progressive, peaceful, and stable democracy.

Government

Politically stable and largely self-governing, Bermuda has the oldest Westminster-style government outside of Britain. Established by the island's English governor and colonists in the 17th century, the first legislative assembly met on August 1, 1620; among the 15 laws passed in its inaugural session was a ban on "idle and unprofitable persons" being shipped to the colony—a credo that paved the way for Bermuda's capitalistic pursuits ever since.

One of the last remaining British Overseas Territories, Bermuda nevertheless manages most of its own affairs—including the passage of all laws. Despite the island's significant autonomy on national matters, the Queen remains the titular "head of state," and responsibility for Bermuda falls to the Foreign & Commonwealth Office in London, which appoints a resident governor, approved by the

Bermuda's national crest depicts a lion holding a shield with an image of the *Sea Venture* shipwreck and the motto, which translates as "Whither the Fates Carry Us."

Queen. As the Crown's voice on security, defense, and international issues, the Governor—who lives in Bermuda at Government House, a grand, rambling old property with towered mansion on the North Shore in Pembroke—acts as a liaison between the Bermuda and U.K. governments. He also appoints the judiciary and police service, though these positions are truly selected by the government; the governor's signature, over the last century at least, has been nothing more than a rubber-stamp. While many of the Governor's day-to-day duties are purely ceremonial, he is a key diplomatic figure as a go-between for Bermuda and London, particularly as the island wrestles with the notion of cutting ties with Britain.

Sir John Vereker, Bermuda governor since April 2002 and a former World Bank executive, is considered something of a new breed of governor for his practical take on corporate issues—a trait much appreciated in an international business mecca like Bermuda. Bermuda participates in the United Nations through British delegations, and the Bermuda government is consulted on all international decisions affecting the island—though relations between Government House and the pro-Independence Progressive Labour Party (PLP) have been frosty at times. Bermuda's interests in the United States are represented by the United Kingdom via its Washington, DC, embassy. In recent years, Bermuda's government has demonstrated some autonomy in international relations, controversially signing a cultural friendship treaty with Cuba in 2003 and becoming an associate member of the Caribbean Community (CARICOM) the same year.

Bermuda has its own Constitution, drawn up on June 8, 1968, and updated in 1989 and 2003. The island's government, in the Westminster tradition, is three-pronged, with executive, legislative, and judicial branches. The executive hierarchy is headed by the Queen, whose role is carried out by the governor; followed by a premier—leader of the party winning the most seats in a general election—and a 13-member Cabinet nominated by the premier from among members of parliament. The 36-seat Legislature or Parliament has two legislative chambers: the House of Assembly, whose members are chosen by eligible voters in general elections held at least every five years, and the appointed 11-member Senate, or Upper House. All laws must be passed by the House and approved by the Senate, and governor. The Senate's 11 members are named by the governor, the premier, and the leader of the opposition.

Bermuda's legal system is its own, dating back to 1612, though it is based on English common law. The judiciary, which enforces laws, is three-tiered: Magistrates Court, or lower court, rules on lesser criminal offences; Supreme Court, or high court, decides more serious criminal cases, as well as civil issues; and the Court of Appeal. Judgments have the right of final appeal to the House of Lords in London. A chief justice, appointed by the governor, heads the Supreme Court, where English tradition goes full-tilt with judges in robes and powdered wigs. All judicial entities are based in Hamilton, with the largest Supreme Court room and the House of Assembly sharing separate floors of the Italianate Sessions House on the hill overlooking Parliament Street. Magistrates Court sits below it.

Two political parties, the governing Progressive Labour Party (PLP) and the Opposition United Bermuda Party (UBP), are represented in Parliament. The government has been headed by Premier Alex Scott, a lawyer, since the PLP won only its second election victory—22 to 14 seats, or 51 percent of the popular vote—in the July 2003 polls (the next election must be held by July 2008). The UBP, as the largest minority political party, is the current Opposition, with its own shadow leader (businessman Wayne Furbert) and shadow cabinet. Bermuda's government is the island's largest employer, with an estimated 15 percent of the population working in its various ministries and departments.

Bermuda has nine parishes—St. George's, Hamilton Parish, Smith's, Devonshire, Paget, Pembroke, Warwick, Southampton,

and Sandys—each further divided for electoral purposes into 36 single-seat voting districts (Pembroke North, Devonshire South) that each elect a Member of Parliament (MP). These constituencies measure roughly half a square mile and hold about 1,000 voters each. The Corporations of Hamilton and St George run the affairs of their respective municipalities, based in Pembroke and St. George's, and parish councils acts as local advisory groups. Voting is universal, at age 18.

British-style pomp and pageantry accompany the official convening of a new Parliamentary session every November (MPs break for three months over the summer). MPs decked out in lounge suits and Ascot bonnets ascend the steps to the House for the reading of the Throne Speech—Prince Andrew did the honors in 2005—a rundown of the government's policy plans for the coming year. Visitors can visit Parliament every Friday when in session (upstairs in the Sessions House, on Parliament Street) to watch island politicos harangue each other over issues ranging from serious (the lack of affordable housing) to purely trivial (whether to allow personalized vehicle license plates). In a society where appearance tops nearly all else, the latter motion was easily passed.

POLITICAL PARTIES

Although it did not win an election for 35 years, the Progressive Labour Party (www.plp.bm) is Bermuda's oldest political party, formed by black activists in May 1963 with a mandate to improve quality of life for the island's blacks. While its socialist-leaning platform called for better healthcare, education, and housing, the PLP's main target was electoral reform and the removal of racial discrimination. Until the late 1960s, voting rights in Bermuda were restricted to property-owners, which eliminated the majority of the black community, as well as most women of both races.

Equal voting and universal adult suffrage finally came about on May 22, 1968, when Bermuda's first election was held. The United Bermuda Party (www.ubp.bm), founded in 1964 and loosely based on the British Conservative party, formed the first government under the island's new Constitution, winning 30 of 40 seats. The party held on to power for eight successive electoral victories, finally losing to the PLP in 1998 in a landslide 26-to-14 defeat. With a founding power base of white, old-family merchants, the UBP was long perceived as a party dedicated to representing the interests of Bermuda's whites; indeed, Bermudians only half-jokingly refer to the virtual "Cabinet meetings" held in the Royal Bermuda Yacht Club, a whites-only male bastion comprised of Front Street's "Forty Thieves"—wealthy shopkeepers who shaped the island's destiny. That history has been hard to shake, despite the fact that in the last 25 years, the party's ranks have been bolstered by middle-class blacks, women, and conservative Portuguese, and two of its leaders, Sir John Swan and Pamela Gordon (the first woman to hold the post of premier) have been black. Indeed, today, most UBP MPs are black Bermudians.

Given the emotive path of party politics, therefore, the PLP's decisive 1998 victory, which claimed 54 percent of the popular vote, was a euphoric milestone for Bermuda's black majority population. The election result also won support from whites who believed democratic change would help heal long-held racial frictions. The party has been increasingly criticized for drifting from its labor roots, but with the UBP proving a surprisingly lackluster Opposition, pundits predict Bermuda's demographics, namely the island population's 60-percent black majority, could ensure the PLP holds on to the reins of government for a long time to come.

Bermudians love talking politics, and everyone from the multinational CEO to the horse-and-buggy driver has a viewpoint, which they usually are more than eager to share. Perhaps due to the comfortable average standard of living, however, the island mostly is anchored in political apathy when it comes time to put words into action. Political protests are almost nonexistent, so the public march along Front Street in 2004 by residents demanding action on the housing crisis was visible testament to the problem's severity. Occasional grassroots petitions—including largely white-

driven campaigns against changing electoral boundaries and against Independence—have won enough support to merit a few days' headlines, but Bermudians generally tend to choose the status quo, as long as their pocketbook benefits. There have been perennial calls for a new political party that would aim to accomplish what neither the UBP nor PLP have been able to over the past century, including unifying black and white communities and appealing to young voters. A third party, the National Liberal Party (NLP), was formed in the 1980s with that intention, but although it scored a few seats in past elections, it has proven mostly inconsequential. Independent candidates have also occasionally won seats, but the current government has no minority MPs. The Gombey Liberation Party, literally a one-man band staged by St. George's resident Gavin Smith in 2003, was more entertainment than crusade, though he did garner 16 votes (2 percent) in his East End constituency.

The island's critical lack of affordable housing, declining tourism, increasing crime (particularly gang violence), systemic problems in public education, and environmental destruction continue to be the most substantial national problems facing the current government. With growing calls for public policy that nurtures more sustainable development, it looks likely these will remain Bermuda's fundamental challenges in the years to come.

THE REGIMENT AND POLICE

As a British territory, Bermuda's security is the domain of the U.K. in the event of serious civil disturbances, terrorism, or other external factors. When street riots erupted in 1977, for example, Britain jetted in 250 Royal Regiment of Fusiliers soldiers, who quickly put an end to the visible chaos. Similarly, Scotland Yard police officers are sometimes called on to investigate serious crimes on the island.

In most circumstances, however, the island's part-time army and police forces handle internal security issues. The 600-strong Bermuda Regiment holds a mostly ceremonial role, marching with its Band and Corps of Drums in "Beating the Retreat" displays and other traditionally British events, such as the Queen's Birthday Parade, Remembrance Day, and Parliament Throne Speech appearances. With the Governor acting as Commander-in-Chief, the battalion has 27 full-time staff. An annual computer ballot selects Bermudian males aged 18 to 25 for three years of compulsory part-time service. Female service is voluntary. The Regiment's mandate is to help the island's police force maintain internal security; its soldiers also carry out hurricane-relief work in Bermuda and storm-struck areas of the Caribbean. Established in 1965, the Regiment brought an end to racial segregation of local forces by amalgamating a white rifle corps and a black militia. It is affiliated with Canada's Lincoln & Welland Regiment, as well as several in the United Kingdom.

The Bermuda Police Service, established in 1879, today has nearly 500 officers, including plainclothes detectives, marine patrols, and narcotics and forensic teams. Headquartered in Prospect, Devonshire, since the British Army garrison withdrew in 1958, the police force has stations in Hamilton, Somerset, St. George, and the airport, as well as marine detachments in Hamilton and St. George.

Police on patrol carry truncheons, but not guns, though special tactical teams within the force are armed. Officers wear traditional British "Bobby" hats—to the amusement of North American visitors—as well as flat-capped versions, both emblazoned with the force's silver crest. One of the island's most photographed sights is the Front Street "Birdcage"—a blue-and-white-spoked kiosk in the center of the road at the Queen Street junction, where an officer is routinely posted to direct traffic, but also to pose for innumerable snapshots.

Economy

If Bermuda's wealth of past centuries was generated in large part by pirates and privateers, today's pursuit of capitalistic rewards from these 21 square miles is no less ambitious or lucrative. Bermuda remains a society of no-holds-barred entrepreneurial spirit, and islanders, no matter their job field, are ever ready to grasp shifting opportunities or run with a good idea. Money—making it, spending it, and, very often, flaunting it—is the lynchpin of island life, and you need relatively more of it here to pay for everything from restaurant tabs and groceries to rent and transport. Because practically everything must be imported—food, clothing, household goods, animals, machinery—and prices reflect high government customs duties, the cost of living in Bermuda is among the world's highest. That is even without traditional sales, income, or wealth taxes, though there exists a 13.75 percent payroll tax split by employer and employee. But if costs are high, so is the standard of living. Gross Domestic Product (GDP) per capita income for 2004 totaled a whopping $69,000, top in the world. Bermudians often work two or three jobs, though sometimes not to make ends meet but to afford more luxury goods and overseas trips. Consumerism is rampant. "Bermuda is not a place of 'haves' and 'have-nots,'" jokes a friend of mine. "There are only 'haves' and 'have-mores.'"

Such a quip is not entirely true—there are homeless Bermudians, seniors struggling to pay for medications, and numerous cases of families sharing apartments to get by. But one would have trouble finding genuine abject poverty here. Bermuda's national GDP in 2004 was $4.5 billion. Of that, the biggest contribution was from international business, with 6.7 percent year-over-year growth, nearing a total $1 billion. Industries that supported the business sector, such as financial services, computer, accounting, and legal services, also fared well, as did the real estate sector, which generated $712 million from sales and rentals. Unemployment is near zero. As a result, the island

REAL ESTATE ON "THE ROCK"

Bermuda claims some of the priciest real estate values in the world, nearly equivalent to North American urban centers such as New York or Los Angeles. It is a source of pride for those fortunate enough to own nest egg properties and a challenge for others who can't afford to rent increasingly "executive"-priced homes ($6,000 to $18,000 per month) or buy even a simple cottage, which, in 2005, averaged $1.2 million. Condominiums don't provide a solution, with an average two-bedroom unit selling for $900,000.

Condo-mania is sweeping the island as landowners turn to developers in a bid to squeeze as much income as possible from their properties. Centuries-old family estates are being divided by the dozen, hotel properties are building time-share luxury villas, and every possible tract of open land is eyed for its rent-or-sell potential. Foreign purchase of Bermuda property has always been curtailed by a price floor of about $2 million on homes offered to non-Bermudians, coupled with sky-high taxes. Some circumvented the system through private trusts that hid their identities – a maneuver the government tried to wipe out in 2005 with a controversial ban on Bermudians selling property to foreigners for the next five years. The following year, however, a Supreme Court judge ruled the ban unlawful, overturning the rule in a landmark case involving a $45 million home it was said Oprah Winfrey had been prevented from buying.

For locals, the housing issue brings mammoth pressures on all fronts – social, economic, natural – as politicians grapple with how to make housing affordable for anyone earning middle-range paychecks or less. Young couples or fresh graduates, for example, hold out little hope of buying property unless they inherit, or are helped by family members or employers. The issue is fueled by highly paid foreign workers in the international business arena, whose ridiculous rents are often covered by the corporation that employs them – a perk aimed at making a move to the island seem more attractive. (Bermudian executives tend not to score such extras, simply because, as nationals, they are more likely to stay put on home turf.)

The trend has had an alarming domino effect on the island's entire real estate market, driving up rents across the parishes thanks to the scarce supply of units. Compounding the lack of affordable units is the fact that many Bermudian landowners are refurbishing and moving out of their own homes so as to charge a hefty rent that will tidily cover renovations or a mortgage – or sock some cash away. These lucky few, riding the wave of economic opportunity, add to the rental shortage because they then join the ranks of potential renters searching for less costly units in which to bide their time. As a result, the days of finding a $1,000 studio have long passed, along with the dream of buying a fixer-upper at a bargain.

Even those with the resources to buy sometimes find themselves out of luck, due to the sellers' market. For every home that comes up for sale, a dozen potential buyers will compete to purchase it, driving up the asking price or laying down even more to seal the deal. Such a nightmare leaves anyone who goes through Bermuda's house-hunting maelstrom with a nasty taste in their mouths – whether they win or lose.

How much hotter can the searing market get? Prices showed no signs of diminishing in 2006, and experts predict that, barring any disastrous economic downturns, the Bermudians who end up laughing all the way to the bank will be those who manage to grab their piece of "The Rock."

has a labor shortage that attracts thousands of foreign workers, the majority from Canada and Britain, to fill mostly white-collar jobs in the international business sector. Statistics from 2004 indicate non-Bermudians made up a significant 22.6 percent of the workforce. Even with that influx, some 1,192 jobs went unfilled, mostly in international business, financial mediation, or business services.

That Bermuda may be a textbook example of unbridled economic success is all the more impressive given its geographic remoteness and the unlikely path of its current prosperity. From tobacco farming to shipbuilding to the sale of winter vegetables, the island's economy flip-flopped from one pursuit to another over the better part of three centuries. In the 1900s, Bermuda reinvented itself twice. With no exportable natural resources, no heavy industry, and few viable exports other than onions, the island cashed in on its physical beauty, launching an enviable tourism industry in the early 20th century that became its economic pillar. An even more dramatic economic makeover was to follow: Beginning in the post-war years, Bermuda simultaneously began to attract foreigners interested in the island for its offshore business benefits—and a behemoth second fiscal mainstay was born. Thousands of insurance "captive" companies, trusts, mutual funds, and most importantly, multi-billion-dollar reinsurance firms, flocked to the island in the 1970s, '80s, '90s, and beyond, turning Bermuda into a blue-chip financial center. International business quickly surpassed tourism as Bermuda's major cash cow, and today, the island's reinsurance sector alone ranks third in the world, behind New York and London, with total assets surpassing $100 billion.

"Bermuda, Inc.," as the number-one industry is dubbed, is, perhaps surprisingly, not all good news. Despite its large and increasingly affluent middle class, Bermuda is witnessing an increasing economic gap between the rich, who benefit from corporate largesse with housing allowances that pave the way for $15,000-per-month waterfront homes, bonuses, and expense accounts, and the less privileged, who work in traditional jobs or service industries—a two-class system that fuels social, economic, and racial rifts. Young black men, particularly, feel shut out of the prosperity enjoyed by the international business sector. A 2005 job market survey indicated blacks earned an average of $43,156 per year, compared with $101,616 earned by non-Bermudians in managerial jobs.

And there are widespread fears Bermuda's inflated economy could burst. In recent years, Bermudians are for the first time beginning to question both the less-tangible costs of success—among them, the dire housing market, overcrowded roads, and environmental destruction—and the reality of a continued surge in their economy's growth. In a July 2005 interview with *Bermuda Insurance Quarterly*, Ross Andrews, coordinator of the government's Sustainable Development Project, said: "One of the reasons businesses are based in Bermuda is the quality of life. But there's the paradox—their presence directly impacts that quality of life."

So far, there is no indication of an economic slowdown of any sort, but most people recognize the tenuous strength of an economy that could be devastated by something as trivial as a change in local work permit rules or overseas tax policy. Critics deplore Bermuda's reliance on international business at the cost of neglecting of other economic generators.

Such fragility of the island's hot economy, and the fact it is driven by non-Bermudians—the captains and owners of island-based multinational corporations—are the downsides of what, on the surface, seems a win-win scenario for the island. In a 2005 report that affirmed the island's "AA" insurance rating, New York agency Standard & Poor's hailed Bermuda as a stable, wealthy democracy, but warned its economy was "highly vulnerable to external factors." Despite some misgivings, Bermudians appear determined to ride the wave of opportunity while it lasts. As for what comes next, their economic spirit seems content to embrace the stoicism of Bermuda's national motto, emblazoned on the island's flag: "Whither the Fates Carry Us."

INTERNATIONAL BUSINESS

Insurance Derivatives Trader. Pricing Actuary. Risk Modeling Technician. Structured Finance Credit Analyst. The arcane job descriptions for international business posts on the island fill most of the employment pages in the daily paper—a visible testament to the extent of the island's economic juggernaut.

What brings so many foreign companies to the island? One of the most business-benign regulatory environments in the world, along with a tax-neutral environment and political stability, are the main attractions. "Exempt" or "permit" corporations—which differ from local companies in that they can be owned by non-Bermudians as long as their business is overseas—are not taxed on their income, and there are no taxes on interest, dividends, unearned income, or capital gains. The island also offers a professional workforce, a sophisticated commercial infrastructure, and cutting-edge telecommunications. While Bermuda has benefited hugely as a result, it has also managed to hone a reputation as a respected offshore financial center, untarnished by the rampant money-laundering, corruption, and dubious bank-secrecy laws that plague many other so-called tax havens.

The international business sector comprises a variety of enterprise: heavily capitalized reinsurance companies (firms insuring against underwritten loss); insurance captives (offshore subsidiaries offering insurance within the parent company or mainland group); financial services firms; mutual and hedge funds; trusts; investment managers; shipping corporations, and commercial traders. All the "top-four" accounting firms—PricewaterhouseCoopers, Deloitte & Touche, KPMG International, and Ernst & Young—have major offices in Hamilton. Banking, investment, and management services; advertising firms; printing houses; computer and data consultants; and many other Bermudian-owned businesses also support and benefit from the industry.

Indeed, the current welfare of all islanders depends heavily on international business, directly or indirectly. For, while the sector's growth has caused its share of social pressures, foreign companies pay for the privilege of an offshore jurisdiction through government fees, by bringing business visitors to the island, providing jobs and revenue to local businesses, and fueling the need for nonstop construction. The trickle-down is felt even on the grassroots level: companies help support island charities, including museums and art galleries; fund summer camps, conservation initiatives, and social projects; even pump cash into private-school budgets—though cynical Bermudians argue the last simply pays for expat children to jump long admissions waiting lists. Though perennial problems such as the threat of work-permit caps, tax hikes, or the politically divisive ramifications of independence from Britain have the potential to undermine the international business sector by driving companies to competing jurisdictions like Dublin, Guernsey, or Cayman, the immediate future of the industry looks as rosy as ever.

TOURISM

Missionaries and military officers were Bermuda's first visitors, their impressions of the island ranging from euphoric descriptions of an earthly paradise to indictments of a disease-ridden backwater. It was not until the late 19th century that the concept of travel as "vacation" was born. It took the 10-week winter sojourn of Queen Victoria's daughter, Princess Louise, in 1883, to officially launch tourism in Bermuda. Following glowing media coverage of her visit, America's elite—politicians, socialites, artists and writers—began to travel to the island to escape North American winters. Woodrow Wilson, Rudyard Kipling, Mark Twain, and Frances Hodgson Burnett were among the most celebrated early visitors, and as hotels and clubs sprang up to accommodate them, Bermudian officials marketed the island as a lotus land for wealthy urban Americans. In 1911, the first guidebook extolled the offerings of Bermuda as "Nature's Fairyland" and the "Isles of Rest"—euphemisms that fixed the island in foreign imaginations as a romantic escape from the real world.

That image—of candy-pink cottages, blossom-sprinkled lanes, and private azure bays—has been Bermuda's calling card ever since, a magnet that made the island the private playground of the super-rich and gradually built a significant industry. The timing was perfect, as Bermuda desperately needed an economic lifeline. Agriculture in the early 1900s was starting to wane, and the chance for a makeover through tourism was welcomed. Early visitors attended garden parties, dances, and military displays, traveling around by bicycle or horse-drawn carriages on unpaved roads (cars were banned until the post-war years). Croquet, tennis, and golf became popular, as well as the popular new pastime of swimming.

Gradually the island became both a winter and summer resort, with ocean liner service to and from the U.S. East Coast, whose residents made up 85 percent of the trade. A steady influx of year-round visitors began to pour in to the island. Critics worried the influx would spoil Bermuda's quaint character, but there was no stopping it. Between the two world wars, tourism developed, and Bermuda's appeal, especially to the glitterati, grew. Visits by Vincent Astor, William Vanderbilt, Charlie Chaplin, and playwright Eugene O'Neill underscored the island's self-perpetuated image as a place for the rich and famous.

Tourism's heyday came in the postwar years, thanks to the new civilian airport, built for World War II by the U.S. military, which opened the island for the first time to large numbers of mainstream visitors from gateway cities. Bermuda was no longer the realm of the elite. The island had modernized, too, allowing private cars and investing in large new hotels. By the mid-1960s, some 200,000 visitors were traveling to the island annually, including many thousands on cruise ships during the summer season. The industry's golden years throughout the 1970s and 1980s saw that figure catapult to a peak of 630,000 in 1985. Tourism employed thousands of Bermudians and represented not only the country's economic lifeblood, but also its sense of identity and national pride.

It was not to last, however. Competing destinations, especially bargain resorts in the Caribbean, coupled with rising costs triggered a slow but steady slump in the industry throughout the 1990s and into the 21st century. Even more alarming to the industry is the continued drop in visitor spending; retailers blame fewer air arrivals compared to cruise passengers, a demographic that traditionally spends less than those who fly to the island.

Claiming they could no longer afford to operate, several well-known hotels closed in the 1980s, 1990s, and 2000s, including Club Med, the Belmont, Lantana, the Palmetto Hotel, the Inverurie, the Newstead, and the Marriott Castle Harbour. The Hamilton-based Bermudiana Hotel, where Woodrow Wilson once slept, was sold to become the headquarters of Bermuda's largest reinsurers. Other former hotel properties have developed upscale time-share and condominium units, with a promise to government include a certain number of hotel rooms in the future. Labor is another challenge: From the mid-1980s onward, the industry has been hemorrhaging young Bermudians to better-paying careers in international business.

Tourism remains Bermuda's second-largest industry, however, and to a large extent business and tourism are codependent on each other, with increasing numbers of business visitors needing accommodations, attractions, and visitor-geared recreation. Indeed, many of the most successful hotels and guesthouses now claim business clientele as their major source of income. Notably, a few closed-down properties are reopening: The waterside Inverurie in Paget was redeveloped as a business hotel-cum-condominium complex; Lantana was purchased with plans for a spa resort; and The Newstead, another Paget landmark, is due to open in 2007 with hotel units as well as condos. Existing properties such as Pompano Beach, Mandarin Oriental's Elbow Beach Hotel, and the Fairmont Southampton have reinvested millions in their properties, though some were forced to do so by the destruction of Hurricane Fabian in 2003.

The majority of Bermuda's visitors still hail from North America, mostly Americans (80 percent), followed by Europeans (11 percent) and Canadians (10 percent). The difference is that more now come from farther afield—the U.S. Midwest and the west coasts of both Canada and the U.S.—and the island is starting to attract people from newer markets such as continental Europe. Generally, Bermuda visitors of all nationalities are affluent (making at least $100,000 a year), mature (air visitors' average age was between 35 and 54 in 2003; cruise-ship passengers were slightly older), and many are "repeat" customers. The island has always enjoyed a solid market of repeat visitors—Bermudaphiles who come every year for decades. Leisure travelers make up 69 percent of the market, business visitors 19 percent, and those who come to visit families and friends who live and work on the island account for 12 percent. Shopping, soft adventure, cultural pursuits, and the more typical beach experience are the norm.

There are constant calls from industry watchers for Bermuda to offer boutique hotels, better service to match prices, and lower airfares to attract more visitors—something that carriers such as JetBlue and USA 3000 are now offering. Having evolved from a winter resort to a midsummer escape in the 20th century, Bermuda is today a multiseasonal destination challenged to offer attractions and events that appeal to visitors looking for more than sunburns and rum swizzles. While travelers still seek relaxation, they also want to know more about the destination they choose, a worldwide trend.

As a result, Bermuda has recently focused on developing cultural and events-oriented tourism, with an emphasis on island heritage, grassroots traditions, and community involvement. The government plans to revamp the chain of centuries-old forts throughout the island, and a foundation is forging ahead with restoration of the UNESCO World Heritage Site of St. George. Down the road, the historic military buildings of the Royal Naval Dockyard may turn into a third major town, complete with loft living and a new slate of retail, craft, and entertainment outlets. And the island's majority black community is beginning to celebrate its cultural roots and milestones through museums, street festivals, poetry, film and theater.

Bermuda's government is focusing on big-draw attractions like October's Music Festival, January's marathon, and March's Bermuda International Film Festival. Eco-tourism is another facet of the industry with largely untapped potential, though there has been growing interest in activities such as whale-watching trips, birding tours, and other outdoor pursuits.

People and Culture

Bermudians grapple with their national identity, which, combining British colonialism, American capitalism, West Indian roots, and dashes of Portuguese and Native American culture, is sometimes incredibly difficult to pin down. Aside from the complicated ethnic and cultural mix, there's the deeper question of how to characterize islanders as a people—stuck somewhere, physically and philosophically, between the sophistication of the world we belong to and the insular self-complacency engendered by living on a remote island.

If generalizations can be made, Bermudi-ans represent a rather quirky combination of small-town vice (islanders love nothing better than to gossip, and it's easy because everyone knows everyone) and cosmopolitan sophistication (most have traveled overseas, many have attended mainland colleges and universities). As survivors in the broadest sense—of the sea, of hurricanes, of utter economic fragility and an unlikely history—Bermudians have evolved as an enigmatic and sometimes contradictory breed, both greedy and freely giving, open-minded and terribly bigoted, standoffish and disarmingly friendly.

They are also an assimilation of many people and cultures over the centuries, creating a diverse society.

The ongoing political debate over Independence has strong social overtones for Bermudians as a people. If we cut our ties to Britain, do we lose or gain? Would Bermudians then have a stronger sense of identity? Can such a small society so far removed from others make it alone... and should we try? While many Bermudians would gladly keep hold of the motherland's apron strings, others feel ready to take the leap. Whatever's decided, it's fair to say that the Bermudian character—stoic, proud, and ultimately charming through so many storms—will remain intact.

DEMOGRAPHICS

Bermuda has been a home of immigrants from its earliest days. Unlike many Caribbean nations, there were no indigenous people here when the first English colonists arrived in the early 17th century, likely due to the island's isolated position in the mid-Atlantic. Since then, Empire-building, more than two centuries of slavery, and labor shortages have brought waves of immigration to the island—notably large numbers of British whites, West Indian blacks, and Portuguese Azoreans. The official language has always been English, though Portuguese is spoken within a restricted community.

According to the most recent census in 2000, the population stands at roughly 65,000, of which 60 percent is black. Seventy-nine percent of the population is Bermuda-born, while 21 percent is foreign-born. U.K. immigrants made up 28 percent of the immigrant population, Americans 20 percent, Canadians 15 percent, Caribbean 12 percent, and Portugal/Azores 10 percent. Until a cap on immigration in the latter half of the 20th century, the most recent immigrants were British teachers, police officers, pharmacists, and nurses in the 1950s and 1960s. West Indian immigration began en masse in the late 1890s when citizens of Jamaica, St. Kitts, Barbados, and Trinidad were fleeing economic depression.

Development of the Royal Naval Dockyard demanded the region's skilled workers, and many West Indian-Bermudian families can trace their roots back to this period. More Caribbean workers were recruited in the 1920s to build the Railway, and later West Indian police were sought to help balance the racial mix of Bermuda's police force. Portuguese have also had a large impact on Bermuda's demographics and culture since the first Azoreans were brought to the island in 1849 to revitalize agriculture. In the past 20 years, Bermuda's East Asian community has developed, thanks to a high demand for Filipino guest-workers as nannies and housekeepers. The number of Indian, Indonesian, and Thai nationals living on the island has also increased as restaurants seek cheaper labor than Bermudians are willing to provide, although their overall numbers remain small. Even today, though immigration laws are far stricter, Bermuda depends on foreign labor to survive, and inevitably many expatriates marry locals and end up living on the island forever.

RACISM AND SOCIAL TENSIONS

The island's mix of races, cultures, and immigrants has not happened without bitter tensions. Slavery—from the earliest record in 1616 to Emancipation in 1834—and its socio-economic fallout has proven the most divisive and emotionally fraught issue among Bermudians, right up to the current day. Slavery in Bermuda was domestic in nature, and very different in scale from the plantation system of the Caribbean or U.S. South—mainly because the islands had no sugarcane or cotton. Bermudian colonists used slaves to farm their land, crew their ships, and look after their homes and children. In a system of conflict and compromise, island whites and blacks influenced each other's lives heavily and shaped the culture and look of modern Bermuda—the generally lighter skin color of Bermudians compared to West Indian or African blacks is an obvious example.

It took until modern times, even up to the 1980s and 1990s, for Bermudians to start openly discussing race and racial tensions in their society. That is largely due to the fact racial segregation here ended just a generation ago, in the early 1960s. One of the biggest issues for the black community remains the ongoing struggle to achieve economic equality, after decades in which even getting a mortgage from white-owned banks was an impossible dream. Racist views still exist in Bermuda, though with a black-run government, a large and growing black middle class, and increasing Bermudian youth receiving higher education in multiethnic urban centers, it continues to recede, and if expressed, is often subtler than in America. "Bermuda's blacks and whites mix very well nine-to-five, and at big community events," comments Charles Barclay, editor of *Bermuda Business Visitor* magazine. "But among some in the older white community, there flourishes what might be described as a benign bigotry; a casual, condescending bias which one could laugh off as the folly of a fading era—were it not for the fact that they retain significant wealth and power."

Complicating the situation is the influx of "expats"—mostly white expatriate workers, many of whom are hired at higher salaries than Bermudian counterparts, black or white. Common resentment against foreign workers is difficult to separate from the issue of race, though more often than not, economic factors are to blame.

Regardless of color or salary, there is a definite pecking order in Bermudian society. Top of the heap in terms of social acceptance are "Born Bermudians," though those with 300-year-old families rather than second-generation status are preferred. Next come the spouses of Born Bermudians, who are accorded respect almost grudgingly. So-called "Paper Bermudians"—those who have won their status—either decades ago, when it was straightforward, or as newly recognized long-term residents—are next down on the list of social importance. Finally, at the bottom of the heap, come the for-

eign workers, the expats. They have no voting rights, but they consider themselves, correctly in most cases, to be standing on shaky ground in a much larger sense. Thanks to Bermuda's work-permit system, which allows one-year or three-year permits to most workers, the expat population remains a largely silent one. Most foreign residents prefer not to speak out publicly about issues of any kind, let alone controversial topics like race or Independence; most feel they would be jeopardizing their chances of remaining on the island. Some Bermudians dislike foreigners because they are seen to consider the island as a place to make loads of money with little care for its people or culture. As a visitor, you will usually be unaware of such complicated social undercurrents, but they do exist and affect daily life for all residents.

RELIGION

Bermuda is often cited as the place with the most churches per square mile of anywhere in the world, something that will soon become apparent as you spot innumerable places of worship around the parishes—from Anglican spires and Roman Catholic grandeur to African Methodist Episcopal congregations and simple gospel halls. Some churches stand on the site of 17th-century origins; others are modernist creations of the new millennium. Baptists, Seventh-Day Adventists, Christian Scientists, Lutherans, Ethiopian Orthodox, Jews, Evangelicals, even non-denominational churches—they are all well represented. The Religion pages in the weekend edition of the *Bermuda Sun* or the Churches listing in the phone book are proof of the island's deep religious roots, as well as the substantial power wielded by church lobby groups.

Visiting Bermuda's churches, either when they're empty or during services, is a fascinating lesson in local history and social studies. Most churches are open to the public at different times during the week. Check schedules with respective church offices or pastors.

ESSENTIALS

Getting There

BY COMMERCIAL AIRLINE

Bermuda has no national airline, despite much discussion over the years about the pros and cons of launching a homegrown carrier. But the island has no shortage of flight service from major cities on the U.S. East Coast, as well as from London and Toronto. Nine commercial airlines flew roundtrip schedules to Bermuda in 2005. JetBlue launched daily service between JFK and Bermuda in 2006, and up to two more carriers are to be added in 2007.

Visitors returning to the island since 2003 will notice numerous updates at **Bermuda International Airport** (2 Kindley Field Rd., St. George's, tel. 441/293-1640,

www.bermudaairport.bm), which had a face-lift in the destructive aftermath of Hurricane Fabian. The airport is located in the East End, in St. George's Parish, which is linked by a half-mile Causeway to the rest of the island. It's a half-hour drive to central hotels.

Travelers flying back to America from Bermuda will appreciate one of the tangible benefits the island reaps from its long, amicable relationship with Uncle Sam. Under a special arrangement since the 1970s, U.S. Customs pre-clearance at Bermuda's airport—a process of a few minutes—basically allows passengers to be treated as domestic arrivals once they reach their American airport destination, thereby

© ROSEMARY JONES

avoiding the long lines of security and Immigration checks imposed on international travelers since September 11, 2001. The airport's executive lounge, located in U.S. Departures, is open to first- and business-class passengers traveling on U.S.-bound flights.

Reservations and Fares

Bermuda tourism's biggest problem has long been the stratospheric cost of air travel to and from the island. Industry officials and locals recognize the high cost as probably the biggest single reason for the slide in visitor numbers over the past two decades and have labored to try to find ways to bring flight prices down.

Bermuda's problem can be attributed to geography and supply-and-demand economics. It is not a major urban center, so airlines serving the island can wield complete monopolies on various gateways. As a result, Bermuda has become something of a cash cow for carriers; the island rates as one of the highest-yield destinations in the world.

Luckily for travelers, including Bermuda residents, more airline and gateway choices are starting to emerge—including money-saving options. In 2003, discount airline USA 3000 began flying to the island, introducing unprecedented $79 fares each way ($159 round-trip) from U.S. East Coast cities—a highly popular move that forced major airlines to compete with occasional special offers. In 2006, JetBlue launched $129 fares with daily service from New York's JFK. Fare sales remain the most cost-effective way for leisure travelers to get to Bermuda, particularly in the peak summer season. If you happen to narrowly miss out on a seat sale after booking a ticket, some airlines will honor the lower price and offer a refund.

Seat availability diminishes (and prices rise accordingly) during the peak summer months and over Christmas, when Bermudians fly home en masse from London, Toronto, and U.S. East Coast cities. Generally, though, you will pay more April–October than during the quieter November–March "off" season. Midweek fares are also less expensive than weekend options, as demand is higher Friday to Sunday, especially

AIRLINES

Major airlines with Hamilton and/or airport ticket offices and local telephone numbers are:

- **Air Canada:** Windsor Place, second floor, Queen St., tel. 441/295-4587, 9 A.M.-5 P.M. Mon.-Fri.; airport office, tel. 441/293-0793, baggage 441/293-0794, flight information 441/293-1777.

- **American Airlines:** 21 Church St., 8:45 A.M.-5:15 P.M. Mon.-Fri.; airport office, reservations tel. 441/293-1420, flight information and baggage 441/293-1556, 8 A.M.-9 P.M. daily.

- **British Airways:** airport office, tel. 441/293-1944, baggage 441/278-6201, 9 A.M.-7:30 P.M. daily.

- **Continental Airlines:** Bermudiana Arcade, 27 Queen St., walk-in service only, 9 A.M.-5 P.M. Mon.-Fri., 9 A.M.-noon Sat.; airport office, flight information and general inquiries tel. 441/293-3092, 9 A.M.-5 P.M. daily.

- **Delta Airlines:** 7 Washington Mall, ground floor, 9 A.M.-5 P.M. Mon.-Fri.; airport office, tel. 441/293-1024, baggage 441/293-1022, 9 A.M.-5:30 P.M. daily.

- **US Airways:** airport office, tel. 441/293-3073, 9 A.M.-4:30 P.M. daily.

holiday weekends, when North American travelers tend to fly down for brief doses of subtropical R&R. Prices from the same gateway city can range dramatically, depending on all these factors. A ticket on American Airlines from New York City to Bermuda, for example, can range anywhere from $250 (during a seat sale) to well over $1,000 if booked last-minute.

Bermuda International Airport's code is BDA; this is the island's only airport. If you search for fares online, try checking different departure airports to win a cheaper fare. Rates from the New York area to Bermuda vary, for instance, depending on whether you fly American Airlines from JFK, US Airways from La

Guardia, or Continental from Newark. Similarly, if you plan to travel from Britain and don't mind stopping, fares from London via New York are sometimes cheaper than Gatwick–Bermuda direct.

One stringent rule about flying to Bermuda: You must have a return ticket. Airlines normally will not sell one-way fares to foreign countries without proof of residency, and if you land here, you will not be permitted through Bermuda Immigration and Customs without proof of return. Even if you are leaving the island by alternative transport (as crew on a private yacht, for instance), it is best to buy an unrestricted round-trip ticket, then get the return refunded.

A $25 tax is charged to all air passengers to Bermuda, both visitors and residents. The charge is incorporated into the airfare and collected in advance. Children younger than two are exempt.

From the United States

There are seven commercial airlines serving Bermuda from the United States. **American Airlines** (tel. 800/433-7300, www.aa.com) flies direct, twice daily from New York (JFK), and five days a week (Wed.–Sun.) from Miami. **Delta Air Lines** (tel. 800/221-1212 or 800/241-4141, www.delta.com) offers daily flights from Boston and Atlanta. **US Airways** (tel. 800/622-1015, www.usairways.com) flies nonstop daily from New York (La Guardia), Boston, Washington, D.C., and Philadelphia; it sporadically offers a direct flight from Orlando. **Continental** (tel. 800/231-0856, www.continental.com) serves Bermuda daily with a direct flight from Newark. **USA 3000 Airlines** (tel. 800/872-3000, 610/359-6545 for group rates, www.usa3000airlines.com) offers daily direct flights from Baltimore, Newark, and Philadelphia. Both **Northwest Airlines** (tel. 800/447-4747, www.nwa.com) and **United Airlines** (tel. 800/241-6522, www.united.com) also fly direct to the island during the summer, from Detroit and Chicago, respectively.

From Canada

Only **Air Canada** (tel. 800/776-3000 or 888/247-2262, www.aircanada.com) flies direct daily to Bermuda from Canada, with a daily flight to and from Toronto. In early September, Air Canada occasionally offers a single, round-trip Halifax–Bermuda flight catering mainly to the many island students heading up to colleges and universities in the eastern provinces.

From the United Kingdom

British Airways (tel. 800/247-9297 from North America, 0181/897-4000 from London, or 0345/222-1111 outside London, www.ba.com) flies direct from London's Gatwick airport five days a week (except Wednesdays and Fridays), with overnight return flights leaving Bermuda on those evenings. The British Airways Executive Club is located in the International Departures Lounge.

From Other Countries

New York, Miami, and London are the key gateway cities for connecting flights to Bermuda from most other points of departure, including the Caribbean and Latin America, continental Europe, Africa, Asia, and Australasia.

BY PRIVATE AIRCRAFT

The use of private jets by corporations and deep-pocketed individuals worldwide has sky-rocketed since September 11, 2001, a timesaving trend fueled by the desire to bypass long security lines endured by commercial airline passengers. Often, civilian aircraft use smaller airports, allowing passengers to avoid the congestion of major hubs and access suburban business centers more easily. In Bermuda, the leasing and purchase of an increasing number of private jets can also be attributed to the gargantuan growth of the island's reinsurance market since September 11.

If the billions of dollars in capital injection isn't actually visible to the average Bermudian, the daily lineup of sleek Gulfstreams, Hawkers, and Lear jets along the airport's northern perimeter presents an undeniable snapshot of the hefty wealth injection. Resident and visiting celebrities (Michael Douglas, Jack Nicholson, and John Travolta) have always traveled this way, and today a handful of Bermudians count themselves among such high-income globetrotters. The bulk of private arrivals are corporate, as CEOs of Hamilton-based multinational corporations zip between meetings in New York, Zurich, and London, or host on-island gatherings. While many Bermuda-headquartered companies own executive aircraft, others opt for lease arrangements, "air shares," or other forms joint ownership.

Passengers arriving by private jet still have to be checked by Immigration and Customs, but they are quickly processed in a small, separate terminal at Bermuda International Airport in an efficient operation run by a private company, Bermuda Aviation Services (BAS) (tel. 441/293-5067). Pilots of private planes liaise with BAS prior to departure from mainland airports.

One Bermuda company, **Longtail Aviation** (tel. 441/293-5971, www.longtailaviation.bm), offers executive charter flights aboard two Bermuda-registered aircraft based on the island. Established in 1999, the company owns a six-seater Westwind II, which flies nonstop to North America, the Caribbean, and Western Europe (cost: $2,600 per hour), and a longer-range Falcon 900 ($5,500 per hour), which can fly up to a dozen passengers anywhere in the world.

BY CRUISE SHIP

Cruising to Bermuda has been a popular mode of getting to the island since the wintering elite used to journey here aboard elegant steamships from snow-bound U.S. cities in the late 1800s. Today, cruise ship passengers to Bermuda are typically American budget travelers, and the season has long switched to summer (avoiding the north Atlantic's fierce winter storms—though hurricane season can still make for turbulent passages). Due to the efficiency of Hamilton-based port agents **Meyer Group of Companies** (35 Church St., Hamilton, HM 12, tel. 441/295-4176, www.meyer.bm), and the well-organized slate of shore excursions, cruising is a good way to experience Bermuda's highlights in just a handful of days.

Cruising is popular, as it offers an all-inclusive package vacation, with transport, meals, and lodging included in a single price. Passengers sleep onboard the ship during their Bermuda stopover, and most also eat onboard—though flexible dine-around programs are now offered by at least one cruise line serving the island. But the all-inclusive arrangement has forged a somewhat ambivalent relationship between Bermudians and visiting ships. While island hoteliers and restaurateurs don't benefit financially from cruise passengers, and high-end retailers bemoan the "T-shirt and ice cream" crowd, cruise ships do pour a substantial amount of revenue into government coffers through passenger head taxes alone (a $60 levy, included in the fare). Additionally, island tour operators, such as water sports companies, do a roaring trade when liners are in port.

The first stop for anyone considering a cruise to the island should be the Department of Tourism's dedicated cruise website, www.cruisingtobermuda.com, where island and embarkation ports, cruise lines, ground-transport options, and seasonal events are all detailed. Most excursions from U.S. ports take the form of weeklong cruises, with three and a half days spent in Bermuda. Cruise ships visiting the island have hailed from dozens of different ports in recent years, including Baltimore, Boston, New York, Charleston, Fort Lauderdale, the Azores, Cuba, Puerto Rico, and other Caribbean islands. Of these, a select few serve Bermuda weekly through the summer season, though ships and schedules change each year.

In 2006, six vessels, operated by two cruise lines, were scheduled to visit the island regularly April–October, a total of up to 26 calls each. **Royal Caribbean Celebrity Line** (www.royalcaribbean.com) sails a trio of ships, *Empress of the Seas, Grandeur of the Seas,* and *Explorer of the Seas,* from Philadelphia and New Jersey, while a fourth RCCL ship, *Zenith,* also travels weekly from New Jersey. **Norwegian Cruise Line**'s (www.ncl.com) *Majesty* leaves from Boston, and the *Crown* from Philadelphia and New York. Princess Cruises' *Crown Princess* scheduled 10 stops in Bermuda in 2006.

Numerous other cruise ships, the majority European vessels sailing trans-Atlantic, 10-day or two-week excursions to or from the Mediterranean, schedule briefer stops at Bermuda, typically a one-day or overnight call. These occasional visitors have also included ships of American lines, such as **Carnival Cruise Lines** (www.carnival.com) and **Radisson Seven Seas Cruises** (www.rssc.com). For updated cruise schedules, with information on specific ships and ports of call, check Bermuda Harbour Radio's website (www.rccbermuda.bm).

Regularly visiting cruise ships arrive in Bermuda on either Monday or Tuesday morning, and depart on Thursday or Friday afternoon. Technology has automated the Customs and Immigration checks; these departments receive the passenger manifest in advance and electronically review them before ships make port. Upon the ship's arrival, Customs officials board for a 30-minute inspection process, including a walkthrough with drug-sniffing dogs, before passengers are free to go. Passengers need their ship's identity card—also usable as a credit card and cabin key on some vessels—plus personal ID, such as a driver's license, to re-board the ship.

Shore excursions, including golf, kayaking, and snorkeling tours, yacht charters, historic walks, and bus tours to the Aquarium, Museum & Zoo and Crystal Caves, may be booked online via cruise ships' websites or arranged after boarding through vessels' shore excursion desks. Alternately, visitors can independently book tours and activities when they disembark at Bermuda, including sports or sightseeing options that may not be available on the ship's prearranged slate. If you prefer doing your own thing, this is the best way to go—but be warned: if you have not pre-booked excursions, you run the risk of sold-out tours and zero tee times.

BY PRIVATE YACHT

Bermuda is a strategic port for private yacht traffic sailing and motoring between North America and the Caribbean. Boats head south from all points on the Eastern Seaboard in the early fall, in preparation for key industry boat shows in St. Thomas, Tortola, Antigua, and other islands, and the start of the winter-

---

OFFSHORE SAFETY

Bermuda Harbour Radio (www.rccbermuda .bm) and the government's **Marine and Ports Department** (www.gov.bm) advise all ocean-going yachts to stow the following safety equipment onboard:

- An Emergency Position Indicating Radio Beacon (EPIRB), preferably one that operates on frequency 406 MHz

- A VHF radio-telephone transceiver capable of 25 watts power output

- A Single Side Band radio-telephone transceiver operating on medium and high frequencies, or satellite telephone

- An ocean-ready life-raft designed to hold the total number of crew aboard your vessel, and a survival or "panic" bag containing prepacked rations and other essential items

- A radar reflector

- Parachute rockets, smoke flares, and dye markers

- Some form of auxiliary power

- Sufficient battery power to keep navigation and communication systems operating for several days to cover engine or generator failure.

---

long charter season in the West Indies. In the spring, a similar migration sees yachts return en masse to North American harbors from Florida to Nantucket for the summer. Bermuda is a convenient halfway point on both annual journeys for refueling, provisioning, making repairs, and taking on crew.

Hundreds of yachts also descend on the island for international races held between May and July, either annually or every other year. These include the Charleston–Bermuda Race (Charleston, North Carolina, to Bermuda) in May of odd years; the Bermuda Ocean Race (Annapolis, Maryland, to Bermuda) in June of even years; the Newport to Bermuda Race (Newport, Rhode Island, to Bermuda) in June of even years, and the Marion–Bermuda Cruising Yacht Race (Marion, Massachusetts, to Bermuda) in June of odd years. The King Edward VII Gold Cup in October and International Race Week in June also attract scores of yachtsmen for world-class match-racing and International One Design events. Skippers off boats visiting the island during these times but not involved in any of these events should make advance arrangements for berthing and other needs.

Anyone traveling to the island by yacht needs to be acutely aware of ocean safety for the Atlantic crossing and also well attuned to the particular dangers of Bermuda's reef-strewn waters. Centuries of shipwrecks attest to the dangers of the area's tricky channels and neck-lace of reefs, which, extending up to 10 miles north of the island, are not taken lightly even by veteran mariners.

Maps and Communications

British Admiralty Hydrographic Office charts for the Bermuda area are available from yacht-ing supply or map and travel outlets throughout the United States and Canada. On the island, contact PW's Marine Centre (110 Wood-lands Rd., Pembroke, tel. 441/295-3232, fax 441/292-5092, www.pwmarine.bm). All charts have been revised and electronically aligned so that satellite positions can be plotted. At the very least, all mariners should have charts de-picting offshore beacons and reef areas, as well as major Eastern approaches (the Narrows and St. George's Harbour).

The island has one marine radio com-munications facility. **Bermuda Harbour Radio** (tel. 441/297-1010, fax 441/297-1530, www.rccbermuda.bm, INMARSAT C AOR [East] 581-431010110, or INMARSAT C AOR [West] 584-431010120) is the Rescue Coordi-nation Centre for the area. Duty officers are in 24-hour contact with U.S. Coast Guards and other sea-air rescue centers in North America, Europe, and the Caribbean, and they maintain a continuous listening watch on international distress frequencies of 2182 kHz, 4125 kHz, Channel 16 VHF, and digital selective call fre-quencies 2187.5 kHz and Channel 70 VHF.

Harbour Radio also broadcasts naviga-tional and weather warnings and information by voice and Navtex to an internationally pub-lished schedule. Radio broadcasts are initially broadcast on 2182 kHz and Channel 16 VHF, before switching to 2582 kHz and Channel 27 VHF. Continuous weather information is also available on VHF Weather Channel 2 (WX 02), frequency 162.4 MHz. Channel 16 VHF is reserved for distress calls, or call and reply. Be sure to stay off VHF Channels 12 (used by piloted ships), 10 (port operations), 22 (Ber-muda Marine Police Section), and 70 (digital selective calling). There are no VHF radio-tele-phone link calls from Bermuda.

Arriving in Bermuda

During an approach to Bermuda, all vessels should make and maintain radio contact with Harbour Radio beginning at 30 miles from the island; duty officers can assist when necessary. Buoys and beacons mark Bermuda's channels, in keeping with international marking systems. Port Hand markers are evenly numbered green can buoys, which flash green when lit. Star-board Hand markers are odd-numbered red conical buoys, which flash red when lit.

Private vessels arriving at Bermuda have to obtain clearance from **Customs, Immigration, and Health** (eastern end of Ordnance Island, St. George, tel. 441/297-1226, VHF Channel 16) in St. George's Harbour before venturing to any other part of the island. Fly code flag "Q" (the yellow quarantine flag) until Cus-toms clearance is granted. Vessels arriving overnight are asked to anchor at Powder Hole, in the southeastern part of St. George's Har-bour, and proceed to Customs/Immigration in the morning.

Anchoring and Berthing

There are safe anchorages in both St. George's and Hamilton harbors; Harbour Radio will provide anchorage and berthing instructions, and clearance must be given to shift berth or sail. Berthing is not permitted at the south side of Ordnance Island or Penno's Wharf, St. George, as these areas are reserved for cruise ships. First-come, first-served is the rule for securing space along the north side of Ordnance Island and Market Wharf, but it comes at a fee. Likewise, berthing carries a fee in Hamilton and is restricted to yacht club berths, boatyards, and marinas. The St. George's Dinghy & Sports Club (24 Cut Rd., St. George, tel. 441/297-1612 or or 441/537-0712, www.stgdsc.bm) can accommodate up to a dozen 100-foot yachts berthed in a Mediterranean mooring style (stern to dock), offering water, electricity, showers, laundry, Internet access, and garbage and waste oil removal. Yachts anchoring in St. George's Harbour are also offered full access to club facilities and can come alongside to fill water tanks ($0.15 a gallon). In Hamilton and the West End, King's Point Marina (Dockyard, tel. 441/234-0300), the Royal Bermuda Yacht Club (Albouy's Point, Hamilton, tel. 441/295-2214, www.rbyc.bm), The Waterfront Marina (96 Pitt's Bay Rd., Pembroke, tel. 441/295-1233), and the Royal Hamilton Amateur Dinghy Club (25 Pomander Rd., Paget, tel. 441/236-2250 or 441/236-4411, www.rhadc.com) all have modern facilities built or updated since 2003 and offer water, electricity, ice, and trash disposal. Trash pickup can also be arranged through the Corporations of Hamilton or St. George. There is a floating dock at Barr's Bay Park, Hamilton, for visiting sailors to tie up dinghies while running errands in the city. The Mariner's Club (22 Richmond Rd., Hamilton, tel. 441/295-5598, fax 441/292-1519) has facilities for naval personnel and other mariners, including a seaman's chapel.

Marine Services and Information

Having arrived safely at Bermuda, you will find a wealth of marine services in the ports of Hamilton, St. George, and Dockyard. Har-

bour Radio can arrange for emergency repairs. **Fuel** (diesel or gasoline/petrol) is easily available at numerous waterfront marinas, including Van Buren's Marine Station (Flatts Village, Smith's Parish, tel. 441/292-2882); St. David's Esso Marine (St. David's Island, St. George's, tel. 441/297-1996); and Dowling's Marina (1 Penno's Dr., St. George, tel. 441/297-1914). For bulk fuel orders, contact Shell Company of Bermuda (tel. 441/297-1577) to supply duty-free fuel via dockside pipeline or tank truck to its all-weather bunkering facility at Ireland Island, Sandys. **Canvas repairs** are done by Dockyard Canvas Co. (Royal Naval Dockyard, tel. 441/234-2678) and Ocean Sails Custom Canvas & Upholstery/Doyle Sailmakers Bermuda (60 Water St., St. George, tel. 441/297-1008, fax 441/297-8330, www.oceansails.com). **Rigging** is handled by Triangle Rigging (tel. 441/297-2155, www.rigging.bm). **Engine repairs** can be handled by West End Yachts Ltd. (tel. 441/234-1303), PW's Marine Centre (Pembroke, tel. 441/295-3232), or Bermuda Marine Supply & Services Ltd. (Pembroke, tel. 441/295-7901). Aristo Ltd. (tel. 441/292-4902) sells and services alternators, starters, and electrical systems.

The Bermuda Yacht Reporting Centre on Ordnance Island in St. George provides four-day forecast charts, tropical warnings, and Gulf Stream analysis. Pre-sail weather briefings can be booked from the Bermuda Weather Service meteorologist (tel. 441/293-5067, ext. 402). For emergencies in port, contact Harbour Radio or call 911 direct for police, fire, or ambulance services. A detailed outline of marine regulations and resources can be found in Ralph Richardson's *Bermuda Boater,* published 2004. The Department of Tourism (tel. 441/292-0023, www.bermudatourism.com) also publishes a comprehensive resource booklet for private yacht travelers.

Getting Around

"This is one of the last refuges now left in the world to which one can come to escape such persons," read a 1908 petition against allowing cars (and their drivers) in Bermuda. The petition was signed by Mark Twain and Woodrow Wilson, among other Bermudaphiles, who staged a successful lobby against the noisy onslaught of 20th-century transport. Alas, such quaint hopes for tranquility are long gone from Bermuda's now-frantic roads. The influence of celebrity visitors managed to keep out automobiles until as late as 1946, but since then, Bermudians have proven as hungry for four-wheeled convenience as anyone else. There are certain restrictions, including a limit of one car per household and a maximum vehicle size, though the government has stretched the limits to allow bulkier SUVs and Cabriolet convertibles, which are all the rage. Given the ever-increasing congestion, it's understandable the island has always denied car rentals to visitors.

The rule poses challenges, however, for movement around the island, particularly for families traveling with babies or small children, or anyone who dare not risk the next best option, mopeds and scooters. But public transport via buses and ferries is comfortable, safe, and efficient and allows a far more leisurely appreciation of Bermuda's picturesque scenery than could be had negotiating hairpins turns and dodging local road hogs.

TAXIS

Your first experience with Bermuda-style transport will most likely be a taxi ride from the airport to your hotel or guesthouse. Taxi drivers have all airport flights covered like clockwork, so there is rarely a problem getting a cab to where you need to go. When you exit Customs, you will be directed through glass sliding doors to an arrivals hall, where taxis line up outside at the curb. (If a resident is collecting you, they will be waving at you from the small corral at arrivals, parked through the door on the right leading from the hall.) All taxis are metered; the

government sets the rates, which are as steep as anything else on the island. A 45-minute ride to the hotel-peppered parish of Southampton, for instance, will set you back at least $25. A tip of 15 to 20 percent of the fare is appreciated—and expected, if there's heavy luggage to schlep. Rates are held by law at $5.75 for the first mile, and $2 for every additional mile. There is also a surcharge of 25 cents per piece of luggage. Fares are 25 percent higher between midnight and 6 A.M. and all day on Sunday and public holidays.

Bermudian taxi drivers are friendly and knowledgeable for the most part, and usually fastidious about cab cleanliness and slamming doors. Some drivers are specifically registered as official tour guides (look for a blue flag atop their vehicle or in their front window, or make a special request from the taxi companies or your hotel concierge). For travel to business meetings, the airport, dinner reservations, or any other time-sensitive appointment, prearranging rides hours in advance, or the night before an early flight, is absolutely advisable. Taxis can take eons to arrive for last-minute reservations islandwide, particularly when it's raining or during peak periods such as Friday or Saturday nights. If you need a taxi in parish extremities such as St. George or Sandys, calling early is again wise. After years of vehemently fighting the Transport Ministry, the island's taxi industry finally relented in 2005 and agreed to the installation of global positioning systems (GPS) in vehicles—a move government hopes will help better regulate the cab service and make drivers more efficient.

If you are touring the parishes, hailing cabs along roadsides rarely succeeds, as most passing you by will already be on calls. Flagging down a passing taxi in Hamilton is more rewarding, and there are also specific cabstands in the city (mainly along Front Street, especially around Number One Shed when cruise liners are in port) and at King's Square in St. George in the busy season. Major hotels always have taxis on hand, and Hamilton's Bermudiana Road,

Bermuda's "Restaurant Row," is a sure bet for cabs on Friday and Saturday evenings.

Two of the largest and most used taxi companies are **Bermuda Taxi Radio Cabs Ltd.** (Trott Rd., Hamilton, tel. 441/295-4141 taxi dispatch, Hamilton branch 441/295-0041, airport branch 441/293-0315) and **Bermuda Industrial Union (BIU) Taxi Co-op Transportation** (40 Union St., Hamilton, tel. 441/292-4476, cooptaxi@cwbda.bm). Others include Bermuda Taxi Operators Company Ltd. (tel. 441/292-4175), and Bermuda Taxi Services Ltd. (tel. 441/295-8294). For West End service, call Sandys Taxi & Transfer Co. Ltd. (4 Hook & Ladder Ln., tel. 441/234-2344 or 441/234-0074) or Southampton-based Gladstone Brown (tel. 441/734-7377 or 441/535-8617, gladstone51@hotmail.com).

Reliable independent drivers, most of whom also conduct tours, include Lloyd J. Smart (VIP Taxi Service, 2 Cloverdale Close, Devonshire, tel. 441/236-2957, cell 441/534-8688, lsmart@northrock.bm); Pre-Arranged Courtesy Taxi Service (tel. 441/297-0651, evenings 441/334-8737, tsimpson@northrock.bm); and Robert Powell (tel. 441/337-1558). Tour guide Keith Simmons (tel. 441/295-9106, keithsimmons@ibl.bm), who

is himself a paraplegic, and First Step Taxi Service (tel. 441/293-0301, cell 441/735-7151), with driver Berlyn Rogers, are two companies with vehicles that are wheelchair-accessible.

Two companies cater specifically to airport transportation: Bermuda Hosts Ltd. (tel. 441/293-1334, www.bermudahosts.bm) offers airport meet-and-greet, golf tours, restaurant drop-off and pickup, and sightseeing trips, with mini-buses big able to handle groups. It is located through the left door of the arrivals hall after clearing Customs. Bee Line Transportation Bermuda Ltd. (tel. 441/293-0303, after hours 441/238-2603 or 441/293-1493, info@beelinetransportltd.bm) is conveniently based at the airport. Island Transfers' John Powell (tel. 441/734-8260, fax 441/236-0074) caters to special prearranged transport requests, particularly those of visiting corporate travelers, with his fleet of six-seater vans, many chauffeured by ex-police or prison officers.

BUSES

Aside from perennial complaints about a few drivers' unfortunate lack of people skills, the island's bus service generally wins great reviews

The central bus terminal on Church Street in Hamilton is the hub for 14 bus routes covering every parish.

from visitors and is also well used by locals, including schoolchildren. Routes cover the main roads and neighborhoods of the entire island, and vehicles are well maintained and air-conditioned. Strollers can be stowed in a rack at the front, and drivers are usually more than willing to alert you to your desired stop.

The candy-pink diesel fleet operates from the renovated central **Bus Terminal** (Church St., Hamilton, tel. 441/295-4311, information and dispatch 441/292-3854), where passes, tokens, books of tickets, plus routes and fare information can be found. From here, buses travel east and west with numerous stops along the way. If you want to save time, opt for the fast ferries instead; buses take an hour between Hamilton and Dockyard, for example, compared to a brief and breezy 20-minute journey across the Great Sound. But buses offer a slice of workaday Bermudiana you won't necessarily find on customized tours or taxi rides. Local custom demands Bermudians boarding the bus call out an all-inclusive "Good Morning!" or "Afternoon!" to the driver and seated congregation as they choose their seat. Students in their various school uniforms pile on board later in the afternoon, as buses take them home or to Hamilton. And views of the South Shore beaches and other scenic areas are worth the long journeys and sometimes-lurching movement as buses stop and start their way through the parishes. For more peaceful trips, avoid the rush hour and travel between 9 A.M. and 3 P.M. or after 5:30 P.M.

For foreigners confused by the island's drive-on the-left rule, bus stop poles offer color clues to let you know which side of the road to stand on. A pole with a pink top indicates a route inbound to Hamilton; if it's blue, passing buses are headed out from the city. One rule all drivers enforce: exact fare (coins only) is needed, so no change is given. Passes, tokens, and tickets are more economical if you plan to make frequent use of the bus or ferry to get around during your stay. The popular Transportation Pass is available for one day ($12), three days ($28), four days ($35), and seven days ($45) of unlimited use, allowing you to get on and off buses and ferries as many times as you wish. These are also sold at the Visitors' Service Bureau in Hamilton, and other authorized outlets.

There are a total of 11 routes covering the island, on most of which buses run every half hour throughout the day. Morning start times vary according to route, but service begins as early as 6:15 A.M. and generally runs until around 6:30 P.M. weekdays. The exceptions are Route 7, 8 and 11, serving Southampton, Dockyard, and St. George's, which keep running until 10 or 11 P.M. There are curtailed schedules and fewer buses weekends and holidays. Fares are based on a possible 14 zones traveled and priced accordingly (each zone is about two miles long). Fares are either $3 and $4.50 (for Hamilton to Dockyard, St. George's, or Hamilton Parish), but special passes and books of tickets cost less per ride. Children under five and resident seniors ride free. Routes, fares, schedules, and running times can be found in public transport brochures available at Visitors Service Bureaus, or, contact the **Public Transportation Board (PTB)** (26 Palmetto Rd., Devonshire, DV 05, tel. 441/292-3851 weekdays, fax 441/292-9996, www.bermudabuses.com). Tours and group charters (tel. 441/292-6704, charters@ptb.bm) can also be arranged.

FERRIES

Bermuda's ferry service, Sea Express (www .seaexpress.bm), has undergone major changes for the better in the past five years. The resulting service has become so fast and efficient, more locals are commuting to work. The government purchased four "fast ferries" beginning in 2000—two-tier air-conditioned, hovercraft-like vessels that practically fly over the Great Sound to Dockyard and along the North Shore to St. George. For the nostalgic, the clunky old iron black-and-white ferries, *Georgia, Corona,* and *Coralita,* still chug along the Hamilton/Paget/Warwick route, while the veteran *Deliverance* and *Patience* make occasional scenic milk runs along the Somerset shore several times a day in the summer.

The four ferry routes are divided by color:

the popular and busiest Blue Route (which also takes scooters aboard) runs between Hamilton and Dockyard; the Pink Route serves the quieter stops of Paget and Warwick; the Green Route, an express service geared mainly to West End commuters, serves Rockaway and Somerset Bridge; and the summer-only Orange Route travels between Hamilton/Dockyard/St. George. The latter represents a wonderfully scenic—and hassle-free—way to do a day trip to the East End. Unfathomably, bikes have not been permitted on this route, so exploring the parish by scooter if you take the ferry has not been an option to date. There are five departures to St. George's daily May–November, but there's talk of increasing the frequency.

The cost of a single fare varies by route; an adult return fare to St. George is $8, to Dockyard $4, across the harbor to Paget and back just $2.50. You can purchase affordable one-($12) to seven-day ($45) passes, or monthlong ($55) and even three-month ($135) passes for longer stays. Books of 15 tickets ($30) are also cost-effective for longer vacations. As is the rule on buses, cash is not accepted on ferries. Children under five and resident seniors ride free. Information, advice, schedules, tokens, tickets, and passes are available at the **Hamilton Ferry Terminal** (8 Front St., tel. 441/295-4506, 6 A.M.–11:30 P.M. Mon.–Fri., 8 A.M.–11:30 P.M. Sat., 8:30 A.M.–8 P.M. Sun. and holidays). Passes, tickets, and tokens are also sold at the Bus Terminal in Hamilton, and at sub post offices, hotels, and guesthouses.

SCOOTERS AND MOPEDS

They are fun, fast, and offer the utmost freedom to explore wherever you will, but never underestimate the very real dangers associated with renting mopeds and scooters. Scores of visitors every year end up in the hospital's Emergency Department for treatment of grazes and gashes—"road rash" in local parlance—which can ruin a vacation. More serious injuries such as broken limbs and head and back injuries, even fatalities, also happen, meaning the decision to rent scooters should not be

made lightly. The problem is such that cruise ships no longer recommend rental bikes to passengers for liability reasons, though livery reps offer their services dockside.

For those visitors who choose to rent bikes, note that children under 16 years may not drive motor scooters, though they can sit on the back as passengers—a highly risky proposition for youngsters. All scooter drivers and passengers are required by law to wear safety helmets securely fastened at all times.

Most gas stations are open 7 A.M.–7 P.M. daily, though some remain open later. The only 24-hour gas station is Esso City Tigermart (37 Richmond Rd., Hamilton, tel. 441/295-3776).

Rentals

There are four liveries. The largest, **Oleander Cycles** (6 Valley Rd., Paget, tel. 441/236-5235, fax 441/236-3916, 24-hour answering service, www.oleandercycles.bm), has six other locations: 15 Gorham Rd., Hamilton (tel. 441/295-0919, fax 441/292-7336); 8 Middle Rd., Southampton (tel. 441/234-0629); The Reefs Resort, South Shore Rd., Southampton (tel. 441/236-5235); The Clock Tower, Royal Naval Dockyard (tel. 441/234-2764), Cambridge Beaches in Sandys (30 Kings Point Rd., tel. 441/234-0331), and 26 York St., St. George (tel. 441/297-0478). All are open 8:30 A.M.–5:30 P.M. daily.

Wheels Cycles (117 Front St., tel. 441/292-2245, fax 441/296-6423, wheels@northrock. bm, 9 A.M.–5 P.M. daily) has another outlet at Grotto Bay Resort in Hamilton Parish (Blue Hole Hill, tel. 441/293-2378). **Eve's Cycles** (114 Middle Rd., Paget, tel. 441/236-6247, fax 441/236-6996, www.evecycles.com, 8 A.M.–5 P.M. daily) has a second location in the East End (1 Water St., St George, tel. 441/236-0839). **Smatt's Cycle Livery** (74 Pitts Bay Rd., outside the Fairmont Princess Hotel, tel. 441/295-1180, fax 441/295-2539, msmatt@ northrock.bm, 8 A.M.–5 P.M. daily) has a second outlet at the Fairmont Southampton Resort (tel. 441/238-7800, 8:30 A.M.–5 P.M. daily).

All the liveries offer a free shuttle between their outlets and locations where visitors are staying, and also pick up clients left stranded

SCOOTER SAFETY

Road traffic accidents (RTAs) are far too common in Bermuda, affecting both locals and visitors. Before you end up a victim of "road rash" – painful grazes after skimming tarmac – or far worse, consider these basic safety tips:

- Drive on the LEFT, and remember the left-hand rule when turning into junctions and navigating city streets. (Roundabouts, or traffic circles, routinely confuse the uninitiated; to negotiate them without a problem, be sure always to give way to traffic approaching on your right.)

- Wear a helmet provided with your scooter rental. It's the law, but it may also keep you alive in an accident. If you forget, as visitors sometimes do, you will notice locals flagging you down, waving their arms and pointing at your bare head.

- Bermudians rarely do, but keep to the speed limit of 35 kilometers per hour (about 22 miles per hour). Take corners especially carefully, and drive defensively at all times: you never know when a local is about to cut across a lane of traffic or throw a car door open in your path. Look out for blind entrances and sharp turns.

- Do not turn around to look at motorists or sights behind you. In a group of scooters touring together, let the slowest driver go in front.

- When it rains, take extra care, as mopeds and scooters skid and slide easily on slick roads. Drive slowly and brake gradually in these conditions, touching the rear break first. The same goes for areas with sand or oil on the road.

- Many scooter and motorbike riders suffer bad calf burns because their legs touch the muffler. After driving, stay clear of your muffler, which becomes dangerously hot; avoid those of parked scooters also when walking between bikes.

- Secure all possessions either inside the scooter compartment or tied with a bungee cord on the rear basket. Bag thefts from bikes are one of the most common island crimes, and you provide an easy target for thieves on bikes if your belongings are not obviously strapped down.

- Park only in legal spaces and lock the scooter, both with its ignition lock and the wheel lock provided. The livery rate insures against accidents, but not theft (though visitors generally do not get nailed for stolen bikes).

- If you do come off and suffer scrapes, Dr. Edward Schultz, head of Bermuda's Emergency Department, recommends treating road rash as you would a second-degree burn: cleanse gently with saline or clean water, then use cream dressings, changed frequently. Don't use Vaseline or leave wounds open and dry. Swimming, long considered by Bermudians to be a healing factor, actually risks infection, says Schultz. Keep injured areas out of the sun, also, as the skin is more prone to damage.

by broken-down vehicles. They also have representatives at No. 1 and No. 6 Sheds and at Dockyard and St. George wharves when cruise ships are in port. All scooters and mopeds have 50 cc engines with electric start and automatic gears. Rates vary, usually starting at around $50 per day, with special rates for longer rentals, but prices are fairly competitive between the companies and include delivery and pick-up, a carry basket, mandatory third-party insurance ($15–25), and the all-important helmet and lock.

BICYCLES

Pedal cycles up the adventure quotient for travelers who want exercise with their sightseeing. Bermuda's hilly terrain, and the ever-popular Railway Trail, has attracted increasing numbers of pedal cyclists, including off-road mountain-bikers. Bikes can be rented from some hotels and liveries, including **Eve's Cycle Livery** (114 Middle Rd., tel. 441/236-6247, 8:30 A.M.–5:30 P.M. daily), but unless you are Ironman-fit, you might want to opt for motorized transport in midsummer heat.

TRAIN TOURS

Bermuda lost its railway in the 1940s, but you will still see trains tootling around on the main roads. **The Bermuda Train Company** (6 Valley Rd., Paget, tel. 441/236-5972) uses colorful mini-trains, like large kids' toys, to conduct tours around Hamilton and Dockyard in the summer. The hour-long trip from Front Street goes to Botanical Gardens and back, for a fee of $30. Open-air carriages allow great sightseeing, but don't believe all the tall tales spun by your tour guide; historic fact tends to fall completely by the wayside in the train tours I've experienced.

Visas and Officialdom

Air passengers arriving at Bermuda International Airport must pass first through Immigration and then Customs controls. There are separate lines for Bermudian residents and arriving foreigners, both of which can be long and tedious. Criticism is perennially leveled at airport officials and staff for the long waits, searches, and sometimes surly officers running both Immigration and Customs operations. Patience, a friendly demeanor, and the correct paperwork will usually get you through. Do not bring drugs with you; the island's authorities and its legal system do not differentiate between drug dealers and those who carry small amounts of drugs for personal consumption. If you are caught, the penalties are stiff.

DOCUMENTS AND REQUIREMENTS
Passports and Visas

Travelers to Bermuda need a return or onward ticket, or other proof of transportation out of the island to a country where right of entry has been granted. One-way tickets are usually questioned by North American check-in staff at airlines serving Bermuda. Open return tickets may have a time limit imposed on their length of stay by island Immigration officials. All visitors must also carry proof of citizenship and personal government-issued photo identification. A passport is the preferred document for entry to the island and is required from all visitors who need passports to re-enter their own

country or enter another country. A driver's license is not considered proof of citizenship.

U.S. travelers must show either a U.S. passport; a birth certificate with a raised seal or official stamp, along with photo I.D. (neither American nor Bermuda Immigration Control officials accept notarized copies of birth certificates, or any other non-government document); a U.S. re-entry permit; a U.S. Naturalization Certificate; or a U.S. Permanent Resident Card. Note that a new policy set by the U.S. in 2005 requires all returning U.S. citizens to have valid passports, as these are now the only recognized document for American travelers.

Visitors from Canada need either a valid Canadian passport; a birth certificate or certified copy, with photo I.D.; a Canadian Certificate of Citizenship or Permanent Resident Card. Travelers from Britain and Western Europe have to present a valid national passport. Women traveling under their married name, but with identification documents in their maiden name, should also bring a marriage certificate or certified copy.

The other key to entering Bermuda without snafus is knowing the name of your hotel or guesthouse, or the street address of the private home where you'll be staying. Keep the name and address of your accommodation handy for officials. If you are staying at a private residence, don't be surprised if the Immigration officer personally knows your host. As you'll soon find out, the island is a *very* small place.

Visas are needed by nationals of these countries—unless they have valid passports and proof of a right to reside: Albania, Algeria, Armenia, Azerbaijan, Belarus, Bosnia-Herzegovina, Bulgaria, China (People's Republic of), Croatia, Cuba, Georgia, Haiti, Iran, Iraq, Jordan, Kampuchea (Cambodia), Kazakhstan, Kirghizstan, Lebanon, Libya, Macedonia, Republic of Moldova, Mongolia, Morocco, Nigeria, North Korea, Pakistan, Romania, Russian Federation, Republic of Slovakia, Slovenia, Soviet Union (former), Sri Lanka, Syria, Tajikistan, Tunisia, Turkmenistan, Ukraine, Uzbekistan, Vietnam (North and South), Yugoslavia (former) and Yugoslavia (Serbian Federal Republic of). Visas are also required of holders of Hong Kong Identity Cards issued after midnight on June 30, 1997, and nationals of Slovakia traveling on Czechoslovakian passports. Citizens of the Czech Republic do not need visas.

Visas can be obtained from a British Embassy, British High Commission, Consulate, or other British Foreign Service office overseas.

Traveling Children

As well as the relevant travel documents, children who are not traveling with their parents must show a letter from their parent(s) authorizing the child to be accompanied by another adult. Parents traveling with adopted children should bring proper documents for their adopted children. Children entering Bermuda for adoption must carry Department of Immigration paperwork.

Length of Stay

The absolute maximum amount of time a visitor may stay in Bermuda is six months, but only through exceptional circumstances; the normal limit is half that. If you want to stay longer than six months, you need special permission from the Immigration Minister to qualify as a bona fide resident. Generally, visitors are allowed to stay on the island for up to 21 days. Permission for an extension on that period may be applied for through an appointment with an Immigration inspector (Department of Immigration Headquarters, Government Administration Building, 30 Parliament St., Hamilton, tel. 441/295-5151). The cost of an extension is $25. Travelers cannot enter Bermuda to live, work, or look for work without work permits or other official documentation, nor will they be allowed in for an indefinite period.

TAXES AND CUSTOMS

Long line-ups and 45-minute waits are not unusual in the Customs Department, especially when several flights arrive at similar times or when crowds of Bermudians are carting back suitcases of shopping. Once you have been cleared by Immigration, you will receive a colored card. If you have nothing to declare, go directly to the baggage conveyor, then continue to the Customs control point in the same hall. Make sure you have completed your Customs declaration form, and hand it over with the Immigration card. A uniformed officer will either give you the all-clear, and wave you through to the exit and ground-transport stands, or direct you to the baggage inspection desk.

Taxes

Residents and visitors are equal under Bermuda's Passenger Tax Act, 1972. Passenger taxes are $25 for all air travelers (included in the airfare) and $60 for cruise ship passengers (collected in advance by cruise lines). Children under the age of two are exempt in both cases.

Duty Free

Visitors are allowed to enter the island with personal clothes and belongings, including sports equipment, cameras, golf bags, and 50 cigars, 200 cigarettes, 0.5 kilogram of tobacco, one liter of liquor and wine, and $30 worth of gifts. Duty of 22.25 percent will be levied on up to 50 pounds of meat and other foodstuffs brought into the island. There are strict rules governing the importation of plants, fruits, and vegetables, and these require an import permit. Live marine animals are not permitted, but fresh, frozen, or cooked fish or shellfish may be brought in, as long as it contains no algae or seaweed.

Animals require proper documentation or they will be returned to their point of origin, since there are no quarantine facilities on the island. They must be accompanied by an import permit issued in advance by the Department of Environmental Protection, as well as a health certificate issued within 10 days of the visit by a licensed vet in the animal's home country. For more details on document requirements, contact the department at tel. 441/236-4201, fax 441/232-0046, www.animals.gov.bm.

Returning Home

Bermuda visitors are allowed to take home duty-free merchandise purchased on the island. U.S. Customs has a pre-clearance facility at Bermuda National Airport, so declaration forms must be filled out in Bermuda before your journey home. Forms are available at airlines and travel agencies. U.S. citizens (www.cbp.goc/xp/cgov/travel) are permitted $800 goods allowance after 48 hours, including 200 cigarettes and 100 non-Cuban cigars. The allowance is good every 30 days.

Canadian citizens (www.cbsa-asfc.gc.ca) are allowed $50 after 24 hours, $200 after 48 hours, or $750 after seven days. U.K. citizens (www.hmce.gov.uk) can take back £145 worth of purchases.

Different countries have varying rates of duty on goods carried back above the duty-free limits. Plants should not be taken back without permission from your own country.

FOREIGN CONSULS

Since Bermuda remains a British dependency, no foreign embassies are located here. Instead, relevant business is conducted through British Embassies in Washington, DC (3100 Massachusetts Ave., NW, Washington, DC 20008, tel. 202/588-6500, fax 202/588-7870) and other centers.

British nationals needing their country's assistance can contact the deputy governor's office at Government House (11 Langton Hill, Pembroke, HM 13, tel. 441/292-2587, fax 441/292-3823, depgov@ibl.bm).

American interests are represented by the American Consulate (Crown Hill, 16 Middle Rd., Devonshire, DV 03, tel. 441/295-1342, duty officer 441/335-3828, fax 441/295-1592, www.hamilton.usconsulate.gov), which has 40 staff headed by an American consul general. The consulate is open Monday–Friday 8 A.M.–4:30 P.M. but closes for all official American and Bermuda holidays. Public services are restricted to certain hours: American citizen services, Monday–Wednesday 1:30–3:30 P.M., Thursday 8:30–10:30 A.M.; non-immigrant visa services, Monday and Wednesday 8:30–11 A.M., Thursday 1:30–3:30 P.M.; immigrant visa services, Tuesday and Thursday 8:30–10:30 A.M. Identification is required to enter the consulate. No parking is provided.

Portugal has recently established a consulate in Bermuda (Melbourne House, 11 Parliament St., Hamilton, HM 12, tel. 441/292-1039), though a full-time consul has yet to be appointed by Portugal. The office acts as a direct liaison with Lisbon, processing passport renewals, ID cards, and paperwork authentication. Close to a quarter of Bermuda's population is of Portuguese origin, most from the Azores; many nationals are children born in Bermuda but without status on the island. There is also a steady stream of Azorean contract workers coming to Bermuda, as well as Portuguese-Bermudian families on the island who maintain strong links to relatives in the Azores, Madeira, and Portugal.

Eighteen other nations, including Norway, France, Italy, and Jamaica, are represented by honorary consuls, who maintain diplomatic links with Bermuda via Britain's Foreign & Commonwealth Office. Honorary consul positions are awarded to resident Bermudians who are natives of or have strong links to represented countries. Canadians can contact Saul Froomkin (Reid House, 31 Church St., Hamilton, HM FX, tel. 441/294-3611, fax 441/296-4229, cdn-con.Bermuda@mindspring.com). Bermuda-related matters are also handled by the Canadian Consulate General in New York (1251 Avenue of the Americas, New York, NY, 10020-1175, tel. 212/596-1700, fax 212/596-1790).

Conduct and Customs

Perhaps due to its British past, the island projects an air of entrenched conservatism, at least on the surface. Loud public demonstrations, big-'L' liberal sentiments, overly revealing clothing—or the lack of it—do not go down well with most Bermudians. Men and women, both black and white, tend to project a polite reserve upon initial contact—until they've sussed you out, anyway. Like their iconic onions, they prefer to reveal themselves gradually.

Generally, things tend to change slowly in Bermuda, including attitudes and the adoption of new ideas. Outsiders are suspect— at least at first. A certain pace and ritual is expected in social encounters: the omission of a requisite "Good Morning," or "Good Afternoon," for example—passkeys to any conversation with locals—can mean the difference between terse unhelpfulness and beaming cooperation. Indeed, there's a darkly humorous local joke that describes how Bermudian air-traffic controllers let a plane crash because the pilot forgets to greet them properly as he makes his descent.

Mostly, playing by the rules goes a long way towards really fitting into the island's sometimes oddball environment—just don't expect Bermudians to. They are flagrant scofflaws, and nowhere is that more apparent than on the island's roads. Local drivers break all speed limits, double-park to have a chat or grab a takeout, dump trash out their car windows, and overtake on blind hairpin bends at 70 miles per hour. These are the same folks who'll shake their heads and tut-tut in disapproval if someone tells a bawdy joke too loudly in a restaurant, or happens to walk down the street in a bikini top.

Punctuality is not as big a problem in Bermuda as in more laid-back island nations to the south, but, aside from the corporate circles of Hamilton, locals often tend not to be overly fastidious about time. Nor are they too worried about returning phone calls immediately, turning up when they said they would, or delivering what was promised. Yet jobs get done, people make a good living, and the economy ticks around. But when 5 o'clock tolls, Bermudians head for the door. Don't try to achieve anything important toward the end of a workday afternoon, particularly in bureaucratic environments. That goes triple if it's a Friday afternoon before a public holiday weekend. Islanders *love* their holidays, and it really doesn't matter whether it's the Queen's Birthday or Cup Match (although the latter sees Bermudian frivolity at the extreme), locals are like children at Christmas in the run-up to such festivities. Driving through Hamilton at such time reveals a free-for-all, a cheerful camaraderie that reverberates through "Town," as people wave, shout, and honk their horns at each other.

FESTIVALS AND EVENTS
January
Bermuda Festival of the Performing Arts: This six-week evening festival running from mid-January through the end of February brings international dance, drama, comedy, music, and even circus performers to City Hall and Arts Centre, Hamilton, and the Ruth Seaton James Centre for the Performing Arts, Devonshire (www.bermudafestival.org).

Bermuda International Race Weekend: Hundreds of locals and visitors take part in this mid-January weekend's quartet of events: an international marathon, half-marathon, 10K run and charity walk, and an invitational mile. The 10K starts and finishes at Devonshire's National Sports Centre; all other events take place on Front Street, Hamilton (www.bermudatracknfield.com).

Annual Bermuda Regional Bridge Tournament: More than 200 players fly in for this prestigious seven-day test of bridge skill, hosted by the Bermuda Bridge Federation and held in the last week of January at the Fairmont Southampton Hotel (www.bermudaregional.com).

February

The Bermuda Festival of the Performing Arts: The festival continues through another month in the City of Hamilton and Devonshire (www.bermudafestival.org).

March

Bermuda Cat Fanciers' Association Cat Show: Pedigreed cats, and household pets, compete before top foreign judges in early March at Harbour Room, No. 1 Shed, Front Street, Hamilton (tel. 441/238-0112).

Zoom Around the Sound: This 7.2-mile circular walking, running, bicycling, and in-line skating race is held mid-month from Flatts around Harrington Sound to raise money for the Bermuda Aquarium, Museum & Zoo (www.bamz.org).

Bermuda International Film Festival: Award-winning films from around the world are screened at island cinemas for 10 days starting mid-month, along with celebrity appearances and filmmaking workshops. Tickets can be purchased online or from the BIFF box office, at No. 6 Passenger Terminal, Front Street, Hamilton (www.biff.bm).

April

Good Friday Kite Festival: Kite-flying contests, fishcakes, gombeys, face-painting, bouncy castles, and tug-of-war make for traditional island fun every Easter Friday at Horseshoe Bay, Southampton (www.ubp.bm).

XL Bermuda Open Tennis: Nine days of tennis exhibitions and competition at the tony Coral Beach & Tennis Club, Paget, feature top international ATP Tour players starting in mid-April. This one sells out early! (For tickets and schedules, see www.xlcapitalbermudaopen.bm.)

Bermuda Annual Exhibition: Held at the Botanical Gardens the last week of April, Paget, this three-day cultural and agricultural showcase, featuring equestrian events, acrobats and school displays, has become a beloved institution (www.agshowbda.com).

Open Houses and Gardens: The Bermuda Garden Club's open-house tour is held every Wednesday afternoon for a month at the end of April and through May, allowing a rare inside look at some of the island's most impressive properties (tel. 441/236-7321).

Virtual Spectator Bermuda Masters: The world's top 31 male squash players battle for $120,000 in prize cash in this prestigious weeklong tournament at the start of April. The venue is an impressive glass court inside the Jessie Vesey Sports Centre, Bermuda High School, Pembroke (www.bermudamasters.com).

PUBLIC HOLIDAYS

New Year's Day	January 1
Good Friday	late March or early April
Bermuda Day	May 24
Queen's Birthday	mid-June
Cup Match	last Thursday and Friday in July or first Thursday and Friday in August
Emancipation Day	last Thursday in July or first Thursday in August
Somers Day	last Friday in July or first Friday in August
Labor Day	early September
Remembrance Day	November 11
Christmas Day	December 25
Boxing Day	December 26

Public holidays falling on a weekend result in public closures of shops and offices on the following weekday. For more information on public holidays, contact the **Bermuda Employers Council** (tel. 441/295-5070).

May

Open Houses and Gardens: The Bermuda Garden Club's Wednesday afternoon open-house tour continues through May (tel. 441/236-7321).

Bermuda Day Parade: Enjoy Bermuda's daylong version of Caribbean Carnival, held throughout the City of Hamilton on May 24, with highlights being a historic half-marathon and an all-out parade of floats, dancers, and marching bands. Bermuda Day also marks the official first day of summer boating and swimming for Bermudians.

Harbour Nights: The summer-long Wednesday night street festival, featuring fun, food, crafts, and late-night shopping on Front Street in the City of Hamilton begins this month and runs through September. Similar festivals are held Tuesday nights in the Town of St. George and Dockyard (www.bermudachamber.bm).

Bermuda Fitted Dinghy Races: Traditional dinghies vie for weekly honors throughout the summer. Races take place every Sunday afternoon in St. George's Harbour, Mangrove Bay, and Granaway Deep (www.rhadc.com).

June

Harbour Nights: The celebrations in the City of Hamilton (Wed.) and St. George's Market Nights and Destination Dockyard evening festivals (Tues.) run through the month (www.bermudachamber.bm).

Newport-Bermuda Race/Marion-Bermuda Ocean Race: The Newport Race, a premier blue water sailing contest from Newport, Rhode Island, to St. David's, marked its 100th anniversary in 2006 (www.rbyc .bm, www.bermudarace.com). The Marion Race, from Buzzard Bay, Massachusetts, to St. David's, is for amateur cruising yachts (www.rhadc.com, www.marionbermuda.com). Run in alternate years, both races bring hundreds of competitors to the island.

Queen's Birthday Parade: A gun salute kicks off the Bermuda Regiment Band and Corps of Drums' march down Front Street in the City of Hamilton in mid-June, a public holiday in tribute to Queen Elizabeth.

July

Harbour Nights: Celebrations in the City of Hamilton (Wed.) and St. George's Market Nights and Destination Dockyard evening festivals (Tues.) offer family fun through the month (www.bermudachamber.bm).

Bermuda Fitted Dinghy Races: Traditional dinghies continue their summer-long Sunday afternoon series at harbors throughout the island (www.rhadc.com).

Canada Day: Canadians gather at Chaplin Bay, Southampton, on July 1 for barbecues, games and music to mark Canada's birthday (www.canadiansinbermuda.com).

Bermuda Big Game Classic: A three-day, big-fish team event in mid-July offers cash and prizes, including a top prize to the largest blue marlin catch (www.bermuda biggameclassic.com).

August

Harbour Nights: Celebrations in the City of Hamilton (Wed.) and St. George's Market Nights and Destination Dockyard evening festivals (Tues.) continue through the month (www.bermudachamber.bm).

Bermuda Fitted Dinghy Races: Continue every Sunday afternoon at various harbors around the island continue through August (www.rhadc.com).

Cup Match Cricket Festival (Emancipation Day and Somers Day): This four-day holiday honoring both the abolition of local slavery and Bermuda's founder, Sir George Somers, stages a historic showdown between East and West End cricket clubs, complete with islandwide campouts, boating and parties galore.

September

Harbour Nights: Celebrations in Hamilton, St. George's Market Nights, and Destination Dockyard weekly festivals wind up as the summer season ends and the cruise ship season winds down (www.bermudachamber.bm).

Bermuda International Sand Sculpture Competition: Grownups and kids get creative and win prizes at this friendly contest of grainy architecture at Horseshoe Bay,

Southampton, the first Saturday in September (vleader@gov.bm).

Labor Day March and Celebration: Participants including gombeys and majorettes march to Bernard Park, Hamilton, for a day-long festival honoring Bermuda's labor movement and organized by the Bermuda Industrial Union (tel. 441/292-0044).

CD&P Bermuda Grand Prix: This four-day international cycling competition is Bermuda's largest professional sporting event, with elite male and female events, as well as amateur races at venues in the City of Hamilton and at Southside, St. David's (www.bermudagrandprix.com).

October

Bermuda Music Festival: Three nights of performances by top international jazz, soul, and R&B artists performing alfresco at Dockyard, Sandys, draws hundreds of visitors to the island (www.bermudamusicfestival.com).

Bermuda Culinary Arts Festival: Celebrity chefs fly in for this four-day tasting festival held in late October in the show ring at Botanical Gardens, Paget, and accompanied by a slate of foodie events at venues around the island (www.bermudaculinaryarts.com).

BIFF Kids Film Festival: A kids' version of Bermuda's popular annual adult showcase, this mid-month weekend event screens child-friendly flicks from around the world, including cartoons and documentaries, at the Liberty Theatre, Hamilton (www.biff.bm).

Bermuda Cat Fanciers' Association Cat Show: A Halloween-themed cat extravaganza, this daylong event at the end of October features pedigree felines along with household pets (tel. 441/238-0112).

November

World Rugby Classic: International former top rugby players compete in 11 matches in this highly popular weeklong event held at National Sports Centre, Devonshire (www.world rugby.bm).

Remembrance Day Parade and Ceremony: The Bermuda Regiment and Band join war veterans in a solemn march down Front Street in the City of Hamilton on November 11, a public holiday.

December

Festival of Lights: Private homes and businesses deck their halls in this islandwide illumination competition, creating fairy-lit neighborhoods throughout the parishes.

Bermuda National Trust Christmas Walkabout: This festive evening street festival takes place the first Friday in December in the Town of St. George. Crowds flock to mingle with friends, sip hot cider, and listen to strolling carolers (www.bnt.bm).

Christmas Boat Parade: Head to Hamilton Harbour to see beautiful illuminated boats of all sorts vie for prizes as they loop the waterfront (www.bermudaboatparade.bm).

Bermuda Musical & Dramatic Society Pantomime: An annual treat for children, the annual BMDS pantomime at Hamilton's City Hall and Arts Centre features the island's amateur actors in a British-style theatrical extravaganza (www.bmds.bm).

New Year's Eve Festival: Revelers ring in the new year at King's Square, St. George, where live music and a street festival atmosphere climax with fireworks and the dropping of a giant disco ball–style onion (nhooper@ stgeorge.bm).

Accommodations

Travelers to Bermuda can take their pick of luxury resorts, quaint cottage colonies, guesthouses, self-catering apartments, or bed-and-breakfasts. The range of accommodations is only matched by the vast price range, from as low as $70 a night (doubles, high season) to a $4,000 penthouse. Generally, most of the resort hotels offer average rooms in the $300–400-a-night price bracket, compared to the $150–250 range of smaller, independent properties. There has been a constant demand over the years for more affordable places to stay in Bermuda, and that call is now increasingly being met by local residents who are renting out rooms, attached apartments, or separate cottages on their properties for far more reasonable rates than those charged by the hotel industry. Some of these are in beautiful homes or historic landmark properties, including several owned by the Bermuda National Trust. Visitors who seek something more private or unusual than standard hotels, or don't mind staying in less-than-five-star surroundings, should check Toronto-based www.bermudarentals.com or www.bermudagetaway.com, which both list scores of well-managed guest accommodations ranging from private villas with swimming pools to pullout-sofa studios. Most of these fall below the radar of the Tourism Department's official listings (only properties with six or more units require government inspection and licenses).

For those who prefer resort pampering, the good news is that many of Bermuda's hotels are heavily reinvesting in their properties, undertaking winterlong renovations to add pools, restaurants, spas, and updated rooms. Hurricane Fabian of 2003 may have been the lightning rod to spur many hotels to renovate in the aftermath of extensive destruction, but by 2005 the storm's effect was no longer felt and many properties continued to pour money into new facilities—a bonus for new or returning visitors to the island. The surge in spas is another trend, with world-class amenities and special spa vacation packages offered by all the major resorts, and even a few of the smaller ones.

The key to choosing a place to stay in Bermuda lies in recognizing the type of vacation you want, as well as the style of accommodations you prefer. Because it's easy to cover the whole island, regional preferences are perhaps less important than, say, whether you plan to spend every day on the beach or shop-'til-you-drop. Most Bermuda properties—even the tiny ones—have websites featuring photos of rooms and amenities, rates, and full descriptions of facilities.

After decades without new hotels, or worse, major hotel closures, there's good news. Several brand new developments are on the horizon, including a boutique hotel promised by the exclusive Tucker Point Club (formerly Castle Harbour) in St. George's Parish; a new wellness center with spa suites and beachfront villas to replace the beloved Lantana Resort in Sandys; and hotel accommodations incorporated into the new Newstead and Belmont developments in Paget and Warwick, slated to open in 2007.

Reservations

Early reservations are highly recommended for all accommodations. Popular hotels and resorts book quickly in the summer months, especially thanks to the very Bermuda phenomenon of repeat visitors who stake out their room sometimes a year in advance. Smaller properties or tiny rentals with just one or two rooms also get booked up quickly. For large properties, you may encounter better deals, including air-and-hotel package options, online; family-run properties with just a few rooms are best contacted directly. Check Bermuda's Tourism Department website (www.bermudatourism.com), www.bermuda.com, and www.bermuda4u.com for full listings of most of the island's major hotels and guesthouses.

Rates

Rates go up during the high season (April–Oct.), typically by a third, but sometimes double what hotel properties charge in the winter season (Nov.–March). With smaller properties, check whether quoted rates are double-occupancy or per-person. Beyond the quoted room rate, expect to pay government tax of 7.25 percent and a 10 percent gratuities, housekeeping, or service charge. Other extra fees might include an extra-person charge, if you're adding a bed, or an extra charge for children, though most kids sleep free. Properties have different deposit requirements and cancellations policies; make sure you know the details before booking. All resorts and major hotels, and most guesthouses, accept major credit cards. Some private residences or apartment rentals only accept cash or travelers checks.

ACCOMMODATION TYPES
Bed-and-Breakfasts

A very cost-effective way to enjoy a Bermuda vacation, bed-and-breakfasts usually comprise a room in a private home or a historic property, with either private or shared bathroom. Breakfast is included in the rate, and ranges from continental croissants to "F.E.B.s" (Full English Breakfast, for example, bacon and eggs). Eating out is normally required for other meals, so this type of accommodation is best suited for short stays.

Private Residences

This is the way to see Bermuda if you are want to live like the locals. Staying in a private home, whether it's a studio apartment beneath the main house, or a separate cottage across the lawn, lends a touch of island authenticity you don't get to experience in resorts. More residents are offering rentals, including long-term rentals to visiting business people. Don't be surprised to find properties with pools, waterfront docks, beautiful gardens, or historic legacies. Like the larger hotels, these nearly always offer amenities such as air-conditioning (a must in the summer months), self-catering kitchens, barbecues, irons, and cable TV. The downside is that no matter how private the place, it is part of the

owner's home, and so total freedom and anonymity may be limited.

Inns and Guesthouses

Bermuda has many inns and guesthouses, some in historic or picturesque neighborhoods, others on the water or featuring a pool. Doubles with king- or queen-size beds and private bathrooms inside a large homestead are the norm. Some allow for self-catering with kitchenettes (mini fridge, microwave, toaster oven, and hot plates); others allow guests to share kitchen facilities. Breakfast, baked goods, or afternoon tea are sometimes served.

Apartments and Cottages

The island has numerous apartment and private cottage rentals that are not part of a local family's property, thereby offering total privacy. Some are stand-alone cottages located on estates in tony neighborhoods—upscale rentals in the $300–400 range for summer double occupancy. Others are less expensive, with several apartments arranged around a pool. All are self-catering, with kitchens and barbecues, but maid service is usually included.

Cottage Colonies

These quaint throwbacks to the elegant vacations of the 1950s and 1960s still hold major appeal for Bermuda visitors. Some are upscale properties, with on-site spas, pools, putting greens, beaches, dining rooms, and concierge services. They feel almost like a private club and often lay claim to beautifully manicured estates dating back many decades. Other cottage colonies offer a more casual approach, with self-catering units and minimum staff.

Small Hotels

Repeat visitors swear by the island's small hotels, which often seem to offer as much in the way of luxurious amenities as their bigger counterparts. Spas, high-end restaurants, and designer bathrooms are slowly becoming the norm for many of these. Yet, they retain an intimate feel and connection with staff and other guests, which many visitors to the island like to experience.

Resort Hotels

Bermuda's major resort hotels are almost all beachfront or harborfront—or, at the very least, have impressive views of the ocean. Most offer pools, tennis courts, putting greens, spas, beauty salons, social desks or concierges, multiple restaurants, room service, porters, nightclubs, entertainment, scuba and water sports centers, and kids' activity clubs during the high season. Some have their own golf course on site, or rights at sister properties. Failing all else, the concierge can arrange pretty much anything.

Food and Drink

BERMUDIAN CUISINE

Is there a true Bermudian cuisine? Gourmands might snigger at such a proposition, but Bermuda has claimed its repertoire of hallmark dishes—usually a melting pot of items from other places adapted for local menus. The amalgam of British, West Indian, African, and Portuguese cultural influences has created a somewhat eclectic collection of local dishes. Many are pure comfort food, and probably not the best for waistlines or arteries, but they are usually delicious. British cuisine has donated fish 'n' chips, shepherd's pie, steak pies, and teatime desserts like scones, pound cake, trifle, and lemon meringue pie. Slavery's legacy is seen in dishes once rejected by Bermudian white society for their poor-man simplicity but now embraced in the fanciest restaurants; these include cassava and farine pie (made from root vegetables), peas 'n' rice and Johnny cakes (common in the Caribbean), fried chicken legs, fried fish sandwiches (made with local catches like grouper or rockfish), butter-baked lobster, macaroni 'n' cheese, and sweets like macaroons, gingerbread, and coconut cake. The immigration of Azorean immigrants over the past 150 years has entrenched certain dishes and snacks into the island's culinary lexicon. Portuguese chorizo (spicy sausage) and malasadas (deep-fried doughnuts) are the most common examples, found islandwide at corner stores where hot snacks are served.

Restaurants dedicated to these assorted nationalities are good places to sample such dishes. Café Acoreano (Hamilton) is owned and staffed by Portuguese-Bermudians. Jamaican Grill (Hamilton and Pembroke) is a very popular family-run café-style eatery with jerk meats and West Indian curries. For the ultimate in British fare, head for any of numerous pubs throughout the island—Henry VIII (Southampton) is the standard-bearer—or attend an afternoon cream tea served at hotels like the Heritage Court at the Fairmont Hamilton Princess Hotel (Pembroke). Down-home Bermudian restaurants are getting fewer these days, as upscale eateries take over, but holdouts like The Spot (Hamilton), The Green Lantern (Pembroke), and Black Horse Tavern (St. David's) are a trio of favorites.

Interestingly, there's been a movement among top chefs over the last decade toward adapting favorite local ingredients and everyman dishes into a more innovative interpretation of Bermudian cuisine on the pricier menus. As a result, there are few top-notch restaurants nowadays that don't serve a gourmet version of Bermudian fish cakes, banana or loquat chutneys, onion tarts, or rum cake. One of the more influential chefs in that vein has been Terence Clark, of the Seahorse Grill at Mandarin Oriental's Elbow Beach Resort (Paget), which has billed itself as the "birthplace of New Bermudian Cuisine."

Bermuda fish is excellent, from the sweet fillets of snapper and rarer rockfish, to the steaks of fresh-caught tuna, wahoo, and swordfish. Lobsters (the spiny variety) are in season September 1–March 31; fishing laws are strict, so you likely won't see lobster over the summer months—at least in restaurants. There are no local shrimps, mussels, clams, or conch, so any of these on local menus have been imported.

Fresh local produce is worth seeking out in season, mainly because imported fruit and vegetables can't compare with straight-from-the-soil versions sold in grocery stores and roadside stands. Large bananas imported from the United States and Central America, overripe by the time they arrive, can't compete with Bermuda's own tiny sweet hands of fruit. Similarly, Bermuda carrots, tomatoes, and potatoes are well worth buying if you're staying in a self-catering unit or simply want to try the local harvest.

Wild fruits are also popular, namely the Surinam "Bermuda" cherry, a more sour version of its North American counterpart that has several harvests throughout the year, and the loquat, which hangs heavy on trees throughout the island in January and February. Help yourself to a taste from trees in local parks or on public land along the Railway Trail. At the height of cherry or loquat season, you often see drivers pulling over to gather a roadside haul or schoolchildren dangling out of trees as they collect a fresh snack.

In the supermarkets, there has been a growing movement among some local farmers to supply organic fare, including organically raised chickens, vegetables, and salad greens. These can be found in most large groceries, and at the weekly Bull's Head Farmers Market in Hamilton, held on Saturdays during the November–June growing season.

Fishermen sell their daily catch, including crawly lobsters in season, at roadside stands islandwide. Sometimes, this is simply a guy with a cooler. The best places are at the foot of Scaur Hill, Sandys; Devonshire Dock and Devonshire Bay in Devonshire; and at the top of Trimingham Hill, Paget, leading out of Hamilton.

The best occasions, outside of restaurants, to sample Bermudian cooking and specialties are public festivals and holidays such as Cup Match, when alfresco gatherings or street fairs usually have foodstalls selling fish sandwiches, fish cakes, homemade pies, and other goodies.

RESTAURANTS

Eating out is a favorite island pastime, and many residents, particularly those who work in Hamilton, and especially young expatriates, frequent local bars and restaurants several evenings a week. With Bermuda's steep tabs, that could bankrupt you pretty easily. Like everyone else, restaurants have to import the majority of their ingredients, a reality reflected in menu prices. On top of that, almost all charge an automatic 15 percent gratuity included on the bill. If you *really* enjoyed the food and service, you can leave an extra 10 percent, but otherwise the built-in surcharge will suffice. Check your tab to make sure it's included.

Bermudians lament the dearth of restaurants that fall between the high-end restaurants (charging $25 per entrée) and the quickie café variety. There are no true diners, for example, nor enough reasonable family-style eateries (though, aside from pricing, most restaurants cater well to children).

All-day breakfasts, once rare, are now more common, though many restaurants, curiously, refuse to make pancakes or eggs after 11 A.M. and even Hamilton-based eateries sometimes have inconsistent opening hours—for instance, closing their doors after lunch at 2:30 P.M. and reopening in the early evening. Late-afternoon diners often find themselves out of luck.

Bermudians would admit the quality of fare, even at the priciest restaurants, is inconsistent, and food and service do not always compare with the offerings of similarly priced establishments in urban centers such as New York or London. But generally, the standard is high, with menus created by award-winning Bermudian and foreign-born chefs.

BARS

Bermudians love to drink—there was even a song with that title released by a local artist in 2005. They also love to drink and drive, though media pressure and police crackdowns in the past 20 years have somewhat curtailed the habit. Don't be tempted to hop on a scooter after a few black rums or Elephant beers; many visitors (and locals) have been killed or badly injured over the years doing just that. But do enjoy Bermuda's bars; they must rank among the most lively in the world, particularly in the busy crush of summer. Happy hours are prevalent, with cheaper drink prices offered for a couple of hours after work, usually on Friday. A full wine list and a good choice of beers, cocktails, and liqueurs can be found at most drinking establishments and licensed restaurants. National favorites Black 'n' Coke (black rum—preferably Gosling's Black Seal—and Coca-Cola) and Cockspur 'n' Coke are party staples.

Tips for Travelers

TRAVELING WITH CHILDREN

There's no end to child-friendly fun in Bermuda, and, best of all, a lot of it is absolutely free. Beaches, public playgrounds, gombey dances, and the serenade of treefrogs—kids fall in love with the island even faster than their parents. Traveling to Bermuda poses no special health risks; the island has no rabies and a standard vaccinations program for infants and children. The short flight from U.S. East Coast cities—a mere couple of hours—is doable for kids (flights from London are about seven hours). Many of the major hotels have special kids' camps during the summer high season; inquire about their activities and age restrictions when you book accommodations. Some hotels and guesthouses can also arrange baby-sitting.

Most childcare products are easily available on the island at drugstores and supermarkets, including diapers, wipes, shampoos, vitamins, sunblock, and children's pain relievers and cold medicines. The majority stock North American brands, except for The Supermart's popular English Waitrose grocery line; if you're traveling from Europe and will miss a favorite product, you might want to bring it with you.

There are numerous toy stores and kids' clothing outlets, though prices generally run at least a third higher than in the United States.

Generally, local eateries are more than willing to try to make young diners happy, with kids' menus, high chairs, and cheery wait staff.

The best public playgrounds are located at Mullet Bay, St. George's; Shelly Bay, Hamilton Parish; Parson's Road, Pembroke; South Shore Road, Warwick (just east of the entrance to Warwick Long Bay); Death Valley, Middle Road, Southampton; and outside Bermuda Maritime Museum at Dockyard. All are equipped with regulation climbing frames, tunnels, swings, and slides, for both toddlers and older children.

WOMEN TRAVELERS

Women will find Bermuda a far more benign traveling environment than many places in the Caribbean, Central America, or even a typical North American city. Bermudians pride themselves on the safety of their island, and violent, arbitrary crime is extremely rare (see *Health and Safety* in this chapter). Female travelers should nevertheless use common sense and practical measures to keep safe, especially at night and if alone or in remoter areas.

Generally, Bermuda is conservative and modern in its attitudes towards women, and women won't notice any gender issues they wouldn't encounter in London or Los Angeles. Women doing business on the island will be treated with the same respect as their male colleagues (the local and international business communities count a growing number of women in top corporate jobs). And women need not feel unsafe or out of place touring most areas of the island, or eating alone in restaurants. They need not expect to encounter unwanted harassment, either, although Bermudian men have the habit of issuing a surreptitious hiss to catch your attention. Whether you smile, wave, or have no reaction, there's rarely any further approach. The exception may be on the beaches, when local men sometimes try to chat up foreign women. If you're not in the mood, just say so.

Women take part in most sports and clubs on the island, and a few annual sporting events are geared to them, such as the **PartnerRe Women's 5K Run & Walk** (www.partnerre5k .bm) in mid-October, a charity event launched in 1998 on behalf of Mid-Atlantic Athletic Club (M.A.A.C.). Top female match-race teams compete in an annual championship qualifier for the prestigious **King Edward VII Gold Cup** International One design competition, also in October.

Should you need help or advice, the **Women's Resource Centre** (58 Reid St., Hamilton, tel. 441/295-3882, crisis hotline 441/295-7273, fax 441/295-9833, 9 A.M.–5 P.M.) is the island's prime advocacy group, and its services include emergency response, counseling, assistance for victims, and a crisis intervention hotline. Other women's support and networking resources include the **Business & Professional Women's Association of Bermuda** (21 Somerset Rd., Sandys, tel. 441/234-5733), and the **Bermuda Junior Service League** (tel. 441/332-2575, www.bjsl.bm).

GAY AND LESBIAN TRAVELERS

While Bermuda has a general tolerance for homosexuality on a grassroots level, politically, the island lags far behind North American and European societies. Until 1994, it was actually illegal to be gay in Bermuda; the House of Parliament finally decriminalized sexual relations between consenting gay men after a private bill was introduced that year (no former law had outlawed lesbians). But the island's gay community is still battling for basic human rights legislation that would prevent discrimination based on sexual orientation.

Gay tourists will probably not experience any overt discrimination, but bear in mind the island is a very conservative society and even open displays of affection among heterosexuals are frowned on, so subtlety is valued.

There is not a true "gay scene" in Bermuda compared to livelier urban centers, but Hamilton has a number of gay-friendly venues. These include Café Cairo, Square One (late night),

and Casey's Lounge. Funky coffeehouse Rock Island Coffee is also gay-friendly, with a very mixed crowd. The new Little Venice Wine Bar and nearby Splash nightclub on Bermudiana Road also attract a mixed crowd.

Washington Mall Magazines in Hamilton stocks numerous gay publications, including *Advocate, Out, Genre, XY,* and *Gay Times.*

Other useful resources include the gay support group **Bermuda Rainbow Alliance** (chairperson Nikki Bowers, tel. 441/297-4105, bermudarainbowalliance@hotmail.com); the **Gay Men's Support Group** (tel. 441/295-0022, gmsg@northrock.bm); and the website www.gaybermuda.com, which covers the island's gay life and carries news and bulletin boards.

TRAVELERS WITH DISABILITIES

Bermuda is far from ideal as a perfectly accessible destination for travelers with disabilities, but improvements have been made in recent years. Many more attractions, city sidewalks, restaurants, nightclubs, and public buildings have been made wheelchair accessible over the past decade. However, many places, including retail stores and restaurants, still pose great physical challenges to people with disabilities. And while the new fast ferries and ramp-fitted Ferry Terminal are a breeze, public buses are not equipped at all for disabled access. Disabled lobby groups have also complained that too few taxis accommodate wheelchairs.

Access Bermuda (1 Loyal Hill, Devonshire, FL 03, tel. 441/295-9016, www.access. bm) provides useful information to physically challenged visitors, including viable modes of transport, including wheelchair-accessible taxis, as well as appropriate sights and activities. **Project Action** is a family-run taxi service offering wheelchair transport. Vehicles are equipped with hydraulic ramps. Contact James Edwards (tel. 441/333-9785), Charles Edwards (tel. 441/535-4349), or RoseAnn Edwards (tel. 441/299-8218 or 441/337-6996).

The WindReach Recreational Village (57 Spice Hill Rd., Warwick, tel. 441/238-2469, fax

441/238-2597, www.windreach.org) is a popular nonprofit community group located on a quiet chunk of rural property surrounded by agricultural fields and residential neighborhoods. It offers numerous special-needs services and activities, including a petting zoo, a wheelchair-accessible playground, and a fully accessible camping area with wheelchair-accommodating cabins, bathrooms, and shower facilities. Located on the same property, **Bermuda Riding for the Disabled** (tel. 441/238-7433, brd@ibl.bm) provides therapeutic riding lessons and programs for children and adults with disabilities.

The **Bermuda Red Cross** ("Charleswood," 9 Berry Hill Rd., Paget, tel. 441/236-8253) rents equipment such as walking frames and wheelchairs. Other resources include the **Association for the Mentally Handicapped** (tel. 441/292-7206); **Bermuda Islands Association of the Deaf** (tel. 441/238-8116, biad@the rock.bm); **Bermuda Physically Handicapped Association** (Summerhaven, South Shore Rd., Hamilton Parish, tel. 441/293-5035); and **Bermuda Society for the Blind** (Beacon House, 3 Beacon St., Hamilton, tel. 441/292-3231).

SENIOR TRAVELERS

Bermuda has long been a favorite destination for older travelers, particularly in the wintertime, when golf, eco-tours, and cultural programs take center stage. While scores of substantial discounts—on public transport, museums, groceries—are offered to resident seniors, unfortunately these are not available to visitors. However, the island's moderate temperatures, easygoing lifestyle, and numerous accessible leisure activities make it popular among senior travelers, and its costliness is often not a deterrent to this increasingly active and well-heeled demographic.

The best dedicated program for senior travelers to the island is offered by **Elderhostel,** through the **Bermuda Biological Station for Research (BBSR)** (17 Biological Ln., Ferry Reach, St. George's, tel. 441/297-1880, fax 441/297-8143, www.bbsr.edu). Based at the station for the past quarter-century, the year-round program includes accommodations, cafeteria-style dining, field trips, lectures, and evening entertainment for $200 a day. Five weeklong courses range from a study of Bermuda homes and gardens to history and heritage to an inside look at the cutting-edge global "science in Bermuda shorts" that goes on at the world-famous station. There is also a "Walking Bermuda's Railway Trail" course, in which hostelers take in the flora, fauna, geology, and cultural history of Bermuda along the way, and an intergenerational course in which grandparents can sign up with a grandchild for summer snorkeling expeditions. Special-interest groups can design their own program, and more than one program may be taken consecutively. All participants should be able to walk a mile (longer for the Walking Bermuda course), enjoy a long bus tour, and feel comfortable on short, smooth boat trips. Access to the lecture hall and dining area is up a single flight of stairs. To register, contact Elderhostel, 11 Avenue de Lafayette, Boston, MA 02111-1746, tel. 617/426-8056.

The November–March period offers a program of daily events geared to visitors of all ages, though these are particularly popular with seniors. Included are glass-blowing demonstrations, bagpipe skirling ceremonies, gombey revues, guided walking tours of Hamilton, and historical re-enactments in St. George. In any season, older travelers who wish to steer clear of scooters should opt for a multiday transportation pass that allows unlimited use of ferries and buses within the designated time frame. One-day, three-day, and monthlong passes can be purchased at Visitor Services Bureaus, or at the Hamilton Bus or Ferry Terminals.

Ocean Isle Concierge (tel. 441/236-5903, fax 441/236-6146, www.oceanisleconcierge.com) provides concierge services and care for elderly tourists traveling to Bermuda, including airport transport, restaurant reservations, sightseeing arrangements, and personal shopping.

VOLUNTEERING

Bermuda's charities and nonprofit organizations depend heavily on volunteers to carry out much of their day-to-day workload. Very often, unpaid volunteers are retired or wealthy

Bermudians, or the wives of expatriate workers who don't hold work permits themselves and are looking for social and professional interaction when they move to the island with their spouse. From walking the canine residents of the S.P.C.A. to CPR instruction or staffing the front desk at an art gallery, volunteers keep the island running smoothly. If you are visiting Bermuda for an extended period and would like to get involved, check the charities' listings in the Bermuda Yellow Pages, or contact the **Centre on Philanthropy** (Par-la-Ville Rd., Hamilton, tel. 441/292-5320) to find out which organizations seek help.

Health and Safety

With one of the highest standards of living anywhere, Bermuda poses none of the health risks found in many exotic destinations, particularly those in the Caribbean or Latin America. Sanitary standards are excellent, and healthcare is modern and professional. The island's freshwater, rain caught on the lime-coated roofs and channeled into tanks below every home, is nearly always potable—except after hurricanes and severe storms, when rotting foliage and other debris in the tanks can cause stomachaches and intestinal problems. Bottled water is available in all groceries, gas stations, drugstores, and restaurants. Bermuda is subtropical, and therefore has no common tropical diseases, such as malaria. Vaccinations are unnecessary.

MEDICAL SERVICES

Good medical services are provided by the island's main health center, **King Edward VII Memorial Hospital** (7 Point Finger Rd., Paget, tel. 441/236-2345, fax 441/236-2213, www.bermudahospitals.bm), simply known as "the hospital" or "KEMH." The 324-bed hospital provides round-the-clock emergency care and islandwide ambulance service; it is equipped with maternity facilities, a children's ward, a hyperbaric recompression chamber for divers and diabetics, and intensive care, dialysis, oncology, and cardiac diagnostic units, as well as other specialty services. Emergency air-ambulance service, organized by the hospital, provides access within 24 hours to U.S. and Canadian cities for treatment of serious conditions, including severe burns and spinal, neurological, and coronary problems. A second local hospital, the newly renamed **Mid-Atlantic Wellness Institute** (formerly St. Brendan's Psychiatric Hospital) (44 Devon Springs Rd., Devonshire, tel. 441/236-3770, www.bermudahospitals.bm), offers professional counseling and treats patients suffering from mental disorders.

Well-stocked pharmacies and drugstores are located throughout the island. Pharmacists can issue a maximum five-day refill of a prescription, including a one-cycle pack of birth-control pills, providing they are satisfied medications and doses are accurate. If a longer supply is needed, you'll have to visit a local doctor who can write a new prescription. Pharmacies do not accept prescriptions from overseas doctors, so any call your home physician might make on your behalf would be wasted. If you need to see a doctor, appointments can be made via your hotel, guesthouse, or host. Most major resorts and hotels have a physician on call who can arrange treatment or phone prescriptions directly to a pharmacy, sometimes without an office visit. Cruise-ship passengers can visit local pharmacies, but it's usually simpler to contact their ship's doctor, who can write a five-day prescription, fillable at an island pharmacy by the ship's agent.

BEFORE YOU GO

Bring all prescription medications you may need with you, including enough for an extra day or two, in case flights are canceled or travel is delayed for any reason. Wear a medical-alert bracelet if you have a health problem, to help medical staff treat you properly in an emergency. Eyewear prescriptions and meds, left in their original containers for ease through customs, are best packed in carry-on luggage in case bags go missing. Keep a detailed written list in your purse or wallet as a backup. Meds are often the last thing packed, and therefore frequently forgotten; put them in an obvious place as you pack so you don't overlook them as you leave home.

Travel and Medical Insurance

Any industry veteran will tell you travel insurance—while often deemed unnecessary—is a prudent investment, particularly if your regular health insurance does not cover overseas expenses or treatment. As well, primary insurers can sometimes take up to a fortnight to verify a patient's policy details—an unworkable delay in an emergency. Bermuda's hospital cannot treat overseas patients who are not covered by insurance, unless they are able to pay on the spot. In an emergency, travelers health insurance avoids logistical nightmares, allowing for confirmation of an overseas hospital bed and immediate air-ambulance transport. Take time to review your healthcare plan before leaving home to find out exactly what is covered, as well as any restrictions that might affect the choice of hospital in an emergency. Remember, it's not just the patient who may need help in an emergency but also relatives or companions who may have to find accommodation while a patient is in the hospital or make other travel plans.

MEDICAL EMERGENCIES

King Edward VII Memorial Hospital has an effective protocol in place for emergency treatment of visitors who may need to be flown off the island for specialized treatment—as long as health insurance or upfront funds are provided. An air-ambulance journey from Bermuda to the U.S. East Coast costs $10,000–15,000. Have handy information about any pre-existing medical condition, as well as the name and contact number of your primary doctor, so that if air ambulance is necessary, hospital staff can arrange for your doctor to be the receiving physician at the destination.

The hospital's social workers now have the time-saving option of using a Bermuda-based air ambulance to fly patients to the mainland in emergency situations. Bermuda Air Medivac Services (tel. 441/295-1963, airambulance@ northrock.bm), a private company set up in the summer of 2005, can fly patients anywhere in Canada, the United States, or the northern Caribbean and can be at a patient's bedside within two hours of contact (compared to the 24-hour wait for a foreign air ambulance to fly in and turn around). Based out of Bermuda International Airport with a local flight crew, the nine-seater Citation SII plane is staffed by doctors and registered nurses, some trained in critical care, and is equipped with defibrillators, ventilators, and other standard lifesaving devices. The basic fee for flights to the U.S. East Coast is $12,900. Cash and credit cards are accepted.

Among their myriad tasks, "Pink Ladies" and "Pink Men" volunteers (whose title refers to their rosy uniforms) help families find emergency accommodation if a relative or traveling companion ends up having to stay in the hospital. Limited space in the nearby nurses' residence is available for such a scenario at minimal cost, about $75 a day. Many island hotels and guesthouses also try to accommodate visitors during emergencies, but space is very tight during the high season.

Patients who have been checked in to the hospital need a "fit-to-fly" document signed by a local doctor in order to leave. The other possibility is for patients or their families to sign an "against medical advice" form, or A.M.A., but departure from the island's airport under such circumstances is difficult to impossible. For cruise ship passengers checking out of the hospital, doctors will confer with the ship's physician to ensure all necessary equipment (oxygen, for example) is aboard the vessel before it leaves port.

The U.S. Consulate General (Crown Hill, 16 Middle Rd., Devonshire, DV 03, tel. 441/295-1342, duty officer 441/335-3828, fax 441/295-1592, www.hamilton.usconsulate .gov) can aid American citizens when things go awry, particularly those lacking travel

EMERGENCY CONTACTS

Ambulance, Fire, Police, and Marine	911
King Edward VII Memorial Hospital	441/236-2345
King Edward VII Memorial Emergency Room	441/239-2009
Bermuda Police Service	441/295-0011
Fire Services Headquarters	441/292-5555
Electricity Power Outage	955
Telephone Repair Service	441/295-1001
Harbor Radio	441/297-1010
Weather Forecast	977
Women's Resource Hotline	441/295-7273
Physical Abuse Hotline	441/297-8278
Crime Stoppers (calls are anonymous)	800/623-8477
Government Emergency Radio Broadcast	FM 100.1 Mhz

insurance. Staff may sometimes contact relatives or credit card companies to help pay out-of-pocket expenses or even extend short-term loans to cover emergency medical care.

HEALTH PROBLEMS
Sunburn and Dehydration

Bermuda's high humidity, coupled with blistering summer temperatures—in the high 90s for much of July and August—can lead to severe sunburns, dehydration, and sunstroke. Even if you have a tan, wear sunscreens with high SPF content; some brands, such as Australia's Bullfrog, make waterproof sunblock of SPF 30 or higher, which protects your skin from harmful UVA and UVB rays for hours, even if you're sweating or in the water.

If you're not accustomed to the heat, cover up. Wear light clothing of natural fibers like cotton or silk that covers easy-to-burn or overexposed areas. Arms, hands, and shoulders can burn while driving a scooter, and even moped passengers end up sporting lobster-red knees and feet after sitting in the same position under scorching skies. Protect your face, including eyes and lips, with shades, a sun hat, and lip balm with sunblock. After too much sun, slather on aloe creams or place paper towels soaked in vinegar on the affected region (an island remedy to draw the heat out). Try to skip a day or two's beaching if you get burned to let your skin recover; visit a museum or go shopping instead.

Stay hydrated in hot weather by drinking lots of water throughout the day, especially if you're exercising. Bermuda's humidity, regularly in the 80 and 90 percent zone, can make it feel like you're moving around inside a greenhouse. Dehydration's onset—including heavy sweating, cramps, and dizziness—mean it's time to get out of the sun to let your body rest. Heat stroke, a potentially fatal condition, happens when the body's self-regulating thermometer shuts down completely. Symptoms include severe headaches and delirium. Get emergency aid and keep heat-stroke patients as cool as possible. Bermuda's hospital emergency department has intravenous treatment to speedily rehydrate and reenergize heat-stroke victims with vital salts and water.

Keep children well protected from the sun, especially toddlers, who are often oblivious to the sun, or youngsters who may not complain about burns until the damage is done. Reapply sunscreen often, particularly if you are swimming, and take a large water bottle to the beach. Many adults and kids in Bermuda wear UV-protective clothing, including hats, bodysuits, and long-sleeved, high-necked tops made of swimsuit fabric to guard against months of destructive sun exposure at the beach or on the water. One local company, **Groovy UV** (tel. 441/232-0527, www.groovy-uv.com), operated by Bermudian sailors Debbie and Adam Barboza, offers a full range of colorful outfits for all ages, including UV goggles and board shorts.

Sexually Transmitted Diseases

AIDS/HIV is not a large threat in Bermuda, but it exists nonetheless, along with less severe sexually transmitted diseases such as gonorrhea, syphilis, and genital warts. Always practice safe sex. Condoms can be purchased in all the island's drugstores and are also available free in some nightclubs. If you have questions or need information about AIDS/HIV while in Bermuda, contact the **Allan Vincent Smith Foundation** (2 Bermuda House Ln., tel. 441/295-6882, hotline tel. 441/295-0002, www.avsf.bm), a local information provider on AIDS/HIV.

Insects and Poison Ivy

Bermuda has no truly dangerous wildlife—no scorpions, snakes, nor even sharks close to shore. (Sharks do frequent local waters but are seen rarely inshore and are almost always docile species. As a result, there has not been a reported shark attack in more than 50 years.) The few hazards that do exist are not serious, and mostly of the insect variety.

Mosquitoes are irritating outdoor pests on summer evenings, and during the day in areas where they breed. Wear a repellent in areas near ponds or marshland, for example, and after dark when they are prevalent. Bermuda's subtropical climate is also conducive to flea infestations; responsible pet-owners treat cats and dogs regularly with prescription flea-killers that stop the little parasites breeding. Bermuda has no ticks.

American cockroaches (the large, flying type)—euphemistically dubbed "Palmetto Bugs" in Florida—can be seen everywhere at night throughout the hot summer months, even on the walls inside elegant homes. They are rather frightening apparitions upon first encounter, but they are harmless; window screens usually serve to keep them outdoors. Savvy scooter riders appreciate shades or, better still, helmets with visors, to keep wayward flying insects from face collisions. Ants by the thousands are a byproduct of summer and are especially apparent after severe storms or hurricanes. Again, they are harmless, but a nuisance. To keep their numbers down, avoid leaving dirty dishes around, including pet bowls, and conquer invasions with a simple household tool: the vacuum cleaner. Some also swear by lemon sprays and baby powder.

The St. David's centipede, or giant centipede, which can grow to a foot in length, is rarely seen these days, but it can inflict a mild bite, so avoid it if you happen to spot one.

Poison ivy *(Rhus radicans)* grows wild in parks and brush areas of the island, including off-trail parts of Paget Marsh and other nature reserves. Stay on boardwalks or main trails to avoid it. Rash, blisters, and itchiness break out once you have been exposed to the plant but usually disappear without treatment within a couple of weeks. Use cool compresses or an antihistamine to soothe the itching.

BEACH HAZARDS
Rip Currents and Undertows

Other than the risk of moped accidents, the sea poses the greatest danger to Bermuda visitors, particularly rip currents and undertows found off the South Shore beaches. Drownings are infrequent—and often caused by neither phenomenon. Bermuda has very few "dangerous surf" days, except around hurricanes, which tend to occur at the season's end in September and October. But inexperienced swimmers should check beach conditions carefully before entering the water and know what to do if they encounter risks.

Rip currents, also called riptides, though they are not tidal, are found at the world's surf beaches, such as those on the South Shore. They occur as water dumped by breakers at the shoreline returns to the deep sea, "ripping" past natural structures such as rocks, reefs, or sandbars. They are intensified by onshore winds coupled with storm conditions. A rip current is recognizable as a sandy stream of fast-moving water flowing seaward, sometimes splashing as it hits incoming waves. It moves at right angles from the beach—a bottleneck of water stretching up to 200 meters. Swimmers trapped in its movement feel helpless as the surge carries them away from the beach. If you find yourself in a rip current, the number-one rule is: keep calm. Swimming against the outward-flowing water is exhausting and unproductive, even for strong swimmers. Instead, try to swim across it, parallel to the beach. Rip currents aren't very wide, so a swimmer can usually reach the tide's edge, escape its pull, then swim back to safety. If you can't, don't panic. The current will eventually release you and will not pull you under.

Undertows or "runbacks," sometimes mistakenly called "rip currents," occur by contrast in the rolling surf at the edge of steep beaches, posing a risk to weak swimmers. As a wave is about to break, water from the beach edge is sucked back beneath it. The force of gravity can be strong enough to sweep swimmers off their feet and beneath the crashing surf. The cycle repeats as more waves break, disperse, and break again. The phenomenon, intensified by the angle of a beach, can make even practiced bodysurfers feel a sense of lost control. If you get swept into a series of waves, try to stand up, climb out, or call for help.

May 1–October 1, lifeguards are stationed 10 A.M.–6 P.M. daily at a few popular and family beaches around the island, including Horseshoe Bay, John Smith's Bay in Smith's, and Clearwater and Turtle Cove, St. George's. They are on the lookout for swimmers in trouble; wave an arm or call out if you need help. Avoid swimming alone or in rough conditions or storm swells; bodysurfing in hurricane surf, for example, can cause spinal fractures and other injuries. Warning signs and flags are posted in particularly stormy conditions at popular beaches, including Horseshoe Bay and Warwick Long Bay. A yellow flag crossed by a black diagonal stripe is a warning: See on-duty lifeguards or read information boards posted at the beach entrance. A red flag, for example, around a hurricane's approach and aftermath, prohibits swimming. A flag atop the lifeguard tower indicates a lifeguard is on duty.

Cliff-Diving

Shallow water and submerged rocks near favorite swimming holes have left Bermudian teenagers paralyzed, in comas, or severely injured over the years. Accidents commonly occur over the summer holidays as youths show off to friends or spectators from the picturesque overhangs at the edge of popular beaches such as Horseshoe Bay. Travelers would be ill-advised to try high-diving from any points around the island where they are not entirely sure of water depth or the possibility of concealed reefs, sunken objects, or other hazards.

Portuguese Man-of-Wars

A translucent, frilly edged, violet balloon, the jellyfish known as the Portuguese man-of-war, might be considered exquisitely beautiful—if it wasn't such a menace.

This invertebrate marine animal *(Physalia physalis)* has a gas-filled, purple-blue float topped by a crest that catches the wind and carries the organism over the ocean. But what you see at the surface is just a fraction of the creature, whose severely poisonous tentacles stretch many meters below. Found in the Gulf Stream and in tropical oceans worldwide, Portuguese man-of-wars travel in schools of hundreds or thousands and can be a swimming hazard on

© ROSEMARY JONES

a Portuguese man-of-war washed up on rocks

Bermuda's South Shore year-round, depending on wind direction and other conditions. Onshore winds blow them in. Look for their balloons washed up on the beach (they are difficult to spot on the sea surface) before you enter the water.

Avoid getting stung by the man-of-war's clinging blue tentacles, which can cause intense pain and occasional blistering, and leave red, whip-like welts on the skin. The impact is rarely more serious, though small children, the elderly, and those with allergies face a greater risk of severe reaction. Notably, the jellyfish is not only harmful when intact, but also when its myriad tentacles are broken into particles by the surf, causing rashes and irritation. Out of the water, their sting is no less severe, so don't be tempted to pick them up.

The best remedy if you do get stung? Treatment and opinion among medical professionals has evolved over the past 20 years, advising everything from meat tenderizer to urine, and there is still no absolute consensus. The key, says Dr. Edward Schultz, director of Bermuda's ER, is to deactivate the venom-firing cells, called nematocysts, released by tentacles on to the skin. Schultz recommends that jellyfish victims:

- Remove any visible bits of tentacle (wipe off with a towel or gloved hand)
- Rinse with seawater
- Soak the area in vinegar (acetic acid soothes pain and reduces inflammation)
- Shave the affected area to remove stinging particles
- Apply a warm compress or immerse in hot water

Lifeguards on Bermuda beaches will assist you with first-aid if you get stung. While a hospital visit isn't usually necessary, go the ER immediately if you have difficulty breathing, feel lightheaded or weak, or if the rash spreads. For emergency aid, call 911.

Fire Coral

Fire coral *(Cnidaria Phylum),* a reddish-brown spongy-looking mass on the island's reefs, can deliver a stinging burn-like sensation. Related to the jellyfish rather than the coral family, it can also scrape the skin. Rule of thumb on the reefs: Don't touch anything—for your comfort, as well as the reef's longevity (real corals can die when touched).

Other Marinelife

Fish to avoid include the porcupine-like lionfish, a poisonous species usually found in Australasia, but which has been spotted in the last few years in Bermuda's waters. The fish usually avoids human contact, but if touched, it releases venom from its puncturing spines. The great barracuda's menacing profile is deceptive; despite its ugly toothy grin, this large fish is usually harmless, though they have been known to snap at shiny metal objects, so keep watches and jewelry out of sight. Moray eels may look fearsome, but they mostly avoid human contact—unless you shove a hand into their lair. Do not touch the flat red bristleworm, or fireworm, whose needles leave a rash. Most corals, sea anemones, and jellyfish deposit a poisonous zap on human skin, so try not to touch them. Spiny sea urchins hidden in sea grass also pose a hazard; wearing fins or surf slippers helps avoid such dangers, as well as nasty reef scrapes and coral cuts.

CRIME

Against Bermuda's bucolic backdrop, the specter of crime—even the petty variety (handbag snatches, break-ins)—may seem out of place. But it is an unfortunate reality of modern life. Every parish has its share of neighborhoods plagued by perennial drug problems, the catalyst for most of the island's criminal activity; gangs and drug abuse appear to be the biggest factors driving an increase in violent crime in Bermuda in recent years. For the visitor, this flip side of local life is usually barely visible, but it is there nonetheless, and sensible measures should be taken to guard against opportunistic crime.

In 2005, closed-circuit surveillance cameras were installed on North Hamilton's Court Street and Pitts Bay Road, Pembroke—two economically divergent neighborhoods, yet both areas where police have recorded a high number of crimes, ranging from bag-snatchings to assaults and drug-related incidents. Cameras in other parts of the city have reduced the number of bike thefts, bag snatches, and public troublemakers.

Bag-Snatching

Protect your belongings and use the same street sense and practical judgment you would anywhere else in the world. The most common crime is bag-snatching, from beaches, scooter baskets, or, on rare occasions, from scooter-riders wearing bags over one arm—sometimes leading to traffic accidents and injuries. Visitors are not the only victims; Bermuda residents are also targets, though most have learned to lock away handbags, knapsacks, or shopping items in compartments attached to the back or under the scooter seat, or to strap down belongings in a rear basket with bungee cords looped through bag handles. Thieves have also targeted tourists strolling through Hamilton's streets at night, notably in quiet, seemingly safe, upscale neighborhoods such as Pitts Bay, where numerous hotels and guesthouses are located.

Take cabs at night if you are traveling alone. Be aware of your surroundings, keep wallets or purses out of sight, and wear long-strapped bags across your body, or hold them firmly to avoid becoming easy prey. On beaches, don't leave belongings unattended, or if you do, don't carry valuables and money. It is not unusual for swimmers to come back from a swim to find belongings gone or bags missing contents.

Break-Ins

Break-ins and home burglaries are frequent throughout the parishes, and again, Bermudian householders face a similar risk. Indeed, while leaving doors open was the oft-touted neighborhood habit of decades past, knowing residents rarely leave homes unlocked anymore when they're out. Most locals also lock doors and windows overnight when they're sleeping to keep intruders out. Tourist properties, particularly guesthouses and rental cottages outside the more secure confines of a hotel, are frequently targeted. Thieves know windows and sliding-glass doors at holiday properties are often left open through ignorance or to let in the breeze if there's no air-conditioning. Easy-to-cut screens are no deterrent. Thieves commonly break into rooms and residences when inhabitants are sleeping, though break-ins have rarely turned violent. Use hotel property safes to store valuables, and lock your room or house at night and when you're not around.

Motorcycle Theft

Scooters are favorite targets of thieves, who go for joyrides or scavenge for spare parts before dumping the remains on the roadside. Lock up your scooter or moped whenever you leave it. Motorscooters sometimes have both an ignition lock and a provided U-lock to place on the back wheel. It's a drag to have to fiddle with several times a day but well worth the effort. Other bikes are safe as long as the ignition key is removed. If your rental scooter or bike is stolen, contact the livery, which will usually collect you if you're stranded and notify the police.

Crimes Against Women

Violence against women in Bermuda has increased in recent years, along with violent crime in general. The Bermuda Police Service advises women traveling alone to choose well-lit routes and areas, to check vehicle gas regularly so you don't find yourself stranded, and to carry a cell phone, flashlight, or warning device such as a small air-horn.

Stay alert if you are walking or running alone—for example, along remote stretches of the Railway Trail or in large parks such as Spittal Pond or Hog Bay. If possible, women should avoid exploring or traveling alone in these areas; for safety, try to join organized groups of runners, walkers, or hikers, or take along a companion.

Harassment

Travelers tired of harassment in the Caribbean will appreciate being left alone in Bermuda; rarely are drugs offered or sold in public, and purveyors of services such as car-washing or hair-braiding generally do not actively seek clients, foreigners included. In recent years, Hamilton has experienced a minor problem with panhandling. Use your own judgment: give spare change if you wish, simply ignore panhandlers, or say no and move on, as most Bermudians do.

SMOKING

Bermuda has joined the growing list of countries to ban smoking in enclosed public places and work areas. New legislation took effect April 1, 2006, outlawing smoking in bars, restaurants, shops, cinemas, or any enclosed workplace—in line with similar crackdowns in North America and Europe. The law also prohibits cigarette vending machines on the island, and the sale of cigarettes to anyone under age 18. Penalties for smokers who defy the law are $250, or $1,000 for repeat offenders.

Information and Services

TOURIST INFORMATION

The website of **Bermuda's Department of Tourism and Transport,** www.bermuda tourism.com, offers a well-researched rundown on immigration rules, wedding resources, general activities, seasonal events, islandwide accommodations, and group and incentive tours, along with a mechanism to book trips online, including air and hotel packages.

The department did away with its various branch offices in North America in 2005 and consolidated into a single North American headquarters based in New York City (675 Third Ave., New York, tel. 212/818-9800, fax 212/983-5289, fdesk@bermudatourism.com). North Americans planning a trip to the island can call the department's toll-free, 24-hour hotline, 800/BERMUDA. An operator will quiz you about any specific interests or preferences, from accommodations to activities, before sending out a package of brochures by mail.

In the United Kingdom and Europe, contact the department's London office (Tulip House, Suite 9, 70 Borough High St., London, tel. 44/(0)207-864-9924, fax 44/(0)207-864-9966, www.bermudatourism.co.uk).

Once on the island, a first stop should be to any of the four **Visitors Service Bureaus,** run by the Bermuda Chamber of Commerce and open 9 A.M.–5 P.M. Monday–Saturday. Find them at these locations: **VSB Hamilton** (1 Point Pleasant Rd., next to the Front Street Ferry Terminal, Hamilton, tel. 441/295-1480); **VSB Dockyard** (across from the ferry stop, tel. 441/234-3824); **VSB St. George** (King's Square, tel. 441/297-1642); **VSB Airport Desk** (Arrivals Hall, Bermuda International Airport, tel. 441/299-4857). The offices are staffed by friendly, knowledgeable locals, who can answer even offbeat questions, such as how to get married and where to trace relatives and college friends living on the island. They also hand out free maps and brochures and help organize day trips, tours, shows, and other activities. The pocket-sized *Handy Reference Map,* an easy-to-read, east-to-west depiction of sights and attractions produced by the Tourism Department, can be picked up here, along with bus and ferry schedules, and brochures on restaurants, shopping, water sports, nature reserves, and the Railway Trail.

There is also a What's On in Bermuda telephone line with daily updates on events and activities around the island (tel. 974).

Don't be surprised, or alarmed, if you are approached on the beach or elsewhere by exuberant young Bermudians waving colorful flags. They are likely part of the "Pop By" campaign launched by Tourism in the summer of 2005 to encourage more interaction between Bermudians and visitors. Flags and six-packs of ginger beer were distributed free to the public, who were invited to share their sodas with tourists and tell them about the island. While the method proved controversial in some corners, and much of the ginger beer predictably went home to local fridges, the flags were wielded on beaches and in nightclubs as Bermudian college kids took up the call to be friendlier.

Under the campaign, the department also hired a handful of youthful "ambassadors" to zip around the island by scooter and interact with visitors at popular attractions like beaches and cruises—one of the world's better summer jobs, one can only imagine.

MONEY

Bermuda's currency, formerly based on the sterling system of shillings, pounds, and pence, went decimal in 1970, adopting colorful dollars and cents issued by the Bermuda Monetary Authority (BMA). Today, Bermuda's money, pegged to the U.S. dollar and interchangeable with it anywhere on the island, incorporates cultural icons in its designs, making the notes and coins sought after by collectors. The currency includes banknotes in denominations of $2 (turquoise, Dockyard Clocktower), $5 (pinkish-red, St. David's Lighthouse), $10 (purple, the cahow), $20 (green, Somerset

Butterfield Bank headquarters on Front Street, one of the island's oldest financial establishments

Bridge), $50 (brown, Santa Lucia wreck site) and $100 (orange, House of Parliament).

Coins are similarly artistic, especially the penny, manufactured in bronze with the image of a wild hog on the back—a tribute to the distinctive and now very rare Hogge money forged for use by settlers in the colony's early years, when tobacco-bartering was also common. Other coin denominations, in nickel, include: five cents (angelfish), 10 cents (lily), 25 cents (longtail), and $1 (in gold, Bermuda fitted dinghy). The latter was introduced in 1988, when a $1 note was discontinued and a $2 introduced. Since her coronation in 1952, all notes and coins have featured Queen Elizabeth II on the front side; the island's note series was updated in 2000 with her portrait redrawn as an older monarch. Because Bermuda notes and coins are restricted to use on the island, U.S. currency is used by all island-based international companies and their non-Bermudian employees, who are paid in U.S. dollars and hold local U.S.-dollar accounts at Bermudian banks.

Counterfeiting has been a minor but peren-nial problem, but Bermuda notes are continually updated with security features such as multicolored inks and watermarks (hold up any note to the light, and a leaping Allison tuna becomes visible).

Changing Money

Travelers are advised to bring credit cards or travelers checks (both are widely used throughout the island), plus a minimum amount of cash for their Bermuda holiday. Since Bermuda currency cannot be exchanged at foreign banks, ask stores for U.S. change where possible before leaving the island (many merchants are happy to comply). Visitors with passports can exchange travelers checks for U.S. cash at any branch of the three licensed retail banks, **Bank of Bermuda HSBC** (6 Front St., tel. 441/295-4000, www.bankofbermuda.bm), **Butterfield Bank** (65 Front St., tel. 441/295-1111, www.butterfieldbank.com), or **Capital G** (19 Reid St., tel. 441/296-6969). Mondays and Fridays are busiest, especially during lunch hours when Bermuda residents do most of their banking; the advent of online banking in recent years, however, has cut down on long bank lines. Many retail stores accept travelers checks. Few merchants cash personal checks, however; if they do, most charge a $15 fee for processing. Personal checks can be cashed for a 3 percent service charge at the **Bermuda Financial Network,** island agent for **American Express** (133 Front St., fourth floor, British-American Building, Hamilton, tel. 441/292-1799). The banks do not cash foreign checks for visitors unless a special prior arrangement has been made.

ATM machines, open 24 hours, are located at each bank's Hamilton headquarters and throughout the island at bank branches, gas stations, and supermarkets. ATMs deal only in Bermuda currency—meaning that if you draw cash from a foreign account, you'll need to spend it during your vacation, or carry it home as a souvenir, since you will not be able to convert it out of the country. The island's ATMs issue a maximum of $2,000 per day (or much less, depending on your home bank's policy, which can be as low as $250 per day) and charge a 1.5 percent transaction fee of the dollar amount withdrawn, with a minimum fee of $2.50. Bermudians can buy foreign currency, including U.S. and Canadian dollars, British pounds, Euros, and special-order currencies, from all the banks. Bank hours vary, but most are open 9 A.M.–4:30 P.M. (Somerset, St. George, and airport branches have restricted hours).

Travelers Checks

Most international travelers checks (Visa, American Express, Barclays) are accepted on the island, but travelers are advised to bring U.S.-dollar checks rather than any other currency. Individual stores and hotels set various limits on amounts that can be cashed at any one establishment. A passport is usually necessary as valid photo I.D. to cash travelers checks, which must be in the visitor's own name.

Credit Cards

All major credit cards (Visa, MasterCard, American Express) are accepted at most hotels,

restaurants, liveries, and retailers and can be used for cash advances at all bank branches. ATMs open 24 hours around the island also distribute cash advances for Visa, MasterCard, American Express, Cirrus, and Plus cards (know your PIN number). The American Express representative is **Bermuda Financial Network** (133 Front St., fourth floor, British-American Building, Hamilton, tel. 441/292-1799), which offers free phone calls and emergency AmEx card-replacement services. AmEx cardholders can also make payments on their cards at this office.

Lost or stolen major credit cards can be reported to these contact numbers:

- American Express: tel. 800/327-1267 (dial 880 from Bermuda)
- MasterCard: tel. 800/247-4623 or 314/275-6690
- Visa: tel. 800/336-8472 or 410/581-0120
- Visa Gold/Business: tel. 441/800/847-2911 or 410/581-9754

Costs

Despite the lack of sales tax, Bermuda rates as one of the priciest destinations in the world, and many visitors are shocked by the high cost of island living, particularly restaurant tabs (which slap on an automatic 15 percent gratuity) and grocery bills. But budget-conscious travelers can save money in a number of ways during their Bermuda vacation.

Booking an apartment or studio via websites such as www.bermudarentals.com or www.bermudagetaway.com can save the great expense of a resort vacation and allow you to live like a local. Shopping—wisely—at grocery stores instead of breaking your budget at pricey restaurants every day can also rein in costs. Shop like Bermudians do: Farmers roadside stands, fishermen's catch of the day, and the Saturday market at Bull's Head Car Park in Hamilton during the winter all deliver the freshest local ingredients in season at very fair prices.

Traveling by bus and ferry is cheaper than renting a moped or taking taxis. Buying passes for public transport saves money, too: a three-day pass allows you to hop on and off buses and ferries all day long. A book of 13 tokens saves money on each ride if you plan to stay a while.

As far as sights and activities go, much of what Bermuda has to offer is free: Explore the chain of forts, trek the Railway Trail and national parks, swim at umpteen beaches, wander the backstreets of Hamilton, St. George, and Somerset—you will not only save money, but leave Bermuda with a truer picture of island life than anyone sequestered in an all-inclusive cruise or fancy resort.

Tipping

Bermudians in the service industries are fond of their tips. Taxi drivers expect a 15- to 20 percent tip on rates, more if heavy luggage or official touring is involved. In nearly all restaurants, a 15 percent gratuity is automatically added to your bill, so there is no need to leave a tip at these establishments unless you feel the service or food is exceptional enough to deserve more; in such circumstances, islanders typically leave an extra $10 or $20. Smaller, homespun eateries tend not to build a tip into the tab; check the menu or bill slip to confirm. In hotels, bellboys and doormen should receive $5 or more. Room service warrants a $5–10 tip. Depending on your length of stay and service, chambermaids typically get $20 or more when you leave. Bermudians tip gas-station attendants $2 or more for a fill-up (all Bermuda's stations are full-serve).

FILM AND PHOTOGRAPHY

Just as it is to artists, Bermuda is a never-disappointing muse to photographers amateur and professional. Lensfolk rhapsodize about the unique softness of the island's light, the diffusion of water and air, the multi-turquoise hues of its ocean, the cornucopia of pastel shades at every turn.

If you shoot film, it's highly advisable to bring a stock with you; the cost of buying film on the island is exorbitant (a canister of 36-exposure Fuji Velvia, for example, costs $24—more than triple the amount it sells for in North America or Britain). Processing is also expensive in Bermuda (85 cents each for 4x6 prints, $1 for 5x7), so you might prefer to wait to develop your film rolls at home. Black-and-white film should be developed off the island for time and cost reasons. For color film, processing is fast and efficient at **Kodak Express** (Washington Mall, at Reid St., Hamilton, tel. 441/295-2519); **Jiffy Photo and Gifts** (5 Burnaby St., Hamilton, tel. 441/4436); and **P-Tech** (5 Reid St., Hamilton, tel. 441/295-5496). Same-day turnaround for standard prints or slide developing is the norm. Most outlets also have digital labs with do-it-yourself kiosks.

Beware the effect of heat on cameras and film—do not store equipment or film inside parked cars or the oven-like canisters on the back of rental mopeds. Bring a polarizing UV lens filter to take the shine off ocean shots, in particular, and be careful of sand and salt exposure at the beach or on the water (keep cameras covered when not in use). Avoid shooting in the harshness of midday if possible; Bermuda's intense sunlight 11 A.M.–2 P.M. fills photos with deep contrasts, burnout, and shadows; dawn or early evening will provide the most alluring light conditions, not to mention soft pink sunrises and sunsets.

Wedding photo specialists include **Sacha Blackburne** (tel. 441/234-5089, www.sacha blackburne.com) and her sister **Amanda Temple** (tel. 441/236-2339, www.amandatemple.com); **Ras Mykkal** (tel. 441/232-2470, or 441/732-3190, www.rasmykkal.com); **Ernie McCreight** (Visual Impact Photography, tel. 441/295-4755, www.viphotograph.com); **Dee Nobles** (Ace Studios, tel. 441/505-1414, www .acestudios.bm); and **Art Simons** (Photographic Associates Ltd., tel. 441/295-5619, www.photobermuda.com).

LookBermuda's digital photographic services (tel. 441/295-3555, www.lookbermuda.com) include shooting special events and panoramas. For more contacts and portfolios, check www.bermudaphotographers.com.

ELECTRICITY

Power losses, both brief and of the lengthier variety, are unfortunately an integral part of island life. Bermuda relies on one power plant, Belco, on Hamilton's outskirts in Pembroke, to serve the island's electricity needs. When something goes awry, Bermudians are made acutely aware of their tenuous connection to modern comforts. One unforgettable such occasion was a massive blaze at the power plant in July 2005, when the entire island—including the vital core of Hamilton—was left powerless for several days.

Heavy winter storms and summer hurricanes usually take Bermudian homes and businesses off the grid at least temporarily. Few Bermuda homes are without flashlights, matches, lighters, candles, or batteries—the essential tools for any semblance of life after dark during power outages. Blackouts are frequent enough that most of the major hotels, both hospitals, many businesses, and increasing numbers of private residences also own gas- and propane-fueled generators, which can be switched on to run at least very basic electric needs such as water pumps, stoves, and refrigerators.

Power surges are common, so make sure to unplug laptops, phones, faxes, and other sensitive equipment after an outage; when the power returns, it sometimes shuts on and off a couple of times during testing before being fully restored. Bring a surge-protector with you, or purchase one at **Complete Office** (17 Reid St., Hamilton, tel. 441/292-4333) or **Computer City** (45 Victoria St., Hamilton, tel. 441/292-1774). Call 955 to report outages via a recorded phone-in system that matches telephone number with affected neighborhood address.

Like North America, Bermuda operates on 110-volts AC, 60 cycles, with U.S. flat-blade (two-pin) plug outlets, so any U.S.-manufactured appliances such as hair dryers and curling irons will not require voltage converters or adaptors. European visitors, however, can either bring these with them or purchase them at stores such as **Radio Shack** (Washington Mall, Church St., Hamilton, tel. 441/292-8008 or 441/292-2920) or **P-Tech** (5 Reid St., Hamilton, at Queen St., tel. 441/295-5496).

BUSINESS HOURS

Most Hamilton offices follow the North American and English counterparts, with an official eight-hour workday Monday to Friday. Staff in retail outlets start winding down at 4:30 P.M., in readiness for a prompt 5 P.M. exit. The "rush hour"—a misnomer, since it is more a motorized crawl through the parishes—typically runs 7:30 A.M.–9:15 A.M. weekday mornings, and 5 P.M.–6:15 P.M. evenings, as residents make their way to and from Hamilton en masse. Traveling to and from the East End in these hours is usually not too difficult. Try to avoid being caught up in the western flow of traffic, however; all three arteries to and from Hamilton (Harbour Road, Middle Road, and South Shore) are crammed with bumper-to-bumper cars, with scooters zipping down the center line to get ahead.

Major Front Street stores stay open during the summerlong Harbour Nights street festival (7–9 P.M.). Stores throughout Hamilton usually keep longer Friday hours (until 9 P.M.) during the Christmas period.

As a conservative, religious society with more churches per square mile than nearly anywhere, Bermuda has been slow to embrace Sunday shopping. The law was finally amended in the late 1990s, and since then, most supermarkets open 1–5 P.M., though you will see their liquor departments roped off (it remains illegal for stores to sell alcohol on Sundays). Most bars stay open until 1 A.M., though nightclubs and a few private after-hours clubs do not shut their doors until 3 A.M.

TIME

Bermuda is on Atlantic Standard Time, one hour ahead of Eastern Standard Time (Toronto, New York, and U.S. East Coast cities) and four hours behind Greenwich Mean Time. Daylight saving time is observed, with clocks jumping forward an hour each spring and back in the fall. DST is stepping in line with the United States energy-saving measures in 2007, starting three weeks earlier (March 11 in 2007) and ending a week later (Nov. 4) than in the past. Dawn varies between 6:15 A.M. and 7:30 A.M. in summer and winter, and dusk falls between 8:30 P.M. and 5:15 P.M. in each season, respectively.

Communications and Media

Bermudians, isolated 670 miles from the nearest landfall (Cape Hatteras, North Carolina) take their communications very seriously. Thanks to a well-developed infrastructure, albeit threatened by seasonal hurricanes, the island provides modern telephone, fax, Internet, wireless, and wireless-roaming services. The mail service is mostly efficient, there's no shortage of couriers, and the island is bombarded with up-to-the-minute media—print, digital, and broadcast.

MAIL AND COURIER SERVICES

Airmail travels to and from the island daily. Mail received by 9:30 A.M. at the **General Post Office** (56 Church St., Hamilton, tel. 441/297-7893, gpo@gov.bm) is sent out the same day but may take several days to reach its destination. Mail sent internationally via the sub-post offices in the parishes must first go to the General Post Office, sometimes taking a day or two to exit the island. Stamps for a postcard to the United States and Canada cost 70 cents; to Europe, 80 cents; to Africa, Asia, and Australasia, 90 cents. Letters weighing 10 grams are five cents more, plus up to 50 cents on top for each additional 10 grams. The General Post Office is open 8 A.M.–5 P.M. Monday–Friday, 8 A.M.–noon Saturday. Parish post offices are open 8 A.M.–5 P.M. Monday–Friday. Surface mail is airlifted to and from Bermuda frequently. **International Data Express** (tel. 441/297-7802), a service offered through the General Post Office, is a 48-hour mail service delivering to most international destinations; it requires mail be posted by 10:30 A.M. for same-day dispatch.

Local company **Mailboxes Unlimited,** at three locations, offers mail and courier services, including boxing and wrapping, as well as full-scale moving services for larger items. The main office (48 Par-la-Ville Rd., Hamilton, tel. 441/292-6563, fax 441/292-6587) sells boxes, envelopes, bubble wrap, labels, tape, and pens. There are also Mailboxes outlets at 12 Church Street, Hamilton (tel. 441/296-5656) and 2 Lovers Lane, Paget (tel. 441/236-5142).

All major international courier services have offices in Bermuda, in some cases several outlets. They include **FedEx** (25 Serpentine Rd., Pembroke, tel. 441/295-3854); **DHL Worldwide Express** (16 Church St., Hamilton, tel. 441/295-3300; 1 Water St., St. George, tel. 441/297-5080; 3 Cahow Way, Bermuda International Airport, St. George's, tel. 441/293-6188, www.dhl.com); **International Bonded Couriers (IBC)** (10 Park Rd., Hamilton, tel. 441/295-2467, fax 441/292-7422, www.ibc.bm); **Sprint International** (22 Reid St., Hamilton, tel. 441/296-7866, fax 441/295-7544, www.sprint.bm); **UPS** (10 Park Rd., Hamilton, tel. 441/295-2467); and **Best Shipping** (6 Addendum Ln. South, Pembroke, tel. 441/292-8080, www.best.bm).

TELEPHONES

Bermuda's phone, fax, and wireless data services, like its Internet capabilities, are modern and efficient, though more costly than in North America or Europe. Increasingly, travelers to Bermuda bring their own cell phones or wireless handhelds. North American models should operate normally here, though adaptors may be needed for others. However, calling via a phone linked to an overseas network can be expensive. Depending on how many calls you intend to make, an alternative is to purchase prepaid SIM cards for your cell phone. **Cingular,** formerly AT&T Wireless (22 Church St., at the Washington Mall, tel. 411/500-5000, info@bm.cingular.com) sells these cards in $10, $20, $50, and $100 denominations and will remove and later put back your current SIM card. Mobile phones can be rented from **Bermuda Cell Rental** (Armoury Building, 37 Reid St., Hamilton, tel. 441/232-2355, www.bermudacellrental.com).

Public phones are located around the island, though often are in a shabby state or out of order—a problem most Bermudians, with their surgically attached mobiles, don't seem to notice or care about these days.

For international calls, **Cable & Wireless** (Burnaby St. at corner of Church St., Hamilton, tel. 441/297-7128, 9 A.M.–4:30 P.M. Mon.–Fri.), **TeleBermuda International** (Reid St. at corner of Queen St., Hamilton, tel. 441/296-9029/9030, 9 A.M.–4:30 P.M. Mon.–Fri.), and **Logic Communications** (12 Burnaby St., tel. 441/294-8888, 8 A.M.–6 P.M. Mon.–Fri., 9 A.M.–5 P.M. Sat.) have retail centers in Hamilton, where prepaid phone cards can be purchased and local or long-distance calls made on the premises.

Bermuda's international access code is '1' followed by 441 (area code) and the phone number. To dial the United States or Canada from Bermuda, simply dial '1' plus the area code and number. For operator-assisted calls, dial '00.' For U.S. or Canada directory assistance, dial '1' plus the area code plus 555-1212. To make U.K. calls, dial '011' followed by '44,' plus a city area code, and a phone number. Caribbean nations take '1' or '011' as international access codes, depending on their nationality, with European islands requiring the latter.

INTERNET ACCESS

Bermuda has been cyber-crazy ever since Internet service was first offered here in the early 1990s. Most hotels and guesthouses offer Internet access to visitors. Larger properties cater to laptop-toting business travelers with high-speed connections in rooms, lobby areas, and dedicated business centers. There are also numerous cybercafés around the island, in the city of Hamilton, at the Dockyard in Sandys, and in the old town of St. George. In 2005, the government launched an initiative to provide free online access to the public via parish post offices; so far, outlets in Sandys and Warwick have been the vanguard of the project.

Computer and communication supplies are extremely expensive to purchase in Bermuda, so try to come equipped, or be prepared to pay two to three times the price you would at home.

Bermuda's Internet domain is .bm, though some Bermuda-based websites have chosen .com URLs for higher visibility.

PUBLICATIONS
Tourist Publications

Preview magazine and *This Week in Bermuda* are fat little booklets published weekly with advertisements and information on seasonal events, tours, cultural sights, and activities, as well as roundups on the island's history, restaurants, nature reserves, and shopping highlights. Both are available throughout the island, at all major hotels, airport and cruise ship terminals, and Visitors Service Bureaus.

Destination Bermuda (tel. 44/1-747-838-378, fax 44/1-747-839-808, ralstonpub@aol.com) is an annual magazine published in the United Kingdom and distributed free of charge to Bermuda-bound airline passengers at check-in at Gatwick, London; New York; Toronto; and other major North American gateways. Copies are also available on-island at all the Visitors Service Bureaus, and on request. Photos and features highlight cultural attractions, activities, history, shopping, and business services.

Experience Bermuda, a glossy, hard-backed advertorial-heavy publication backed by the Bermuda Hotel Association, can be found in hotel rooms island-wide. Included are photo features and write-ups on things to see and do, wining and dining, and weddings and honeymoons. Check its companion website (www.experiencebermuda.com) for seasonal deals on accommodation packages.

Dining Out in Bermuda (tel. 441/295-2412 or 441/292-1459, www.dininginbermuda.com), produced and published locally, covers the island's foodie scene, with menus, prices, dress codes, reservation phone numbers, features on local dishes and chefs, and other restaurant information, including hours and credit-card details. Meal reservations can be made through the magazine's website.

Newspapers

Bermuda has one daily newspaper, *The Royal Gazette* ($0.75); one biweekly, the *Bermuda Sun* ($0.80); and one weekly, *Mid-Ocean News* ($0.75). All three are available at island newsstands and hotels.

The Royal Gazette (tel. 441/295-5881, www

.royalgazette.bm) dates back to 1828 and is owned and printed by Bermuda Press Holdings. While the professionalism of its writing and design ebbs and flows, it is a morning must-read for most locals, even those who perennially criticize the paper for its white roots and conservative slant on social issues. Indeed, the *Gazette* is an essential ingredient of life in Bermuda, where staying atop national truths and small-town gossip is considered imperative for dinner-party conversation.

The *Gazette* covers local news, sports, the arts scene, and the business community, its pages padded by wire stories for coverage of overseas events. Aside from the funeral listings, the *Gazette*'s best-read section is the daily "Letters to the Editor," on page 4, where views of all persuasions—sometimes signed, more often not—wax loudly on everything from political scandals to scolding over traffic violations.

For visitors, the *Gazette* is a barometer of island life. It also offers concrete resources including movie listings, a community calendar listing events, activities, shows, art and museum openings, plus advertisements for auctions, end-of-season sales in Hamilton stores, and other services. The otherwise slim Saturday paper provides a rundown of restaurants and other businesses open on Sunday. If you are planning a trip and want to get a sense of what's making headlines, check out the *Gazette*'s online edition before you arrive.

The revamped **Bermuda Sun,** a tabloid owned and printed by the rival Island Press, publishes twice a week, on Wednesdays and Fridays, and is worth reading for what the *Gazette* leaves out. With a raft of columnists and feature writers, the *Sun* takes a decidedly more human-interest slant, with analyses of the island's multiethnic population, and earnest examinations of politically fraught issues like Independence, racism, and the lack of affordable housing. Its investigative reporting gives the *Gazette* a run for its money, too.

The broadsheet **Mid-Ocean News** is the *Gazette*'s sister paper, which publishes on Friday, with a weekly circulation of 13,000. A thinner publication than either the *Gazette* or *Sun,* it

can be disregarded for its soft news and overly sensational front-page headlines, but the long inside features, columnists, and personality profiles are entertaining.

Local Magazines

For such a small market, Bermuda has a plethora of glossy magazines, all fighting for a diminishing pot of advertising dollars. **RG** magazine, published six times a year and distributed free inside *The Royal Gazette,* offers newsy features, profiles of local personalities, and a comprehensive calendar of seasonal events. **The Bermudian** ($4), launched in 1930 in the vein of *The New Yorker,* finally downsized after its 75th anniversary in 2005 from a monthly to a quarterly. Produced by the Bermudian Publishing Company, it features Bermuda history, architecture, and traditions, and a well-perused party section. The magazine's popular "Best of Bermuda Awards" issue each summer provides a well-vetted insider's list of the island's favorite shops, attractions, and services—a very useful resource for visitors.

Other magazines include Bermuda Media's annual **New Resident Guide** ($4.95), a resource for newcomers to the island; **Who's Who,** a listing of Bermuda personalities; and **Bermuda Real Estate Handbook,** which offers advice on buying and selling property in Bermuda and advertises local realtors.

Business travelers should pick up a copy of **Bermudian Business** ($4.95), a Bermudian Publishing Company magazine, which counts many of the island's CEOs as subscribers; **Bottom Line,** the Royal Gazette Ltd.'s free quarterly assessment of domestic and international company news, including in-depth corporate profiles; and **Bermuda Insurance Quarterly,** produced by Bermuda Media and sponsored by PricewaterhouseCoopers. As well, **dot.bm** magazine provides a rundown on ISPs, new technology, high-tech hardware, and communications service providers.

Local lifestyle mags include **Bermuda Homes & Gardens** (tel. 441/295-5845, www .bdahomesandgardens.bm, $4) and the style and fashion magazine *Show Off* (tel. 441/296-7503, fax 441/295-0972, www.showoffmagazine.net, $4.95).

International Publications

Major American, Canadian, and British newspapers are available at the large **Phoenix Centre** (3 Reid St., near Queen Street junction, tel. 441/295-3838, phoenixstores.com, 8 A.M.–6 P.M. Mon.–Sat., noon–6 P.M. Sun.), and at some of its islandwide outlets, though the cost of flying them in makes for elevated prices. American daily papers like *The New York Times* ($2.50), *USA Today* ($1.50), and *Boston Globe Sunday* ($5.95) are flown in daily but do not end up on the shelves until the afternoon. Weekend editions of Canadian papers, including the *Toronto Star* ($4.95) and *Globe & Mail* ($4.25), are available Sundays. British editions such as *The Sunday Times* ($10.95), *Telegraph* ($5.25), *Mirror* ($2.50), and *Daily Mail* ($3.25) come to the island aboard British Airways' evening flights on Tuesdays, Thursdays, and Saturdays, appearing in stores the following morning. Some of the resort hotels fly in copies of *The New York Times, Wall Street Journal, Financial Times,* and *USA Today* on afternoon flights to Bermuda, or distribute condensed versions of those publications downloaded daily from respective websites.

Magazine racks at the Phoenix and other pharmacies, as well as **Washington Malls Magazines** (lower level Washington Mall, Hamilton, tel. 441/292-7420, www.bda books.bm, 8:15 A.M.–5:15 P.M. Mon.–Fri., 8:45 A.M.–5:15 P.M. Sat.) and most large grocery stores display weekly editions such as *People, Time, Newsweek, US Weekly, New York,* and *The New Yorker*—though typically a week late. All the major monthly U.S. glossies, from fashion to shelter magazines, as well as a few Canadian ones, are also sold at these stores, along with U.K. counterparts. Prices, particularly for the British editions once translated back into dollars (*British Vogue* $8.95, *Hello* $6.15), can be daunting for magazine junkies.

BROADCASTING
Television
North American—mostly U.S.—television fare is on the menu; major U.S. networks are affiliated with Bermuda stations, which air their programming daily, and the island's two cable companies offer hundreds of mainly American channels.

Three broadcast stations represent the U.S. television networks and also offer some local, though amateur quality, programming. Established in 1947, **Bermuda Broadcasting Company** (Fort Hill, Devonshire, tel. 441/295-2828) today has two commercial TV stations, ZFB-TV channel 7 (cable channel 2) is the affiliate of ABC, while ZBM-TV channel 9 (cable channel 3) airs CBS network programming. Both stations also air locally produced daily evening news, talk shows, and sports programs. **Defontes Broadcasting Television** (94 Reid St., Hamilton, tel. 441/295-1450) operates VSB-TV channel 11, the island's NBC affiliate. Local news, weather, and sports air at 7 P.M. nightly, and local productions, including educational and community-oriented shows, are also carried weekly.

Two companies offer digital and standard cable television service islandwide. **Bermuda Cablevision** (19 Laffan St., Hamilton, tel. 441/292-5544) offers nearly 200 24-hour channels from the United States, Canada, and Portugal. Newcomer **WOW (World on Wireless) TV** (Washington Mall, Church St., Hamilton, tel. 441/292-1969) has 110 channels, 84 of which are available in digital.

The Bermuda Channel (Bermuda Media, Suite 310, International Centre, 26 Bermudiana Rd., Hamilton, tel. 441/292-7279, www.bermudamedia.bm) is a closed-circuit service aired in the majority of major resorts and hotel rooms. The 60-minute show, which broadcasts in guest rooms on a continual loop on cable channels 6 and 77, carries features on sightseeing, sports, transportation, shopping, and restaurants.

Radio
The island has 10 radio channels, with eclectic,

sometimes homespun announcers, DJs, news-readers, and programming.

For locals and visitors, daytime talk shows, featuring call-in segments and vociferous debates about all things Bermudian, are a highly entertaining slice of island life. **Gold AM (VSB-1) 1450-AM,** with host Shirley Dill, carries such programs throughout the afternoon, along with easy-listening music, while **ZBM-2 1340-AM,** with host David Lopes, also broadcasts lively local chitchat. Other AM channels include: **VSB-2 1280-AM,** which offers religious and gospel programming, **ZFB 1230-AM,** offering an easy listening mix and local programming, and **VSB-3 1160-AM,** the British Broadcasting Corporation (BBC World) feed.

FM channels are: **ZBM 89.1-FM,** piped-in syndicated programming from the United States, with mellow chart favorites from the 1970s onward, and **VSB-4 106.1-FM (Mix 106),** which broadcasts a mixture of old and new rock, along with teen pop and rap hits.

ZFB Power 95-FM has a popular morning host ("The Captain") and carries a mix of reggae, rap, and R&B.

Hott 107.5-FM, launched in 2004 and targeting the island's black population, offers the most slickly produced programming, thanks to its Chicago connections—one of its founders was the former program director of WGCI in the city.

Bermuda's newest radio station, launched in September 2005, is **KJAZ 98.1-AM,** broadcasting live to online listeners with streamed jazz, blues, and world music programming.

RESOURCES

Suggested Reading and Viewing

ISLAND LIFE AND TRAVEL

Barritt, Fred and Smith, Peter. *Bermewjan Vurds: A Dictionary of Conversational Bermudian*. Bermuda: Lizard Press, seventh edition, 2005. Hilarious collection of amazing-but-true local idiom and slang, updated periodically.

Berg, Daniel and Denise. *Bermuda Shipwrecks: A Vacationing Diver's Guide to Bermuda's Shipwrecks*. East Rockway, New York: Aqua Explorers Inc., 1991. An A-to-Z rundown of legendary wrecks discovered off Bermuda, with a brief history, plus photos of wreck sites, artifacts, and the divers who found them.

Caswell, Tracey. *Tea With Tracey: The Woman's Survival Guide to Bermuda*. Bermuda: Print Link, 1994. A cockroaches-and-all view of Bermuda by a resident expat whose introduction to island life is a highly entertaining read for anyone interested in what it's really like to live in a so-called paradise.

Emery, Llewellyn. *Nothin' But a Pond Dog*. Bermuda: Bermudian Publishing Company, 1996, reprinted 1999. Businessman, cedar craftsman, and author Emery paints both a humorous and poignant portrait of back o' town life as a child in the 1950s.

Richardson, Ralph. *The Bermuda Boater*. Second edition. Bermuda: Pyro Press, 2004. Written by a seasoned Bermudian navigator and boating enthusiast, this edition is an extremely useful resource for yachties and commercial or recreational boaters in Bermuda. Complete with navigation and safety basics, local chart references, and island knowledge on weather, tides, emergency resources, and other tips.

Smith, Molly. *Discovering Bermuda with Paintbrush and Bike*. Bermuda: Bermudian Publishing Company, 2005. An island tour through the eyes of Bermudian watercolorist Smith, whose sketches, paintings, and observations along the way—including recipes, herbal remedies, and poems—paint a rich portrait of a whimsical island.

Watlington, Frank. *Bermuda Kites: How to Make and Fly Them*. Reprint. Bermuda, 1960. A 101 primer on tried-and-true methods to create the colorful tissue-paper concoctions that grace island skies over the Easter weekend. Easy-to-follow diagrams describe basic designs, papering, and looping tricks that have become a beloved Bermudian tradition.

HISTORY & FOLKLORE

Bermuda's Architectural Heritage Series. Devonshire, St. George's, Sandys, Hamilton Parish, Smith's. Bermuda: Bermuda National Trust, 1995–2005. In-depth parish histories researched and written by local historians, full of photos and illustrations.

Bernhard, Virginia. *Slaves and Slaveholders in Bermuda, 1616–1782*. Columbia, Missouri:

University of Missouri Press, 1999. Historical analysis of the complex relationship between slavery and racism in the second-oldest colony of the New World.

Cox, John. *Bermuda's Favourite Haunts.* Bermuda: John Cox, 1991. Spooky chronicle of haunted houses around the island and the ghosts that inhabit them.

Deichmann, Catherine Lynch. *Rogues & Runners: Bermuda and the American Civil War.* Bermuda: Bermuda National Trust, 2003. Companion booklet to the fascinating exhibit in the Bermuda National Trust Museum at the old Globe Hotel building in St. George.

Harris, Edward Cecil. *Bermuda Forts: 1612–1957.* Bermuda: Bermuda Maritime Museum Press, 1997. Written by archaeologist, historian, and director of the Bermuda Maritime Museum, this comprehensive overview of the island's chain of fortifications, their history, and archaeology, is especially topical now that government plans to restore many of these decaying landmarks as cultural attractions.

Jones, Rosemary. *Bermuda: Five Centuries.* Bermuda: Panatel VDS Ltd., 2004. Full-color, reader-friendly history of the island from its discovery in 1505 to the 21st century. A companion to a DVD series by the same name, the book contains timelines, contemporary accounts, and more than 360 historic images, from private and public collections.

McDowall, Duncan. *Another World, Bermuda and the Rise of Modern Tourism.* London: Macmillan Education, 1999. Canadian history professor and longtime Bermudaphile McDowall describes the economic makeover tourism effected in Bermuda, in a highly readable, anecdotal edition.

Zuill, W. S. *The Story of Bermuda and Her People.* London: Macmillan Caribbean, third edition 1999. Concise paperback history of the island, written by a former editor of the daily newspaper.

NATURE AND THE ENVIRONMENT

The Bermuda Rose Society. *Roses in Bermuda.* Bermuda: Bermudian Publishing Company, 1997. Packed with color photos to make identification easy, this edition highlights the wealth of roses and where to find them throughout the island, from ramblers and hybrid teas to the so-called mystery varieties. One section even details where to find Bermuda roses in the United States.

Dobson, Andrew. *A Birdwatching Guide to Bermuda.* Shrewsbury, England: Arlequin Press, 2002. A detailed birding guide written by the president of the island's Audubon Society.

Phillips-Watlington, Christine. *Bermuda's Botanical Wonderland: A Field Guide.* MacMillan Education, 1996. Whimsically illustrated edition with renditions of typical island habitats and the abundant flora within them.

Frith, Kathleen and Jonathan; Constable, James and Jennifer; James Cooper. *Sporty Little Field Guide to Bermuda.* Bermuda: 2 Halves Publishing, 1997. A comprehensive paperback guide to the island's main plant and animal life, with artful illustrations and brief, informative text for each.

Sterrer, Wolfgang. *Bermuda's Marine Life.* Bermuda: Bermuda Zoological Society, 1992. A comprehensive, and highly readable, look at all forms of island sealife by a former curator of the Bermuda Zoological Society's Natural History Museum in Flatts.

Thomas, Martin L. H. *A Natural History of Bermuda.* Bermuda: Bermuda Zoological Society, 2004. Comprehensive full-color coffee-table edition by a Canadian professor and research scientist who studied the island's flora and fauna for more than 30 years. Photos and detailed text on marine and terrestrial habitats and wildlife, along with threats to the island's delicate ecosystem. It is available at the Bermuda Aquarium, Museum & Zoo shop, as well as bookstores in Hamilton and St. George.

COLLECTORS

Williams, Malcolm and Sousa, Peter T. (Eds.). *Coins of Bermuda*. Bermuda: Bermuda Monetary Authority, 1997. A history of island coinage, from the first Hogge money and sterling coins to the decimal system.

ART AND ARCHITECTURE

Calnan, Patricia. *The Masterworks Bermudiana Collection*. Bermuda: The Bermudian Publishing Company, 1994. Lavish edition showcasing the repatriated island artworks of Winslow Homer, Georgia O'Keeffe, and other art-world luminaries, as collected by Bermuda's Masterworks Foundation.

Shorto, Sylvia and MacDonald-Smith, Ian. *Bermuda Gardens & Houses*. New York: Rizzoli International, 1996. Informative coffee-table volume written by Bermudian art historian Shorto and photographed by much-published island lensman MacDonald-Smith.

FOOD

Bottone, Edward. *Spirit of Bermuda: Cooking with Gosling's Black Seal Rum*. Bermuda: The Bermudian Publishing Company, 1998. Vibrantly illustrated cookbook by Philadelphia chef and former resident Bottone, with all the island's favorite recipes (cod fish cakes, cassava pie), as well as colorful descriptions of holiday traditions and culinary folklore.

Island Thyme: Tastes and Traditions of Bermuda. Bermuda: Junior Service League, 2004. Collection of recipes, menus, and table settings from island residents and restaurants in a full-color volume produced to raise money for one of Bermuda's core social agencies.

Ming, Fred. *Bermuda Favourites*. Bermuda: 2004. A compendium of recipes from one of the island's best-known chefs and cooking teachers, including red snapper fillets, red bean soup, and nasturtium salad.

Wadson, Judith. *Bermuda: Traditions and Tastes*. Bermuda: Judith Wadson, 1998. A history of Bermudian holidays, including Cup Match and Good Friday, and the typical dishes that accompany the celebrations.

PHOTOGRAPHY

Airey, Theresa and Marshall, Edward. *Bermuda: The Quiet Years 1883–1953*. Bermuda: 2004. A fascinating collection of 147 restored nitrate negatives published for the first time in this edition, the book portrays the island before the advent of automobiles. Photographs taken by a handful of the island's professional lensmen capture street scenes, city restaurants, lily festivals, the railway, and pristine landscapes many Bermudians would barely recognize anymore.

MacDonald-Smith, Ian. *A Scape to Bermuda*. Third edition. Bermuda, 2004. All-season Bermuda, with studies of clouds, rocks, flower-strewn lanes, architecture, rainbows, and Christmas lights.

Skinner, Roland. *Picturesque Bermuda I and II*. Bermuda, 1996 and 1999. Landscapes, seascapes and aerial shots of Bermuda by prolific lensman Skinner, a former Bermuda News Bureau staffer who now owns one of the largest Bermuda stock photo libraries and sells large-scale prints of his work.

Spurling, Ann. *Nine Parishes*. Bermuda, 2003. Pricey ($80), but satisfying photographic tour of the island by the island's premier homes-and-gardens photographer. Entertainingly written and laden with informative captions and parish intros, its lush spreads feature Bermudian homes, people, cultural traditions, and pastimes. For its scope and local knowledge, it is one of the best Bermuda pictorials available.

BUSINESS

Duffy, Catherine R. *Held Captive: A History of International Insurance in Bermuda.* Toronto: Oakwell Boulton, 2004. Definitive 516-page tome outlining in detailed CEO interviews, photos, glossaries, and corporate profiles, the creation of "Bermuda, Inc."

Stewart, Robert. *A Guide to the Economy of Bermuda.* Toronto: Oakwell Boulton, 2003. An analysis of why Bermuda has been one of the most successful economies in the world for the past half century by economics teacher and former Shell Group C.E.O. who now is director of several international Bermuda companies and investment funds.

CHILDREN

Surprisingly, perhaps, Bermuda boasts a number of well-produced children's books, which local and visiting kids enjoy for their stories about island animals, icons, and traditions, including treefrogs, cedars trees, and sailboats. Great souvenirs for kids back at home, too.

Booth, Mark. Illustrated by Patricia DeCosta. *Bermuda's Sidney the Sailboat.* Bermuda: Bermudian Publishing Company, 1994. Compelling Cinderella tale of a neglected sailboat and its adventures. Perfect for ages four and up.

Cooper, Dana. *My Bermuda ABC.* New York: Worzalla Publishing Company, 1991. Bermudian commercial artist Cooper's whimsical counting and alphabet guides, inhabited by tropical touchstones like loquats, limestone, and lizards.

Donkin, Andrew. *Bermuda Triangle.* New York: Dorling Kindersley (DK), 2000. Eerily illustrated and vividly told, this DK Readers Program book, with large text for easy reading, is a kid-pleasing synopsis of the legendary phenomenon.

Jacobs, Francine. *Bermuda Petrel: The Bird that Would Not Die.* New York: William Morrow & Co., 1981. The story of the endemic Bermuda petrel, or cahow.

Karwoski, Gail Langer. *Miracle: The True Story of the Wreck of the Sea Venture.* Plain City, Ohio: Darby Creek Publishing, 2004. Very professionally produced edition by Georgia-based writer Karwoski that's sure to captivate young imaginations with the story of Bermuda's first colonists. Kid-friendly design includes scores of illustrations, photos, and graphics, along with digestible, yet historically detailed text and provoking sidebars on early navigation, island traditions, birds, and animals. A great buy for inquisitive kids of all ages.

Mulderig, A. Elizabeth. *Tiny the Treefrog Tours Bermuda.* Bermuda: Bermudian Publishing Company, 1992. A charmingly illustrated rhyme about a quixotic treefrog and his Bermuda sightseeing exploits.

Stevenson, Kevin. Illustrated by Daniel, Helen. *The Story of the Bermuda Cedar Tree.* Bermuda: Bermudian Publishing Company, 1997. Artfully illustrated with gouache plates, the book tells the story of Bermuda's iconic tree and its multiple use throughout the centuries.

RARE OR OUT-OF-PRINT BOOKS

Some of the best books on Bermuda are now out of print, but copies can be found for sale at various stores around the island, including Bermuda Bookstore and Bermuda Craft Market at Dockyard. Or, contact dealers directly:

Anthony Pettit, by appointment, tel. 441/292-2482, fax 441/295-5416, www.anthonypettit.com; Twice-Told Tales, 34 Parliament St., Hamilton, tel. 441/296-1995. Some rare editions often can be found online for competitive prices at sites like eBay, alibris, and other rare-book sites.

Beebe, William. *Half Mile Down.* New York: Duell, Sloan & Pearce, 1951. In his own words, the story of deep-ocean pioneer Beebe's underwater explorations in a revolutionary bathysphere off Bermuda in the 1930s.

Dorr, Julia. Bermuda: *An Idyl of the Summer Islands.* New York: Charles Scribner & Sons, 1884. Amusing Victorian travelogue written by a wintering American at the time of tourism's debut, her island sojourn coinciding with that of Princess Louise.

Hutchings Smith, Louisa. *Bermuda's Oldest Inhabitants: Tales of Plant Life.* Sevenoaks, England: J. Salmon Ltd., 1963. Gardeners and naturalists will enjoy this beautifully illustrated account of the island's flora, with nine color plates by artist May Middleton.

Winchester, Simon. *Outposts, Journeys to the Surviving Relics of the British Empire.* London: Sceptre, 1986. Witty observations of journalist Winchester's 1970s visit to Bermuda, among other remaining British colonial "pink" spots on the map.

BERMUDA ON FILM

Bermuda: Five Centuries, Panatel VDS Ltd., 1999. Six-part documentary series using contemporary interviews and historic and modern footage to trace the island's history via major social themes over 500 years. With companion book.

The Bermuda Depths, Rankin-Bass, 1978. A made-for-TV motion-picture adventure written by Arthur Rankin, Jr., a Bermuda resident and Canadian cartoon producer of *Rudolph the Red-Nosed Reindeer* and *Frosty the Snowman.* Directed by Shussei Kotani, the film stars Burl Ives, Leigh McCloskey, Carl Weathers, and Connie Selleca in a ghost yarn about scientists terrorized by a giant turtle as they investigate the Bermuda Triangle. McCloskey and Selleca's kid versions are played by Bermudian children.

The Deep, Columbia Pictures, 1977. Peter Benchley's underwater thriller, directed by Peter Yates and starring Nick Nolte, Jacqueline Bisset, and Lou Gossett, Jr., was inspired by Benchley's visits to the island and was filmed in Bermuda. A romantic interlude turns to adventure when a couple discovers gold coins and mysterious glass ampoules on a sunken World War II wreck. The film features many familiar sights—including lots of Bermudian extras. Based on Benchley's 1976 book of the same title, one of its hallmark elements was the theme song sung by Donna Summer.

Neptune's Daughter, Warner Studios, 1949. This Oscar-winning musical-comedy-romance directed by Edward Buzzell and starring aquatic goddess Esther Williams, Red Skelton, and Ricardo Montalban was filmed at a pool on Agar's Island, in Bermuda's Great Sound. The production was fraught with problems, but the film ended up as the 10th-grossing movie of that year, propelled by the popular song, "Baby, It's Cold Outside."

Internet Resources

GENERAL INFORMATION

www.bermuda4u.com

This concise independent guide to Bermuda by former English resident David Mottershead offers a frank and witty overview of Bermuda life, services, attractions, and regulations for visitors, along with a trip-booking facility. Best are the brief, but keenly accurate, discussions of life on "The Rock," both good and bad.

www.bermudatourism.com

The sleekly navigable Bermuda Tourism Department website encompasses facts, figures, and useful resources for travelers, including events, sights, customs and immigration rules, licensed accommodations, activities, and a reservations system.

www.bermuda.com

Boasting the most hits of any Bermuda site, this comprehensive portal is owned and run by a local printery, the Island Press Ltd. Thorough but advertising-driven listings for accommodations, dining, and activities understandably read like a tourism brochure.

www.bermuda-online.org

Comprising a portal linking to 128 websites, plus a digital library compiled by local resident and author Keith Forbes, the regularly updated website is now owned and supported by *The Royal Gazette*. Overwritten and cumbersomely designed, it remains a useful repository of information—from census figures to resources for new residents.

www.cia.gov/cia/publications/factbook/geos/bd.html

The Central Intelligence Agency's online fact book is crammed with constantly updated information on Bermuda, including land-use, population, literacy, and electricity-consumption statistics.

www.travel.state.gov

The U.S. Department of State's website posts a Consular Information Sheet on Bermuda, which gives an accurate overview of crime, communications, traffic safety, and customs issues, as well as links relevant to U.S. travelers.

www.access.bm

A website created by wheelchair-bound Bermudian Keith Simmons as a resource for physically challenged visitors, it is sparse but contains useful resources and information about islandwide transport and the accessibility of certain areas and sights.

GOVERNMENT

www.gov.bm

The official Bermuda government website is a portal to all ministries, departments, and related bodies, including the National Anti-Money Laundering Committee (NAMLC).

www.bermudaairport.bm

Bermuda International Airport's website gives flight, check-in, customs, retail, and restaurant details, plus links to airlines and major travel agents.

ISLAND LIFE AND EVENTS

www.boxoffice.bm

Buy tickets online to all Bermuda's major entertainment events via this site, a favorite timesaver for thousands of island residents.

www.limeyinbermuda.com

This highly popular blog—a favorite of resident expats—was created by Yorkshireman Phillip Wells, who also writes a weekly column for *The Royal Gazette*. Married to a Bermudian, he vents, often satirically, on thorny island issues—politics, expat relations, racial tensions—and represents the rare non-Bermudian point of view in public debates.

www.bermynet.com

Covering the home-from-college scene, this popular site features photos from Front Street happy hours, as well as the summer club scene, beach parties, DJs, and live web radio.

www.bermuda.e-moo.com

A morning must-see for thousands of residents, this classifieds website carries information on public events, yard sales, and stuff for sale galore, from jewelry and pianos to boats and furniture.

ACCOMMODATIONS

www.bermudarentals.com

Toronto-based Bermudian Fiona Campbell is a broker for a list of islandwide vacation properties of various sizes and rates, including historic homes and long-term rentals. Most are studios or apartments attached to local homes. Prices range from under $100 to $300 a night (double). It also contains useful contacts and links to activities and services, from hiring a gourmet chef to scuba tours and grocery deliveries.

www.bermudagetaway.com

This website provides a listing of information, photos, and contacts for Bermuda vacation rentals, but does not broker reservations.

www.bermuda-reservations.com

A portal to large North American-based travel sites selling Bermuda vacations, with flight-hotel and cruise packages, including www.travelocity, www.expedia, www.tripadvisor, www.orbitz.com and www.cruises.com.

WEDDINGS

www.bermudabride.com

Highly-rated wedding planner Nikki Begg's stylish website encapsulates pretty much anything prospective brides and grooms might want to know about getting married in Bermuda—paperwork, photographers, flowers, and more.

www.bridalsuitebermudaweddings.com (Allistair Simmons)

Long-established wedding consultants Carmen and Allister Simmons dish out the romance, with details (and photos) of recommended wedding locations, towering cakes, marriage license regulations, travel tips, and glowing testimonials from the sub-tropically married.

MEDIA

www.theroyalgazette.com

The online edition of Bermuda's daily paper carries recent major headlines, plus classifieds, TV listings, and opinion polls, accessible through the site's effective search engine.

www.bermudasun.bm

The website of popular weekly, *Bermuda Sun* dishes up news, sports and entertainment, along with TV listings, local ads and links to scores of island websites, from bus schedules to resorts.

BUSINESS INFORMATION

www.bma.bm

The official website of the Bermuda Monetary Authority (BMA), the island's main regulatory body, which supervises the financial services industry, approves incorporations, oversees licenses to financial institutions, and issues banknotes and coinage. The site offers text of public legislation, and a "warning" list of bogus companies not licensed to do business on the island.

www.biba.org

The Bermuda International Business Association (BIBA) uses its website to promote the island as a blue-chip business jurisdiction and represent members ranging from financial services to accounting, legal, and IT companies. Included is basic information about Bermuda's highly developed corporate infrastructure, communications, and regulations. Text of Bermuda laws can also be downloaded.

www.bermudacommerce.com

The Bermuda Chamber of Commerce's website represents its members, from e-business to construction companies. Included is information on how to acquire permits to sell and showcase products on the island, as well as contacts for its Visitors Service Bureaus, and weekly Harbour Nights summer street festivals in Hamilton, Dockyard, and St. George.

www.bermuda-insurance.org

The online home of the booming Bermuda insurance market, with links to many of its 1,600 members, global reinsurance giants responsible for island-based assets totaling over $200 billion. The site also offers information on conferences and related associations, exchange-control, and tax regulations.

www.bsx.com

The website of the 34-year-old Bermuda Stock Exchange, which bills itself as the largest offshore electronic securities market. The site features market highlights, news, a daily trade report for the domestic market, plus links to trading members.

TELEPHONE DIRECTORIES

www.bermudayp.com

The searchable Bermuda Yellow Pages website, listing thousands of island businesses, community agencies, and services, also provides free classifieds, movie listings, weather updates, and a visitor section with links to bus and ferry schedules, restaurant menus, wedding planner resources, a video tour of the island, and the Ministry of Works & Engineering's Internet-based address-finder.

www.bermudabusiness.com

The website of Yellow Pages rival, Bermuda Communications Directory, has an effective search engine and well-grouped categories, from government and community listings to event planners, fishermen, and realtors. A visitor information section includes links to activities reservations, restaurants, and public transport information.

WEATHER

www.weather.bm

The official site of the Bermuda Weather Service offering current conditions, weeklong forecasts, marine conditions, climate data, and satellite imagery.

www.sharkoil.bm

A succinct, well-designed site (named for the homespun storm predictor) details everything from Bermuda hurricane folklore to a homeowner's hurricane prep list. It includes Atlantic storm synopses and satellite storm-tracking imagery.

Index

HISTORIC SITES

PARKS AND NATURE RESERVES

Acknowledgments

As this, the first edition of *Moon Bermuda*, came together, it relied heavily on the advice, tips, insider secrets, scientific explanations, and historical trivia contributed by numerous individuals, without whom I could never have completed the project. Thanks to Dr. Edward Harris, director of the Bermuda Maritime Museum, and Dr. Wolfgang Sterrer, former curator of the Bermuda Natural History Museum, for their patient explanations of everything from the science of shark oil to the engineering of 18th-century forts.

The Bermuda Department of Tourism's Terri Greenslade generously gave of her time and impressive Rolodex to fill me in on useful resources in every area of my research. My thanks also go to Jo Ann MacMillan and the efficient team at the Department of Statistics, who speedily fulfilled my late requests for accurate recent data on the economy, population, and other key figures. Mike Osborn at Bermuda International Airport described the vagaries of local aviation; Carl Paiva took me on an interesting journey behind the scenes of the local travel industry. Alison Outerbridge revealed the local secrets of the Town of St. George. Jack Ward and Jennifer Conklin-Gray explained the Department of Conservation's great efforts to protect endangered species. Bev Morfitt juggled a slew of government-related queries. Former Botanical Gardens curator Lisa Outerbridge provided details and history on one of the most beautiful parks in the world. And sports editor Adrian Robson brought me up to speed on the island's golfing scene.

Much appreciation goes to the dynamic Elmore Warren, of Fresh Creations, whose friendship, energy, in-depth knowledge, and innovative ideas for rejuvenating his beloved North Hamilton were incredibly inspiring. I wish all your big dreams for the neighborhood and its residents come true.

To all my "foodie" friends, including Edward Bottone, Pennie Lamb, Myra Brayham, Hilary Evans-Turner, Melissa Kizer, Noelle Heckscher, Sacha Blackburne, and Tim and Christine Patton, I owe you big time for all the recommendations, opinions, and out-of-the-way directions to both Bermuda's gourmet and down-home surprises. I'm also indebted to Karen Robinson, Kristen Linberg, and Christopher Edwards for their very helpful perspective on young Bermuda, local nightlife, and the scoop on some of their favorite attractions.

Heartfelt thanks to all who encouraged me along the way, including supportive friends and fellow Mums Noelle, Christine, Sacha, Ali, Frances, Karina, Karen, and Katrina. Your constant interest in the project kept me going.

A lot of my research depended on digesting the scholarship of others. The published works of Dr. Edward Harris, Dr. Martin Thomas, Dr. Duncan McDowall, Dr. Wolfgang Sterrer and the Bermuda National Trust provided me with useful background for contextual writings on the island's history, both human and natural. Published material by editors Charles Barclay, Tony McWilliam, Chris Gibbons, Bill Zuill, and Tim Hodgson were also enlightening. Helpful snippets from other authors are credited in the guide.

As a Bermudian, I'd particularly like to acknowledge the good humor, stoicism, indefatigable optimism, and utmost professionalism demonstrated by so many in the island's hospitality industry. While Bermuda's tourism statistics may have suffered in recent years, the dedication of those in the field to what they do and those for whom they do it promises exciting new avenues for tourism here—not to mention dream vacations for so many who decide to travel to one of the most unusual little communities in the world.

I am proud to have worked under the patient guidance of Avalon Travel Publishing's team, including Rebecca Browning, who encouraged this project from the start; Editor Kathryn Ettinger, whose sage suggestions and calm hand on the tiller were much appreciated; and Graphics Coordinator Tabitha Lahr and Cartography Editor Kevin Anglin, who offered their enthusiastic support.

Above all, my love and thanks go to Paul and Gabriel, who indulged me in my wish to undertake this ultimately fulfilling project, and bore the brunt of my constant research and writing disappearances for the better part of a year.

Lastly, for my mother, a curious and vicarious traveler ever ready for spontaneous adventure: thank you for choosing Bermuda—and for sharing the thrill of discovering new places. This book is dedicated to you.

www.moon.com

For helpful advice on planning a trip, visit www.moon.com for the **TRAVEL PLANNER** and get access to useful travel strategies and valuable information about great places to visit. When you travel with Moon, expect an experience that is uncommon and truly unique.

HANDBOOKS | METRO | OUTDOORS | LIVING ABROAD

MAP SYMBOLS

▨▨▨ Expressway	**⊂** Highlight	✗ Airfield	⚲ Golf Course
▨▨▨ Primary Road	○ City/Town	✗ Airport	**P** Parking Area
▨▨▨ Secondary Road	◉ State Capital	▲ Mountain	▟ Archaeological Site
▫▫▫ Unpaved Road	⊛ National Capital	✚ Unique Natural Feature	⬗ Church
------- Trail	★ Point of Interest		▯ Gas Station
··········· Ferry	● Accommodation	⑃ Waterfall	⬭ Glacier
⊢⊢⊢ Railroad	▼ Restaurant/Bar	▲ Park	Mangrove
▨▨▨ Pedestrian Walkway	▪ Other Location	▯ Trailhead	Reef
▨▨▨ Stairs	Λ Campground	⛷ Skiing Area	Swamp

CONVERSION TABLES

°C = (°F - 32) / 1.8
°F = (°C x 1.8) + 32
1 inch = 2.54 centimeters (cm)
1 foot = 0.304 meters (m)
1 yard = 0.914 meters
1 mile = 1.6093 kilometers (km)
1 km = 0.6214 miles
1 fathom = 1.8288 m
1 chain = 20.168 m
1 furlong = 201.168 m
1 acre = 0.4047 hectares
1 sq km = 100 hectares
1 sq mile = 2.59 square km
1 ounce = 28.35 grams
1 pound = 0.4536 kilograms
1 short ton = 0.90718 metric ton
1 short ton = 2,000 pounds
1 long ton = 1.016 metric tons
1 long ton = 2,240 pounds
1 metric ton = 1,000 kilograms
1 quart = 0.94635 liters
1 US gallon = 3.7854 liters
1 Imperial gallon = 4.5459 liters
1 nautical mile = 1.852 km

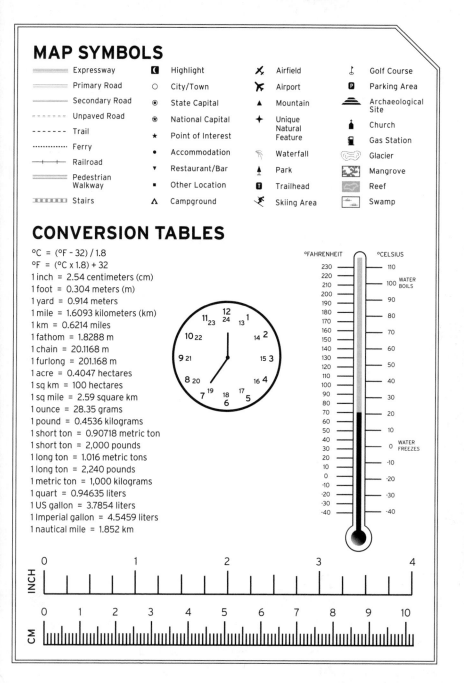

MOON BERMUDA

Avalon Travel Publishing
An Imprint of
Avalon Publishing Group, Inc.

AVALON
publishing group incorporated

1400 65th Street, Suite 250
Emeryville, CA 94608, USA
www.moon.com

Editor and Series Manager: Kathryn Ettinger
Acquisitions Manager: Rebecca K. Browning
Copy Editor: Valerie Sellers Blanton
Graphics Coordinator: Tabitha Lahr
Production Coordinator: Tabitha Lahr
Cover & Interior Designer: Gerilyn Attebery
Map Editor: Kevin Anglin
Cartographer: Suzanne Service
Proofreader: Candace Hilbert
Indexer: Rachel Kuhn

ISBN-10: 1-56691-902-9
ISBN-13: 978-1-56691-902-9
ISSN: 1932-7870

Printing History
1st Edition – October 2006
5 4 3 2 1

KEEPING CURRENT

If you have a favorite gem you'd like to see included in the next edition, or see anything
that needs updating, clarification, or correction, please drop us a line. Send your comments via email to feedback@moon.com, or use the address above.